MOTOCOURSE™

THE WORLD'S LEADING GRAND PRIX & SUPERBIKE ANNUAL

CONTENTS

MOTOCOURSE 2023-2024

is published by:
Icon Publishing Limited
2 Redesdale House,
85 The Park,
Cheltenham,
Gloucestershire
GL50 2RP
United Kingdom

Tel: +44 (0)1242 245329

Editorial office:
Park Farm Barn,
New Street,
Deddington,
OX15 0SS
United Kingdom

Tel: +44 (0)7836 271998

Email: info@motocourse.com
Website: www.motocourse.com

Printed in the United Kingdom by
Gomer Press Ltd
Llandysul Enterprise Park,
Llandysul,
Ceredigion,
SA44 4JL
Tel: 01559 362371
email: sales@gomer.co.uk

© Icon Publishing Limited 2024.
No part of this publication may be reproduced, stored in a retrieval system or transmitted, in any form or by any means, electronic, mechanical, photocopying, recording or otherwise, without prior permission in writing from Icon Publishing Limited.

ISBN: 978-1910584-59-0

DISTRIBUTORS

Gardners Books
1 Whittle Drive, Eastbourne,
East Sussex, BN23 6QH
Tel: +44 (0)1323 521555
email: sales@gardners.com

Chaters Wholesale Ltd
25/26 Murrell Green Business Park,
Hook, Hampshire, RG27 9GR
Tel: +44 (0)1256 765443
Fax: +44 (0)1256 769900
email: books@chaters.co.uk

NORTH AMERICA
NATIONAL BOOK NETWORK
NBN
4501 Forbes Boulevard,
Suite 200,
Lanham, MD 20706
Tel: (301) 459-3366
Fax: (301) 429-5746

Dust jacket: Jorge Martin became MotoGP world champion for the independent Pramac Ducati Team.

Title page: Toprak Razgatlioglu, 2024 World Superbike champion for BMW.

Photos: Gold & Goose

FOREWORD by 2024 MotoGP World Champion Jorge Martin	5
EDITOR'S INTRODUCTION	6
THE TOP TEN RIDERS OF 2024 Ranked by the Editor	8
THE STATE OF RACING by Michael Scott	14
LIBERTY MEDIA: IS MOTOGP'S FUTURE IN SAFE HANDS? Dorna is set to be bought by F1 owners Liberty Media. What does that mean for MotoGP? Dario De Wet examines the prospects	22
THE RETURN OF THE MASTER Marc Marquez's recovery from career meltdown was the highlight of 2024. How did he do it? Neil Morrison has the inside story	26
A NEW MOTOGP FOR 2027 What will the new 2027 regulations mean for MotoGP racing? And why does it matter? Kevin Cameron analyses the details	30
INSIDE MOTOGP'S AI REVOLUTION Artificial Intelligence is in its infancy and this powerful technology is already transforming MotoGP. Mat Oxley reports	36
BIKE BY BIKE The MotoGP machines of 2024 analysed by Jack Gorst	42
MOTOGP RIDERS AND TEAMS Guide to the grid by Peter McLaren and Adrian Dean	50
MOTO2 RIDERS AND TEAMS by Peter McLaren	74
MOTO3 RIDERS AND TEAMS by Peter McLaren	78
2024 GRANDS PRIX by Michael Scott and Neil Morrison	82
WORLD CHAMPIONSHIP RIDERS' POINTS TABLES Compiled by Peter McLaren	244
MOTOE REVIEW by Neil Morrison	248
RED BULL ROOKIES CUP REVIEW by Peter Clifford	252
SUPERBIKE WORLD CHAMPIONSHIP REVIEW by Gordon Ritchie	256
SUPERBIKE CHAMPIONSHIP RESULTS AND POINTS TABLES Compiled by Peter McLaren	288
WORLD SUPERSPORT CHAMPIONSHIP REVIEW by Gordon Ritchie	296
ISLE OF MAN TT REVIEW by Michael Guy	300
SIDECAR CHAMPIONSHIP REVIEW by John McKenzie	310
BRITISH SUPERBIKE REVIEW by Josh Close	312
US RACING REVIEW by Larry Lawrence	330
MAJOR RESULTS WORLDWIDE compiled by Peter McLaren	339

Acknowledgements

The Editor and staff of MOTOCOURSE wish to thank the following for their assistance and support: Marc Balsells, Matt Birt, Peter Clifford, Simon Crafar, Lucia Gabani, Michael Guy, Isabelle Lariviere, Harry Lloyd, Neil Morrison, Mat Oxley, David Pato, Laura Perez, Ignacio Sagnier, Paolo Scalera, Federico Tonelli, Frine Vellila, Artur Vilalta, Mike Webb, Gunther Wiesinger, Fran Wyld and numerous others. The usual apologies to colleagues if I ignored their helpful comments and advice.

Photographs published in MOTOCOURSE 2024–2025 have been contributed by:
Chief photographers: Gold & Goose.

Other photographs contributed by: Aprilia Racing, Bennetts Superbike Championship, Gavan Caldwell, Clive Challinor Motorsport Photography, David Collister, Photography, Ducati Corse, Bernd Fischer - motoarchive.com, Jack Gorst, Gresini Racing, Hackrod, HRC, Liberty Media, Stephen McClements, Mercedes AMG Petronas F1 Team, Monster Energy Yamaha MotoGP, MotoAmerica/Brian J. Nelson, MotoGP, MSV, Mat Oxley, Pramac Ducati, David Purves, Red Bull Content Pool, Red Bull KTM, Repsol Honda, University of Nebija, Mark Walters, Bryn Williams, Andrea Wilson.

---

publisher
STEVE SMALL
steve.small@iconpublishinglimited.com

commercial director
BRYN WILLIAMS
bryn.williams@iconpublishinglimited.com

editor
MICHAEL SCOTT

text editor
IAN PENBERTHY

results and statistics
PETER McLAREN

chief photographers
GOLD & GOOSE
David Goldman
Gareth Harford
David 'Chippy' Wood

www.goldandgoose.com
Tel: +44 (0)208 444 2448

MotoGP bike and circuit illustrations
ADRIAN DEAN
f1artwork@blueyonder.co.uk

www.motocourse.com

FOREWORD
by JORGE MARTIN

IT'S one thing to have a childhood dream.

It's something incredible for that dream to come true.

Especially when you have worked so hard and for so long.

In 2023, I experienced the feeling of leading the championship, and then the feeling of losing that lead. Of facing defeat at the final race.

Processing those feelings really helped my approach in 2024. In the previous year, I couldn't enjoy the final part of the season. I was too tense, too anxious. In 2024, I relished the occasion. And I think it showed.

That didn't make winning the championship any easier. It was a really strong battle. The level was incredible, and I want to say thank you to Pecco for that. It was a privilege fighting with a great champion every week. I think I can be proud of beating such an accomplished opponent, and he can be proud for the fight we had all year. The advantage went back and forward. He made it a hell of a fight.

It meant a lot that we could race each other so hard and still be good with each other. Back in 2015 and 2016, we were team-mates with Mahindra in Moto3. We were teenagers, our grand prix journeys just beginning, and we were really good friends.

As rivals, we can't be exactly like that any more, but we were able to laugh and joke together, and to respect each other. I hope it will always be like that.

There are others I must thank: my family for their support from the beginning, and for the many sacrifices they made for me. My team, for their dedication and work, never becoming tired, never giving up.

Ducati, of course, for making such a fantastic motorcycle – a Desmosedici won almost every race.

The Red Bull Rookies Cup, for showing me the way into the championship, also my Moto3 and Moto2 teams. Dorna, for putting on this incredible show. And, of course, the fans. Their support means so much to me and to this sport that we all love.

It is an honour to write the foreword to this book, the premier record of motorcycle championship racing since the 1970s, before I was born. The reports and articles, and fantastic pictures are the best way for fans and riders to keep the memories alive.

Now it is time to enjoy the title – and prepare for a new challenge. To try to do it again in 2025 on another bike would be even more special.

EDITOR'S INTRODUCTION
IN AT THE DEEP END

THE 2024 season was memorable, in several ways. At the deep end, serious technical development, a plethora of lap records and a Ducati duel that went to the final flag. At the shallow, a celebration of the trivial that peaked when a cosplay Sonic the Hedgehog was recruited to wave the chequered flag at a blingy US GP. (Who next? Ronald McDonald? Kim Kardashian? Hannibal Lecter?)

MotoGP can probably expect more of this lowest-common-denominator indulgence with the Liberty Media takeover – heralded by a 'rebranding exercise' (i.e., new logo), which met a reception as mixed as its typefaces. For example, if the 'oto' in MotoGP is to represent two wheels and a racing rider, why keep the 't' vertical, like a pizza delivery boy on a bicycle?

But it can also expect more of what matters. Great racing. The continued return of the master, Marc Marquez, versus a flourishing supply of talented rookies, personified by Pedro Acosta.

And two more years of a golden era – the 1000cc MotoGP monsters that arrived in 2012, and – once production-based CRT bikes had run their course – came to booming good health, with Aprilia and KTM joining, while increasingly restrictive technical regs guaranteed close racing.

Stealthily, another new era has already begun.

Motorcycles have always responded to individual genius. In the long-gone two-stroke days, gifted tuners with a musical ear and a rat-tail file would make the motors sing. With four-strokes, the likes of Ducati's inspired Gigi Dall'Igna.

These gifted eccentrics are in danger of being rendered redundant by the advent of Artificial Intelligence, which can think faster outside an almost infinite number of boxes. MOTOCOURSE analyses the start of this phenomenon, and much else, within these pages.

MICHAEL SCOTT
West Sussex
November, 2024

Main: Fans flocked to MotoGP's celebration of reality at Aragon. Alex Espargaro left the party early.
Photo: Monster Energy Yamaha

Left: A class act – twice. Defeated double-champion Pecco Bagnaia congratulates his 2024 nemesis Jorge Martin.

Below left: Marquez and Dall'Igna – a marriage made in heaven?
Photos: Gold & Goose

FIM WORLD CHAMPIONSHIP 2024

TOP TEN RIDERS

THE EDITOR'S CHOICE

Rider Portraits by Gold & Goose

1 MARC MARQUEZ

MARQUEZ was an unknown quantity for 2024. Not to himself, though. His wicked grin after his first taste of Ducati at Valencia in 2023 foretold a rapid return to the form that had won him eight championships. Not in 2024, but mainly because his year-old GP23, all GP23s, struggled with the new back tyre. The next best on the older bike, brother Alex, didn't score half as many points. Marc, though, was a constant threat to the title-leading GP24 riders, in spite of giving away an estimated two-tenths per lap. He won as many Sunday races as Martin, and though the practice-crash tally was high, he no-scored only twice, once through mechanical failure. Simply the best.

2 JORGE MARTIN

MARTIN was a deserving winner of a season-long toe-to-toe with the defending champion. He did it not by racking up race wins – only three from 20, although a more impressive seven sprints – but by backing them up with ten seconds, three thirds and just two Sunday crashes, both out of the lead. He was never anything but spectacularly fast, but more importantly – Jerez and Sachsenring apart – he was spectacularly reliable. That's what really mattered. Martin came up the hard way, and in the past had shown signs of temperament. But in 2024, he demonstrated calmness and maturity that served him well. Ducati must regret losing him. And vice versa.

3 PECCO BAGNAIA

WHEN Pecco dubbed the contest "a championship of mistakes", he was referring to his own errors, those by other riders he blamed for making him crash (the Marquez brothers) and tyres that didn't always perform as he expected. On error-free weekends, he was magnificent – and he finished the year with a dominant double in Catalunya. It was his fifth of the season. He showed great depth of talent, the first to get the measure of the latest Desmosedici and difficult Michelin rear. He progressed steadily through each weekend to maximise his performance in qualifying and the race. Perhaps he did deserve to join the list of riders with three in a row, but unfortunately he didn't do quite enough.

4 PEDRO ACOSTA

BURDENED with expectations and supercharged with ambition, Acosta didn't quite make the level predicted by even Marc Marquez, whose 'youngest-ever' records he threatened. What the teenager did do was mightily impressive, getting up among the fastest from the first races, and on the full-race podium at the second and third rounds. He found the going tough after that, with too many tumbles, but he got back on the podium twice more on Sunday and a total of four times in sprints. And he kept learning, even if sometimes it was from the gravel trap. He'll be threatening Marquez again in 2025.

5 ENEA BASTIANINI

THE second factory Ducati rider seemed to have one blind spot: qualifying. On the front row at Qatar and on pole for round two in Portugal, he then lost the knack of the single fast lap, with a solitary front row in the next 11 races, and a worst grid position of 11th. The exception was at Silverstone, where he qualified third and rode to a brilliant double to briefly regain championship momentum. He only claimed one other Sunday win, and the sprint in Thailand. In spite of reliably being the best at nursing tyres and achieving late-race pace, too often he left himself too much to do. A flawed campaign.

6 FABIO QUARTARARO

THE French former champion didn't have much going for him in 2024, least of all a factory Yamaha that simply wasn't up to snuff. Did that discourage him? Well, sometimes, yes. But other times, most times, his efforts to exceed the possibilities were exhausting to watch. And they often bore fruit, with seven top-tens, including a best of sixth at Sepang. As revealing was that the other Yamaha rider, the highly talented Alex Rins, admittedly hampered by injury, was seldom anywhere near his team-mate. Quartararo remained true to Yamaha, staying on in the hope of a revival. They are lucky to have such loyalty.

7 JOHANN ZARCO

BAFFLINGLY, in 144 MotoGP starts, Zarco has only won once. Perhaps the cards just didn't fall right for the only double Moto2 champion; then he knocked the table over by storming out of KTM halfway through 2019. Apart from that year, 17th overall was his worst ever result. Yet 2024 was a year when he showed real quality and depth, riding for Honda in the company's extraordinary nadir. Zarco far exceeded his RC213V stablemates, turning his faith in HRC's certain recovery into astonishingly strong qualifying positions – the only Honda in Q2 all year, five times, with a best of seventh in Indonesia. His contribution to the stricken racing giant's morale cannot be underestimated.

8 AI OGURA

A CALM and measured campaign won in MotoGP. Ogura's steady march towards the Moto2 crown was even more so. He'd left his long-time Honda Team Asia and Kalex to join MT Helmets on a Boscoscuro, and won only three races, with four seconds and one third. Yet in volatile Moto2, good points scored in all but one of the 19 races he started (the exception being Malaysia, due to a mechanical failure) gave a very clear overall win. Ogura never became flustered, and even if he'd qualified poorly, he would always come through strongly. And he crashed only twice all year. Next test – MotoGP.

9 DAVID ALONSO

MOTOCOURSE almost always includes the Moto3 champion in this list, because to prevail in such febrile conditions suggests a special quality. Often, but not always, dominant champions go on to greater success in MotoGP – Rossi and Marquez being two examples. But nobody in lightweight (or any other) class history has been as dominant as Alonso, with a record 14 wins. Spanish-born and resident, but racing as a Colombian, the affable teenager won fans galore as well as races, and he moves to Moto2 for 2025. Will he prove to be another major talent?

10 ARON CANET

IF grand prix racing is as much entertainment as sport, then the entertainers merit inclusion, even if they have performance flaws that undermine their results. Not that second in the championship is by any means shabby, but the spectacularly inked Spaniard made it spectacularly difficult for himself, with a gift for seizing defeat from the jaws of victory. The way he lost a race-long lead to Dixon on the last lap at Silverstone was just one example. His first Moto2 win came in his 70th start, after seeming to have a stranglehold on second. Canet always entertained, however, and always enjoyed himself, even when he didn't win. So did his fans.

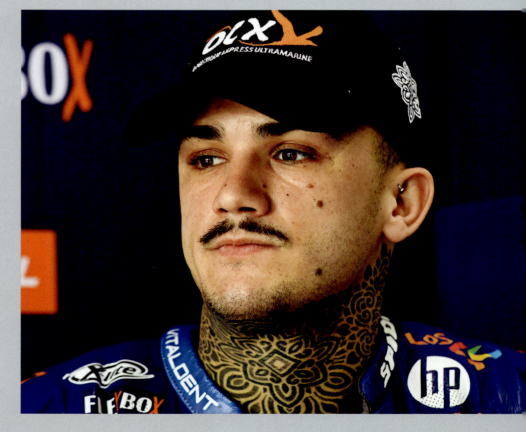

THE STATE OF RACING
FAST FORWARD

Both MotoGP and WorldSBK experienced considerable evolution during 2024, which is set to continue in the immediate future. Editor MICHAEL SCOTT reviews the progress…

Above: Bagnaia and Martin – the main event.

Top right: Hugging rivals. Ducati's Dall'Igna provided the machinery that allowed Pramac's Campinoti to realise his dream.

Above right: Toprak Razgatlioglu was lured to BMW and gave them the WorldSBK title they had craved for years. Will they now make the move to MotoGP?

Right: WorldSBK laid on a varied and hard-fought season.
Photos: Gold & Goose

IF there was a sense of *fin de siècle* as the last exhaust bellows died away at the final round in November, it was a little premature. There are two more seasons of MotoGP-As-We-Know-It before that happens. Two more seasons of crazy horsepower and crazy aerodynamics, and the crazy racing they have created.

Racing where overtaking is considered almost impossible. Unless you are Marc Marquez, Brad Binder, Pedro Acosta, or one or two others. Where too much conformity flattens the profile, without actually cutting the elite down to size. And where for 20 often unforgettable races, a championship battle for the ages attracted record crowds and enhanced the sport's image – not only of itself, but also to the outside world – in spite of any cavils, quibbles and the carping complaints of the never-happy.

The 1000cc era, which took over from the unloved 800s in 2007, has taken the machines to an extraordinary level, where (to the dismay of some and the delight of others) they look like manga-drawn earth-bound rocket ships.

They will continue to do so, although perhaps slightly toned down from 2027, when sweeping regulation changes come into effect – among them a reduction in front wing width, from 600 to 550mm, mounted 50mm further back. Although the past couple of seasons have shown that regulations intended to limit aero developments by freezing fairing design have simply driven the winglets elsewhere – front mudguard and forks, rear swing-arms, seats…

More significant, the reduction in engine size – from 1000cc to 850, a cut of 15 per cent. But maximum bore size, currently 81mm, is to drop to 75mm, a reduction of only 7.4 per cent. Which means that the new cylinder size is notably less oversquare and the piston stroke reduced only slightly. Piston speeds, and thus the rev ceiling, remain similar. This should avoid the pitfall of the shrieky 800cc generation, preserving a similar torque curve. There will be less power, but currently there is much more than enough, needing to be tamed electronically in the lower gears.

Top speeds will probably suffer or at least be stopped from continuing to increase – but this is for another reason as well. The banning of ride-height devices will make a difference. Without lowering the centre of gravity, corner exit acceleration will be slower.

Will lap times be slower? By a second or maybe two at first is the consensus. That won't affect the quality of the racing, but there is another concern. It would bring the exotic prototypes within reach of production-based WorldSBK – an embarrassing outcome.

All-time circuit records at directly comparable tracks put Superbikes at 2.4 seconds slower (Portimao and Assen), 1.6 seconds at Jerez and just 1.3 at Catalunya.

FIM president Jorge Viegas promised at the announcement, "We will make Superbikes slower, too". The first steps will begin in 2025, with the adoption of fuel-flow restrictions that will not only balance the differences between Superbikes, but also potentially slow all of them by however much is needed.

MOTOGP in 2024 was not quite a one-make series. But it came close. While Ducati Desmosedicis, both new and old, ran rampant, rivals were reduced to competing to be best of the rest. For formerly dominant Japanese pair Yamaha and Honda, even that was out of reach.

Ducati's almost complete domination of the season was a measure of engineering and strategic excellence, steered by Gigi Dall'Igna.

Since his time at Aprilia, Dall'Igna has shown nothing short of genius in his comprehension and ability to exploit regulations to advantage – whether it be by confrontation or sidestep. Ducati has led the way in pioneering ride-height adjustments and in aerodynamics, with Aprilia and KTM coming close in the latter at times.

The desmodromic-valve motors have played a major role in giving the Desmos a top-speed advantage, although a bit less so in 2024 than previously; more important is the usability of the power, for the punch out of corners.

But if there was a key, it was that the Ducatis could make the best use of Michelin's super-grippy 2024 rear slick. This consolidated the accelerative powers.

Ducati have won the riders' title for three years in a row, the constructors' every year since 2020. Success is easy to admire, but what does this domination mean for the other constructors? Does it inspire them to greater efforts (which usually means greater investment), or make them wonder whether to follow Suzuki to the exit?

All have pledged to stay, but the Ducati-owning VW group were dealing with financial hardship, and news broke as MOTOCOURSE went to press that KTM, facing a shortfall of an estimated 500,000-million euros, had retrenched some 300 staff and were filing for voluntary insolvency in an attempt to rescue the company. It remains to be seen whether racing promises can be kept.

Will MotoGP owners Liberty act to break the deadlock? As well as the threat of losing current factories, there is a feeling that new ones might be difficult to attract. This applies particularly to BMW, already welcomed into the fold for more than two decades as suppliers of official track vehicles and sponsors of the fastest qualifier's award. They have long been courted as potential MotoGP participants, and there were fresh hopes after the German manufacturer's eventual and long-awaited victory with Toprak Razgatlioglu in World Superbikes.

Above: The end of a (mostly) glorious three decades for Honda and Repsol.
Photo: Repsol Honda

Top right: Breaking the Kalex Moto2 stranglehold. Fermin Aldeguer was just one of four to win on a Boscoscuro chassis.
Photo: Gold & Goose

Above right: The new MotoGP logo met a mixed reception.
Graphic: MotoGP

Right: Tyres – always a perplexing problem.
Photo: Gold & Goose

More likely, fresh names will come from the East, particularly given that motorcycle sales (of scooters and commuters) are booming in India and Southeast Asia in particular. In 2024, Chinese manufacturers were involved in the smaller classes in WorldSBK, and in name also in Moto3, under the Pierer Mobility Group (KTM) umbrella.

Dynasties don't last forever. One example is the end of the Repsol Honda team. The Spanish petroleum giant had backed the factory Honda team since 1995. Poor results – just four wins over the past five years – were one reason, as well as the loss of Marquez; but discomfort had grown from Honda's side as well.

Then there's the case of Moto2, dominated by the Kalex chassis since 2013. The upset was achieved by the Italian Boscoscuro chassis, formerly Speed Up, itself a close descendant of the British TSR. Things changed quickly. In 2023, there were just two on the grid, but ridden by Alonso Lopez and Fermin Aldeguer, who won five races. In 2024, Sergio Garcia and Ai Ogura doubled the numbers with the new MT Helmets team. The four riders won six races between them, and Ogura the championship, breaking the Kalex stranglehold. In 2025, the new Pramac Yamaha team will use the Italian chassis, and the multi-successful Elf Marc VDS team will switch.

Earlier history does put Ducati's achievement into some kind of proportion.

Having won every main race bar one (Vinales's Aprilia won in the USA) and all but three sprints, their best of the year was to take the top eight places in the Thai sprint – the first time this had been done in the MotoGP era. But not in GP racing's 75-year history.

The greatest domination was achieved by Suzuki, during their purple patch, when the disc-valve, square-four RG500 reigned supreme: the top ten in Belgium and top nine at Mugello in 1976. Top eights have gone to Yamaha in the 1974 TT, Suzuki at Imatra in 1976 and Honda in Catalunya in 1996. And on each occasion, other constructors bounced back and racing survived.

THE Liberty Media Group's takeover of Dorna – and thence MotoGP and WorldSBK – remained to be confirmed as MOTOCOURSE went to press, but a successful outcome was confidently expected.

So too that the injection of capital and commercial nous would secure a growth spurt. In general, recovery from the double post-Rossi and pandemic slump had been positive, with a trackside footfall of more than three million over the full year a new record. But many felt that the focus on the emergent markets – Malaysia, Indonesia and Thailand on the calendar (the last set to open the 2025 season), and India expected to return – was at the expense of the traditional European base, and that the USA was badly under-represented.

Much remained to be seen. In the interim, a rebranding exercise was revealed after the final GP. It's easy to make fun of marketing speak, but the launch announcement made it particularly easy to do so. Especially when habitually gruff Dorna CEO Carmelo Ezpeleta, talking of working with the design studio Pentagram, was said to have described it as "an incredible adventure".

"Come with us to the edge of possibility and the edge of your seat," continued a breathless announcement of "more than a logo … a complete evolution of the brand."

The 'M' of the new mixed-typeface MotoGP logo "takes inspiration from two bikes, at a lean, close to each other on track as is unique to the sport. The 'O's suggest the wheels' geometry, and the 't' the rider between them. Human and machine."

Really?

THE long-standing front tyre scandal – a consequence, arguably, of having a single tyre supplier facing no competition – not only continued through 2024, but also, it was confirmed after a late-season Michelin test, would carry on through the 2025 season.

The new tyre needed further development, the French tyre company said, then further testing. It would not be available until 2026.

So the unpopular and sometimes more than faintly absurd punishments will continue.

It is a consequence of ever-increasing aerodynamic developments, supplemented by ride-height devices. Greater downforce, increased braking and faster cornering overload the front tyre. Even heat off the carbon discs is a factor, while running closely behind another bike not only robs the wheel of cooling air, but worse than that also keeps it in the heat coming off the one in front.

Michelin's slick, of a construction in use for a decade or more, is not up to the task. It has been overtaken by technology; however, attempts to develop a new construction have been overtaken by events – plans for first tests in 2020/21 were thwarted by Covid. So the situation dragged on.

Riders are tempted to start with under-inflated tyres, so that the inevitable pressure rise during the race will bring them up to a good working range. Michelin view this as risky, in terms of both potential damage to the carcase and the possibility of crashes. They decreed a minimum safe pressure. Regulations were put in place, but not enforced while a monitoring infrastructure was developed, finally fit for purpose midway through 2023.

The year began with a comforting crumb: the previous threat of disqualification for a repeat offender was rescinded; now a still punitive time penalty (16 seconds for a full race, eight for the sprint) would be the same each time. The minimum pressure was slightly reduced, from 1.88 bar to 1.80, but the proportion of the race during which it was permissible to be below that was cut, from 50 per cent to 40 per cent.

Above: A tyre-pressure issue meant that Quartararo lost a sprint podium to Pedrosa at Jerez.

Above right: Punishment czar Freddie Spencer's contentious reign came to an end.

Above far right: Simon Crafar takes over in 2025.

Right: Honda's tough times put them with Yamaha in concession category D. New LCR rider Somkiat Chantra tries out the latest bike at the Barcelona MotoGP Test.

Photo: Gold & Goose

Seventeen times during the year, riders fell foul, in sprints and the GP, and lost positions every time. Five were punished in the Jerez sprint, three in the races in Germany and Aragon. One to suffer was Fabio Quartararo, robbed of a single podium in the Jerez sprint, being dropped from third to fifth. Another, Marc Marquez at Assen. He was dropped from fourth to tenth, losing seven points, after the unedifying spectacle of waving another rider past to try to heat his tyre. Which is not real racing.

Then there was the pantomime in Indonesia, where Acosta's podium celebrations were spoiled under the pall of an investigation, only for him to be declared innocent some time later. His tyre pressure had been below regulation, but due to a technical fault rather than by intention. And obviously not that dangerous after all.

Infringements are not deliberate rule breaking, but the consequence of guesswork gone wrong. Teams know that inevitably pressure will rise, distorting the profile to diminish the contact patch and reduce grip.

Back when there was competition between Michelin, Dunlop and Bridgestone, Michelin made special event- and weather-specific 'Rossi tyres' during race weekends, and shipped them to the star rider overnight. Much to the dismay of Casey Stoner and others, who missed out.

This had more to do with compound. What is needed now is a different construction – changing this is not an overnight affair. Yet it should be manageable within, say, a few months. Or a year. But with Michelin racing only against themselves, the pressure just isn't there.

It's difficult to imagine MotoGP's commercially minded new owners Liberty tolerating this sort of nonsense. It needs to be fixed.

By contrast, Pirelli's arrival, as replacement for Dunlop in Moto2 and Moto3, went much more smoothly than anyone had expected.

After a shaky start in the admittedly peculiar conditions in Qatar, most riders rapidly adapted. Literally so, with a profusion of new ultimate fastest laps and race lap records at almost every track.

Providing tyres for the much faster, heavier and hugely more powerful MotoGP bikes is a different level of challenge; but it would be interesting to see what sort of a fist Pirelli might make of it.

MOTOGP'S new four-tier system of concessions operated successfully in its first season. At one end, Ducati in category A – very limited testing, no wild-cards and frozen engine development. At the opposite end, in category D, the two Japanese factories, with extra engines, and unrestricted wild-cards and testing, and most importantly, free engine development. Between the two extremes, KTM and Aprilia entrants, with frozen engines and limited testing, but up to six wild-cards.

It changed nothing for Ducati, in terms of increased domination, while it gave a little room for its two European challengers. Enough for Aprilia to record four wins, and for KTM at least to talk about how they were continuing to improve, although in fact, results took a step backwards – two sprint wins in 2023, none in 2024.

It proved most significant for Honda and Yamaha, however. Most importantly in giving them heart, at a time when there are certainly elements within both companies questioning the continued expense, set against serially disappointing results.

Both Honda and Yamaha pursued vigorous testing regimes, including joint tests at Mugello and Misano, with a continuous stream of aero, chassis and engine updates. Only towards the end of the season did these appear to be bearing any fruit, giving improved qualifying and race results.

As significantly, each turned to Europe for senior personnel, as reported in these pages, seeking a fresh approach as well as detailed knowledge. They recruited expertise particularly from former Ducati staff. The latest such brain-poaching exercise, late in 2024, was by Honda, hiring Romano Albes-

iano as their first non-Japanese technical director. The Italian had been the technical architect of Aprilia's advancement from also-rans to race-winning potential.

THE FIM Stewards Panel had another busy year, over and above their tyre-pressure duties, with particular attention being paid to the dangerous practice of dithering out on track during qualifying, awaiting a faster rider or group of riders for a tow. This is particularly prevalent, but not exclusively confined to Moto3, where on a track with a long straight, a slipstream can make a very significant difference to lap time.

A cumulative punishment regime starts with a warning and escalates via a single long-lap penalty to an eventual pit-lane start or even disqualification. There seemed to have been some success in this exercise in 'herding cats', in that no Moto3 rider offended often enough to be given more than two long-laps. There were 12 sanctions at the US GP, exceeded in Germany by 16, but generally fewer, and at some races, none – including, rather surprisingly, the Thai GP, with its long straight.

There were also slightly fewer of the much-hated track-limits sanctions, which cost race results for last-lap infringements. They are triggered automatically by trackside sensors at particular points, so there is equally no room for error, but also no room for exercise of judgement. However, a different way of dissuading riders from seeking advantage by using more than the official track came into play, and it was both popular and effective.

The so-called 'Misano Kerbs', which appeared also at Jerez, Thailand and several other circuits, have a saw-tooth cross-section – each block acts as a ramp before dropping to the next one – that becomes increasingly exaggerated the further from the track edge. A rider can use a bit of kerb (the paint can offer better grip than the asphalt) if he can cope with the vibration, but the further he strays, the more severe the rumble-strip effect becomes. The escalating punishment better fits the crime.

Inevitably, the panel attracts criticism from riders, generally focused on the chairman. Since October, 2018, that role was filled by former triple champion Freddie Spencer (1983 and 1985, 500cc; 1985, 250cc), who maintained a lordly silence in the face of continual brickbats, and declined also to blame the opprobrium for his decision to resign.

For 2025, there will be a new volunteer for this unenviable role. One-time GP winner, and more recently technical analyst and TV commentator Simon Crafar takes over. Riders

APPRECIATIONS

PAT HENNEN, 1953–2024

PAT HENNEN, the first American to win a 500cc GP, died on 6th April, 2024, aged 70. His victory in Finland in 1976 was a seminal event in the history of American racing. It helped change the face of GP racing and opened the door for the many American riders who followed in his footsteps.

Hennen honed his skills riding regional dirt-track and scrambles races across Northern California in the late 1960s and early '70s. He rapidly became one of the top up-and-coming riders in the region, becoming an AMA 'Expert' in 1975. Signed with Suzuki and focused primarily on road racing, he earned his first major podium in the Daytona 200 in 1976.

Later that year, on 1st August, riding for Suzuki as team-mate to Barry Sheene, Hennen made history by winning the Finnish GP at Imatra. An American victory was so unexpected that the organisers didn't have a recording of the US national anthem; an exultant Hennen wore a cowboy hat on the podium.

He finished the season third in the championship and repeated the feat in 1977, again on a works Suzuki, scoring a second win in the British GP and four other podium finishes.

In 1978, Hennen was reaching his prime. He opened the season with a dominant performance in the Trans-Atlantic Match Races, beating Kenny Roberts and Barry Sheene to become top scorer. Then he won the Spanish GP at Jarama and took the championship points lead.

By mid-season, the two Americans, Roberts and Hennen, were leading the championship. Hennen was just eight points behind Roberts after five of 11 rounds.

After the Italian GP, there was a break in the schedule, and Hennen agreed to race the Isle of Man at the request of Suzuki Great Britain. It would be his final race, a crash at Bishopscourt leaving him with a career-ending head injury that produced lasting effects.

Although his racing life had been ended prematurely, his short, but brilliant career was an inspiration to all US road racers of his era, proving that an American could win in the highest echelon of motorcycle racing at a time when few thought it could be done.

Larry Lawrence

ANTHONY GOBERT, 1975–2024

ANTHONY GOBERT was the antithesis of a modern professional racer. In every way, except for one. He was really, really fast..

His roller-coaster career and cruelly short life – he was 48 when he died – could have been so different. Supremely talented, but ultimately fatally flawed, he was addicted to drugs and alcohol, which undermined every triumph.

Born in the Sydney suburb of Camden on 5th March, 1975, Gobert's first teenage successes were on the dirt, winning numerous motocross and short-circuit races, and titles in Australia and New Zealand.

Moving to asphalt, he made rapid progress to his first national Superbike win at Phillip Island in 1992, earned a full-time ride in the national series in 1993 and took the title in 1994, adding a striking wild-card win in the season-ending World Superbike race – at 19, the youngest SBK winner so far.

In 1995, he was fourth overall in the World Superbike championship on a Muzzy Kawasaki. The 'Go-Show' became famous for lavish podium celebrations. In 1996, by now with flamboyant Ronald McDonald red hair, he took a double win at the home circuit, but injury and missed races spoiled his title bid.

The big time came with a 1997 factory Suzuki contract, alongside compatriot Daryll Beattie. According to crew chief Stuart Shenton, "If he hadn't had his demons, he'd have been as good as Valentino Rossi." He managed five top-tens, but serial drug-test failures tried the patience of team, the FIM and sponsors Lucky Strike, and he was sacked before the end of the season.

Too fast to disappear, Gobert found a more tolerant atmosphere in the United States, where track successes – including an injury-hit near miss for the 1999 AMA championship – were marked by wild parties and more failed drug tests.

But his career was starting to unravel, and success thereafter was spasmodic: a single wet WorldSBK win on an uncompetitive Bimota in 2000, and one-off GP rides on a MuZ-Weber and Modenas.

His US career ended in 2002 after a drink-driving conviction. In 2006, he admitted that he was addicted to heroin; in 2008, he was jailed in Australia for small-time mugging offences.

In 2024, after a video emerged showing a barely recognisable figure, his family revealed that he had been admitted to a hospice for palliative care, for an undisclosed condition. Days later, on 17th January, he died.

"At times, he was challenging to say the least," his mother, Suzanne Gobert, wrote. "But he always had a kind heart and cared for everyone. Sadly, he was a victim of addiction."

Michael Scott

GARRY TAYLOR, 1949–2024

GARRY TAYLOR, former manager of the Suzuki Grand Prix Team, was the last great British GP team manager, at the head of the last English-based factory team, in the golden years of the 500cc class.

A noted paddock character and gifted raconteur, he was an instantly recognisable figure, who had worked with Barry Sheene at the height of his fame, taken over the Suzuki team after his retirement, and steered Kevin Schwantz and later Kenny Roberts Junior to world championships.

To many, the affable and unflappable Englishman's most notable success was to keep the Suzuki team alive and a major player for three years after the factory pulled out abruptly at the end of 1983.

It involved more than just keeping a crack pit crew out of the dole queue. Diplomacy and influence within the factory ensured a trickle of parts necessary to keep the obsolescent RG500 square-four marginally competitive. Taylor also commissioned a revolutionary carbon honeycomb-sandwich chassis, nicknamed 'the cardboard box', years ahead of its time, and hand-picked rising British riders Rob McElnea and Niall Mackenzie, giving them their first chance in the premier class.

When Suzuki returned with a new V4 in 1987, the English team was ready to continue the quest. Schwantz was signed full time from 1988, and he took the first of his 25 wins at the opening round in Japan. In 1993, the Texan won the World Championship.

In the next phase, Kenny Roberts Jr repeated the feat in 2000.

Taylor retired at the end of 2004, returning briefly to head the short-lived Huawei Moto3 team, figure-headed by long-standing ally John Surtees.

Thereafter, Taylor enjoyed the life of a retired gentleman on the rural Kent/Sussex border, indulging in country pursuits, including clay-pigeon shooting, at which he was an expert.

He died after a long illness on 30th January, 2024.

Michael Scott

Above: Girl power – Sara Sanchez (64) leads the WorldWCR race at Estoril in October.
Photo: Gold & Goose

welcomed the appointment, since Crafar is still an active rider and racing instructor with more recent track experience, and he is expected to offer increased transparency. But not leniency: he has promised to expand the focus on on-track loitering to include Moto2 and MotoGP.

DORNA and the FIM expanded motorcycle racing in new ways during 2024, perhaps most notably with the first steps of the new female-only series, which ran through six races alongside WorldSBK as a full world championship, under the title Women's Circuit Racing (WorldWCR).

It was a one-make series, à la Red Bull Rookies Cup, with teams allowed to make set-up adjustments to the race-kitted 690cc Yamaha YZF-R7 motorcycles supplied and maintained by the organisers.

The first year went to seasoned Spanish competitors with wide-ranging prior experience, and the different levels of ability can be gauged by a qualifying regulation that requires only 110 per cent of the fastest lap time, as against 107 per cent for other classes. But the series made a promising start, and surely will improve to become more competitive and popular.

Another innovation was the biennial FIM Intercontinental Games, open to eight-rider international teams competing in Supersport and Supersport 300 classes, also on Yamahas provided by the organisers. Forty-eight riders from 19 countries were due to participate at Jerez over the last weekend in November. An interesting experiment.

FINALLY, despite vastly improved rider safety equipment and rigorously homologated circuits, any season without serious injury earns a sigh of relief. Motorcycle racing is intrinsically dangerous.

Efforts to improve safety have born fruit, with mandatory rider-suit airbags a major contributor.

It might be impossible to mitigate the danger of collisions between motorcycles and fallen riders, but there remains at least one other notable blind spot, concerning head injuries, and in particular concussion and its cumulative effects.

In rugby, players wear gum-shields with impact monitors to keep an official check on this danger. It is high time something similar was introduced to MotoGP.

THE STATE OF RACING

LIBERTY MEDIA: IS MOTOGP'S FUTURE IN SAFE HANDS?

On 1st April, 2024, it was announced that Dorna would be bought by F1 owners Liberty Media. What does that mean for the premier motorcycle racing series? DARIO DE WET unpicks the details...

Above: One-make series? Ducati domination will need addressing to broaden the appeal to entrants, fans and sponsors.
Photo: Ducati Corse

Top right: Fabio Quartararo signs for his eager fans at Le Mans, but who outside the sport really knows anything about the 2021 world champion?

Above centre right: Crashes sell clips. Dorna restrict access to crash footage (this is Dani Pedrosa in Spain). Liberty are expected to free it up.

Above right: Carmelo Ezpeleta with post-Rossi talisman Marc Marquez.
Photos: Gold & Goose

Right: The seat of power. Liberty's headquarters in Englewood, Colorado.
Photo: Liberty Media

IN 2024, a seismic shift occurred in the MotoGP World Championship's history, as Bridgepoint Group's 18-year tenure as majority owner came to an end with the sale of Dorna Sports to Liberty Media.

This monumental acquisition promises to reshape MotoGP's future, sparking intense anticipation and concern among its dedicated fanbase. With Liberty poised to bring its entertainment and media expertise to the global stage of motorcycle racing, 2025 will begin a new era – one that could redefine MotoGP's trajectory in thrilling and unforeseen ways.

Is this the dawn of unparalleled opportunity, or a departure from tradition as fans fear? Let's dive into the transformative impact ahead.

It's no secret that MotoGP has been in desperate need of new shareholders. While Formula One has soared to new heights on the global stage, MotoGP has struggled to capture the same momentum, resulting in a widening gap in appeal and reach. An over-reliance on now-retired, nine-times world champion Valentino Rossi has left the championship in dire need of sustained media attention. Marc Marquez has served as a convenient stopgap for Dorna, but a series of injuries and absences from the championship has proved to be a significant setback in recent years. To put it mildly, there has been an outright disregard for storytelling, succession planning, and maximising entertainment value through effective marketing and promotion.

UNTAPPED POTENTIAL

Enter Liberty Media. There is no denying that the US-based company has fundamentally transformed Formula One from an elitist, European-centric sport into a globally celebrated entertainment powerhouse. Its takeover injected fresh blood into Bernie Ecclestone's brainchild, maximising brand exposure through its *Drive to Survive* Netflix partnership, and kickstarting a new wave of global fan engagement and increased intergenerational spectatorship. Purists might argue that commercialising the sport detracts from its exclusivity, but at the same time, it has brought a flurry of new sponsorship opportunities, an expanded race calendar across the United States and the Middle East, and a much-needed cash injection into the four-wheeled ecosystem for drivers, teams and others.

Will Liberty's involvement be good for MotoGP and the world of motorcycle racing? Yes. This is a delicate situation, however, and a thoughtful approach is certainly required. Unquestionably, MotoGP offers an unrivalled racing product, a sophisticated ecosystem and an impressive talent pipeline, but the task will not be as simple as applying a copy-and-paste Formula One strategy.

What we can all agree on is that MotoGP has a passionate global fanbase, and Bridgepoint's Dorna has poorly executed the maximisation of the United States and South American markets. Instead, they have focused on emerging

market economies and leading motorcycle markets, and while this diversification is welcomed, it is not enough.

For all of Dorna's marketing and promotional shortcomings, Liberty is the answer. The proof lies in their track record, having brought much-needed entertainment value through a media strategy that emphasises storytelling in the digital era.

Until now, Dorna has not allowed its intellectual property (IP) to be freely shared online outside official channels, which has hurt the sport. For example, a knee-down cornering spectacle or a sensational crash presents stellar opportunities for viral online debate, but unless these are shared via Dorna affiliates, content is removed. Should fans be allowed to share as much content as possible? Liberty understands that content creation and media engagement are key to attracting younger, more diversified audiences, and it is almost certain that they will immediately overhaul this IP restriction.

This alone opens up the spectacle of MotoGP. In the world of big tech, more eyeballs mean more opportunity. Enter Silicon Valley and global technology players.

One of the biggest advantages to the sport is that Liberty's media-centric strategy should usher in a new wave of sponsors – moving away from an over-reliance on energy-drink brands and bringing a welcome change that could restore the sport to the heydays of tobacco money. The domino effect could fundamentally reshape motorcycle racing by introducing fresh investment into the sport, resulting in fully-subscribed, high-quality grids supported by diversified talent pools. This shift could also help move the sport away from predatory 'pay-to-play' practices, where riders are forced to scrape together sponsorship money to secure sub-par rides, in the hope of being noticed by established teams.

A HISTORY OF OWNERSHIP

How did we get to this point? To understand this, it's important to look at the history of MotoGP's ownership and what this has meant for the championship over the years.

In the late 1980s, Banco Banesto, a major Spanish bank, founded Dorna Promoción del Deporte (now Dorna Sports) to manage its sports-related ventures. The first of these was the acquisition of the FIM Road Racing World Championship Grand Prix (now MotoGP). Carmelo Ezpeleta became CEO of Dorna in 1994 after an extensive career in motorsports management, particularly in Formula One and MotoGP in Spain during the 1980s. This acquisition, combined with Ezpeleta's expertise, led to the emergence of the MotoGP World Championship that we have all come to love.

CVC Capital Partners

In 1998, Banco Banesto sold Dorna Sports to CVC Capital Partners for US$86 million. The move made strategic and financial sense for Banesto, as it shifted its focus to banking entities rather than sports promotion, while helping to reduce Dorna's debt burden. CVC was identified as the best-placed private equity group to enhance MotoGP's global reputation – something that had stagnated under Banco Banesto's ownership.

You might be wondering why a private equity group would have wanted to acquire MotoGP in the first place. There were four main factors behind this decision:

- Growth potential: MotoGP was (and still is) an emerging sport with room for growth.
- Portfolio diversification: Reduces portfolio risk and encourages portfolio synergies.
- Commercial rights and branding: Broadcasting and sponsorship deals.
- Management expertise: They trusted Carmelo Ezpeleta to continue running the business.

Bridgepoint Group

Fast forward to 2006, which marked the next monumental shift in the history of Dorna Sports' ownership. That year, CVC sold its stake to Bridgepoint for approximately US$2.8 billion, representing around a 33-fold increase on their initial investment of US$86 million in 1998, with Carmelo Ezpeleta continuing to lead the company. Interestingly, the sale was influenced by anti-trust concerns from European regulators due to CVC's dual ownership of both Dorna Sports and Formula One. This became a focal point in the 2024 Liberty Media deal.

Six years later, in 2012, Bridgepoint decided to sell 39 per cent of its stake in Dorna Sports to the Canada Pension Plan Investment Board (CPPIB) for US$518 million. The transaction proved mutually beneficial: Bridgepoint was looking for a long-term strategic partner, while CPPIB wanted to invest in premier global sports franchises. This allowed Bridgepoint to realise some of its investment gains while still retaining significant control over Dorna.

In 2013, Bridgepoint transferred the remaining stake in Dorna Sports to itself, by moving it to a newer flagship fund, Bridgepoint Europe IV. The original fund had reached its seven-year close, but Bridgepoint believed that there was untapped value in Dorna. This ownership transfer allowed them to maintain control while benefiting from fresh capital under the new fund, focused on high-value investments in growth sectors like sports and entertainment.

Above: Trackhouse Racing is the new American team in MotoGP, but still there is no American rider.

Top left: There were record crowds in 2024, but it's sponsorship that pays the bills.

Above right: Feel the noise. The thunder of MotoGP bikes at close quarters has an irresistible appeal to fans. And to Liberty, who have already raised the profile of Formula 1.
Photos: Gold & Goose

Right: Carmelo Ezpeleta continues to be hands-on as Dorna CEO.

Far right, top: Outgoing Liberty president Greg Maffei, who instigated the purchase before announcing his departure at the end of 2024.

Far right, bottom: Liberty founder John C. Malone. The 83-year-old will act as interim CEO.
Photos: Liberty Media

IT'S A DEAL

Despite a higher bid from Ari Emanuel's TKO Group Holdings – parent company of both WWE (World Wrestling Entertainment) and UFC (Ultimate Fighting Championship) – offering US$200 million more, Bridgepoint agreed to sell Dorna Sports to Liberty Media in a deal valued at US$4 billion.

The deal was announced on 1st April, 2024, but this was no April Fool's joke. Liberty would acquire 86 per cent of MotoGP, with the existing Dorna management remaining in place, but foregoing seven per cent of their pre-transaction ownership, resulting in a cumulative 14 per cent pro-forma ownership stake.

The deal was structured as a straight equity consideration, comprising:

- 65 per cent cash – funded with a mix of cash and debt.
- 21 per cent FWONK (Formula One Group) common non-voting stock – with an option for Liberty to pay with cash instead.
- The existing US$1 billion MotoGP debt balance remaining outstanding.

Liberty chose to pay cash rather than use FWONK stock, while still issuing US$949 million in non-voting Formula One shares at a four per cent discount to market price. Additionally, CEO Greg Maffei – due to step down by the end of 2024 – confirmed that all necessary transactions to fund the planned acquisition of Dorna Sports had been completed. He would be succeeded by chairman John Malone, who would serve as interim CEO of Liberty Media.

AND SO IT BEGINS...

Liberty's first move was the introduction of the all-new MotoGP brand identity after the final round of the 2024 championship, with a strong focus on fan engagement around the revamped MotoGP Awards ceremony. While there wasn't much new information when MOTOCOURSE went to press, the real concern was the potential disallowance of the deal by the European Competition Commission – the issue that had plagued CVC in 2006.

Renewed concerns about a potential breach of European competition laws had emerged, and while the landscape had shifted, it remained uncertain that the transaction would be approved. What is undeniable, however, is that a pivotal moment is on the horizon for motorcycle racing – inevitably, MotoGP will come under new ownership, whether by Liberty Media or some other entity.

The question remains. Is the future of this iconic sport in safe hands? The potential for transformation is clear, but the true measure of success lies in how a new owner navigates the challenges ahead. With the right vision and execution, MotoGP could rise to become a global leader in motorsports. Only time will tell if this ambitious vision is realised.

The stakes are high, and the world is watching.

THE RETURN OF THE MASTER

Marc Marquez's recovery from career meltdown was the highlight of 2024. How did he do it? NEIL MORRISON spoke to those closest to him – team-mates, family, technicians and managers – to get the inside story...

Above: The thousand-day wait for his 60th MotoGP win ended in Aragon. The fans had remained faithful.
Photo: Gresini Racing

Above right, from top: The 2021 return – shattered in Portugal in his first race back; victorious two months later at the Sachsenring; and celebrating a second win with second-placed team-mate Pol Espargaro and HRC's Shinichi Kokubu at Misano.

Right: Never give up. Marquez put in the hard yards to regain the strength in his right arm.
Photos: Repsl Honda

NOTHING grabs the attention quite like a comeback story. And at the close of 2024, a year when he was back to approaching his very best, there's reason to state that Marc Marquez's recovery from a number of career-threatening injuries can stand among those mustered by the sport's toughest characters.

The respective returns of Barry Sheene and Mick Doohan to the pinnacle of grand prix racing are rightly lauded and celebrated, not just for a gritty resilience to pain, but also their sheer bloody-minded refusal to give in. The Briton claimed a maiden 500cc title just 17 months on from a horrific 175mph smash at Daytona, while Doohan was triumphant two years and one month on from suffering a grisly tibia break in June, 1992, which at one point led to his legs being sewn together to recover circulation.

And while Marquez didn't lift the championship trophy in 2024, the travails he faced since that fateful summer afternoon outside Jerez in July, 2020, are as painful as those his predecessors endured – and arguably more prolonged.

For four years, Marquez lived a personal hell. The comeback from one injury was curtailed by another. He returned only to find his strength and mobility greatly diminished, and the threat to his career was never far away. As former team-mate Pol Espargaro spelled out, "At one stage, he was risk-ing losing the arm. It wasn't ready, and one more crash on it and it'd be super, super critical."

Such complications coincided with Honda's worst spell in grand prix racing since the late 1970s. When the worst of the injuries were behind him, there was the unwelcome sight of Marquez struggling to make the top six.

In many ways, 2024 was vindication of his seismic decision to quit MotoGP's most successful manufacturer for Gresini Ducati in October, 2023. And while he didn't quite match Jorge Martin or Pecco Bagnaia through the year, his 21 podiums (including sprints), three grand prix wins and third in the championship achieved on a year-old machine would have caused some rivals to fear what's coming next.

Now Marquez finds himself in Ducati's factory team for 2025, where many are tipping him to complete the comeback circle. This is how he got there.

It's no exaggeration to say that Marquez's career was on the rocks. The humerus bone in his right arm, which he had broken in a dramatic high-side at Jerez, was plated two days after the 2020 Spanish GP. And he was back on the bike four days later. Yet it soon became clear that all was not well. Subsequently, the plate snapped when he was opening a patio door, sending him back under the knife for a replacement 13 days from the first op. It became worse. A third intervention

was needed that December, when a bone was grafted from his hip to aid healing. Doctors soon discovered that it was infected, however, requiring further hospital time.

Publicly, at least, Marquez was philosophical about the decision to attempt to ride in the Andalusian GP six days after the initial break. "In the end, it was a decision of everybody," he said at the beginning of 2021. "The last decision is mine. When me, Honda and my team received a good feeling from the doctors, I felt I was able to try. But what I felt was not what my body needed." When eventually he returned to the track in April, 2021, he was rarely comfortable.

It wasn't all doom and gloom during that period, however. Marquez won three races in 2021 and came seventh overall – not bad, considering that he had finished only ten of 18 races. Yet his upper arm had healed in such a way that the bone was rotated at 34 degrees below the break. "I feel a big limitation," he said in June, 2022. "A lot of pain. No power. I can't ride like I want." It was decided that a fourth operation was needed, and doctors in Rochester, USA, carried out a humeral osteotomy to rotate the bone back by "approximately 30 degrees."

How had he been even competing before that, let alone winning? "People are not aware of what it means to live with a humeral and circumoral rotation as big as Marc had," said Carlos Garcia, Marquez's physio at that time. "With 34 degrees of rotation, day-to-day tasks at home are complicated. So imagine what it's like on a MotoGP bike. With his talent and with his work, Marc found a way to get a little levitation to be able to get to Sunday. For me, it's something that escapes logic and reasoning."

In his absence – Marquez raced at only 50 per cent of the 52 GPs from 2020 to 2022 – Honda had not only lost his leadership, but also there was a feeling that the team's issues would be resolved once the six-times premier-class champ returned. "We had Marc covering the weakness of the bike," said LCR Honda technical director Christophe Bourguignon. "Probably, HRC was waiting too much on him to find his good moment and thinking all would be beautiful when he did."

As the European manufacturers aggressively sought gains in new areas of development for MotoGP – namely aerodynamics, start and ride-height devices – their Japanese counterparts stood still. Race times fell by 20–30 seconds over the space of two years as Ducati fine-tuned an already remarkably complex package. Unable to marshal its vast resources and expertise in a coherent direction, Honda went from the benchmark to also-rans – a further challenge to Marquez's vast depths of self-belief.

"What was missing was co-ordination between all parties," explained Espargaro, Marquez's team-mate at Repsol Honda in 2021 and 2022. "Honda has amazing muscle, but this is the power of the Europeans. They're so small, they're so in control of what they do, and how they invest all their resources and move forward.

"Instead of bringing new, small parts to move the package forward, they were bringing completely new concepts. At one stage, I realised they were not understanding the problems. MotoGP reached a level now where everything is so on the limit and tough, you have to adjust everything little by little. Now it's something Honda is doing. But I think it was a matter or co-ordination and organisation."

When Marc was riding, there was the unfamiliar sight of him contesting sixth, seventh and eighth place. "He was struggling," said Espargaro. "It's not just about the pain. It's about all the muscles. They need to come back. He was dropping a lot the rhythm in the last laps. I remember I was fighting against him in Qatar [2022] and I beat him. I knew he was fast there, but it was not the Marc I wanted. Somehow, he knew to reach that level, he needed to risk so much, and his physical condition was so critical, he was not able to do it."

The stats bear this out. Marquez was MotoGP's top crasher in 2021 (22) and 2023 (29). Only 18 in 2022 couldn't

THE RETURN OF THE MASTER 27

Above: Celebrating Ducati victory number two in Misano.

Top right: A kiss for Gresini team owner Nadia Padovani in Australia.

Top centre right: The first 2024 win, in Aragon.
Photos: Gresini Racing

Top far right: Marc and crew chief Frankie Carchedi gelled from the beginning.
Photo: Gold & Goose

Above right: Bagnaia was beaten fair and square in Misano.
Photo: Gresini Racing

Right: Red shift. Marquez starts his new life in the Ducati factory team at the post-season test in Valencia. Rivals beware.
Photo: Gold & Goose

be considered low, as he competed in just 12 rounds. That brought further injuries. After missing the final two races of 2021 due to diplopia, which causes double vision, from a training accident, his terrifying warm-up crash in Indonesia in 2022 ruled him out of two further races with the same issue – another stress to add to the dramas he was facing with his arm. And all to score his worst championship finishes (seventh in 2021, 13th in 2022, 14th in 2023) since his days riding 125s.

"Marc saw he was crashing way too much," said Espargaro. "The bike wasn't ready to do the job. He kept pushing, but got injured a couple of times. He realised to get back to the top, he needed to risk too much, which wasn't possible any more."

"The toughest decision of my career," Marquez called his departure from Honda. But by the second half of 2023, it was becoming clear that there was no other option. Despite its lead rider's repeated threats to leave, the Japanese giant was slipping further from the front, often appearing to be without direction.

That year's German GP was a particular nadir. Fully expected to continue a winning run at the Sachsenring that stretched back to 2010, Marquez crashed five times, the last of which ruled him out of the race. That he gave his RC213V the middle finger after a scary moment on Friday afternoon was telling. HRC's decision to replace outgoing technical director Shinichi Kokubu internally suggested that improvements wouldn't arrive at the necessary speed. And another underwhelming test at Misano in September appeared to push the Catalan towards a move that would have been unthinkable previously.

Even though it was expected that eventually an 11-year stint with Honda would come to an end, the news was no less shocking when it arrived. Gresini, Ducati's third satellite team, was a better prospect than the group that had yielded all of his six world titles and 59 previous wins. "Sometimes, you need to go out of your comfort zone, and my comfort zone was Honda," he explained. "It's been a long time, I've been suffering a lot. I did a change to enjoy racing again. If not, there was no meaning for me to continue."

Marquez saw the potential of the satellite package after a first contact in Valencia, that November. "In that test, I realised that we would have our opportunities," he said. It was only then "I think, when Marc faced riding in optimal physical condition," said Garcia. And he was fully up to speed by the second round, no mean feat considering that he had the ways of a new bike and team to learn, with the exception of his tyre and fuel technician, Javi Oritz, who followed him from Honda.

As he saw his name towards the front, that happiness returned. "That was straight away," said his new crew chief, Frankie Carchedi, speaking of his rider's new-found comfort. "In the first race, he was fourth in the GP. We were clearly not too far straight away, but it was then about ironing out the details."

As the speed returned on track, so did the happiness off it. "When you have tough moments at work, you don't lose the motivation, but it's harder to be smiling all day," said brother Alex of Marc's mood change in 2024. "When everything is going in the right direction, you're happier. That's changed. Maybe the Marc from 2019 has come back in terms of character. It's super-nice to see."

While Ducati's GP23 was no match for Martin and Bagnaia's GP24s, Marquez and Carchedi discovered a solid base in Austria: "We went in one direction with the set-up from Red Bull Ring, when we found something for his style, when he felt comfortable straight away." From there, three wins and a sprint followed, including a crucial first GP victory in 1,043 days in Aragon. Even if he didn't have enough to fight for the title, he often repeated, "I've achieved all of my targets for this year," in ending his losing streak and finding the joy once more.

Later, he reflected on how Gresini's small, familiar outfit had offered the environment in which to regain his confidence. "I found the perfect atmosphere to be reborn, to feel again that I'm competitive," he said at the season finale. "And I found the perfect family, the perfect atmosphere, with my brother as a team-mate."

A few details from 2024 that stand out. Those who have access to the eight-times champion's data have stated that he can maintain the front tyre temperature at around 20 degrees cooler than his rivals. Another startling note: after his Phillip Island success, when he reeled in eventual champ Jorge Martin in the closing laps, his team was stunned to find that he still had roughly half of his rear tyre left. He also demonstrated that his cunning was alive and well, edging Martin out of Ducati by refusing the opportunity to switch to Pramac and insisting on the factory team instead. Does this all point to trouble on the horizon for the rest of MotoGP in 2025?

Espargaro has no doubt: "Marc has shown he can face those guys with an older and, in theory, worse bike. Next year, Marc can be a potential world champion. I'd bet my money on that for sure." And Carchedi agrees: "He's going to have a two-spec upgrade. I'd be worried if I was the others!"

So, after four operations, two serious eye injuries, 95 crashes and a major manufacturer switch in the past five years, how has Marquez done it? Anyone who's crossed him attests to a mental toughness that even Sheene and Doohan would have applauded.

"His mental side is like something I've never, ever seen," said Carchedi. Riders he'd worked with previously "weren't even close. We've had a few occasions we've crashed both bikes in qualifying, and in the race, it's like nothing happened… phenomenal." Former team manager Alberto Puig agrees: "It's been a real nightmare for this guy. But his comeback didn't surprise me at all. He's a really special person with clear determination. He never gave up."

THE RETURN OF THE MASTER   29

TECHNICAL ESSAY
A NEW MOTOGP FOR 2027

Less engine, less fuel and less aero. What will the new 2027 regulations mean for MotoGP racing? And why does it matter? KEVIN CAMERON analyses the details and concludes that racing really does improve the breed...

Above: MotoGP bikes will undergo many changes for 2027, aimed at reducing speeds. But will less turn out to be more?
Photo: Gresini Racing

Above right: Will the bikes look different? Dorna's imagined 2027 show bike illustrates forthcoming changes: engine capacity reduced, engine allocation cut.
Photos: MotoGP

Right: Too fast? Brad Binder clocked a top speed of 227mph in 2023.
Photo: Gold & Goose

DORNA tell us that the motivation for the new formula – most obvious of which is a 15 per cent reduction in displacement from the present 1000cc to 850cc – is to moderate performance just a bit.

This is understandable. At Mugello in 2023, Brad Binder's KTM reached 366km/h (227mph), and at recent GPs, riders have been saying that even the biggest carbon front brake discs – 355mm in diameter – are becoming marginal. At Motegi, Marc Marquez's discs glowed bright red *in daylight*.

Not relevant to top speed, but a rising concern for more than a decade is that the steady rise in tyre grip is now making it possible in corners for riders to drag their entire upper arm on the track (Jorge Martin at Motegi). The higher the corner speed, the wider the gravel trap required for a safe stop after a fall. Where is such real estate to come from?

The manner in which the 2027 displacement reduction is made tells us more about Dorna's intentions. For 2007–11, MotoGP displacement was cut from the original 2002 990cc to 800. The result was that at the first pre-2007 test, run after the season-ending Valencia race, the 800s were already competitive with the 990s, and an expensive rpm race resulted. When the 2007 formula was replaced by 1000cc for 2012, bore size was limited to 81mm, mandating a minimum stroke of 48.5mm.

The physical limit to rpm is peak piston acceleration, as pistons stop and start again at the ends of each stroke. In the 1950s, peak piston acceleration of Britain's classic Manx Norton singles was around 4,000 g. Today, if rumours of MotoGP engines touching 20,000rpm can be believed, peak piston acceleration would be close to 11,000 g. This acceleration stresses the aluminium from which pistons are made, causing cumulative damage that eventually produces cracking (usually around the piston-pin bosses).

For the new 2027 formula, bore size is specified at 75mm, setting a minimum stroke of 48mm – very close to the existing 48.5. Notionally, this will hold rpm at the present level.

In the past, racing formulae reflected the nature of the motorcycle industry. The 1949 FIM GP formula of 125, 250, 350, 500 and sidecar was based on the existence at that time of many small manufacturers. The first MotoGP formula of 2002 was created in a world of larger manufacturers, each building a full range of motorcycles. Moto3 and Moto2 are training classes, steps leading to MotoGP. The choice of 990cc was probably influenced by the strong popularity at that time of litre-sized production bikes, and also by the need to ensure that the new four-stroke class was faster than the 500cc two-strokes it replaced.

Today, sportbikes have lost popularity (giant insurance bills!) and the most active production category covers less expensive middleweights (650–850cc), parallel twins.

Engine rpm races occur because the variables determining horsepower are displacement, stroke-averaged net combustion pressure and rpm. Since displacement is set by rule and combustion pressure in unsupercharged engines is limited by atmospheric pressure, raising rpm is the most rewarding path to higher power. At any given rpm, piston acceleration is proportional to stroke, so to keep pistons from excessive stress, shorter strokes and higher rpm are partners.

Some have spoken of a possible alignment of the new MotoGP formula with exhaust emissions limits, such as Euro 5. For years, production engines were given bigger bores and shorter strokes. Now that trend is reversed. Bores are becoming smaller and strokes shorter. The reason is that unburned hydrocarbons can hide in piston ring crevice volumes. The shorter the total length of an engine's top piston rings (if they were straightened out and placed end to end), the lower the emissions. A first step was a switch from four cylinders to two; the next was to reduce bore and increase stroke. MotoGP's bore reduction from 81 to 75mm aligns with this trend.

Another rule further discourages teams from seeking higher revs. At present, each rider is allotted seven engines per season (there were 20 events in 2024), but that will drop to six in 2027. Fewer engines requires pistons to survive more stress cycles. That will keep engineers busy in just making their engines finish all the races, not pushing revs up.

Why not just impose adjustable rev limits as in World Superbike? The answer here is partly linked to history. Honda engineer Shuhei Nakamoto, during his time as that company's MotoGP tech manager, let it be known that if rev limits were imposed, Honda would withdraw from the series.

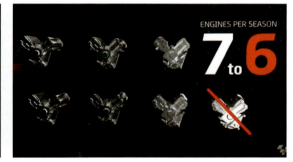

Above: Practice makes perfect – Yamaha and Ducatis hunkered down for practice starts at Misano.
Photo: Gold & Goose

Top right: Fairing nose will be 50mm further back in 2027. Original rules had it another 50mm further back, in line with the front axle.
Photo: MotoGP

Above, right and far right: Fairing design was frozen, with limited updates, in 2024 – but seat aero was free. Honda and KTM had similar solutions, among other ideas.

Right: Bastianini moves out of Marquez's slipstream in search of cooler air.
Photos: Gold & Goose

Corrado Cechinelli, Dorna's director of technology, has said that rev limits are contrary to the spirit of GP racing, which is to explore the limits of performance rather than to set them.

Variable-ride-height (VRH) systems will be banned from 2027, on the basis that once all teams have workable systems, it offers no advantage. On rider command, a VRH bike lowers itself to resemble a dragster, enabling faster acceleration. For turning, the system raises the bike for corner clearance.

There is talk of spectator dissatisfaction. Often seen in print is "Not enough passing"; another grouch is dislike of the less traditional appearance of MotoGP bikes, which now carry multiple small downforce airfoils, spoons, ducts and even fairing sides shaped to form downforce-producing venturis when close to the track surface during turning.

When considering passing, we must remember that this requires the rider to plan a pass that will be sufficiently faster or more clever than the opponent to make the risk of moving off the clean racing line worth taking. Yet Dorna have worked relentlessly and successfully to achieve both rider and equipment parity to avoid 'Doohan's Syndrome' – one superior rider/machine combination dominating the results. By reducing skill and performance differences, this in itself makes passing less likely. All riders in MotoGP are promoted through the Moto3 and Moto2 classes, and all ride factory-engineered bikes of closely equal specification.

A frequently mentioned cause of too little passing is that riders might encounter unusual turbulence from the aero devices on an opponent's bike, sufficient in some cases to affect control. Another hazard – more frequently mentioned by riders – is the hot air streaming back from the exhaust, and from water and oil radiators of a bike ahead. Some have said that they avoid being closer than 0.5 of a second while directly behind a bike because the hot slipstream can push front tyre pressure and temperature high enough to make front wheel locking occur. This is why, so often at present, races are won by taking the lead either off the start or on the first lap, the cool air up front making it easier to preserve tyre grip through to the last lap. There are certainly exceptions to this, such as when a top rider qualifies poorly, yet is able to come through the field to a podium finish. Enjoy the passing this requires!

No rule banning aero downforce devices has been made, but measures to reduce their size are in the 2027 formula. The imaginary vertical plane, parallel with the front axle, behind which all bodywork must be located, will move back 50mm from its present position, 100mm ahead of the front axle (the original FIM rule placed this vertical plane through the centreline of the front axle). In addition, the minimum width of the upper fairing has been narrowed by 50mm.

At present, the rider's seatback is a garden of small airfoils, which are unregulated, but from 2027, seatback aero will be subject to tech approval.

Bear in mind that aero devices produce drag as well as lift – the familiar lift-over-drag or L/D ratio. The most powerful of the present 1,000cc MotoGP engines have power to spare for this, but the 15 per cent power reduction expected from the 2027 engines (i.e., 255hp rather than the 300hp informally estimated) will offer less to drive aero.

Why not just ban aero devices, as some traditionalists propose? There is a real safety issue in this respect. At very high speeds, aero drag considerably reduces front wheel load. Especially at undulating tracks like CoTA in the USA, this reduces control, evidenced by a 'floaty' feeling. Some downforce is desirable to counter this.

At present, 40 per cent of any fuel used in MotoGP engines must be of sustainable origin (i.e., not derived from fossil precursors such as natural gas, petroleum or coal). From 2027, that rises to 100 per cent. There are short-term and longer-term paths to this goal. In the short term, alcohol from corn fermentation is chemically reformable into the required variety of hydrocarbons. This has a limited future and greenwashing value because it requires the burning of food that someone might like to eat. At present, 40 per cent of the US corn crop is consumed in this way.

In the longer term, liquid hydrocarbon fuels will be synthesised in large volumes for applications that cannot be electrified – notably for long-range commercial and military

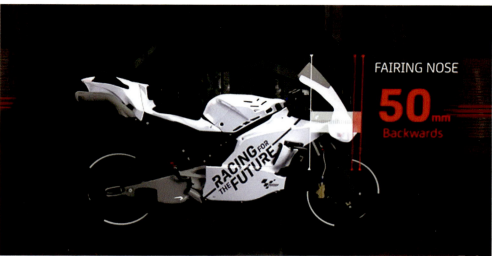

FAIRING NOSE
50mm Backwards

Above: KTM complexity. Engineers strive to find advantage within regulations that require a high degree of conformity.
Photo: Gold & Goose

Right: From 2027, fuel for all classes will be fully sustainable, with zero fossil content.

Centre right: Fuel allowance will be reduced for both race formats.
Photos: MotoGP

Facing page:
Top, left and right: Ducati and KTM carbon discs at rest. At some tracks, they can be seen glowing bright red in full daylight.
Photos: Gold & Goose

Above right: Petronas supplied 40-per cent non-fossil fuel for Moto2 and Moto3.
Photo: Petronas

Above far right: Natural shrinkage – the frontal area of the Aprilia has narrowed since it was introduced in 2017.
Photo: Aprilia Racing

Right: Honda, like Yamaha, had the benefit of full concessions in 2024 to help them regain momentum. The concession system will be given a fresh start for 2027.
Photo: Gold & Goose

aviation. European planning calls for the employment of a notional future surplus of renewable electric power (from wind, solar, etc) to drive the synthesis of 'carbon net zero' liquid hydrocarbon fuels.

Raw materials are to be carbon, separated from atmospheric carbon dioxide, and 'green' hydrogen (hydrogen separated from water by electrolysis, using electricity from renewable sources only). Both of these processes require power because they are effectively 'unburning' the products of hydrocarbon fuel combustion. Significant amounts of excess renewable electric power are forecast to become available circa 2050. As the production of such synthetic fuels increases, petroleum-based fuels will be displaced from that market. Presently available synthetics are significantly more expensive than petroleum-based equivalents.

The fuel allowance for GPs will be cut from the present 22 litres to 20 (a nine per cent reduction) with 11 litres for the Saturday sprint races. With engine displacement cut by 15 per cent, this provides some extra fuel on a per-displacement basis. That is needed, for in some races in 2024, engines ran out of fuel on the cool-down lap, and even before.

We know that fuel restrictions are necessary to show that Dorna are a responsible organisation, mindful of the need to limit climate change. It is ironic to recall that when, in the mid-1970s, the US AMA shortened the Daytona 200-mile road race to 180 miles for similar reasons (saving about 70 gallons of fuel in the race) that Dutch race fans chartered a Boeing 747 airliner to fly them to and from Daytona – a total of 19 hours flying time, consuming 475,000lb of fuel.

Minimum weight will be reduced by 4kg (8.8lb) and the suite of alternative transmission ratios cut to 16. (It used to be normal to carry five alternate ratios for each transmission speed, to best match engine torque curve to corner speeds on particular tracks.) In addition, four alternate primary ratios are permitted. Such alternates exist in GP racing because they make it easier to provide the desired drive ratio from engine to rear wheel without changing the angle between the upper chain run and the central plane of the swing-arm. That angle determines the balance between the motorcycle's natural tendency to squat at the rear during acceleration and the opposing lift force generated by chain tension. The desired result is a controlled chassis attitude that prevents rear 'squat' from taking load off the front wheel, causing the bike to run wide as it accelerates off corners.

Teams will be required to share GPS data, and a new system of concessions (to allow under-performing teams temporary opportunities to hasten their return to competitiveness) will begin. Initially, all teams will be ranked 'B', and concessions will be granted at specified intervals to those who are deemed in need of them. Those who excel will lose concessions. This allows underperforming teams to continue engine development, while successful teams must forego it.

Does racing still improve the breed? Since at least the 1920s, respected authorities have claimed that racing's specialised nature has lost all connection with production vehicles for street and highway use.

The facts disagree – if anything, MotoGP and production motorcycles are more closely linked than ever. The first ex-

ample is the rapid adoption of rider-aid electronics (anti-spin, anti-wheelie, virtual powerband, multiple engine modes). Such systems, inspired by NASA's 1960s development of digital flight control for Apollo, began to appear in the two-stroke era of 500 GP. Why? Because the FIM threatened to impose weight minimums and even intake restrictions if the late-1980s rash of high-side crash injuries did not abate. The FIM went as far as imposing a minimum weight, but soon the new electronics significantly smoothed off-corner acceleration. The near-doubled displacement of the MotoGP formula of 2002 drove rapid development of electronic rider aids.

Very quickly, such electronic systems began to appear on production bikes – first those from Europe and later on Japanese machines. As the cost of such technologies dropped with rising volume, added capabilities appeared – such as the use of an inertial measuring unit (IMU – developed from inertial guidance for aerospace) to link throttle opening to lean angle. After some complaints about the rider's control being taken away, motorcyclists began to enjoy the new capabilities.

Another spin-off from MotoGP is the wide, flat torque delivered by today's production bikes.

Developing flatter, less sudden torque was a necessity for MotoGP, as US Superbike builder Rob Muzzy once noted: "The harder you tune a four-stroke, the more it comes to resemble a two-stroke."

A simple four-stroke engine resembles an air pump, but to increase its power, tuners resorted to higher rpm, and to wave effects in the intake and exhaust pipes. Sportbikes (RIP) were given their 'everything-on-top' torque curves by leaving the intake valves open for longer and longer after bottom dead centre; an additional kick could be had by adding valve overlap combined with exhaust wave action. There are drawbacks. Putting all the torque up high with late intake valve closing leaves the bottom and mid-range weak. Top speed is strong, but acceleration suffers. Adding valve overlap with exhaust-wave effects makes torque depend upon whether the wave hitting the cylinder during valve overlap is negative or positive. The more you use the 'good' negative wave, the more you lose just a few hundred revs below peak torque, where a positive wave blows the intake system full of exhaust gas. The result can be such a steep torque rise – from flat spot up to peak – that no human throttle hand can keep the back tyre from breaking traction.

MotoGP has been forced to find another way to make power – shorter valve timing, greater valve lift and faster valve acceleration. That's why MotoGP engines designed by F1 constructors (who have acres of tyre to absorb those torque spikes) have failed.

MotoGP methods for smoothing torque are now transforming the drivability of production bikes, making them much easier to ride well than the peaky sportbikes of the recent past, with their need for frantic gear-changing to stay in a narrow torque zone.

Rather than devolving into specialised sports equipment, MotoGP design is continuing its partnership with production motorcycle design.

TECHNICAL ESSAY 35

INSIDE MOTOGP'S AI REVOLUTION

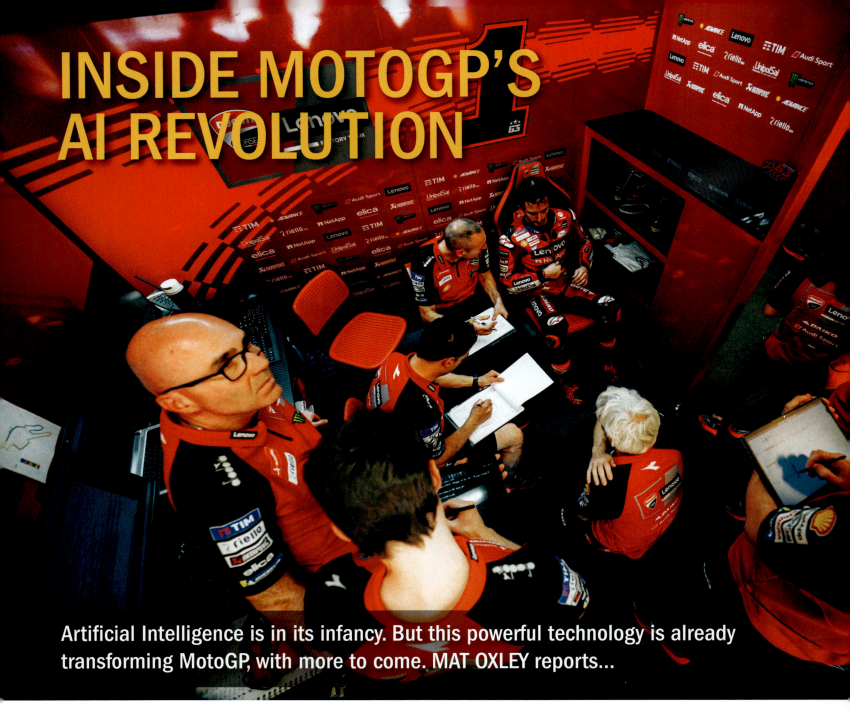

Artificial Intelligence is in its infancy. But this powerful technology is already transforming MotoGP, with more to come. MAT OXLEY reports…

Above: **Debrief at Ducati – Bagnaia watches the boffins.**
Photo: Ducati Corse

Above right, from top: **Riccardo Savin, Ducati vehicle dynamics and design manager; Aprilia's chief engineer, Romano Albesiano; F1 engineer Mike Elliott.**
Photos: Ducati, Gold & Goose & Mercedes

Right: **No rider required. Alternative cornering lines are analysed.**
Photo: Aprilia Racing

MOTOGP is in the grip of a high-tech revolution. Downforce aerodynamics and ride-height adjusters are visible and obvious. This revolution is invisible. It's virtual, taking place on computer servers and data clouds in the garages of MotoGP teams and in manufacturers' race departments.

This is AI, artificial intelligence and its close relations – computer simulations, neural networks, machine learning and geometric deep learning.

These crunch the numbers, and think better, faster and more originally than humans can. And it's only happening now because of developments that permit the vast amount of data required to be captured, analysed and acted upon incredibly quickly. MotoGP bikes record data through approximately 500 channels, from engine, chassis and ECU, plus many more 'calc' channels, which combine different data inputs.

Your smart phone has more computing power than Apollo 11, which took mankind to the moon in 1969. But exactly how much more?

"Eleven-trillion times more," says Michael Russell, who races classic bikes and works at ESI, one of Britain's biggest automotive computer simulations companies. To put that in proportion, "a million seconds ago is eight days ago, a billion seconds is 1980, a trillion seconds is 30,000 years ago, so 11 trillion seconds is 330,000 years ago. So you can imagine how much computing power MotoGP teams have at their disposal."

AI and its relations are vital tools for all five MotoGP manufacturers. These computing technologies are so good that engineers can ask them specific questions to help with bike set-up and development: How do we make the bike quicker through sector two this afternoon? What does the bike need to go faster next season?

There are so many parameters in each motorcycle – engine, chassis, electronics, aero and so on – that even with unlimited practice time, you'd probably never find the optimum combination. But computers can.

Manufacturers produce computer models – also called physical models and virtual models – of their motorcycles and of the race-tracks, created via mathematical models, computer simulations and physical experiments. Running physical and virtual models together gives a simulation of actual riding.

If you play MotoGP on PlayStation, you are operating basic simulations, created through computer modelling. The game employs AI based on neural networks (a type of AI whereby computers process data in a manner inspired by the human brain).

The motorcycle computer model combines multiple elements: engine and parts thereof, suspension and parts thereof, aerodynamics, tyres and on and on and on. A computer model of a race-track consists of a scan of the circuit, including its layout, camber and adhesion, plus weather conditions.

"Most of the modelling in F1 and MotoGP is based on our

knowledge of the physics," says F1 engineer Mike Elliott, who has worked with the Mercedes, McLaren and Renault F1 teams. "We create physical models of the aerodynamics, vehicle handling, the tyres and so on – and that's what we run in our simulations.

"In the case of aerodynamics, the physical model comes from a mixture of measurements taken on the track, the wind tunnel and in CFD [computational fluid dynamics]."

Aprilia, like the other manufacturers in MotoGP, have been working in this direction "for the last seven or eight years, so the level of simulations we can apply to the real world is quite okay," says chief engineer Romano Albesiano. "But the job isn't finished. There are some aspects of the machine we can't yet realistically simulate, but we are working on that.

"We are already applying simulations to aerodynamics, fuel consumption, gear shifting and so on. We mostly use these simulations before each weekend, because by the time the weekend starts, it's time attack, time attack… you can't test anything."

However, computer models can run into problems when modelling the most crucial components of an F1 car or MotoGP bike: the tyres.

"It's difficult to make a physical simulation of the tyres because you don't know all the properties of the materials in the tyre," explains Riccardo Savin, Ducati's MotoGP vehicle dynamics and design manager. "Michelin know, but we don't know all the physical properties, so we build some equations, we put in some data and parameters, trying to estimate the force the tyre gives you, depending on the average temperature, the average speed, the slip ratio and the slide angle."

There's another problem area. "The most difficult part is trying to simulate the rider as a control system that guides the bike. That's very difficult," says Albesiano.

The next big breakthrough in MotoGP simulations will be strain gauges on the handlebars and footpegs, and sensors on the riders, so the engineers know how much force a rider puts into the motorcycle and how their body position affects the loading of the tyres.

In the film industry, actors wearing sensor-bedecked suits are filmed. Then an alternative creature – Gollum in Lord of the Rings, for example – is uploaded to inhabit the actor's movements.

Aprilia use the same technology, and likewise VW Group-owned Ducati, as revealed by Volkswagen Data Lab scien-

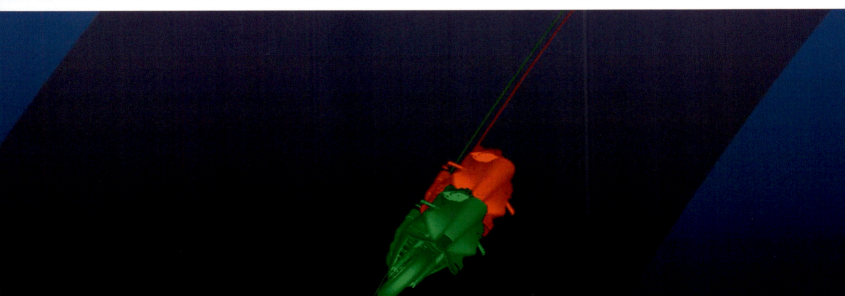

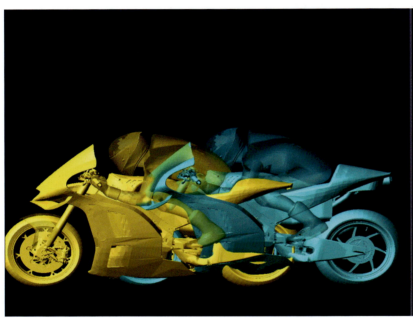
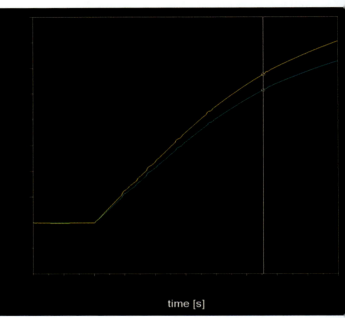

Above: Yellow beats blue. AI-generated graph plots potential acceleration.
Photo: Aprilia Racing

Top: Ducati's Gigi Dall'Igna benefits from a reliance on science.
Photo: Ducati Corse

Top right: Body sensors help to model rider position.
Photo: Aprilia Racing

Top far right: Robin Tuluie, whose simulations company, PhysicsX, works with Ducati.
Photo: Chippy Wood

Above right: Petrucci digitised – sensors plot rider movement and shifting centre of gravity.

Above far right: Screen time for Bagnaia and crew chief Gabarrini. Data tells all.
Photos: Ducati Corse

Right: Aprilia engineers scan the Red Bull Ring.
Photo: Gold & Goose

tist Marc Hilbert in a recent interview: "Ducati approached us with a task that they could not solve with conventional means, to make the rider's movement measurable and to use it to simulate the race.

"These movements are not linear, and are very individual. They cannot be recorded with conventional measurement technology. That's why we were asked whether the problem could be solved with artificial intelligence."

The data comes from mega-high-definition forward-facing seat cameras. Filming the rider's every movement with excellent clarity.

Videos are analysed frame by frame by a deep-learning algorithm, which works out the centre of gravity from each rider's position – torso, arms and legs – at every point of the race-track. This helps engineers to make better decisions and also allows riders to compare their riding position to their fellow Desmosedici riders, potentially improving their riding technique.

Top Formula 1 teams, like Mercedes, do more than a hundred thousand simulation laps before each race weekend, "working out roughly what set-ups we might want to run at the weekend," says Elliott. "We also test new components in the virtual world. Then we'll try those with a driver in the simulator and dial in a set-up they're happy with.

"But of course, that estimate is based on your estimate of what the tyres will do, which will be affected by track conditions, temperature, wind and so on, so you don't know everything before the weekend. So then you run on Friday, download loads of data, which you feed back into your simulations, rerun them and come up with some ideas to try on Saturday."

Recent trends – in F1 and MotoGP – towards reducing testing and practice, and increasing the number of races only increases the need for modelling and simulations. "The more we can do in the virtual world and in simulations, the better," explains Elliott. Hence the constant push to improve the virtual tools and methodologies.

No one in MotoGP will say exactly what they're doing, but Ducati leads the way, followed by KTM, then the rest. The fact that Ducati has eight bikes on the grid is a huge factor, because the more data you have, the more accurate your models and simulations.

Elliott again: "Most of all, it's about the quality and quantity of the data you feed into your systems. If you look at deep-learning systems at companies like Amazon, they're based on having vast amounts of data. Then the 'noise' isn't such an issue, because it gets averaged out. But in our world, and I suspect it's the same in MotoGP, you've got so many variables at play."

Nonetheless, Ducati's MotoGP boss, Gigi Dall'Igna, believes that his engineers are making increasingly better use of these technologies: "AI has increased a lot in the last three years. We also did many things like this in the past, but the results weren't good, because you need to build up the data. Now AI is really important for us to achieve our results."

The technology is so advanced that it can be a faster, cheaper and safer way to go testing – no broken bikes or riders. And it compresses the time scale, cramming a week's work into a few minutes.

Computer lap-time optimisers – you literally ask the computer to work out how to make your bike go faster – are nothing new, but they're much more powerful now, because they use machine learning to offer better answers to questions.

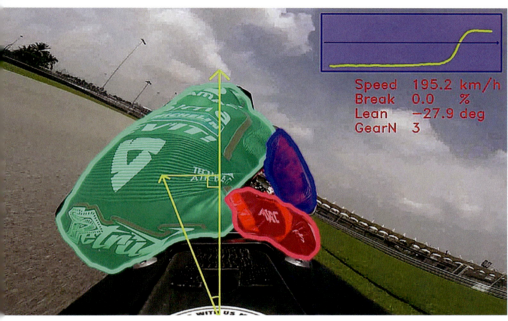

"You may want to adjust your suspension," says Robin Tuluie, founder of simulations company PhysicsX ('Equations for a better world'), who worked with the Renault and Mercedes F1 teams, and now works with Ducati in MotoGP. "Let's say you have ten different springs to try, so you change one at a time in your lap-time optimiser and go stiffer, stiffer, stiffer, and the lap time gets quicker, quicker, quicker. Then you go stiffer again and the lap time gets slower, so you find the optimum.

"Or you can simultaneously try a dozen different experiments with a dozen settings on various parts of the bike, which you would never do in reality."

Geometric deep learning – the newest manifestation of machine learning – takes this technology to the next level, allowing engineers to come up with answers between 5,000 and 10,000 times faster than with programs like CFD. That's a game changer during race weekends and in respect of longer-term development.

Of course, motorcycles are more complicated than cars, because their dynamics are so varied – they do so many things that cars don't. They wheelie, they lean, they lift the rear wheel and so on.

"Also, motorcycle racing is more human related, which makes it difficult to find clear answers, so we are not at the level of F1 in simulations," says Takahiro Sumi, Yamaha Motor Racing president. "That's why the vehicle-dynamics model of a motorcycle is maybe a never ending job! However, we all live according to the same laws of physics, so, even with rider interaction, the same physics are there."

One of AI's main jobs in this revolution is to make sense of the huge amount of data captured by MotoGP bikes, which

Above: Plug me in and watch me go-go. A final electronics check for Bagnaia's Ducati.
Photo: Gold & Goose

Top right: Organic shapes in a generative-design chassis for a BMW S1000RR.
Photo: Hackrod

Above right: KTM's 2024 carbon-fibre chassis – strain gauges can be built in.
Photo: Gold and Goose

Above far right: Bare bones – generative-design Moto3 chassis made by Corbera Sergio at the University of Nebija, Spain.
Photo: University of Nebija

Right: Four of the eight Ducatis on the 2024 grid. Lots of bikes meant lots of data.
Photo: Gold and Goose

would require hundreds or even thousands of computer technicians to hunt through. AI zooms into areas of data where there are interesting connections and ignores others, so it speeds up the process massively.

It's the same away from the race-track. Oncologists use AI to treat cancer because it can recognise patterns within patient data that humans cannot see.

KTM races its RC16 with a carbon-fibre frame, and Aprilia hopes to race its own carbon frame for the first time in the near future. The obvious advantages of carbon fibre are more strength, less weight, and the ability to fine-tune rigidity and flex with different fibres and weaves. But, thanks to the new age of data, carbon-fibre chassis parts offer another benefit, which could revolutionise chassis design. When fabricators lay up chassis components, they can include electrical-conducting plastic fibres, which become strain gauges when you pass a current through them, so engineers can see exactly how the frame is twisting and moving all around the track.

The most important factor in all motorsports is grip, the ultimate determinant of lap speed. Therefore, tyres are the most important parts on a MotoGP bike, and tyre performance the most important area of computer modelling and data analysis.

"In F1, it's pretty much the only question they ask," says Russell. "Everything else is: what compromise do you make to keep the tyres in their operating window? What kind of load do you want on the tyre and how do you achieve that load through changes to geometry, suspension, whatever?

"In F1, the engineers tell drivers stuff like, 'Please turn into Turn Seven three metres later,' and that's probably to make the tyres last longer. You may lose 0.001 seconds in that corner, but the tyres stay in their operating window for three or four laps longer, which is much more important."

Generative design is design and engineering led by AI and machine learning. This allows engineers to look very quickly at what they call total universe solutions, which create radical answers to questions.

"Large, cloud-based computing power allows us to look at all possible answers," explains Russell. "When I worked at Autodesk, we made a generative-design chassis with Hackrod [two high-tech software companies] for BMW in competition with the [limited-edition] HP4 carbon chassis. BMW decided customers weren't ready for something so different, so they released the carbon chassis instead.

"Our design had a lot to do with something called biomimicry. Mother Nature has been showing off for millions of years, leading the way in engineering. Look at any animal bone, and it's not a straight line with a nice chamfer or radius, because it's the best-designed shape for the task in hand with the material in use. Humans only created these angular engineering shapes because they're easier to engineer and make.

"I think this is how Gigi Dall'Igna approaches MotoGP – it allows engineers to look for answers in places they've never looked, because humans don't have the time or skills to do that."

Hand in hand, there is a potential revolution in materials. Aprilia recently started collaborating with Italian company RINA, which works in material sciences, across the aerospace, space and other industries.

Smart materials change when subjected to external stimuli, like heat or electricity. RINA believes that this technology could help Aprilia's RS-GP go faster.

"It's about transfer of technology," explains RINA's Ugo Salerno. "For example, we work with smart metals used in satellites, which change shape when subjected to an electrical charge to open and close solar panels. We were approached by a company that mines quartz. They used explosives, which obviously damage a lot of quartz, so they wanted a better way. We suggested these smart metals, which are inserted into the quartz to break it apart in a less damaging way."

Exactly how will smart metals help the RS-GP? Aprilia and RINA won't say!

2024 MOTOGP · BIKE BY BIKE
CUT THE CHATTER

Enhanced ground effect, on-track vapour trails and extra help for struggling teams, but old-fashioned chatter was the bugbear of 2024. JACK GORST reports...

Above: What the rivals saw. The rear view of Ducati's Desmosedici GP24.
Photo: Ducati Corse

Above centre right: Ducati's new lower exhaust.
Photo: Pramac Racing

Above right: The rear-wheel ground-effect add-on improved grip, but spoiled feeling.
Photo: Jack Gorst

MOTOGP entered the new season with a revised concessions system, aimed at helping those struggling to catch up to benchmark manufacturer Ducati. With open engine development for some, greater testing and wild-card benefits for all except Ducati, it should have been a season when the Bologna Bullets were pulled back towards the pack. If anything, however, it turned out to be the opposite.

Ducati's GP24 wasn't perfect, but it was extremely good. It had made a step forward in its main weakness and bolstered its strengths even more. As the others ran into unforeseen problems in their attempts to catch the Desmos, the season turned into a story of a one-man band, with Ducati hitting all the high notes and providing the backing vocals.

That doesn't mean that the others didn't make progress. KTM, particularly with Acosta, showed that they could fight, and at times, Aprilia similarly played their part, the only other factory to claim a victory all season.

Further behind, Honda and Yamaha were locked in their own war, and with the new concessions on their side, the groundwork to unlock hopeful future riches really began in 2024. The development race was fierce once again, but the most intriguing part was the tactical chess game of mechanical minds behind the scenes.

On track and in action, however, a new grippier rear Michelin was one possible cause for mysterious chatter, which afflicted all teams to a greater or lesser extent.

Left: New aero development added ground-effect side fairings behind the downwash ducts.

Far left: Good, but not enough to go round. Ducati's new chassis was withheld from Bagnaia for the remainder of 2024.
Photos: Jack Gorst

Below: GP24 was the pick of the bunch.
Photo: Ducati Corse

DUCATI DESMOSEDICI GP24

THANKS to the new concession system, Ducati were under more pressure than ever to get their pre-season development right. Not so luckily for their rivals, they did.

Visually, the GP24 was a minor upgrade of the GP23. Ducati changed the profile of the main set of wings, giving them more surface area, but a reduced angle of attack, as well as enlarging their 'dino' wings at the back. The most significant change, though, was combining their two side fairing options from 2023.

Ducati created an extremely clean way to incorporate their downwash ducts into the bulging ground-effect side fairings. It was a best-of-both-worlds idea, the ducts working in a larger range of lean angles and speeds, but not quite creating the same strength of ground effect mid-corner. Back-to-back world champion Pecco Bagnaia was convinced straight away, but 2023 runner-up Jorge Martin took a little more time, admitting that he had to tweak his set-up to really experience the benefit of the greater corner speed.

Ducati also changed their lower exhaust for 2024, but the bigger factor was what it was paired with – their 2024 engine. With their relative restriction under the new concessions, it was paramount that Ducati nailed their engine spec to prevent the troubles that they had encountered in 2022. The 2023 engine had been good, but there was one issue that made it slightly problematic – its engine braking character. This was an issue that had plagued Enea Bastianini, who had suffered from the same things that Bagnaia and Martin had commented on, but who had managed to tame – for the most part. The 2024 engine, though, was much better in that critical engine braking aspect.

The GP24 did have some teething issues, however, mainly rear-end chatter. Martin suffered from it most in testing, but when racing began, Bagnaia also suddenly found himself with rear vibration. Michelin's rear slick for 2024 added much more edge grip than its predecessor, and that paired with Ducati's new engine seemed to give them problems. Both Bagnaia and Martin had said that the issue came from too much rear edge grip. Ducati managed to reduce the problem, but it never went away completely.

An aero upgrade arrived for the September Misano test. The downwash ducts had been reprofiled and a new element added to the rear. Mirroring the change they had made to their front wheel aero earlier in the year, they added a small ground-effect piece that was suspended from the rear axle block. It added rear grip, but felt slightly more numb. Martin like the added performance, but Bagnaia preferred the greater movement and feel without the piece.

A new chassis was also debuted at that test. Bagnaia asked if he could use it in the remaining rounds, but Ducati refused, the reason reportedly being that they couldn't build enough units to provide it to all four GP24 riders at the same time before the end of the season. Consequently, he would have to wait until 2025 to get a taste of it again.

Right: Late-season version – Aprilia at Phillip Island.
Photo: Gold & Goose

Left: Aprilia's new front wing added downforce.

Below left: The underseat diffuser unit was difficult to get along with.

Bottom left: Mid-season aero upgrade modified the sidepod and created a channel behind it.
Photos: Jack Gorst

Below: The 2024 RS-GP.
Photo: Aprilia Racing

APRILIA RS-GP

YOU could argue that Aprilia's 2024 season was the first to muddy their year-on-year impressive progress – ever since the switch to a 90-degree V4 in 2020. There was progress, but perhaps not quite as cleanly or as much as they'd have liked.

Aprilia made a fairly substantial change for the new season to address their biggest weakness – straight-line braking and corner entry. Weight was shifted ever so slightly forwards to reduce rear traction, to allow the bike to slide into the corner. Thus the rear tyre could glide over the tarmac, stepping out of line more easily to help start the turn with the rear, rather than being planted perfectly in line.

It sounds odd to want to reduce traction, but team principal Paolo Bonora admitted that for the RS-GP to become a better package overall, they had to take away from their outright strongest point – incredible rear traction in low-grip conditions.

As usual, Aprilia updated their engine, chassis and swing-arm for 2024, as well as developing a new aero package. The front wing gained more surface area and thus downforce, with an extra connection point to the main fairing. The side fairings looked identical but for the addition of a small sidepod winglet.

One big change was a radical new under-seat diffuser integrated into the tail unit. It looked epic, but the benefits seemed questionable. Maverick Viñales dismissed it almost instantly in pre-season testing, citing a lack of front-end feel and confidence. Aleix Espargaro persisted, and when he could make it work, he was fast. Really fast. But when he couldn't, he struggled, and after switching back and forth between the 2024 and '23 tail for several races early on, eventually he switched back to the '23 spec as well.

For the second half of the season, Aprilia introduced an updated aero package and a revised set of exhausts. The aero incorporated further small tweaks to the side fairings only, improving their efficiency. The result was a bike that provided a fraction more grip in the mid-corner, but that was heavier to change direction. When Raul Fernandez graduated to the 2024 RS-GP after the summer break, he switched back to the 2023 aero, explaining that it was less physical to ride.

Interestingly, Aprilia suffered with late-race rear grip midway through the season. This perhaps is where their new exhausts came in, the most significant difference being that the lower exhaust, which served the front bank of cylinders, was much longer than before. One possible consequence could have been a slightly smoother power curve in an attempt to treat the rear tyre with more care.

Worryingly, Aprilia have lost their technical guru and lead, Romano Albesiano, to Honda for 2025. Albesiano had led Aprilia from strength to strength. In his place, steps Fabiano Sterlacchini after parting ways with KTM mid-2024. Before that, Sterlacchini had spent 17 years at Ducati, rising to the role of technical director. There's no doubt that he has the credentials to fill Albesiano's shoes, but with three new riders on the RS-GP, there'll be a lot of change.

Right: Pol Espargaro's test bike had different engine, aero and exhausts, with a large balance-pipe between the upper and lower tailpipes.
Photo: Jack Gorst

Below: KTM's swing-arm 'bat-wing' added rear stability.
Photo: Gold & Goose

Bottom: The new seat aero package added a trio of winglets to the side.
Photo: Jack Gorst

Below right: KTM fettled at the Thai MotoGP in October.
Photo: Gold & Goose

KTM RC16

GOING into 2024, KTM stuck with their pioneering carbon-fibre chassis, which had appeared late in 2023. However, at that stage, it hadn't been updated.

One major focus was on fine-tuning power delivery. In pre-season testing, they tried two different exhaust configurations, the first being the familiar design we'd seen over the previous year or so. The second featured the same upper exhaust, but paired it with a much shorter lower exhaust. KTM's 'kryptonite' had been wheelspin as the bike began to stand up, so the hope for the new exhaust was that it would reduce that. The riders liked it and started the season with it.

KTM also reworked their aero for 2024. The new side fairings displayed a different concept – to extend the sidepod wings all the way back along the top of the fairing flanks, creating a channel. With the large side fairings becoming an ever more important component for mid-corner speed, the channel helped to separate air flows, gaining efficiency. There was also an updated air intake in the new pre-season aero, but the riders opted to stick with the older version.

Despite KTM's developments, problems occurred after the early part of the season, causing results to drop off for a while – incidentally coinciding with the timing of the departure of vice-president of technology Fabiano Sterlacchini. The main culprit was rear chatter. Just as Ducati had experienced, the added edge grip from the new rear slick seemed to create issues, and Jack Miller particularly was at a loss to find a solution.

After the summer break, KTM made some changes, and their lost performance did begin to return. They reverted to the longer lower exhaust as well as introducing their first carbon-fibre chassis update. This appeared to help the chatter issues, but not solve them entirely. Their crashes seemed to give that away: riders found that they tended not to lose the front at the apex, but a little afterwards, suggesting that chatter was a factor.

In the latter part of the year, Miller began using an entirely new aero package, while Acosta adopted the rather radical 'batwing' aero. These swing-arm-mounted elements were large, and a more complex version of what Aprilia had tested briefly pre-season. With a small horizontal winglet on each side, it's likely that they helped with the issue of the KTM spinning as the bike stood up.

KTM's minor resurrection in the latter half of the season indicated that they'd found the direction they had lost earlier in the year. And, with a new bike waiting in the wings, things looked more positive for 2025.

The new bike, which Pol Espargaro used in his wild-card rides at the Red Bull Ring and Misano, featured a totally revised engine that probably had different firing intervals. It also had a large balance pipe between the two exhaust outlets, something not seen very often. Pol admitted that the bike was clearly better for one-lap pace, but there was still work to be done in respect of race pace. A better 2025 beckoned.

Right: Yamaha's V1 aero had a large swooping wing.

Centre right: V2's wider side fairing improved lap times.

Below right: Yamaha's V3 slimmed the fairing and gained a triplane wing.

Bottom right: Long exhaust and winged seat unit provided another solution.
Photos: Jack Gorst

Below: The 2024 Yamaha YZR-M1.
Photo: Monster Yamaha

YAMAHA YZR-M1

AFTER Yamaha found that their 2023 engine was too aggressive, for 2024, they brought an updated specification with a smoother power delivery. However, it didn't go far enough. The riders found that despite its better characteristics, it was still too aggressive. Yamaha's concession rank allowed them to bring engine upgrades throughout the year, and they made the most of that luxury.

The 2024 YZR-M1 was also much different visually. In what was probably the biggest overhaul the bike had had, it featured a redesigned aero package with a much larger, Aprilia-like front wing. There was also a set of very boxy sidepods, along with downwash ducts. The sidepods were soon ditched, though.

A new tail unit sat boldly with a race-car-style horizontal wing initially, although later this was replaced by a trio of 'dino' wings. The new tail was heavily concaved underneath, the idea being to drop the bike lower when activating a revised rear ride-height system, allowing for more acceleration and punch off the corner.

Through the year, the main point with Yamaha was their engine. Not long after the summer break, they had reportedly brought seven different engine specs to the track in 2024, through their own private testing and official events. During that time, the bike became slower in a straight line, but faster in corners.

The new specs helped turning, as did a new chassis. Finally, Yamaha recovered a fraction of their mid-corner prowess – a fabled trait of the M1 that had been lost in recent seasons. But as with all upgrades, there was a trade-off. Once again, Yamaha's main man, Fabio Quartararo, was happy with the improved turning, but now he hoped that they could regain some top speed.

Along with engine developments, Yamaha returned to their trusty, slash-cut short exhaust instead of the longer one they had debuted at the start of the year. It seemed an easy choice for Quartararo once he'd reverted to it, but Rins wasn't quite so sure and kept the longer one for a spell, before ultimately agreeing with the Frenchman's choice.

Another concession benefit allowed two aero upgrades during the season. The first arrived for the Jerez test and made its grand prix debut in Barcelona. The front wing had evolved, while the fairing became much slimmer, meaning that less horsepower was needed to push the bike through the air.

The major aspect was the side fairings. Adopting the ground-effect ethos, Yamaha joined KTM in creating a channel behind the sidepod winglet to increase efficiency. It worked, and according to the riders, the new aero gained them two-tenths a lap. The second update introduced a reprofiled main wing and front fairing, which was slightly slimmer and more angular.

Despite Yamaha's gains during the season, they didn't manage to tackle their biggest issue – rear grip. Thus 2024 was another season when their riders were at the mercy of track conditions. When grip was plentiful, they could be strong. When it wasn't, they couldn't.

Left: Yamaha went big with aero during testing.
Photo: Jack Gorst

Below: Michelin remained in the firing line over their troublesome front tyre.
Photo: Gold & Goose

THE FRONT TYRE SCANDAL, AND WHY IT CAME TO PASS

FRONT tyre pressure regulations and attendant swingeing penalties were a cause of several upsets in 2024, interfering with results, and leaving teams and riders guessing in the dark about the pressures to choose.

Michelin's new front slick tyre was meant to solve the problem. Initially promised for 2025, it has been delayed until 2026.

The current front tyre is too susceptible to temperature and pressure changes, but that is only because of the increased demands on it. More horsepower, corner speed and ride-height devices have pushed front tyre forces beyond the limit. So too an improved Michelin rear slick.

The issues are familiar. When riding aggressively or behind another bike, temperature and pressure soar, leading to ballooning of the profile. The contact patch reduces in size, removing feel and grip when braking and tipping in – an unpleasant feeling that makes overtaking a nightmare.

The new 2026 front slick has a different profile and construction. The larger contact patch provides greater braking stability, feel and grip, but makes it harder to change direction. However, riders felt that it would be less susceptible to temperature and pressure changes when behind another rider.

Despite the positive feedback after the test in Misano in September, Michelin delayed its release. Why?

The primary reason was a lack of testing time. The riders only tried the tyre for 30 minutes, and Michelin deemed that not enough to approve it for 2025. More tests with the official riders were needed to further prove the tyre before its introduction.

The tyre had been in development for over a year, and speaking at the start of the season, Michelin motorsport manager Piero Taramasso said that to develop a new front, they need a year. So why wasn't it ready? In truth, Michelin had been chasing moving goal posts.

During the new front's development cycle, their own improvements to the rear tyre allowed faster corner speeds, asking more of the front, and also reaching the ends of straights faster.

Aerodynamic loads in MotoGP are also increasing every year.

It takes only a few months to design and produce a new aero package. Michelin's tyre development was outpaced by bike development.

With active riders strictly limited in the number of tests allowed, which in any case are primarily devoted to machine development, tyres have been left out in the cold.

Right: Honda unmasked at the Qatar test in February.
Photo: Gold & Goose

Below: Misano test aero improved mid-corner grip and speed.
Photo: Jack Gorst

Below right: This at Assen was the most complex seat aero.
Photo: Gold & Goose

Centre right, top to bottom:
Spot the difference. Honda slightly modified the swing-arm…

…The later version improved grip.

LCR tried a different, simpler seat wing early in the European season.

Honda clearly took a lot of inspiration from Ducati.
Photos: Jack Gorst

Far right: Marini's late-season development Honda.
Photo: Gold & Goose

HONDA RC213V

THE 2024 RC213V was believed to be 8kg lighter and, at least in the early stages of testing, things did seem to be positive. Johann Zarco believed that the new bike was eight-tenths quicker, and the test times bore that out. But while Honda were going quicker, so was everyone else, and so the tail-chasing began.

One of the new bike's big positives was its engine. The character was smoother and more user friendly, although it was far from perfect, However, it was a beginning.

Elsewhere, the new chassis was a big change, displaying very different design features compared to Honda's usual offering. It gained them some better front-end feel, the bike receiving the most favourable comments for its straight-line braking. Some work was still needed, however, and despite doing away with the Kalex swing-arm in favour of their own, rear grip – especially on corner exit with lean angle – was poor.

Initially, the riders asked for more downforce, so Honda added larger wings to the front as well as a double-stacked rear wing. Coupled with the new, large ground-effect side fairings, it was Honda's most extensive aero package yet, but the riders still said that there was a lot of room for improvement aerodynamically.

Honda quickly introduced a slightly updated swing-arm, which removed some material from beneath the rear axle. The greater chassis change, though, was the update that arrived for Jerez. It was clear that Honda had focused on finding better flex characteristics for turning. Luca Marini liked it and opted for it immediately, but Mir took more convincing. It wasn't until several rounds later that he switched to it full time and Honda had enough units to give to the LCR duo.

The first aero update also arrived at Jerez. Gone were the bulging side fairings in favour of downwash ducts, although they didn't seem as aggressive as those on the Ducati or elsewhere. The bigger difference was the rework of the sidepods, which had significantly more surface area to provide the bulk of the downforce.

The change also came with a brand-new seat/tail unit, which incorporated a very large rear wing. While the LCR duo went for the new aero straight away, the Repsol pairing preferred to wait for a further upgrade to make a bigger step forward. Eventually, though, they also made the switch.

Engine changes came, too. The riders were left hoping for more, however, the initial engine mods being minor and external. In the meantime, Honda updated their exhausts, which did produce better initial throttle contact, but the bike was still plagued by a lack of turning and rear grip.

Honda's turning point came at the Misano test, where they debuted a new aero package and swing-arm, which finally offered better turning and rear grip. This combined downwash ducts with large ground-effect side fairings, the result being positive, with improved turning, while the updated swing-arm gave rear grip on corner entry and exit with high lean angle. But again, they admitted that there was room for improvement.

The riders found that with the new aero less downforce at the rear worked better. Mir and Marini ditched the horizontal elements of their rear wings, keeping just the vertical 'dino' wings. Zarco also removed one of the two elements on his preferred wing, while only Nakagami kept the same rear wing set-up as before – preferring the extra rear contact when braking.

In the last races, Zarco showed significant improvement, especially one-lap pace in qualifying.

There's no doubt that Honda finally found some positive progress, but as in 2023, many still felt that an engine revolution could stand them in better stead for 2025.

HOW JAPAN INC FACED ITS PROBLEMS

AFTER two years of increasingly dire results, the new 2024 concessions system ranked Honda and Yamaha joint bottom – the only constructors in the lowest 'D' category. This conferred open engine development, an extra aero upgrade and additional tests for full-time riders, as well as extra test tyres. Both took advantage, but did that translate into actual progress?

First, the problems. In 2023, Honda had suffered from a terrible lack of front feel while trail braking, along with issues with rear grip. Their new chassis seemed to improve the former, but the lack of rear grip remained chronic, not so much in a straight line, but spin accelerating with lean angle severely damaged lap times. Improved, but still aggressive engine character compounded the problem.

Yamaha's M1 suffered similar engine-spec issues, and both chased similar solutions, bringing numerous new-spec engines.

The Yamaha progressively lost top speed, but gained improved turning and rideability.

Honda's engine upgrades improved the initial touch of the throttle, but made less impact on turning. Their second aero upgrade made the difference. Ducati-style side fairings added mid-corner and exit grip, helping the rider to get on the power earlier; and with a new swing-arm, riders felt that it was a half-second improvement. Yamaha riders claimed a two-tenths step from their aero update.

The 2024 stories became interesting off-track. Yamaha had already made one move, signing Massimo Bartolini from Ducati as technical director. His influence was in its infancy at the start of the season, but already evident. The changes to the 2024 M1 were perhaps the biggest overhaul in its existence. Aero was more complex and extensive, while the revised tail unit and ride-height device were evidence of a willingness to find every possible percentage within the rules – a stark change from Yamaha's previous more conservative approach.

No sign was more telling of Yamaha being open to bold change than their announcement that they were working on a V4 engine. It suggests a huge change in mind-set, and no doubt this was one of the main reasons why Quartararo decided to stay.

Twenty of 22 bikes on the grid were V4s, providing data to Michelin that allowed them to develop tyres that worked better on such bikes. It's a racing truth that if you are doing something different from your competitors, it's possible that you are doing something wrong. Even if not, there's safety in numbers.

Honda's late-season bombshell, another step-change in philosophy, was the recruitment from Aprilia of technical director Romano Albesiano, an open admission that they needed outside influence to change their working methods, and to gain knowledge and experience from rivals. Albesiano had overseen Aprilia's relentless progress since switching to a 90-degree V4 in 2020, and he would be Honda's first non-Japanese technical lead ever.

Furthermore, Honda will expand their test team considerably for 2025, bringing in crucial talent. Aleix Espargaro, well known to Albesiano, will head an expanded European test team, and in Japan, Taka Nakagami will transition from full-time rider to test rider – two riders still properly MotoGP fast. Aleix's fiery and passionate feedback will be a change from the generally mild-mannered Stefan Bradl. While also mild-mannered, Nakagami's frustration quota is near full after recent seasons riding a bike with few strong points. He will be pushing them for results, while closer to the factory than ever.

So both manufacturers made behind-the-scenes changes with the potential for improvement. On the track, the verdict is more split.

Yamaha had the higher highs, but again Quartararo's magnificence masked underlying problems. If the primary reason for his improvement was down to the bike improving, you'd have expected to see Alex Rins' results improve, too. But that wasn't always the case.

At the same time, there was little progress in gaining time on a new tyre in qualifying, a troublesome issue since 2022.

By contrast, Honda ultimately showed more uniform progress in the latter third of the season, after the Misano test. Clear gains in one-lap and race pace were evident, and it wasn't always just with one rider.

Honda, perhaps, were a little behind in terms of outright one-lap and even race pace, but appeared to make more unified progress. They could be at the bottom of an Aprilia 2020-like arc, which could result in them leaving Yamaha at the bottom of MotoGP's manufacturer war. But there is always that V4 project…

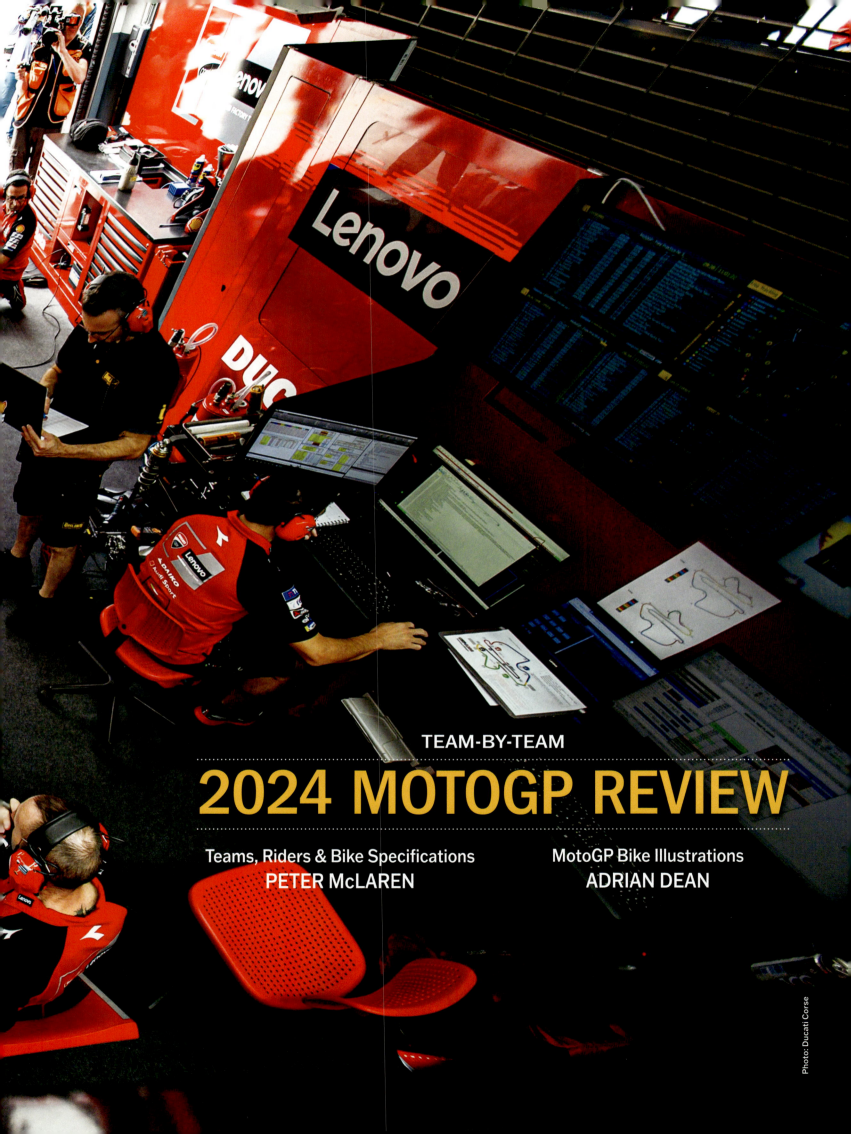

TEAM-BY-TEAM

2024 MOTOGP REVIEW

Teams, Riders & Bike Specifications
PETER McLAREN

MotoGP Bike Illustrations
ADRIAN DEAN

Photo: Ducati Corse

DUCATI LENOVO TEAM

TEAM STAFF

Luigi DALL'IGNA: General Manager
Mauro GRASSILLI: Sporting Director
Davide BARANA: Ducati Corse Technical Director
Davide TARDOZZI: Team Manager
Riccardo SAVIN: Chassis & Vehicle Dynamics Engineer
Gabriele CONTI: Electronic Systems Manager
Leonardo SIMONCINI: Track Technical Co-ordinator
Nicolo MANCINELLI: Vehicle Performance Engineer
Andrea GIAVARINI: Data Analyst
Manuel POGGIALI: Rider Coach
Artur VILALTA: MotoGP Press Manager
Julie GIOVANOLA: MotoGP Press Officer
Davide GIBERTINI: Team Co-ordinator

FRANCESCO BAGNAIA PIT CREW

Cristian GABARRINI: Track Engineer
Tommaso PAGANO: Electronics Engineer
Marco VENTURA: Chief Mechanic
Ivan BRANDI, Massimo TOGNACCI, Lorenzo CANESTRARI, Tommaso PELI: Mechanics
Giacomo MASSAROTTO: Ohlins Technician

ENEA BASTIANINI PIT CREW

Marco RIGAMONTI: Track Engineer
Dario MASSARIN: Electronics Engineer
Michele DUCOLI: Chief Mechanic
Marco POLASTRI, Fabio MORANDINI, Federico COLOMBO, Giuliano POLETTI: Mechanics
Rhys HOLMES: Ohlins Technician

FRANCESCO BAGNAIA
Born: 14 January, 1997 – Torino, Italy
GP Starts: 211 (106 MotoGP, 36 Moto2, 69 Moto3)
GP Wins: 39 (29 MotoGP, 8 Moto2, 2 Moto3)
World Championships: 3 (2 MotoGP, 1 Moto2)

ENEA BASTIANINI
Born: 30 December, 1997 – Rimini, Italy
GP Starts: 190 (69 MotoGP, 33 Moto2, 88 Moto3)
GP Wins: 13 (7 MotoGP, 3 Moto2, 3 Moto3)
World Championships: 1 Moto2

DUCATI reached new heights of dominance in 2024, winning all but one grand prix, headlined by 11 victories for reigning double champion Francesco Bagnaia. It was a record for the Italian, with more wins than all other riders combined, and it towered over the three GP victories for Pramac rival Jorge Martin. But Bagnaia's title hopes were sunk by eight DNFs in what he would call "a championship of mistakes."

The last, and costliest, occurred in the Sepang sprint, after which, victories alone were no longer enough to defend his crown. He won the remaining three races, stuck to his principles by refusing to engage in "dirty" go-slow tactics and finished ten points short of Martin.

Changes to the MotoGP concession system resulted in Ducati being hit with new restrictions on testing tyres and wild-cards, after scoring a near-perfect 96 per cent of the maximum constructors' points in 2023. It made no noticeable impact. However, there was plenty of off-track drama as Ducati ripped up its established succession order of bringing young riders through to the factory team, by picking Marc Marquez to partner Bagnaia in 2025.

The fallout cost Ducati three of its young stars – eventual world champion Martin, Enea Bastianini and

DUCATI Desmosedici GP24

Engine: 1000cc liquid-cooled, 90-degree V4, counter-rotating crankshaft, DOHC, four valves per cylinder, Desmodromic valve system
Power: More than 250bhp
Electronics: Official MotoGP electronic control unit (ECU), inertial measurement unit (IMU) and unified software; ride-by-wire fuel injection
Transmission: Six-speed seamless-shift cassette-type gearbox
Frame: Aluminium alloy twin-spar with carbon-fibre swing-arm, front and rear ride-height devices • *Suspension:* Ohlins inverted front fork and rear shock absorber
Ancillaries: Akrapovic exhaust • *Lubrication:* Shell Advance • *Tyres:* Michelin
Brakes: Brembo 320, 340 and 355mm carbon twin front discs, single stainless steel rear disc, thumb and foot levers available

Pecco Bagnaia

Luigi Dall'Igna

Mauro Grassilli

Davide Tardozzi

Davide Barana

Enea Bastianini

Marco Bezzecchi – and the satellite Pramac team.

The first major personnel changes occurred over the winter, with long-time sporting director Paolo Ciabatti moved to the factory's new off-road project, and being replaced by marketing and sponsorship manager Mauro Grassilli.

Technically, the defection of esteemed vehicle performance engineer Massimo Bartolini to Yamaha was acknowledged as a significant loss. But on the rider front, it was business as usual, to begin with. Bagnaia signed a new two-year contract on the eve of the Qatar opener. Then a deal was done to place Fermin Aldeguer, the dominant force at the end of the 2023 Moto2 championship, on a satellite Desmosedici.

So far, so good. Then came the question of Bagnaia's team-mate. Although Enea Bastianini had rebounded from an injury-wrecked 2023 campaign, his chances of keeping the factory seat were slim. With VR46's Marco Bezzecchi floundering on the GP23, Pramac star Martin was the obvious choice. His only opposition was Marc Marquez.

Martin made it clear that he would join another manufacturer if overlooked by Ducati yet again, while Marquez seemed willing to accept promotion to a factory-spec bike, with the Gresini team. Perhaps giving Bezzecchi a factory machine at VR46 and offering Bastianini a place at Pramac would have been one possible way of retaining all four riders.

Heading into Ducati's home Mugello round, rumours emerged that Martin had been given the Lenovo nod. The twist, however, was that Marquez's factory-bike upgrade would mean him leaving Gresini for Pramac – something a stony-faced Marquez very publicly ruled out.

Exactly what happened behind the scenes then, during the Mugello weekend, is unclear, but by Sunday evening, a dramatic U-turn had resulted in Marquez heading for the factory team. Martin jumped before he was pushed, hastily signing for Aprilia at the Monday test. Marquez's two-year factory contract was confirmed shortly afterwards, with Bastianini named at Tech3 KTM.

Bezzecchi signed to join Martin at Aprilia while, following Marquez's Mugello rejection, Pramac headed into the arms of Yamaha.

"Unfortunately, we had to choose one rider out of three," Ducati Corse general manager Gigi Dall'Igna said. "All could be in the official team. It was a very difficult decision to make from a professional and sporting point of view, but also a human one."

Ever the engineer, Dall'Igna was won over by what he had seen in Marquez's data, the Spaniard standing out from his very first laps on the Desmosedici: "In the end, our choice fell on an unquestionable talent like Marc Marquez," he said. "In just a few races, he has managed to adapt perfectly to our Desmosedici GP, and his innate ambition pushes him to grow continuously." He reminded critics that the Bagnaia/Marquez line-up would be Ducati's strongest ever: "Two riders who together hold 11 world championships."

Dall'Igna rebuffed any accusations that Ducati had abandoned its practice of developing young talent. "We have not changed our philosophy," he said. "We have a contract with Aldeguer. We would like to do with him exactly what we did with Pecco, Enea and Martin."

Ducati CEO Claudio Domenicali acknowledged, "The choice of Marquez is divisive. Much more so in Italy due to his way of riding and what happened in the past [with Valentino Rossi]. But no one questions his talent."

Bagnaia – the star member of Valentino Rossi's VR46 Academy – clashed with Marquez at Portimao, leaving them both on the ground. Then he left Marquez with rubber on his shoulder during a no-holds-barred pass for victory at Jerez. "Bagnaia responded immediately to his overtakes, this is very important," a proud Rossi stated afterwards. "Because if Marc sees you bleeding, he devours you."

Just a few weeks later, the long-simmering relations between the Bagnaia/VR46 camp and the Marquez family reignited when he tangled with Alex Marquez at the end of a nightmare Aragon weekend.

Bagnaia would come to rue the points lost during clashes with other riders, and other seemingly unforced errors. Victory in the Qatar opener was followed by mishaps during the Portimao, Jerez, Le Mans (technical) and Catalunya weekends. But in performance terms, he didn't look back after a breakthrough at Jerez, where Ducati appeared to have solved chatter issues caused by the revised Michelin rear tyre.

"We needed time to understand it, but maybe the fact we have eight bikes means we understood before the others," said Bagnaia, who also had the new forks and swing-arm removed. "As soon as we went back, I was more fast."

Ducati insisted that Martin would be supported equally until the end. Many were sceptical, but Bagnaia cited the decision to delay a new chassis until 2025 as proof that he wasn't receiving special treatment. "If Ducati wanted to help me, from Misano, I could have something better," he said. "We tried a new chassis in the test. But it's not ready for everybody, so we are not using it, because it's fair like this. Gigi was always clear: Lenovo and Pramac have the same package. Nothing more, nothing less. It's a different strategy compared to other manufacturers, but it's what helps make Ducati so competitive."

Bagnaia, who married during summer break, celebrated notable milestones by surpassing Casey Stoner's 23 MotoGP wins to become Ducati's most successful MotoGP rider, then Kevin Schwantz's 25 victories.

On the other side of the garage, Bastianini delivered the kind of form expected when he had been promoted from Gresini at the end of 2022.

It was too late to save his Ducati seat, but a perfect double at Silverstone, followed by a brutal last-lap pass on Martin for another victory in Misano, hinted at a title challenge. That ended with a crash at Mandalika, leaving the 'Beast' to battle Marquez for third in the world championship.

The Bagnaia and Bastianini crews, led by Cristian Gabarrini and Marco Rigamonti respectively, remained unchanged for 2024.

With Pramac departing, Ducati grid numbers will not only be cut from eight to six, but also their roster of factory bikes reduced from four to three.

PRIMA PRAMAC DUCATI

TEAM STAFF
Paolo CAMPINOTI: Team Principal
Gino BORSOI: Team Manager
Roma LOPEZ BLANCO: Team Co-ordinator
Jacopo MENGHETTI: Marketing & Sponsorship
Alberto DORIS: Marketing & Sponsorship Specialist
Lucia GABANI: Media Manager & Press Officer
Alessandro TOMASI: Video maker
Adrien DELFORGE: Social Media Specialist
Paolo ZANELLA: Hospitality Manager
Fonsi NIETO: Rider Performance Coach
Massimiliano SABBATANI: Rider Track Analyst

JORGE MARTIN PIT CREW
Daniele ROMAGNOLI: Crew Chief
Cristian BATTAGLIA: Data Engineer
Nicola MANNA: Chief Mechanic
David GALACHO, Daniele PENZO,
Jarno POLASTRI: Mechanics
Luca PARTIGLIANI: Fuel & Tyre Technician

FRANCO MORBIDELLI PIT CREW
Massimo BRANCHINI: Crew Chief
Erik CHIARVESIO: Data Engineer
Fabrizio MALAGUTI: Chief Mechanic
Tiziani VERNIANI, Andrea ZAMPIERI,
Riccardo PEPE: Mechanics
Moris GRASSI: Fuel & Tyre Technician

FRANCO MORBIDELLI
Born: 4 December, 1994 – Rome, Italy
GP Starts: 193 (122 MotoGP, 71 Moto2)
GP Wins: 11 (3 MotoGP, 8 Moto2)
World Championships: 1 Moto2

JORGE MARTIN
Born: 29 January, 1998 – Madrid, Spain
GP Starts: 173 (74 MotoGP, 32 Moto2, 67 Moto3)
GP Wins: 18 (8 MotoGP, 2 Moto2, 8 Moto3)
World Championships: 2 (1 MotoGP, 1 Moto3)

BEATEN to the world championship by Francesco Bagnaia in the final race of 2023, Jorge Martin raised his game to make history as the first Independent rider to win the MotoGP title.

Having led the world championship for 24 hours in the previous season, the 26-year-old Spaniard bore the pressure of being top of the standings for much of 2024. Crediting a mental coach for new inner calmness, he only won three grands prix, but held his nerve during critical end-of-season moments, when Bagnaia ultimately cracked.

"Last season was great. Even after being second, I was quite happy. But in January, I was struggling with my mental health," Martin said after winning the title. "I was really scared, thinking, 'I will never be MotoGP champion'. So thanks to my coach, I improved a lot. I became more focused on the hope of winning than on the fear of losing. If I lose, life is not ending."

But Martin's heroics weren't enough to seal promotion to the factory Ducati team. The fallout from that snub not only sent him into the arms of Aprilia, but also contributed to Pramac calling time on its 20-year Ducati association for a new era with Yamaha.

While Bagnaia floundered in some early rounds,

DUCATI Desmosedici GP24

Engine: 1000cc liquid-cooled, 90-degree V4, counter-rotating crankshaft, DOHC, four valves per cylinder, Desmodromic valve system
Power: More than 250bhp

Electronics: Official MotoGP electronic control unit (ECU), inertial measurement unit (IMU) and unified software; ride-by-wire fuel injection

Transmission: Six-speed seamless-shift cassette-type gearbox, Regina chain

Frame: Aluminium alloy twin-spar with carbon-fibre swing-arm, front and rear ride-height devices • *Suspension:* Ohlins inverted front fork and rear shock absorber

Ancillaries: Akrapovic exhaust • *Lubrication:* Motul • *Tyres:* Michelin

Brakes: Brembo 320, 340 and 355mm carbon twin front discs, single stainless steel rear disc, thumb and foot levers available.

Paolo Campinoti

Gino Borsoi

Jorge Martin

The Pramac team celebrate their championship success in Barcelona.

Martin proved that he would be a major title force by finishing off the podium just once in the opening seven races. The first chink in his armour came when he fell from the lead at Jerez, but he rebounded with a perfect double in France and arrived at Mugello a massive 39 points clear of Bagnaia.

Ducati's home round was the deciding point for the factory ride, and Martin was all smiles on Thursday as reports emerged that he had been picked to partner Pecco for 2025. But those smiles turned to apprehension as the weekend progressed, not helped by a crash in the sprint, and by Sunday evening, all the signs pointed to Marc Marquez being on the factory Ducati in 2025.

Martin, who had been overlooked by Ducati in favour of Bastianini for 2023, acted swiftly and signed for Aprilia at the Monday test. "I arrived in Mugello with some information… which then changed a lot!" he said of his disappearing factory Ducati deal. "Difficult to explain from my side. I spoke with Ducati after Montmelo and everything seemed quite clear.

"But on the Sunday at Mugello, I saw it wasn't that clear… Something or someone changed the idea. It was a bit frustrating to miss out again, after four years trying to get the official bike. Some things in life don't go as you want. So I took the best opportunity I could [at Aprilia] and think I will be much happier, where they really want me and will give 100 per cent for me."

Martin's close friendship and shared management with Aleix Espargaro helped expedite the Aprilia deal, but "the decision was 100 per cent on me."

Did he feel fired up to show that Ducati had made the wrong decision? "Not at all. Even if I had a 100-point lead, I wouldn't be their choice. So it's not about proving anything."

Did he fear a loss of support from Ducati for his title challenge? "No, I'm not scared about this. I'm a professional, paid by Ducati. It's my home until Valencia. I'll do my best to win, and they've told me I will have the same material. So I'm confident it won't be an issue."

The Mugello weekend was also pivotal in Pramac's future, with Marc Marquez shooting down rumours that he would join the team to ride a factory-spec bike. Thus Pramac faced not only the loss of star rider Martin, who had long made it clear that he would join another factory if Ducati weren't interested, but also no 'superstar' replacement.

With VR46 resisting Yamaha's advances, reigning teams' champions Pramac had been courted by the Japanese manufacturer for months. But there were serious doubts over whether Pramac could be persuaded to give up the best bikes on the grid for the struggling M1s. With no results to attract Pramac, Yamaha needed to rely on off-track incentives and faith in their future aspirations. But perhaps the Martin factory-team snub was the final straw.

Despite Pramac being Ducati's official satellite team, raising a young rider to lead the world championship, Ducati had again favoured a Gresini rider (Bastianini also came from the Italian squad). And while Marquez had been at Gresini only for 2024, Martin's whole MotoGP career had been spent under a direct Ducati contract.

"The choice not to take Martin, who is leading the world championship, is certainly not a choice that we agree with," Pramac team principal Paolo Campinoti said. "It seems that Ducati changed priorities. Our project was to help young riders grow and join the factory team, like Iannone, Petrucci, Miller, Bagnaia.

"When Marquez was chosen instead of Martin, it made me make different considerations. Namely that there was no longer any need for a 'Junior team', and so honestly, I no longer felt an integral or fundamental part of this project."

However, Campinoti played down reports that Ducati's jubilant celebrations when Bastianini had overtaken Martin at the final corner in Mugello had been a factor.

Subsequently, a Pramac/Yamaha deal, with access to factory-spec M1s, was confirmed and is set to run for seven years. It also includes a Moto2 project.

Ducati thanked Pramac for contributing, "to the sporting growth of Ducati and its riders in the premier class, achieving eight victories, 55 podiums and 20 pole positions."

A wide range of riders were linked with the new Pramac M1 seats. Quartararo gave a running commentary on his preferred candidates, adding weight to speculation that the satellite team would target a proven rider and a rookie. The Frenchman did his best to help Yamaha tempt Fabio Di Giannantonio, but when the Italian re-signed for VR46, Quartararo fed growing speculation that Miguel Oliveira was now Yamaha's main target: "He's doing a really great job, he's really experienced and he's won quite a lot of races. He can be a really good rider for the project."

Moto2 front-runners Sergio Garcia, Ai Ogura, Tony Arbolino and Alonso Lopez had been among those on the 'rookie' list, but a sudden change of tack resulted in Yamaha plumping for experience over youth and signing popular ex-Pramac rider Jack Miller.

Martin's 2024 team-mate Franco Morbidelli had moved in the opposite direction, from Yamaha to Ducati. But the former Petronas title runner-up had his preparations wrecked by a troublesome concussion while training on a superbike at Portimao, when the Marquez brothers came to his aid as he lay unconscious on the track.

Making up for the loss of hundreds of testing laps was a formidable task, but the Italian became a top-six contender from mid-season onwards. Sticking with Pramac for a return to Yamaha was unthinkable after his previous struggles at the factory team. However, his MotoGP future was secured when VR46 slotted him into the ex-Marco Bezzecchi seat alongside Di Giannantonio.

Again, Martin's crew was run by Daniele Romagnoli, who had moved from Yamaha to Ducati with Cal Crutchlow in 2014, but would leave with the Spaniard to join Aprilia in 2025. Like Morbidelli, Massimo Branchini will move to VR46 for the coming season, albeit to work with Di Giannantonio.

GRESINI RACING MOTOGP

TEAM STAFF
Nadia PADOVANI: Team Owner & Team Principal
Carlo MERLINI: Commercial & Marketing Director
Michele MASINI: Sporting Director
Sandra VILCHEZ: Team Co-ordinator
Cristian MASSA: Communication Director
Manuel POGGIALI: Rider Coach
MIKE WATT: Ohlins Suspension Technician
Sergio VERBENA: Technical Co-ordinator
Luca BELLOSI: Spare Parts Co-ordinator

MARC MARQUEZ PIT CREW
Frankie CARCHEDI: Track Engineer
Mattia SERENI: Electronics Engineer
Filippo TOGNONI: Chief Mechanic
David CASTANEDA, Marco ROSA GASTALDO, Mirko FIUZZI, Javier ORTIZ, Marco BONAZZI: Mechanics

ALEX MARQUEZ PIT CREW
Donatello GIOVANOTTI: Track Engineer
Andrea MATTIOLI: Electronics Engineer
Rafael LOPEZ: Chief Mechanic
Claudio EUSEBI, Alberto PRESUTTI, Joan TORTOSA, Francesco SCIUSCO: Mechanics

MARC MARQUEZ
Born: 17 February, 1993 – Cervera, Spain
GP Starts: 267 (189 MotoGP, 32 Moto2, 46 125cc)
GP Wins: 88 (62 MotoGP, 16 Moto2, 10 125cc)
World Championships: 8 (6 MotoGP, 1 Moto2, 1 125cc)

ALEX MARQUEZ
Born: 23 April, 1996 – Cervera, Spain
GP Starts: 224 (89 MotoGP, 89 Moto2, 46 Moto3)
GP Wins: 12 (8 Moto2, 4 Moto3)
World Championships: 2 (1 Moto2, 1 Moto3)

Photos: Gold & Goose

THE arrival of Marc Marquez thrust Gresini, one of MotoGP's smallest teams, firmly into the limelight in 2024.

The eight-times world champion's shock switch from Repsol Honda to ride a year-old Desmosedici alongside younger brother Alex had been the talk of the winter, some predicting that he would dominate the new season. "If Marc goes on the Ducati, the rest may as well not turn up," former Honda colleague Cal Crutchlow said in late 2023.

The reality wasn't quite that spectacular, but the Gresini gamble paid off handsomely for Marquez. The Spaniard, 31, soon adapted his riding style from the front-end Honda to the rear-grip Ducati, remained well clear of the other GP23 riders and proved a regular thorn in the side of the factory GP24s.

As early as Mugello, Gigi Dall'Igna had seen enough and picked Marquez over Ducati's roster of young stars, including title leader Jorge Martin, to be Francesco Bagnaia's future factory team-mate.

Then Marc and Alex made history at Sachsenring, becoming the first brothers to stand on the premier-

DUCATI Desmosedici GP23

Engine: 1000cc liquid-cooled, 90-degree V4, counter-rotating crankshaft, DOHC, four valves per cylinder, Desmodromic valve system
Power: More than 250bhp

Electronics: Official MotoGP electronic control unit (ECU), inertial measurement unit (IMU) and unified software; ride-by-wire fuel injection

Transmission: Six-speed seamless-shift cassette-type gearbox

Frame: Aluminium alloy twin-spar with carbon-fibre swing-arm, front and rear ride-height devices • *Suspension:* Ohlins inverted front fork and rear shock absorber

Ancillaries: Akrapovic exhaust • *Lubrication:* Federal Oil • *Tyres:* Michelin

Brakes: Brembo 320, 340 and 355mm carbon twin front discs, single stainless steel rear disc, thumb and foot levers available

A double podium for the team at Sachsenring.

Michele Masini

Frankie Carchedi

class podium together since Nobuatsu and Takuma Aoki in 1997.

Although the GP24s of Bagnaia and Martin stretched their advantage as the season progressed, Marquez's renaissance was complete when he broke a 1,000-day MotoGP win drought with a perfect weekend in Aragon.

Two more grand prix victories followed, at Misano and Phillip Island, but his slim title hopes went up in smoke with an engine failure in Mandalika. Nevertheless, Marquez finished on a high by snatching third in the world championship from Enea Bastianini.

The difference in performance between the GP24s (Lenovo/Pramac) and GP23s (Gresini/VR46) was a hot topic for much of the season. The benchmark for year-old Ducatis had been set by Marco Bezzecchi (three wins) and Fabio Di Giannantonio (one) in 2023, with Alex Marquez also victorious in two sprints.

But the gap grew in 2024. Not only was the GP23 fickle to set up and ride, but also it was designed to work with the previous-generation rear Michelin. As a result, the extra grip from the new rear caused turning issues with the front.

Ducati also appeared to offer the satellite teams an older spec relative to the previous campaign. "Last year was different because I had the bike that they finished [2022 with] in Valencia," explained Alex Marquez. "This year, we started with the bike that they started the season with in 2023."

The Lenovo and Pramac machines also benefited from a factory ride-height device that dropped their machines by around an extra 20mm.

Marc Marquez estimated the overall GP23/GP24 difference at "two-tenths per lap, four seconds in a race." It's unclear whether Gigi Dall'Igna thought the same, but by Mugello, where Ducati made its decision on Bagnaia's team-mate, Marquez had finished within four seconds of victory at four GPs… That included losing out to Bagnaia by just 0.372 of a second at Jerez, then 0.446 of a second to Martin at Le Mans.

The backdrop to the Jerez duel was a fierce Bagnaia/Marquez clash at Portimao, as the reigning champion attempted to thwart the Spaniard's overtake. In Spain, Bagnaia went on the offensive again, levering Marquez from the lead with his front wheel.

It was exactly the kind of move that Marquez is famous for. But the No.93 rider seemed to be holding back in his battles with Bagnaia, while putting hard moves on others, such as former Honda team-mate Joan Mir.

Was Marquez playing the long game, already setting his sights on the factory team and aware that taking down Bagnaia would veto his chances?

While many riders roll their eyes at silly-season rumours, Marquez had revelled in the modern 24-hour news cycle during 2023's Repsol Honda split,

Nadia Padovani

and played the game to perfection again in 2024. An insight into his headline-making mindset came when addressing eyebrow-raising reports that Lewis Hamilton was interested in buying the Gresini team.

"If it's real, it's good for our sport. And even if it's not real, it's good for our sport!" Marquez said. "Because MotoGP needs people talking about it… Maybe I'm thinking about buying an F1 team!"

With only a single-year deal at Gresini, Marquez insisted that his priority was to see if he was still competitive. When that was proven, his intentions emerged drip-feed style during May. "I decided to go to the best bike [Ducati, at Gresini] to see what I was capable of. Because even I had my doubts, about if I was finished or not," he said at Le Mans.

"But seeing that I'm still competitive, logically, next year I want – whatever colour it may be, whatever bike it may be – the latest spec. Because it gives you a better chance of fighting for the world championship."

Marquez arrived at the crucial Mugello weekend, long touted as a deadline for Ducati's decision, insisting that he had multiple options. Then, in Italy, reports claimed that Ducati had chosen Martin for the factory team and Marquez for factory support at Pramac. That solution was promptly shot down in flames by an unusually grouchy Marquez: "Pramac is not an option for me. I'm not going to change from one satellite team to another."

Did Ducati misjudge Marquez's stance or wrongly think that he would cave in and compromise? Either way, his plans were now crystal clear: the factory Ducati team, Gresini on a factory bike, or the threat of moving to KTM or Aprilia.

By the end of the weekend, Ducati had dramatically swung its support behind Marquez for the 2025 factory ride and cast title leader Martin adrift.

"I'm super-happy and very thankful to Ducati Corse. Especially because one year ago, I was close to saying, 'It's the end of my career,'" Marquez said. "Thanks also to Honda, who understood my situation and allowed me to go to Gresini, which was the perfect team to renew a rider that was in some way lost.

"I was clear and honest with Ducati about what I wanted: the latest bike in Gresini or at the official team. I just did my 100 per cent on the racetrack, and finally on Sunday night [at Mugello], they informed me I will be the rider."

The only thing still missing from Marquez's season was a return to the top step of the podium, dating back to his final Honda win at Misano in 2021. He played down the significance: "It doesn't matter if it's 1,000 days, 1,100 or 1,200 days. The most important thing is we're getting closer. This year is a building year, and victory – if not this year – will arrive next year."

Marquez's first Ducati win did arrive soon after, at Aragon, but it was partly overshadowed by a controversial incident between Bagnaia and Alex Marquez.

The FIM stewards declared that neither rider was predominantly responsible, although in time-honoured tradition, each felt that the other should have given more room. The incident escalated when Bagnaia suggested that Alex's contact with him was deliberate, calling the move "unacceptable and dangerous".

Alex issued a social-media post of his own: "I would never deliberately crash with another rider." Bagnaia apologised, but as Alex emphasised, the damage had been done.

Marc Marquez's arrival might have filled the winter headlines, but it resulted in very few changes within the Gresini set-up. Team owner Nadia Padovani, widow of the late Fausto Gresini, continued to count on commercial and marketing director Carlo Merlini and sporting director Michele Masini for the team's day-to-day operations (Masini's title being upgraded from team manager).

Likewise, Marc Marquez took just one mechanic, Javier Ortiz, with him from Honda, as he slotted into the ex-Fabio Di Giannantonio crew run by Frankie Carchedi.

Ducati usually keeps rider/crew-chief partnerships intact during team changes, but Carchedi – who had helped Joan Mir to the 2020 title at Suzuki, and Di Giannantonio to become a race winner in 2023 – wouldn't join Marquez in red. Instead, Marc will work with ex-Bastianini crew chief Marco Rigamonti, his third different crew chief in three seasons.

While Marc bounced in and out of Gresini, Alex committed to a further two seasons in July, effectively becoming team leader alongside rookie Fermin Aldeguer in 2025.

Crew chief Donatello Giovanotti, who had switched from Di Giannantonio's side of the garage for 2023, again catered for Alex's technical needs, alongside electronics engineer Andrea Mattioli and chief mechanic Rafael Lopez.

The German Grand Prix podium alongside Marc was the highlight of Alex's season, Aragon having proved his best chance of a podium return. Nonetheless, Alex claimed a new career high of eighth in the world championship.

MotoGP • TEAM REVIEW 57

APRILIA RACING TEAM

TEAM STAFF

Massimo RIVOLA: Aprilia Racing CEO
Romano ALBESIANO: Technical Director
Paolo BONORA: Team Manager
Victoria ORTEGA CABRERA: Press Officer
Mitia DOTTA: Team Co-ordinator
Stefano ROMEO: Electronics Engineer
Michele FANTINI: Engine Engineer
Pasquale VALENTE: Vehicle Engineer
Elena DE CIA: Strategy Engineer

MAVERICK VINALES PIT CREW

Manuel CAZEAUX: Crew Chief
Luca CONTI: Electronics Engineer
Francesco VENTURATO: Performance Engineer
Matteo FRISON: Data Analysis
Davide MANFREDI: Chief Mechanic
Gianluca PERETTI, Cristian CONTE,
Carlo CORRADINI: Mechanics
Inigo GARCIA: Tyres & Fuel
Ben POPPERWELL: Suspension Tech (Ohlins)

ALEIX ESPARGARO PIT CREW

Antonio JIMENEZ: Crew Chief
Renato PENNACCHIO: Electronics Engineer
Michele BERTELLI Performance Engineer
Andrea ILARIO: Data Analysis
Carlo TOCCAFONDI: Chief Mechanic
Salvador FRANCO, Roberto MARINONI,
Simone ALESSANDRINI: Mechanics
Oscar MARTINEZ: Tyres & Fuel
Oscar BOLZONELLA: Suspension Tech (Ohlins)

ALEIX ESPARGARO
Born: 30 July, 1989 – Granollers, Spain
GP Starts: 339 (255 MotoGP, 61 Moto2/250cc, 23 125cc)
GP Wins: 3 MotoGP

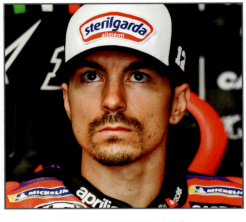

MAVERICK VINALES
Born: 12 January, 1995 – Figueres, Spain
GP Starts: 247 (180 MotoGP, 18 Moto2, 49 Moto3/125cc)
GP Wins: 26 (10 MotoGP, 4 Moto2, 12 Moto3/125cc)
World Championships: 1 Moto3

Photos: Gold & Goose

APRILIA were the only manufacturer to defeat Ducati in 2024, but they still dropped behind KTM as best-of-the-rest in the rider and constructor standings.

The team's bittersweet fortunes continued off-track, where Aprilia signed eventual world champion Jorge Martin, but lost not only riders Aleix Espargaro and Maverick Vinales, but also technical director Romano Albesiano.

While Espargaro was instantly fast on the 2024-spec RS-GP in pre-season testing, revelling in the extra downforce, even though it made the machine physically demanding, Vinales (like Miguel Oliveira) soon moved away from the 'batmobile' rear aero, and Espargaro joined them in running the standard rear unit after the European season began. Doubts over the aero package lingered for much of the campaign.

Nonetheless, Vinales looked every inch a title contender as he romped to three early wins in a row, including a perfect double at CoTA, his Sunday victory the sole interruption to a Ducati clean sweep. But his success disappeared as quickly as it had arrived, and he finished on the grand prix podium just once more as he faded behind the KTM duo of Brad Binder and Pedro Acosta, plus the top four Ducatis.

"When I finished 2023, I asked for two things. Bet-

Aprilia RS-GP24

Engine: 1000cc liquid-cooled, 90-degree V4, counter-rotating crankshaft, DOHC, four valves per cylinder, pneumatic valve system
Power: More than 270hp

Electronics: Official MotoGP electronic control unit (ECU), inertial measurement unit (IMU) and unified software; ride-by-wire fuel injection

Transmission: Six-speed seamless-shift cassette-type gearbox

Frame: Aluminium alloy twin-spar with carbon-fibre swing-arm, front and rear ride-height devices • *Suspension:* Ohlins inverted front fork and rear shock absorber

Ancillaries: SC-Project exhaust • *Lubrication:* Castrol • *Tyres:* Michelin

Brakes: Brembo 320, 340 and 355mm carbon twin front discs, single stainless steel rear disc, thumb and foot levers available

LORENZO SAVADORI
Born: 4 April, 1993 – Cesena, Italy
GP Starts: 60 (29 MotoGP, 31 125cc)

Maverick Vinales took two brilliant wins at Circuit of The Americas.

Massimo Rivola

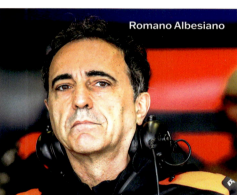

Romano Albesiano

Fabianio Sterlacchini

Paulo Bonora

ter starts and the same bike," Vinales revealed during his final Aprilia appearance. "I loved that bike, but then [the 2024 bike] was another story.

"It's the only thing I regret, because I think with the '23 bike and a little more downforce, we could be, I don't know about fighting with Ducati, but top four for sure. Because we knew the set-up, we knew everything.

"So I needed to ride all year with a bike that I didn't like. We worked really hard, but we still don't understand why Portimao and Austin were so good… Braking consistency was one of the problems."

His assessment ignores the game-changing impact of the new Michelin rear tyre construction, which, as Espargaro admitted, only Ducati mastered: "We had information from the '23 bike on the new tyres at some circuits with Raul. But there is something we cannot put together. We don't have enough traction, grip. Only Ducati [fully understands it] and we were struggling a lot."

Aprilia's heat weakness also re-emerged during the flyaways – "not just the riders, but the engine," said Espargaro.

The Spaniard might not have claimed a Sunday podium, but he delighted the local fans with a sprint win from pole after announcing his retirement plans in Catalunya. Signing off at the same track in November, he helped defend his friend Martin in the title decider, ensuring that Aprilia would welcome a reigning world champion for 2025.

At 35, the oldest on the grid, Espargaro's emotional retirement announcement had been expected. The twist in the tale was that his future as a test rider would be with Honda, not Aprilia. Nevertheless, wearing a fresh 'Captain' tattoo, he played the role of intermediary as Aprilia pulled off a major coup by signing Martin as his replacement.

"Jorge stayed in my motorhome until midnight on Sunday [at Mugello], asking a lot of questions," Espargaro recalled. "Obviously, he was quite disappointed with Ducati, so he was very interested in the human side of the team. Then on Monday, he signed. It was fast, quite exceptional."

Espargaro brushed off concerns that Martin, who had only ever ridden a Ducati in MotoGP, might not adapt to the Aprilia. "With the Aprilia, you can push a lot with the front, and Jorge is a rider who loves to ride with the front brake. They have some front locking problems with the Ducati under braking, and this will also be easier on the Aprilia. Maybe on the engine side, he will struggle a bit more because the Aprilia is not as strong. But when you're talented, it's a bike, with an engine and two wheels!"

A potent Martin/Vinales line-up looked assured, with Vinales set to inherit Espargaro's 'Captain' armband at the end of his fourth year. But Maverick by name, Maverick by nature, and the surprise of the silly season was that the Suzuki, Yamaha and Aprilia race winner had signed for Tech3 KTM.

Vinales explained, "I was thinking about it since Jerez. I didn't feel like continuing, because after Austin, I was a little bit shocked, because I can only do that in one race out of 20. "Obviously, Jorge and I could make a really good team, but I had already made up my mind before Mugello."

Asked why he felt that KTM could offer him a brighter future than Aprilia, his home since a dramatic split from Yamaha in mid-2021, he replied, "I just tried to understand what is going to be the best for me. And I think the KTM is much more suitable for my riding style."

The loss of Vinales at least allowed Aprilia to achieve its ambition of having an Italian rider, but with Enea Bastianini also picking Tech3, VR46 rising star Marco Bezzecchi was chosen to partner Martin.

Aprilia Racing CEO Massimo Rivola said, "My feeling is that the real Bez is the one of last year and not this year. The signs of talent are unequivocal. You can see this guy has something special. But I'm sorry to lose Maverick. I think he wants to be the only one winning with so many different manufacturers, and he has the talent to do it."

Rivola also praised the input of test rider Lorenzo Savadori, who made several wild-card appearances in 2024.

Aprilia's off-track drama continued with a bizarre incident at the Austrian MotoGP, where the factory parted ways with a rogue contractor accused of spying by brazenly filming rival machines at close range in the pit lane. A far more dangerous pit-lane incident occurred at Misano, where a Moto2 bike veered into the Aprilia garage. "We were lucky because Antonio [Jimenez] and my data guy went out for a coffee," Espargaro said. "It destroyed part of the garage."

A similar order of surprise was the late-season news that Albesiano, leader of the RS-GP project since Gigi Dall'Igna's defection to Ducati in 2014, had signed to join Honda. Beating HRC's announcement by minutes, Aprilia named ex-Ducati and KTM manager Fabiano Sterlacchini as its future technical director. He attended the final rounds as an observer.

"Fabiano's arrival is another important step in further strengthening of the MotoGP project, following the signing of two young and talented riders, Jorge Martín and Marco Bezzecchi," read a team statement. "Aprilia Racing wish to thank Romano Albesiano for his 11 years as Technical Director of the Team, as well as for his 20 years within the Piaggio Group."

PERTAMINA ENDURO VR46 RACING TEAM

TEAM STAFF

Valentino ROSSI: Team Owner
Alessio SALUCCI: Team Director
Pablo NIETO: Team Manager
Barbara MAZZONI: Financial Officer
Luca BRIVIO: Team Co-ordinator
Pol BERTRAN: Head of Communication
Laura BERETTA: Senior Press Officer
Giorgia FRATESI: PR and Team Co-ordinator
Idalio GAVIRA: Coach
Andrea MIGNO: Coach Assistant and Video Analysis

FABIO DI GIANNANTONIO CREW

David MUNOZ: Track Engineer
Claudio RAINATO: Electronics Engineer
Jacques ROCA: Chief Mechanic
Gianluca FALCONI, Giacomo SILVESTRI,
Pasquale POTITO: Mechanics
Guillem RODRIGUEZ: Tyres & Fuel

MARCO BEZZECCHI PIT CREW

Matteo FLAMIGNI: Track Engineer
Sergio MARTINEZ: Electronics Engineer
Alex JOAQUIN: Chief Mechanic
Miguel PERURENA, Antonio BALLESTIN,
Luca CASALI: Mechanics
Filippo BERTI: Tyres & Fuel
Luca FERRACCIOLI, Mattia SERENI,
Giulio DE BLASI: Ducati Technicians

FABIO DI GIANNANTONIO
Born: 10 October, 1998 – Rome, Italy
GP Starts: 164 (57 MotoGP, 52 Moto2, 55 Moto3)
GP Wins: 4 (1 MotoGP, 1 Moto2, 2 Moto3)

MARCO BEZZECCHI
Born: 12 November, 1998 – Rimini, Italy
GP Starts: 152 (60 MotoGP, 52 Moto2, 40 Moto3)
GP Wins: 9 (3 MotoGP, 3 Moto2, 3 Moto3)

AFTER race wins and the early MotoGP title lead in 2023, Valentino Rossi's team had far less to celebrate in 2024. But there were more important 'results' off-track, VR46 signing to replace Pramac as Ducati's official satellite team.

Rossi continued to maintain a hands-off approach, entrusting lifelong friend Alessio Salucci and former racer Pablo Nieto with running the project, but both insisted that Rossi is involved in all key decisions.

Pertamina, Indonesia's state-owned oil and gas corporation, took over from Mooney as title sponsor, resulting in an impossible-to-miss fluorescent yellow and white livery.

New signing Fabio Di Giannantonio moved into the ex-Luca Marini squad commanded by former Rossi crew chief David Munoz. Marco Bezzecchi kept his Matteo Flamigni-led group for a third season.

A triple MotoGP winner, and behind only Francesco Bagnaia and Jorge Martin in the 2023 world championship, Bezzecchi would have been firmly in the title fight had he been able to continue his trajectory. But the 25-year-old suffered a Bastianini-style slump on the GP23, the characteristics of which didn't play to his natural strengths.

"I struggle with the first touch of gas, the bike doesn't turn, I'm losing speed and often go wide,"

DUCATI Desmosedici GP23

Engine: 1000cc liquid-cooled, 90-degree V4, counter-rotating crankshaft, DOHC, four valves per cylinder, Desmodromic valve system
Power: More than 250bhp
Electronics: Official MotoGP electronic control unit (ECU), inertial measurement unit (IMU) and unified software; ride-by-wire fuel injection
Transmission: Six-speed seamless-shift cassette-type gearbox
Frame: Aluminium alloy twin-spar with carbon-fibre swing-arm, front and rear ride-height devices • *Suspension:* Ohlins inverted front fork and rear shock absorber
Ancillaries: Akrapovic exhaust • *Lubrication:* Pertamina Enduro • *Tyres:* Michelin
Brakes: : Brembo 320, 340 and 355mm carbon twin front discs, single stainless steel rear disc, thumb and foot levers available

ANDREA IANNONE
Born: 9 August, 1989 – Vasto, Italy
GP Starts: 247 (119 MotoGP, 51 Moto2, 77 125cc)
GP Wins: 13 (1 MotoGP, 8 Moto2, 4 125cc)

MICHELE PIRRO
Born: 5 July, 1986 – San Giovanni Rotondo, Italy
GP Starts: 116 (69 MotoGP, 18 Moto2, 29 125cc)
GP Wins: 1 Moto2

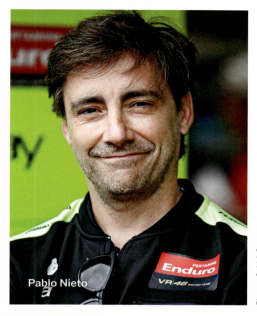

Pablo Nieto

Fabio Di Giannantonio

Bezzecchi said. "All the GP23 Ducati riders complain about the same problem. There are some tracks where I was able to adjust a bit, and some tracks where I struggled more."

"The window with this [GP23] bike is very small, and it's hard to keep it in that window," said Nieto. "I think it goes in cycles. Last year, the difference between [the GP23 and GP22] was not so big. This year, they have taken that little step [with the GP24], but more than anything, I think it's the way of riding the bike. The GP24 is much smoother. On the GP23, the engine is more aggressive. And that ultimately makes the bike harder to ride."

A podium at Jerez, VR46's only silverware of the season, proved a false dawn, and Bezzecchi found himself outside the world championship top ten and ranked last of the Ducati riders. The Italian's poor form had many questioning the wisdom of having turned down a GP24 seat at Pramac in favour of remaining loyal to VR46.

Fortunately for Bez, Aprilia had longer memories and, with Maverick Vinales departing for KTM, were searching for a young Italian for 2025. Thus Bezzecchi follows in the footsteps of Franco Morbidelli, Francesco Bagnaia and Luca Marini in joining a factory MotoGP team, the VR46 Academy's stated goal.

With Bezzecchi floundering, VR46's challenge was led by an 'outsider' in the form of Di Giannantonio – the team's first rider who had not been a member of the actual Academy. After Luca Marini signed for Honda, VR46 initially had ruled out signing Diggia as his replacement, until his stunning late-2023 charge, which culminated in victory in Qatar, made him impossible to ignore.

"I said, 'Not Di Giannantonio', because our project is a little bit more for rookie riders, but in the last two or three races, Fabio was unbelievable," conceded Salucci on the eve of the 2023 Valencia finale, just before Di Giannantonio's deal was signed.

Although separated from Gresini crew chief Frankie Carchedi, he quickly adapted to his new VR46 surroundings, establishing himself as erstwhile next-best GP23 rider after Marc Marquez and posing a challenge to the multi-champion at certain events.

He also caught the notice of other teams, and Fabio Quartararo was openly pushing Di Giannantonio for one of the new Pramac Yamaha rides. Grateful for the praise, Diggia politely maintained that "Plan A was to stay", and he sealed a new two-year VR46 deal via a Ducati Corse contract and promotion to factory-spec bikes.

The machinery upgrade marked VR46 taking over from Pramac at the head of Ducati's satellite queue, as the official factory-supported team. But VR46 began the year still linked with a Yamaha deal. The Iwata factory was becoming increasingly desperate to sign a satellite team to aid its MotoGP recovery, and the Rossi connection made VR46 the obvious choice.

But VR46 management were adamant that the decision had to be based on results, not sentiment, and – despite the step back in form with the GP23 – rumours suggested that VR46 was manoeuvring itself for closer future ties with Ducati. When Yamaha clinched a deal with Pramac, it opened the door for VR46 to inherit the factory support.

"If they had said [we could do this deal] a few years ago, I wouldn't have believed it," Salucci said. "It's a truly significant moment for the entire group: having achieved this result in just three years, with a young team, with so many guys with us from Moto3, is something extraordinary."

Di Giannantonio took a pair of season-best fourth places at Phillip Island and Buriram, then reluctantly abandoned his eighth place in the championship to undergo major shoulder surgery, the legacy of a practice accident at the Red Bull Ring.

Rossi called up an old friend to take Di Giannantonio's place for Sepang in the form of Andrea Iannone, who returned to the scene of his failed 2019 anti-doping test. The 35-year-old admitted that his upper body was destroyed by the physicality of a modern MotoGP prototype, but despite having no knowledge of the GP23, he wound back the clock with flashes of speed.

"It's another MotoGP, completely another story compared to 2019," said the 2024 Aragon WorldSBK race winner. "Now you have a lot of aerodynamics. The braking point, entry and corner speed are the biggest differences. It's unbelievable."

Ducati test rider Michele Pirro took over for the Barcelona season finale, where he concluded that the GP23's front-end issues were related to the new Michelin rear tyre. The '23 bike, Pirro highlighted, had been designed around the previous generation of rear tyre.

With the Pramac Ducati seats gone, Morbidelli was the obvious choice to replace Bezzecchi in 2025. The former Petronas Yamaha title runner-up, who had never raced for a VR46 team, would remain on a Desmosedici GP24.

"Franco was the first rider to enter the VR46 Riders Academy, we have known him years, we have seen him grow in Tavullia and now, with great satisfaction, we can say that he will join the team," announced Salucci.

Di Giannantonio will have a new crew chief in 2025, David Munoz moving back to the factory Yamaha MotoGP team. Pramac's Massimo Branchini will join Morbidelli in moving to VR46, but to work with Diggia, while Franky settles into the ex-Bezzecchi crew of Matteo Flamigni.

RED BULL KTM RACING

TEAM STAFF
Stefan PIERER: KTM CEO
Hubert TRUNKENPOLZ: KTM CMO
Pit BEIRER: KTM Motorsports Director
Jens HAINBACH: Vice President Sports Management Road Racing
Fabiano STERLACCHINI: Vice President Technology Road Racing
Francesco GUIDOTTI: Team Manager MotoGP
Sebastian RISSE: Technical Manager MotoGP
Alberto GIRIBUOLA: Track Performance Manager
Mika KALLIO: Rider Coach
Sebastian KUHN: Head of Sponsorship & PR
Beatriz GARCIA: Team Co-ordinator
Jeremy WILSON: Logistics Manager

JACK MILLER PIT CREW
Cristhian PUPULIN: Crew Chief
Alessandro DAMIA: Strategy Engineer
Giovanni PIRAS: Data Engineer
Christophe LEONCE: Chief Mechanic
Michele BUBBOLINI, Xavi QUEIXALOS, Mark BARNETT: Mechanics

BRAD BINDER PIT CREW
Andres MADRID: Crew Chief
Errki SIUKOLA: Strategy Engineer
Tex GEISSLER: Data Engineer
Mark LLOYD: Chief Mechanic
Daniel PETAK, John EYRE, Florian FERRACCI: Mechanics

BRAD BINDER
Born: 11 August, 1995 – Potchefstroom, South Africa
GP Starts: 236 (91 MotoGP, 52 Moto2, 93 Moto3/125cc)
GP Wins: 17 (2 MotoGP, 8 Moto2, 7 Moto3)
World Championships: 1 Moto3

JACK MILLER
Born: 18 January, 1995 – Townsville, Queensland, Australia
GP Starts: 231 (176 MotoGP, 55 Moto3/125cc)
GP Wins: 10 (4 MotoGP, 6 Moto3)

RED BULL KTM felt ready for a title challenge in 2024, but the reality was far more sobering. They failed to win a race (sprint or grand prix) for the first time since 2019 and were in danger of losing best-of-the-rest status behind Ducati to Aprilia.

The GasGas entry of Tech3 rookie Pedro Acosta also outshone the factory riders for much of the season, but Brad Binder restored pride by narrowly beating his future team-mate to fifth in the championship.

The season began with high hopes as Binder took his RC16 to a pair of second places in Qatar. That was KTM's highest-scoring weekend of the year, and the only time an 'orange' rider was technically seen on a podium, with wild-card Dani Pedrosa's third at the damp Jerez sprint the product of a post-race penalty.

Binder slipped to eighth in the early standings, and team-mate Jack Miller as far back as 16th by Mugello, where his factory seat was confirmed as going to Acosta in 2025.

Miller was tipped to swap places with Acosta and move to Tech3, a decision he was comfortable with, given Acosta's flying form. But the Australian was in for a shock, KTM instead announcing the dual signing of Enea Bastianini and Maverick Vinales for the French team.

"The last I heard [from KTM] was, 'Don't bother talking to anybody, we want to keep you in the family,'" Miller revealed. "And then you get a phone call three

KTM RC16

Engine: 1000cc liquid-cooled, 86-degree V4, DOHC, counter-rotating crankshaft, four valves per cylinder, pneumatic valve system
Power: More than 270bhp
Electronics: Official MotoGP electronic control unit (ECU), inertial measurement unit (IMU) and unified software; ride-by-wire fuel injection
Transmission: Six-speed seamless-shift cassette-type gearbox
Frame: Carbon-fibre chassis with carbon-fibre swing-arm, front and rear ride-height devices • *Suspension:* WP inverted front fork and rear shock absorber
Ancillaries: Akrapovic exhaust • *Lubrication:* Mobil 1 • *Tyres:* Michelin
Brakes: Brembo 320, 340 and 355mm carbon twin front discs, single stainless steel rear disc, thumb and foot levers available

DANI PEDROSA
Born: 29 September, 1985 – Sabadell, Spain
GP Starts: 299 (221 MotoGP, 32 250cc, 46 125cc)
GP Wins: 54 (31 MotoGP, 15 250cc, 8 Moto3)
World Championships: 3 (2 250cc, 1 125cc)

POL ESPARGARO
Born: 10 June, 1991 – Granollers, Spain
GP Starts: 291 (169 MotoGP, 51 Moto2, 71 125cc)
GP Wins: 15 (10 Moto2; 5 125cc)
World Championships: 1 Moto2

Pit Beirer

hours before the press release saying you're not getting a contract. So I was surprised, to say the least."

The decision meant that Miller, whose fifth place at Portimao was his only top ten by the post-Mugello decision, no longer had to pick his words when describing what had gone wrong for KTM in 2024. "Last year, the information we brought [from Ducati] to improve the bike was a big addition. And now we've hit a bit of a wall," he said.

"We need to develop more, simple as that. In terms of the base stuff, we're on the same as Misano last year."

That included the carbon-fibre chassis, fast-tracked into use at the end of the previous season after a strong Misano wild-card performance by Pedrosa. "We're still on the very first model of the carbon-fibre chassis," Miller said. "So I think something needs to be done there. Even the swing-arm length, we're maxed out at the back end of the bike."

Miller's pre-break verdict that KTM had simply fallen behind was shared by motorsport director Pit Beirer. "I want to protect our riders," he said. "We need to make a step in the summer break and give the riders better tools."

The technical side of KTM's road racing activities was forced to regroup following the news that Fabiano Sterlacchini – the most senior of several key Ducati-to-KTM signings in recent years – would not be renewing his contract. The Italian, who had risen to the role of MotoGP technical co-ordinator in 17 years at Ducati, had been responsible for KTM's overall road racing activities, alongside fellow vice-president Jens Hainbach. The only people above them in the KTM hierarchy were CEO Stefan Pierer, CMO Hubert Trunkenpolz and Beirer. Subsequently, Sterlacchini would sign for Aprilia.

"It was a stormy week for us," Beirer said at the Sachsenring. "Fabiano was at the end of his contract. We were working on a new three-year contract. But we just couldn't agree to some things. That's why we mutually agreed to split up. The distance from his home was one part, but I don't want to use this as our main excuse."

At Misano, rumours spread that another key figure was to depart, team manager Francesco Guidotti, who had been hired from Pramac Ducati to replace Mike Leitner at the end of 2021. "After three years with Francesco and a lot of positive progress and working methods, we are moving the team with a different leadership approach," Beirer said. "Making these changes is never an easy process and we can only thank Francesco warmly for what he has done in our MotoGP story."

KTM's long-time Moto2 and Moto3 team manager, Aki Ajo, was confirmed in the role for 2025.

As well as the rider and management turnover, worrying financial news emerged about the Pierer Mobility Group, which KTM insisted would not impact the MotoGP project.

Brad Binder

Meanwhile, KTM's technical response to its mid-season woes appeared at its home Austrian round, where wild-card Pol Espargaro rode a prototype RC16. "We have revised the entire motorcycle: the aero package, the engine, the chassis," Beirer said.

Initially reluctant to step back from racing, Espargaro revelled in his new role as test rider and wild-card (Mugello, Red Bull Ring, Misano), which he combined with TV work. But while KTM's 'C' concession ranking allowed Espargaro to race a modified engine, the official riders were stuck with the homologated 2024 design.

Miller returned from the summer break with grim news about his future, saying that even rumoured WorldSBK options were false: "I've got nothing. The phone's not ringing. I could be heading home for an early shower." Fortunately for the 29-year-old, the phone did ring eventually. And the call was from his former Pramac team, who wanted him alongside Miguel Oliveira for its new Yamaha era.

The extent of Miller's season-long vibration woes was caught on camera during practice at Motegi, where his RC16 could be seen to be shaking violently. "That's been my life for the last ten months," the Australian said of the video clip.

"We haven't been able to solve it. It was really good for the engineers to see it so clearly. I'm not making this shit up! It's been doing it ever since we put this [revised 2024 rear] tyre in. The only solution is trying to ride through it, but it's like a wall you keep hitting your head against."

A much more violent head-banging incident occurred at the start of the Malaysian Grand Prix, where Miller was knocked down at Turn Two, and then became entangled in Fabio Quartararo's rear wheel. Repsol Honda's Joan Mir ran over his legs. He lay worryingly prone as the race was stopped.

"I feel lucky to walk away from that one, seeing some of the images," Miller said.

"That gives you a slight indication of how [sticky] these tyres are when they can grab the helmet, pick it up off the ground and pull it around like that. Then Joan used my legs as a double jump!"

Binder was also taken down in the incident, injuring his shoulder, meaning that no Red Bull KTMs were present for the restart.

The South African joined Acosta on the revised chassis, but Miller received no new parts for the end of the season. The former Honda and Ducati race winner matched his season-best fifth in the Buriram rain and signed off his RC16 career be securing 14th in the standings.

RED BULL GASGAS TECH3

TEAM STAFF

Herve PONCHARAL: Team Owner
Nicolas GOYON: Team Manager
Fabien ROPERS: Parts/Design Manager
Jordi MELENDO: Parts
Mathilde PONCHARAL: Communications
Amelie JOURDAIN: Co-ordinator & Social Media
Laura BACHELET: Assistant Press Officer
Riccardo SANCASSAN: GasGas Engineer
Edward HENRY: GasGas Support Engineer
Evangelia SISSIS: GasGas PR Manager
Gregory REBEYRAT: Mechanic Assistance

PEDRO ACOSTA PIT CREW

Paul TREVATHAN: Crew Chief
Alessio CAPUANO: Strategy Engineer
Marco CACCIANIGA: Data Engineer
Steve BLACKBURN, Herve GOURCY,
Brice GROSSIN: Mechanics
Adrian JIMENEZ CALDERO: Fuel & Tyres Manager

AUGUSTO FERNANDEZ PIT CREW

Alexandre MERHAND/Alberto GIRABOLA:
Crew Chief
Flavio NAPOLI: Strategy Engineer
Adria CASTILLA VALERO: Data Engineer
Eric LABORIE, Thomas BRUN, David LIEBERT:
Mechanics
Roberto LA CORTE: Fuel & Tyres Manager

PEDRO ACOSTA
Born: 25 May, 2004 – Mazarron, Spain
GP Starts: 75 (19 MotoGP, 38 Moto2, 18 Moto3)
GP Wins: 16 (10 Moto2; 6 Moto3)
World Championships: 2 (1 Moto2, 1 Moto3)

AUGUSTO FERNANDEZ
Born: 23 September, 1997 – Madrid, Spain
GP Starts: 134 (40 MotoGP, 94 Moto2)
GP Wins: 7 Moto2
World Championships: 1 Moto2

PEDRO ACOSTA might not have won a race in 2024, but the rookie delivered Tech3's best season in over a decade, and provided KTM with some much-needed highlights in an otherwise disappointing year.

MotoGP's most exciting rookie since title-winner Marquez in 2013, Acosta secured nine podiums (sprint and grand prix) and a pole position, and was in the lead for 13 laps. But a debut victory slipped away, as he topped the fallers list with 28 accidents and endured a barren run of five consecutive no-scores. Then he lost fifth place in the world championship – and top KTM honours – to Brad Binder on the last lap of the season.

"There were many mistakes, many difficult moments," Acosta admitted. "On the other side, many good moments, fighting for victories, improving a lot, understanding MotoGP. For this, I'm more happy than sad."

Pol Espargaro having been persuaded to step aside, Acosta settled into his fellow Spaniard's place in the Paul Trevathan-run crew. The arrival of data engineer Marco Caccianiga was the only significant change to the crew.

GAS GAS – Tech3

Engine: 1000cc liquid-cooled, 86-degree V4, DOHC, counter-rotating crankshaft, four valves per cylinder, pneumatic valve system
Power: More than 270bhp
Electronics: Official MotoGP electronic control unit (ECU), inertial measurement unit (IMU) and unified software; ride-by-wire fuel injection
Transmission: Six-speed seamless-shift cassette-type gearbox
Frame: Carbon-fibre chassis with carbon-fibre swing-arm, front and rear ride-height devices • *Suspension:* WP inverted front fork and rear shock absorber
Ancillaries: Akrapovic exhaust • *Lubrication:* Motul • *Tyres:* Michelin
Brakes: Brembo 320, 340 and 355mm carbon twin front discs, single stainless steel rear disc, thumb and foot levers available

Pedro Acosta

Augusto Fernandez

Team-mate Augusto Fernandez also had a new data engineer, Adria Castilla Valero, to replace ex-Suzuki engineer Yuta Shimabukuro, who had moved to Yamaha.

Overseeing both sides of the garage was Nicolas Goyon, in his second year as team manager, while Red Bull returned as title sponsor for the final edition of GasGas branding.

Twice a world champion, Acosta's arrival in MotoGP was highly anticipated. He played down expectations over the winter, although Marquez seemed happy to pile on the pressure: "He will achieve podiums, victories this year, and let's see if he can fight for the championship straight away."

The Marquez comparisons continued when racing got under way. A swashbuckling, if tyre-punishing debut in Qatar was followed by a new record as the youngest rider to take back-to-back MotoGP podiums – in Portimao and CoTA.

Acosta also led a race in America, leaving victory as the next logical step. And the teenager still had until Sachsenring to beat Marquez's record as the youngest MotoGP winner.

But it didn't happen, before or after Germany.

Acosta's talent was not in doubt, and a new multi-year KTM contract was announced at Mugello, confirming his move to the factory team for 2025.

Although KTM made good on its promise to back Acosta with equal factory-spec machinery to Binder and Miller, the RC16 lost touch with Ducati after returning from the USA.

Following a sobering Sachsenring, where "we were in another world to the guys winning", Acosta made a fact-finding summer-break visit to Austria. "For me, it was difficult to understand what changed from the beginning of the season to now. Do you know? Because I don't!" Acosta asked the media as the second half of the year began at Silverstone.

Persistent chatter issues triggered by the new Michelin rear tyre were a known problem, but Acosta hinted that KTM had persisted in going down the wrong path: "When somebody has difficult moments, we need to stop and go one step back, rather than continue. It's better to remake the way."

He emphasised that it was "not about the people around me" and suggested that the main aim should be to make the RC16 more consistent over a full season, even if that means surrendering its slow-corner strengths. "From the beginning of [KTM's] history in MotoGP, we were strong in braking and tight corners," he explained. "And all four riders are really pushing the braking, because it is our best point.

"The problem is in fast and flowing tracks: we can't ride like that. Because if you brake hard, you break the corner speed and you're done. We need to improve the bike a little bit, for example in turning, to not be so bad on the bad days, even if we are not so good

Paul Trevathan

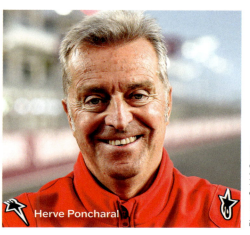
Herve Poncharal

on the good days. When we can fight for ten victories and ten top-fives in a season, we are in the game for the championship. This will be a process, but we will arrive."

After hitting a low with 13th in KTM's home Austrian round, Acosta reverted to his start-of-season settings. He was straight back on the podium at a slippery Aragon. "With the changes we've been introducing to the bike, the riding style has also gone in a different direction," he explained. "Now, going back, I'm riding the way I know. Maybe it's not the fastest bike, but it's the bike that I know.

"It's a bit like what happened in my first year in Moto2. Then we only changed the riding style. Now we have to go back, with myself and the bike, to go forward again."

A new chassis for Indonesia accelerated Acosta's return to form, matching his season best of second after being cleared of a tyre-pressure penalty due to a leaking rim. Pole position followed at Motegi, but a double disaster in the races sank his best chances of victory. Then came a shoulder ligament injury at Phillip Island, which ruled him out of the grand prix, and a 12th no-score of the year in the Buriram sprint

Acosta was still three points clear of Binder heading into the Barcelona finale, but drama in both races resulted in him losing fifth in the championship.

On the opposite side of the pit box, Fernandez rarely looked comfortable during his second and (for now) final MotoGP season. Whether it was the carbon-fibre chassis, which Tech3 received over the winter, or the 2024 rear tyre construction was a mystery for Fernandez, who admitted to copying Acosta's settings in search of progress.

It was to no avail, however, and with 2023's fourth place at Le Mans a distant memory, Fernandez found himself without a ride when Enea Bastianini and Maverick Vinales were named at Tech3 for 2025. The former Moto2 champion had mulled over Moto2 and WorldSBK options before being approached by Fabio Quartararo over a Yamaha test and wild-card deal. "The first thing that came into my mind was 'retirement'. But it's the best opportunity to get back into this paddock. I love World Superbike, but I'm not ready to close MotoGP yet. I'll give my 200 per cent as a test rider to try and be back in MotoGP in 2027."

His best of the season was tenth in Sepang. From Aragon, he worked with a new crew chief, Alberto Girabola replacing Alex Merhand. Girabola had left Ducati to become KTM's track performance manager, but he will be reunited with Bastianini at Tech3 in 2025, and he used the end-of-season rounds to settle back into the crew-chief role.

The rider line-up won't be the only change at Tech3 for 2025, as the French team will return to Red Bull KTM branding. "We made great publicity for GasGas," said KTM motorsport director Pit Beirer. "It's the youngest brand in our family and, through Pedro and Jorge Prado in motocross, is now famous around the world. On the other side, the market is facing a difficult moment and we decided to commit fully to KTM.

"We feel the project is strongest if it's a line-up with four factory riders, all in orange, all racing for Red Bull KTM. Our ultimate goal is that riders wouldn't really care which of our four places they pick. We spoke to all four boys about how we're going to work next year. It's not the usual MotoGP situation where a factory team gets new parts before a satellite team.

"It's racing, so the strongest will be the captain. If we only have enough new parts for one rider, then our best rider will get it, whichever team they are in."

Beirer added that Acosta's heroics had helped KTM pull off the biggest surprise of the silly season by signing multi-race winners Vinales and Bastianini to Tech3, despite interest from rival factory teams. "Pedro helped us show the potential of our Tech3 operation. That it's full factory. I'm sure without Pedro, we couldn't convince [Vinales and Bastianini]."

MONSTER ENERGY YAMAHA MOTOGP

TEAM STAFF

Lin JARVIS: Managing Director, Yamaha Motor Racing & Team Principal
Takahiro SUMI: General Manager, Yamaha Motor Co. & President, Yamaha Motor Racing
Kazuhiro MASUDA: YMC MotoGP Group Leader & YZR-M1 Project Leader
Massimo BARTOLINI: Technical Director, MotoGP Operations
Massimo MEREGALLI: Team Director
William FAVERO: Communications Manager
Maider BARTHE, Alen BOLLINI: Press Officers
Julian SIMON: Rider Performance Analyst
Alessandro VERONESI: Team Co-ordinator

FABIO QUARTARARO PIT CREW

Diego GUBELLINI: Crew Chief
Davide MARELLI: Data Engineer
Shinya YADA: Yamaha Engineer
Bernard ANSIAU, Achim KARIGER, Daniele GRELLI, Mark ELDER: Mechanics

ALEX RINS PIT CREW

Patrick PRIMMER: Crew Chief
Yuta SHIMABUKURO: Data Engineer
Hitoshi HOSHINO, Daisuke SUGIYAMA: Yamaha Engineers
Ian GILPIN, Jurij PELLEGRINI, Julien ARMENGAUD, Juan MADURGA REVILLA: Mechanics

FABIO QUARTARARO
Born: 20 April, 1999 – Nice, France
GP Starts: 178 (111 MotoGP, 36 Moto2, 31 Moto3)
GP Wins: 12 (11 MotoGP, 1 Moto2)
World Championships: 1 MotoGP

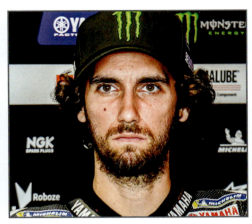

ALEX RINS
Born: 8 December, 1995 – Barcelona, Spain
GP Starts: 211 (123 MotoGP, 36 Moto2, 52 Moto3)
GP Wins: 18 (6 MotoGP, 4 Moto2, 8 Moto3)

YAMAHA suffered its worst MotoGP season in 2024, with not one podium and star rider Fabio Quartararo only 13th in the championship. But if the final season under the leadership of Lin Jarvis failed to deliver on-track, where they beat only Honda, the Englishman scored several major coups.

The first was re-signing Quartararo. The second, was tempting future world champions Pramac away from Ducati to become Yamaha's new satellite team. Not to mention news of a major technical endeavour in the form of a V4 engine.

Jarvis had been at the helm of Yamaha's MotoGP project since the late 1990s, including the glory years with Valentino Rossi. But speaking on the sidelines at February's Sepang test, he revealed that after 25 years, 2024 would be the last season he would spend in his current role.

Subsequently, Paolo Pavesio, director of marketing and motorsport for Yamaha Motor Europe, was named as Jarvis's successor. Takahiro Sumi, promoted from M1 group leader after Quartararo's 2021 title, continued to head the Japanese side as general manager of motorsports development and president of Yamaha Motor Racing. However, a variety of staff changes for the 2024 season began with Kazuhiro Masuda replacing Kazutoshi Seki as MotoGP group

YAMAHA YZR-M1

Engine: 1000cc liquid-cooled, inline 4, counter-rotating cross-plane crankshaft, DOHC, four valves per cylinder, pneumatic valve system
Power: More than 270bhp
Electronics: Official MotoGP electronic control unit (ECU), inertial measurement unit (IMU) and unified software; ride-by-wire fuel injection
Transmission: Six-speed seamless-shift cassette-type gearbox
Frame: Aluminium alloy twin-spar with aluminium/CFRP swing-arm, front and rear ride-height devices • *Suspension:* Ohlins inverted front fork and rear shock absorber
Ancillaries: Akrapovic exhaust • *Lubrication:* ENEOS • *Tyres:* Michelin
Brakes: : Brembo 320, 340 and 355mm carbon twin front discs, single stainless steel rear disc, thumb and foot levers available

REMY GARDNER

Born: 24 February, 1998 – Sydney, Australia
GP Starts: 137 (23 MotoGP, 93 Moto2, 21 Moto3)
GP Wins: 6 Moto2
World Championships: 1 Moto2

Fabio Quartararo

Massimo Meregalli

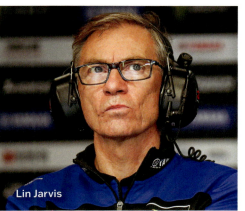

Lin Jarvis

leader and YZR-M1 project leader, plus the headline grabbing signing of Max Bartolini from Ducati.

Bartolini was assigned the new role of technical director of MotoGP operations, in charge on GP weekends. It was an unusually high technical position for someone who was not Japanese and sign of Yamaha's recognition that change was needed.

Bartolini impressed Quartararo from their first meeting. He encouraged a more aggressive European mind-set, such as extreme set-up parameters and less linear thinking. Significantly, his leadership was a major factor in securing Quartararo's continued presence in the team.

At the early test, Jarvis labelled the arrival of Bartolini as the final stage of a three-phase plan, "a process that started in 2022 when we took the contract with Luca Marmorini to help us develop the engine. To look outside of Japan, take in new knowledge and additional manpower. That was the first phase.

"The second phase was in August, 2023, when we started the collaboration with Dallara to assist us with aerodynamics. Because, honestly, we are pretty behind with aerodynamics.

"The third part of the process was when we took Marco Nicotra from Ducati last October as head of our new aerodynamics department. And then we were able to get Max Bartolini, who joined us in January.

"We know we need to change. We know we need to speed up. We know we need to be less conservative. We need to open our minds and especially the efficiency that we work in a test or a race weekend. Max will bring us that knowledge and experience from outside to create, not the Ducati system, but a new-generation Yamaha system.

"He is on an equal level with Masuda. This has never happened in my experience in Yamaha, or any Japanese manufacturer probably, to have a European on equal level with the project leader. Max will take decisions in the race-weekend environment. And Masuda will take that race-weekend knowledge and make sure it's integrated with Yamaha Japan."

Jarvis was "realistic" about Yamaha's 2024 goals: "We know the level in particular of Ducati. But we must come back to frequent podiums. I think we can win some races." That proved wildly optimistic – despite access to new technical concessions – and when star rider Quartararo began the season even worse than in 2023, the Frenchman's departure was widely rumoured.

But Jarvis wasn't about to throw in the towel: "You don't sign a contract for the bike you have now. You sign for the bike you expect to have in the future." That pitch proved crucial in retaining Quartararo, somewhat against the odds, who surprised by signing a new two-year deal in early April.

"I had the opportunity to go to every brand," said Quartararo, who had been particularly linked with Aprilia, "but I was not ready to leave Yamaha. First, to be loyal, for what they did for me in the past. And I started to really believe in the project. The investment in engineers during the pre-season was huge.

"Max Bartolini was a big factor. I believe in him and I know the plans he has with the bike. I am pretty confident. I'm still young, we've been to the top with Yamaha, now the bottom and I want to go to the top again with them." A rumoured bumper 12-million euros annual pay deal also wouldn't have done any harm.

Quartararo explained Yamaha's descent. "I think we fell asleep a bit," he said. "In 2021, our engine was much slower than Ducati, but our turning was better. Now they have the turning that we had, plus more power, using the aero and everything."

Fabio's pit crew was run by Diego Gubellini, at his side since his debut 2019 MotoGP season at Petronas. The only notable change was the arrival of data engineer Davide Marelli from the former Franco Morbidelli side of the garage.

The Frenchman's best result of the season, third in the damp Jerez sprint, was whipped away due to a post-race tyre-pressure penalty. He also experienced the sour side of Yamaha's aggressive new approach when twice he ran out of fuel on the final lap, at Misano and Motegi.

But the M1's performance took a clear step forward from September onwards, culminating in a sixth place in Malaysia.

New team-mate Alex Rins kept Morbidelli's crew chief Patrick Primmer. Helping the Spaniard to adapt to his third different MotoGP machine in as many seasons was former Suzuki engine management engineer Yuta Shimabukuro, who had spent 2023 with GasGas Tech3.

Still limping from his 2023 Mugello leg fractures, Rins might have had little to celebrate on-track during the first half of the season, but he impressed Yamaha enough to complete a new two-year deal during the summer break. Said Jarvis, "Alex is not only very talented and fast, he is also technically savvy, a hard worker and a real team player."

The relentless pace of MotoGP progress was illustrated when Rins crossed the finish line 15th at Mugello with a race time that would have ensured a win the previous year. His season-best result was eighth in Malaysia. Meanwhile, his knowledge of rival machines allowed him to highlight electronics as an area in need of improvement, while also warning that they might only mask problems "coming more from the engine".

A series of new engine specifications was duly introduced during the season, albeit at the expense of top speed. But the biggest Yamaha engine news concerned the V4 project, announced on the eve of the second Misano round.

"The inline four still has plenty of capacity to be developed, but when all of your competitors are using V4s, and looking towards the 2027 [850cc] regulations, it's important to fully understand the potential of V4 versus inline four," said Jarvis. "I don't know when you will see it racing, but track testing will not be so far away."

"In terms of pure power, a V4 shouldn't be a big difference," Bartolini explained. "But there are some ways to manage the layout of the bike, to make the tyres work better, that we think will be a little bit easier."

Former Tech3 KTM rider and current Yamaha WorldSBK podium finisher Remy Gardner stood in for the injured Rins at Sachsenring, then replaced test rider Cal Crutchlow for wild-cards at Silverstone and Motegi. Crutchlow had also missed a planned Mugello wild-card due to complications following hand surgery, triple MotoGP title runner-up Andrea Dovizioso being brought in to assist Quartararo and Rins during a private test at Misano.

TRACKHOUSE RACING

TEAM STAFF

Justin MARKS: Team Owner
Davide BRIVIO: Team Principal
Wilco ZEELENBERG: Team Manager
Robin SPIJKERS: Team Co-ordinator
Mats MELANDER: Parts Manager
Guido FONTANA: Electronics Engineer
Matteo FRIGO: Ohlins Specialist
Roberto SIMIONATO: Gearbox & Clutch Technician
Jeremy APPLETON: Director of Communications
Maria POHLMANN: Press Officer
Patrick TIGTIG: Content Creator

MIGUEL OLIVEIRA PIT CREW

Giovanni MATTAROLLO: Crew Chief
Andy GRIFFITH: Data Engineer
Stewart MILLER, Matthew LLOYD, Benjamin FRY, Francesco VARDANEGA: Mechanics
Calum WILLEY: Tyre Manager

RAUL FERNANDEZ PIT CREW

Noe HERRERA: Crew Chief
Daniel BONMATI: Data Engineer
Jorge MORELL, Martin ZABALA, Hibbatuulah FUAD, Francisco NOGUEIRA: Mechanics
Fernando MENDEZ: Tyre Manager

MIGUEL OLIVEIRA
Born: 4 January, 1995 – Pragal, Portugal
GP Starts: 228 (99 MotoGP, 50 Moto2, 79 Moto3/125cc)
GP Wins: 17 (5 MotoGP, 6 Moto2, 6 Moto3)

RAUL FERNANDEZ
Born: 23 October, 2000 – Madrid, Spain
GP Starts: 117 (57 MotoGP, 18 Moto2, 42 Moto3)
GP Wins: 10 (8 Moto2, 2 Moto3)

MOTOGP hasn't had a full-time American rider since Nicky Hayden in 2015, but it did gain an American team in 2024 when Trackhouse took over from CryptoDATA RNF.

After keeping a lid on growing financial issues for much of the 2023 season, CryptoDATA RNF suddenly unravelled at the Valencia finale. Founder Razlan Razali (40 per cent shareholder) announced his departure on the eve of the event, which was swiftly followed by rumours of unpaid bills and American investors ready to take over the grid slots.

The first of several combative statements by CryptoDATA's Romanian management (60 per cent shareholder) insisted that it was business as usual. However, the FIM, IRTA and Dorna promptly announced that the team had not been selected for the 2024 season due to "repeated infractions and breaches of the Participation Agreement affecting the public image of MotoGP."

NASCAR team Trackhouse, owned by former racer Justin Marks and Grammy award-winning rapper Pitbull, swiftly completed a deal with MotoGP and Aprilia on 5th December to fill the vacancy.

"Joining the MotoGP World Championship is a very exciting moment for our young company," said Marks. "Trackhouse has worked from day one to recognise unique and compelling motorsport opportunities, and being able to expand to a global series like MotoGP is

APRILIA RS-GP24

Engine: 1000cc liquid-cooled, 90-degree V4, counter-rotating crankshaft, DOHC, four valves per cylinder, pneumatic valve system
Power: More than 270bhp
Electronics: Official MotoGP electronic control unit (ECU), inertial measurement unit (IMU) and unified software; ride-by-wire fuel injection
Transmission: Six-speed seamless-shift cassette-type gearbox
Frame: Aluminium alloy twin-spar with carbon-fibre swing-arm, front and rear ride-height devices • *Suspension:* Ohlins inverted front fork and rear shock absorber
Ancillaries: SC-Project exhaust • *Lubrication:* Castrol • *Tyres:* Michelin
Brakes: Brembo 320, 340 and 355mm carbon twin front discs, single stainless steel rear disc, thumb and foot levers available

LORENZO SAVADORI
Born: 4 April, 1993 – Cesena, Italy
GP Starts: 60 (29 MotoGP, 31 125cc)

Wilko Zeelenberg

Justin Marks

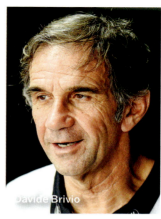
Davide Brivio

Celebrating Oliveira's German sprint podium.

a massive step in scaling the company." Dorna, IRTA and CryptoDATA announced that they had amicably solved their differences on the same day. The truce didn't last long, however. In May, 2024, CryptoDATA CEO Ovidiu Toma issued a statement claiming that RNF would initiate formal legal proceedings against Dorna and IRTA.

Trackhouse avoided the team's past controversy while inheriting RNF's bike and rider contracts, and retaining the RNF mechanics. A clear line was drawn between the team's former existence, however, with only Wilco Zeelenberg remaining from the management side.

After year-old RNF machines in 2023, Trackhouse made an early statement of intent by securing factory RS-GP24s for Miguel Oliveira and pledging to upgrade Raul Fernandez as soon as logistically possible.

Trackhouse followed that with another big announcement during their track debut at February's Sepang test. Former Yamaha and Suzuki team principal Davide Brivio, who had left MotoGP for F1 after Joan Mir's 2020 title triumph, was rumoured to be interested in a return to two-wheelers and linked with several factory projects.

"You thought you'd be talking to Davide Brivio today!" joked Yamaha's Lin Jarvis at a team presentation a few days earlier. Instead, Trackhouse was revealed as Brivio's destination, replacing short-lived team director PJ Rashidi.

Previously, Brivio and Zeelenberg had worked on different sides of the garage during Yamaha's glory days with Rossi and Lorenzo. Ex-Alpinestars and Triumph manager Jeremy Appleton was another familiar face in a new role, as the Trackhouse director of communications.

After a fourth (Oliveira) and fifth (Fernandez) in 2023, podiums seemed a realistic goal for Trackhouse. However, while Oliveira and Maverick Vinales suffered similar initial struggles on the 2024 Aprilia, the former took much longer to threaten the podium.

Oliveira's moment came at Sachsenring, where, after finishing no higher than eighth in the previous rounds, the five-times KTM winner was fastest in final practice, qualifying on the front row and hounding Jorge Martin for victory in the sprint.

Although the Ducatis stretched away on Sunday, Oliveira was best-of-the-rest again. But it was back down to earth at Silverstone, and it became increasingly obvious that Oliveira was looking elsewhere for 2025. The Portuguese rider's place at the new Pramac Yamaha project was officially confirmed in September, meaning that Fernandez would be the only Aprilia rider to start the 2025 season with previous RS-GP race experience.

It wasn't just continuity that secured Fernandez's new Trackhouse contract. The Spaniard delivered career-saving performances on the '23 bike – leading in Catalunya and joining Oliveira on the German front row – before his chassis and aerodynamics were upgraded to '24 spec in the summer break.

"I'm a super-fan of Raul," said Aprilia Racing boss Massimo Rivola, who nonetheless insisted that ultimately it was down to Trackhouse to choose its riders. "We have data that shows the speed of Raul, more than people can see from the races or lap times."

Alongside Fernandez in 2025 will be a MotoGP rookie – but not Joe Roberts. Rumours of the American stepping up to the premier class had flourished since Trackhouse's arrival: an American MotoGP rider in an American team, just as Dorna was trying to grow the US market – a key priority for the sport's future commercial rights owner Liberty Media.

The Roberts/Trackhouse rumours ramped up a gear when the 27-year-old took the early Moto2 title lead, then won at Mugello. But Trackhouse didn't follow that script. Instead, another Moto2 rider caught the attention of Brivio, who previously had given MotoGP debuts to Maverick Vinales, Alex Rins and Joan Mir at Suzuki.

Backed by Marks, Brivio surprised many by selecting Ai Ogura for the remaining Trackhouse seat. "It would be nice to have an American rider in the American team. And, of course, Joe Roberts was on our shortlist," Brivio said. "But we made our evaluation, our analysis and we decided that Ai was a better choice for our project, from a potential sporting performance point of view. Regardless of the passport."

"Ai has won races, but he also has a kind of resilience. Maybe he doesn't have a good start, but he recovers and never gives up. We also think his riding style can evolve well to a MotoGP bike."

Ogura repaid Trackhouse's faith by winning the Moto2 title at Buriram.

The ensuing Malaysian round was the last of five events that Oliveira skipped while recovering from surgery for a fractured right wrist, which had been sustained due to a traction-control glitch in practice for Mandalika.

During his absence, Fernandez had matched his season-best sixth place in the Phillip Island sprint. Then he had the wings removed from his RS-GP for the Sunday grand prix. "It was like a joke in the middle of the season – 'Maybe in a test, we can try the bike with no wings.' But in the end, it was not a joke!" Fernandez said.

Aprilia had taken advantage of an exception to the aero homologation rules for Phillip Island, allowing wings to be removed due to the possibility of strong crosswinds. "It was a nice surprise," Fernandez added after finishing tenth. "We understood a lot of things about the bike, that we're struggling with a lot. So it was a good test for the future."

The extreme move illustrated the doubts hanging over the RS-GP's aerodynamics, with Fernandez less competitive on the 2024-spec parts than he had been in the first half of the season on the '23 bike.

Aprilia test rider Lorenzo Savadori replaced the injured Oliveira for four grands prix, but – as with his factory Aprilia wild-cards – he didn't score a point.

Oliveira was not the only key Trackhouse departure for 2025. In September, news leaked that Zeelenberg would not be retained as team manager. "It's the last MotoGP race of this season and maybe also the final one of my career," the 1990 West German 250 GP winner confirmed at the Barcelona finale.

Zeelenberg has been in MotoGP since 2010, when he enjoyed instant title success overseeing Jorge Lorenzo at the factory Yamaha team. Lorenzo and Zeelenberg had won three MotoGP world championships and 43 races together by the time the Spaniard left for Ducati in 2017. Subsequently, the Dutchman worked with Maverick Vinales before joining the new Petronas Yamaha project for 2019. He continued to run the garage as it morphed into RNF, followed by a switch to Aprilia and finally Trackhouse.

LCR HONDA

TEAM STAFF

Lucio CECCHINELLO: Team Manager

Christophe BOURGUIGNON: Technical Director

Irene ANEAS: Press Officer

JOHANN ZARCO PIT CREW

David GARCIA: Crew Chief

Jaume CARRAU: Electronics Engineer

Albert TALAMINO: Data Engineer

Joan CASAS, Christopher RICHARDSON,

Michele ANDREINI, Sergi SANGRA: Mechanics

TAKAAKI NAKAGAMI PIT CREW

Klaus NOHLES: Crew Chief

Eric PEREZ: Electronics Engineer

Patricia PACHECO MARIN: Data Engineer

Federico VICINO, Filippo BRUNETTI,

Marc CANELLAS, Willibrord KLEINE: Mechanics

JOHANN ZARCO

Born: 16 July, 1990 – Cannes, France

GP Starts: 282 (144 MotoGP, 88 Moto2, 50 125cc)

GP Wins: 17 (1 MotoGP, 15 Moto2, 1 125cc)

World Championships: 2 Moto2

TAKAAKI NAKAGAMI

Born: 9 February, 1992 – Chiba, Japan

GP Starts: 262 (123 MotoGP, 105 Moto2, 34 125cc)

GP Wins: 2 Moto2

NEW LCR signing Johann Zarco carried Lucio Cecchinello's team above the factory Repsol Honda squad in the rider and team standings, during an otherwise grim year for the RC213V.

Although often fighting for crumbs left by the European machines, the Frenchman featured in Q2 five times and took Honda's only top-ten finishes.

Zarco deserved much more than his 17th place in the championship. And with team-mate Takaaki Nakagami also outscoring the Repsol riders in his final MotoGP campaign, the LCR duo collected almost triple the points of the official team. A feat that would have been unthinkable a few years previously.

Fresh from breaking his MotoGP win drought and helping Pramac Ducati to the 2023 teams' title, Zarco arrived to fill the void left by CoTA 2023 winner Alex Rins's switch to Yamaha. With the Frenchman's mid-2019 split from an uncompetitive KTM still relatively fresh in the memory, Zarco insisted that he knew the size of the task ahead and had learned from the Austrian experience.

True to his word, he showed patience in the face of Honda's woes, making the best of what was available and clawing his way forward. "To get points in the

HONDA RC213V – LCR

Engine: 1000cc liquid-cooled, 90-degree V4, counter-rotating crankshaft, DOHC, four valves per cylinder, pneumatic valve system

Power: More than 240bhp

Electronics: Official MotoGP electronic control unit (ECU), inertial measurement unit (IMU) and unified software; ride-by-wire fuel injection

Transmission: Six-speed seamless-shift cassette-type gearbox

Frame: Aluminium alloy twin-spar with aluminium swing-arm, front and rear ride-height devices • *Suspension:* Ohlins inverted front fork and rear shock absorber

Ancillaries: Akrapovic exhaust • *Lubrication:* Castrol/Idemitsu • *Tyres:* Michelin

Brakes: Brembo 320, 340 and 355mm carbon twin front discs, single stainless steel rear disc, thumb and foot levers available

Lucio Cecchinello

HONDA RC213V – LCR

Johann Zarco

Takaaki Nakagami

sprint is like a victory," he said after securing eighth in Indonesia, where he also qualified a head-turning seventh on the grid: "A few races ago, we were struggling to be in the top 15." The top ten had been Zarco's goal. "It took a bit of time, but better late than never," he said with a smile. "I did a huge step forward in the overseas races."

The 34-year-old Frenchman, whose eagerness to fight for every point meant that he gained a reputation for some ruthless mid-pack moves, magnified Honda's steady technical gains by improving his own braking skills. "We've improved a lot in the fast corners. We got a bike that was turning better because of the new aero," Zarco said of his late-season form.

"Then braking is really about technique, it's a skill that not many riders have totally mastered. I tried to develop this skill because once you can unlock it, then you can enjoy more on the bike. I also tried to work on it with the supermoto, even with my CBR. It's not about forcing the brakes more, it's about playing with the lean angle, slide and brake pressure."

While traction and turning issues continued to dog the RCV, Zarco had pinpointed the weaknesses more precisely by the end of the year. "It's too easy to just say 'rear grip,'" he explained. "It's the entry of the corner where we need to get more control of the bike, and then it will be easier to work on the traction on the exit."

Joining Honda after four years with MotoGP's dominant manufacturer, Ducati, Zarco welcomed the arrival of Aprilia's Romano Albesiano to HRC for 2025. "It's important to get information from other engineers and other brands to make bigger changes. We need something different to understand the direction. Albesiano will bring new ideas, which can be very interesting if we combine them with the high quality of the Japanese engineering."

The highlight of Zarco's season was arguably outside MotoGP, winning the Suzuka 8 Hours as part of the HRC team at his first attempt.

He slotted into the ex-Rins crew run by David Garcia, with team-mate Takaaki Nakagami continuing alongside Klaus Nohles.

Results-wise, 2024 was Nakagami's worst MotoGP season. But he was still the leading Honda rider in the standings by August, and his intention to stay at LCR was clear. "My plan A is to stay here with this team because, honestly speaking, it is not fair to judge my potential this season when all four [Honda] riders are struggling. Not only me," he said at Silverstone.

Young countryman Ai Ogura's decision to sign for Trackhouse, rather than Honda, briefly strengthened Nakagami's chances of a contract renewal. But rumours of a surprise deal for Thai Moto2 rider Somkiat Chantra grew ever stronger and, at Aragon, it was announced that Nakagami would make way for Chantra, switching to an HRC test-riding role in 2025.

"I was very happy when I knew that I would be in MotoGP next year," said Chantra, wearing his heart on his sleeve. "I was crying when I called my mum!"

Nakagami said of his future role, "It's a new chapter, I'm very excited and happy also for Chantra. The main thing I want to do is help speed up bike development in Japan and try to connect [Japan] with the paddock. We need to share many things… At the moment, no one here in the paddock knows what HRC is testing in Japan."

Upon reflection, Nakagami pinpointed when and why MotoGP's most successful manufacturer had lost its way. "From 2022," he said. "Why? Because in 2022, they changed completely the concept of the bike. I remember when I jumped on this different concept of bike I thought, 'Wow, this is not a Honda bike anymore!' Because in the past, it was a small bike and its really strong point was braking, but always the front [was] the limit. So they changed a lot of concepts to try to improve rear grip and after this, we lost the way. Then things like the aero and [ride-height] devices made more confusion, and we couldn't find a good balance for the bike."

Nakagami is expected to join HRC's other new testing recruit, Aleix Espargaro, in some MotoGP wildcard appearances in 2025.

REPSOL HONDA TEAM

TEAM STAFF

Taichi HONDA: HRC Director, General Manager Race Operations Management Division

Alberto PUIG: Repsol Honda Team Manager

Ken KAWAUCHI/Mikihiko KAWESE: HRC Technical Manager

Harry LLOYD: Head of Communications, Marketing & Sponsorship

LUCA MARINI PIT CREW

Giacomo GUIDOTTI: Chief Engineer

Masashi OGO: Chief Mechanic

Daniel VILLAR: Electronics Engineer

Eneko HEMANDO: Data Engineer

Emanuel BUCHNER, Felix KERTZSCHER, Carles LURBE, Juan LLANSA: Mechanics

JOAN MIR PIT CREW

Santi HERNANDEZ: Chief Engineer

Carlos LINAN: Chief Mechanic

Carlo LUZZI: Electronics Engineer

Ricardo CARRASCOSA: Data Engineer

Roberto CLERICI, Yuchiro SEGAWA, Jose BARBER, Liam BORONAT: Mechanics

LUCA MARINI

Born: 10 August, 1997 – Urbino, Italy

GP Starts: 163 (75 MotoGP, 87 Moto2, 1 Moto3)

GP Wins: 6 Moto2

JOAN MIR

Born: 1 September, 1997 – Palma de Mallorca, Spain

GP Starts: 154 (99 MotoGP, 18 Moto2, 37 Moto3)

GP Wins: 12 (1 MotoGP, 11 Moto3)

World Championships: 2 (1 MotoGP, 1 Moto3)

IF Marc Marquez questioned his decision to leave Repsol Honda, such doubts would soon be erased in 2024. Despite new technical concessions, the RC213V scored fewer than half of the previous year's points, remained at the bottom of the constructors' table and rarely broke into the top ten.

Without Marquez, the once mighty Repsol Honda team fell furthest, shrinking from 122 to just 35 points and dropping to last place in the teams' standings. Similarly, Joan Mir and new team-mate Luca Marini finished 21st and 22nd in the riders' classification, last of the full-time riders.

By Misano, Repsol had seen enough and pulled the plug on its historic three-decade title sponsorship. However, Honda – criticised for doing too little, too late to keep Marquez – was responding. More senior Japanese personnel were reassigned, while European influence was bolstered by future deals with Romano Albesiano and Aleix Espargaro.

The RCV did show signs of progress as the season went on. With the axe having fallen on technical manager Takeo Yokoyama and technology director Shinichi Kokubu during 2023, the next reshuffle resulted in HRC general manager Tetsuhiro Kuwata – the of-

HONDA RC213V – Repsol

Engine: 1000cc liquid-cooled, 90-degree V4, counter-rotating crankshaft, DOHC, four valves per cylinder, pneumatic valve system

Power: More than 240bhp

Electronics: Official MotoGP electronic control unit (ECU), inertial measurement unit (IMU) and unified software; ride-by-wire fuel injection

Transmission: Six-speed seamless-shift cassette-type gearbox

Frame: Aluminium alloy twin-spar with aluminium swing-arm, front and rear ride-height devices • *Suspension:* Ohlins inverted front fork and rear shock absorber

Ancillaries: Akrapovic exhaust • *Lubrication:* Repsol • *Tyres:* Michelin

Brakes: Brembo 320, 340 and 355mm carbon twin front discs, single stainless steel rear disc, thumb and foot levers available

STEFAN BRADL

Born: 29 November, 1989 – Augsburg, Germany
GP Starts: 218 (131 MotoGP, 33 Moto2, 54 125cc)
GP Wins: 7 (5 Moto2, 2 125cc)
World Championships: 1 Moto2

Luca Marini

Alberto Puig

Santi Hernandez

ficial head of the MotoGP project – moved to a 'new role' in early 2024.

Taichi Honda, from HRC's off-road department, was parachuted into Kuwata's place, but he maintained a low-key presence in the paddock. As did former Suzuki technical boss Ken Kawauchi, in his second season at Honda after replacing Yokoyama.

While Yamaha went on a winter hiring spree for European influence, HRC's only comparable recruitment was Alex Baumgartel, or 'Alex from Kalex', as a 'technical advisor'. HRC had contracted Kalex to build its swing-arms since 2022, followed by a full chassis in 2023. But any hope that Baumgartel would inspire a wave of rapid development was soon quashed, and he had departed by Aragon.

After a torrid debut Honda season, 2020 Suzuki world champion Joan Mir moved to the other side of the garage to join the ex-Marquez crew, led by Santi Hernandez. Thus new HRC signing Marini was inserted into Mir's old crew, run by Giacomo Guidotti.

Winter testing on a heavily revised machine brought cautious optimism, but soon it emerged that the chosen engine design had been a mistake.

"We've been a bit unlucky because the engine character looked pretty good in the pre-season Sepang test, but then gave a lot of unexpected problems," Mir explained.

"We started even more behind than last season," confirmed Marini. "And nobody expected this."

After three seasons on a Desmosedici, Marini also pinpointed aerodynamics as a fundamental weakness: "Because the aero is about everything. If you play with the aero, you can find more grip, more turning, better stopping. It doesn't give you more horsepower, but it can give you less drag, so you are faster on the straights.

"The manufacturers that started to work on aerodynamics first have an advantage and it's clear we are struggling on that side. Plus, for sure, with the engine [character]."

After scoring 201 points and two podiums in his final VR46 Ducati season, Marini didn't score a single Honda point until Sachsenring, where he was promoted to 15th by post-race tyre-pressure penalties. But Valentino Rossi's younger brother reacted angrily to rumours that dire results might prompt him to seek an early exit from Honda.

"We are only at the beginning," said Marini, who had signed a two-year deal. "It's true, last year, I was fighting for podiums and now fighting for one point is tough. But I'm really satisfied with the people I am working with at Honda and we are getting better."

By contrast, Mir – whose contract expired at the end of 2024 – openly questioned his future. "The reality is that recently, nobody goes out of Honda in a better [career] situation than they went in," he said.

"When I came to Honda, I had many offers. And now it's not like this."

Nobody could accuse Mir of not trying. A rider who had crashed 12 times as a Suzuki rookie hit the ground 24 times in his first Honda season. He added another ten accidents in the early part of 2024, while trying to extract more than the RCV could offer.

"I have no idea how long my body can take this. I'm trying to do my best, but you can't expect miracles," said Mir, whose 9th and 12th finishes at Jerez were Honda's best results in the first half of the season.

The 27-year-old openly considered following Marquez's footsteps and jumping ship to a competitive bike, even if that meant riding for a satellite team. "I spoke many times with Marc," he said. "I have an example that I can follow, or I can stay in this situation." His manager painted a more positive picture: "Joan doesn't like to exit from the back door. He likes to fight and help [Honda] build a competitive bike".

To some surprise, Mir signed a new two-year HRC contract during the summer break. That deal followed hot on the heels of official confirmation that Aleix Espargaro would join HRC as a test and wild-card rider in 2025.

The biggest Aprilia-to-Honda surprise was still to come. During Honda's home grand prix at Motegi, Romano Albesiano was announced as its 2025 technical director, hired to "oversee HRC's MotoGP project and the continued development of the Honda RC213V machine."

It's the first time that a European has held such a level of technical authority in HRC. "Romano will bring us a lot of experience, a lot of knowledge," said Marini. "Aprilia did a fantastic job in recent years, and I'm super-happy about this news."

Kawauchi's absence from the front line was also explained at Motegi: he had moved to the MotoGP test team and been replaced by Mikihiko Kawese.

"We will keep all the same engineers as now, with Romano as an addition," Marini continued. "I don't think it will change the philosophy of Honda… We just need a bit more co-ordination and communication sometimes. A direct link between what's happening in the garage and Japan."

Honda's Albesiano deal followed Yamaha's signing of Max Bartolini at the start of 2024. But Marini argued that it's not as simple as hiring a top European, since "The results for Yamaha are not coming yet. And they were not starting as far behind as Honda. We started two seconds [a lap] from Ducati. Now we are closer to one second, but it's still not enough. I think next year will be much better."

Marini scored points in five of the last seven rounds, including a best of 12th at Emilia-Romagna and Thailand. "The latest fairing helps with turning, and the new swing-arm is better on corner-entry feeling," Marini said of his progress. "The engine is also in the correct direction now, more rideable. But still, there is a lack of grip compared to other manufacturers."

Mir also took his season-best 11th at 'Misano 2'. But the Spaniard's vibration issues with the new Michelin rear tyre were never cured. "It's disturbing me a lot. I lose four-tenths in just two corners," he said of the chatter at Mandalika. "The good thing is that the other Honda riders seem to have it much less."

Honda finished its worst MotoGP season without a confirmed replacement for sponsor Repsol, whose logos have adorned the factory team since 1994. "The Repsol Honda Team is the most successful team in the history of the championship, with 11 team titles, 15 rider titles and 183 victories in the premier class of motorcycling", reminded a Repsol statement confirming its exit. Coincidence or not, the announcement came minutes after former rider Marquez had won the San Marino Grand Prix for Gresini, a race no Repsol Honda rider even started, due to illness.

Marquez had visited his former Honda crew earlier in the weekend, just days after his debut Ducati victory at Aragon. "I gathered all the group together and said, 'You are part of this victory'. Because they all suffered with me and helped me through a lot of dark moments," said Marquez, who had taken what will go down in history as Repsol Honda's final race win at Misano in 2021.

FIM MOTO2 WORLD CHAMPIONSHIP

2024 TEAMS AND RIDERS

By PETER McLAREN

AI OGURA ruled the inaugural season of Pirelli tyres to become Japan's first world champion of the Moto2 era and first non-Kalex champion since Marc Marquez. He did it with a new team and chassis, having split from Honda Team Asia to join the new MT Helmets-MSI squad (formerly Pons), taking Boscoscuro to its first Moto2 crown.

The change from Dunlop to Pirelli tyres produced a major shake-up in the chassis hierarchy, with Kalex – chasing 12 riders' and constructors' titles in a row – beaten by Boscoscuro in seven of the opening nine races.

Aided by overwhelming grid numbers, however, the German manufacturer staged a determined fight-back to retain its constructors' crown. It was led by Fantic's Aron Canet, who smashed his victory drought by claiming the most race wins and finishing title runner-up to Ogura.

Fermin Aldeguer's dominant end to 2023 had resulted in a Ducati MotoGP contract being signed before the start of the season. But while other Boscoscuro riders revelled in the Pirelli era, kicking off with a round-one victory by team-mate Alonso Lopez, Aldeguer sunk to sixth in the early standings and never recovered.

Joe Roberts was next to be tipped for a MotoGP move. The American fought for the early title lead, but Trackhouse surprised by picking Ogura over its 'home' rider. Sergio Garcia, the first repeat winner of the year, was another whose MotoGP dream disappeared.

By contrast, Thai star Somkiat Chantra sealed the final 2025 MotoGP seat at LCR Honda, despite not featuring on the Moto2 podium.

Ogura was the last of the four Boscoscuro riders to win in 2024, while Jake Dixon, Manuel Gonzalez and Celestino Vietti joined Roberts and Canet on the top step for Kalex. It was a bittersweet debut victory for Gonzalez, whose unwitting 'headband' gesture at Motegi resulted in a split with Gresini's title sponsor.

Diogo Moreira snatched a podium from under the nose of Ogura at the season finale to seal Rookie of the Year over Senna Agius. Deniz Oncu made it three rookies to reach the podium, but reigning Moto3 champion Jaume Masia had only half a dozen points.

Third chassis manufacturer Forward made headlines for the wrong reasons at Misano, where a track worker crossed the pit lane in front of stand-in rider Unai Orradre. The collision sent Orradre's bike swerving into the Aprilia MotoGP garage.

Marc VDS reacted swiftly to Boscoscuro's early dominance by signing a chassis deal for 2025, but its lead rider, Tony Arbolino, would switch to the new Pramac Yamaha Moto2 project. Pramac also chose Boscoscuro's chassis.

Exclusive engine supplier Triumph planned to introduce a new racing gearbox for the 2025 season.

2024 MOTO 2 RIDERS

#	Rider	Team
3	Sergio Garcia	MT Helmets - MSI - Boscoscuro
4	Simone Corsi	KLINT Forward Factory Team - Forward
5	Jaume Masia	Pertamina Mandalika GAS UP Team - Kalex
6	Andrea Migno	Yamaha VR46 Master Camp Team - Kalex
7	Barry Baltus	RW-Idrofoglia Racing GP - Kalex
9	Jorge Navarro	KLINT Forward Factory Team - Forward
10	Diogo Moreira	Italtrans Racing Team - Kalex
11	Alex Escrig	KLINT Forward Factory Team - Forward
11	Matteo Ferrari	QJMOTOR Gresini Moto2 - Kalex
12	Filip Salac	Elf Marc VDS Racing Team - Kalex
13	Celestino Vietti	Red Bull KTM Ajo - Kalex
14	Tony Arbolino	Elf Marc VDS Racing Team - Kalex
15	Darryn Binder	Liqui Moly Husqvarna Intact GP - Kalex
16	Joe Roberts	OnlyFans American Racing Team - Kalex
17	Daniel Munoz	Pertamina Mandalika GAS UP Team - Kalex
18	Manuel Gonzalez	QJMOTOR Gresini Moto2 - Kalex
19	Mattia Pasini	Team Ciatti Boscoscuro - Boscoscuro
20	Xavi Cardelus	Fantic Racing - Kalex
21	Alonso Lopez	Sync SpeedUp - Boscoscuro
22	Ayumu Sasaki	Yamaha VR46 Master Camp Team - Kalex
24	Marcos Ramirez	OnlyFans American Racing Team - Kalex
28	Izan Guevara	CFMOTO Aspar Team - Kalex
29	Harrison Voight	Preicanos Racing Team - Kalex
31	Roberto Garcia	Fantic Racing - Kalex
32	Marcel Schrotter	Red Bull KTM Ajo - Kalex
34	Mario Aji	IDEMITSU Honda Team Asia - Kalex
35	Somkiat Chantra	IDEMITSU Honda Team Asia - Kalex
40	Unai Orradre	KLINT Forward Factory Team - Forward
43	Xavier Artigas	KLINT Forward Factory Team - Forward
44	Aron Canet	Fantic Racing - Kalex
52	Jeremy Alcoba	Yamaha VR46 Master Camp Team - Kalex
53	Deniz Oncu	Red Bull KTM Ajo - Kalex
54	Fermin Aldeguer	Sync SpeedUp - Boscoscuro
55	Helmi Azman	PETRONAS MIE Racing RW - Kalex
62	Stefano Manzi	Yamaha VR46 Master Camp Team - Kalex
64	Bo Bendsneyder	Pertamina Mandalika GAS UP Team - Kalex
67	Alberto Surra	Sync SpeedUp - Boscoscuro
71	Dennis Foggia	Italtrans Racing Team - Kalex
75	Albert Arenas	QJMOTOR Gresini Moto2 - Kalex
79	Ai Ogura	MT Helmets - MSI - Boscoscuro
81	Senna Agius	Liqui Moly Husqvarna Intact GP - Kalex
84	Zonta van den Goorbergh	RW-Idrofoglia Racing GP - Kalex
89	Khairul Idham Pawi	PETRONAS MIE Racing RW - Kalex
96	Jake Dixon	CFMOTO Aspar Team - Kalex

Ai Ogura Aron Canet

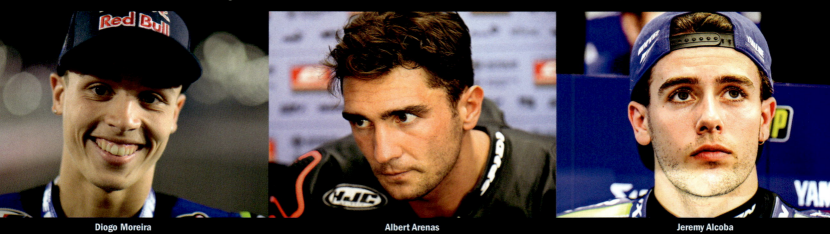

Diogo Moreira Albert Arenas Jeremy Alcoba

Filip Salac Izan Guevara Senna Agius

Sergio Garcia Manuel Gonzalez

Photos: Gold & Goose

Celestino Vietti   Jake Dixon

Zonta van den Goorbergh   Jorge Navarro   Dennis Foggia

Mario Aji   Xavi Cardelus   Alex Escrig

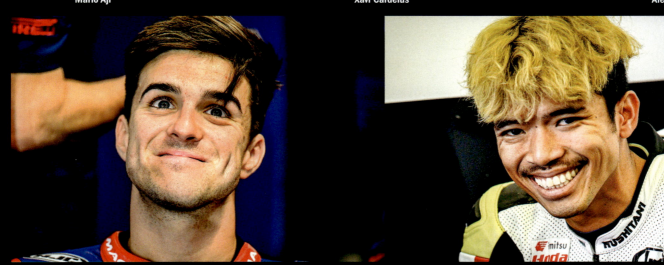

Marcos Ramirez   Somkiat Chantra

Photos: Gold & Goose

FIM MOTO3 WORLD CHAMPIONSHIP
2024 TEAMS AND RIDERS

By PETER McLAREN

DAVID ALONSO made history as the first Colombian to win a grand prix title, his 14 wins also breaking Valentino Rossi's record for most Moto3/125 victories in a season.

The 18-year-old continued the momentum from his rookie campaign to wrap up the title by the Japanese GP. Alonso was Aspar's third champion in five seasons, after Albert Arenas (2020) and Izan Guevara (2022), but first with a CFMoto-branded KTM.

Of the 26 full-time entries, ten were for Honda, with KTM filling the remainder of the grid, branded as either KTM (10), GasGas (2), Husqvarna (2) or CF-Moto (2).

After being locked at 2021-spec for two seasons, Moto3 machines also began a fresh development cycle in 2024.

KTM came out on top from the redesign, with reigning champion Honda winless for the opening 12 rounds and absent from the final championship top five.

The mid-season review introduced an agreed bike freeze until 2026, but with KTM giving consent for Honda to use engine modifications as its one available first-year upgrade. However, those changes resulted in overheating issues at Sepang.

Rookies Angel Piqueras and Luca Lunetta provided the Honda highlights. Riding for reigning champions Leopard, Piqueras took Honda's only win (despite two long-laps) on his way to Rookie of the Year. Lunetta also featured on the podium for Sic58.

With Alonso grabbing the lion's share of trophies, Ivan Ortola was the only other repeat winner. Alonso's distant title rival, Dani Holgado, plus Collin Veijer and Jose Antonio Rueda joined Piqueras with a single victory each.

Alonso and Holgado would become Aspar team-mates in Moto2 for 2025. Ortola and Veijer would also step up to the intermediate class.

KTM announced a slimming down of its rebranding for 2025, resulting in the GasGas and Husqvarna names disappearing from the Moto3 grid.

2024 MOTO3 RIDERS

#	Rider	Team
5	Tatchakorn Buasri	Honda Team Asia - Honda
6	Ryusei Yamanaka	MT Helmets - MSI - KTM
7	Filippo Farioli	SIC58 Squadra Corse - Honda
8	Eddie O'Shea	FleetSafe Honda - MLav Racing - Honda
10	Nicola Carraro	LEVELUP - MTA - KTM
12	Jacob Roulstone	Red Bull GASGAS Tech3 - GASGAS
18	Matteo Bertelle	Rivacold Snipers Team - Honda
19	Scott Ogden	FleetSafe Honda - MLav Racing - Honda
21	Vicente Perez	Red Bull KTM Ajo - KTM
22	David Almansa	Rivacold Snipers Team - Honda
24	Tatsuki Suzuki	Liqui Moly Husqvarna Intact GP - Husqvarna
31	Adrian Fernandez	Leopard Racing - Honda
32	Rei Wakamatsu	FleetSafe Honda - MLav Racing - Honda
34	Jakob Rosenthaler	Liqui Moly Husqvarna Intact GP - Husqvarna
36	Angel Piqueras	Leopard Racing - Honda
48	Ivan Ortola	MT Helmets - MSI - KTM
54	Riccardo Rossi	CIP Green Power - KTM
55	Noah Dettwiler	CIP Green Power - KTM
57	Danial Shahril	SIC58 Squadra Corse - Honda
58	Luca Lunetta	SIC58 Squadra Corse - Honda
64	David Munoz	BOE Motorsports - KTM
66	Joel Kelso	BOE Motorsports - KTM
70	Joshua Whatley	FleetSafe Honda - MLav Racing - Honda
71	Hamad Al Sahouti	Rivacold Snipers Team - Honda
72	Taiyo Furusato	Honda Team Asia - Honda
78	Joel Esteban	CFMOTO Aspar Team - CFMOTO
80	David Alonso	CFMOTO Aspar Team - CFMOTO
82	Stefano Nepa	LEVELUP - MTA - KTM
83	Alvaro Carpe	Red Bull KTM Ajo - KTM
85	Xabi Zurutuza	Red Bull KTM Ajo - KTM
89	Marcos Uriarte	CFMOTO Valresa Aspar Team - CFMOTO
93	Arbi Aditama	Honda Team Asia - Honda
95	Collin Veijer	Liqui Moly Husqvarna Intact GP - Husqvarna
96	Daniel Holgado	Red Bull GASGAS Tech3 - GASGAS
99	Jose Antonio Rueda	Red Bull KTM Ajo - KTM

David Alonso Daniel Holgado

Stefano Nepa Tatsuki Suzuki Jacob Roulstone

Matteo Bertelle Joel Esteban Riccardo Rossi

Collin Veijer Ivan Ortola

Photos: Gold & Goose

David Munoz   Adrian Fernandez

Filippo Farioli

Scott Ogden

Nicola Carraro

Tatchakorn Buasri

Noah Dettwiler

Eddie O'Shea

Joel Kelso

Taiyo Furusato

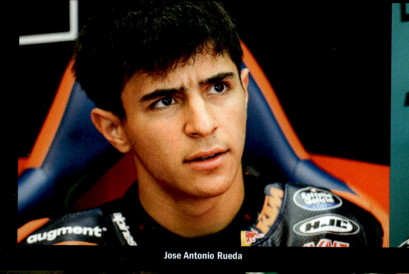
Jose Antonio Rueda

Angel Piqueras

David Almansa — Xabi Zurutuza — Vicente Perez

Joshua Whatley — Rei Wakamatsu — Arbi Aditama

Ryusei Yamanaka — Luca Lunetta

Photos: Gold & Goose

MOTOGP · MOTO2 · MOTO3
GRANDS PRIX 2024
Reports by MICHAEL SCOTT & NEIL MORRISON
Statistics compiled by PETER McLAREN

Main: Something old, something new – Bagnaia, Binder, Martin and Marquez lead a precocious Acosta.

Inset: All smiles on the first Sunday podium of the new year.
Photos: Gold & Goose

Above: Martin took control in the sprint race.

Top right: The challenger and the champ. Acosta started the year at Marquez's shoulder.

Above right: Tyre headaches for Michelin's Piero Taramasso.

Above far right: Back from F1 with Alpine, Davide Brivio was in charge at Trackhouse.

Right: Echelons of power. The MotoGP gang poses for the new season's group photo.

Photos: Gold & Goose

THIS could be no routine season-opener, thanks to two major questions, both of which concerned Marc Marquez.

The first directly: would a switch to Ducati revive the fortunes of the formerly dominant superstar, or would his advancing years (he had turned 31 in February), and the toll of three years of crashes and injuries tip the balance?

The second was beyond his influence: would star rookie Pedro Acosta emulate his progress? Would those dubbing him "the next Marc" be correct? There were some specific targets: Marc had been on the podium at his first attempt, and had won his second race, aged 20 and 63 days. Having started at a slightly earlier age, Acosta had until the summer break to depose his compatriot as the youngest ever winner.

Pre-season tests had fuelled the speculation. Marquez's wicked grin following his first Ducati ride at the November Valencia test had been an early portent, and he'd been strong at the 2024 tests. He was sixth at the Sepang 2024 opener, more than half a second off Bagnaia and fourth (to Bagnaia again) by four-tenths at the Qatar outing. Acosta had the advantage of an extra three days at Sepang – as a rookie, he could join factory testers in the so-called 'shakedown', where he was fastest. Up against the full-timers, he was ninth. At Qatar, 15th and a second away was still impressive, but seemed more realistic.

All were agog to see what would happen when they began riding in anger.

Neither made the podium, but both showed potential aplenty. Marc was fifth in the sprint and fourth on Sunday, just 1.8 and 3.4 seconds behind double winner Bagnaia: "My bike is working well, but they are riding better than me." Adaptation was a work in progress: "I need to improve my riding style in some points. Round two will be important. Normally, I take time to arrive with a good lap time. A test here two weeks ago helped me a lot this weekend."

Acosta's eighth and ninth belied his prowess. He challenged for the podium on Sunday before eventually falling back after burning his tyres. He'd looked completely at home among the top names, carrying high corner speed and braking late: "Only one or two mistakes … it's not so much. We need to be happy."

But it was not just about them.

At Ducati, there was some relief at no repeat of the previous year's misstep with the new bike, although all riders of the GP24 experienced some chatter problems that would continue to haunt them. Aprilia's new bike also showed all-round improvement, being more predictable and sporting upgraded aero, while KTM had definitely come back stronger, according to Brad Binder, after a double podium. Braking and corner entry showed "huge steps compared to here last year."

Yamaha and Honda remained in the doldrums, in spite of new chassis and engine upgrades for both, for the opposition had become still faster. The timings on a track that admittedly was in good condition, and well rubbered after tests and the 1,812km World Endurance sports car race the previous weekend, underlined development.

With race length cut by a lap after a delayed start, the overall time was not directly comparable to the previous November's GP, but winner Bagnaia's lap time was faster by better than seven-tenths a lap. The 11-lap sprint was even more impressive, 11.3 seconds faster. Ducati had improved by 11 seconds, Aprilia by 14, and KTM by 16. Honda's Mir was 7.8 seconds quicker than Marquez had been in 2023, but Quartararo bettered his time by only 4.8 seconds.

There was welcome relief at the easing, if only partially, of the front tyre-pressure strictures, after repeated calls to Michelin. Not only was the minimum permitted pressure lower, at 1.80 bar instead of the original 1.88 bar, but also the ultimate sanction of disqualification had been rescinded. In its place was a new penalty of 16 seconds. But the other hand took something away – in 2023, riders could get away with being under minimum pressure for 50 per cent of the race; in 2024, only 40 per cent of it.

Michelin's head of two-wheel motorsport, Piero Taramasso, explained that in response to teams and riders' requests, "We ran simulations track by track and looked at the data from last year. We decided it was possible to lower the front tyre pressure." The change to 60 per cent reflected the greater risk of the lower limit. "When you run lower, the carcass is moving and you risk damaging it."

Riders could control the situation via onboard pressure monitors. According to 2023 Qatar winner Di Giannantonio,

FIM WORLD CHAMPIONSHIP | 1

"We have a countdown of laps, how many laps you have to be in to be in the regulation. Once you are okay, you are free to be in front." But if the pressure was too low, "slipstream, slipstream, slipstream! It's the only way … and to brake as hard as possible to get the pressure up to the necessary level again."

Pirelli's first race as new supplier to the smaller classes produced mixed results. The Moto3 race was a stunning 30 seconds faster than the previous November's. Yet the Moto2 outing was 13 seconds slower, with a number of high-profile names suffering from a serious lack of rear tyre performance. Manager Giorgio Barbier professed satisfaction for "our first grand prix … [at] one of the most demanding tracks for tyres." In tests and practice, bad weather had limited track time, complicating tyre choice. "It will take a few GP rounds to set up the bikes, and the riders will also need a bit of time to adapt to our tyres."

MOTOGP SPRINT RACE – 11 laps

Martin secured the first pole of the season, with fellow GP24 rider Bastianini third. Between them was Aleix Espargaro on "the best Aprilia yet". Binder led row two from Bagnaia and Marc Marquez; Acosta was in the middle of row three, between Di Giannantonio and Alex Marquez. Zarco was top Honda, 13th fastest, Quartararo 16th.

The sprint was predictably intense, but Martin was in control throughout, leading into the first corner and successfully fending off fast-starting Binder's early attack. The order of the first two remained unchanged.

Close behind, Bagnaia was quickly past Bastianini into third, with Espargaro following him through. Next past the second factory Ducati was Marc Marquez on lap five, the top six still close.

Marc's next victim was Espargaro, and he was leaning on Bagnaia, eye on a podium finish. But it didn't last, and three laps later, Espargaro was back ahead after the Ducati ran slightly wide.

Now it was the Aprilia challenging for the podium, and while the first attack failed, with Bagnaia straight back in front, with two laps to go, Espargaro was ahead for good. The Aprilia's corner speed outweighed any top-speed advantage Bagnaia might claw back.

Marc was still close, Bastianini half a second down; Alex Marquez succeeded in holding Acosta at bay. Vinales took the last point; Miller and off-song Bezzecchi were spaced out behind, the Italian back ahead of Quartararo on the final lap. Di Giannantonio was an early faller.

MOTOGP RACE – 21 laps (shortened)

The start was delayed after Raul Fernandez's Aprilia stalled on the line. He would start the shortened race from the pit lane, but last only four laps.

Ten minutes later, Bagnaia started his second title defence in emphatic fashion, making the final ten laps something of an anticlimax. Was this really a new year? So many aspects of his weekend performance mirrored 2023: Friday disappointing, Saturday underwhelming. But, as he had done seven times during the previous season, he saved his best for the feature race. Binder was never more than 1.3 seconds behind, but never got a sniff.

Bagnaia left his rivals trailing from the opening exchanges. No one had an answer. "We worked in silence," he grinned soon after, referring to his unfancied pre-race status. His pace throughout was ferocious and the key to his 19th premier-class win came early. During the sprint, he'd experienced the implications of sitting in another bike's slipstream, as first he suffered from rising front tyre pressure, and by the end, rear chatter issues. The latter were also of concern to Martin, after a relatively subdued third place.

Martin got the jump from Binder; Bagnaia passed the South African at Turn Two before barrelling under Martin two

Above: KTM started strong, with a pair of second places for Binder.

Top right: Barry Baltus narrowly missed the Moto2 win, but was overjoyed with his first podium.

Above right: Alonso Lopez took his first win in more than a year.

Above far right: Japanese teenager Furusato celebrated a second career podium with his Honda Team Asia.

Right: First blood to Boscoscuro as Lopez holds off the determined charge of Baltus's Kalex.

Below right: Alonso, heading Holgado, Furusato and Rossi, timed it perfectly.

Photos: Gold & Goose

corners later. Soon, he had edged out half a second. From there, his rhythm was relentless. He couldn't really break clear, but with his lead never under 0.9 of a second, the contest was a formality from half-distance.

It was left to Acosta to bring the noise. There was a semblance of a contest during the first ten laps, after Miller crashed out of eighth at the beginning of lap two. Marc Marquez, Bastianini, Alex Marquez, Di Giannantonio, Espargaro and the class rookie all gathered behind the battling Binder and Martin.

Acosta soon began to move forward, twice with late-braking prowess at the final turn, passing Di Giannantonio and Bastianini on laps two and three. By the fifth, he'd passed Alex Marquez at Turn Ten, at the second attempt. On the 12th, he even bustled past Marc on the run to Turn One. With third-placed Martin just a tenth of a second clear, it was looking like a giant-killing performance. But while the leaders were carefully conserving their rear rubber, the cavalier approach would have consequences. A first sign of this came through Turn 13 on the 14th lap, where he ran off-track to let Marc back through. Soon the big names behind were poised to pounce.

Martin and Binder had been exchanging places repeatedly, the South African taking advantage of the KTM's much improved braking stability and corner entry speed. That helped Bagnaia to escape.

Over the last five laps, the leading quintet edged apart. Rising front tyre temperatures were a common complaint, making it more comfortable to trail several bike lengths back. Marc did get to within two-tenths of Martin on lap 18, but he'd been saving rubber for a final push. He moved clear of Marquez and back within range of Binder, just three-tenths off the South African starting the final lap. In the end, he was never close enough to pass.

Marc Marquez was content with fourth; Acosta had slipped back to ninth, after succumbing in turn to Bastianini, Alex Marquez, Di Giannantonio and Espargaro (complaining of a sub-standard rear tyre). Vinales was a muted tenth.

Another four seconds away, both Quartararo and Zarco had overtaken Mir in the last two laps, the trio still close, with Bezzecchi less than a second behind. Oliveira took the last point, having served a much-delayed long-lap penalty – incurred at the same track in 2023 during a sprint-race crash with Espargaro.

Rins made an undistinguished Yamaha debut, back ahead of Augusto Fernandez's GasGas on the last lap; Morbidelli, in 18th, was invisible on his first Pramac Ducati appearance, after missing all the tests injured, a second ahead of Nakagami. Honda new boy Marini was miles behind, four-tenths ahead of the remounted Miller.

MOTO2 RACE – 18 laps

Even without limited testing and Friday's practice being rained off, Pirelli's first race was fraught with unknowns. But few expected the result to be so distorted.

Not only did Alonso Lopez take a first win since 2022, his career third, but also second- and third-placed Barry Baltus and Sergio Garcia were podium first-timers. Meanwhile, pre-race favourites Aldeguer and Arbolino limped home in 16th and 20th, miles behind.

Moreover, Aron Canet, who had taken the first pole of the season ahead of Lopez and Albert Arenas, slumped from a strong early lead to a distant and disconsolate tenth. All were victims of an ill-advised choice of hard rear tyre, which went down badly as the laps wore on.

Canet made a poor start, finishing lap one behind early leader Alonso, Manu Gonzalez, Arenas and Arbolino. However, he fought through to the lead on lap three with such authority that victory seemed a formality. Yet three laps on, the Spaniard was clearly in trouble, having quickly dropped behind Lopez and Gonzalez, before losing further ground to Baltus two laps on.

Those on the softer rear rubber thrived. As Gonzalez dropped away, after briefly leading on lap ten, new Boscoscuro riders Ogura and Garcia – 13th and 18th on the grid – advanced, the latter seizing third on lap 13 to make a three-way fight with six laps to play.

The lead trio was marginally clear of Ogura starting the final lap, with very little to choose between them. On numerous occasions, Baltus tried to muscle by Lopez for a maiden victory, through the final turns in particular. Then a slide exiting Turn Five on the final lap gave Lopez enough to win his first race since October, 2022, by barely five-hundredths of

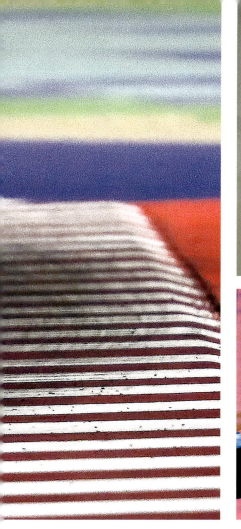

a second. Garcia was seven-tenths behind, content with a maiden podium in the class. It was a strong debut on a new chassis in a new team.

The same could be said for Ogura, a lonely fourth, while Gonzalez just held off Marcos Ramirez's Kalex on the closing lap, after the American Racing Team rider had mounted a spirited recovery from 17th on lap seven. In the final five laps, no rider was as quick as the Andalusian.

Team-mate Roberts was a disappointed seventh, lamenting poor qualifying and a set-up gamble that had hampered his chances at a personal favourite track. But it was a respectable comeback from 14th on lap four, to beat the fading Arenas. Celestino Vietti took ninth off Canet on the last lap.

Oncu was the best of six ex-Moto3 rookies, taking the last point. Champion Masia was 25th behind fellow newcomers Moreira and Aji; Sasaki crashed out early.

MOTO3 RACE – 16 laps

Pirelli's first Moto3 race was very different from Moto2 – as frantic as it ever had been with Dunlop rubber. In an opening-round classic, Columbian boy-wonder David Alonso took a thrilling last-corner win after starting the final lap eighth. Four-tenths of a second covered the top six.

Holgado was on pole, ahead of fellow Spaniards Ortola and Rueda. He led the first lap from the last named, although as usual this was by so little as to be notional.

Then Rueda took down Ortola on lap three, leaving Holgado to capably set the pace, although never more than half a second ahead of an 11-rider group.

Starting the last lap, he led Furusato, Rossi and Adrian Fernandez. Alonso recovered three places through the first two corners. By the fourth, he was ahead of Fernandez, who promptly high-sided out at Turn Five, taking down Vicente Perez. The Colombian made two further overtakes at Turns Ten and 12 before coolly snatching the lead from Holgado at the final turn. Four-hundredths covered the top two, with Furusato 0.14 of a second back in third, his second podium.

Rossi, Veijer and Nepa completed the top six. A remounted Ortola came through from last on lap three to ninth, splitting the Australian pair, with Joel Kelso eighth and impressive rookie Jacob Roulstone tenth.

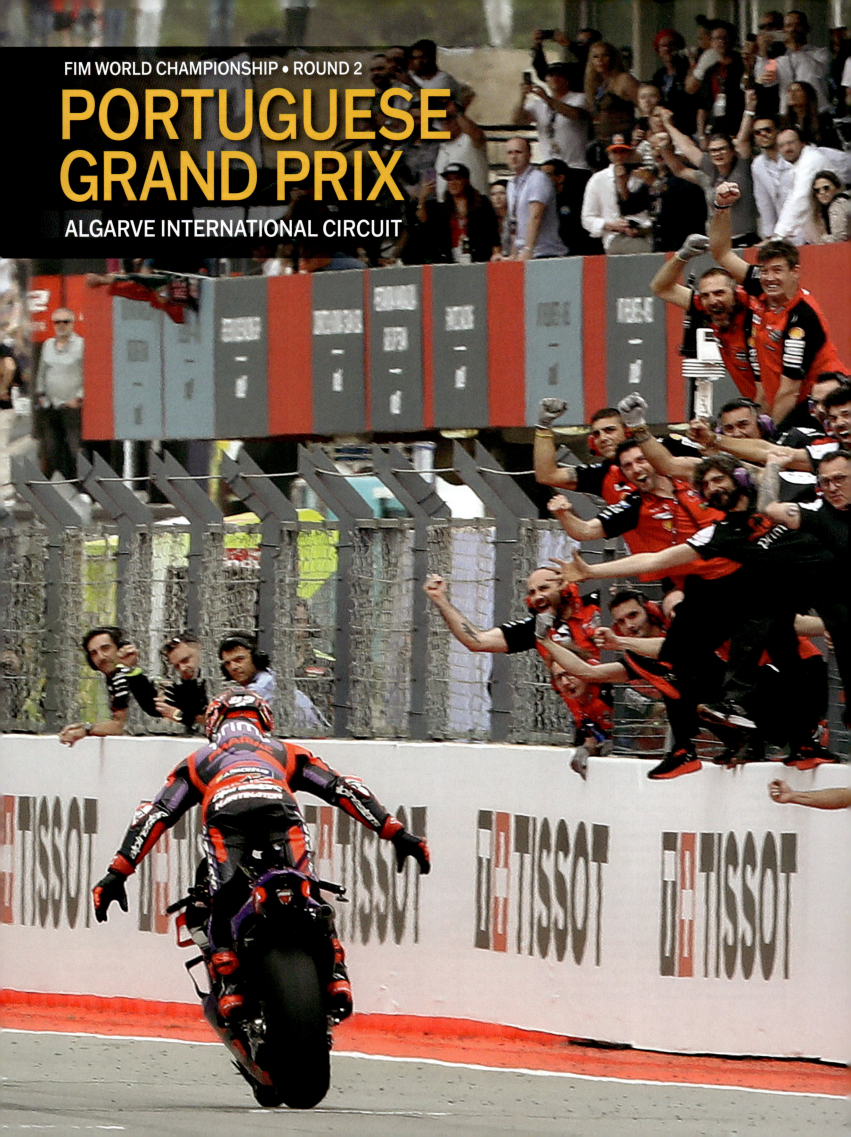

a second. Garcia was seven-tenths behind, content with a maiden podium in the class. It was a strong debut on a new chassis in a new team.

The same could be said for Ogura, a lonely fourth, while Gonzalez just held off Marcos Ramirez's Kalex on the closing lap, after the American Racing Team rider had mounted a spirited recovery from 17th on lap seven. In the final five laps, no rider was as quick as the Andalusian.

Team-mate Roberts was a disappointed seventh, lamenting poor qualifying and a set-up gamble that had hampered his chances at a personal favourite track. But it was a respectable comeback from 14th on lap four, to beat the fading Arenas. Celestino Vietti took ninth off Canet on the last lap.

Oncu was the best of six ex-Moto3 rookies, taking the last point. Champion Masia was 25th behind fellow newcomers Moreira and Aji; Sasaki crashed out early.

MOTO3 RACE – 16 laps

Pirelli's first Moto3 race was very different from Moto2 – as frantic as it ever had been with Dunlop rubber. In an opening-round classic, Columbian boy-wonder David Alonso took a thrilling last-corner win after starting the final lap eighth. Four-tenths of a second covered the top six.

Holgado was on pole, ahead of fellow Spaniards Ortola and Rueda. He led the first lap from the last named, although as usual this was by so little as to be notional.

Then Rueda took down Ortola on lap three, leaving Holgado to capably set the pace, although never more than half a second ahead of an 11-rider group.

Starting the last lap, he led Furusato, Rossi and Adrian Fernandez. Alonso recovered three places through the first two corners. By the fourth, he was ahead of Fernandez, who promptly high-sided out at Turn Five, taking down Vicente Perez. The Colombian made two further overtakes at Turns Ten and 12 before coolly snatching the lead from Holgado at the final turn. Four-hundredths covered the top two, with Furusato 0.14 of a second back in third, his second podium.

Rossi, Veijer and Nepa completed the top six. A remounted Ortola came through from last on lap three to ninth, splitting the Australian pair, with Joel Kelso eighth and impressive rookie Jacob Roulstone tenth.

QATAR AIRWAYS GRAND PRIX OF QATAR 89

FIM WORLD CHAMPIONSHIP: ROUND 1
QATAR AIRWAYS GRAND PRIX OF QATAR

8-10 MARCH, 2024

LOSAIL INTERNATIONAL CIRCUIT
21 laps
Length: 5.380km / 3,343 miles
Width: 12m

MOTOGP: RACE DISTANCE: 21 laps, 70.203 miles/112.980km
WEATHER: Dry (air 22°, humidity 66%, track 26°)

Pos.	Rider	Nat.	No.	Entrant	Machine	Race tyre choice	Laps	Time & speed
1	Francesco Bagnaia	ITA	1	Ducati Lenovo Team	Ducati Desmosedici GP24	F: Medium/R: Medium	21	39m 34.869s 106.4mph/171.2km/h
2	Brad Binder	RSA	33	Red Bull KTM Factory Racing	KTM RC16	F: Medium/R: Medium	21	39m 36.198s
3	Jorge Martin	SPA	89	Prima Pramac Racing	Ducati Desmosedici GP24	F: Medium/R: Medium	21	39m 36.802s
4	Marc Marquez	SPA	93	Gresini Racing MotoGP	Ducati Desmosedici GP23	F: Medium/R: Medium	21	39m 38.298s
5	Enea Bastianini	ITA	23	Ducati Lenovo Team	Ducati Desmosedici GP24	F: Medium/R: Medium	21	39m 40.022s
6	Alex Marquez	SPA	73	Gresini Racing MotoGP	Ducati Desmosedici GP23	F: Medium/R: Medium	21	39m 41.660s
7	Fabio Di Giannantonio	ITA	49	Pertamina Enduro VR46 Racing	Ducati Desmosedici GP23	F: Medium/R: Medium	21	39m 44.030s
8	Aleix Espargaro	SPA	41	Aprilia Racing	Aprilia RS-GP24	F: Medium/R: Medium	21	39m 46.111s
9	Pedro Acosta	SPA	31	Red Bull GASGAS Tech3	KTM RC16	F: Medium/R: Medium	21	39m 46.464s
10	Maverick Vinales	SPA	12	Aprilia Racing	Aprilia RS-GP24	F: Medium/R: Medium	21	39m 48.066s
11	Fabio Quartararo	FRA	20	Monster Energy Yamaha MotoGP	Yamaha YZR-M1	F: Medium/R: Medium	21	39m 52.570s
12	Johann Zarco	FRA	5	CASTROL Honda LCR	Honda RC213V	F: Medium/R: Medium	21	39m 52.944s
13	Joan Mir	SPA	36	Repsol Honda Team	Honda RC213V	F: Medium/R: Medium	21	39m 53.306s
14	Marco Bezzecchi	ITA	72	Pertamina Enduro VR46 Racing	Ducati Desmosedici GP23	F: Medium/R: Medium	21	39m 54.063s
15	Miguel Oliveira	POR	88	Trackhouse Racing	Aprilia RS-GP24	F: Medium/R: Medium	21	39m 55.586s
16	Alex Rins	SPA	42	Monster Energy Yamaha MotoGP	Yamaha YZR-M1	F: Medium/R: Medium	21	39m 58.962s
17	Augusto Fernandez	SPA	37	Red Bull GASGAS Tech3	KTM RC16	F: Medium/R: Medium	21	39m 58.975s
18	Franco Morbidelli	ITA	21	Prima Pramac Racing	Ducati Desmosedici GP24	F: Medium/R: Medium	21	39m 59.510s
19	Takaaki Nakagami	JPN	30	IDEMITSU Honda LCR	Honda RC213V	F: Soft/R: Medium	21	40m 00.425s
20	Luca Marini	ITA	10	Repsol Honda Team	Honda RC213V	F: Medium/R: Medium	21	40m 17.291s
21	Jack Miller	AUS	43	Red Bull KTM Factory Racing	KTM RC16	F: Medium/R: Medium	21	40m 17.630s
	Raul Fernandez	SPA	25	Trackhouse Racing	Aprilia RS-GP23	F: Medium/R: Medium	17	DNF-ret in pit

Fastest lap: Pedro Acosta, on lap 2, 1m 52.657s, 106.8mph/171.9km/h.
Lap record: Enea Bastianini, 1m 52.978s, 106.5mph/171.4km/h (2023).
Event maximum speed: Jack Miller, 223.7mph/360.0km/h (sprint).

Qualifying: Weather: Dry **Air:** 26° **Humidity:** 63% **Track:** 33°
1 Martin 1m 50.789s, 2 A. Espargaro 1m 50.872s, 3 Bastianini 1m 50.875s, 4 Binder 1m 50.913s,
5 Bagnaia 1m 50.928s, 6 M. Marquez 1m 50.961s, 7 Di Giannantonio 1m 51.019s, 8 Acosta 1m 51.130s,
9 A. Marquez 1m 51.266s, 10 Vinales 1m 51.306s, 11 Miller 1m 51.340s, 12 R. Fernandez 1m 51.521s.
Q1: 13 Zarco 1m 51.537s, 14 Oliveira 1m 51.565s, 15 Bezzecchi 1m 51.864s, 16 Quartararo 1m 51.918s,
17 Mir 1m 52.026s, 18 A. Fernandez 1m 52.204s, 19 Nakagami 1m 52.228s, 20 Rins 1m 52.327s,
21 Marini 1m 52.952s, 22 Morbidelli 1m 52.980s.

SPRINT RACE: 11 laps, 36.773 miles/59.180km
WEATHER: Dry (air 21°, humidity 52%, track 27°)

Pos.	Rider	Race tyre choice	Laps	Time & speed
1	Jorge Martin	F: Medium/R: Medium	11	20m 41.287s 106.6mph/171.6km/h
2	Brad Binder	F: Medium/R: Medium	11	20m 41.835s
3	Aleix Espargaro	F: Medium/R: Medium	11	20m 42.016s
4	Francesco Bagnaia	F: Medium/R: Medium	11	20m 42.912s
5	Marc Marquez	F: Medium/R: Medium	11	20m 43.159s
6	Enea Bastianini	F: Medium/R: Medium	11	20m 43.609s
7	Alex Marquez	F: Medium/R: Medium	11	20m 44.441s
8	Pedro Acosta	F: Medium/R: Medium	11	20m 45.718s
9	Maverick Vinales	F: Medium/R: Medium	11	20m 48.025s
10	Jack Miller	F: Soft/R: Medium	11	20m 53.957s
11	Marco Bezzecchi	F: Medium/R: Medium	11	20m 54.122s
12	Fabio Quartararo	F: Medium/R: Medium	11	20m 54.150s
13	Miguel Oliveira	F: Medium/R: Medium	11	20m 54.382s
14	Raul Fernandez	F: Medium/R: Medium	11	20m 55.082s
15	Joan Mir	F: Medium/R: Medium	11	20m 55.383s
16	Johann Zarco	F: Medium/R: Medium	11	20m 56.127s
17	Alex Rins	F: Medium/R: Medium	11	20m 56.916s
18	Augusto Fernandez	F: Medium/R: Medium	11	20m 58.998s
19	Takaaki Nakagami	F: Soft/R: Soft	11	21m 04.020s
20	Franco Morbidelli	F: Medium/R: Medium	11	21m 04.554s
21	Luca Marini	F: Medium/R: Medium	11	21m 06.840s
	Fabio Di Giannantonio	F: Medium/R: Medium	2	DNF-crash

Fastest race lap: Marc Marquez, on lap 3, 1m 52.040s.

Fastest race laps
1 Acosta 1m 52.657s, 2 Bagnaia 1m 52.667s, 3 Binder 1m 52.729s, 4 Martin 1m 52.742s,
5 M. Marquez 1m 52.773s, 6 A. Marquez 1m 52.811s, 7 A. Espargaro 1m 52.887s, 8 Bastianini 1m 52.890s,
9 Di Giannantonio 1m 52.909s, 10 Vinales 1m 52.932s, 11 A. Fernandez 1m 53.214s, 12 Rins 1m 53.270s,
13 Bezzecchi 1m 53.342s, 14 Oliveira 1m 53.401s, 15 Zarco 1m 53.410s, 16 Mir 1m 53.457s,
17 Quartararo 1m 53.468s, 18 Morbidelli 1m 53.630s, 19 R. Fernandez 1m 53.638s,
20 Nakagami 1m 53.704s, 21 Miller 1m 53.927s, 22 Marini 1m 54.306s.

Grid order	1	2	3	4	5	6	7	8	9	10	11	12	13	14	15	16	17	18	19	20	21
89 MARTIN	1	1	1	1	1	1	1	1	1	1	1	1	1	1	1	1	1	1	1	1	1
41 A. ESPARGARO	89	33	33	89	89	89	89	33	33	89	33	33	33	33	33	33	33	33	33	33	2
23 BASTIANINI	33	89	89	33	33	33	33	89	89	33	89	89	89	89	89	89	89	89	89	89	3
33 BINDER	93	93	93	93	93	93	93	93	93	31	31	93	93	93	93	93	93	93	93	93	4
1 BAGNAIA	23	23	73	73	31	31	31	31	31	93	93	31	31	73	73	73	73	23	23	23	5
93 M. MARQUEZ	49	73	31	31	73	73	73	73	73	73	73	73	73	31	23	23	23	73	73	73	6
49 DI GIANNANTONIO	73	31	23	23	23	23	23	23	23	23	23	23	23	23	31	31	31	49	49	49	7
31 ACOSTA	43	49	49	49	49	49	49	49	49	49	49	49	49	49	49	49	49	31	41	41	8
73 A. MARQUEZ	41	41	41	41	41	41	41	41	41	41	41	41	41	41	41	41	41	41	31	31	9
12 VINALES	31	20	20	20	20	20	20	12	12	12	12	12	12	12	12	12	12	12	12	12	10
43 MILLER	20	12	36	36	12	12	12	20	20	20	20	20	20	36	36	36	36	20	20	20	11
25 R. FERNANDEZ	12	36	5	12	36	36	36	36	36	36	36	36	36	20	20	20	20	36	36	36	12
5 ZARCO	36	5	12	5	5	5	5	5	42	42	42	42	42	42	5	5	5	5	5	5	13
88 OLIVEIRA	5	72	72	72	72	42	42	42	5	5	5	5	5	5	72	72	72	72	72	72	14
72 BEZZECCHI	88	88	88	88	42	37	37	37	37	37	37	37	72	72	72	42	42	88	88	88	15
20 QUARTARARO	37	37	42	42	37	72	72	72	72	72	72	72	37	37	37	37	88	37	42		
36 MIR	72	42	37	37	25	25	25	25	25	25	25	25	88	88	88	88	37	42	37		
37 A. FERNANDEZ	42	25	25	25	21	21	21	88	88	88	88	88	25	25	42	42	42	21			
30 NAKAGAMI	0	21	21	21	88	88	88	21	21	21	21	21	42	42	25	25	25				
42 RINS	25	30	30	30	30	30	30	30	30	30	30	30	30	30	30	30					
10 MARINI	21	10	10	10	10	10	10	43	43	43	43	43	10	43	43	43	43				
21 MORBIDELLI	30	43	43	43	43	43	43	10	10	10	10	10	25								

Championship Points
1	Bagnaia	25	(6)	31
2	Binder	20	(9)	29
3	Martin	16	(12)	28
4	M. Marquez	13	(5)	18
5	Bastianini	11	(4)	15
6	A. Espargaro	8	(7)	15
7	A. Marquez	10	(3)	13
8	Di Giannantonio	9	(0)	9
9	Acosta	7	(2)	9
10	Vinales	6	(1)	7
11	Quartararo	5	(0)	5
12	Zarco	4	(0)	4
13	Mir	3	(0)	3
14	Bezzecchi	2	(0)	2
15	Oliveira	1	(0)	1

Constructor Points
1	Ducati	25	(12)	37
2	KTM	20	(9)	29
3	Aprilia	8	(7)	15
4	Yamaha	5	(0)	5
5	Honda	4	(0)	4

MOTO2: 18 laps, 60.174 miles/96.840km

RACE WEATHER: Dry (air 22°, humidity 71%, track 29°)

Pos.	Rider	Nat.	No.	Entrant	Machine	Laps	Time & Speed
1	Alonso Lopez	SPA	21	Sync SpeedUp	Boscoscuro	18	35m 45.595s / 100.9mph/162.4km/h
2	Barry Baltus	BEL	7	RW-Idrofoglia Racing GP	Kalex	18	35m 45.650s
3	Sergio Garcia	SPA	3	MT Helmets - MSI	Boscoscuro	18	35m 46.337s
4	Ai Ogura	JPN	79	MT Helmets - MSI	Boscoscuro	18	35m 47.109s
5	Manuel Gonzalez	SPA	18	QJMOTOR Gresini Moto2	Kalex	18	35m 50.695s
6	Marcos Ramirez	SPA	24	OnlyFans American Racing Team	Kalex	18	35m 50.915s
7	Joe Roberts	USA	16	OnlyFans American Racing Team	Kalex	18	35m 54.653s
8	Albert Arenas	SPA	75	QJMOTOR Gresini Moto2	Kalex	18	35m 54.805s
9	Celestino Vietti	ITA	13	Red Bull KTM Ajo	Kalex	18	35m 56.305s
10	Aron Canet	SPA	44	Fantic Racing	Kalex	18	35m 56.474s
11	Somkiat Chantra	THA	35	IDEMITSU Honda Team Asia	Kalex	18	36m 00.661s
12	Jeremy Alcoba	SPA	52	Yamaha VR46 Master Camp Team	Kalex	18	36m 04.581s
13	Zonta van den Goorbergh	NED	84	RW-Idrofoglia Racing GP	Kalex	18	36m 04.633s
14	Bo Bendsneyder	NED	64	Pertamina Mandalika GAS UP	Kalex	18	36m 07.933s
15	Deniz Oncu	TUR	53	Red Bull KTM Ajo	Kalex	18	36m 08.163s
16	Fermin Aldeguer	SPA	54	Sync SpeedUp	Boscoscuro	18	36m 10.815s
17	Senna Agius	AUS	81	Liqui Moly Husqvarna Intact GP	Kalex	18	36m 12.655s
18	Darryn Binder	RSA	15	Liqui Moly Husqvarna Intact GP	Kalex	18	36m 14.110s
19	Dennis Foggia	ITA	71	Italtrans Racing Team	Kalex	18	36m 15.694s
20	Tony Arbolino	ITA	14	Elf Marc VDS Racing Team	Kalex	18	36m 15.951s
21	Filip Salac	CZE	12	Elf Marc VDS Racing Team	Kalex	18	36m 26.798s
22	Diogo Moreira	BRA	10	Italtrans Racing Team	Kalex	18	36m 28.713s
23	Xavi Cardelus	AND	20	Fantic Racing	Kalex	18	36m 28.780s
24	Mario Aji	INA	34	IDEMITSU Honda Team Asia	Kalex	18	36m 28.854s
25	Jaume Masia	SPA	5	Pertamina Mandalika GAS UP	Kalex	18	36m 29.218s
26	Alex Escrig	SPA	11	KLINT Forward Factory Team	Forward	17	36m 52.644s
27	Xavier Artigas	SPA	43	KLINT Forward Factory Team	Forward	17	36m 52.744s
	Izan Guevara	SPA	28	CFMOTO Aspar Team	Kalex	12	DNF-ret in pit
	Ayumu Sasaki	JPN	22	Yamaha VR46 Master Camp Team	Kalex	6	DNF-crash

Fastest lap: Aron Canet, on lap 3, 1m 57.661s, 102.3mph/164.6km/h.
Lap record: Sam Lowes, 1m 57.366s, 102.5mph/165.0km/h (2023).
Event maximum speed: Deniz Oncu, 185.4mph/298.3km/h (race).

Qualifying
Weather: Dry
Air: 22° **Humidity:** 52% **Track:** 29°

1	Canet	1m 56.788s
2	Lopez	1m 56.890s
3	Arenas	1m 57.025s
4	Gonzalez	1m 57.027s
5	Arbolino	1m 57.214s
6	Baltus	1m 57.336s
7	Aldeguer	1m 57.362s
8	Ramirez	1m 57.396s
9	Guevara	1m 57.463s
10	V d Goorbergh	1m 57.579s
11	Binder	1m 57.584s
12	Alcoba	1m 57.610s
13	Ogura	1m 57.690s
14	Roberts	1m 57.720s
15	Chantra	1m 57.762s
16	Vietti	1m 57.777s
17	Bendsneyder	1m 57.795s
18	Garcia	1m 58.618s
Q1		
19	Salac	1m 57.982s
20	Oncu	1m 58.004s
21	Agius	1m 58.345s
22	Masia	1m 58.412s
23	Foggia	1m 58.464s
24	Escrig	1m 58.493s
25	Sasaki	1m 58.654s
26	Moreira	1m 58.817s
27	Cardelus	1m 59.161s
28	Aji	1m 59.388s
29	Artigas	2m 01.328s

Fastest race laps

1	Canet	1m 57.661s
2	Guevara	1m 57.957s
3	Garcia	1m 58.026s
4	Ogura	1m 58.075s
5	Chantra	1m 58.097s
6	Arenas	1m 58.162s
7	Gonzalez	1m 58.165s
8	Aldeguer	1m 58.226s
9	Baltus	1m 58.240s
10	Lopez	1m 58.244s
11	V d Goorbergh	1m 58.268s
12	Binder	1m 58.299s
13	Arbolino	1m 58.328s
14	Salac	1m 58.617s
15	Oncu	1m 58.640s
16	Bendsneyder	1m 58.657s
17	Alcoba	1m 58.665s
18	Vietti	1m 58.668s
19	Roberts	1m 58.692s
20	Ramirez	1m 58.826s
21	Agius	1m 58.829s
22	Foggia	1m 58.921s
23	Escrig	1m 59.053s
24	Cardelus	1m 59.224s
25	Aji	1m 59.263s
26	Moreira	1m 59.291s
27	Sasaki	1m 59.466s
28	Masia	1m 59.603s
29	Artigas	2m 00.445s

Championship Points

1	Lopez	25
2	Baltus	20
3	Garcia	16
4	Ogura	13
5	Gonzalez	11
6	Ramirez	10
7	Roberts	9
8	Arenas	8
9	Vietti	7
10	Canet	6
11	Chantra	5
12	Alcoba	4
13	Van den Goorbergh	3
14	Bendsneyder	2
15	Oncu	1

Constructor Points

1	Boscoscuro	25
2	Kalex	20

MOTO3: 16 laps, 53.488 miles/86.080km

RACE WEATHER: Dry (air 24°, humidity 49%, track 33°)

Pos.	Rider	Nat.	No.	Entrant	Machine	Laps	Time & Speed
1	David Alonso	COL	80	CFMOTO Aspar Team	CFMOTO	16	33m 19.778s / 96.3mph/154.9km/h
2	Daniel Holgado	SPA	96	Red Bull GASGAS Tech3	GASGAS	16	33m 19.819s
3	Taiyo Furusato	JPN	72	Honda Team Asia	Honda	16	33m 19.921s
4	Riccardo Rossi	ITA	54	CIP Green Power	KTM	16	33m 19.964s
5	Collin Veijer	NED	95	Liqui Moly Husqvarna Intact GP	Husqvarna	16	33m 20.116s
6	Stefano Nepa	ITA	82	LEVELUP - MTA	KTM	16	33m 20.194s
7	Tatsuki Suzuki	JPN	24	Liqui Moly Husqvarna Intact GP	Husqvarna	16	33m 20.922s
8	Joel Kelso	AUS	66	BOE Motorsports	KTM	16	33m 29.243s
9	Ivan Ortola	SPA	48	MT Helmets - MSI	KTM	16	33m 29.797s
10	Jacob Roulstone	AUS	12	Red Bull GASGAS Tech3	GASGAS	16	33m 30.404s
11	Joel Esteban	SPA	78	CFMOTO Aspar Team	CFMOTO	16	33m 30.605s
12	Angel Piqueras	SPA	36	Leopard Racing	Honda	16	33m 30.711s
13	Scott Ogden	GBR	19	MLav Racing	Honda	16	33m 32.706s
14	Nicola Carraro	ITA	10	LEVELUP - MTA	KTM	16	33m 32.724s
15	Luca Lunetta	ITA	58	SIC58 Squadra Corse	Honda	16	33m 33.305s
16	David Munoz	SPA	64	BOE Motorsports	KTM	16	33m 35.731s
17	Noah Dettwiler	SWI	55	CIP Green Power	KTM	16	33m 48.704s
18	Joshua Whatley	GBR	70	MLav Racing	Honda	16	33m 48.904s
19	Tatchakorn Buasri	THA	5	Honda Team Asia	Honda	16	33m 54.398s
	Vicente Perez	SPA	21	Red Bull KTM Ajo	KTM	15	DNF-crash
	Adrian Fernandez	SPA	31	Leopard Racing	Honda	15	DNF-crash
	Ryusei Yamanaka	JPN	6	MT Helmets - MSI	KTM	14	DNF-crash
	Filippo Farioli	ITA	7	SIC58 Squadra Corse	Honda	4	DNF-crash
	Matteo Bertelle	ITA	18	Rivacold Snipers Team	Honda	4	DNF-crash
	Jose Antonio Rueda	SPA	99	Red Bull KTM Ajo	KTM	2	DNF-crash

Fastest lap: Tatsuki Suzuki, on lap 3, 2m 3.135s, 97.7mph/157.2km/h.
Lap record: Romano Fenati, 2m 5.403s, 95.9mph/154.4km/h (2019).
Event maximum speed: Taiyo Furusato, 155.7mph/250.5km/h (race).

Qualifying
Weather: Dry
Air: 23° **Humidity:** 51% **Track:** 31°

1	Holgado	2m 02.276s
2	Ortola	2m 02.541s
3	Rueda	2m 02.596s
4	Fernandez	2m 02.632s
5	Bertelle	2m 02.672s
6	Kelso	2m 02.691s
7	Rossi	2m 03.020s
8	Alonso	2m 03.059s
9	Perez	2m 03.166s
10	Veijer	2m 03.249s
11	Farioli	2m 03.327s
12	Piqueras	2m 03.370s
13	Munoz	2m 03.389s
14	Lunetta	2m 03.390s
15	Yamanaka	2m 03.462s
16	Nepa	2m 03.551s
17	Roulstone	2m 03.760s
18	Furusato	2m 04.071s
Q1		
19	Suzuki	2m 04.468s
20	Ogden	2m 04.716s
21	Whatley	2m 04.858s
22	Carraro	2m 05.163s
23	Esteban	2m 05.355s
24	Buasri	2m 05.634s
25	Dettwiler	2m 05.738s

Fastest race laps

1	Suzuki	2m 03.135s
2	Nepa	2m 03.194s
3	Furusato	2m 03.202s
4	Yamanaka	2m 03.224s
5	Alonso	2m 03.383s
6	Perez	2m 03.419s
7	Ortola	2m 03.427s
8	Veijer	2m 03.459s
9	Kelso	2m 03.490s
10	Rueda	2m 03.490s
11	Holgado	2m 03.594s
12	Fernandez	2m 03.645s
13	Rossi	2m 03.708s
14	Roulstone	2m 03.779s
15	Lunetta	2m 03.845s
16	Piqueras	2m 03.900s
17	Ogden	2m 03.933s
18	Bertelle	2m 04.042s
19	Farioli	2m 04.107s
20	Munoz	2m 04.313s
21	Esteban	2m 04.391s
22	Carraro	2m 04.492s
23	Buasri	2m 05.085s
24	Dettwiler	2m 05.107s
25	Whatley	2m 05.467s

Championship Points

1	Alonso	25
2	Holgado	20
3	Furusato	16
4	Rossi	13
5	Veijer	11
6	Nepa	10
7	Suzuki	9
8	Kelso	8
9	Ortola	7
10	Roulstone	6
11	Esteban	5
12	Piqueras	4
13	Ogden	3
14	Carraro	2
15	Lunetta	1

Constructor Points

1	CFMOTO	25
2	GASGAS	20
3	Honda	16
4	KTM	13
5	Husqvarna	11

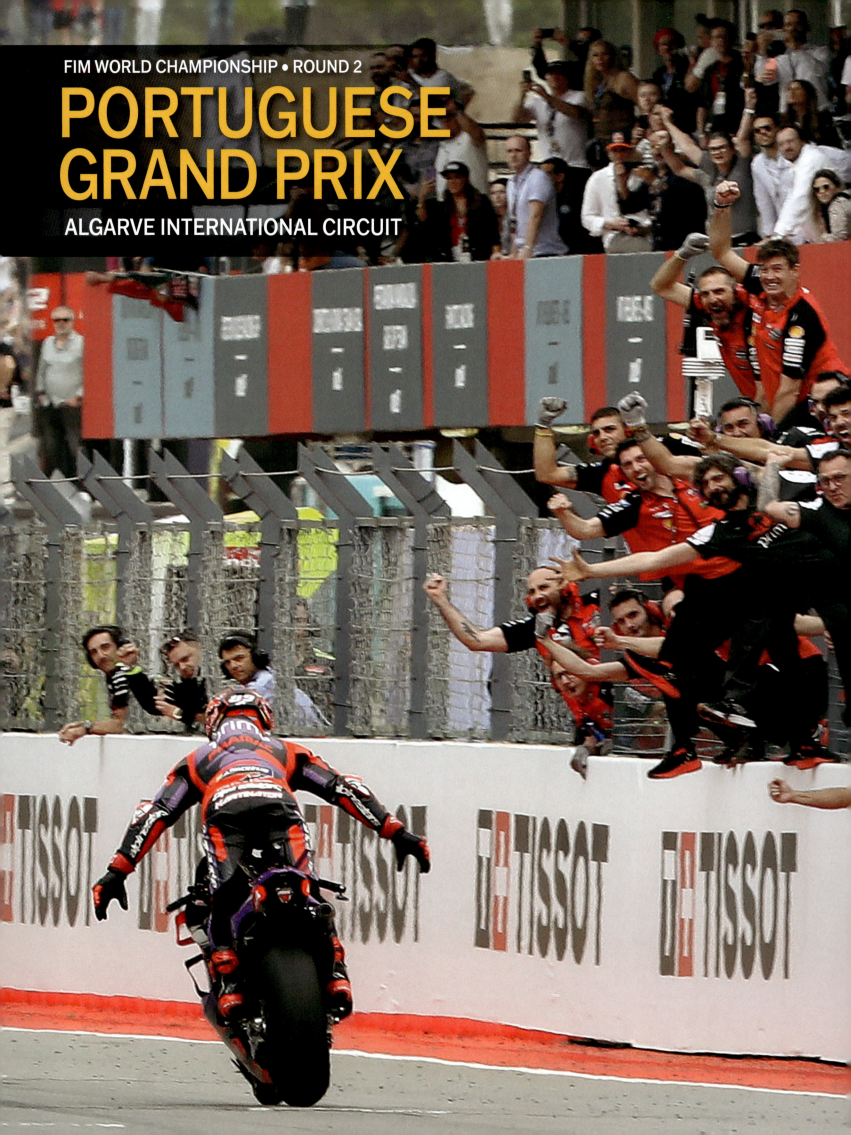

Above: Mix of makes: Vinales's Aprilia (12), Miller's KTM (43) and Martin's Ducati (89) lead away in the sprint. Marquez and Bezzecchi give chase.

Right: Leading lights on the deck: Marquez and Bagnaia collided for zero points.

Opening spread: Take a bow. Martin wins the main race for Pramac.
Photos: Gold & Goose

TWO races in, and the battle lines were already becoming clear. And not only in the championship table. Personal rivalry between Bagnaia and Marquez was given a major boost when the pair collided and exchanged harsh opinions; Acosta's blazing beginning burned brighter still; while the fortune of Vinales and Aprilia played yet another cruel trick.

The racing was not especially exciting at the spectacular track, but the undercurrents were. Specifically, a who-goes-where controversy that started early and would intensify over the coming weeks.

The trigger was confirmation that Moto2 favourite Fermin Aldeguer had been snapped up by Ducati, evidence no doubt of corporate dismay at the way in which KTM had snaffled Acosta. Aldeguer, considered by many to be the next big thing, confirmed a two-year deal starting in 2025. This followed a contract tussle in 2023 between Ducati and his Moto2 employer, Luca Boscoscuro, determined to keep him in his eponymous team, and ended the badgering of the rider about his future. "Now it's time to focus on Moto2," he said. Which he did with his first points of the year, although not yet living up to pre-season expectations.

It switched the frenzied speculation to Pramac, Ducati and, by extension, all the other European teams. Jorge Martin continued to insist that he wanted a factory ride for 2025, but would Ducati have room for him? If they did, what would happen to Bastianini, who hadn't done much wrong except suffer serial bad luck in the previous season? And what about Marc Marquez – wouldn't he be a tempting choice to ride in red alongside Bagnaia?

The ramifications extended to KTM and Aprilia – possible destinations for Martin. And perhaps even Honda, which at least was a factory team, if not at the time a very tempting destination. The scuttlebutt would intensify, with talk of Pramac in any case abandoning Ducati in favour of Yamaha.

Thoughts of a Bagnaia-Marquez pairing were spiced by a spat between them, after a clash in the main race. Bagnaia had been losing ground in fifth, Marquez pushing forward, both having been passed by rookie Acosta. Marquez made a hard pass through Turn Four and was wide into the next tight left; Bagnaia, rather desperately, tried to cut back underneath. Bang! They collided. Both fell. Unsurprisingly, they disagreed over who had been to blame. "He overtook me, then went wide," said Bagnaia. "So what do you want to do? From my side, it wasn't a risky move." Marquez was adamant that "it was a mistake from Pecco, too optimistic ... but not just the incident. Because we were fighting for fifth. Two more points, two less. And when three or four laps remain, you know that you will lose the position, so it's not necessary to come back in that aggressive mode. But he decided this; the consequence to Ducati is zero points."

Acosta was on his way to a first podium after another stunning ride, overcoming inexperience with daring, confidence and huge talent, and becoming the third-youngest premier-class top-three finisher in history. Only Randy Mamola (second in Finland, 1979) and Argentinean Eduardo Salatino (second in Buenos Aires in 1961) had been younger. His experienced crew chief, Paul Trevathan, dubbed his prowess amazing: "Every time he rides the bike, he improves. He makes little changes to his riding, and I haven't seen the limit yet."

There was an element of luck – good for Pedro, bad for compatriot Vinales, who scored a convincing first sprint win on Saturday, then lost a seemingly assured second on Sunday, just a lap away from crowning the best weekend of his Aprilia career. He suffered a gear malfunction over the finish line. "I tried to put sixth, but it didn't go in," he said. "The bike went into neutral and hit the limiter." A leg wave warned the pursuing Bastianini as he slowed, continuing to search for a gear. At the bottom of the hill, as he ran on to the kerb, "it suddenly went into second"; the rear wheel locked and he high-sided. He revealed that he'd been having trouble for most of the race, and that the gremlin was "maybe a call to attention, trying to improve reliability". The intriguing question over whether it had been caused by his novel switchable dual-purpose clutch/rear-brake lever on his left handlebar remained unanswered.

It all played out against a background of an uncertain future, with growing interest in the forthcoming 2027 rule changes. Talk of power-down smaller engines, reduced aero, and the elimination of up-and-down suspension met with guarded approval. Marquez spoke for many when he illuminated the difference between a show for the spectators and having "the perfect bike … more aerodynamics means lap times will be faster. But the people at home don't realise if we'll be faster or slower, on TV. I will go that way … less aero, everything more manual. For the show, it will be better." KTM's Pit Beirer agreed that reduced performance was a goal, though at first "not our wish. But after discussion with our colleagues, we are also in favour now. The crash zones and everything are becoming a problem because the bikes are just getting too fast."

MOTOGP SPRINT RACE – 12 laps

Bastianini snitched pole ahead of Vinales and Martin; Bagnaia headed row two from Miller and Bezzecchi. Acosta had come through Q1 to lead the third from Marquez and Quartararo, in a moderately encouraging showing for Yamaha.

Miller led the first lap, but Bagnaia took over on the second, and the KTM gradually dropped back, losing second to an aggressive Marc Marquez on lap three, and then dropping behind Vinales and Martin two laps later.

For the first eight laps, it looked like Bagnaia's race as Vinales and Marquez traded blows, Martin joining in, after pushing past Bastianini on the second lap.

As they started the ninth, Vinales was striving to close a gap, Bagnaia holding his lead by three-quarters of a second. Then his Ducati snapped viciously as he braked going into the first corner, and the champion was wide in the run-off, rejoining fourth.

Vinales's lead looked precarious as Martin pushed hard in the slower corners, but the Aprilia's fast-corner prowess won the day, and on the last lap, Marquez put a strong block-pass on Martin to claim second, his first podium on a Ducati.

Bagnaia was three seconds adrift, narrowly holding off Miller, Bastianini and Acosta. Espargaro was another second down; then Quartararo matched his grid position for the final point, a second ahead of Raul Fernandez, the lacklustre Bezzecchi and the rest.

Rins, Di Giannantonio, a troubled Binder and Zarco crashed out.

MOTOGP RACE – 25 laps

Nineteen laps into the race, the fight up front wasn't quite befitting of the self-titled 'Rollercoaster' venue. Martin had controlled affairs, keeping Vinales and pole-starter Bastianini at arm's length throughout.

Then a thrilling finale offered enough drama to last a full weekend. The surprises came thick and fast. Bagnaia clashed with Marc Marquez at Turn Five, taking both men down with three laps to play. Then Vinales's stellar weekend came to a cruel conclusion when a transmission issue initially forced him off track and subsequently out of second place at the start of the final lap, before promptly high-siding out.

Aprilia's latest implosion cleared Acosta to collect a stunning third in his second MotoGP race, another breathtaking display. Having started seventh, he tore through the field, his tenacious arcing lines and audacious late braking leaving KTM colleagues Miller and Binder, as well as Marquez and Bagnaia, trailing.

His rise through the pack excepted, this was a fairly mundane contest. Both Martin and Vinales jumped pole-sitter Bastianini on the run to Turn One to establish an early he-

gemony, with Bagnaia initially battling Marquez for fourth, after Marc had jumped three places on the first lap. A ferocious early rhythm was established, with Martin edging the lead quintet apart. Starting lap three, he already had six-tenths in hand over Vinales.

Then Acosta started to move forward. Eighth on lap three, and behind Miller and Binder, he began a run of passes that made a number of MotoGP's elite appear ordinary. First, both he and Binder moved by Miller at Turn One on the fifth lap, then he did the same to the South African two laps later. Not content as top KTM, he soon breezed by Marquez with the same move. Bagnaia – trailing Martin by 1.8 seconds – was just three-tenths ahead.

Having miraculously saved a crash when trying to pass Bagnaia on the kerbs around the outside of Turn One on lap 12, Acosta continued to harry the champion as they lost ground to the leading trio, edging clear at around two-tenths per lap. By lap 21, he was close enough for another bite, and a late lunge into Turn Three was enough for fourth, Bagnaia unable to respond.

Then Marquez sensed his moment. As Acosta tore clear, Bagnaia's rear tyre had run its race and he was in damage-limitation mode. Marquez had a first bite at Turn 13, only for the official Ducati to close the door, nearly taking the Gresini Ducati's front tyre away.

It wasn't over. Marquez attacked again at Turn Four, forcing past inside the Ducati. He was ahead as they arrived at the next left, but a little wide on entry, before cutting back to the apex. Unwilling to give early ground to a certain title adversary, Bagnaia accelerated under him into a gap that didn't really exist. He tucked the front after contact, taking both of them down.

Up front, Martin's lead over Vinales and Bastianini yoyoed between five- and nine-tenths in the final ten laps, the Aprilia repeatedly losing two-tenths on the straight – he'd been struggling to engage sixth gear from the sixth lap, he explained later. Subsequently, that issue had dreadful consequences when he couldn't shift up at the beginning of the final lap. As Bastianini breezed by, the RS-GP cruelly spat Vinales off as he kicked down the box and unexpectedly engaged second gear. Now Acosta was on the podium.

This drew attention from Martin, whose ride to victory was flawless. Eight-tenths separated him and Bastianini at the flag, with Acosta another 5.3 seconds back in third. Binder and Miller meekly accepted fourth and fifth behind their new colleague, with Bezzecchi achieving a cheering improvement on early form, heading a tight trio that included Quartararo and Espargaro to take sixth.

Oliveira was next, having dropped back from a late-race top-ten by running wide, only to be promoted again by the Marquez-Bagnaia contretemps. He was narrowly ahead of Augusto Fernandez. A second behind, Mir was top Honda after a spirited recovery.

Rins, Nakagami and Zarco trailed in to wrap up the points; a second behind them, a remounted Marc Marquez just missed out.

Morbidelli was 18th and last, also remounted after a first-lap shunt had dropped him to 21st; Raul Fernandez fell, too; Alex Marquez retired.

MOTO2 RACE – 21 laps

Manuel Gonzalez took a maiden pole for Kalex, ahead of Aldeguer's Boscoscuro – on the warpath to compensate for his poor start to the season. They were joined up front by Canet, on the brink of a long-awaited first win, after 69 starts had yielded a frustrating 15 near-miss second places.

Lopez, Roberts and Arenas were on row two; two more

Boscoscuro riders headed row three – team-mates Ogura and Garcia.

Jake Dixon had withdrawn, still suffering from his Qatar injuries after placing seventh on Friday.

Canet had some unwitting help. Aldeguer ruined his chances with a jumped start, a pair of long-laps his reward. Then at half-distance, Qatar winner Lopez crashed out of the lead at Turn 13, leaving Canet, Roberts, Gonzalez and Ogura to fight it out.

Yet when Gonzalez passed Roberts for second, six laps from the flag, it was clear that Canet's relentless rhythm meant that he would not be caught. Even when the American retook second three laps from the flag, and immediately upped his pace, the Spaniard never wavered. He went on to his first class win and the first in any class since September, 2019, by two seconds.

Gonzalez now had his hands full with Aldegeur, back through after dropping to 13th on lap seven after his penalties. A string of fastest times thereafter allowed him to quickly dispose of Arbolino, Alcoba, Ramirez and Arenas. By lap 14, he was fifth and haring after the leaders.

He caught up, but had used up the best of his tyres. From there, he could just hang on, hoping for a mistake ahead. Luckily for him, that happened on the final lap. Ogura really should have had third, but a failed move on Gonzalez at Turn Three the last time around pushed him wide at the following corner, allowing Aldeguer through. Roberts claimed second by six-tenths; Gonzalez's second GP podium was a hard-fought affair. With Ogura on Aldeguer's rear wheel, second to fifth was covered by barely 1.7 seconds.

Margins were tight all the way, with less than nine seconds covering the top ten.

Garcia's typical late speed secured sixth after he had loitered as low as 13th in the early laps, clearing a close fight for seventh, eventually won by Vietti, with Arenas and Ramirez not far behind. Chantra was tenth, narrowly ahead of Alcoba and Arbolino, still struggling to get a handle on the Pirelli rubber, but just clear of Baltus.

Rookie Agius was 14th after a long-lap penalty (overtaking under a yellow flag), with Darren Binder securing the last point, just ahead of Bendsneyder. Moto3 champion Masia was a distant 21st; erstwhile title rival and fellow rookie Sasaki crashed out for a second race in a row.

Above: Moto2 formation flying – Canet leads Gonzalez and Roberts.

Left: At last. Moto2 victory was a long time coming for Aron Canet.

Far left: Acosta charged to third in just his second MotoGP race.

Below: Colombian David Alonso (80) looks for an opening in the Spanish Armada of Rueda (99), Holgado (96) and Ortola (48).
Photos: Gold & Goose

MOTO3 RACE – 19 laps

Rueda secured pole ahead of Kelso and Alonso; Holgado, Rossi and Veijer right behind. And it was Rueda who led away and for the first nine laps – at least over the line. It was the usual scramble, with Alonso next to take over and Holgado among those in close attendance.

At half-distance, Veijer had caught up from an indifferent start to make a lead group of seven, with Ortola, Kelso and Rossi – the last named losing touch after an error and crashing out while trying to catch up.

Yet Alonso didn't look as comfortable out front as he did lurking in the pack. Despite holding a lead of four-tenths on lap 13, Holgado and Rueda had reeled him in two laps later and assumed control of the contest. All race, Rueda could make up full tenths of a second exiting Turn 14. That's where he launched his victory attack on the final lap, only for Holgado to ably defend, notching up a fourth career victory by four-hundredths.

Ortola escaped for third, eight-tenths back, while intense infighting between Alonso and Veijer allowed the Colombian to claim fourth, and Kelso to jump ahead of the Dutchman for a well-earned fifth.

Nepa and Esteban were out of touch; then Munoz led a gang of four, from Fernandez, impressive Australian rookie Jacob Roulstone and Bertelle. The last named was disqualified after the race for a fuel infringement, which promoted Suzuki, Perez, Ogden and Carraro into improved points positions.

FIM WORLD CHAMPIONSHIP • ROUND 3

UNITED STATES GRAND PRIX

CIRCUIT OF THE AMERICAS

TALES of the unexpected – at a track that, for once, laid on a brilliantly close race, including ecstasy for Vinales, a turnaround for former track master Marquez and a cosplay culture shock possibly foretelling a cartoonish future.

No longer unexpected – that Pedro Acosta would do astonishingly well, a second successive podium making the teenager the youngest rider ever to achieve such a distinction.

The cosplay included Sonic the Hedgehog waving the chequered flag, after a tassel-clad country-singer National Anthem had started the race. The cultural overload continued with a troop of pompom-waving cheerleaders lining the silver steps to the podium to a triumphal soundtrack, where the top three riders were invited to address an adoring crowd. Very unlike, say, an austere prefab Brno podium in the rain.

Double winner Vinales was so overcome with the rock-star atmosphere that he actually shouted, "I love you, America!" But who could blame him, after by far his best weekend in his third full season with Aprilia.

It was full circle after disappointing tests, where "I had a very strange crash in Malaysia, so I had no confidence with the new bike." Work on settings and weight distribution, step by step, turned that around. "Now I have the same feeling as last year, but better because of the better aerodynamics." He added that ex-Suzuki crew chief Jose Manuel Cazeaux "took one full year to understand really the bike and what we needed." Stability was key. "The flowing part, like section one or the three right-hand corners, was where I was making the difference."

The razzmatazz came directly upon the official confirmation that US media, communications and entertainment company Liberty Media had committed to purchase a controlling (86 per cent) interest in Dorna, a big increase on the 39 per cent of previous majority owners Bridgepoint. It would not take effect until ratified in October, but given the upscaling of marketing applied to F1 since Liberty took over in 2016, this race's very American promo could be taken as a foretaste of what could be expected.

Marquez continued to underplay his chances as he continued to adapt, but if he secretly harboured hopes at a track where he had won seven times in nine visits, they were abruptly dashed just a couple of corners after taking the lead, following braking problems all race, "which gave me a lot of difficulties" and explained a wild dive under Jorge Martin at the final turn. "Even like this, I was in the top group because the pace was not very fast. I tried to lead as soon as possible to see if the temperature of the brake changed … but when I arrived at Turn 11, I braked and nothing was there. I tried a second time, but I had too much speed."

The Japanese discomfort continued. For Honda, at a track where once they had dominated, and where even in 2023, their worst season, Alex Rins had added a win to Marquez's previous seven, earnest development work went unrewarded. No rider scored any points, with Marini the only one to finish both races, well last in each of them. Double-crasher Mir explained that the changes to the RC213V had caused the loss of its one previous strong point, without yet producing any others: "Last year, it was a bike that was stopping, and with brakes you were able to turn. Then we requested too much on this good point, and the crashes started. This is a track that this bike had something positive in the past, and now we don't have any positives. We are a little bit lost…"

The news was a little brighter at Yamaha, where Quartararo garnered four points on Sunday. Earlier, he had confirmed an extension to his contract, until the end of 2026, bringing to an end speculation of a possible switch to Aprilia, or indeed anywhere. A rumoured and hefty $12 million per year aside, his previously often expressed disgruntlement had been mollified by plans to set Yamaha back on track: "There are some really interesting things, still confidential, in the works. New people are joining, the project is going to be huge. So the decision was made in Portugal." Although on-track struggles continued, Yamaha's aggressive hiring of top Ducati personnel – Max Bartolini (technical director) and Marco Nicotra (senior aerodynamics engineer) – and change in development approach were other factors behind Quartararo's decision: "What really made me want to stay was that we totally changed the way of working." He confirmed contact with MotoGP's other four factories, Aprilia being the most hyped, but able to offer only a fraction of Yamaha's rumoured millions.

Doubtless unrelated was the news that Lin Jarvis, long-standing MD of Yamaha Motor Racing, would be departing at the end of the 2024 season. At 66, he'd decided it was time to retire.

Inset, top left: Vinales loved America, and America loved Vinales.

Inset, below left: Fringed cowgirl Kimberly Dunn sang the *Star-Spangled Banner*…

Inset, below far left: …and Sonic the Hedgehog waved the chequered flag at a razzmatazz race weekend. Another flag was shown at pit-wall level, just in case.

Main: Vinales overcame a bad start to secure his first main-race win since 2021, and his first for Aprilia.

Photos: Gold & Goose

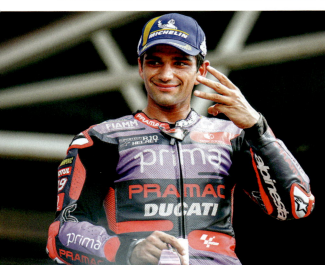

Was there a crumb of comfort for the beleaguered Japanese teams in continuing talk of niggling problems at both ends of the 2024 Ducati? Chatter issues persisted for Martin and Bagnaia. Said the latter, "I was thinking before lap six I could fight for a win, but I started to have a lot of vibration on the left … and I completely destroyed the front tyre on the right. It is similar to 2022, when at the start of the season, I had to race in defence."

The stewards had a busy weekend, with multiple cases of slow riding in practice and qualifying in Moto3, at a track where slipstreaming is paramount on the long straight. In all, nine riders received first-offence warnings, several then re-offending to be among eight long-lap penalties, including two double long-laps.

MOTOGP SPRINT RACE – 10 laps

Vinales set the pace during the first free practice and in qualifying to sit on pole. Acosta, undaunted by a new bike on a complex track, started out third and eventually became second, with Marc Marquez completing the front row. It was all Ducati behind them, with Bagnaia and team-mate Bastianini heading Martin.

The race started much as it would go on. Vinales led into the first corner, and was in control throughout for a second straight sprint win, this one by better than two seconds – a margin he had gained by half-distance.

Marquez led the pursuit, fending off early pressure from Acosta and breaking free on lap six, when Martin had caught up, after taking two laps to displace Bastianini from fourth.

The Gresini rider had escaped by the time Martin finally got the better of the rookie at Turn 11 on lap six, whereafter the GasGas dropped back. Acosta described his race as "a complete mess", as he'd used up his rear tyre fighting with the two senior riders. A day later, he would prove a fast learner from that mistake.

A little way back, Espargaro had passed Bastianini on lap six, with Miller – off the fourth row – following him through a lap later. The Aprilia rider escaped to close right up on Acosta. Bastianini got back ahead of Miller on the last lap for sixth, heading a close gang, with Bagnaia a tenth behind the KTM, then last-points-scorer Raul Fernandez, Morbidelli and Binder, seventh to 12th all within just over 1.5 seconds. Bagnaia had recovered from an awful start, tenth on lap one.

Nakagami crashed on the first lap; Di Giannantonio suffered a smoky retirement, his Ducati damaged in early contact with Alex Marquez. Augusto Fernandez, Zarco and Mir also crashed out.

MOTOGP RACE – 20 laps

The third round laid on the race of the year so far. Marquez proved fallible at one of his best tracks, and Vinales recovered from 11th at Turn One to record a first feature-race victory in 1,113 days.

It took 12 laps for Vinales to join an epic victory fight that included Marquez, Martin, Acosta, Bagnaia and Bastianini. With podium places changing hands almost by the corner, it slowed the pace, allowing Vinales to catch up. The way he cut through all of them after Marquez's surprise crash took the breath away, and dispelled some of the long-held doubts about his temperament. He made history as just the fifth rider to win premier-class races on three makes of machinery.

He wasn't the only star. For the third weekend in a row, Acosta lived up to his much-hyped reputation, leading six laps while passing and repassing the leading names. In the closing laps, the rookie pushed Vinales the hardest.

After pole and the sprint win on Saturday, at first it looked like another case of potential unfulfilled for Vinales. A poor getaway due to an all-to-familiar clutch issue left him fourth entering Turn One, and Martin's lunge on Bagnaia caused him to lift and run off track.

Rejoining 11th, all appeared lost. Yet the frenetic exchanges were in his favour.

Above: Vinales led into the first corner and was never headed for a second straight sprint win.

Top left: No return to CoTA dominance for faller Marc Marquez, who hitched a ride back to the pits.

Above left: Count the fingers. Martin took third in the sprint…

Left: …but lost third to Bastianini in Sunday's main race.
Photos: Gold & Goose

Above: Acosta went one better with second. Could there be a first win coming soon?

Top right: David Alonso was the convincing Moto3 winner.

Above right: A podium for rookie Angel Piqueras in only his third race.

Above far right: Roberts flies the flag, but the home win was tantalisingly out of reach.

Right: Garcia leads Roberts, Foggia, Lopez, Aldeguer and Dixon in Moto2.
Photos: Gold & Goose

Acosta led away, and the first three laps, under incessant pressure from Martin, who twice lunged under the rookie at Turn 11, only to run wide. Behind, Bagnaia and Marquez made short work of fast-starting Miller. Marquez had made contact exiting the final corner, knocking off his left front aero pod. Bastianini watched, just behind.

Martin finally made a move stick on Acosta on the Turn Nine cutback on lap four. Marquez (Turn 11) and Bagnaia (Turn 12) quickly flashed through, raising the question of whether the rookie – the only leader along with Vinales to have chosen Michelin's medium-compound rear rather than the soft – had done too much, too soon. Not so. He took advantage of Marquez's lap-five rub with Martin at the final turn to grab third, before pushing Bagnaia out at Turn One for second.

Having disposed of Rins and Alex Marquez, Vinales was now in the front seven, two seconds behind the leader. At this point, Martin appeared capable of escape, eight-tenths clear on lap eight.

A lap later, however, Acosta and Marquez had reeled him back into range.

They attacked with pizzazz on lap ten. First, Acosta dived under Martin at Turn 11, Marquez following suit at the next corner, after they'd run down the back straight three abreast. Thanks to this, Vinales suddenly found himself in the victory fight after smart moves on Bastianini, Miller (lap seven), and Bagnaia (lap nine). The Aprilia was clearly superior through the flowing final sector.

Then Marquez made his play. Passing Acosta for the lead starting lap 11, he immediately sought to break clear. Yet the race-long braking issues caused him to lock the front, falling at Turn 11. Acosta led again, but at the end of that lap, Vinales pounced on Martin at the final corner. Acosta's half-second lead was soon wiped out, the Aprilia decisively hitting the front at Turn 11 on lap 13, after a failed attempt the lap before.

From there, the top three stretched apart, while a familiar late charge by Bastianini gained him third. He'd passed Bagnaia earlier, and Martin on the penultimate lap.

Di Giannantonio was a lone sixth, having moved forward from tenth on lap one. Espargaro remained a second clear of Bezzecchi and the pursuing Binder; then came Raul Fernandez, Oliveira and Quartararo, all spaced out.

Miller was a disappointed 13th, having lost 12th on the last lap. His flying start from the fourth row to third on lap one went sour when he ran into ever-worsening tyre issues as the race wore on.

Marini's bike, 17th, was the only Honda to finish: Zarco retired early, Nakagami and Mir crashed. So too Morbidelli and Alex Marquez, the latter out of a creditable seventh, the former still catching up on lost pre-season testing.

MOTO2 RACE – 16 laps

Canet's Kalex claimed pole ahead of Boscoscuro pair Aldeguer and Garcia; home hope Roberts was in the middle of an all-Kalex second row, between Arenas (through from Q1) and Ramirez. Dennis Foggia was seventh, a best yet; Ogura a downbeat 17th.

Hopes for a first US home victory since Nicky Hayden at Laguna Seca in 2006 were narrowly denied. Garcia led away and did just enough to keep Roberts at bay, by less than half a second. To rub it in, the Spaniard also took over the championship lead.

Aldeguer and Canet became mired in the pack after making lousy getaways – exiting Turn One seventh and tenth respectively.

Garcia made the early running, Roberts, Foggia and an inspired Dixon – taking a flier from 14th on the grid – gave

chase. Gonzalez was a close fifth, but had jumped the start, destined for a double long-lap; Lopez had passed him and Dixon on lap two.

The recovering Aldeguer was also past on lap four, and the Briton crashed next time around.

Garcia's unerring pace was stretching the front five. Yet the Spaniard was never completely comfortable. Struggling to engage first on the track's low-gear hairpins, he found neutral several times, most notably on lap 12 as he outbraked himself entering Turn 11. From trailing by 2.8 seconds, home hero Roberts was now less than 1.3 seconds behind.

But the American suffered a similar fate the following lap at Turn 12, handing a second back to the leader and briefly losing second to Aldeguer. Roberts credited braking feel offered by Pirelli's front as he reeled in Garcia lap by lap.

Sadly for the home fans, he ran out of time to deny Garcia a first class win.

As at the previous race, Aldeguer's recovery had punished his tyres, and he was frustrated at being unable to join the victory fight. Some consolation came from beating teammate Lopez, 3.5 seconds away in fourth.

For the second race in three, Marcos Ramirez was among the fastest late on. The Andalusian botched his start, made a mess of the first lap and overshot Turn 12 on lap two, leaving him 17th. Stress caused him to throw up inside his helmet on lap three, but his recovery was formidable, carving through to fifth. He even passed Lopez at the penultimate turn on the final lap, only to run wide and relinquish the place. Foggia was just behind in sixth, his best Moto2 race to date.

Ogura was a subdued seventh ahead of Alcoba, after another disappointing qualifying; Canet was despondent in ninth, not once having replicated his practice pace.

Vietti regained tenth from the still troubled Arbolino on the final lap, both having passed Arenas in the closing stages. Gonzalez had climbed back to 13th at the end, having displaced top rookie Moreira and Salac; Baltus and Agius narrowly missed the points.

Dixon and fellow faller Binder remounted, Aji did not. Van den Goorbergh retired.

MOTO3 RACE – 14 laps

David Alonso was utterly invincible in usually the most volatile class, topping every practice session, then cruising to a second win in three races, massively reinforcing his title credentials while several of his rivals imploded.

Yet the Colombian's five-second victory couldn't take attention away from rookie sensation Angel Piqueras. The 2023 Red Bull Rookies and Junior world champion claimed a stunning maiden podium in just his third race, after qualifying 18th.

Alonso had help. First, opening-lap chaos worked in his favour as second-row qualifier Kelso tagged the back of third-fastest Holgado, pushing both men wide, before Ivan Ortola crashed out at Turn 15 after hitting Collin Veijer. There were a number of long-lap penalties, notably for Kelso, Rossi and Bertelle. And second-fastest Jose Antonio Rueda missed the start after undergoing emergency surgery for appendicitis on Saturday night.

The early melee handed Alonso a commanding early advantage of 4.5 seconds by lap six. But Veijer, Holgado, Piqueras and Yamanaka started to chase him down, almost halving his lead by lap ten. Then came a scary Turn Five fall for group leader Veijer. Bike and rider slid back across the track in the to-and-fro section, scattering the other three in a narrow escape for the Dutchman.

Dropped to fourth, Holgado quickly passed Yamanaka before prevailing in an entertaining last-lap scrap for second with rookie Piqueras.

More than seven seconds away, Munoz led Suzuki, with the Australians next. Kelso was three seconds away, then Roulstone, narrowly in front of Esteban, with Bertelle completing the top ten.

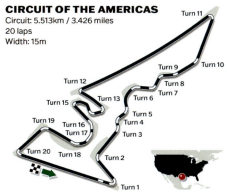

FIM WORLD CHAMPIONSHIP: ROUND 3
RED BULL GRAND PRIX OF THE AMERICAS
12–14 APRIL, 2024

CIRCUIT OF THE AMERICAS
Circuit: 5.513km / 3.426 miles
20 laps
Width: 15m

MOTOGP: RACE DISTANCE: 20 laps, 68.512 miles/110.260km

RACE WEATHER: Dry (air 27°, humidity 56%, track 42°)

Pos.	Rider	Nat.	No.	Entrant	Machine	Race tyre choice	Laps	Time & speed
1	Maverick Vinales	SPA	12	Aprilia Racing	Aprilia RS-GP24	F: Medium/R: Medium	20	41m 09.503s, 99.9mph/160.7km/h
2	Pedro Acosta	SPA	31	Red Bull GASGAS Tech3	KTM RC16	F: Medium/R: Medium	20	41m 11.231s
3	Enea Bastianini	ITA	23	Ducati Lenovo Team	Ducati Desmosedici GP24	F: Medium/R: Soft	20	41m 12.206s
4	Jorge Martin	SPA	89	Prima Pramac Racing	Ducati Desmosedici GP24	F: Medium/R: Soft	20	41m 14.193s
5	Francesco Bagnaia	ITA	1	Ducati Lenovo Team	Ducati Desmosedici GP24	F: Medium/R: Soft	20	41m 16.895s
6	Fabio Di Giannantonio	ITA	49	Pertamina Enduro VR46 Racing	Ducati Desmosedici GP23	F: Medium/R: Soft	20	41m 19.483s
7	Aleix Espargaro	SPA	41	Aprilia Racing	Aprilia RS-GP24	F: Medium/R: Soft	20	41m 21.711s
8	Marco Bezzecchi	ITA	72	Pertamina Enduro VR46 Racing	Ducati Desmosedici GP23	F: Medium/R: Soft	20	41m 22.846s
9	Brad Binder	RSA	33	Red Bull KTM Factory Racing	KTM RC16	F: Medium/R: Soft	20	41m 24.434s
10	Raul Fernandez	SPA	25	Trackhouse Racing	Aprilia RS-GP23	F: Medium/R: Medium	20	41m 26.159s
11	Miguel Oliveira	POR	88	Trackhouse Racing	Aprilia RS-GP24	F: Medium/R: Medium	20	41m 28.045s
12	Fabio Quartararo	FRA	20	Monster Energy Yamaha MotoGP	Yamaha YZR-M1	F: Medium/R: Soft	20	41m 32.402s
13	Jack Miller	AUS	43	Red Bull KTM Factory Racing	KTM RC16	F: Medium/R: Soft	20	41m 33.514s
14	Augusto Fernandez	SPA	37	Red Bull GASGAS Tech3	KTM RC16	F: Medium/R: Soft	20	41m 37.155s
15	Alex Marquez	SPA	73	Gresini Racing MotoGP	Ducati Desmosedici GP23	F: Medium/R: Medium	20	41m 42.358s
16	Luca Marini	ITA	10	Repsol Honda Team	Honda RC213V	F: Medium/R: Medium	20	41m 43.032s
	Marc Marquez	SPA	93	Gresini Racing MotoGP	Ducati Desmosedici GP23	F: Medium/R: Soft	10	DNF-crash
	Alex Rins	SPA	42	Monster Energy Yamaha MotoGP	Yamaha YZR-M1	F: Medium/R: Medium	10	DNF-crash
	Joan Mir	SPA	36	Repsol Honda Team	Honda RC213V	F: Medium/R: Medium	8	DNF-crash
	Franco Morbidelli	ITA	21	Prima Pramac Racing	Ducati Desmosedici GP24	F: Medium/R: Soft	7	DNF-crash
	Takaaki Nakagami	JPN	30	IDEMITSU Honda LCR	Honda RC213V	F: Medium/R: Medium	6	DNF-crash
	Johann Zarco	FRA	5	CASTROL Honda LCR	Honda RC213V	F: Medium/R: Medium	6	DNF-technical

Fastest lap: Maverick Vinales, on lap 14, 2m 2.575s, 100.6mph/161.9km/h.
Lap record: Alex Rins, 2m 3.126s, 100.1mph/161.1km/h (2023).
Event maximum speed: Brad Binder, 220.7mph/355.2km/h (sprint).

SPRINT RACE: 10 laps, 34.256 miles/55.130km

WEATHER: Dry (air 26°, humidity 50%, track 40°)

Pos.	Rider	Race tyre choice	Laps	Time & speed
1	Maverick Vinales	F: Medium/R: Soft	10	20m 27.825s, 100.4mph/161.6km/h
2	Marc Marquez	F: Medium/R: Soft	10	20m 30.119s
3	Jorge Martin	F: Medium/R: Soft	10	20m 32.224s
4	Pedro Acosta	F: Medium/R: Soft	10	20m 34.305s
5	Aleix Espargaro	F: Medium/R: Soft	10	20m 34.482s
6	Enea Bastianini	F: Medium/R: Soft	10	20m 36.446s
7	Jack Miller	F: Medium/R: Soft	10	20m 37.062s
8	Francesco Bagnaia	F: Medium/R: Soft	10	20m 37.174s
9	Raul Fernandez	F: Medium/R: Soft	10	20m 37.462s
10	Franco Morbidelli	F: Medium/R: Soft	10	20m 37.719s
11	Miguel Oliveira	F: Medium/R: Soft	10	20m 38.189s
12	Brad Binder	F: Medium/R: Soft	10	20m 38.549s
13	Marco Bezzecchi	F: Medium/R: Soft	10	20m 39.374s
14	Alex Marquez	F: Medium/R: Soft	10	20m 43.293s
15	Fabio Quartararo	F: Medium/R: Soft	10	20m 43.399s
16	Alex Rins	F: Medium/R: Soft	10	20m 45.971s
17	Luca Marini	F: Medium/R: Soft	10	20m 50.814s
	Johann Zarco	F: Medium/R: Soft	6	DNF-crash
	Joan Mir	F: Medium/R: Soft	3	DNF-crash
	Fabio Di Giannantonio	F: Medium/R: Soft	0	DNF-technical
	Augusto Fernandez	F: Medium/R: Soft	0	DNF-crash
	Takaaki Nakagami	F: Medium/R: Soft	0	DNF-crash

Fastest race lap: Maverick Vinales, on lap 3, 2m 2.275s.

Qualifying: Weather: Dry Air: 23° Humidity: 62% Track: 33°

1 Vinales 2m 00.864s, 2 Acosta 2m 01.192s, 3 M. Marquez 2m 01.266s, 4 Bagnaia 2m 01.352s, 5 Bastianini 2m 01.439s, 6 Martin 2m 01.511s, 7 A. Espargaro 2m 01.562s, 8 Di Giannantonio 2m 01.667s, 9 Morbidelli 2m 01.737s, 10 Bezzecchi 2m 02.279s, 11 Miller 2m 02.297s, 12 A. Marquez No Time.
Q1: 13 R. Fernandez 2m 01.726s, 14 Oliveira 2m 01.844s, 15 Rins 2m 01.893s, 16 Quartararo 2m 02.089s, 17 Binder 2m 02.140s, 18 A. Fernandez 2m 02.223s, 19 Zarco 2m 02.380s, 20 Mir 2m 02.829s, 21 Nakagami 2m 03.114s, 22 Marini 2m 03.249s.

Fastest race laps

1 Vinales 2m 02.575s, 2 Bagnaia 2m 02.901s, 3 Acosta 2m 02.966s, 4 Bastianini 2m 03.051s, 5 Martin 2m 03.100s, 6 M. Marquez 2m 03.149s, 7 Oliveira 2m 03.179s, 8 Morbidelli 2m 03.197s, 9 Di Giannantonio 2m 03.212s, 10 R. Fernandez 2m 03.314s, 11 A. Espargaro 2m 03.329s, 12 Binder 2m 03.463s, 13 A. Marquez 2m 03.466s, 14 Miller 2m 03.468s, 15 Bezzecchi 2m 03.503s, 16 A. Fernandez 2m 03.803s, 17 Quartararo 2m 03.938s, 18 Mir 2m 03.939s, 19 Rins 2m 04.115s, 20 Zarco 2m 04.211s, 21 Marini 2m 04.425s, 22 Nakagami 2m 04.577s.

Grid order / Lap chart

Grid order	1	2	3	4	5	6	7	8	9	10	11	12	13	14	15	16	17	18	19	20
12 VINALES	31	31	31	89	89	89	89	89	89	31	31	12	12	12	12	12	12	12	12	1
31 ACOSTA	89	89	89	93	1	1	31	31	31	93	12	12	31	31	31	31	31	31	31	2
93 M. MARQUEZ	43	1	1	1	93	31	93	93	93	89	89	89	89	89	89	89	89	23	23	3
1 BAGNAIA	93	93	93	31	31	93	1	1	12	12	1	23	23	23	23	23	23	89	89	4
23 BASTIANINI	1	43	43	43	43	43	12	12	1	1	23	23	1	1	1	1	1	1	1	5
89 MARTIN	23	23	23	23	23	23	43	23	23	23	49	49	49	49	49	49	49	49	49	6
41 A. ESPARGARO	42	73	73	12	12	12	23	43	43	73	43	43	41	41	41	41	41	41	41	7
49 DI GIANNANTONIO	73	12	12	73	73	73	73	73	73	49	41	41	43	72	72	72	72	72	72	8
21 MORBIDELLI	12	42	42	49	49	49	49	49	49	43	72	72	72	43	33	33	33	33	33	9
72 BEZZECCHI	49	49	49	21	21	21	21	41	41	41	25	25	33	33	25	25	25	25	25	10
43 MILLER	21	21	21	41	41	41	41	72	72	72	33	33	25	25	88	88	88	88	88	11
73 A. MARQUEZ	41	41	41	42	72	88	88	25	25	25	88	88	88	88	43	43	43	43	20	12
25 R. FERNANDEZ	72	72	72	72	42	72	72	33	33	33	37	20	20	20	20	20	20	20	43	13
88 OLIVEIRA	30	33	33	88	88	25	25	37	88	88	20	37	37	37	37	37	37	37	37	14
42 RINS	33	88	88	33	33	42	42	88	37	37	10	10	10	10	10	10	73	73	73	15
20 QUARTARARO	25	25	37	37	25	33	33	42	20	20	73	73	73	73	73	73	10	10	10	
33 BINDER	88	37	25	25	37	37	20	42	42											
37 A. FERNANDEZ	37	30	30	20	20	20	20	36	10	10										
5 ZARCO	10	20	20	30	30	30	36													
36 MIR	20	5	5	5	36	36	10													
30 NAKAGAMI	5	36	36	36	10	10														
10 MARINI	36	10	10	10	5	5														

Championship Points

1	Martin	54 (26)	80
2	Bastianini	47 (12)	59
3	Vinales	31 (25)	56
4	Acosta	43 (11)	54
5	Bagnaia	36 (14)	50
6	Binder	40 (9)	49
7	A. Espargaro	25 (14)	39
8	M. Marquez	13 (23)	36
9	Di Giannantonio	25 (0)	25
10	Miller	14 (8)	22
11	Bezzecchi	20 (0)	20
12	Quartararo	18 (1)	19
13	A. Marquez	11 (3)	14
14	Oliveira	13 (0)	13
15	R. Fernandez	6 (1)	7
16	A. Fernandez	7 (0)	7
17	Mir	7 (0)	7
18	Zarco	5 (0)	5
19	Rins	3 (0)	3
20	Nakagami	2 (0)	2

Constructor Points

1	Ducati	66 (30)	96
2	KTM	56 (20)	76
3	Aprilia	41 (31)	72
4	Yamaha	18 (1)	19
5	Honda	8 (0)	8

MOTO2: RACE DISTANCE: 16 laps, 54.810 miles/88.208km

RACE WEATHER: Dry (air 26°, humidity 49%, track 39°)

Pos.	Rider	Nat.	No.	Entrant	Machine	Laps	Time & Speed
1	Sergio Garcia	SPA	3	MT Helmets - MSI	Boscoscuro	16	34m 25.954s
							95.5mph/153.7km/h
2	Joe Roberts	USA	16	OnlyFans American Racing Team	Kalex	16	34m 26.446s
3	Fermin Aldeguer	SPA	54	Beta Tools SpeedUp	Boscoscuro	16	34m 29.247s
4	Alonso Lopez	SPA	21	Beta Tools SpeedUp	Boscoscuro	16	34m 32.921s
5	Marcos Ramirez	SPA	24	OnlyFans American Racing Team	Kalex	16	34m 33.056s
6	Dennis Foggia	ITA	71	Italtrans Racing Team	Kalex	16	34m 33.104s
7	Ai Ogura	JPN	79	MT Helmets - MSI	Boscoscuro	16	34m 35.823s
8	Jeremy Alcoba	SPA	52	Yamaha VR46 Master Camp	Kalex	16	34m 35.990s
9	Aron Canet	SPA	44	Fantic Racing	Kalex	16	34m 36.958s
10	Celestino Vietti	ITA	13	Red Bull KTM Ajo	Kalex	16	34m 38.705s
11	Tony Arbolino	ITA	14	Elf Marc VDS Racing Team	Kalex	16	34m 39.183s
12	Albert Arenas	SPA	75	QJMOTOR Gresini Moto2	Kalex	16	34m 40.688s
13	Manuel Gonzalez	SPA	18	QJMOTOR Gresini Moto2	Kalex	16	34m 43.463s
14	Diogo Moreira	BRA	10	Italtrans Racing Team	Kalex	16	34m 43.913s
15	Filip Salac	CZE	12	Elf Marc VDS Racing Team	Kalex	16	34m 43.948s
16	Barry Baltus	BEL	7	RW-Idrofoglia Racing GP	Kalex	16	34m 44.572s
17	Senna Agius	AUS	81	Liqui Moly Husqvarna Intact GP	Kalex	16	34m 45.414s
18	Bo Bendsneyder	NED	64	Pertamina Mandalika GAS UP	Kalex	16	34m 52.139s
19	Jaume Masia	SPA	5	Pertamina Mandalika GAS UP	Kalex	16	34m 52.226s
20	Izan Guevara	SPA	28	CFMOTO Asterius Aspar Team	Kalex	16	34m 52.305s
21	Somkiat Chantra	THA	35	IDEMITSU Honda Team Asia	Kalex	16	34m 55.740s
22	Deniz Oncu	TUR	53	Red Bull KTM Ajo	Kalex	16	34m 59.164s
23	Jake Dixon	GBR	96	CFMOTO Asterius Aspar Team	Kalex	16	35m 09.775s
24	Alex Escrig	SPA	11	KLINT Forward Factory Team	Forward	16	35m 10.938s
25	Xavier Artigas	SPA	43	KLINT Forward Factory Team	Forward	16	35m 11.125s
26	Xavi Cardelus	AND	20	Fantic Racing	Kalex	16	35m 26.037s
27	Darryn Binder	RSA	15	Liqui Moly Husqvarna Intact GP	Kalex	16	35m 43.245s
	Zonta van den Goorbergh	NED	84	RW-Idrofoglia Racing GP	Kalex	7	DNF-ret in pit

Fastest lap: Alonso Lopez, on lap 6, 2m 8.210s, 96.1mph/154.7km/h.
Lap record: Aron Canet, 2m 9.312s, 95.3mph/153.4km/h (2022).
Event maximum speed: Celestino Vietti, 181.3mph/291.8km/h (race).

Qualifying
Weather: Dry
Air: 29° **Humidity:** 67% **Track:** 44°

1	Canet	2m 07.631s
2	Aldeguer	2m 07.740s
3	Garcia	2m 07.819s
4	Arenas	2m 07.865s
5	Roberts	2m 07.868s
6	Ramirez	2m 07.911s
7	Foggia	2m 08.031s
8	Lopez	2m 08.063s
9	Gonzalez	2m 08.074s
10	Bendsneyder	2m 08.112s
11	Arbolino	2m 08.127s
12	Baltus	2m 08.142s
13	Alcoba	2m 08.147s
14	Dixon	2m 08.281s
15	Vietti	2m 08.311s
16	Moreira	2m 08.365s
17	Ogura	2m 08.461s
18	Masia	2m 08.512s
Q1		
19	Chantra	2m 08.479s
20	Salac	2m 08.599s
21	Oncu	2m 08.601s
22	Agius	2m 08.617s
23	Guevara	2m 08.870s
24	V d Goorbergh	2m 08.930s
25	Aji	2m 09.419s
26	Artigas	2m 10.408s
27	Cardelus	2m 10.735s
28	Escrig	2m 11.109s
29	Binder	2m 08.733s

Fastest race laps

1	Lopez	2m 08.210s
2	Aldeguer	2m 08.251s
3	Garcia	2m 08.317s
4	Roberts	2m 08.387s
5	Foggia	2m 08.518s
6	Ramirez	2m 08.684s
7	Canet	2m 08.749s
8	Alcoba	2m 08.787s
9	Ogura	2m 08.788s
10	Dixon	2m 08.793s
11	Vietti	2m 08.997s
12	Arbolino	2m 09.011s
13	Baltus	2m 09.068s
14	Arenas	2m 09.074s
15	Moreira	2m 09.127s
16	Gonzalez	2m 09.332s
17	Bendsneyder	2m 09.402s
18	Salac	2m 09.429s
19	Agius	2m 09.437s
20	Chantra	2m 09.440s
21	Guevara	2m 09.540s
22	Masia	2m 09.640s
23	V d Goorbergh	2m 09.874s
24	Binder	2m 09.898s
25	Oncu	2m 10.024s
26	Aji	2m 10.320s
27	Artigas	2m 10.684s
28	Escrig	2m 10.734s
29	Cardelus	2m 11.010s

Championship Points

	Rider	Pts
1	Garcia	51
2	Roberts	49
3	Lopez	38
4	Canet	38
5	Ogura	33
6	Gonzalez	30
7	Aldeguer	29
8	Ramirez	28
9	Baltus	23
10	Vietti	22
11	Arenas	20
12	Alcoba	17
13	Chantra	11
14	Foggia	10
15	Arbolino	9
16	Van den Goorbergh	3
17	Bendsneyder	2
18	Agius	2
19	Moreira	2
20	Binder	1
21	Oncu	1
22	Salac	1

Constructor Points

		Pts
1	Kalex	65
2	Boscoscuro	63

MOTO3: RACE DISTANCE: 14 laps, 47.959 miles/77.182km

RACE WEATHER: Dry (air 22°, humidity 78%, track 27°)

Pos.	Rider	Nat.	No.	Entrant	Machine	Laps	Time & Speed
1	David Alonso	COL	80	CFMOTO Valresa Aspar Team	CFMOTO	14	31m 38.427s
							90.9mph/146.3km/h
2	Daniel Holgado	SPA	96	Red Bull GASGAS Tech3	GASGAS	14	31m 43.590s
3	Angel Piqueras	SPA	36	Leopard Racing	Honda	14	31m 43.603s
4	Ryusei Yamanaka	JPN	6	MT Helmets - MSI	KTM	14	31m 44.103s
5	David Munoz	SPA	64	BOE Motorsports	KTM	14	31m 51.712s
6	Tatsuki Suzuki	JPN	24	Liqui Moly Husqvarna Intact GP	Husqvarna	14	31m 52.157s
7	Joel Kelso	AUS	66	BOE Motorsports	KTM	14	31m 55.390s
8	Jacob Roulstone	AUS	12	Red Bull GASGAS Tech3	GASGAS	14	31m 57.553s
9	Joel Esteban	SPA	78	CFMOTO Valresa Aspar Team	CFMOTO	14	31m 57.752s
10	Matteo Bertelle	ITA	18	Rivacold Snipers Team	Honda	14	31m 59.084s
11	Adrian Fernandez	SPA	31	Leopard Racing	Honda	14	31m 59.116s
12	Nicola Carraro	ITA	10	LEVELUP - MTA	KTM	14	32m 01.212s
13	Xabi Zurutuza	SPA	85	Red Bull KTM Ajo	KTM	14	32m 01.296s
14	Noah Dettwiler	SWI	55	CIP Green Power	KTM	14	32m 06.002s
15	Filippo Farioli	ITA	7	SIC58 Squadra Corse	Honda	14	32m 10.574s
16	Riccardo Rossi	ITA	54	CIP Green Power	KTM	14	32m 17.380s
17	Joshua Whatley	GBR	70	MLav Racing	Honda	14	32m 23.351s
18	Stefano Nepa	ITA	82	LEVELUP - MTA	KTM	14	32m 23.502s
19	Luca Lunetta	ITA	58	SIC58 Squadra Corse	Honda	14	32m 58.179s
	Collin Veijer	NED	95	Liqui Moly Husqvarna Intact GP	Husqvarna	11	DNF-crash
	Ivan Ortola	SPA	48	MT Helmets - MSI	KTM	11	DNF-crash
	Taiyo Furusato	JPN	72	Honda Team Asia	Honda	3	DNF-crash
	Scott Ogden	GBR	19	MLav Racing	Honda	-	DSQ

Fastest lap: Daniel Holgado, on lap 9, 2m 14.866s, 91.4mph/147.1km/h.
Lap record: Aron Canet, 2m 15.583s, 90.9mph/146.3km/h (2017).
Event maximum speed: Joel Kelso, 151.4mph/243.7km/h (practice).

Qualifying
Weather: Dry
Air: 25° **Humidity:** 52% **Track:** 37°

1	Masia	2m 16.250s
2	Sasaki	2m 16.351s
3	Ortolá	2m 16.556s
4	Moreira	2m 16.866s
5	Holgado	2m 16.912s
6	Nepa	2m 17.016s
7	Yamanaka	2m 17.330s
8	Bertelle	2m 17.348s
9	Artigas	2m 17.372s
10	Suzuki	2m 17.407s
11	Rueda	2m 17.683s
12	Salvador	2m 17.708s
13	Fenati	2m 17.752s
14	Oncu	2m 17.998s
15	Toba	2m 18.001s
16	Munoz	2m 17.507s
17	Rossi	2m 17.984s
18	Azman	2m 17.542s
Q1		
19	Furusato	2m 17.946s
20	Farioli	2m 18.065s
21	Veijer	2m 18.129s
22	Alonso	2m 18.178s
23	Ogden	2m 18.181s
24	Migno	2m 18.257s
25	Aji	2m 18.363s
26	Carrasco	2m 18.667s
27	Whatley	2m 19.710s
	Almansa	No Time

Fastest race laps

1	Holgado	2m 14.866s
2	Yamanaka	2m 14.906s
3	Alonso	2m 14.948s
4	Piqueras	2m 15.007s
5	Veijer	2m 15.007s
6	Kelso	2m 15.038s
7	Fernandez	2m 15.508s
8	Furusato	2m 15.578s
9	Roulstone	2m 15.583s
10	Bertelle	2m 15.588s
11	Munoz	2m 15.679s
12	Ogden	2m 15.788s
13	Nepa	2m 15.817s
14	Suzuki	2m 15.832s
15	Esteban	2m 15.862s
16	Carraro	2m 16.188s
17	Zurutuza	2m 16.204s
18	Dettwiler	2m 16.532s
19	Farioli	2m 16.591s
20	Rossi	2m 17.210s
21	Ortola	2m 17.248s
22	Lunetta	2m 17.566s
23	Whatley	2m 17.835s

Championship Points

	Rider	Pts
1	Holgado	65
2	Alonso	63
3	Kelso	28
4	Ortola	23
5	Suzuki	23
6	Veijer	21
7	Rueda	20
8	Piqueras	20
9	Esteban	20
10	Nepa	19
11	Roulstone	19
12	Munoz	18
13	Furusato	16
14	Rossi	13
15	Yamanaka	13
16	Fernandez	11
17	Carraro	7
18	Bertelle	6
19	Ogden	5
20	Zurutuza	3
21	Perez	3
22	Dettwiler	2
23	Farioli	1
24	Lunetta	1

Constructor Points

		Pts
1	GASGAS	65
2	CFMOTO	63
3	KTM	46
4	Honda	38
5	Husqvarna	31

FIM WORLD CHAMPIONSHIP · ROUND 4

SPANISH GRAND PRIX
JEREZ-ANGEL NIETO CIRCUIT

Inset: Pecco and Marc trade paint.

Main: When you're smiling – Marquez, bearing tyre marks on his leathers, knew exactly how much second place meant in his fourth Ducati race.
Photos: Gold & Goose

Above: Alex Marquez bounced back to fourth on Sunday after crashing out of the sprint.

Top right: An over-ambitious Espargaro took Zarco down in the feature race.

Above right: Dani Pedrosa shares his belated gong with KTM's Pit Beirer.

Right: Quartararo held off Pedrosa for third in the sprint, but subsequently was demoted for a tyre-pressure infringement.

Photos: Gold & Goose

DEFENDING his crown amid the heightened competition of 2024 might have been Bagnaia's toughest challenge so far, but he proved up for the fight after resisting a series of powerful late attacks by Marquez to score a thrilling victory in a classic Spanish Grand Prix. One month on from their controversial clash in Portugal, this had the feel of a heavyweight rematch. Twice Marquez pushed through at the circuit's stadium section, only for Bagnaia to respond with equal aggression, leaving tyre marks on both bike and rider.

It was hard to know what was more impressive: that slow-starting Marquez had annihilated Bagnaia's 1.2-second lead in just six laps; or the way that the Italian responded to his attacks. Bagnaia hushed a voluble sold-out crowd, clinically regaining control. The ruthlessness that gave him his 30th win doubtless reflected the teachings of mentor Valentino Rossi, who had watched from the sidelines. "If Marquez sees that you're bleeding, he bites you harder," Rossi said later. His protege responded in kind, before decisively setting fastest lap three from the flag for his finest victory yet.

It was also Marquez's best yet on a Ducati, tempered as it was by maturity, after qualifying on pole. "I was smart enough and gave up at the correct time, because if not, Pecco or me, or both would have crashed," he said.

The return to Europe marked the intensification of rider and team contract rumours, with an added element – with Liberty Media's takeover of Dorna, there was increased emphasis on the USA. In timely fashion, Joe Roberts took a third consecutive second in Moto2, regaining the championship lead to enhance his appeal to a potential Americanisation of the US-owned Trackhouse Aprilia squad. "The possibility could be there if the results are. What stays is what you do on the track," the 26-year-old Californian said. "If I could fit in somewhere, that'd be pretty sweet."

Honda were fresh from two days of testing at Barcelona, making the most of their full concessions, although progress could only be measured by research completed rather than any immediate improvement. Full-time riders Mir and Marini opined that HRC needed a total rethink, and that in the quest to improve traction, the RC213V had sacrificed front-end performance. "The concept of this bike is not the right one," said Mir. "Probably, braking is the weakest point we have at the moment. The advantage that we had last year in that phase, that Marc was very good at, you don't have it with this bike." Clutching at straws perhaps, he offered some positives in the post-race test at Jerez. A new engine format, thought to be revised crankshaft inertia, was "more positive than you could see! We tried a different concept, and I think it is working. We have more turning now."

Iffy weather on Saturday led to a chaotic sprint, with some riders criticising race direction for letting it continue after 15 crashes and nine riders failing to finish – alarming numbers for a 12-lap race. It was sunny, but hard-to-see wet patches repeatedly caught riders out at Turns Five, Eight and Nine. Marini also blamed fierce gusts: "It was a lot, so easy to make a mistake. And in the sprint, everybody is pushing, and there is a little bit of chaos every time."

Vinales said, "Race Direction should understand that if we are 25 riders and 15 crash, it's because of something. Put a red flag and check the conditions." Bagnaia had a different criticism, after being knocked down by Binder at the first corner on lap three. Riled by Race Direction's decision not to punish the South African, he said, with heavy irony, "Racing incident? To overtake two riders on the [inside] kerb, you're out of the current line."

The officials also stoked the ire of Zarco, not for a bad decision, but for failing to make one at all. Called before the stewards, after being knocked out of Sunday's main event in a failed overtake by Espargaro, he had to be restrained by his on-track assailant after blowing his top, infuriated by panel chief Freddie Spencer's response: "Freddie was watching the action with us. And it seems he was looking to me, that he wanted to know what I wanted. But I said to him that he is not good for this job because he doesn't take the right decision in the right moment. So don't ask me what you have to do! Freddie Spencer is not the right guy in this place."

But they had no choice in another bad-friends exercise,

bound by rules to penalise five riders by eight seconds for front tyres that were below pressure in the sprint. That dropped Quartararo from third to fifth, Raul Fernandez from eighth to 12th and out of the points, but it didn't have any effect on the lower positions of Di Giannantonio, Miller and Rins.

Dani Pedrosa was back again as a wild-card, taking a podium with a survivor's third in the depleted sprint, after qualifying 16th, but crashing out of the main race. Semi-team-mate Acosta secured another podium in the sprint, but spoiled his main-race chances with a very fast and bruising crash at Turn Seven in morning warm-up.

MOTOGP SPRINT RACE – 12 laps

Bagnaia set a new all-time record on Friday afternoon, but Saturday was wet and he ended up seventh on a grid that was led for the first time in the season by Marc Marquez, from Bezzecchi and Martin. Binder, through from Q1, led the second, from Diggia and Alex Marquez.

The sun had dried most of the track for the sprint, but it remained highly treacherous, and almost every rider had difficulties. This included Marc Marquez, at the same Turn Nine where he had seized the lead at half-distance from eventual winner Martin.

Binder led away convincingly, only for Martin to close the gap and take over before the first lap was done.

The mayhem had already started, with Espargaro and Miller falling. Bagnaia was jostling for position into Turn One as they started lap three, only to be squeezed between Bezzecchi and an ambitious Binder, crashing out.

The crowd were ecstatic when Marquez had closed on Martin, then profited by a wobble at Turn Eight to seize the lead at Nine, and he looked secure for two laps, until he crashed at the same corner.

By the finish, Martin was comfortably clear of the survivors, with Acosta taking yet another podium, but Quartararo (from 23rd on the grid) was robbed of third place in Pedrosa's favour by the tyre-pressure rule.

Likewise, Morbidelli was promoted; the remounted Marc Marquez was sixth, with Augusto Fernandez, Oliveira and Mir rounding out the points.

Miller, Di Giannantonio, Savadori, Rins, Marc Marquez and Zarco had all fallen and remounted; Espargaro, Bagnaia, Binder, Alex Marquez, Bastianini (all three crashing together without any contact), Bezzecchi, Vinales, Marini and Bradl did not manage to do so.

MOTOGP RACE – 24 laps

Marquez led away, chased by Martin, Bezzecchi and Bagnaia. As they reached the end of the back straight for the first time, the defender released his brakes on the outside kerb, brilliantly swooping to gain two places, then managed to make the apex.

That left only Marquez ahead. Wary of track conditions after crashing out of the lead on a damp patch the previous day, the Spaniard was cautious on his way into the final Turn 13 hairpin. Bagnaia pounced, completing a fine first lap in the lead and setting the tone for his race.

It wasn't all clear running from there, however. Bagnaia himself fell victim to the slippery Turn 13 on the following lap, allowing Martin and briefly also Marquez through. Martin, who had won on Saturday by keeping his head while others lost theirs, soon settled into a rhythm, seeking to pull the group apart.

But there would be no escape. Bagnaia remained within two-tenths for the first nine laps. Martin managed to add half a second to that over the next two, but hopes of a famous home double tumbled when he tucked the front at Turn Six on lap 11. "I arrived with the same speed and I was braking at the same point," shrugged the perplexed Spaniard. The fault, it seemed, lay in being slightly off line.

FIM WORLD CHAMPIONSHIP: ROUND 4
GRAN PREMIO ESTRELLA GALICIA 0,0 DE ESPAÑA
26-28 APRIL, 2024

CIRCUITO DE JEREZ
25 laps
Length: 4.423km / 2.748 miles
Width: 11m

MOTOGP: 25 laps, 68.708 miles/110.575km
RACE WEATHER: Dry (air 20°, humidity 37%, track 39°)

Pos.	Rider	Nat.	No.	Entrant	Machine	Race tyre choice	Laps	Time & speed
1	Francesco Bagnaia	ITA	1	Ducati Lenovo Team	Ducati Desmosedici GP24	F: Medium/R: Medium	25	40m 58.053s 99.9mph/160.7km/h
2	Marc Marquez	SPA	93	Gresini Racing MotoGP	Ducati Desmosedici GP23	F: Medium/R: Medium	25	40m 58.425s
3	Marco Bezzecchi	ITA	72	Pertamina Enduro VR46 Racing	Ducati Desmosedici GP23	F: Medium/R: Medium	25	41m 01.956s
4	Alex Marquez	SPA	73	Gresini Racing MotoGP	Ducati Desmosedici GP23	F: Medium/R: Medium	25	41m 05.258s
5	Enea Bastianini	ITA	23	Ducati Lenovo Team	Ducati Desmosedici GP24	F: Medium/R: Medium	25	41m 05.306s
6	Brad Binder	RSA	33	Red Bull KTM Factory Racing	KTM RC16	F: Medium/R: Medium	25	41m 05.854s
7	Fabio Di Giannantonio	ITA	49	Pertamina Enduro VR46 Racing	Ducati Desmosedici GP23	F: Medium/R: Medium	25	41m 08.116s
8	Miguel Oliveira	POR	88	Trackhouse Racing	Aprilia RS-GP24	F: Medium/R: Medium	25	41m 09.032s
9	Maverick Vinales	SPA	12	Aprilia Racing	Aprilia RS-GP24	F: Medium/R: Medium	25	41m 09.270s
10	Pedro Acosta	SPA	31	Red Bull GASGAS Tech3	KTM RC16	F: Medium/R: Medium	25	41m 18.815s
11	Raul Fernandez	SPA	25	Trackhouse Racing	Aprilia RS-GP23	F: Medium/R: Medium	25	41m 21.561s
12	Joan Mir	SPA	36	Repsol Honda Team	Honda RC213V	F: Medium/R: Medium	25	41m 21.637s
13	Alex Rins	SPA	42	Monster Energy Yamaha MotoGP	Yamaha YZR-M1	F: Medium/R: Medium	25	41m 26.505s
14	Takaaki Nakagami	JPN	30	IDEMITSU Honda LCR	Honda RC213V	F: Medium/R: Medium	25	41m 27.102s
15	Fabio Quartararo	FRA	20	Monster Energy Yamaha MotoGP	Yamaha YZR-M1	F: Medium/R: Medium	25	41m 30.068s
16	Stefan Bradl	GER	6	HRC Test Team	Honda RC213V	F: Medium/R: Soft	25	41m 39.486s
17	Luca Marini	ITA	10	Repsol Honda Team	Honda RC213V	F: Medium/R: Medium	25	41m 41.376s
	Augusto Fernandez	SPA	37	Red Bull GASGAS Tech3	KTM RC16	F: Medium/R: Medium	19	DNF-crash
	Jack Miller	AUS	43	Red Bull KTM Factory Racing	KTM RC16	F: Medium/R: Medium	17	DNF-crash
	Franco Morbidelli	ITA	21	Prima Pramac Racing	Ducati Desmosedici GP23	F: Medium/R: Medium	17	DNF-crash
	Lorenzo Savadori	ITA	32	Aprilia Racing	Aprilia RS-GP24	F: Medium/R: Medium	11	DNF-crash
	Jorge Martin	SPA	89	Prima Pramac Racing	Ducati Desmosedici GP24	F: Medium/R: Medium	10	DNF-crash
	Johann Zarco	FRA	5	CASTROL Honda LCR	Honda RC213V	F: Medium/R: Medium	9	DNF-crash
	Aleix Espargaro	SPA	41	Aprilia Racing	Aprilia RS-GP24	F: Medium/R: Medium	9	DNF-crash
	Daniel Pedrosa	SPA	26	Red Bull KTM Factory Racing	KTM RC16	F: Medium/R: Medium	3	DNF-crash

Fastest lap: Francesco Bagnaia, on lap 23, 1m 37.449s, 101.5mph/163.3km/h.
Lap record: Francesco Bagnaia, 1m 37.669s, 101.3mph/163.0km/h (2022).
Event maximum speed: Daniel Pedrosa, 186.4mph/300.0km/h (race).

Qualifying: Weather: Wet Air: 15° Humidity: 84% Track: 17°
1 M. Marquez 1m 46.773s, 2 Bezzecchi 1m 47.044s, 3 Martin 1m 47.381s, 4 Binder 1m 47.730s,
5 Di Giannantonio 1m 47.778s, 6 A. Marquez 1m 47.840s, 7 Bagnaia 1m 47.962s, 8 Morbidelli 1m 48.116s,
9 Bastianini 1m 48.362s, 10 Acosta 1m 48.528s, 11 Vinales 1m 48.595s, 12 A. Espargaro 1m 49.417s.
Q1: 13 Zarco 1m 48.102s, 14 Oliveira 1m 48.418s, 15 Miller 1m 48.672s, 16 Pedrosa 1m 48.699s,
17 R. Fernandez 1m 48.728s, 18 A. Fernandez 1m 49.229s, 19 Bradl 1m 49.659s, 20 Mir 1m 49.765s,
21 Savadori 1m 49.860s, 22 Marini 1m 49.978s, 23 Quartararo 1m 50.100s, 24 Nakagami 1m 50.245s,
25 Rins 1m 50.302s.

SPRINT RACE: 12 laps, 34.240 miles/55.104km
WEATHER: Dry (air 23°, humidity 46%, track 39°)

Pos.	Rider	Race tyre choice	Laps	Time & speed
1	Jorge Martin	F: Medium/R: Soft	12	19m 52.682s 99.5mph/160.2km/h
2	Pedro Acosta	F: Medium/R: Soft	12	19m 55.652s
3	Daniel Pedrosa	F: Medium/R: Soft	12	19m 59.784s
4	Franco Morbidelli	F: Medium/R: Soft	12	20m 01.163s
5	Fabio Quartararo	F: Medium/R: Soft	12	20m 07.734s*
6	Marc Marquez	F: Medium/R: Soft	12	20m 10.813s
7	Augusto Fernandez	F: Medium/R: Soft	12	20m 10.960s
8	Miguel Oliveira	F: Medium/R: Soft	12	20m 11.100s
9	Joan Mir	F: Medium/R: Soft	12	20m 11.235s
10	Takaaki Nakagami	F: Medium/R: Soft	12	20m 13.818s
11	Johann Zarco	F: Medium/R: Soft	12	20m 14.630s
12	Raul Fernandez	F: Medium/R: Soft	12	20m 16.564s*
13	Fabio Di Giannantonio	F: Medium/R: Soft	12	20m 24.160s*
14	Jack Miller	F: Medium/R: Soft	12	20m 38.583s*
15	Alex Rins	F: Medium/R: Soft	12	21m 02.970s*
16	Lorenzo Savadori	F: Medium/R: Soft	12	21m 15.661s
	Luca Marini	F: Medium/R: Soft	11	DNF-crash
	Stefan Bradl	F: Medium/R: Soft	11	DNF-crash
	Maverick Vinales	F: Medium/R: Soft	9	DNF-crash
	Alex Marquez	F: Medium/R: Soft	8	DNF-crash
	Brad Binder	F: Medium/R: Soft	8	DNF-crash
	Enea Bastianini	F: Medium/R: Soft	8	DNF-crash
	Marco Bezzecchi	F: Medium/R: Soft	8	DNF-crash
	Francesco Bagnaia	F: Medium/R: Soft	2	DNF-crash
	Aleix Espargaro	F: Medium/R: Soft		DNF-crash

* Fabio Quartararo, Raul Fernandez, Fabio di Giannantonio, Jack Miller, Alex Rins: 8s penalty for technical infringement.

Fastest race lap: Marc Marquez, on lap 6, 1m 37.812s.

Fastest race laps:
1 Bagnaia 1m 37.449s, 2 M. Marquez 1m 37.637s, 3 Martin 1m 37.884s, 4 Bezzecchi 1m 37.910s,
5 Morbidelli 1m 37.943s, 6 Di Giannantonio 1m 37.967s, 7 A. Marquez 1m 37.982s, 8 Vinales 1m 37.999s, 9 Binder 1m 38.001s, 10 Bastianini 1m 38.048s, 11 Oliveira 1m 38.105s,
12 R. Fernandez 1m 38.253s, 13 Acosta 1m 38.318s, 14 Miller 1m 38.350s, 15 A. Espargaro 1m 38.415s, 16 Zarco 1m 38.433s, 17 Mir 1m 38.484s, 18 Quartararo 1m 38.641s, 19 Rins 1m 38.648s, 20 Pedrosa 1m 38.767s, 21 Nakagami 1m 38.819s, 22 A. Fernandez 1m 38.918s
23 Marini 1m 39.210s, 24 Bradl 1m 39.227s, 25 Savadori 1m 39.542s.

Grid order / Lap-by-lap leaderboard

Grid order	1	2	3	4	5	6	7	8	9	10	11	12	13	14	15	16	17	18	19	20	21	22	23	24	25
93 M. MARQUEZ	1	89	89	89	89	89	89	89	89	89	1	1	1	1	1	1	1	1	1	1	1	1	1	1	1
72 BEZZECCHI	93	1	1	1	1	1	1	1	1	1	72	72	72	93	93	93	93	93	93	93	93	93	93	93	2
89 MARTIN	89	93	93	72	72	72	72	72	72	72	93	93	93	72	72	72	72	72	72	72	72	72	72	72	3
33 BINDER	72	72	72	93	93	93	93	93	93	93	73	73	73	73	73	73	73	73	73	73	73	73	73	73	4
49 DI GIANNANTONIO	73	73	73	73	73	73	73	73	73	73	33	33	33	33	33	33	33	33	33	33	33	33	33	23	5
73 A. MARQUEZ	33	33	33	33	33	33	33	33	33	33	88	23	23	23	23	23	23	23	23	23	23	23	23	33	6
1 BAGNAIA	49	88	88	88	88	88	88	88	88	88	23	88	88	88	88	88	88	88	49	49	49	49	49	49	7
21 MORBIDELLI	88	43	43	23	23	23	23	23	23	23	49	49	49	49	49	49	49	49	88	88	88	88	88	88	8
23 BASTIANINI	43	23	23	43	43	43	49	49	49	49	12	12	12	12	12	12	12	12	12	12	12	12	12	12	9
31 ACOSTA	23	49	49	49	49	49	43	43	43	12	43	43	25	43	31	31	31	31	31	31	31	31	31	31	10
12 VINALES	26	26	25	25	25	25	25	25	25	43	25	25	43	31	31	43	43	43	25	25	25	25	25	25	11
41 A. ESPARGARO	12	25	26	12	12	12	12	12	12	21	21	21	31	21	25	25	25	25	36	36	36	36	36	36	12
5 ZARCO	21	12	12	21	21	21	21	21	25	31	31	31	21	25	25	20	20	20	42	42	42	42	42	42	13
88 OLIVEIRA	25	36	21	36	36	36	31	31	31	36	36	36	36	36	36	36	42	42	42	20	30	30	30	30	14
43 MILLER	41	21	36	31	31	31	36	36	36	20	20	20	20	20	20	42	42	30	30	30	20	20	20	20	15
26 PEDROSA	36	5	5	5	5	5	5	20	42	42	42	42	42	6	6	6	6	6	6	6					
25 R. FERNANDEZ	5	41	31	41	41	41	41	41	42	30	30	30	30	30	30	10	10	10	10	10	10	10			
37 A. FERNANDEZ	31	31	41	20	20	20	20	20	30	6	6	6	6	37	37										
6 BRADL	20	20	20	42	42	42	42	42	6	10	10	10	10												
36 MIR	42	42	42	37	30	30	30	30	10	37															
32 SAVADORI	37	37	37	30	37	37	37	37	32																
10 MARINI	6	30	30	6	6	6	6	10																	
20 QUARTARARO	30	6	6	32	32	32	32																		
30 NAKAGAMI	10	32	32	10	10	10																			
42 RINS	32	10	10																						

Championship Points

1	Martin	54 (38)	92
2	Bagnaia	61 (14)	75
3	Bastianini	58 (12)	70
4	Acosta	49 (20)	69
5	Vinales	38 (25)	63
6	M. Marquez	33 (27)	60
7	Binder	50 (9)	59
8	A. Espargaro	25 (14)	39
9	Bezzecchi	0	36
10	Di Giannantonio	34 (0)	34
11	A. Marquez	24 (3)	27
12	Quartararo	19 (6)	25
13	Oliveira	21 (2)	23
14	Miller	14 (8)	22
15	R. Fernandez	11 (1)	12
16	Mir	11 (1)	12
17	A. Fernandez	7 (3)	10
18	Pedrosa	0 (7)	7
19	Rins	6 (0)	6
20	Morbidelli	0 (6)	6
21	Zarco	5 (0)	5
22	Nakagami	4 (0)	4

Constructor Points

1	Ducati	91 (42)	133
2	KTM	66 (29)	95
3	Aprilia	49 (33)	82
4	Yamaha	21 (6)	27
5	Honda	12 (1)	13

MOTO2: RACE DISTANCE: 21 laps, 57.715 miles/92.883km
RACE WEATHER: Dry (air 17°, humidity 55%, track 33°)

Pos.	Rider	Nat.	No.	Entrant	Machine	Laps	Time & Speed
1	Fermin Aldeguer	SPA	54	Beta Tools SpeedUp	Boscoscuro	21	35m 36.316s
							97.2mph/156.5km/h
2	Joe Roberts	USA	16	OnlyFans American Racing Team	Kalex	21	35m 37.603s
3	Manuel Gonzalez	SPA	18	QJMOTOR Gresini Moto2	Kalex	21	35m 37.884s
4	Sergio Garcia	SPA	3	MT Helmets - MSI	Boscoscuro	21	35m 42.542s
5	Albert Arenas	SPA	75	QJMOTOR Gresini Moto2	Kalex	21	35m 44.375s
6	Ai Ogura	JPN	79	MT Helmets - MSI	Boscoscuro	21	35m 48.806s
7	Tony Arbolino	ITA	14	Elf Marc VDS Racing Team	Kalex	21	35m 49.662s
8	Jeremy Alcoba	SPA	52	Yamaha VR46 Master Camp	Kalex	21	35m 49.805s
9	Celestino Vietti	ITA	13	Red Bull KTM Ajo	Kalex	21	35m 50.824s
10	Somkiat Chantra	THA	35	IDEMITSU Honda Team Asia	Kalex	21	35m 56.009s
11	Filip Salac	CZE	12	Elf Marc VDS Racing Team	Kalex	21	35m 56.361s
12	Izan Guevara	SPA	28	CFMOTO Aspar Team	Kalex	21	35m 58.095s
13	Zonta van den Goorbergh	NED	84	RW-Idrofoglia Racing GP	Kalex	21	36m 04.249s
14	Deniz Oncu	TUR	53	Red Bull KTM Ajo	Kalex	21	36m 08.462s
15	Matteo Ferrari	ITA	23	QJMOTOR Gresini Moto2	Kalex	21	36m 17.474s
16	Mario Aji	INA	34	IDEMITSU Honda Team Asia	Kalex	21	36m 18.269s
17	Xavi Cardelus	AND	20	Fantic Racing	Kalex	21	36m 18.907s
18	Jorge Navarro	SPA	9	KLINT Forward Factory Team	Forward	21	36m 23.249s
19	Darryn Binder	RSA	15	Liqui Moly Husqvarna Intact GP	Kalex	20	37m 08.185s
20	Xavier Artigas	SPA	43	KLINT Forward Factory Team	Forward	17	36m 10.407s
	Jaume Masia	SPA	5	Pertamina Mandalika GAS UP	Kalex	20	DNF-crash
	Jake Dixon	GBR	96	CFMOTO Aspar Team	Kalex	20	DNF-crash
	Alonso Lopez	SPA	21	Beta Tools SpeedUp	Boscoscuro	17	DNF-crash
	Marcos Ramirez	SPA	24	OnlyFans American Racing Team	Kalex	15	DNF-crash
	Alex Escrig	SPA	11	KLINT Forward Factory Team	Forward	13	DNF-crash
	Diogo Moreira	BRA	10	Italtrans Racing Team	Kalex	11	DNF-crash
	Barry Baltus	BEL	7	RW-Idrofoglia Racing GP	Kalex	6	DNF-crash
	Dennis Foggia	ITA	71	Italtrans Racing Team	Kalex	4	DNF-crash
	Senna Agius	AUS	81	Liqui Moly Husqvarna Intact GP	Kalex	1	DNF-crash
	Bo Bendsneyder	NED	64	Pertamina Mandalika GAS UP	Kalex	1	DNF-crash

Fastest lap: Joe Roberts, on lap 9, 1m 41.020s, 97.9mph/157.6km/h.
Lap record: Sam Lowes, 1m 41.313s, 97.6mph/157.1km/h (2021).
Event maximum speed: Somkiat Chantra, 159.0mph/255.9km/h (race).

Qualifying
Weather: Dry
Air: 19° Humidity: 55% Track: 29°

1	Aldeguer	1m 40.673s
2	Arenas	1m 41.111s
3	Dixon	1m 41.466s
4	Gonzalez	1m 41.554s
5	Moreira	1m 41.657s
6	Garcia	1m 41.706s
7	Vietti	1m 41.741s
8	Arbolino	1m 41.759s
9	Alcoba	1m 41.771s
10	Ramirez	1m 41.788s
11	Roberts	1m 41.799s
12	Chantra	1m 41.889s
13	Baltus	1m 41.973s
14	Salac	1m 42.245s
15	Guevara	1m 42.262s
16	Lopez	1m 42.347s
17	Ogura	1m 42.705s
18	V d Goorbergh	No Time
	Q1	
19	Agius	1m 42.416s
20	Bendsneyder	1m 42.458s
21	Binder	1m 42.542s
22	Oncu	1m 42.590s
23	Foggia	1m 42.908s
24	Navarro	1m 42.922s
25	Masia	1m 43.016s
26	Ferrari	1m 43.090s
27	Aji	1m 43.433s
28	Escrig	1m 43.438s
29	Cardelus	1m 43.818s
30	Artigas	1m 45.002s
	Sasaki	No Time

Fastest race laps

1	Roberts	1m 41.020s
2	Gonzalez	1m 41.028s
3	Aldeguer	1m 41.037s
4	Garcia	1m 41.176s
5	Ramirez	1m 41.301s
6	Arenas	1m 41.330s
7	Moreira	1m 41.514s
8	Vietti	1m 41.515s
9	Dixon	1m 41.556s
10	Alcoba	1m 41.577s
11	Ogura	1m 41.578s
12	Arbolino	1m 41.617s
13	Lopez	1m 41.621s
14	Chantra	1m 41.724s
15	Baltus	1m 41.771s
16	Salac	1m 41.815s
17	Guevara	1m 41.949s
18	Binder	1m 41.956s
19	Masia	1m 42.028s
20	V d Goorbergh	1m 42.052s
21	Navarro	1m 42.130s
22	Oncu	1m 42.243s
23	Foggia	1m 42.254s
24	Aji	1m 42.323s
25	Escrig	1m 42.344s
26	Cardelus	1m 42.579s
27	Ferrari	1m 42.618s
28	Artigas	1m 43.174s

Championship Points

	Rider	Pts
1	Roberts	69
2	Garcia	64
3	Aldeguer	54
4	Gonzalez	46
5	Ogura	43
6	Lopez	38
7	Canet	38
8	Arenas	31
9	Vietti	29
10	Ramirez	28
11	Alcoba	25
12	Baltus	23
13	Arbolino	18
14	Chantra	17
15	Foggia	10
16	Salac	6
17	Van den Goorbergh	6
18	Guevara	4
19	Oncu	3
20	Bendsneyder	2
21	Agius	2
22	Moreira	2
23	Binder	1
24	Ferrari	1

Constructor Points

		Pts
1	Boscoscuro	88
2	Kalex	85

MOTO3: 19 laps, 52.218 miles/84.037km
RACE WEATHER: Dry (air 15°, humidity 63%, track 27°)

Pos.	Rider	Nat.	No.	Entrant	Machine	Laps	Time & Speed
1	Collin Veijer	NED	95	Liqui Moly Husqvarna Intact GP	Husqvarna	19	33m 29.725s
							93.5mph/150.5km/h
2	David Munoz	SPA	64	BOE Motorsports	KTM	19	33m 29.770s
3	Ivan Ortola	SPA	48	MT Helmets - MSI	KTM	19	33m 30.596s
4	Ryusei Yamanaka	JPN	6	MT Helmets - MSI	KTM	19	33m 34.574s
5	Joel Kelso	AUS	66	BOE Motorsports	KTM	19	33m 39.903s
6	Adrian Fernandez	SPA	31	Leopard Racing	Honda	19	33m 40.078s
7	Daniel Holgado	SPA	96	Red Bull GASGAS Tech3	GASGAS	19	33m 40.125s
8	Nicola Carraro	ITA	10	LEVELUP - MTA	KTM	19	33m 40.372s
9	Stefano Nepa	ITA	82	LEVELUP - MTA	KTM	19	33m 41.125s
10	Angel Piqueras	SPA	36	Leopard Racing	Honda	19	33m 44.610s
11	David Alonso	COL	80	CFMOTO Gaviota Aspar Team	CFMOTO	19	33m 48.877s
12	Jacob Roulstone	AUS	12	Red Bull GASGAS Tech3	GASGAS	19	33m 49.646s
13	Filippo Farioli	ITA	7	SIC58 Squadra Corse	Honda	19	33m 50.148s
14	Matteo Bertelle	ITA	18	Rivacold Snipers Team	Honda	19	33m 50.266s
15	David Almansa	SPA	22	Rivacold Snipers Team	Honda	19	33m 50.387s
16	Vicente Perez	SPA	21	Red Bull KTM Ajo	KTM	19	33m 52.107s
17	Taiyo Furusato	JPN	72	Honda Team Asia	Honda	19	33m 52.607s
18	Riccardo Rossi	ITA	54	CIP Green Power	KTM	19	33m 52.911s
19	Scott Ogden	GBR	19	MLav Racing	Honda	19	33m 55.274s
20	Luca Lunetta	ITA	58	SIC58 Squadra Corse	Honda	19	34m 01.995s
21	Noah Dettwiler	SWI	55	CIP Green Power	KTM	19	34m 02.208s
22	Xabi Zurutuza	SPA	85	Red Bull KTM Ajo	KTM	19	34m 15.071s
23	Joshua Whatley	GBR	70	MLav Racing	Honda	19	34m 15.567s
24	Tatchakorn Buasri	THA	5	Honda Team Asia	Honda	19	34m 16.570s
25	Tatsuki Suzuki	JPN	24	Liqui Moly Husqvarna Intact GP	Husqvarna	18	35m 03.492s
	Joel Esteban	SPA	78	CFMOTO Gaviota Aspar Team	CFMOTO	18	DNF-crash

Fastest lap: Ryusei Yamanaka, on lap 8, 1m 45.105s, 94.1mph/151.4km/h.
Lap record: Ryusei Yamanaka, 1m 46.016s, 93.3mph/150.1km/h (2023).
Event maximum speed: Daniel Holgado, 137.5mph/221.3km/h (race).

Qualifying:
Weather: Dry
Air: 19° Humidity: 50% Track: 31°

1	Alonso	1m 44.954s
2	Munoz	1m 45.174s
3	Veijer	1m 46.013s
4	Kelso	1m 46.053s
5	Yamanaka	1m 46.152s
6	Piqueras	1m 46.477s
7	Ortola	1m 46.495s
8	Esteban	1m 46.600s
9	Suzuki	1m 46.797s
10	Carraro	1m 46.963s
11	Nepa	1m 47.018s
12	Fernandez	1m 47.152s
13	Ogden	1m 47.182s
14	Rossi	1m 47.366s
15	Farioli	1m 47.561s
16	Almansa	1m 47.603s
17	Roulstone	No Time
18	Holgado	No Time
	Q1	
19	Bertelle	1m 48.406s
20	Lunetta	1m 48.579s
21	Furusato	1m 48.651s
22	Whatley	1m 49.203s
23	Dettwiler	1m 49.228s
24	Perez	1m 49.523s
25	Buasri	1m 50.340s
26	Zurutuza	1m 51.460s

Fastest race laps

1	Yamanaka	1m 45.105s
2	Esteban	1m 45.116s
3	Ortola	1m 45.127s
4	Alonso	1m 45.127s
5	Veijer	1m 45.163s
6	Munoz	1m 45.179s
7	Kelso	1m 45.242s
8	Piqueras	1m 45.309s
9	Fernandez	1m 45.380s
10	Nepa	1m 45.521s
11	Holgado	1m 45.538s
12	Carraro	1m 45.595s
13	Bertelle	1m 45.743s
14	Rossi	1m 45.794s
15	Furusato	1m 45.836s
16	Almansa	1m 45.846s
17	Farioli	1m 45.861s
18	Roulstone	1m 45.863s
19	Perez	1m 45.928s
20	Dettwiler	1m 46.104s
21	Ogden	1m 46.222s
22	Lunetta	1m 46.304s
23	Suzuki	1m 46.829s
24	Whatley	1m 46.852s
25	Zurutuza	1m 47.121s
26	Buasri	1m 47.203s

Championship Points

	Rider	Pts
1	Holgado	74
2	Alonso	68
3	Veijer	46
4	Ortola	39
5	Kelso	39
6	Munoz	38
7	Piqueras	26
8	Yamanaka	26
9	Nepa	26
10	Suzuki	23
11	Roulstone	23
12	Fernandez	21
13	Rueda	20
14	Esteban	20
15	Furusato	16
16	Carraro	15
17	Rossi	13
18	Bertelle	8
19	Ogden	5
20	Farioli	4
21	Perez	3
22	Zurutuza	3
23	Dettwiler	2
24	Lunetta	1
25	Almansa	1

Constructor Points

		Pts
1	GASGAS	74
2	CFMOTO	68
3	KTM	66
4	Husqvarna	56
5	Honda	48

Main: Jorge Martin did the double.

Inset, top right: Dorna's Carlos and Carmelo Ezpeleta take the stage with FIM president Jorge Viegas *(second right)* and IRTA president Herve Poncharal *(right)* at the announcement of sweeping rule changes for 2027.
Photos: Gold & Goose

Inset, right: Honda factory new boy Luca Marini was still waiting for a first championship point.
Photo: Repsol Honda

Inset, far right: Zarco rowed back on his criticism of the stewards.

Inset, below right: Fans and their phones flocked to the Sarthe circuit in record numbers.
Photos: Gold & Goose

FIM WORLD CHAMPIONSHIP • ROUND 5

FRENCH GRAND PRIX

LE MANS BUGATTI CIRCUIT

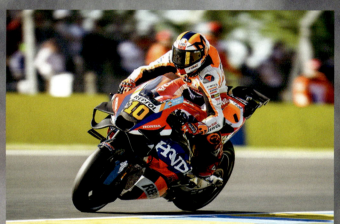

Above: Martin leads Bagnaia, Marquez and Vinales in the main race.

Top right: No home-race joy for Quartararo, who had his recalcitrant Yamaha up to a heroic sixth before crashing out.

Above right: Bezzecchi crashed out of both races.

Right: Marquez in the sprint. He was second on Saturday and Sunday.

Photos: Gold & Goose

WHILE the speculation about Ducati's choice for the second factory seat remained as feverish as ever, there was a new talking point in the paddock at Le Mans. It followed the formal announcement of new regulations to come into force in 2027 at a briefing hosted by Dorna and the FIM.

There were no real surprises, thanks to previous leaks. But having it laid out in black and white finally turned rumour into fact, and opinions could be based on something more than speculation. And concern about losing speed had become real.

This would definitely happen, with engine size reduced from 1000cc to 850, along with aerodynamic forces reduced (front wing width cut from 600mm to 550, mounted 50mm further back), going at least some way to reducing stress on front tyres – ride-height changes would be banned altogether. These moves would hand back more to the rider, at least in theory.

Do lap times matter? Why hurry a good race? MotoGP riders aren't going for the land-speed record, only to go faster than one another. And ever-increasing speeds needed to be brought back under control for safety. As Marquez insisted, doubtless correctly, neither trackside nor TV viewers would be affected were lap times to be slowed or top speeds shaved, as long as the contest was preserved.

Thus there was cautious approval in the paddock – cautious, because the last time engine size had been cut (from 990cc to 800 in 2007), for similar reasons, the consequences were universally unpopular. Speeds were barely affected, but higher revs and reduced torque killed the wheelspin and rear-wheel steering that had made 990 racing so spectacular. The return to 1000cc in 2012, along with a rev limit (applied indirectly by limiting maximum bore size), came as a huge relief. But top speed continued to rise, while aero and ride-height developments impinged, with dirty air and reduced braking distances making overtaking harder, as well as stressing front tyres.

What about the power loss? The capacity drop from 1000cc to 850 represented a reduction of 15 per cent. But maximum bore size, currently 81mm, would be cut to 75mm, a reduction of only 7.4 per cent. Thus the cylinder dimensions would be notably less oversquare, and the piston stroke only slightly reduced. Piston speeds, and thence the rev ceiling, should remain similar. This should preserve torque characteristics, and avoid the pitfall of the shrieky and detested 800s. Power would be reduced, but currently there is such a surplus that it needs to be tamed electronically in the lower gears, and still would be, even if there is less.

Lap times would be slower by a second or maybe two, engineers thought, leading to concerns that Superbikes would threaten MotoGP. At comparable tracks in 2023, differences were more than two seconds, except at Catalunya, where Bautista's Superbike was just 1.625 seconds off Bagnaia's pole, both set by V4 Ducatis. Questioned at the formal announcement, FIM chief Jorge Viegas was reassuring: "We will slow down the Superbikes, too."

Not that MotoGP was in much danger of running out of fans – at least if the numbers at a scorching Le Mans were anything to go by, setting a new record of 297,471 over the weekend. This came directly after a claim of a record 296,741 at the previous round at Jerez, although that was swiftly withdrawn when Dorna realised that 125,000-odd ghost spectators had somehow swelled the total. Some old-timers grumbled that, since spectators who had started a weekend of trackside festivity early were counted four times for the Thursday-to-Sunday figure, it fell short of the estimated 400,000 or more who had thronged the Sachsenring back when it was a long road circuit in the old East Germany, providing rare entertainment behind the Iron Curtain; also the 445,000 Sunday-only crowd for the German GP at Solitude in 1964. All the same, a race-day figure of 119,145 was impressive.

There was news of changes of heart within the beleaguered Honda camp. From Zarco came a modicum of

backtracking after his explosive outburst at the stewards, and Freddie Spencer in particular, at Jerez. Not in what he had said, but in how he had allowed himself to become overheated and "to get a high voice". It was unprofessional, he admitted.

In the factory team, where Marini remained yet to score a single point and Mir suffered a second zero after a race crash, the latter was contemplating his future, including a possible switch to World Superbikes. He'd had an offer to stay with HRC, but had also been linked with a possible move to Trackhouse Aprilia, where his manager at his former Suzuki team, Davide Brivio, had recently taken the reins. The Majorcan would not elaborate. "I have options, but I need a bit more time to understand and take a good decision," he said.

An unusual technical infringement by evocatively named Moto3 rookie Xabi Zurutuza resulted in him being disqualified from Q2. The diminutive Spaniard was below the minimum bike/rider weight limit of 152kg, by 1.8kg.

MOTOGP SPRINT RACE – 13 laps

Martin was on form, leading free practice and taking a second pole of the year ahead of Bagnaia and Vinales; Di Giannantonio, Bezzecchi and Espargaro on row two. Quartararo secured a best-so-far eighth at home, but Zarco fell in Q1 to languish 15th.

More significantly, Marc Marquez was finding the going tough after a fall in practice meant that he would face Q1 for the first time on a Ducati. "I was fighting the bike," he admitted. It became worse when Bastianini and Oliveira consigned him to third in that session and 15th on the grid. That gave him the chance to display his genius when the flag fell for the sprint. He gained three places into Turn One, two more into Turn Three, the Dunlop Chicane. Di Giannantonio, divebombed into Turn Six, was his seventh victim in 30 seconds – the Marquez of old.

Martin led away, keenly pursued by Bezzecchi, the gap slowly stretching to 1.2 seconds by the start of lap ten. The Italian would get no further, sliding off at Garage Vert. This handed second to Marquez, who had battled for third with Espargaro in the early stages, before the Aprilia rider took the first of two long-laps for a jumped start, letting teammate Vinales past as well.

By half-distance, Bastianini was also ahead after Espargaro completed his second long loop, although erstwhile companion Miller had dropped away, suffering another troublesome race.

Acosta secured sixth after finishing the first lap tenth; Diggia, Miller and Raul Fernandez took the last points; Quartararo narrowly missed out. Both Mir and Rins crashed out.

Bagnaia's race was disastrous. He retired after losing places hand over fist on the first lap, blaming "something dangerous", believed to be a faulty rear tyre.

MOTOGP RACE – 27 laps

The sunshine of the preceding two days had gone, to be replaced by overcast skies that threatened rain, and the crews made ready for a possible bike change that turned out to be unnecessary.

Bagnaia pushed to assert his authority early on, coming out ahead of Martin in a first-lap scrap. Espargaro, Di Giannantonio, Vinales and Acosta followed, the rookie passing Vinales on lap two, only to crash out at Garage Vert on lap three after being squeezed between him and Diggia. "Today, I had the bike to win," he said later, but couldn't prove it.

The early drama promoted Marquez to sixth – he'd been eighth on the first lap thanks to further heroics through the Dunlop Chicane – after getting by Bastianini. The early order

Above: Bastianini was fast enough for the podium – just too late.

Top right: Roberts, Canet and Lopez fight for inches in Moto2.

Above right: Ai Ogura leads Lopez, Roberts *(hidden)*, Chantra, Canet and Aldeguer in their pursuit of Moto2 winner Garcia.

Right: Another fast Moto3 rookie. Joel Esteban took an impressive fourth place.

Below right: Alonso, Holgado and Veijer emerged as top dogs after a ten-bike tussle.

Photos: Gold & Goose

was set, Martin working hard to keep up with Bagnaia, with a five-way fight for third on lap nine, Espargaro and Di Giannantonio caught by Vinales, Marquez and Bastianini.

Then Espargaro's race started to fall apart. Di Giannantonio took third, before Vinales and Marquez pounced next time around. Desperate to keep up, Bastianini squeezed under Espargaro at Turn Nine, taking both wide and forcing the Aprilia down the slip road. As the factory Ducati didn't lose one second after running across the chicane, as the rules dictate, he was handed a long-lap. Espargaro was now seventh, behind home hero Quartararo, working minor miracles on his awkward, heavy-steering M1.

Having taken advantage of a Garage Vert mistake by Vinales on lap 14, Marquez started working on Di Giannantonio for third. They nearly came together at the Dunlop Chicane on lap 17, the Italian forcing Marquez to shut off down the hill. A similarly full-blooded move followed on the next lap at Turn Two. This forced Di Giannantonio off track to rejoin behind Vinales. Like Bastianini, he hadn't lost the requisite one second – a long-lap penalty ensued.

By now, thoughts of a Marquez victory charge seemed fanciful. The skirmishes had allowed the leading pair to escape by better than two seconds. Earlier, Martin had seemed to be clinging on desperately, but now he appeared more comfortable in Bagnaia's slipstream. Yet two events worked in the pursuer's favour. First, his own electric rhythm, which began dropping Vinales. Then the leaders began their own fight. Martin took a first bite of his rival entering the Dunlop Chicane on lap 20, only for Bagnaia to cut it tight and exit first. Not to worry; a second attempt on the following lap bore fruit. Now Martin had clean air.

Starting lap 22, it had become a three-way fight. Martin's attempts to break clear came undone with minor mistakes on laps 25 (Turn Three) and 26 (Turn Seven). And his defensive line into the chicane on the final lap brought all three tantalisingly together. And even though Marquez had spent heavily closing the gap, he still had enough to rob Bagnaia of second at the Chemin aux Boeuf, five corners from the chequered flag.

All three were fortunate that the race hadn't been two laps longer, as Bastianini's ferocious late-race rhythm could have eclipsed them all. After taking his penalty on lap 14, dropping to ninth behind Espargaro and Oliveira, he'd clawed 3.7 seconds out of the leaders. He gained two places – first when Oliveira slowed to retire, then on lap 17 when Quartararo's superhuman efforts in sixth sadly ended in a crash.

Bastianini dealt with Espargaro, passed Di Giannantonio as he took his penalty, and was barely 1.6 seconds behind Bagnaia at the flag.

Vinales was fifth, well clear of Di Giannantonio, who in turn was less than half a second clear of Morbidelli, whose last-lap lunge had pushed Espargaro back to ninth, behind also Binder. The South African had started 22nd after three crashes on Friday had wrecked his pre-race strategy, then came through from 13th on the first lap.

Alex Marquez was a lone tenth; Raul Fernandez, Zarco, Augusto Fernandez, Nakagami and Rins trailed in for the rest of the points; Marini was a distant last once again. With Bezzecchi and Miller crashing out, there were only 16 finishers.

Maximum points meant that Martin increased his lead over Bagnaia to 38, with Marquez and Bastianini only two points behind the defending champion.

MOTO2 RACE – 22 laps

Canet's third pole of the season had a heroic quality, considering that he'd broken a bone in his left ankle just 16 days before, and had been a dubious starter before being declared fit. And that he'd come through from Q1.

Roberts and Garcia were alongside; Arenas, Lopez and Gonzalez next. Agius was eighth behind Guevara, both also

Ogura was by Canet on the penultimate lap, then Lopez on the final circuit. Roberts soon followed the Japanese rider past Canet and set up a brilliant last-corner lunge on Lopez. Only it didn't pay off, the Spaniard cutting it tight and nabbing third on the run to the line, for the first all-Boscoscuro podium in Moto2 history.

Behind Roberts, Chantra also got by Canet on the final lap, demoting the suffering Spaniard down to sixth. Title hopeful Aldeguer capped a subdued weekend in seventh, with the Boscoscuro chassis less than five seconds behind the winner.

Arbolino fought through to eighth from a terrible start, blaming a new clutch setting. At one point, he'd been 17th, but rallied to pass Arenas four laps from the end. Guevara was a lone tenth; Alcoba led Salac, Agius, Binder and Ramirez in a gang disputing the final points.

Jake Dixon, still adapting to White Power suspension, had a downbeat weekend, qualifying 11th and finishing 17th. Baltus, Munoz, van den Goorberg, Gonzalez and Artigas crashed out.

MOTO3 RACE – 20 laps

Colombian David Alonso dominated all practice sessions again before going for a third consecutive pole, ahead of points leader Holgado and Rueda. Fernandez, facing a double long-lap for a fourth slow-sections offence, led the second row from Veijer and Ortola; Kelso headed the third from Munoz and rookie Piqueras.

It was another fine Moto3 scrap, a lead group of ten headed over the line for the first eight laps by Holgado, before Veijer took over for a couple. As usual, it was rather notional, so close that it was still anybody's race. At half-distance, the top nine were still within nine-tenths. By then, early pace-setter Munoz had taken out Riccardo Rossi at Turn 12, leading to a double long-lap penalty, followed by a crash when he was trying to recover.

Alonso signalled his intentions as he dived under both Holgado and Veijer at Turn Nine with two laps to go. Holgado drafted back past to lead at the start of the penultimate lap; Alonso returned the favour on the final circuit, producing a thrilling pass at Turn One to jump back ahead. The coolest of last laps followed as he led Holgado home by a tenth of a second, while Veijer was another quarter of a second back in third.

Rookie Joel Esteban mugged Ortola on the last lap to claim fourth, while Fernandez recovered to sixth in spite of his penalties.

It was close all the way, the top 15 all but inside ten seconds, with Yamanaka, Rueda, Suzuki and Piqueras completing the top ten, the last named only 2.1 seconds off the lead.

There were numerous penalties for short cuts at the chicane, reliably involuntary in the heat of close combat, and surprisingly only three fallers – Scott Ogden and Nicola Carraro as well as Munoz.

Alonso's third victory closed him to within one point of Holgado in the championship.

from Q1; Ogura was in an increasingly familiar 17th, this time because his team had mistakenly fitted the wrong sprocket after the final tyre change in Q2.

The race offered much variety. Garcia took advantage of some early chaos to establish an early advantage, eking out a comfortable lead over Roberts, Lopez and Canet. The last had come through brilliantly to second on lap seven after fluffing his start.

Then, with the top four gradually spacing out, the race was in danger of becoming processional. Until Canet started to take chunks out of Garcia's lead. Inevitably, though, he tired, leaving Garcia free for a comfortable second win in three races, by better than three seconds.

Lopez caught and passed Canet with three laps to go after a tough move on Roberts ten laps before, but soon he was left reeling by a stunning late attack from Ogura, after typically stealthy progress from 17th on the grid, up to 11th on lap one. He joined the fight for second with only a handful of laps to go, Roberts and fellow late-charger Somkiat Chantra also in the mix.

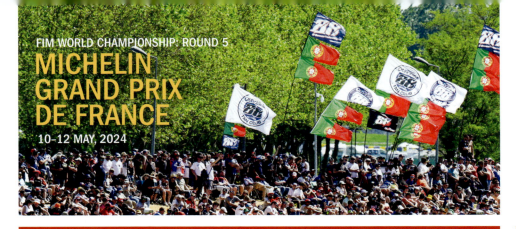

MICHELIN GRAND PRIX DE FRANCE
FIM WORLD CHAMPIONSHIP: ROUND 5
10–12 MAY, 2024

LE MANS – BUGATTI
27 laps
Length: 4.185km / 2.600 miles
Width: 13m

MOTOGP: RACE DISTANCE: 27 laps, 70.212 miles/112.995km
WEATHER: Dry (air 21°, humidity 68%, track 29°)

Pos.	Rider	Nat.	No.	Entrant	Machine	Race tyre choice	Laps	Time & speed
1	Jorge Martin	SPA	89	Prima Pramac Racing	Ducati Desmosedici GP24	F: Hard/R: Soft	27	41m 23.709s 101.7mph/163.7km/h
2	Marc Marquez	SPA	93	Gresini Racing MotoGP	Ducati Desmosedici GP23	F: Hard/R: Soft	27	41m 24.155s
3	Francesco Bagnaia	ITA	1	Ducati Lenovo Team	Ducati Desmosedici GP24	F: Hard/R: Soft	27	41m 24.294s
4	Enea Bastianini	ITA	23	Ducati Lenovo Team	Ducati Desmosedici GP24	F: Hard/R: Soft	27	41m 25.915s
5	Maverick Vinales	SPA	12	Aprilia Racing	Aprilia RS-GP24	F: Hard/R: Soft	27	41m 27.762s
6	Fabio Di Giannantonio	ITA	49	Pertamina Enduro VR46 Racing	Ducati Desmosedici GP23	F: Hard/R: Soft	27	41m 33.189s
7	Franco Morbidelli	ITA	21	Prima Pramac Racing	Ducati Desmosedici GP24	F: Hard/R: Soft	27	41m 33.577s
8	Brad Binder	RSA	33	Red Bull KTM Factory Racing	KTM RC16	F: Hard/R: Soft	27	41m 34.062s
9	Aleix Espargaro	SPA	41	Aprilia Racing	Aprilia RS-GP24	F: Hard/R: Soft	27	41m 35.101s
10	Alex Marquez	SPA	73	Gresini Racing MotoGP	Ducati Desmosedici GP23	F: Hard/R: Soft	27	41m 37.151s
11	Raul Fernandez	SPA	25	Trackhouse Racing	Aprilia RS-GP23	F: Hard/R: Soft	27	41m 47.910s
12	Johann Zarco	FRA	5	CASTROL Honda LCR	Honda RC213V	F: Hard/R: Soft	27	41m 50.518s
13	Augusto Fernandez	SPA	37	Red Bull GASGAS Tech3	KTM RC16	F: Soft/R: Soft	27	41m 51.135s
14	Takaaki Nakagami	JPN	30	IDEMITSU Honda LCR	Honda RC213V	F: Hard/R: Soft	27	41m 53.735s
15	Alex Rins	SPA	42	Monster Energy Yamaha MotoGP	Yamaha YZR-M1	F: Hard/R: Soft	27	41m 54.645s
16	Luca Marini	ITA	10	Repsol Honda Team	Honda RC213V	F: Hard/R: Soft	27	42m 03.709s
	Fabio Quartararo	FRA	20	Monster Energy Yamaha MotoGP	Yamaha YZR-M1	F: Hard/R: Soft	16	DNF-crash
	Jack Miller	AUS	43	Red Bull KTM Factory Racing	KTM RC16	F: Hard/R: Soft	16	DNF-crash
	Miguel Oliveira	POR	88	Trackhouse Racing	Aprilia RS-GP24	F: Hard/R: Soft	16	DNF-technical
	Joan Mir	SPA	36	Repsol Honda Team	Honda RC213V	F: Hard/R: Soft	14	DNF-crash
	Marco Bezzecchi	ITA	72	Pertamina Enduro VR46 Racing	Ducati Desmosedici GP23	F: Hard/R: Soft	3	DNF-crash
	Pedro Acosta	SPA	31	Red Bull GASGAS Tech3	KTM RC16	F: Hard/R: Soft	2	DNF-crash

Fastest lap: Enea Bastianini, on lap 23, 1m 31.107s, 102.7mph/165.3km/h.
Lap record: Francesco Bagnaia, 1m 31.778s, 102.0mph/164.1km/h (2022).
Event maximum speed: Enea Bastianini, 201.8mph/324.8km/h (Sprint).

Qualifying: Weather: Dry Air: 22° Humidity: 50% Track: 33°
1 Martin 1m 29.919s, 2 Bagnaia 1m 30.111s, 3 Vinales 1m 30.313s, 4 Di Giannantonio 1m 30.436s, 5 Bezzecchi 1m 30.553s, 6 A. Espargaro 1m 30.572s, 7 Acosta 1m 30.650s, 8 Quartararo 1m 30.686s, 9 Morbidelli 1m 30.782s, 10 Bastianini 1m 30.786s, 11 Miller 1m 31.007s, 12 Oliveira 1m 31.075s
Q1: 13 M. Marquez 1m 30.586s, 14 R. Fernandez 1m 30.676s, 15 Zarco 1m 30.891s, 16 Rins 1m 31.067s, 17 A. Marquez 1m 31.148s, 18 Mir 1m 31.186s, 19 Nakagami 1m 31.274s, 20 A. Fernandez 1m 31.473s, 21 Marini 1m 31.837s, 22 Binder 1m 32.228s.

SPRINT RACE: 13 laps, 33.806 miles/54.405km
WEATHER: Dry (air 22°, humidity 62%, track 37°)

Pos.	Rider	Race tyre choice	Laps	Time & speed
1	Jorge Martin	F: Hard/R: Soft	13	19m 49.694s 102.3mph/164.6km/h
2	Marc Marquez	F: Hard/R: Soft	13	19m 51.974s
3	Maverick Vinales	F: Hard/R: Soft	13	19m 53.868s
4	Enea Bastianini	F: Hard/R: Soft	13	19m 54.492s
5	Aleix Espargaro	F: Hard/R: Soft	13	19m 57.392s
6	Pedro Acosta	F: Hard/R: Soft	13	19m 58.879s
7	Fabio Di Giannantonio	F: Hard/R: Soft	13	20m 00.884s
8	Jack Miller	F: Soft/R: Soft	13	20m 01.210s
9	Raul Fernandez	F: Hard/R: Soft	13	20m 01.951s
10	Fabio Quartararo	F: Hard/R: Soft	13	20m 02.393s
11	Miguel Oliveira	F: Hard/R: Soft	13	20m 03.186s
12	Franco Morbidelli	F: Hard/R: Soft	13	20m 05.272s
13	Johann Zarco	F: Hard/R: Soft	13	20m 06.133s
14	Alex Marquez	F: Hard/R: Soft	13	20m 06.510s
15	Brad Binder	F: Hard/R: Soft	13	20m 06.663s
16	Takaaki Nakagami	F: Hard/R: Soft	13	20m 08.817s
17	Augusto Fernandez	F: Hard/R: Soft	13	20m 13.312s
18	Luca Marini	F: Hard/R: Soft	13	20m 17.548s
	Marco Bezzecchi	F: Hard/R: Soft	9	DNF-crash
	Alex Rins	F: Hard/R: Soft	6	DNF-crash
	Joan Mir	F: Hard/R: Soft	4	DNF-crash
	Francesco Bagnaia	F: Hard/R: Soft	3	DNF-technical

Fastest race lap: Marco Bezzecchi, on lap 3, 1m 30.852s.

Fastest race laps
1 Bastianini 1m 31.107s, 2 Di Giannantonio 1m 31.403s, 3 A. Espargaro 1m 31.447s, 4 M. Marquez 1m 31.463s, 5 Bagnaia 1m 31.531s, 6 Martin 1m 31.557s, 7 Vinales 1m 31.561s, 8 Oliveira 1m 31.615s, 9 Quartararo 1m 31.686s, 10 Morbidelli 1m 31.829s, 11 Binder 1m 31.865s, 12 Acosta 1m 31.877s, 13 A. Marquez 1m 31.940s, 14 Mir 1m 31.952s, 15 Miller 1m 31.978s, 16 R. Fernandez 1m 32.005s, 17 A. Fernandez 1m 32.011s, 18 Rins 1m 32.038s, 19 Bezzecchi 1m 32.156s, 20 Zarco 1m 32.287s, 21 Nakagami 1m 32.311s, 22 Marini 1m 32.739s.

Grid order / Lap chart

Grid order	1	2	3	4	5	6	7	8	9	10	11	12	13	14	15	16	17	18	19	20	21	22	23	24	25	26	27
89 MARTIN	1	1	1	1	1	1	1	1	1	1	1	1	1	1	1	1	1	89	89	89	89	89	89	89	89	89	89
1 BAGNAIA	89	89	89	89	89	89	89	89	89	89	89	89	89	89	89	89	89	1	1	1	1	1	1	93			
12 VINALES	41	41	41	41	41	41	41	41	41	49	49	49	49	49	49	49	49	93	93	93	93	93	93	93	93	1	
49 DI GIANNANTONIO	49	49	49	49	49	49	49	49	49	12	12	12	93	93	93	93	12	12	12	12	12	12	12	12	23		
72 BEZZECCHI	12	31	12	12	12	12	12	12	12	93	93	93	12	12	12	12	49	49	23	23	23	23	23	23	12		
41 A. ESPARGARO	31	12	93	93	93	93	93	93	93	41	23	23	20	20	23	49	23	23	49	49	49	49	49	49			
31 ACOSTA	23	23	23	23	23	23	23	23	23	20	20	41	41	23	41	41	41	41	41	41	41	41	21				
20 QUARTARARO	93	93	72	20	20	20	20	20	20	41	41	88	88	23	21	21	21	21	21	21	21	21	33				
21 MORBIDELLI	72	72	20	88	88	88	88	88	88	88	88	23	23	21	33	33	33	33	33	33	33	33	41				
23 BASTIANINI	20	20	88	43	43	43	33	33	33	33	33	21	21	21	73	73	73	73	73	73	73	73					
43 MILLER	43	43	43	33	33	33	21	21	21	21	21	33	33	73	25	25	25	25	25	25	25	25					
88 OLIVEIRA	88	88	33	21	21	21	43	43	43	73	73	73	73	25													
93 M. MARQUEZ	33	33	21	25	25	25	25	25	73	43	43	43	30	37	37	37	30	37	37	37	37						
25 R. FERNANDEZ	21	21	25	36	73	73	73	73	25	25	25	25	88	37	37	37	37	30	30	30	30						
5 ZARCO	73	25	36	73	36	36	36	36	36	36	5	42	42	42	42	42	42	42	42	42	42						
42 RINS	25	73	73	5	5	5	5	5	5	5	30	10	10	10	10	10	10	10	10	10							
73 A. MARQUEZ	36	36	5	30	30	30	30	30	30	30	37	37															
36 MIR	5	5	10	10	37	37	37	37	37	37	42	42															
30 NAKAGAMI	10	10	30	37	10	10	10	10	10	42	10	10															
37 A. FERNANDEZ	30	30	42	42	42	42	42	42	42	10	10																
10 MARINI	42	42	37																								
33 BINDER	37	37																									

Championship Points

1	Martin	79 (50)	129
2	Bagnaia	77 (14)	91
3	M. Marquez	53 (36)	89
4	Bastianini	71 (18)	89
5	Vinales	49 (32)	81
6	Acosta	49 (24)	73
7	Binder	58 (9)	67
8	A. Espargaro	32 (19)	51
9	Di Giannantonio	44 (3)	47
10	Bezzecchi	36 (0)	36
11	A. Marquez	30 (3)	33
12	Quartararo	19 (6)	25
13	Miller	14 (10)	24
14	Oliveira	21 (2)	23
15	R. Fernandez	16 (2)	18
16	Morbidelli	9 (6)	15
17	A. Fernandez	10 (3)	13
18	Mir	11 (1)	12
19	Zarco	9 (0)	9
20	Rins	0 (7)	7
21	Pedrosa	7 (0)	7
22	Nakagami	6 (0)	6

Constructor Points

1	Ducati	116 (54)	170
2	KTM	74 (33)	107
3	Aprilia	60 (40)	100
4	Yamaha	22 (6)	28
5	Honda	16 (1)	17

MOTO2: RACE DISTANCE: 22 laps, 57.210 miles/92.070km

RACE WEATHER: Dry (air 21°, humidity 65%, track 31°)

Pos.	Rider	Nat.	No.	Entrant	Machine	Laps	Time & Speed
1	Sergio Garcia	SPA	3	MT Helmets - MSI	Boscoscuro	22	35m 20.709s
							97.1mph/156.2km/h
2	Ai Ogura	JPN	79	MT Helmets - MSI	Boscoscuro	22	35m 23.883s
3	Alonso Lopez	SPA	21	Folladore SpeedUp	Boscoscuro	22	35m 24.413s
4	Joe Roberts	USA	16	OnlyFans American Racing Team	Kalex	22	35m 24.473s
5	Somkiat Chantra	THA	35	IDEMITSU Honda Team Asia	Kalex	22	35m 24.644s
6	Aron Canet	SPA	44	Fantic Racing	Kalex	22	35m 25.220s
7	Fermin Aldeguer	SPA	54	Folladore SpeedUp	Boscoscuro	22	35m 25.520s
8	Tony Arbolino	ITA	14	Elf Marc VDS Racing Team	Kalex	22	35m 27.520s
9	Albert Arenas	SPA	75	QJMOTOR Gresini Moto2	Kalex	22	35m 29.540s
10	Izan Guevara	SPA	28	CFMOTO Inde Aspar Team	Kalex	22	35m 34.924s
11	Jeremy Alcoba	SPA	52	Yamaha VR46 Master Camp	Kalex	22	35m 38.504s
12	Filip Salac	CZE	12	Elf Marc VDS Racing Team	Kalex	22	35m 38.753s
13	Senna Agius	AUS	81	Liqui Moly Husqvarna Intact GP	Kalex	22	35m 38.900s
14	Darryn Binder	RSA	15	Liqui Moly Husqvarna Intact GP	Kalex	22	35m 39.058s
15	Marcos Ramirez	SPA	24	OnlyFans American Racing Team	Kalex	22	35m 40.395s
16	Jaume Masia	SPA	5	Pertamina Mandalika GAS UP	Kalex	22	35m 42.169s
17	Jake Dixon	GBR	96	CFMOTO Inde Aspar Team	Kalex	22	35m 47.648s
18	Deniz Oncu	TUR	53	Red Bull KTM Ajo	Kalex	22	35m 51.342s
19	Dennis Foggia	ITA	71	Italtrans Racing Team	Kalex	22	35m 51.513s
20	Jorge Navarro	SPA	9	KLINT Forward Factory Team	Forward	22	35m 58.450s
21	Xavi Cardelus	AND	20	Fantic Racing	Kalex	22	35m 58.703s
22	Ayumu Sasaki	JPN	22	Yamaha VR46 Master Camp	Kalex	22	35m 59.677s
23	Daniel Munoz	SPA	17	Pertamina Mandalika GAS UP	Kalex	21	36m 10.351s
24	Manuel Gonzalez	SPA	18	QJMOTOR Gresini Moto2	Kalex	20	36m 09.258s
25	Zonta van den Goorbergh	NED	84	RW-Idrofoglia Racing GP	Kalex	20	36m 13.568s
26	Diogo Moreira	BRA	10	Italtrans Racing Team	Kalex	19	36m 24.486s
	Xavier Artigas	SPA	43	KLINT Forward Factory Team	Forward	15	DNF-crash
	Barry Baltus	BEL	7	RW-Idrofoglia Racing GP	Kalex	2	DNF-crash

Fastest lap: Aron Canet, on lap 5, 1m 35.796s, 97.7mph/157.2km/h.
Lap record: Pedro Acosta, 1m 36.068s, 97.4mph/156.8km/h (2023).
Event maximum speed: Ai Ogura, 169.3mph/272.4km/h (race).

Qualifying
Weather: Dry **Air:** 26° **Humidity:** 40% **Track:** 38°

1	Canet	1m 35.037s
2	Roberts	1m 35.173s
3	Garcia	1m 35.248s
4	Arenas	1m 35.377s
5	Lopez	1m 35.437s
6	Gonzalez	1m 35.453s
7	Guevara	1m 35.599s
8	Agius	1m 35.610s
9	Salac	1m 35.653s
10	Arbolino	1m 35.775s
11	Dixon	1m 35.808s
12	Aldeguer	1m 35.834s
13	Chantra	1m 35.849s
14	Alcoba	1m 35.849s
15	V d Goorbergh	1m 35.864s
16	Baltus	1m 35.960s
17	Ogura	1m 36.088s
18	Ramirez	1m 37.148s

Q1

19	Binder	1m 35.947s
20	Masia	1m 36.020s
21	Moreira	1m 36.067s
22	Oncu	1m 36.252s
23	Sasaki	1m 36.443s
24	Munoz	1m 36.476s
25	Cardelus	1m 36.622s
26	Navarro	1m 37.215s
27	Foggia	1m 37.236s
28	Artigas	1m 37.498s

Fastest race laps

1	Canet	1m 35.796s
2	Ogura	1m 35.871s
3	Chantra	1m 35.881s
4	Garcia	1m 35.907s
5	Lopez	1m 35.952s
6	Arbolino	1m 35.953s
7	Gonzalez	1m 35.978s
8	Roberts	1m 36.020s
9	Aldeguer	1m 36.035s
10	Guevara	1m 36.175s
11	Arenas	1m 36.198s
12	Salac	1m 36.351s
13	V d Goorbergh	1m 36.364s
14	Alcoba	1m 36.365s
15	Dixon	1m 36.373s
16	Ramirez	1m 36.468s
17	Masia	1m 36.530s
18	Agius	1m 36.559s
19	Binder	1m 36.571s
20	Moreira	1m 36.628s
21	Foggia	1m 36.763s
22	Oncu	1m 37.050s
23	Cardelus	1m 37.105s
24	Navarro	1m 37.297s
25	Munoz	1m 37.426s
26	Sasaki	1m 37.426s
27	Baltus	1m 37.464s
28	Artigas	1m 37.697s

Championship Points

1	Garcia	89
2	Roberts	82
3	Aldeguer	63
4	Ogura	63
5	Lopez	54
6	Canet	48
7	Gonzalez	46
8	Arenas	38
9	Alcoba	30
10	Ramirez	29
11	Vietti	29
12	Chantra	28
13	Arbolino	26
14	Baltus	23
15	Foggia	10
16	Guevara	10
17	Salac	10
18	Van den Goorbergh	6
19	Agius	5
20	Binder	3
21	Oncu	3
22	Bendsneyder	2
23	Moreira	2
24	Ferrari	1

Constructor Points

1	Boscoscuro	113
2	Kalex	98

MOTO3: RACE DISTANCE: 20 laps, 52.009 miles/83.700km

RACE WEATHER: Dry (air 20°, humidity 67%, track 28°)

Pos.	Rider	Nat.	No.	Entrant	Machine	Laps	Time & Speed
1	David Alonso	COL	80	CFMOTO Gaviota Aspar Team	CFMOTO	20	34m 00.058s
							91.8mph/147.7km/h
2	Daniel Holgado	SPA	96	Red Bull GASGAS Tech3	GASGAS	20	34m 00.163s
3	Collin Veijer	NED	95	Liqui Moly Husqvarna Intact GP	Husqvarna	20	34m 00.300s
4	Joel Esteban	SPA	78	CFMOTO Gaviota Aspar Team	CFMOTO	20	34m 00.534s
5	Ivan Ortola	SPA	48	MT Helmets - MSI	KTM	20	34m 00.670s
6	Adrian Fernandez	SPA	31	Leopard Racing	Honda	20	34m 00.855s
7	Ryusei Yamanaka	JPN	6	MT Helmets - MSI	KTM	20	34m 01.016s
8	Jose Antonio Rueda	SPA	99	Red Bull KTM Ajo	KTM	20	34m 01.093s
9	Tatsuki Suzuki	JPN	24	Liqui Moly Husqvarna Intact GP	Husqvarna	20	34m 01.159s
10	Angel Piqueras	SPA	36	Leopard Racing	Honda	20	34m 02.221s
11	Luca Lunetta	ITA	58	SIC58 Squadra Corse	Honda	20	34m 06.773s
12	Jacob Roulstone	AUS	12	Red Bull GASGAS Tech3	GASGAS	20	34m 06.961s
13	Joel Kelso	AUS	66	BOE Motorsports	KTM	20	34m 07.275s
14	Taiyo Furusato	JPN	72	Honda Team Asia	Honda	20	34m 10.834s
15	David Almansa	SPA	22	Kopron Rivacold Snipers Team	Honda	20	34m 11.408s
16	Xabi Zurutuza	SPA	85	Red Bull KTM Ajo	KTM	20	34m 13.333s
17	Stefano Nepa	ITA	82	LEVELUP - MTA	KTM	20	34m 16.258s
18	Noah Dettwiler	SWI	55	CIP Green Power	KTM	20	34m 27.999s
19	Nicola Carraro	ITA	10	LEVELUP - MTA	KTM	20	34m 28.857s
20	Tatchakorn Buasri	THA	5	Honda Team Asia	Honda	20	34m 34.226s
21	Joshua Whatley	GBR	70	MLav Racing	Honda	20	34m 47.845s
	David Munoz	SPA	64	BOE Motorsports	KTM	16	DNF-ret in pit
	Matteo Bertelle	ITA	18	Kopron Rivacold Snipers Team	Honda	15	DNF-technical
	Scott Ogden	GBR	19	MLav Racing	Honda	10	DNF-crash
	Riccardo Rossi	ITA	54	CIP Green Power	KTM	7	DNF-crash
	Filippo Farioli	ITA	7	SIC58 Squadra Corse	Honda	1	DNF-ret in pit

Fastest lap: Joel Esteban, on lap 14, 1m 41.059s, 92.6mph/149.0km/h.
Lap record: Ayumu Sasaki, 1m 41.476s, 92.2mph/148.4km/h (2023).
Event maximum speed: Stefano Nepa, 143.7mph/231.3km/h (race).

Qualifying
Weather: Dry **Air:** 26° **Humidity:** 42% **Track:** 38°

1	Alonso	1m 40.114s
2	Holgado	1m 40.125s
3	Rueda	1m 40.426s
4	Fernandez	1m 40.777s
5	Veijer	1m 40.793s
6	Ortola	1m 40.860s
7	Kelso	1m 40.878s
8	Munoz	1m 41.025s
9	Piqueras	1m 41.040s
10	Yamanaka	1m 41.056s
11	Roulstone	1m 41.092s
12	Ogden	1m 41.135s
13	Rossi	1m 41.160s
14	Suzuki	1m 41.204s
15	Lunetta	1m 41.221s
16	Esteban	1m 41.365s
17	Furusato	1m 41.382s
18	Zurutuza	DSQ
19	Bertelle	1m 41.746s
20	Carraro	1m 41.755s
21	Farioli	1m 41.771s
22	Almansa	1m 41.902s
23	Nepa	1m 42.008s
24	Dettwiler	1m 42.466s
25	Whatley	1m 42.495s
26	Buasri	1m 42.670s

Fastest race laps

1	Esteban	1m 41.059s
2	Nepa	1m 41.211s
3	Fernandez	1m 41.228s
4	Carraro	1m 41.286s
5	Rossi	1m 41.300s
6	Rueda	1m 41.331s
7	Yamanaka	1m 41.337s
8	Piqueras	1m 41.342s
9	Suzuki	1m 41.384s
10	Alonso	1m 41.412s
11	Holgado	1m 41.412s
12	Zurutuza	1m 41.414s
13	Ortola	1m 41.418s
14	Lunetta	1m 41.435s
15	Veijer	1m 41.447s
16	Bertelle	1m 41.480s
17	Almansa	1m 41.532s
18	Munoz	1m 41.587s
19	Kelso	1m 41.649s
20	Furusato	1m 41.662s
21	Roulstone	1m 41.672s
22	Ogden	1m 41.774s
23	Dettwiler	1m 42.605s
24	Buasri	1m 42.654s
25	Whatley	1m 43.187s

Championship Points

1	Holgado	94
2	Alonso	93
3	Veijer	62
4	Ortola	50
5	Kelso	42
6	Munoz	38
7	Yamanaka	35
8	Esteban	33
9	Piqueras	32
10	Fernandez	31
11	Suzuki	30
12	Rueda	28
13	Roulstone	27
14	Nepa	26
15	Furusato	18
16	Carraro	15
17	Rossi	13
18	Bertelle	8
19	Lunetta	6
20	Ogden	5
21	Farioli	4
22	Zurutuza	3
23	Perez	3
24	Dettwiler	2
25	Almansa	2

Constructor Points

1	GASGAS	94
2	CFMOTO	93
3	KTM	77
4	Husqvarna	72
5	Honda	58

FIM WORLD CHAMPIONSHIP • ROUND 6

CATALAN GRAND PRIX

BARCELONA-CATALUNYA CIRCUIT

FOR a second race in a row, Ducatis took all three podium positions. The order was shuffled, the personnel the same – three riders with a special advantage, they agreed: the company's policy of an open book for data.

Notionally, Marquez, on an older bike, might have benefited slightly less than winner Bagnaia and Martin, but not necessarily. The older Spaniard credited checking Bagnaia's data for a turnaround from a second poor practice, missing out on Q2 again, to strong race results. Martin explained in greater detail: "It's amazing to watch. I can see Pecco is stronger on braking. Marc is stronger on entry. I am faster on exit. So at the end of the day, you try to take details from everyone. I think it is key that we have the others' data and we can learn where we struggle. But it's also a pity that when you have an advantage, they catch up!"

Bagnaia's turnaround was even more noteworthy, in a zero-to-hero move that had become something of a trademark. A careless crash out of the lead on Saturday left observers questioning his temperament, and how a champion of his obvious quality continued to make so many mistakes. Once again, he silenced them with a flawless Sunday.

The weekend opened with an "exceptional" press conference, where a tearful Aleix Espargaro announced his end-of-season retirement to an audience of reporters and a rogues' gallery of top grand prix riders past and present, several of them equally lachrymose. "There are many riders that won a lot more than me, but I gave it everything that I had. Sometimes, I felt I didn't have the talent of others, but by working hard, I reached quite a high level. These last two or three seasons, I was dreaming. This was one reason why I stopped. I've already had a lot of fun and I'd like to retire at a good time," he said. The oldest rider on the grid had made his debut in the final round of 2004 in the 125 class, but had to wait until 2022 for the first of three wins so far, in the Argentine GP, which launched a creditable title challenge, finishing fourth overall. Sunday marked his 327th GP start.

Both troubled Japanese companies had been using their concessions to carry out extra testing at Mugello, and they arrived with visible changes. For Yamaha, new aero, with a triplane 'moustache' front wing and a copycat 'stegosaurus' seat. Honda also had revised aero, particularly at the rear of the bike, as well as a shorter exhaust, said to give a different, potentially better response to the first touch of the throttle.

Results were not conspicuously improved, but Quartararo was bullish, promising "something big" from Yamaha after the forthcoming Italian GP. In turn, Marini, yet to score a point, reacted angrily to a report in Italy that he was seeking an early exit from Repsol Honda. Not true, he insisted: "I really trust in this project. We have had only five races … we are at the beginning and many things can change, because Honda is pushing and working a lot, bringing a lot of parts, big parts, every test. It's true it's hard because last year I was fighting for the podium every race, and now fighting for one point is tough. But we are coming better."

Main: After a zero-points Saturday, Pecco Bagnaia was back in control in the MotoGP race.
Photo: Ducati Corse

Inset, right: Pecco celebrates.

Inset, below left: Winner Espargaro and rookie Acosta (third) shared the sprint podium.

Inset, below: Bagnaia's sprint ends in a trip to the gravel.
Photos: Gold & Goose

Inset, below right: Frustration. Bastianini tangled with Alex Marquez and lost all his points defying the stewards.
Photo: Ducati Corse

There was more open rebellion against the stewards, this time an act of defiance by Bastianini. He wilfully ignored a long-lap penalty, then a resultant double long-lap, with a consequent 32-second hit to his results, the equivalent of a ride-through. That dropped him from ninth to 18th, but he was unrepentant.

The penalty was for failing to lose one second after taking a short cut at the first corner set, where he'd been bumped wide by Alex Marquez after passing him on the straight. He was quite clear that it was undeserved. Not only was he an innocent victim, but he believed that he had lost the time, having rejoined two or three hundred metres behind his assailant. "I was waiting for the 'drop position' for Alex for two or three laps, but then arrived the long-lap for me. I did not agree, and I decided to continue. I know it's not correct, but we have to do something, because nothing changes. Every race, there is something to explain with the stewards, and it is not correct." Both rider and Ducati said that the stewards had admitted their error, but by the rules, there is no right of appeal and no post-race reversal of decisions. Nor are the stewards obliged to explain themselves. Added Bastianini, "This is crazy, but it's like this!"

Above: Sprint to the flag. Espargaro leads Marquez and Acosta home after Bagnaia crashed out.

Above right, from top: A study in styles by KTM riders – Fernandez, Binder, Acosta.

Right: Flat out. Spectacular Jorge Martin scrapes everything.
Photos: Gold & Goose

MOTOGP SPRINT RACE – 12 laps

Complaints about the slippery surface notwithstanding, the all-time record was broken on three occasions, the last two by pole-sitter Espargaro, on a day of some surprises. One was Raul Fernandez, who qualified third alongside Bagnaia, crediting an electronics update to his year-old Aprilia for a radical upturn that would persist in the afternoon, only to be cruelly cut short.

Binder led row two after another crash-heavy Friday, with two falls, Acosta and Di Giannantonio alongside. Diggia and Fernandez were through from Q1, the pair denying Marc Marquez, between brother Alex and Oliveira on row five.

The race was full of as many surprises.

Bagnaia led away, changing places with Acosta twice over the first two laps before the inspired Fernandez got the better of Binder and took to the front on lap three.

He appeared to be pulling away when he lost the front into the notorious Turn Ten at the end of the back straight.

That left Acosta up front, only for Binder and Bagnaia to pounce. The South African led lap six, then he too paid the price, falling at Turn Five, the tricky downhill-entry first left after a string of rights.

Espargaro had skirmished with Martin, but had passed him by half-distance. Now he was joined by a charging old-style Marc Marquez, who had gained six places on the first lap.

As the pair caught and dealt with Acosta, Bagnaia took over up front, Espargaro chasing, some seven-tenths behind. Acosta and Marquez lost ground as they traded blows behind.

The defender seemed to be in control, if only narrowly. Until he reached Turn Five, where it was his turn to lose the front and the lead, handing the win to Espargaro.

Marquez prevailed over his young challenger by four-tenths; Martin was a close and controlled fourth, Bastianini on his tail. Diggia, Miller, Vinales and Bezzecchi wrapped up the points, the last deposing Quartararo on the final lap. Zarco and Oliveira joined the crash list.

MOTOGP RACE – 24 laps

Bagnaia signalled his intentions from the start, safely making his way through the first chicane on the first lap for the first time in a feature race at this track since 2021. Acosta, Binder, Martin, Espargaro and Miller were in tow.

Martin's expert pass on Binder at Turn Ten gave the top two a half-second gap. But the championship leader was with them within minutes after Acosta's failed attempt on Bagnaia at the same corner, which put him wide.

By lap four, the top six were running together, Raul Fernandez recovering from a bad start to join on the back. Then a 1.5-second gap to Morbidelli and Marquez, fighting for seventh, after another trademark brawling first lap from the latter.

The front order changed when Martin made his play, passing Acosta at Turn Ten on lap four before snatching the lead from Bagnaia at the same place the following time around.

Acosta followed his compatriot's lead. No sooner had he pounced on Bagnaia at Turn Ten on lap six than he began chasing down the leader, posting the race's fastest lap on the seventh. Incredibly, in the trickiest track conditions of

the year, the rookie was harrying Martin, seeking a way by. However, a front brake issue contributed to him tucking the front as he pitched into Turn Ten on lap 11. "We just threw a podium in the trash," he lamented later, a second consecutive victory challenge thwarted.

The faster pace meant that Martin suddenly found himself with better than a second of space, with Bagnaia also clear of Espargaro and Fernandez, now 3.5 seconds behind. Binder's charge was slowed by front tyre concerns, with Marquez past on lap 12. This set up a grandstand finale between Ducati's two lead men as Bagnaia got to work on reducing Martin's lead.

In reality, though, it wasn't a contest. Bagnaia had slashed Martin's advantage in seven laps and was primed to pass as they began lap 19. The Italian's redemption was complete when he outbraked his rival entering Turn Five, scene of his *faux pas* the previous day. "Overtaking there was the best place," he said. "I was just praying I didn't lose the front, but it went well." On a heavily worn front tyre, his rhythm was exceptional and he cruised to a 1.7-second victory.

Martin was a comfortable second. Nearly nine seconds back came Espargaro and Marquez, two Catalans vying for a home podium. Marquez gained the place braking for Turn One with four laps to go. Frustrated by his medium rear tyre's lack of performance (Marquez was on the soft), the Aprilia rider was powerless to respond.

Di Giannantonio had been moving forward steadily, from tenth at half-distance. He battled with Bastianini for several laps; then, over the last five, he picked off Binder and Alex Marquez to nab fifth off Fernandez on the final lap. Marquez cleared Binder for eighth.

Quartararo made up for his sprint disappointment, coming out best from a three-handed battle with Oliveira and Bezzecchi on the final lap for an impressive ninth. In fact, Bastianini was ahead of the trio, but his penalty dropped him out of the points.

Vinales was a second adrift for a subdued 12th. Acosta had remounted to rescue three points, ahead of Nakagami and Mir; then three more Hondas trailed in – Zarco, Marini and wild-card Bradl.

Miller's tough run continued, after a fair start. From ninth

Above: First-time front-row starter Raul Fernandez was slow away and almost swamped.

Top right: Back to victory – Ai Ogura's Moto2 title bid got a boost.

Top far right: Fourth place for Jeremy Alcoba.

Above right: First Moto2 points for rookie Jaume Masia.

Above far right: Boscoscuros in command, with a one-two finish for team-mates Ogura and Garcia.

Centre right: Young Moto3 rookies Jacob Roulstone (12) and Luca Lunetta (58) both impressed with rides into the top ten.

Right: Further down the field, Zurutusa (85), Ogden (19), Bertelle (18) and Carraro (10) battled in vain for the final points on offer.

Photos: Gold & Goose

on the grid, he was up to seventh on lap three when he tucked the front at Turn Ten. "I trusted the front too early. A silly mistake," he said.

Augusto Fernandez fell on lap six, from 14th; and Morbidelli on lap 18, having worked his way to a strong sixth.

MOTO2 RACE – 21 laps

Former Moto3 and Moto2 race winner Jorge Navarro was a wild-card entry, and he topped P1, an unusual position for one of the ill-favoured Forward chassis. It didn't last, and he ended up 21st, on row seven.

More familiarly, there were two Boscoscuros up front, Garcia and Aldeguer, then Vietti for his first front row of the season. Canet, through from Q2, led row two from Arenas and Gonzalez. Roberts was on the far end of row three; Ogura led the fourth from Dixon.

The race was wild and surprising, as title contenders fell away. Low grip made it difficult to stay within track limits, a total of eight riders being handed penalties. And a rider who had been 2.6 seconds off the front at mid-race eventually won by nearly four seconds.

It looked like being an all-Spanish duel between Garcia and Aldeguer, after both had cleared third-placed Arenas by lap two. Aldeguer threatened to break clear in those early laps, but Garcia was managing his rear tyre carefully.

As he began turning the screw, reducing the deficit to three-tenths, Aldeguer was handed a long-lap for exceeding track limits. He seemed far from the rider who had won four straight races at the end of 2023 when he crashed out navigating the penalty lane on lap 15.

He wasn't alone in cursing a stupid mistake. Moments later, Canet crashed out of third at Turn Five, after pulling through from eighth on lap one. This didn't put Garcia in the clear, however. Team-mate Ogura had homed in after spending the early laps sixth. Just as Bagnaia had reeled in Martin with the minimum of fuss, he appeared to be in another class as he breezed by Garcia on the run to Turn One with four laps to go, for his first win since his home GP in October, 2022.

Garcia's second extended his championship lead in a second successive one-two for the MSI squad, new to the class in 2024. Third-placed Dixon, through from 12th on lap one, was nine seconds away – a solid ride from the Englishman, who was recovering from concussion and adapting to the new WP suspension.

The late-charging Alcoba rose to fourth in the latter stages, with Agius a career-best fifth, both past Arenas in the final lap. The Australian was furious to be handed a long-lap for exceeding track limits when he had been punted wide by Vietti, who crashed out.

Not as angry as Marcos Ramirez, however, who finished seventh, only to be disqualified after a mix-up in the pits led to his bike being fitted with one of his Only Fans team-mate Roberts's allocated tyres. That promoted Lopez to the position, two seconds behind Ramirez, after fading from third mid-race.

Roberts also gained a position to a lone eighth, lucky to avoid disaster when involved in a first-corner tangle with Chantra, Guevara and Sasaki. Arbolino was ninth after a long-lap, and Navarro a creditable tenth. Masia was the top rookie in 13th, his first points. Moreira, substitute Daniel Munoz and Foggia crashed; Gonzalez was last after crashing, remounting, pitting and then rejoining.

MOTO3 RACE – 18 laps

As so often, Alonso led all the practice sessions, but was sixth in qualifying thanks to yellow flags, on the far end of row

two. Ortola was on pole, from Veijer and Rueda, with Furusawa and Yamanaka fourth and fifth. Munoz led row three, through from Q1.

Come the race, the Colombian's superiority was on full display as he dismantled his rivals for a fourth win of the year, taking the title lead.

This was a race of two halves. The first was shambolic, a lead group of 14 straying dangerously close to disaster on the long front straight, with Munoz nearly causing chaos on the first run to Turn One.

Ortola led the first two laps over the line before Veijer took over, then briefly Holgado. But it was a matter of inches, swerving and slipstreams, with positions swapping madly by the time they reached the first corner and over the rest of the lap.

But once Alonso hit the front on lap 12, the pack became stretched apart. First, the group was whittled down to Ortola, Veijer, Holgado, Rueda and impressive rookie Luca Lunetta. Yet one by one, they slipped away, leaving just Ortola and Veijer holding on with two to go.

Rueda's fastest lap on the penultimate circuit allowed him to rejoin the lead trio. However, Alonso demonstrated accomplished late-braking skill to maintain just enough of a margin between himself and Ortola to prevent the Spaniard from attempting a move. Rueda displaced Veijer to claim third with an aggressive pass in Turn Four. Munoz and Holgado followed.

Lunetta was barely a second away, while fellow rookie Roulstone was an impressive eighth, having fended off Farioli and Fernandez. Ogden missed out on the points by less than a second.

Kelso, Furusato and Rossi crashed, as did Almansa.

Alonso now displaced Holgado from the championship lead, by 14 points.

FIM WORLD CHAMPIONSHIP: ROUND 6
GRAN PREMI MONSTER ENERGY DE CATALUNYA
24–26 MAY, 2024

CIRCUIT DE CATALUNYA
24 laps
Length: 4.657km /2.894 miles
Width: 12m

MOTOGP: RACE DISTANCE: 24 laps, 69.449 miles/111.768km
WEATHER: Dry (air 26°, humidity 42%, track 47°)

Pos.	Rider	Nat.No.	Entrant	Machine	Race tyre choice	Laps	Time & speed
1	Francesco Bagnaia	ITA 1	Ducati Lenovo Team	Ducati Desmosedici GP24	F: Medium/R: Medium	24	40m 11.726s 103.6mph/166.8km/h
2	Jorge Martin	SPA 89	Prima Pramac Racing	Ducati Desmosedici GP24	F: Medium/R: Medium	24	40m 13.466s
3	Marc Marquez	SPA 93	Gresini Racing MotoGP	Ducati Desmosedici GP23	F: Medium/R: Soft	24	40m 22.217s
4	Aleix Espargaro	SPA 41	Aprilia Racing	Aprilia RS-GP24	F: Medium/R: Medium	24	40m 22.269s
5	Fabio Di Giannantonio	ITA 49	Pertamina Enduro VR46 Racing	Ducati Desmosedici GP23	F: Medium/R: Medium	24	40m 27.167s
6	Raul Fernandez	SPA 25	Trackhouse Racing	Aprilia RS-GP23	F: Medium/R: Medium	24	40m 27.642s
7	Alex Marquez	SPA 73	Gresini Racing MotoGP	Ducati Desmosedici GP23	F: Medium/R: Soft	24	40m 28.608s
8	Brad Binder	RSA 33	Red Bull KTM Factory Racing	KTM RC16	F: Medium/R: Medium	24	40m 30.304s
9	Fabio Quartararo	FRA 20	Monster Energy Yamaha MotoGP	Yamaha YZR-M1	F: Medium/R: Medium	24	40m 32.203s
10	Miguel Oliveira	POR 88	Trackhouse Racing	Aprilia RS-GP23	F: Medium/R: Medium	24	40m 32.615s
11	Marco Bezzecchi	ITA 72	Pertamina Enduro VR46 Racing	Ducati Desmosedici GP23	F: Medium/R: Medium	24	40m 32.749s
12	Maverick Vinales	SPA 12	Aprilia Racing	Aprilia RS-GP24	F: Medium/R: Medium	24	40m 33.863s
13	Pedro Acosta	SPA 31	Red Bull GASGAS Tech3	KTM RC16	F: Medium/R: Soft	24	40m 43.693s
14	Takaaki Nakagami	JPN 30	IDEMITSU Honda LCR	Honda RC213V	F: Medium/R: Medium	24	40m 44.713s
15	Joan Mir	SPA 36	Repsol Honda Team	Honda RC213V	F: Medium/R: Medium	24	40m 44.858s
16	Johann Zarco	FRA 5	CASTROL Honda LCR	Honda RC213V	F: Medium/R: Medium	24	40m 46.280s
17	Luca Marini	ITA 10	Repsol Honda Team	Honda RC213V	F: Medium/R: Medium	24	40m 48.415s
18	Enea Bastianini	ITA 23	Ducati Lenovo Team	Ducati Desmosedici GP24	F: Medium/R: Medium	24	41m 02.341s*
19	Stefan Bradl	GER 6	HRC Test Team	Honda RC213V	F: Medium/R: Medium	24	41m 07.021s
20	Alex Rins	SPA 42	Monster Energy Yamaha MotoGP	Yamaha YZR-M1	F: Medium/R: Medium	24	41m 15.154s
	Franco Morbidelli	ITA 21	Prima Pramac Racing	Ducati Desmosedici GP24	F: Medium/R: Medium	17	DNF-crash
	Augusto Fernandez	SPA 37	Red Bull GASGAS Tech3	KTM RC16	F: Medium/R: Medium	5	DNF-crash
	Jack Miller	AUS 43	Red Bull KTM Factory Racing	KTM RC16	F: Medium/R: Soft	2	DNF-crash

Enea Bastianini 32s post-race penalty for failing to comply with ride through penalties.

Fastest lap: Pedro Acosta, on lap 7, 1m 39.664s, 104.5mph/168.2km/h.
Lap record: Johann Zarco, 1m 39.939s, 104.2mph/167.7km/h (2021).
Event maximum speed: Franco Morbidelli, 221.5mph/356.4km/h (warm-up).

Qualifying: Weather: Dry Air: 21° Humidity: 52% Track: 28°
1 A. Espargaro 1m 38.190s, 2 Bagnaia 1m 38.221s,3 R. Fernandez 1m 38.261s, 4 Binder 1m 38.334s, 5 Acosta 1m 38.369s, 6 Di Giannantonio 1m 38.400s, 7 Martin 1m 38.401s, 8 Rins 1m 38.692s, 9 Miller 1m 38.763s, 10 Morbidelli 1m 38.778s, 11 Bastianini 1m 38.860s, 12 Vinales 1m 38.972s.
Q1: 13 A. Marquez 1m 38.530s, 14 M. Marquez 1m 38.536s, 15 Oliveira 1m 38.551s, 16 Bezzecchi 1m 38.662s, 17 Quartararo 1m 38.705s, 18 Zarco 1m 38.978s, 19 A. Fernandez 1m 39.120s, 20 Nakagami 1m 39.156s, 21 Mir 1m 39.524s, 22 Marini 1m 39.621s, 23 Bradl 1m 40.276s.

SPRINT RACE: 12 laps, 34.725 miles/55.884km
WEATHER: Dry (air 25°, humidity 44%, track 46°)

Pos.	Rider	Race tyre choice	Laps	Time & speed
1	Aleix Espargaro	F: Medium/R: Soft	12	20m 01.478s 104.0mph/167.4km/h
2	Marc Marquez	F: Medium/R: Soft	12	20m 02.370s
3	Pedro Acosta	F: Medium/R: Soft	12	20m 02.647s
4	Jorge Martin	F: Medium/R: Soft	12	20m 03.625s
5	Enea Bastianini	F: Medium/R: Soft	12	20m 04.458s
6	Fabio Di Giannantonio	F: Medium/R: Soft	12	20m 06.101s
7	Jack Miller	F: Medium/R: Soft	12	20m 09.562s
8	Maverick Vinales	F: Medium/R: Soft	12	20m 09.723s
9	Marco Bezzecchi	F: Medium/R: Soft	12	20m 10.121s
10	Fabio Quartararo	F: Medium/R: Soft	12	20m 10.719s
11	Franco Morbidelli	F: Medium/R: Soft	12	20m 11.015s
12	Alex Rins	F: Medium/R: Soft	12	20m 14.523s
13	Takaaki Nakagami	F: Medium/R: Soft	12	20m 14.677s
14	Alex Marquez	F: Medium/R: Soft	12	20m 14.856s
15	Joan Mir	F: Medium/R: Soft	12	20m 17.916s
16	Luca Marini	F: Medium/R: Soft	12	20m 19.478s
17	Augusto Fernandez	F: Medium/R: Soft	12	20m 26.740s
18	Stefan Bradl	F: Medium/R: Soft	12	20m 35.229s
	Francesco Bagnaia	F: Medium/R: Soft	11	DNF-crash
	Miguel Oliveira	F: Medium/R: Soft	9	DNF-crash
	Johann Zarco	F: Medium/R: Soft	7	DNF-crash
	Brad Binder	F: Medium/R: Soft	6	DNF-crash
	Raul Fernandez	F: Medium/R: Soft	4	DNF-crash

Fastest race lap: Raul Fernandez, on lap 4, 1m 38.991s.

Fastest race laps
1 Acosta 1m 39.664s, 2 Martin 1m 39.717s, 3 Bagnaia 1m 39.749s, 4 R. Fernandez 1m 39.849s, 5 Binder 1m 39.913s, 6 M. Marquez 1m 39.959s, 7 Morbidelli 1m 39.974s, 8 A. Espargaro 1m 39.998s, 9 A. Marquez 1m 40.235s, 10 Di Giannantonio 1m 40.269s, 11 Bastianini 1m 40.339s, 12 A. Fernandez 1m 40.359s, 13 Oliveira 1m 40.397s, 14 Quartararo 1m 40.480s, 15 Vinales 1m 40.485s, 16 Bezzecchi 1m 40.688s, 17 Miller 1m 40.857s, 18 Zarco 1m 40.894s, 19 Rins 1m 40.939s, 20 Mir 1m 41.062s, 21 Marini 1m 41.068s, 22 Nakagami 1m 41.087s, 23 Bradl 1m 41.139s.

Grid Order	1	2	3	4	5	6	7	8	9	10	11	12	13	14	15	16	17	18	19	20	21	22	23	24	
41 A. ESPARGARO	1	1	1	1	89	89	89	89	89	89	89	89	89	89	89	89	89	89	1	1	1	1	1	1	1
1 BAGNAIA	31	31	31	89	1	31	31	31	31	31	1	1	1	1	1	1	1	1	89	89	89	89	89	89	2
25 R. FERNANDEZ	89	89	89	31	31	1	1	1	1	1	41	41	41	41	41	41	41	41	93	93	93	93	93	93	3
33 BINDER	33	33	33	33	33	33	33	33	33	25	25	25	25	25	25	25	25	93	93	41	41	41	41	41	4
31 ACOSTA	41	41	41	41	25	25	25	41	41	41	93	93	93	93	93	25	25	25	25	25	25	25	25	49	5
49 DI GIANNANTONIO	43	25	25	25	41	41	41	25	25	25	93	33	21	21	21	21	33	73	73	73	49	49	49	25	6
89 MARTIN	25	43	21	21	21	21	21	21	21	21	33	33	33	33	33	73	33	33	49	49	73	73	73	73	7
42 RINS	23	23	93	93	93	93	93	93	93	93	73	73	73	73	73	73	49	49	49	33	33	33	33	33	8
43 MILLER	21	21	23	23	73	73	73	73	73	23	23	23	23	23	49	49	23	88	88	23	23	23	23	23	9
21 MORBIDELLI	93	93	73	73	23	23	23	23	23	49	49	49	49	49	23	23	49	20	20	23	88	88	88	20	10
23 BASTIANINI*	49	73	49	49	49	49	49	49	49	88	88	88	88	88	88	88	23	23	20	72	72	72	72	88	11
12 VINALES	73	49	88	88	88	88	88	88	88	20	20	12	12	12	12	12	72	72	72	72	20	20	20	72	12
73 A. MARQUEZ	20	88	20	20	20	20	20	20	12	12	12	20	20	20	20	72	12	12	12	12	12	12	12	12	13
93 M. MARQUEZ	88	20	37	37	37	12	12	12	20	72	72	72	72	72	72	20	30	30	30	31	31	31	31	31	14
88 OLIVEIRA	72	72	72	72	12	72	72	72	72	42	42	42	42	42	36	31	31	31	31	30	30	30	30	30	15
72 BEZZECCHI	37	37	12	12	72	30	42	42	42	30	30	30	30	30	30	42	36	36	36	36	36	36	36	36	
20 QUARTARARO	30	30	30	30	30	42	30	30	30	30	10	10	10	10	36	36	36	36	31	42	5	5	5	5	
5 ZARCO	12	12	42	42	42	10	10	10	10	10	36	36	36	36	5	5	5	5	42	5	42	10	10	10	
37 A. FERNANDEZ	10	10	10	10	10	36	36	36	5	5	5	5	5	31	31	10	10	10	10	10	10	4	6	6	
30 NAKAGAMI	5	42	36	36	36	5	5	5	5	31	31	31	31	31	10	10	6	6	6	42	42				
36 MIR	36	36	6	6	5	6	6	6	6	6	6	6	6												
10 MARINI	42	6	6	5	6																				
6 BRADL	6	5																							

BASTIANINI* finished 9th on the road – placed 18th after 32s post-race penalty.

Championship Points

1	Martin	99	(56)	155
2	Bagnaia	102	(14)	116
3	M. Marquez	69	(45)	114
4	Bastianini	71	(23)	94
5	Vinales	53	(34)	87
6	Acosta	52	(31)	83
7	A. Espargaro	45	(31)	76
8	Binder	66	(9)	75
9	Di Giannantonio	55	(7)	62
10	Bezzecchi	41	(1)	42
11	A. Marquez	39	(3)	42
12	Quartararo	26	(6)	32
13	Oliveira	27	(2)	29
14	R. Fernandez	26	(2)	28
15	Miller	14	(13)	27
16	Morbidelli	9	(6)	15
17	A. Fernandez	10	(3)	13
18	Mir	12	(1)	13
19	Zarco	9	(0)	9
20	Nakagami	8	(0)	8
21	Rins	0	(7)	7
22	Pedrosa	7	(0)	7

Constructor Points

1	Ducati	141	(63)	204
2	Aprilia	73	(52)	125
3	KTM	82	(40)	122
4	Yamaha	29	(6)	35
5	Honda	18	(1)	19

MOTO2: RACE DISTANCE: 21 laps, 60.768 miles/97.797km
RACE WEATHER: Dry (air 25°, humidity 47%, track 40°)

Pos.	Rider	Nat.	No.	Entrant	Machine	Laps	Time & Speed
1	Ai Ogura	JPN	79	MT Helmets - MSI	Boscoscuro	21	36m 33.540s
							99.7mph/160.5km/h
2	Sergio Garcia	SPA	3	MT Helmets - MSI	Boscoscuro	21	36m 37.356s
3	Jake Dixon	GBR	96	CFMOTO Inde Aspar Team	Kalex	21	36m 42.726s
4	Jeremy Alcoba	SPA	52	Yamaha VR46 Master Camp	Kalex	21	36m 45.781s
5	Senna Agius	AUS	81	Liqui Moly Husqvarna Intact GP	Kalex	21	36m 46.133s
6	Albert Arenas	SPA	75	QJMOTOR Gresini Moto2	Kalex	21	36m 47.206s
7	Alonso Lopez	SPA	21	MB Conveyors SpeedUp	Boscoscuro	21	36m 51.216s
8	Joe Roberts	USA	16	OnlyFans American Racing Team	Kalex	21	36m 54.330s
9	Tony Arbolino	ITA	14	Elf Marc VDS Racing Team	Kalex	21	36m 52.425s
10	Jorge Navarro	SPA	9	KLINT Forward Factory Team	Forward	21	36m 54.789s
11	Zonta van den Goorbergh	NED	84	RW-Idrofoglia Racing GP	Kalex	21	36m 55.975s
12	Filip Salac	CZE	12	Elf Marc VDS Racing Team	Kalex	21	36m 56.613s
13	Jaume Masia	SPA	5	Pertamina Mandalika GAS UP	Kalex	21	36m 58.080s
14	Darryn Binder	RSA	15	Liqui Moly Husqvarna Intact GP	Kalex	21	36m 58.287s
15	Mario Aji	INA	34	IDEMITSU Honda Team Asia	Kalex	21	36m 58.366s
16	Xavi Cardelus	AND	20	Fantic Racing	Kalex	21	37m 01.448s
17	Mattia Pasini	ITA	19	Team Ciatti Boscoscuro	Boscoscuro	21	37m 03.964s
18	Alex Escrig	SPA	11	KLINT Forward Factory Team	Forward	21	37m 11.801s
19	Deniz Oncu	TUR	53	Red Bull KTM Ajo	Kalex	21	37m 12.130s
20	Xavier Artigas	SPA	43	KLINT Forward Factory Team	Forward	21	37m 12.754s
21	Barry Baltus	BEL	7	RW-Idrofoglia Racing GP	Kalex	21	37m 24.145s
22	Manuel Gonzalez	SPA	18	QJMOTOR Gresini Moto2	Kalex	19	37m 02.109s
	Celestino Vietti	ITA	13	Red Bull KTM Ajo	Kalex	15	DNF-crash
	Fermin Aldeguer	SPA	54	MB Conveyors SpeedUp	Boscoscuro	14	DNF-crash
	Aron Canet	SPA	44	Fantic Racing	Kalex	14	DNF-crash
	Daniel Munoz	SPA	17	Pertamina Mandalika GAS UP	Kalex	14	DNF-crash
	Dennis Foggia	ITA	71	Italtrans Racing Team	Kalex	13	DNF-crash
	Diogo Moreira	BRA	10	Italtrans Racing Team	Kalex	1	DNF-crash
	Izan Guevara	SPA	28	CFMOTO Inde Aspar Team	Kalex	0	DNF-crash
	Somkiat Chantra	THA	35	IDEMITSU Honda Team Asia	Kalex	0	DNF-crash
	Marcos Ramirez	SPA	24	OnlyFans American Racing Team	Kalex	-	DSQ

Fastest lap: Fermin Aldeguer, on lap 2, 1m 42.688s, 101.4mph/163.2km/h.
Lap record: Raul Fernandez, 1m 43.757s, 100.4mph/161.5km/h (2021).
Event maximum speed: Deniz Oncu, 187.4mph/301.6km/h (race).

Qualifying
Weather: Dry
Air: 23° Humidity: 47% Track: 42°

1	Garcia	1m 41.894s
2	Aldeguer	1m 42.134s
3	Vietti	1m 42.182s
4	Canet	1m 42.193s
5	Arenas	1m 42.309s
6	Gonzalez	1m 42.325s
7	Munoz	1m 42.328s
8	Lopez	1m 42.328s
9	Roberts	1m 42.364s
10	Ogura	1m 42.439s
11	Dixon	1m 42.458s
12	Agius	1m 42.623s
13	Guevara	1m 42.697s
14	Arbolino	1m 42.707s
15	V d Goorbergh	1m 42.781s
16	Chantra	1m 42.795s
17	Salac	1m 42.845s
18	Binder	1m 43.348s
Q1		
19	Ramirez	1m 43.086s
20	Pasini	1m 43.089s
21	Navarro	1m 43.108s
22	Alcoba	1m 43.135s
23	Foggia	1m 43.153s
24	Moreira	1m 43.392s
25	Sasaki	1m 43.400s
26	Oncu	1m 43.481s
27	Aji	1m 43.508s
28	Masia	1m 43.900s
29	Cardelus	1m 44.019s
30	Baltus	1m 44.066s
31	Escrig	1m 44.199s
32	Artigas	1m 44.225s

Fastest race laps

1	Aldeguer	1m 42.688s
2	Vietti	1m 43.066s
3	Lopez	1m 43.157s
4	Garcia	1m 43.274s
5	Ogura	1m 43.293s
6	Arenas	1m 43.329s
7	Dixon	1m 43.454s
8	Canet	1m 43.463s
9	Agius	1m 43.495s
10	Gonzalez	1m 43.537s
11	Roberts	1m 43.664s
12	Navarro	1m 43.725s
13	Alcoba	1m 43.780s
14	Salac	1m 43.865s
15	Ramirez	1m 43.915s
16	V d Goorbergh	1m 43.932s
17	Binder	1m 43.943s
18	Aji	1m 44.077s
19	Arbolino	1m 44.087s
20	Masia	1m 44.109s
21	Oncu	1m 44.146s
22	Baltus	1m 44.185s
23	Munoz	1m 44.215s
24	Pasini	1m 44.344s
25	Cardelus	1m 44.486s
26	Foggia	1m 44.668s
27	Escrig	1m 44.874s
28	Artigas	1m 44.960s

Championship Points

Pos	Rider	Pts
1	Garcia	109
2	Roberts	90
3	Ogura	88
4	Aldeguer	63
5	Lopez	63
6	Canet	48
7	Arenas	48
8	Gonzalez	46
9	Alcoba	43
10	Arbolino	33
11	Ramirez	29
12	Vietti	29
13	Chantra	28
14	Baltus	23
15	Dixon	16
16	Agius	16
17	Salac	14
18	Van den Goorbergh	11
19	Foggia	10
20	Guevara	10
21	Navarro	6
22	Binder	5
23	Masia	3
24	Oncu	3
25	Bendsneyder	2
26	Moreira	2
27	Aji	1
28	Ferrari	1

Constructor Points
Pos	Constructor	Pts
1	Boscoscuro	138
2	Kalex	114
3	Forward	6

MOTO3: RACE DISTANCE: 18 laps, 52.087 miles/83.826km
RACE WEATHER: Dry (air 21°, humidity 59%, track 22°)

Pos.	Rider	Nat.	No.	Entrant	Machine	Laps	Time & Speed
1	David Alonso	COL	80	CFMOTO Gaviota Aspar Team	CFMOTO	18	32m 25.084s
							96.4mph/155.1km/h
2	Ivan Ortola	SPA	48	MT Helmets - MSI	KTM	18	32m 25.326s
3	Jose Antonio Rueda	SPA	99	Red Bull KTM Ajo	KTM	18	32m 25.597s
4	Collin Veijer	NED	95	Liqui Moly Husqvarna Intact GP	Husqvarna	18	32m 25.644s
5	David Munoz	SPA	64	BOE Motorsports	KTM	18	32m 26.732s
6	Daniel Holgado	SPA	96	Red Bull GASGAS Tech3	GASGAS	18	32m 28.474s
7	Luca Lunetta	ITA	58	SIC58 Squadra Corse	Honda	18	32m 29.875s
8	Jacob Roulstone	AUS	12	Red Bull GASGAS Tech3	GASGAS	18	32m 32.332s
9	Filippo Farioli	ITA	7	SIC58 Squadra Corse	Honda	18	32m 32.533s
10	Adrian Fernandez	SPA	31	Leopard Racing	Honda	18	32m 32.569s
11	Ryusei Yamanaka	JPN	6	MT Helmets - MSI	KTM	18	32m 33.142s
12	Angel Piqueras	SPA	36	Leopard Racing	Honda	18	32m 33.188s
13	Stefano Nepa	ITA	82	LEVELUP - MTA	KTM	18	32m 33.231s
14	Joel Esteban	SPA	78	CFMOTO Gaviota Aspar Team	CFMOTO	18	32m 33.244s
15	Tatsuki Suzuki	JPN	24	Liqui Moly Husqvarna Intact GP	Husqvarna	18	32m 45.419s
16	Scott Ogden	GBR	19	MLav Racing	Honda	18	32m 46.381s
17	Matteo Bertelle	ITA	18	Kopron Rivacold Snipers Team	Honda	18	32m 46.443s
18	Nicola Carraro	ITA	10	LEVELUP - MTA	KTM	18	32m 46.502s
19	Xabi Zurutuza	SPA	85	Red Bull KTM Ajo	KTM	18	32m 47.411s
20	Joshua Whatley	GBR	70	MLav Racing	Honda	18	33m 05.617s
21	Noah Dettwiler	SWI	55	CIP Green Power	KTM	18	33m 05.636s
22	Tatchakorn Buasri	THA	5	Honda Team Asia	Honda	18	33m 05.684s
23	Arbi Aditama	INA	93	Honda Team Asia	Honda	18	33m 11.769s
	David Almansa	SPA	22	Kopron Rivacold Snipers Team	Honda	12	DNF-crash
	Taiyo Furusato	JPN	72	Honda Team Asia	Honda	5	DNF-crash
	Joel Kelso	AUS	66	BOE Motorsports	KTM	5	DNF-crash
	Riccardo Rossi	ITA	54	CIP Green Power	KTM	5	DNF-crash

Fastest lap: Jose Rueda, on lap 17, 1m 46.748s, 97.6mph/157.0km/h.
Lap record: Darryn Binder, 1m 48.209s, 96.3mph/154.9km/h (2021).
Event maximum speed: Tatsuki Suzuki, 157.1mph/252.9km/h (race).

Qualifying:
Weather: Dry
Air: 23° Humidity: 50% Track: 40°

1	Ortola	1m 46.749s
2	Veijer	1m 46.768s
3	Rueda	1m 47.011s
4	Furusato	1m 47.137s
5	Yamanaka	1m 47.178s
6	Alonso	1m 47.299s
7	Munoz	1m 47.395s
8	Fernandez	1m 47.468s
9	Holgado	1m 47.549s
10	Lunetta	1m 47.563s
11	Nepa	1m 47.564s
12	Bertelle	1m 47.621s
13	Piqueras	1m 47.645s
14	Kelso	1m 47.989s
15	Esteban	1m 48.039s
16	Roulstone	1m 48.054s
17	Almansa	1m 48.249s
18	Rossi	1m 47.003s
Q1		
19	Ogden	1m 48.557s
20	Farioli	1m 48.683s
21	Suzuki	1m 48.752s
22	Buasri	1m 48.799s
23	Zurutuza	1m 48.876s
24	Dettwiler	1m 49.204s
25	Carraro	1m 49.220s
26	Whatley	1m 49.406s
27	Aditama	1m 50.528s

Fastest race laps

1	Rueda	1m 46.748s
2	Munoz	1m 46.894s
3	Alonso	1m 47.030s
4	Ortola	1m 47.057s
5	Veijer	1m 47.105s
6	Holgado	1m 47.245s
7	Lunetta	1m 47.369s
8	Yamanaka	1m 47.389s
9	Furusato	1m 47.488s
10	Farioli	1m 47.504s
11	Suzuki	1m 47.637s
12	Fernandez	1m 47.720s
13	Roulstone	1m 47.722s
14	Esteban	1m 47.735s
15	Piqueras	1m 47.835s
16	Nepa	1m 47.891s
17	Kelso	1m 47.929s
18	Carraro	1m 48.342s
19	Bertelle	1m 48.359s
20	Ogden	1m 48.498s
21	Almansa	1m 48.504s
22	Zurutuza	1m 48.598s
23	Rossi	1m 48.891s
24	Buasri	1m 49.082s
25	Whatley	1m 49.406s
26	Dettwiler	1m 49.525s
27	Aditama	1m 49.646s

Championship Points

Pos	Rider	Pts
1	Alonso	118
2	Holgado	104
3	Veijer	75
4	Ortola	70
5	Munoz	49
6	Rueda	44
7	Kelso	42
8	Yamanaka	40
9	Fernandez	37
10	Piqueras	36
11	Esteban	35
12	Roulstone	35
13	Suzuki	31
14	Nepa	29
15	Furusato	18
16	Lunetta	15
17	Carraro	15
18	Rossi	13
19	Farioli	11
20	Bertelle	8
21	Ogden	5
22	Zurutuza	3
23	Perez	3
24	Dettwiler	2
25	Almansa	2

Constructor Points
Pos	Constructor	Pts
1	CFMOTO	118
2	GASGAS	104
3	KTM	97
4	Husqvarna	85
5	Honda	67

ITALIAN GRAND PRIX

FIM WORLD CHAMPIONSHIP • ROUND 7

MUGELLO CIRCUIT

Above: Bagnaia quickly overcame a three-place grid penalty to stamp his authority.
Photo: Gold & Goose

Top right: Quartararo's Yamaha was better, but not better enough.
Photo: Monster Yamaha

Above right: Back to form, Morbidelli enjoyed a strong weekend.

Right: Feeling unloved by Ducati, Jorge Martin contemplates his future.
Photos: Gold & Goose

Opening spread: Ducati pursued the all-blue *Azzurro* football theme to celebrate their one-two triumph.
Photo: Ducati Corse

MUSICAL chairs had nothing on the Mugello merry-go-round. A series of shocks over and shortly after the weekend shuffled the pack in some very unexpected ways, with six top riders switching teams, resolving the who-goes-where questions that had been occupying the paddock all year.

The shock waves dominated news and social media, and rather unfairly overshadowed a weekend of perfect redemption for Bagnaia – a double win at astonishing speed. On Sunday, he overcame a three-position grid penalty to lead every lap and win a full 25 seconds faster than he had the year before – an average improvement of better than a second a lap.

Set to stay at Ducati's factory team until 2026, his ironic comment on race eve, when the gossip was beginning to peak, defined his position: "I'm jealous that I don't have any options."

It was a riposte to Jorge Martin, who until then had been expected to be promoted from Pramac to the factory, until suddenly that became impossible on Sunday evening. On Thursday, he had said, "I have three different scenarios that I feel comfortable with. It's not like I have one option."

That was one race after Pramac team manager Gino Borsoi had temporarily (and falsely) ended speculation that they might switch from Ducati to Yamaha, confirming that they expected the usual two factory-level bikes for 2025. One was earmarked for Marquez, fulfilling his wish for a factory bike. Then Marc stopped the music. He would not, he said, ride for another satellite team.

Unwilling to lose his services to a rival, by Sunday evening, Ducati had bitten the bullet. Ignoring any loss of face for Bagnaia and sweeping aside any policy of encouraging youth, they slotted in Marquez alongside him.

That left Martin with the option of staying at Pramac or switching – to either KTM or Aprilia (or indeed Honda or Yamaha). Out of the blue, he chose Aprilia, going, he said at the next race, "to a place where they really want me."

This preceded an entirely unexpected move by Vinales to KTM, with the possibility of him becoming the first rider in history to win on four different makes. It hadn't been triggered by Martin's arrival, he said later, but by Aprilia's inconsistency: "I was thinking about it in Jerez. After [winning in] Austin, I knew what I could do, and not only in one race in 20. I'd made up my mind before Mugello."

Bezzecchi leapt at the chance of the second Aprilia seat, fulfilling their desires for an Italian rider and his for a factory ride. Bastianini was the final surprise, rejecting a demotion to Pramac to join KTM – he and Vinales would be in the second full-factory team run by Tech3, dropping the GasGas name.

There was no surprise, however, that Pedro Acosta was signed up for KTM's Red Bull team, switching from Tech3 to join Brad Binder in the direct factory squad.

One race later, at Assen, Pramac would drop their own bombshell. They too were to dump Ducati.

That left some riders with uncertain futures, notably GP winners Jack Miller and Di Giannantonio, as well as Augusto Fernandez, and the satellite Aprilia pair Raul Fernandez and Miguel Oliveira.

The race was followed by an official test, but it was washed out after a weekend of fine weather. Yamaha and Honda had tested at the track before the previous round, and continued to play with aerodynamic variations. Mir and Marini used the

latest fairing, but only Nakagami the fairing and seat combination. Yamaha riders seemed to benefit more, with Quartararo second fastest in FP1 (when it didn't matter very much) and Rins second in practice, so he made it into Q2 for the first time, at the track where he had been so badly hurt in 2023. To little avail – he qualified tenth and made a single point. Both riders said that the new aero was difficult to manage through the fast chicanes, to the extent that heaving on the bars had given Quartararo arm-pump.

Pol Espargaro, in his first KTM wild-card appearance, had the same front mudguard wing that Pedrosa had used at Jerez. Coincidentally, he also set the highest top speed of the weekend, exactly matching fellow KTM rider Brad Binder's 2023 record of 227.5mph (366.1km/h). If the latest aero tweaks weren't affecting top speed, they provided much improved stability over the circuit's infamous top-speed crest at the end of the straight, where the wheelies of the past were notably absent.

There was a welcome return to form for Morbidelli, still recovering lost ground after missing the pre-season tests through injury. Fourth in the sprint and sixth on Sunday made this his best weekend since 2021, when he had been on a Yamaha.

There was more trouble involving the stewards, Quartaro being miffed after Oliveira had gone unpunished for taking him out on the sprint's first lap – an about-face echo of Jerez in 2023, when the Frenchman had been sanctioned for taking the Portuguese rider down. "For five years, they ask us, 'What do you think about this incident – penalty or not?' They say, 'Thank you, it was really helpful.' But at the end, I go out more confused than when I come in. It looks like I'm talking to someone that has never been racing. This is sad. I think we have to get more professional people."

He was not the only dismayed champion. In practice, Alex Marquez came upon Bagnaia riding slowly on line, spoiling a fast lap, and reacted with extravagantly theatrical arm waving and head shaking. Bagnaia felt unjustly accused and that Marquez could easily have ridden around him. The stewards took the Spaniard's part, however, and issued a three-position grid penalty for the main race, though not the sprint. "No one is happy," he said. "We have no consistency."

MOTOGP SPRINT RACE – 11 laps

Martin grabbed pole, ahead of Bagnaia and Vinales. Marc Marquez was back on form, leading row two from Bastianini and Morbidelli, through from Q1. Acosta led the third; Raul Fernandez was impressive again, if only for escaping Q1 ahead of Binder, Di Giannantonio and Quartararo. He ended up 12th.

Martin had smashed the all-time record in the morning, but Bagnaia was unbeatable in the afternoon, taking a

flier off the line to lead Bastianini, Martin, Binder and Marc Marquez into the first corner, the South African shooting through from 13th on the grid to fourth.

Martin was up to second by the end of the lap, his battle with Bastianini giving the leader a bit of breathing room. On the second, after Oliveira had knocked Quartararo off at the Scarperia right-left, Marquez got ahead of Binder, now coming under pressure from Acosta.

Then, into Turn One, Martin and Bastianini touched, the latter crashing out. This was not the only misfortune to take place at that point. Martin had lost second to Marquez on lap six, then two laps later also crashed out there.

Bagnaia was a second clear and untroubled for his first sprint win of the season, after three zero scores in a row; likewise, Marquez was safe in second, with Acosta and then Morbidelli each more than a second behind. Binder had faded to lose fifth to Vinales with three laps to go, narrowly holding off Di Giannantonio, Alex Marquez and Aleix Espargaro, with Raul Fernandez just a second down, but out of the points.

Pol Espargaro was 14th; Mir was an early retirement.

MOTOGP RACE – 23 laps

Wearing an oddly retro-looking light blue *Azzurro* livery, a tribute to Italian sporting teams a couple of weeks before the UEFA Euro championship, the factory Ducatis swamped fast-away starter Martin into the first corner, with Bagnaia shuffling Bastianini and the Spaniard aside to take the lead into the second. Demoted to the second row of the grid, he was determined to stamp his authority.

Now he embarked on setting an awesome pace, cutting more than 25 seconds off his previous year's winning race time and pulling the field along in his wake, so that the top 15 all finished inside that time – reflecting determination as well as improved tyre and machine performance.

Speed, however, doesn't always equal excitement. For long stretches, this was a processional race, low on incident. Although the spacing between the top four – Bagnaia, Martin, Bastianini and Marc Marquez – was minimal (1.5 seconds covered the lead quartet for 16 of the race's 23 laps), for most of it, they were too far apart to attempt a pass.

Acosta was behind Marquez and seemed ready to challenge at the end of lap two. But it came to nothing, and by the eighth, he had lost touch. Vinales was next, but he succumbed to the finally on-form Morbidelli on lap three, then dropped away, his hands full in fending off Alex Marquez.

The pattern up front was soon established. An early exchange of fastest laps meant that Bagnaia's advantage over Martin stood at four-tenths starting the fourth. Four laps on, and he'd doubled that. Fears he'd completely detach himself were eased as the Spaniard brought it back down to four-tenths – yet it was clear that the leader was controlling the pace at will.

By lap 16, Marquez was climbing all over Bastianini, almost getting close enough to pass by the track's looping final turn, only to lose vital ground to the faster GP24 on to the back straight. He finally got by at San Donato with five laps to go. But any hopes of reeling in the lead duo were dashed by lap 19 as his progress stalled.

As the laps ticked down, Martin made one last rally. On lap 21, he was a full four-tenths faster than the leader, to close to within a quarter of a second. Bagnaia responded immediately, however, increasing his advantage to eight-tenths by the final lap. By then, Martin had burned up his rear tyre in the late attack.

Left: Bastianini stole past Martin to grab second on the last corner.

Right: Alonso leads the Moto3 gang of Ortola, Veijer and Furusato.

Below: It was celebration time for John Hopkins and the Only Fans American Racing crew with Moto2 winner Joe Roberts.

Below left: Friend or foe? Pramac's Campinoti and Ducati's Tardozzi go face to face.

Bottom: Wise words – KTM wild-card Pol Espargaro being interviewed on the grid.

Photos: Gold & Goose

The action was taking place behind, with Bastianini showing trademark late pace. He passed Marquez at Scarperia with two laps to go and began closing on Martin. And the championship leader ran a slightly wide line through the last turn for the final time, giving the second factory bike just enough space to accelerate through for second. "A rookie mistake," Martin lamented.

Marquez was two seconds adrift of the winner in fourth, insisting that he was content to be scrapping with the GP24s on his year-old GP23. Acosta was another four seconds away in a lone fifth, deploring, "one of the most boring races of my life." Meanwhile, Morbidelli just resisted a late attack by Di Giannantonio, the VR46 Ducati rider having come through from 14th on the grid. Vinales was alone in eighth, well clear of Alex Marquez.

Binder was tenth after another unspectacular ride, having tussled for a spell mid-race with Aleix Espargaro before outdistancing him; Raul Fernandez and Bezzecchi were together; Oliveira was next after losing touch, narrowly ahead of Rins.

Miller's problematic season continued, out of the points with a vibration issue "that starts in the rear then transfers to the front". Pol Espargaro was alone; Quartararo, Zarco and Marini all close. Quartararo, fighting fatigue, had lost two places in the last four laps.

Aprilia tester Savadori was a long way back. Augusto Fernandez retired; Mir and Nakagami suffered the Honda curse, crashing out.

Martin's advantage had been trimmed to 18 points, and was starting to look precarious.

MOTO2 RACE – 12 laps

The rejigged schedule after the Moto3 red flag delayed the Moto2 race by an hour and shortened it from 19 laps to 12, making it more of a sprint.

The all-time record had fallen on Saturday morning, to Lopez, and again in the afternoon to Roberts, for his first pole position of the season. Garcia and Lopez were alongside; Gonzalez led row two from Binder and Ramirez, both through from Q1. Canet was ninth, Ogura 12th and Dixon 15th.

In a fresh blow to the favourite's hopes, Aldeguer was absent. Second in the morning, he had been stricken with severe neck pain that ruled him out of qualifying. He started 18th, and the weekend continued to disappoint with a second successive no-score, after he was taken out by Jeremy Alcoba on the fourth lap, having climbed to 12th.

Roberts led away on his Kalex, chased by Lopez's Boscoscuro, then the Kalexes of on-form Binder, Gonzalez and Canet. Team-mates Garcia and Ogura, who had jumped six places on the first lap, added two more Boscoscuros to the pack.

Binder crashed at the halfway point. And Roberts's victory hopes came under threat with three to go when Canet, Gonzalez and Lopez all got by. The American's response was swift, however, as he climbed three places on lap ten, but he saved the best until last. As Gonzalez outbraked him into San Donato for the final time, the Californian responded with a fine aggressive move into the following turn.

He held on by six-hundredths, the sixth different winner in seven races. Lopez was third and Garcia fourth. Ogura was less than a tenth behind, Canet another half-second away, dropped to sixth after crossing the line third two laps before. It was more like a Moto3 race than Moto2.

Less than a second away, Vietti led the next trio, from Guevara and Chantra. Ramirez was tenth, narrowly ahead of Moreira, the top rookie. The next was Oncu, 13th, sandwiched between Dixon and van den Goorbergh. Arbolino missed the points by three-tenths, beyond Aji, yet another fast rookie.

Mattia Pasini, in a second wild-card appearance on his private Boscoscuro, dropped from 12th to a distant last after falling and remounting on the final lap. Salac and the luckless Sasaki also crashed.

Roberts closed to within seven points of Garcia, with Ogura another 16 down. Aldeguer's continuing misfortune dropped him to sixth, 59 points adrift.

MOTO3 RACE – 11 laps (restarted, shortened)

Alonso led every practice and qualifying, with new records in the first three outings. He headed Ortola and Rueda; Veijer led row two from Holgado and impressive rookie Luca Lunetta, fastest Honda on a track that favours KTM and its derivatives. Another strong rookie, Australian Roulstone, led row three from Furusato and Kelso.

Alonso won by the biggest ever Mugello Moto3 margin. But it was still only 0.142 of a second.

He led the first three laps, hotly pursued by Furusato, Veijer and Ortola, but then an ugly crash between Farioli and Zurutuza brought out the red flags. Zurutuza, tangled with his bike, was lucky to escape with only relatively minor scapula and humerus fractures.

Alonso led away again from the restart almost half an hour later, but Veijer pushed the Colombian harder than anyone had expected.

Munoz, Ortola and Yamanaka were also involved early on. Lap eight was crucial, as Alonso slipstreamed his way to the front on the run to San Donato, while Veijer was shuffled back to sixth. At the end of that circuit, Alonso had put six-tenths into the rest.

Veijer responded with a series of fastest laps, regaining second on the penultimate, halving the deficit. Alonso held on for his fifth win in seven, with Yamanaka claiming a maiden podium courtesy of Ortola's last-lap spill at Correntaio; Furusato was denied by less than half a second.

Munoz was almost four seconds down and alone in fifth; the hastily remounted Ortola was just clear of Lunetta, who passed Fernandez and Roulstone on the final lap. Bertelle, Piqueras and Kelso were right behind.

Rossi was a lonely 13th; Holgado gained two places on the last lap for 14th ahead of Rueda, his race ruined by a double long-lap after taking down Rueda on the first lap. Nepa crashed out, while Tatsuki Suzuki crashed in both first and second legs.

FIM WORLD CHAMPIONSHIP • ROUND 8
DUTCH TT
ASSEN CIRCUIT

HERESY at the Cathedral! Was the Pope perhaps not a Catholic after all? And was Pramac, for two decades the first acolyte of the hallowed Ducati, really turning its back on MotoGP's true religion?

At Mugello three weeks earlier, Pramac team manager Gino Borsoi had told Spanish TV that they would be continuing with Ducati in 2025, with two GP25 machines. However, that was when they still expected Marc Marquez to be on the team. Two days later, however, everything had changed. About face…

At Assen, it was confirmed. Long-standing rumours of a flirtation with Yamaha proved solid. The covert relationship was consummated very suddenly, in response to Ducati hiring Marquez at the expense of Martin, and in defiance of Pramac's long-established role of polishing future factory-team riders, including Bagnaia.

Pramac principal Paolo Campinoti said, in a TV interview, "They [Yamaha] believe in the project of the young rider, which it seems Ducati don't believe any more." He rather undermined the youth bias elsewhere, naming Miller and Oliveira (both 30 in the coming season) as prime candidates for the team, plus the more likely Di Giannantonio (25).

The decision appeared precipitate, but was "the result of many months of discussion and negotiation," said Yamaha boss Lin Jarvis. "The first important step was to keep Fabio with us. The second was more bikes on the grid. Rather than a satellite team, we will be providing them with bikes of the same specification as the Monster Energy team." As to Pramac's change of loyalty, "I'd say we were in the right place at the right time."

The comeback quest continued with new engines, both riders using one version at Assen. Not the right version, said Quartararo, still complaining of aggressive response. The other, also tested at Valencia the previous week, "improved a lot on agility and turning, and I think this will be a big, big help for the future." He also praised the new working method. Previously, "if we tested an engine in Valencia on Friday, we would never have the opportunity to have it here. Normally, it would've been maybe for Silverstone."

Honda's recovery was slower, however, after taking a wrong direction in development. Riders still awaited significant updates. "Maybe in September, we will make a step," said Joan Mir. "Not the definitive one, but probably a big one, and we will also understand the direction for next year. This season, we've been a bit unlucky because one engine character that looked pretty good in the Sepang test then gave a lot of unexpected problems. We had to come back. We lost time there." Mir was close to extending his stay at Repsol Honda, feeling that abandoning the project without a single good result would be an unacceptable failure.

There was another kind of heresy on Sunday, for those who think that going faster than rivals is the essence of racing. For the first time, we saw a rider deliberately wave another one past, to tuck in behind so as to heat up his front tyre. Notably, it was Marc Marquez, in the podium battle. A dashboard warning had revealed that he was in danger of being below the 1.8-bar limit for more than 60 per cent of the race. Following Di Giannantonio, staying there even when the Italian made an error, might have solved the problem. Frustratingly, later in the race, he was pushed wide by Bastianini, and he blamed running alone again briefly for the pressure dropping once more, to an apparent 0.01 bar below the limit for a single lap. His appeal to the stewards for clemency fell on deaf ears, and he was dropped from a hard-won fourth to tenth.

On a weekend with several injuries and a plethora of slow-

Above: Start to finish. Bagnaia was in charge in the sprint.

Top right: After you, Claude. Marquez dropped behind Di Giannantonio, trying in vain to heat his tyre and avoid a penalty.

Above right: Oliveira, Acosta and Bezzecchi scrap in the sprint.

Right: Zero progress. Mir and his Honda crew remained nonplussed.

Opening spread: MotoGP theatre, as Bagnaia leads Vinales, Martin, Alex Marquez, Morbidelli and the gang.
Photos: Gold & Goose

riding punishments in Moto3, an unpleasant incident in MotoGP qualifying was a talking point for TT star John McGuinness in Britain's *MCN* – a near miss between a slowing Martin and an inattentive Miller, approaching from behind in a slow group looking for a tow. "Martin looked over his shoulder, Miller looked over his, and glanced into him. These are the freak accidents that can kill you."

Luckily, they got away with it. Other riders were less fortunate, however.

Moto2 title contender Joe Roberts fell heavily at the fast Ruskenhoek in P1 and broke his collarbone. Quickly reassembled, he hoped to race on Sunday, but was ruled unfit, since he was still within the 72-hour minimum ban after a general anaesthetic.

Aleix Espargaro arrived with his hair bleached white, and blamed that for jinxing his weekend. He'd essayed the same tonsorial misadventure in 2022 at Silverstone and had suffered a painful heel injury. Already in pain after a jolting fall on Friday afternoon, he was hit with a very fast low-sider in the sprint, which broke a bone in his right hand. Out for Sunday, he shaved his head to ward off any further ill fortune.

Aprilia tester Lorenzo Savadori's wild-card weekend came to a painful end in the sprint, with back injuries that ruled him out on Sunday.

The final victim was Rins, with a spectacular first-corner fling on Sunday. He walked away, but flew home for surgery to wrist and ankle fractures that ruled him out until after the end of the upcoming summer break.

MOTOGP SPRINT RACE – 13 laps

Eschewing his usual "working in secret" slow start, Bagnaia dominated every session except morning warm-up, breaking the record on Friday afternoon and again in qualifying to claim an emphatic first pole of the year.

Martin and Vinales were alongside; an on-form Alex Marquez led row two from Espargaro and Di Giannantonio, through from Q1. Also through, Acosta, down in tenth. Marc Marquez led row three.

Bagnaia made a perfect start, then fended off an early-laps challenge from Martin, who was eventually almost two-and-a-half seconds behind. Vinales, who passed Alex Marquez on lap two, was similarly outpaced in third.

Any hopes Marc might have entertained were scotched when he clipped the inside kerb at Turn Two on the second lap and crashed.

The action was for fourth. Alex Marquez and Binder were joined before half-distance by Espargaro and Bastianini, again hampered by his tenth-place grid position.

On lap nine, Bastianini took Binder at the Strubben, then Marquez at the chicane, and immediately escaped, but too late to catch Vinales.

By that point, Di Giannantonio had caught up, while erstwhile group leader Marquez was hit with a track-limits long-lap. With two laps left, Diggia dive-bombed to the front at the chicane, followed through by Espargaro.

More drama followed after Marquez dropped to the back of the group. Last time through the Ramshoek, a feisty Espargaro went flying at high speed in the gravel.

That left Binder sixth behind Diggia, while a steadfast lone pursuit by Quartararo was rewarded with seventh after three seconds were added to Alex Marquez's time.

Morbidelli took the last point; a downbeat Acosta was almost three seconds down, narrowly ahead of Bezzecchi and Oliveira. Savadori and Rins crashed out, the former suffering spinal fractures.

MOTOGP RACE – 26 laps

Bagnaia was irresistible, leading every lap and posting the fastest, to smash the race record by a staggering 30 seconds and beat Martin by three. "I have no excuses today," conceded Martin. "I just have to congratulate Pecco."

The pair were in a class of their own in both outings. As at Mugello, the superiority of Ducati's GP24 was clear to see, challenges from Ducati's GP23 contingent, as well as Aprilia and KTM, falling well short.

Bagnaia led away from Vinales, Martin and the Marquez brothers, Marc ahead of Alex after a neat move at De Strubben. Martin was also on the move, passing Vinales for second at Turn Eight. Fastest laps on the third and fourth hinted at a possible victory challenge, but Bagnaia's response was swift: fastest laps on lap five, ten and 12 built his lead to more than a second.

His pace was difficult to believe for some rivals. "I could see on the big screen outside Turn Five he did a 1.31 on lap 12, and I honestly thought I was seeing things. It was demoralising," said Miller.

Martin stayed within two seconds until three laps from the chequered flag and pulverised the rest of the field, but Bagnaia's 23rd victory for Ducati – the same number that Casey Stoner had notched up in Bologna red – was never in doubt.

Focus shifted to the fight for third. Initially, Marc Marquez held the place thanks to a nice pass on Vinales at De Strubben on lap two. Acosta and Di Giannantonio were also in the running, however, with the latter climbing to fourth by lap six thanks to a tidy move on Vinales at the final chicane.

Things took an unexpected turn two laps on, when Marquez glanced over his shoulder and waved Di Giannantonio by at Turn Nine. His front tyre pressure was worryingly low

Above: From Les Graham to Pecco Bagnaia Dorna's 75-year pantheon of world champions.
Photo: DORNA

Top right: Ogura and Aldeguer disputed a close Moto2 race.

Above right: Marcel Schrotter deputised for the injured Oncu at Red Bull KTM Ajo.

Right: Flying Dutchman. Collin Veijer suffered a major high-side in Moto3 qualifying.

Far right: Breaking Alonso's run of three wins, Ivan Ortola celebrated his first of the season.

Below right: Rookie Piqueras ended up with the Tissot watch after a maiden pole in Moto3.

Below far right: Local hero Veijer looked set for a home win until Ortola pounced on the last lap.
Photos: Gold & Goose

and he needed to make it legal by following and heating the tyre. He even refused to pass Di Giannantonio when the Italian made an error exiting Turn Nine on lap 19. Vinales took full advantage, breezing by the pair into third.

This was an unfamiliar and unedifying kind of racing.

By then, the group had grown to five. Bastianini, on row four after another lacklustre qualifying, had gradually built up speed from a sleepy tenth on lap one, making stealthy, but irresistible progress toward the podium fight. He passed Acosta on lap 18, then Di Giannantonio next time around.

Then a crucial moment: he outbraked Marquez into Turn One starting lap 21, which pushed the Catalan off track, before passing Vinales for third on lap 22. Crucially, Marquez lost the tow for two laps, causing his front tyre pressure to drop again, which had a grave impact on his final result, although he soon found his way back into the podium fight. Vinales proved obliging, running off line at Ramshoek on the final lap, which put Marc fourth. But his tyre pressure had been too low for too long. The 16-second penalty dropped him to tenth.

That put Di Giannantonio fourth, behind Bastianini, after Vinales was judged to have exceeded track limits at the final chicane and dropped one place. Behind, Acosta had lost touch with five laps to go, and the dangers of riding in clear air and cooler temperatures soon emerged as his front tyre lost temperature on the left side, causing him to crash at high speed at Turn Seven on the final lap, luckily unhurt.

That elevated Binder to a distant sixth, with Alex Marquez and Raul Fernandez seventh and eighth. An early mistake put Morbidelli back in the pack, and he came home ninth, with Marquez tenth. Miller gained some front-end confidence in 11th, with Quartararo up close in 12th. The Yamaha was 24 seconds behind the winner, but still six seconds faster than 2023's race-winning time.

Zarco was narrowly ahead of Raul Fernandez; Oliveira out of touch for the last point. Rins crashed out at the first corner, Bezzecchi and Mir three and six laps later respectively.

MOTO2 RACE – 22 laps

Records fell in every practice session, to Ogura and Aldeguer on Friday, Chantra and Aldeguer again on Saturday, with the last named claiming a second pole of the year. Alongside him, Ogura, in by far his best qualifying of the year, and teammate Garcia, an all-Boscoscuro front row.

Gonzales led row two from Lopez and Arenas, through from Q1. Roberts, third fastest on Friday, was absent, though in the pits, ripping the 'Get Well Soon' message from his parked bike, having been thwarted in his desire to ride.

For the second race in three, track limits would determine the result, for Aldeguer couldn't keep his bike within them. This earned him a long-lap and ultimately cost him victory.

Ogura led away, but Aldeguer took over before the end of the lap, with a revived Arbolino in pursuit. Garcia finished the first lap fifth behind Lopez, but by the fourth was through to second ahead of Ogura.

The Boscoscuro trio swiftly broke clear, Aldeguer's lead growing to 1.6 seconds after a mistake by Garcia on lap 12 put Ogura back in second place.

Aldeguer was hit with the long-lap penalty on the 14th, as he had been in Barcelona, and also at the Dutch track a year before. That demoted him to third next time around, half a second in arrears – though at least he didn't fall off this time.

He was on the back of the MSI team-mates in no time, for a tight three-way fight. Garcia briefly took the lead from Ogura at the GT chicane on lap 18 before immediately losing it on the run to Turn One. Soon his victory chances were run, as he encountered front tyre issues, which caused him to run wide at De Strubben.

That left Ogura to defend from Aldeguer over the last three laps. With the Spaniard's tyres shot after his late push, the Japanese rider hung on for his second win in three races, by half a second, which left the pre-season favourite to contemplate another case of what could have been.

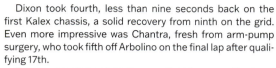

Dixon took fourth, less than nine seconds back on the first Kalex chassis, a solid recovery from ninth on the grid. Even more impressive was Chantra, fresh from arm-pump surgery, who took fifth off Arbolino on the final lap after qualifying 17th.

Ramirez headed a close five-way fight for seventh, ahead of the disappointing Lopez, Gonzalez, Vietti and strong rookie Senna Agius, the group three abreast approaching the GT Chicane on the final lap.

Foggia was close; Alcoba (who had run a long-lap carry-over from his crash with Aldeguer at Mugello) took 13th off home rider Bendsneyder on the last lap; Binder led Moreira for the last point.

Marcel Schrotter, back in place of Oncu – injured in training – missed the points by three places and ten seconds.

Van den Goorbergh, Arenas, Canet and Sasaki all crashed out in the early laps.

MOTO3 RACE – 20 laps

For the first time since March, Alonso was not fastest on Friday morning, nor for any session, ending up 13th at an unfavoured track.

Instead, the omens pointed to a famous home triumph, even after Collin Veijer was robbed of pole by a spectacular high-side exiting the chicane. He had to watch as Honda riders Furusato and finally rookie Piqueras took over.

Veijer started the race as favourite, took time to find his rhythm as Ortola led Furusato and Piqueras, then seized control of a 13-rider gang on lap 11. Immediately, he set about building a lead. By lap 16, he had a four-tenths advantage over Alonso, Munoz, Fernandez and Ortola, who would prove the danger man.

The Spaniard had made his way back up to second on lap 18, with a deficit of eight-tenths to the leader.

At that point, a first Dutch triumph on home soil since 1989 seemed a formality. Yet Ortola hushed the rowdy grandstand as they started the last lap, now just four-tenths behind. Veijer's rear tyre was completely spent, and Ortola continued to close as they rounded the Ramshoek. As Veijer went defensive into the GT Chicane, Ortola's brilliant round-the-outside pass was good enough for the lead at the death, and a first victory of the year by 0.012 of a second.

Munoz and Rueda passed Alonso for third and fourth at the final chicane, with impressive rookie Luca Lunetta sixth, through to head fellow Honda riders Fernandez and Piqueras at a track that finally suited the Japanese bikes.

Nepa and Yamanaka were still up close to complete the top ten; Furusato had dropped to 13th.

Seven riders were hit with long-lap penalties for cruising during qualifying – Farioli, Bertelle, Whatley and Esteban with doubles; Carraro, Detweiler and Zurutusa singles. More long-laps for exceeding track limits were given to Almansa, plus Whatley and Zurutusa again. Suzuki and Almansa crashed out.

FIM WORLD CHAMPIONSHIP: ROUND 8
MOTUL TT ASSEN
28–30 JUNE, 2024

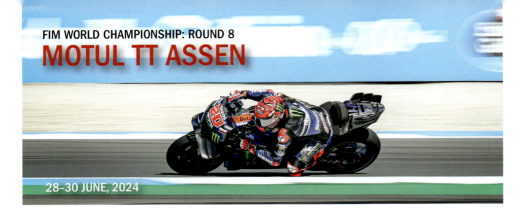

TT ASSEN — 26 laps, Length: 4.542km / 2.822 miles, Width: 14m

MOTOGP: RACE DISTANCE: 26 laps, 73.379 miles/118.092km
WEATHER: Dry (air 22°, humidity 50%, track 39°)

Pos.	Rider	Nat. No.	Entrant	Machine	Race tyre choice	Laps	Time & speed
1	Francesco Bagnaia	ITA 1	Ducati Lenovo Team	Ducati Desmosedici GP24	F: Hard/R: Medium	26	40m 07.214s 103.6mph/166.8km/h
2	Jorge Martin	SPA 89	Prima Pramac Racing	Ducati Desmosedici GP24	F: Medium/R: Medium	26	40m 10.890s
3	Enea Bastianini	ITA 23	Ducati Lenovo Team	Ducati Desmosedici GP24	F: Hard/R: Medium	26	40m 14.287s
4	Fabio Di Giannantonio	ITA 49	Pertamina Enduro VR46 Racing	Ducati Desmosedici GP23	F: Hard/R: Medium	26	40m 15.513s
5	Maverick Vinales*	SPA 12	Aprilia Racing	Aprilia RS-GP24	F: Hard/R: Medium	26	40m 15.472s
6	Brad Binder	RSA 33	Red Bull KTM Factory Racing	KTM RC16	F: Hard/R: Soft	26	40m 23.219s
7	Alex Marquez	SPA 73	Gresini Racing MotoGP	Ducati Desmosedici GP23	F: Hard/R: Medium	26	40m 28.309s
8	Raul Fernandez	SPA 25	Trackhouse Racing	Aprilia RS-GP23	F: Hard/R: Medium	26	40m 29.582s
9	Franco Morbidelli	ITA 21	Prima Pramac Racing	Ducati Desmosedici GP24	F: Hard/R: Medium	26	40m 30.627s
10	Marc Marquez**	SPA 93	Gresini Racing MotoGP	Ducati Desmosedici GP23	F: Hard/R: Medium	26	40m 31.082s
11	Jack Miller	AUS 43	Red Bull KTM Factory Racing	KTM RC16	F: Hard/R: Soft	26	40m 31.218s
12	Fabio Quartararo	FRA 20	Monster Energy Yamaha MotoGP	Yamaha YZR-M1	F: Hard/R: Soft	26	40m 31.271s
13	Johann Zarco	FRA 5	CASTROL Honda LCR	Honda RC213V	F: Medium/R: Medium	26	40m 49.981s
14	Augusto Fernandez	SPA 37	Red Bull GASGAS Tech3	KTM RC16	F: Hard/R: Medium	26	40m 50.085s
15	Miguel Oliveira	POR 88	Trackhouse Racing	Aprilia RS-GP24	F: Hard/R: Medium	26	40m 51.643s
16	Takaaki Nakagami	JPN 30	IDEMITSU Honda LCR	Honda RC213V	F: Medium/R: Medium	26	40m 53.460s
17	Luca Marini	ITA 10	Repsol Honda Team	Honda RC213V	F: Medium/R: Medium	26	41m 18.151s
	Pedro Acosta	SPA 31	Red Bull GASGAS Tech3	KTM RC16	F: Hard/R: Soft	25	DNF-crash
	Joan Mir	SPA 36	Repsol Honda Team	Honda RC213V	F: Medium/R: Medium	6	DNF-crash
	Marco Bezzecchi	ITA 72	Pertamina Enduro VR46 Racing	Ducati Desmosedici GP23	F: Hard/R: Medium	5	DNF-crash
	Alex Rins	SPA 42	Monster Energy Yamaha MotoGP	Yamaha YZR-M1	F: Hard/R: Medium	0	DNF-crash
	Aleix Espargaro	SPA 41	Aprilia Racing	Aprilia RS-GP24	–	–	DNS-injured
	Lorenzo Savadori	ITA 32	Aprilia Racing	Aprilia RS-GP24	–	–	DNS-injured

*Vinales 1 position penalty - track limits on last lap. ** Marc Marquez 16s penalty - technical infringement.

Fastest lap: Francesco Bagnaia, on lap 12, 1m 31.866s, 110.5mph/177.9km/h.
Lap record: Aleix Espargaro, 1m 32.500s, 109.8mph/176.7km/h (2022).
Event maximum speed: Aleix Espargaro, 196.5mph/316.2km/h (Sprint).

Qualifying: Weather: Dry Air: 21° Humidity: 50% Track: 39°
1 Bagnaia 1m 30.540s, 2 Martin* 1m 30.621s, 3 Vinales 1m 30.951s, 4 A. Marquez 1m 30.979s, 5 A. Espargaro 1m 31.077s, 6 Di Giannantonio 1m 31.274s, 7 M. Marquez 1m 31.378s, 8 Morbidelli 1m 31.405s, 9 Binder 1m 31.479s, 10 Acosta 1m 31.482s, 11 Bastianini 1m 31.628s, 12 R. Fernandez 1m 31.928s.
Q1: 13 Quartararo 1m 31.620s, 14 Miller 1m 31.903s, 15 Bezzecchi 1m 31.997s, 15 Bezzecchi 1m 31.997s, 16 Rins 1m 32.108s, 17 Oliveira 1m 32.123s, 18 Savadori 1m 32.243s, 19 Zarco 1m 32.260s, 20 Mir 1m 32.497s, 21 Marini 1m 32.627s, 22 A. Fernandez 1m 32.669s, 23 Nakagami 1m 33.030s.
*Jorge Martin three-place grid penalty for the grand prix.

SPRINT RACE: 13 laps, 36.689 miles/59.046km
WEATHER: Dry (air 25°, humidity 40%, track 49°)

Pos.	Rider	Race tyre choice	Laps	Time & speed
1	Francesco Bagnaia	F: Hard/R: Soft	13	19m 58.090s 110.2mph/177.4km/h
2	Jorge Martin	F: Hard/R: Soft	13	20m 00.445s
3	Maverick Vinales	F: Hard/R: Soft	13	20m 02.193s
4	Enea Bastianini	F: Hard/R: Soft	13	20m 04.467s
5	Fabio Di Giannantonio	F: Hard/R: Soft	13	20m 06.959s
6	Brad Binder	F: Hard/R: Soft	13	20m 07.817s
7	Fabio Quartararo	F: Hard/R: Soft	13	20m 08.918s
8	Alex Marquez*	F: Hard/R: Soft	13	20m 11.286s
9	Franco Morbidelli	F: Medium/R: Soft	13	20m 11.650s
10	Pedro Acosta	F: Hard/R: Soft	13	20m 14.062s
11	Marco Bezzecchi	F: Hard/R: Soft	13	20m 14.126s
12	Miguel Oliveira	F: Hard/R: Medium	13	20m 14.172s
13	Jack Miller	F: Hard/R: Soft	13	20m 16.829s
14	Joan Mir	F: Medium/R: Soft	13	20m 19.881s
15	Augusto Fernandez	F: Hard/R: Soft	13	20m 20.540s
16	Johann Zarco	F: Medium/R: Medium	13	20m 21.780s
17	Raul Fernandez	F: Hard/R: Soft	13	20m 22.520s
18	Takaaki Nakagami	F: Medium/R: Soft	13	20m 27.658s
19	Alex Rins	F: Medium/R: Soft	13	21m 21.643s
	Aleix Espargaro	F: Hard/R: Soft	12	DNF-crash
	Lorenzo Savadori	F: Hard/R: Soft	4	DNF-crash
	Luca Marini	F: Hard/R: Soft	4	DNF-technical
	Marc Marquez	F: Hard/R: Soft	1	DNF-crash

Fastest race lap: Francesco Bagnaia, on lap 2, 1m 31.698s.
*Alex Marquez 3s penalty - failed to comply with long-lap.

Fastest race laps
1 Bagnaia 1m 31.866s, 2 Martin 1m 31.919s, 3 Di Giannantonio 1m 32.099s, 4 Bastianini 1m 32.160s, 5 M. Marquez 1m 32.184s, 6 Vinales 1m 32.231s, 7 Acosta 1m 32.253s, 8 Binder 1m 32.344s, 9 A. Marquez 1m 32.541s, 10 Miller 1m 32.702s, 11 Oliveira 1m 32.728s, 12 R. Fernandez 1m 32.746s, 13 Morbidelli 1m 32.783s, 14 Quartararo 1m 32.796s, 15 A. Fernandez 1m 33.191s, 16 Marini 1m 33.259s, 17 Zarco 1m 33.316s, 18 Mir 1m 33.374s, 19 Nakagami 1m 33.412s, 20 Bezzecchi 1m 33.583s.

Grid order / Lap chart

Grid order	1	2	3	4	5	6	7	8	9	10	11	12	13	14	15	16	17	18	19	20	21	22	23	24	25	26
1 BAGNAIA	1	1	1	1	1	1	1	1	1	1	1	1	1	1	1	1	1	1	1	1	1	1	1	1	1	1
12 VINALES*	89	89	89	89	89	89	89	89	89	89	89	89	89	89	89	89	89	89	89	89	89	89	89	89	89	2
73 A. MARQUEZ	12	93	93	93	93	93	49	49	49	49	49	49	49	49	49	12	12	12	23	23	23	23	23	23		3
49 DI GIANNANTONIO	93	12	12	12	12	49	49	93	93	93	93	93	93	93	93	93	93	23	12	12	12	12	12	93		4
89 MARTIN	73	31	31	49	49	12	12	12	12	12	12	12	12	12	49	23	93	93	93	93	93	93	12			5
93 M. MARQUEZ**	21	73	49	31	31	31	31	31	31	31	31	31	31	31	23	49	49	49	49	49	49	49				6
21 MORBIDELLI	31	49	73	73	73	73	73	23	23	23	23	23	23	23	23	31	31	31	31	31	31	31	33			7
33 BINDER	49	33	33	33	33	33	33	73	33	33	33	33	33	33	33	33	33	33	33	33	33	33	73			8
31 ACOSTA	33	23	23	23	23	23	33	33	73	73	73	73	73	73	73	73	73	73	73	73	73	73	25			9
23 BASTIANINI	23	25	25	25	25	25	25	25	25	25	25	25	25	25	25	25	25	25	25	25	25	25	21			10
25 R. FERNANDEZ	25	21	21	43	43	21	21	21	21	21	21	21	21	21	21	21	21	21	21	21	21	21	43			11
20 QUARTARARO	43	43	43	21	21	43	43	43	43	43	43	43	43	43	43	43	43	43	43	43	43	43	20			12
43 MILLER	20	20	20	88	20	20	20	20	20	20	20	20	20	20	20	20	20	20	20	20	20	20	5			13
72 BEZZECCHI	88	88	88	20	88	88	88	88	88	88	88	88	88	37	37	37	37	37	37	37	37	37	37			14
42 RINS	72	72	72	36	36	36	5	5	5	5	5	5	37	5	5	5	5	5	5	5	5	5	88			15
88 OLIVEIRA	36	36	36	5	5	5	37	37	37	37	37	37	5	5	88	88	30	88	88	88	88	88	30			
5 ZARCO	5	5	5	37	37	37	30	30	30	30	30	30	88	30	30	30	88	30	30	30	30	30	10			
36 MIR	10	30	30	30	30	30	10	10	10	10	10	10	30	10	10	10	10	10	10	10	10	10	10			
10 MARINI	37	37	37	72	10	10																				
37 A. FERNANDEZ	30	10	10	10	72																					
30 NAKAGAMI																										

VINALES* finished 5th on the road – placed 5th after 1-position penalty for exceeding track limits on final lap and Marquez penalty.
M. MARQUEZ** finished 3rd on the road – placed 10th after a 16s penalty for technical infringement.

Championship Points

1	Martin	135 (65)	200
2	Bagnaia	152 (38)	190
3	M. Marquez	88 (54)	142
4	Bastianini	107 (29)	136
5	Vinales	72 (46)	118
6	Acosta	63 (38)	101
7	Binder	82 (17)	99
8	Di Giannantonio	77 (15)	92
9	A. Espargaro	50 (32)	82
10	A. Marquez	55 (7)	62
11	Bezzecchi	44 (1)	45
12	R. Fernandez	38 (2)	40
13	Morbidelli	30 (9)	39
14	Quartararo	26 (13)	39
15	Miller	19 (13)	32
16	Oliveira	30 (2)	32
17	A. Fernandez	12 (3)	15
18	Mir	12 (1)	13
19	Zarco	12 (0)	12
20	Rins	8 (0)	8
21	Nakagami	8 (0)	8
22	Pedrosa	0 (7)	7

Constructor Points

1	Ducati	191 (87)	278
2	Aprilia	92 (64)	156
3	KTM	103 (51)	154
4	Yamaha	34 (9)	43
5	Honda	21 (1)	22

MOTO2: RACE DISTANCE: 22 laps, 62.090 miles/99.924km
RACE WEATHER: Dry (air 22°, humidity 52%, track 40°)

Pos.	Rider	Nat.	No.	Entrant	Machine	Laps	Time & Speed
1	Ai Ogura	JPN	79	MT Helmets - MSI	Boscoscuro	22	35m 27.293s
							105.1mph/169.1km/h
2	Fermin Aldeguer	SPA	54	Folladore SpeedUp	Boscoscuro	22	35m 27.864s
3	Sergio Garcia	SPA	3	MT Helmets - MSI	Boscoscuro	22	35m 31.545s
4	Jake Dixon	GBR	96	CFMOTO Inde Aspar Team	Kalex	22	35m 36.278s
5	Somkiat Chantra	THA	35	IDEMITSU Honda Team Asia	Kalex	22	35m 37.242s
6	Tony Arbolino	ITA	14	Elf Marc VDS Racing Team	Kalex	22	35m 37.362s
7	Marcos Ramirez	SPA	24	OnlyFans American Racing	Kalex	22	35m 39.781s
8	Alonso Lopez	SPA	21	Folladore SpeedUp	Boscoscuro	22	35m 39.885s
9	Manuel Gonzalez	SPA	18	QJMOTOR Gresini Moto2	Kalex	22	35m 40.027s
10	Celestino Vietti	ITA	13	Red Bull KTM Ajo	Kalex	22	35m 40.279s
11	Senna Agius	AUS	81	Liqui Moly Husqvarna Intact	Kalex	22	35m 40.238s
12	Dennis Foggia	ITA	71	Italtrans Racing Team	Kalex	22	35m 41.982s
13	Jeremy Alcoba	SPA	52	Yamaha VR46 Master Camp	Kalex	22	35m 44.340s
14	Bo Bendsneyder	NED	64	Preicanos Racing Team	Kalex	22	35m 44.916s
15	Darryn Binder	RSA	15	Liqui Moly Husqvarna Intact	Kalex	22	35m 50.296s
16	Diogo Moreira	BRA	10	Italtrans Racing Team	Kalex	22	35m 50.815s
17	Barry Baltus	BEL	7	RW-Idrofoglia Racing GP	Kalex	22	35m 56.935s
18	Marcel Schrotter	GER	32	Red Bull KTM Ajo	Kalex	22	36m 00.528s
19	Izan Guevara	SPA	28	CFMOTO Inde Aspar Team	Kalex	22	36m 00.604s
20	Daniel Munoz	SPA	17	Preicanos Racing Team	Kalex	22	36m 09.954s
21	Alex Escrig	SPA	11	KLINT Forward Factory Team	Forward	22	36m 17.816s
22	Mario Aji	INA	34	IDEMITSU Honda Team Asia	Kalex	22	36m 19.324s
23	Xavier Artigas	SPA	43	KLINT Forward Factory Team	Forward	22	36m 19.762s
24	Jaume Masia	SPA	5	Preicanos Racing Team	Kalex	22	36m 19.824s
	Ayumu Sasaki	JPN	22	Yamaha VR46 Master Camp	Kalex	7	DNF-crash
	Aron Canet	SPA	44	Fantic Racing	Kalex	5	DNF-crash
	Albert Arenas	SPA	75	QJMOTOR Gresini Moto2	Kalex	5	DNF-crash
	Zonta van den Goorbergh	NED	84	RW-Idrofoglia Racing GP	Kalex	4	DNF-crash

Fastest lap: Sergio Garcia, on lap 8, 1m 35.977s, 105.8mph/170.3km/h.
Lap record: Raul Fernandez, 1m 36.690s, 105.1mph/169.1km/h (2021).
Event maximum speed: Izan Guevara, 165.0mph/265.5km/h (race).

Qualifying
Weather: Dry
Air: 24° **Humidity:** 42% **Track:** 50°

1	Aldeguer	1m 35.269s
2	Ogura	1m 35.499s
3	Garcia	1m 35.623s
4	Gonzalez	1m 35.640s
5	Lopez	1m 35.745s
6	Arenas	1m 35.824s
7	Arbolino	1m 35.873s
8	Moreira	1m 35.901s
9	Dixon	1m 35.983s
10	Vietti	1m 36.046s
11	Agius	1m 36.130s
12	Ramirez	1m 36.139s
13	Canet	1m 36.157s
14	V d Goorbergh	1m 36.163s
15	Binder	1m 36.271s
16	Alcoba	1m 36.361s
17	Chantra	1m 36.396s
18	Guevara	No Time
Q1		
19	Foggia	1m 36.237s
20	Bendsneyder	1m 36.284s
21	Munoz	1m 36.393s
22	Schrotter	1m 36.655s
23	Baltus	1m 36.682s
24	Sasaki	1m 36.799s
25	Aji	1m 36.920s
26	Masia	1m 37.252s
27	Artigas	1m 37.254s
28	Escrig	1m 37.595s

Fastest race laps

1	Garcia	1m 35.977s
2	Aldeguer	1m 35.985s
3	Ogura	1m 36.098s
4	Lopez	1m 36.161s
5	Chantra	1m 36.261s
6	Canet	1m 36.317s
7	Gonzalez	1m 36.325s
8	Vietti	1m 36.375s
9	Dixon	1m 36.386s
10	Arbolino	1m 36.402s
11	Ramirez	1m 36.407s
12	Agius	1m 36.436s
13	Moreira	1m 36.503s
14	Alcoba	1m 36.588s
15	Foggia	1m 36.602s
16	Bendsneyder	1m 36.615s
17	Arenas	1m 36.669s
18	Binder	1m 36.742s
19	Baltus	1m 36.771s
20	V d Goorbergh	1m 36.787s
21	Munoz	1m 37.311s
22	Guevara	1m 37.439s
23	Schrotter	1m 37.517s
24	Masia	1m 37.754s
25	Escrig	1m 37.858s
26	Sasaki	1m 37.987s
27	Artigas	1m 38.011s
28	Aji	1m 38.067s

Championship Points

1	Garcia	138
2	Ogura	124
3	Roberts	115
4	Lopez	87
5	Aldeguer	83
6	Gonzalez	73
7	Canet	58
8	Arenas	48
9	Alcoba	46
10	Chantra	46
11	Ramirez	44
12	Vietti	44
13	Arbolino	43
14	Dixon	33
15	Baltus	23
16	Agius	21
17	Guevara	18
18	Foggia	14
19	Salac	14
20	Van den Goorbergh	13
21	Moreira	7
22	Navarro	6
23	Oncu	6
24	Binder	6
25	Bendsneyder	4
26	Masia	3
27	Aji	2
28	Ferrari	1

Constructor Points

1	Boscoscuro	179
2	Kalex	152
3	Forward	6

MOTO3: RACE DISTANCE: 20 laps, 56.445 miles/90.840km
RACE WEATHER: Dry (air 20°, humidity 61%, track 34°)

Pos.	Rider	Nat.	No.	Entrant	Machine	Laps	Time & Speed
1	Ivan Ortola	SPA	48	MT Helmets - MSI	KTM	20	33m 45.971s
							100.3mph/161.4km/h
2	Collin Veijer	NED	95	Liqui Moly Husqvarna Intact GP	Husqvarna	20	33m 45.983s
3	David Munoz	SPA	64	BOE Motorsports	KTM	20	33m 48.168s
4	Jose Antonio Rueda	SPA	99	Red Bull KTM Ajo	KTM	20	33m 48.401s
5	David Alonso	COL	80	CFMOTO Gaviota Aspar Team	CFMOTO	20	33m 48.431s
6	Luca Lunetta	ITA	58	SIC58 Squadra Corse	Honda	20	33m 48.458s
7	Adrian Fernandez	SPA	31	Leopard Racing	Honda	20	33m 48.502s
8	Angel Piqueras	SPA	36	Leopard Racing	Honda	20	33m 48.660s
9	Stefano Nepa	ITA	82	LEVELUP - MTA	KTM	20	33m 48.848s
10	Ryusei Yamanaka	JPN	6	MT Helmets - MSI	KTM	20	33m 48.903s
11	Daniel Holgado	SPA	96	Red Bull GASGAS Tech3	GASGAS	20	33m 51.038s
12	Joel Kelso	AUS	66	BOE Motorsports	KTM	20	33m 55.391s
13	Taiyo Furusato	JPN	72	Honda Team Asia	Honda	20	34m 05.987s
14	Jacob Roulstone	AUS	12	Red Bull GASGAS Tech3	GASGAS	20	34m 13.839s
15	Joel Esteban	SPA	78	CFMOTO Gaviota Aspar Team	CFMOTO	20	34m 13.911s
16	Nicola Carraro	ITA	10	LEVELUP - MTA	KTM	20	34m 14.111s
17	Scott Ogden	GBR	19	MLav Racing	Honda	20	34m 14.172s
18	Riccardo Rossi	ITA	54	CIP Green Power	KTM	20	34m 14.232s
19	Xabi Zurutuza	SPA	85	Red Bull KTM Ajo	KTM	20	34m 17.073s
20	Tatchakorn Buasri	THA	5	Honda Team Asia	Honda	20	34m 18.417s
21	Matteo Bertelle	ITA	18	Kopron Rivacold Snipers Team	Honda	20	34m 19.702s
22	Filippo Farioli	ITA	7	SIC58 Squadra Corse	Honda	20	34m 19.849s
23	Noah Dettwiler	SWI	55	CIP Green Power	KTM	20	34m 34.277s
24	Joshua Whatley	GBR	70	MLav Racing	Honda	20	34m 38.815s
	David Almansa	SPA	22	Kopron Rivacold Snipers Team	Honda	14	DNF-crash
	Tatsuki Suzuki	JPN	24	Liqui Moly Husqvarna Intact GP	Husqvarna	2	DNF-crash

Fastest lap: Adrian Fernandez, on lap 3, 1m 40.405s, 101.2mph/162.8km/h.
Lap record: John McPhee, 1m 41.190s, 100.4mph/161.5km/h (2022).
Event maximum speed: Daniel Holgado, 138.5mph/222.9km/h (race).

Qualifying:
Weather: Dry
Air: 23° **Humidity:** 45% **Track:** 49°

1	Piqueras	1m 39.746s
2	Furusato	1m 39.820s
3	Veijer	1m 40.055s
4	Ortola	1m 40.073s
5	Yamanaka	1m 40.113s
6	Nepa	1m 40.146s
7	Rueda	1m 40.189s
8	Fernandez	1m 40.254s
9	Esteban	1m 40.284s
10	Lunetta	1m 40.298s
11	Munoz	1m 40.379s
12	Kelso	1m 40.392s
13	Alonso	1m 40.457s
14	Kelso	1m 40.468s
15	Holgado	1m 40.476s
16	Bertelle	1m 40.735s
17	Ogden	1m 41.139s
18	Almansa	1m 41.570s
Q1		
19	Rossi	1m 41.028s
20	Roulstone	1m 41.063s
21	Zurutuza	1m 41.152s
22	Carraro	1m 41.497s
23	Farioli	1m 41.548s
24	Whatley	1m 42.025s
25	Dettwiler	1m 42.264s
26	Buasri	1m 42.411s

Fastest race laps

1	Fernandez	1m 40.405s
2	Munoz	1m 40.477s
3	Ortola	1m 40.501s
4	Rueda	1m 40.510s
5	Yamanaka	1m 40.523s
6	Alonso	1m 40.528s
7	Holgado	1m 40.561s
8	Piqueras	1m 40.610s
9	Veijer	1m 40.633s
10	Furusato	1m 40.658s
11	Lunetta	1m 40.692s
12	Kelso	1m 40.702s
13	Nepa	1m 40.711s
14	Suzuki	1m 40.861s
15	Ogden	1m 41.373s
16	Roulstone	1m 41.397s
17	Bertelle	1m 41.443s
18	Farioli	1m 41.605s
19	Esteban	1m 41.675s
20	Carraro	1m 41.686s
21	Almansa	1m 41.781s
22	Zurutuza	1m 41.845s
23	Rossi	1m 41.902s
24	Buasri	1m 41.972s
25	Dettwiler	1m 42.201s
26	Whatley	1m 42.347s

Championship Points

1	Alonso	154
2	Veijer	115
3	Holgado	111
4	Ortola	105
5	Munoz	76
6	Yamanaka	62
7	Rueda	58
8	Fernandez	54
9	Kelso	50
10	Piqueras	49
11	Roulstone	44
12	Esteban	36
13	Nepa	36
14	Furusato	34
15	Lunetta	34
16	Suzuki	31
17	Rossi	16
18	Carraro	15
19	Bertelle	14
20	Farioli	11
21	Ogden	5
22	Zurutuza	3
23	Perez	3
24	Dettwiler	2
25	Almansa	2

Constructor Points

1	CFMOTO	154
2	KTM	138
3	Husqvarna	125
4	GASGAS	116
5	Honda	90

FIM WORLD CHAMPIONSHIP • ROUND 9

GERMAN GRAND PRIX
SACHSENRING CIRCUIT

Main: Bagnaia took an early lead in the feature race, heading Martin, Morbidelli, Oliveira and Alex Marquez at the start of lap two.

Inset: Martin would regain control – only to crash out.
Photos: Gold & Goose

Above: Three into one – Bagnaia, Oliveira and Martin in the sprint.

Top left: Brotherly love. Alex and Marc Marquez shared the podium for the first time.

Top centre: Remy Gardner filled in for the injured Rins at Monster Yamaha.

Top right: Oliveira celebrates second in the sprint.

Above right: A front-row start for Raul Fernandez.

Right: Two for Nakagami and one for Marini in a Honda battle for the final points.

Photos: Gold & Goose

MARC MARQUEZ couldn't retain his perfect Sachsenring record – winning every race he started in every class, but neither did he willingly concede the throne. Bagnaia might have taken a fourth win in a row, but Marc was second, having shrugged off painful injuries after a very fast crash on Friday to blaze through from the fifth row of the grid. It was heroic.

His crash was one of several at the notorious Ralf Waldmann curve – first right-hander after a series of seven increasingly rapid lefts. Riders tip on to the well-cooled right side of the tyre at around 180mph. Mostly they get away with it, thanks to dual-compound front tyres (a development directly triggered by this corner). When they don't, the consequences are in the lap of the gods.

Marc's crash was particularly nasty – a vicious high-side after he had tried, but failed to save the front-end slip with his knee, in trademark style. Had he let it go, he might have escaped injury – as did Bezzecchi and Bastianini at the same spot in the same session. But he had his reasons, in the sole session deciding automatic entry into Q2: "I went out with a bike that was supposed to be the good one, but had a mechanical problem. We switched the tyres to the other bike, and the tyre temperature became colder and colder. I tried to save it, because I knew that the other bike was not ready. If not, at that point, you just jump from the bike and that's it."

His only actual fracture was to the index finger of his left hand (painful enough to make riding difficult), but the heavy thump injured his ribs. In 2023, he had withdrawn from this race after a succession of crashes; this time, he suffered further misfortune when baulked on his fast Q1 lap by slowing Honda wild-card Stefan Bradl, missing the cut for Q2. He hailed second place as being "as good as a win".

This crash, another nasty fall for Vinales, plus a number of others in other classes raised the question once again of whether Sachsenring's cramped confines are fit for MotoGP. Bradl baulking Marc wasn't really his fault, just a function of too many tight corners in too small a space. In MotoE, a collision in the same spot – Turns One/Two – brought out the red flag, but luckily caused no serious injury, then triggered the absurdity of perpetrator Oscar Gutierrez having two more long-laps added to two already incurred, making four long-laps in a shortened five-lapper (he fell off anyway). Equally absurd, 16 riders, more than half the Moto3 field, were pulled up for slow riding in qualifying – proof positive that the punishment system is not an effective deterrent. The worrying part, with 14 long-lap penalties to be served, was that the punishment loop fed riders at slow speed directly back on to the racing line for the final-corner exit, there being no space for a better long-lap anywhere else. There was at least one very, very close call, making the punishment more dangerous than the crime.

Bagnaia laid some ghosts of his own. In 2022, he'd left in despair, after throwing away his chances; in 2023, Martin had added a Sunday win to his sprint in an inch-close last-corner fight. On this occasion, Bagnaia watched the same rider emulate his own 2022 Turn One crash. Martin lost a lead that had shrunk alarmingly in the closing stages, denying fans (said Bagnaia) another tough last-lap fight. And handing the defending champion the lead on points, for the first time since March.

For his part, Martin admitted a summer of soul searching lay ahead: "It's time to learn from this. I think my Jerez and Mugello crashes were completely the same, so there is something: I don't know if it's my style … in my head. Something is making me crash. So I need to take time and analyse, learn and get back up."

Vinales's crash occurred on Saturday at Turn Ten. With Espargaro and Savadori injured, he was the sole factory Aprilia rider at a track where the RS-GP performed well. It was left to the Trackhouse satellite team, where Oliveira made the most of it, with a front-row start (team-mate Raul Fernandez alongside) and a Saturday podium.

Rins was also off injured, Yamaha Superbike rider Remy Gardner in his place, testing, among other things, a revised pre-selector ride-height system.

Out of the limelight, there was interesting contract news. First, that Aleix Espargaro had signed to become HRC's second official test rider, alongside Bradl; second, that KTM technical director Fabiano Sterlacchini had quit. The Italian had been a high-profile recruit from Ducati in 2021, where he had been Gigi Dall'Igna's right-hand man. They were parting on friendly terms insisted motorsport director Pit Beirer, describing "a stormy week for us". Sterlacchini's contract had been up for renewal and "we were working on a new three-year contract. But at the end, we couldn't agree on some things. For him, the distance from his home was one part … we mutually agreed to split up."

MOTOGP SPRINT RACE – 15 laps

The all-time record fell to Vinales on Friday, and again to Martin on Saturday, for his fourth pole of the year. The Aprilias of Oliveira and Raul Fernandez were alongside; Bagnaia led row two from Alex Marquez and Morbidelli, with the battered Vinales next. Marc Marquez was 13th, having failed to escape from Q1 after Raul Fernandez and Bezzecchi had knocked him off the top.

Martin led away from Oliveira, but Bagnaia went around both at Turn One, shuffling Martin to third.

Next time into the first corner, Martin pushed past into second, and on the following occasion, passed Bagnaia to lead briefly, the Italian moving back inside on the exit. Not to be denied, a daring inside swoop at Turn Eight put the Spaniard in front for good. Then Bagnaia lost second to Oliveira into the last corner.

Close behind, Vinales had stolen fourth from Fernandez, with Bastianini following him through, Fernandez soon losing more places as his front tyre pressure soared.

Bastianini was ahead of Vinales on lap four and closed up to make a leading quartet. He was pressing Bagnaia hard by the end, but Oliveira held both at bay, while Martin escaped in the closing laps to win by six-tenths.

Another five seconds away, Morbidelli had won a mid-race skirmish with Vinales, who lost another place on the final lap to the steadily advancing Marc Marquez.

Binder remained clear of Alex Marquez by a couple of tenths; the Spaniard had seen off Acosta in the early stages and he secured the last point better than 1.5 seconds clear of Bezzecchi.

Acosta had been ahead of the Italian, but ran off and dropped to last after locking the front. Miller was narrowly ahead of Di Giannantonio; Quartararo next, with the fading Raul Fernandez dropping to 14th in the last three laps, a tenth ahead of Marini on the best Honda.

There were no crashes; Remy Gardner took 20th off Mir on the last lap.

MOTOGP RACE – 30 laps

Martin grabbed early control from surprise front-row starter Oliveira, with Bagnaia jumping a place to sit third. Keen to avoid his failings of the previous day, he pounced on Oliveira for second at Turn 13, before passing Martin at the same spot on the second lap.

Morbidelli, Alex Marquez, Vinales, Raul Fernandez and Marc Marquez followed. The last named gained four places on the first lap and passed Bastianini on the second.

Martin studied his chief rival for five laps, then regained the initiative at Turn One on lap seven. Soon he was trying to stretch his lead. To the surprise of all, it was team-mate Morbidelli who went with him initially, thanks to neat first-corner moves on Oliveira, on lap three, and Bagnaia, on the ninth.

At this point, Bagnaia appeared to be in trouble. An off-track excursion at Turn Eight for Vinales on lap seven, and Fernandez losing places steadily had cut two from the pursuing pack, but Alex Marquez and Oliveira were still snapping impatiently at his heels, and as he dropped seven-tenths behind Morbidelli, Marquez was catching up.

It was soon clear, however, that Bagnaia was sticking ably to a plan. "I decided to slow down a bit," he said, to preserve his rear tyre. By lap 15, half-distance, Morbidelli had encountered tyre problems of his own, and his compatriot was able to ease under him at Turn 12 for second. With Martin now 1.2 seconds ahead, his target was clear. He'd taken three-tenths back on lap 17, and another two by lap 25. He was edging ever closer by lap 29, having got to within half a second when he watched Martin tuck the front and slide off into the gravel. "For sure, this is the best way to go with a big smile into the summer," he beamed soon after – his wedding scheduled during the three-weekend break.

Behind, Alex Marquez had stolen third off Morbidelli by lap 17, just as Marc Marquez and Bastianini relegated Oliveira to seventh, making it an all-Ducati top six. Marc's progress didn't end there, however, in spite of contact with Morbidelli exiting Turn One causing his airbag to inflate. That only fired him up all the more: "After that, I said, 'Now it's time to go!'"

He fought off Bastianini's first-corner attack on lap 23, then disposed of Morbidelli at Turn 13 with six laps to go, before catching and cruising past his younger brother – at one point 1.8 seconds ahead – on the penultimate circuit. "If you said to me on Thursday, 'You won't win, but you'll share the podium with your brother,' I would've said, 'Okay!'" Marc said.

It was an additional footnote to history – their first time together in the top three was the first time siblings had

Above: Marquez, screen broken after an air-bag-inflating collision, congratulates winner Bagnaia.

Top right: Pre-season Moto2 title favourite Aldeguer shrugged of his lows with a first win in five races.

Above right: Taiyo Furusato had to be content with second in Moto3.

Above far right: Under-performing Celestino Vietti took a surprise pole in Moto2.

Right: Alonso leads Rueda, Ortola and Furusato. Leopard Honda pair Piqueras and Fernandez give chase.

Photos: Gold & Goose

shared a premier-class podium since brothers Nobuatsu and Takuma Aoki at Imola in 1997.

Combined with Martin's unscheduled exit, this added to a breathless finale, with Bastianini taking fourth from Morbidelli with three laps to spare. Oliveira was a season's-best sixth.

Pedro Acosta's last chance to oust Marquez as youngest-ever winner ended with seventh, after a difficult start: his ride-height device had failed to disengage, forcing him to ride the track's first three turns with the front lowered. Ending the first lap 14th, he fought through the pack to lead home Bezzecchi and Binder by a tenth, Raul Fernandez and Quartararo close behind.

Vinales was less than two seconds away, followed by a close quintet – Miller, Augusto Fernandez, Nakagami, Marini and Zarco. Then Fernandez, Zarco and Bradl were hit with 16-second tyre-pressure penalties, which promoted Marini to 15th and in the points for the first time in his maiden Repsol Honda season.

Gardner was 20th and last on the road, promoted to 19th by Bradl's time penalty; Di Giannantonio retired with tyre-pressure issues.

And Bagnaia had regained control of the championship fight, ten points ahead of Martin and 56 from Marquez.

MOTO2 RACE – 25 laps

Pirellis brought another all-time record – to Marcos Ramirez on Friday morning, then Chantra in the afternoon. But it was Vietti, through from Q1, on his first pole of the year, with Dixon and Aldeguer alongside. Rookie Agius, also from Q1, led row two from Gonzalez and Arbolino. Roberts, nursing his freshly broken collarbone, was a determined 11th, one place ahead of points leader Garcia.

An exciting race delivered a much-needed victory to Aldeguer, after his misdemeanours and misfortunes. The first half was like Moto3, with a quintet comprising the Spaniard, Vietti, Arbolino, Agius and Dixon swapping continually over the first 14 laps.

Aldeguer made the decisive move on lap 15, passing Arbolino for the lead. Three laps later, the Italian suffered a huge rear slide, which sent him way wide, allowing Vietti and Dixon through. By the time the Englishman had passed the late-braking Vietti, the leader was 1.9 seconds up the road – an advantage he held to the flag.

The drama wasn't over. He was under investigation for "a potential tyre-pressure infraction", but was cleared within the hour to celebrate a second win of the year.

The track's unique layout, notorious for torturing the left side of front and rear tyres, was always going to be tough for circuit virgins Pirelli. It was no surprise to see some names fall away later. Both Arbolino and Agius ran into serious rear tyre issues in the closing laps.

By contrast, Ogura, ninth early on, and white-hot rookie Diogo Moreira climbed through to pounce on the slowing Vietti late on for third and fourth on the final lap; Dixon a safe second ahead. For Ogura to score a podium at a historically difficult track was the strongest sign yet that his championship aspirations were to be taken seriously.

A Saturday-morning crash ruined Friday pace-setter Chantra's chances, but he fought through admirably from 17th to sixth, passing Garcia on the last lap. Third place to seventh – Ogura, Moreira, Vietti, Chantra and Garcia – was covered by just over a second.

Garcia's worst result of the year was a relief for Roberts, still grimacing when donning his leathers on Friday morning. He moved steadily forward from 12th on lap one to eighth, showing podium pace in the closing laps.

Arbolino slipped to a frustrating ninth, with Lopez a second behind, struggling with front tyre wear all weekend. Agius eventually slumped to 11th, his rear tyre so far gone by the end that it was spinning in a straight line.

A downbeat Gonzalez was next, with Alcoba and Masia taking the rest of the points, narrowly ahead of Foggia and second-time replacement Schrotter.

Canet's early title chances were dealt a major blow when he retired from 16th eight laps from the end; Garcia's lead was cut to seven over the closing Ogura; Roberts and Aldeguer were still in the hunt, 24 and 39 points adrift respectively.

MOTO3 RACE – 23 laps

Veijer came through to take pole ahead of Alonso, who had emerged unhurt from a very fast Turn 11 spill on Friday. The track showed some welcome favour to Honda riders, with rookie Luca Lunetta completing the front row, Fernandez heading the second, Ogden and Furusato leading the third.

But the main news from qualifying was sanctions for 15 of the 26-strong entry for slow riding in qualifying, with another three (Ogden, Suzuki and Furusata) on warning after a first offence. Repeat offenders Ortola, Yamanaka, Almansa and Nepa faced single long-laps; double offenders Buasri, Carraro, Rossi, Lunetta and Zurutuza double long-laps; triple offenders Farioli, Bertelle, Whatley and Esteban pit-lane starts. Fourth-timers faced disqualification, but there had been none so far.

This messed with the results for a number of riders, but didn't detract from a typical all-action race.

Veijer's tactics were clear: break away from pole position and establish an early lead. But the Dutchman tucked the front at Turn 11 on just the second lap. He remounted, but finished out of the points.

By lap four, Alonso had taken over from Munoz, but Furusato and Rueda were harrying, with eight others just behind. Rueda's challenge ended two laps from home when he crashed at Turn One. Then Furusato's late wobble through Turn 11 forestalled any final attack. Alonso won by less than two-tenths; Ortola recovered from his penalty for third.

Fernandez and Piqueras led the next group, making three Hondas in the top five. They were closely chased by Yamanaka and Holgado.

Alonso's sixth win put him 58 points clear; Ortola, Holgado and Veijer now appeared to be contesting second.

FIM WORLD CHAMPIONSHIP: ROUND 9
LIQUI MOLY MOTORRAD GRAND PRIX DEUTSCHLAND

5–7 JULY, 2024

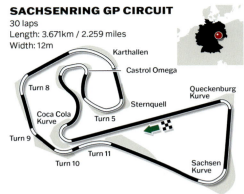

SACHSENRING GP CIRCUIT
30 laps
Length: 3.671km / 2.259 miles
Width: 12m

MOTOGP: 30 laps, 68.432 miles/110.130km
WEATHER: Dry (air 19°, humidity 41%, track 32°)

Pos.	Rider	Nat.	No.	Entrant	Machine	Race tyre choice	Laps	Time & speed
1	Francesco Bagnaia	ITA	1	Ducati Lenovo Team	Ducati Desmosedici GP24	F: Hard/R: Medium	30	40m 40.063s
								100.9mph/162.4km/h
2	Marc Marquez	SPA	93	Gresini Racing MotoGP	Ducati Desmosedici GP23	F: Hard/R: Medium	30	40m 43.867s
3	Alex Marquez	SPA	73	Gresini Racing MotoGP	Ducati Desmosedici GP23	F: Hard/R: Medium	30	40m 44.397s
4	Enea Bastianini	ITA	23	Ducati Lenovo Team	Ducati Desmosedici GP24	F: Hard/R: Medium	30	40m 45.380s
5	Franco Morbidelli	ITA	21	Prima Pramac Racing	Ducati Desmosedici GP24	F: Hard/R: Medium	30	40m 45.620s
6	Miguel Oliveira	POR	88	Trackhouse Racing	Aprilia RS-GP24	F: Hard/R: Medium	30	40m 50.544s
7	Pedro Acosta	SPA	31	Red Bull GASGAS Tech3	KTM RC16	F: Hard/R: Medium	30	40m 54.809s
8	Marco Bezzecchi	ITA	72	Pertamina Enduro VR46 Racing	Ducati Desmosedici GP23	F: Hard/R: Medium	30	40m 54.993s
9	Brad Binder	RSA	33	Red Bull KTM Factory Racing	KTM RC16	F: Hard/R: Medium	30	40m 55.147s
10	Raul Fernandez	SPA	25	Trackhouse Racing	Aprilia RS-GP23	F: Hard/R: Medium	30	40m 56.447s
11	Fabio Quartararo	FRA	20	Monster Energy Yamaha MotoGP	Yamaha YZR-M1	F: Hard/R: Medium	30	40m 57.298s
12	Maverick Vinales	SPA	12	Aprilia Racing	Aprilia RS-GP24	F: Hard/R: Medium	30	40m 58.928s
13	Jack Miller	AUS	43	Red Bull KTM Factory Racing	KTM RC16	F: Hard/R: Medium	30	41m 05.488s
14	Takaaki Nakagami	JPN	30	IDEMITSU Honda LCR	Honda RC213V	F: Hard/R: Medium	30	41m 05.880s
15	Luca Marini	ITA	10	Repsol Honda Team	Honda RC213V	F: Hard/R: Medium	30	41m 05.917s
16	Augusto Fernandez*	SPA	37	Red Bull GASGAS Tech3	KTM RC16	F: Hard/R: Medium	30	41m 21.558s
17	Johann Zarco*	FRA	5	CASTROL Honda LCR	Honda RC213V	F: Hard/R: Medium	30	41m 22.015s
18	Joan Mir	SPA	36	Repsol Honda Team	Honda RC213V	F: Hard/R: Medium	30	41m 23.208s
19	Remy Gardner	AUS	87	Monster Energy Yamaha MotoGP	Yamaha YZR-M1	F: Hard/R: Medium	30	41m 30.178s
20	Stefan Bradl*	GER	6	HRC Test Team	Honda RC213V	F: Hard/R: Medium	30	41m 39.110s
	Jorge Martin	SPA	89	Prima Pramac Racing	Ducati Desmosedici GP24	F: Hard/R: Medium	28	DNF-crash
	Fabio Di Giannantonio	ITA	49	Pertamina Enduro VR46 Racing	Ducati Desmosedici GP23	F: Hard/R: Medium	9	DNF-technical

* Augusto Fernandez, Johann Zarco, Stefan Bradl each given 16s penalties – technical infringements.

Fastest lap: Jorge Martin, on lap 6, 1m 20.667s, 101.8mph/163.8km/h.
Lap record: Johann Zarco, 1m 21.225s, 101.1mph/162.7km/h (2023).
Event maximum speed: Pedro Acosta, 190.6mph/306.8km/h (practice).

Qualifying: Weather: Dry **Air:** 26° **Humidity:** 42% **Track:** 36°

1 Martin 1m 19.423s, 2 Oliveira 1m 19.471s, 3 R. Fernandez 1m 19.643s, 4 Bagnaia 1m 19.749s, 5 A. Marquez 1m 19.791s, 6 Morbidelli 1m 19.946s, 7 Vinales 1m 19.950s, 8 Di Giannantonio 1m 19.957s, 9 Bastianini 1m 19.978s, 10 Acosta 1m 20.348s, 11 Binder 1m 20.446s, 12 Bezzecchi 1m 20.713s,
Q1: 13 M. Marquez 1m 20.263s, 14 Quartararo 1m 20.310s, 15 A. Fernandez 1m 20.419s, 16 Miller 1m 20.515s, 17 Nakagami 1m 20.553s, 18 Marini 1m 20.565s, 19 Zarco 1m 20.799s, 20 Mir 1m 21.162s, 21 Bradl* 1m 21.270s, 22 Gardner 1m 21.297s.

*Stefan Bradl three-place grid penalty for the grand prix.

SPRINT RACE: 15 laps, 34.216 miles/55.065km
WEATHER: Dry (air 30°, humidity 37%, track 43°)

Pos.	Rider	Race tyre choice	Laps	Time & speed
1	Jorge Martin	F: Hard/R: Soft	15	20m 18.904s
				101.0mph/162.6km/h
2	Miguel Oliveira	F: Hard/R: Soft	15	20m 19.580s
3	Francesco Bagnaia	F: Hard/R: Soft	15	20m 20.215s
4	Enea Bastianini	F: Hard/R: Soft	15	20m 20.362s
5	Franco Morbidelli	F: Hard/R: Soft	15	20m 24.504s
6	Marc Marquez	F: Hard/R: Soft	15	20m 25.185s
7	Maverick Vinales	F: Hard/R: Soft	15	20m 25.188s
8	Brad Binder	F: Hard/R: Soft	15	20m 27.965s
9	Alex Marquez	F: Hard/R: Soft	15	20m 28.105s
10	Marco Bezzecchi	F: Hard/R: Soft	15	20m 29.704s
11	Jack Miller	F: Hard/R: Soft	15	20m 32.719s
12	Fabio Di Giannantonio	F: Hard/R: Soft	15	20m 32.864s
13	Fabio Quartararo	F: Hard/R: Soft	15	20m 33.336s
14	Raul Fernandez	F: Hard/R: Soft	15	20m 34.233s
15	Luca Marini	F: Hard/R: Soft	15	20m 34.334s
16	Augusto Fernandez	F: Hard/R: Soft	15	20m 34.397s
17	Johann Zarco	F: Hard/R: Medium	15	20m 35.109s
18	Takaaki Nakagami	F: Hard/R: Medium	15	20m 39.225s
19	Stefan Bradl	F: Hard/R: Soft	15	20m 42.637s
20	Remy Gardner	F: Hard/R: Soft	15	20m 45.270s
21	Joan Mir	F: Hard/R: Soft	15	20m 45.572s
22	Pedro Acosta	F: Hard/R: Soft	15	20m 45.619s

Fastest race lap: Miguel Oliveira, on lap 4, 1m 20.609s.

Fastest race laps

1 Martin 1m 20.667s, 2 M. Marquez 1m 20.809s, 3 Bagnaia 1m 20.822s, 4 Morbidelli 1m 20.877s, 5 Bastianini 1m 20.881s, 6 Oliveira 1m 20.952s, 7 A. Marquez 1m 20.978s, 8 Vinales 1m 21.028s, 9 Acosta 1m 21.061s, 10 R. Fernandez 1m 21.117s, 11 Binder 1m 21.144s, 12 Di Giannantonio 1m 21.154s, 13 Bezzecchi 1m 21.158s, 14 Quartararo 1m 21.414s, 15 A. Fernandez 1m 21.441s, 16 Miller 1m 21.542s, 17 Nakagami 1m 21.575s, 18 Marini 1m 21.631s, 19 Zarco 1m 21.740s, 20 Bradl 1m 21.874s, 21 Mir 1m 21.936s, 22 Gardner 1m 22.142.

Lap Chart

Grid Order	1	2	3	4	5	6	7	8	9	10	11	12	13	14	15	16	17	18	19	20	21	22	23	24	25	26	27	28	29	30
89 MARTIN	89	1	1	1	1	1	89	89	89	89	89	89	89	89	89	89	89	89	89	89	89	89	89	89	89	89	89	89	1	1
88 OLIVEIRA	88	89	89	89	89	89	1	1	21	21	21	21	21	1	1	1	1	1	1	1	1	1	1	1	1	1	1	1	93	93
25 R. FERNANDEZ	1	88	21	21	21	21	21	21	1	1	1	1	1	21	73	73	73	73	73	73	73	73	73	73	73	73	73	73	73	73
1 BAGNAIA	73	21	88	88	73	73	73	73	73	73	73	73	73	73	21	21	21	21	21	21	21	21	21	21	93	93	93	93	23	23
73 A. MARQUEZ	21	73	73	73	88	88	88	88	88	88	88	88	88	88	93	93	93	93	93	93	93	93	93	93	21	23	23	23	21	21
21 MORBIDELLI	12	12	12	12	12	12	93	93	93	93	93	93	93	93	88	88	88	88	88	88	88	88	88	88	23	21	21	21	88	88
12 VINALES	25	25	25	25	93	93	23	23	23	23	23	23	23	23	23	23	88	88	88	88	88	88	88	88	88	88	88	88	33	31
49 DI GIANNANTONIO	23	93	93	93	25	25	25	25	25	25	25	25	25	25	25	25	25	25	25	25	25	25	31	31	31	31	31	31	72	
23 BASTIANINI	93	23	23	23	23	23	33	33	31	31	31	31	31	31	31	31	31	31	31	31	31	31	33	33	33	33	72	33		
31 ACOSTA	33	33	33	33	33	31	31	31	33	33	33	33	33	33	33	33	33	33	33	33	25	72	72	72	72	72	25	25		
33 BINDER	49	49	49	49	49	31	72	72	72	72	72	72	72	72	72	72	72	72	72	72	72	25	25	25	25	25	20	20		
72 BEZZECCHI	20	20	20	72	31	49	72	20	20	20	20	20	20	20	20	20	20	20	20	20	20	20	20	20	20	20	12	12		
93 M. MARQUEZ	72	72	72	31	72	72	20	43	43	43	37	37	37	37	37	37	37	37	37	37	12	12	12	12	12	12	43	43		
20 QUARTARARO	31	31	31	20	20	20	43	43	37	37	37	43	12	12	12	12	12	12	12	12	43	43	43	43	43	43	37	37		
37 A. FERNANDEZ*	37	43	43	43	43	43	37	37	30	30	30	30	30	12	43	43	43	43	43	43	37	37	37	37	37	37	10	30		
43 MILLER	43	37	37	37	37	37	30	30	12	12	12	12	43	30	30	30	30	30	30	30	30	10	10	10	10	10	30	10		
30 NAKAGAMI	30	30	30	30	30	30	12	12	10	10	10	10	10	43	10	10	10	10	10	10	10	30	30	30	30	30	5	5		
10 MARINI	10	10	10	10	10	12	12	10	5	5	5	5	5	10	5	5	5	5	5	5	5	5	5	5	5	5	6	6		
5 ZARCO*	36	36	36	36	36	36	5	5	36	36	36	36	36	5	36	36	36	36	36	36	36	36	36	36	36	36	36	36		
36 MIR	87	87	87	5	5	5	36	36	87	87	87	87	87	36	87	87	87	87	87	87	87	87	87	87	87	87	87	87		
87 GARDNER	6	5	5	87	87	87	87	87	6	6	6	6	6	87	6	6	6	6	6	6	6	6	6	6	6	6				
6 BRADL*	5	6	6	6	6	6	49																							

A FERNANDEZ* finished 14th on the road – placed 16th after a 16s penalty for technical infringement.
ZARCO* finished 17th on the road – placed 17th after a 16s penalty for technical infringement.
BRADL* finished 18th on the road – placed 20th after a 16s penalty for technical infringement.

Championship Points

1	Bagnaia	177	(45)	222
2	Martin	135	(77)	212
3	M. Marquez	108	(58)	166
4	Bastianini	120	(35)	155
5	Vinales	76	(49)	125
6	Acosta	72	(38)	110
7	Binder	89	(19)	108
8	Di Giannantonio	77	(15)	92
9	A. Espargaro	50	(32)	82
10	A. Marquez	71	(8)	79
11	Morbidelli	37	(18)	55
12	Bezzecchi	52	(1)	53
13	Oliveira	40	(11)	51
14	R. Fernandez	44	(2)	46
15	Quartararo	35	(9)	44
16	Miller	22	(13)	35
17	A. Fernandez	12	(3)	15
18	Mir	12	(1)	13
19	Zarco	12	(0)	12
20	Nakagami	10	(0)	10
21	Rins	8	(0)	8
22	Pedrosa	0	(7)	7
23	Marini	1	(0)	1

Constructor Points

1	Ducati	216	(99)	315
2	Aprilia	102	(73)	175
3	KTM	112	(53)	165
4	Yamaha	39	(9)	48
5	Honda	22	(1)	23

MOTO2: RACE DISTANCE: 25 laps, 57.026 miles/91.775km

RACE WEATHER: Dry (air 19°, humidity 41%, track 32°)

Pos.	Rider	Nat.	No.	Entrant	Machine	Laps	Time & Speed
1	Fermin Aldeguer	SPA	54	MB Conveyors SpeedUp	Boscoscuro	25	35m 07.384s
							97.4mph/156.7km/h
2	Jake Dixon	GBR	96	CFMOTO Polarcube Aspar Team	Kalex	25	35m 09.543s
3	Ai Ogura	JPN	79	MT Helmets - MSI	Boscoscuro	25	35m 11.802s
4	Diogo Moreira	BRA	10	Italtrans Racing Team	Kalex	25	35m 11.917s
5	Celestino Vietti	ITA	13	Red Bull KTM Ajo	Kalex	25	35m 11.927s
6	Somkiat Chantra	THA	35	IDEMITSU Honda Team Asia	Kalex	25	35m 12.035s
7	Sergio Garcia	SPA	3	MT Helmets - MSI	Boscoscuro	25	35m 12.809s
8	Joe Roberts	USA	16	OnlyFans American Racing Team	Kalex	25	35m 13.698s
9	Tony Arbolino	ITA	14	Elf Marc VDS Racing Team	Kalex	25	35m 14.402s
10	Alonso Lopez	SPA	21	MB Conveyors SpeedUp	Boscoscuro	25	35m 15.639s
11	Senna Agius	AUS	81	Liqui Moly Husqvarna Intact GP	Kalex	25	35m 16.609s
12	Manuel Gonzalez	SPA	18	QJMOTOR Gresini Moto2	Kalex	25	35m 17.087s
13	Izan Guevara	SPA	28	CFMOTO Polarcube Aspar Team	Kalex	25	35m 18.074s
14	Jeremy Alcoba	SPA	52	Yamaha VR46 Master Camp Team	Kalex	25	35m 20.194s
15	Jaume Masia	SPA	5	Preicanos Racing Team	Kalex	25	35m 21.229s
16	Dennis Foggia	ITA	71	Italtrans Racing Team	Kalex	25	35m 21.669s
17	Marcel Schrotter	GER	32	Red Bull KTM Ajo	Kalex	25	35m 21.867s
18	Marcos Ramirez	SPA	24	OnlyFans American Racing Team	Kalex	25	35m 22.412s
19	Daniel Munoz	SPA	17	Preicanos Racing Team	Kalex	25	35m 23.880s
20	Barry Baltus	BEL	7	RW-Idrofoglia Racing GP	Kalex	25	35m 24.624s
21	Albert Arenas	SPA	75	QJMOTOR Gresini Moto2	Kalex	25	35m 28.941s
22	Alex Escrig	SPA	11	KLINT Forward Factory Team	Forward	25	35m 34.457s
23	Xavier Artigas	SPA	43	KLINT Forward Factory Team	Forward	25	35m 36.735s
24	Ayumu Sasaki	JPN	22	Yamaha VR46 Master Camp Team	Kalex	25	35m 45.896s
25	Darryn Binder	RSA	15	Liqui Moly Husqvarna Intact GP	Kalex	25	36m 20.846s
	Mario Aji	INA	34	IDEMITSU Honda Team Asia	Kalex	22	DNF-crash
	Aron Canet	SPA	44	Fantic Racing	Kalex	18	DNF-ret in pit
	Zonta van den Goorbergh	NED	84	RW-Idrofoglia Racing GP	Kalex	15	DNF-ret in pit
	Roberto Garcia	SPA	31	Fantic Racing	Kalex	11	DNF-crash
	Bo Bendsneyder	NED	64	Preicanos Racing Team	Kalex	7	DNF-technical

Fastest lap: Tony Arbolino, on lap 2, 1m 23.449s, 98.4mph/158.3km/h.
Lap record: Pedro Acosta, 1m 23.673s, 98.1mph/157.9km/h (2023).
Event maximum speed: Somkiat Chantra, 162.9mph/262.1km/h (race).

Qualifying:
Weather: Dry
Air: 29° **Humidity:** 38% **Track:** 41°

1	Vietti	1m 22.778s
2	Dixon	1m 22.825s
3	Aldeguer	1m 22.905s
4	Agius	1m 22.941s
5	Gonzalez	1m 22.992s
6	Arbolino	1m 23.037s
7	Ogura	1m 23.040s
8	Moreira	1m 23.042s
9	Ramirez	1m 23.083s
10	Lopez	1m 23.127s
11	Roberts	1m 23.173s
12	Garcia	1m 23.182s
13	Guevara	1m 23.217s
14	Canet	1m 23.282s
15	Bendsneyder	1m 23.308s
16	Binder	1m 23.330s
17	Chantra	1m 23.340s
18	Foggia	1m 23.446s
Q1		
19	Masia	1m 23.367s
20	Munoz	1m 23.441s
21	Sasaki	1m 23.443s
22	Schrotter	1m 23.506s
23	Alcoba	1m 23.507s
24	Garcia	1m 23.514s
25	Aji	1m 23.589s
26	Arenas	1m 23.595s
27	Baltus	1m 24.071s
28	V d Goorbergh	1m 24.097s
29	Artigas	1m 24.181s
30	Escrig	1m 24.544s

Fastest race laps

1	Arbolino	1m 23.449s
2	Roberts	1m 23.487s
3	Gonzalez	1m 23.545s
4	Agius	1m 23.548s
5	Aldeguer	1m 23.632s
6	Ramirez	1m 23.654s
7	Chantra	1m 23.669s
8	Vietti	1m 23.674s
9	Garcia	1m 23.692s
10	Moreira	1m 23.698s
11	Dixon	1m 23.718s
12	Binder	1m 23.788s
13	Aji	1m 23.817s
14	Lopez	1m 23.842s
15	Guevara	1m 23.866s
16	Canet	1m 23.873s
17	Ogura	1m 23.894s
18	Schrotter	1m 23.991s
19	Munoz	1m 24.077s
20	Alcoba	1m 24.119s
21	Masia	1m 24.143s
22	Baltus	1m 24.163s
23	Bendsneyder	1m 24.177s
24	Foggia	1m 24.265s
25	Sasaki	1m 24.331s
26	Arenas	1m 24.366s
27	Garcia	1m 24.502s
28	Escrig	1m 24.532s
29	Artigas	1m 24.568s
30	V d Goorbergh	1m 24.738s

Championship Points

1	Garcia	147
2	Ogura	140
3	Roberts	123
4	Aldeguer	108
5	Lopez	93
6	Gonzalez	77
7	Canet	58
8	Chantra	56
9	Vietti	55
10	Dixon	53
11	Arbolino	50
12	Alcoba	48
13	Arenas	48
14	Ramirez	44
15	Agius	26
16	Baltus	23
17	Guevara	21
18	Moreira	20
19	Foggia	14
20	Salac	14
21	Van den Goorbergh	13
22	Navarro	6
23	Oncu	6
24	Binder	6
25	Masia	4
26	Bendsneyder	4
27	Aji	2
28	Ferrari	1

Constructor Points
1	Boscoscuro	204
2	Kalex	172
3	Forward	6

MOTO3: RACE DISTANCE: 23 laps, 52.464 miles/84.433km

RACE WEATHER: Dry (air 17°, humidity 42%, track 26°)

Pos.	Rider	Nat.	No.	Entrant	Machine	Laps	Time & Speed
1	David Alonso	COL	80	CFMOTO Gaviota Aspar Team	CFMOTO	23	33m 02.956s
							95.2mph/153.2km/h
2	Taiyo Furusato	JPN	72	Honda Team Asia	Honda	23	33m 03.143s
3	Ivan Ortola	SPA	48	MT Helmets - MSI	KTM	23	33m 03.295s
4	Adrian Fernandez	SPA	31	Leopard Racing	Honda	23	33m 05.318s
5	Angel Piqueras	SPA	36	Leopard Racing	Honda	23	33m 05.394s
6	Ryusei Yamanaka	JPN	6	MT Helmets - MSI	KTM	23	33m 06.742s
7	Daniel Holgado	SPA	96	Red Bull GASGAS Tech3	GASGAS	23	33m 06.825s
8	David Munoz	SPA	64	BOE Motorsports	KTM	23	33m 08.417s
9	Tatsuki Suzuki	JPN	24	Liqui Moly Husqvarna Intact GP	Husqvarna	23	33m 08.641s
10	Scott Ogden	GBR	19	MLav Racing	Honda	23	33m 08.773s
11	Joel Kelso	AUS	66	BOE Motorsports	KTM	23	33m 08.977s
12	Stefano Nepa	ITA	82	LEVELUP - MTA	KTM	23	33m 16.041s
13	Filippo Farioli	ITA	7	SIC58 Squadra Corse	Honda	23	33m 27.957s
14	Joel Esteban	SPA	78	CFMOTO Gaviota Aspar Team	CFMOTO	23	33m 28.025s
15	Matteo Bertelle	ITA	18	Kopron Rivacold Snipers Team	Honda	23	33m 28.027s
16	Xabi Zurutuza	SPA	85	Red Bull KTM Ajo	KTM	23	33m 41.745s
17	Nicola Carraro	ITA	10	LEVELUP - MTA	KTM	23	33m 42.133s
18	Collin Veijer	NED	95	Liqui Moly Husqvarna Intact GP	Husqvarna	23	33m 42.343s
19	Riccardo Rossi	ITA	54	CIP Green Power	KTM	23	33m 42.206s
20	David Almansa	SPA	22	Kopron Rivacold Snipers Team	Honda	23	33m 42.390s
21	Joshua Whatley	GBR	70	MLav Racing	Honda	23	33m 42.508s
22	Tatchakorn Buasri	THA	5	Honda Team Asia	Honda	23	33m 49.847s
23	Noah Dettwiler	SWI	55	CIP Green Power	KTM	23	34m 11.223s
	Jose Antonio Rueda	SPA	99	Red Bull KTM Ajo	KTM	21	DNF-crash
	Luca Lunetta	ITA	58	SIC58 Squadra Corse	Honda	19	DNF-crash
	Jacob Roulstone	AUS	12	Red Bull GASGAS Tech3	GASGAS	13	DNF-crash

Fastest lap: Ivan Ortola, on lap 5, 1m 25.467s, 96.1mph/154.6km/h.
Lap record: Daniel Holgado, 1m 25.694s, 95.8mph/154.2km/h (2023).
Event maximum speed: Xabi Zurutuza, 136.6mph/219.9km/h (practice).

Qualifying:
Weather: Dry
Air: 28° **Humidity:** 39% **Track:** 43°

1	Veijer	1m 24.885s
2	Alonso	1m 25.221s
3	Lunetta	1m 25.222s
4	Fernandez	1m 25.386s
5	Rueda	1m 25.388s
6	Munoz	1m 25.430s
7	Ogden	1m 25.437s
8	Furusato	1m 25.488s
9	Suzuki	1m 25.654s
10	Nepa	1m 25.706s
11	Yamanaka	1m 25.707s
12	Ortola	1m 25.787s
13	Holgado	1m 25.811s
14	Piqueras	1m 25.932s
15	Kelso	1m 26.058s
16	Esteban	1m 26.163s
17	Roulstone	1m 26.429s
18	Bertelle	1m 26.977s
Q1		
19	Zurutuza	1m 26.757s
20	Whatley	1m 26.810s
21	Farioli	1m 26.920s
22	Rossi	1m 27.427s
23	Carraro	1m 27.560s
24	Buasri	1m 27.618s
25	Almansa	1m 27.849s
26	Dettwiler	1m 27.897s

Fastest race laps

1	Ortola	1m 25.467s
2	Piqueras	1m 25.486s
3	Yamanaka	1m 25.505s
4	Furusato	1m 25.545s
5	Rueda	1m 25.559s
6	Holgado	1m 25.597s
7	Lunetta	1m 25.606s
8	Esteban	1m 25.672s
9	Munoz	1m 25.681s
10	Roulstone	1m 25.718s
11	Kelso	1m 25.740s
12	Fernandez	1m 25.787s
13	Nepa	1m 25.821s
14	Alonso	1m 25.854s
15	Ogden	1m 25.895s
16	Suzuki	1m 25.899s
17	Farioli	1m 26.053s
18	Bertelle	1m 26.190s
19	Carraro	1m 26.206s
20	Veijer	1m 26.279s
21	Dettwiler	1m 26.539s
22	Whatley	1m 26.580s
23	Almansa	1m 26.766s
24	Rossi	1m 26.890s
25	Zurutuza	1m 26.891s
26	Buasri	1m 26.930s

Championship Points

1	Alonso	179
2	Ortola	121
3	Holgado	120
4	Veijer	115
5	Munoz	84
6	Yamanaka	72
7	Fernandez	67
8	Piqueras	60
9	Rueda	58
10	Kelso	55
11	Furusato	54
12	Roulstone	44
13	Nepa	40
14	Esteban	38
15	Suzuki	38
16	Lunetta	34
17	Rossi	16
18	Carraro	15
19	Bertelle	15
20	Farioli	14
21	Ogden	11
22	Zurutuza	3
23	Perez	3
24	Dettwiler	2
25	Almansa	2

Constructor Points
1	CFMOTO	179
2	KTM	154
3	Husqvarna	132
4	GASGAS	125
5	Honda	110

FIM WORLD CHAMPIONSHIP • ROUND 10

BRITISH GRAND PRIX

SILVERSTONE CIRCUIT

Above: Silverstone belonged to Bastianini.

Top: One man, two trophies.

Right: Bastianini donned a Mike Hailwood replica helmet for Sunday's triumph.
Photos: Ducati Corse

Left: Consulting the bible. Enea verifies that MOTOCOURSE always spells his name correctly.
Photo: Mat Oxley

CELEBRATING 75 YEARS OF RACING

Above: Martin, Bastianini and Espargaro race clear as Bagnaia falls during the sprint.
Photo: Gold & Goose

Top: Remembrance of things past: title-winning 1949 AJS is flanked by current MotoGP machines, clothed in retro liveries.

Above right: Best looking? Zarco's classic Castrol Honda.
Photos: Bryn Williams

Above far right (from top): Miller's MotoGP tenure was in doubt; Remy Gardner sported a Lawson tribute helmet; bowing out, FIM chief steward Freddie Spencer.
Photos: Gold & Goose & Repsol Honda

Right: Aleix Espargaro, 2023 winner, gave Aprilia a podium in the sprint.
Photo: Clive Challinor Motorsport Photography

RESUMPTION of racing after the summer break also concluded the first half of the season, and introduced an intriguing new phase in the championship, as Martin regained a narrow lead when Bagnaia faltered and fell in the sprint; but Bastianini came into play as a third force, with two clear wins.

Dorna chose Silverstone to celebrate 75 years of motorcycle grand prix racing. For some, it was a year late (2023 had been the 75th year) and a few dollars short. A museum display of historic bikes was impressive, but accessible only to those with a paddock pass rather than the general fans (a disappointing 42,529 there on race-day). A single AJS on the starting grid, winner of the inaugural 1949 title, was somewhat underwhelming. So, too, the absence of such historic multi-champions as Agostini, Roberts, Doohan, Rainey, Rossi *et al*.

Rather more jolly was race-day's commemorative MotoGP paintwork. Honda and Yamaha had eyecatching classic themes, faithful even to the black-on-yellow numbers of the old 500 class; Aprilia revived Max Biaggi's mid-'90s black 250 Chesterfield livery. Those with shorter histories chose other themes – KTM with a retro blue-and-white; Pramac revived Angel Nieto's 1983 red-and-black Garelli colours, including leathers and helmet for Spaniard Martin; Marc and Alex Marquez's Ducatis reprised team founder Fausto Gresini's white-and-*tricolore* Garelli paint; US team Trackhouse's Aprilia had portraits of American world champions. Ducati's red-and-white fairings echoed the Desmosedici's early days, but undermined the impression by replacing the iconic black-on-white Marlboro flanks with a sponsor-friendly white-out-of-black Lenovo block.

Rather unexpectedly, Remy Gardner – present as Yamaha test rider because Crutchlow was unfit – stuck with his '87' number, referencing father Wayne's 1987 title, but opted for a helmet design that paid tribute to his greatest rival, Eddie Lawson.

But racing is less about history, and more about the present and future. There was plenty of both at Silverstone, where the blazing heat of Friday gave way to cooler, overcast conditions that clearly suited Bastianini. In both races, his well-known ability for late pace gave him two clear wins and put him third overall, and a serious title candidate. He consigned Marquez to fourth, 2024 hopes dwindling, the senior rider admitting that at this and other fast tracks, the extra top speed of the GP24 Ducati was worth four or five seconds of race time, try as he might to extract the most from the GP23.

There were several future settlements.

Rins had renewed his Yamaha contract for 2025 and '26, but cut a sorry figure as he withdrew from the meeting, limping heavily from his Assen injuries after an otherwise benign Friday crash.

Ducati confirmed that VR46 would take over Pramac's role

as top satellite team, with a single GP25 for Di Giannantonio (had they given this bike to Marc at Gresini, their whole upheaval would have been avoided). Morbidelli would partner him, replacing Bezzecchi; Aldeguer would take Marc's place at Gresini. Meanwhile, an overtly depressed Jack Miller's future was in doubt after "a summer break without a single phone call – I think I still have more to offer in this class." His mood was reversed the next week, as a candidate for Pramac Yamaha, probably alongside Oliveira. This ended hopes that Moto2 points-leader Garcia would join the squad.

The biggest surprise was for the second Trackhouse Aprilia seat, seemingly earmarked for US rider Joe Roberts. Instead, now it would go to another Moto2 star, Ai Ogura, an unexpected choice for the American team.

The other news was also unexpected: that from 2025, 500cc GP winner Simon Crafar would take over from Freddie Spencer as chairman of the FIM stewards panel – the much-derided body that issues sanctions and penalties on behalf of Race Direction.

Crafar is a popular paddock figure, where he has filled the roles of pit-lane technical reporter, track tester and race commentator since 2018. A former SBK and GP racer, who beat Mick Doohan for his single 500 GP victory in 1998, Crafar is also active as a track instructor for both amateurs and professionals. His new role would be as risky as anything he had undertaken so far, after much outspoken criticism of Spencer. But the news was welcomed generally, with hopes that he would be willing to offer better explanations of controversial decisions.

Bagnaia, a frequent critic of the stewards, said, "It's one of the hardest jobs in the paddock, but one of the good things with Simon is we can have good dialogue with him. We speak a lot every weekend. If he can always take the same line, he could do a really good job." Jorge Martin added, "He's still riding, so he'll understand better how the bike moves."

Crafar promised a particularly tough stance on dawdling in practice, another aspect that found favour with Bagnaia, who deplored MotoGP riders setting a bad example for Moto3 when he spoke out against "ridiculous" and "unprofessional" antics in qualifying, with several riders awaiting a tow in the closing minutes. "The stewards need to be more focused about the important things and less about the things that don't matter. We are at the top of our sport … the fastest riders in the world. I don't understand why some riders need a tow."

MOTOGP SPRINT RACE – 10 laps

A recovered Espargaro, 2023's winner, took the Aprilia to his second pole and third front row of the season, with the factory Ducatis alongside. Third was Bastianini's best after a disappointing spell. Martin had led three practice sessions, and now headed the second row from Alex Marquez (from Q2) and Binder. Marc led row three, with a disappointed Vinales alongside, then Acosta, also from Q2.

Martin took an early lead from Bagnaia, but by the end of the lap, Bastianini had pushed through to second, from Espargaro and Bagnaia. Bezzecchi and Morbidelli crashed together at the first corner, the latter being blamed and sanctioned with a double long-lap for Sunday.

Marquez was seventh, behind Binder and Acosta, but ahead of both by the end of lap two. On the fifth, he was promoted to fourth, as Bagnaia slipped off, his fourth sprint no-score of the year, shortly after setting fastest lap. But Marquez, whose switch to a hard front tyre on the grid proved ill judged, couldn't close on the leading trio, and he was more than three seconds adrift when he also fell, on lap eight.

Up front, Martin had repulsed Bastianini's first attack at Copse on lap six, but succumbed at the end of the Hangar straight. That was it for the first three, over the line separated by a second apiece.

Another six seconds away, Binder held off Acosta and Alex Marquez; Miller did the same to Vinales and a closing Di Giannantonio for the last points.

MOTOGP RACE – 20 laps

Binder had a lucky escape at the start. In the middle of row two, he hit a clutch problem, those behind dodging to either side as he crawled away last, unable to finish the first lap.

Eye-catching colours apart, there wasn't a great deal worth celebrating in the race's first half, before Bastianini's inspired charge forward. Bagnaia, ignoring rain spots on the grid, had called the tune, passing Espargaro into the first corner. Martin and Bastianini also cleared the Aprilia out of Turn Four, with the Italian ahead on lap one, but Martin pushing straight past.

The pole-sitter also got back ahead of the Ducati on lap three, setting a new lap record in the process. The Marquez brothers were close, and Di Giannantonio ahead of Acosta by lap six; Miller gradually losing ground behind.

The front eight were doing more than just running line astern. Now Marquez began to nibble at Bastianini, who seemed to be struggling with Bagnaia's early pace; while a gap opened behind him as Di Giannantonio and Alex Marquez fought to and fro, the Italian eventually emerging victorious; Acosta was a close spectator.

By mid-distance, it was clear that Espargaro was suffering with fading rear grip. At the same time, Bastianini came to life, taking third on the run down to Stowe on lap 11. Immediately, he set about closing the 1.2-second gap to the Bagnaia/Martin duo up ahead.

The way he did so impressed Espargaro: "He reminded me of Dani Pedrosa on his best days. Slowing, accelerating, really, really smooth, taking care of the rear tyre. The feeling from outside is that it was very easy for him."

Out front, dictating the pace, Bagnaia had appeared comfortable. Now he was on the defensive as his front grip began to fade. Having preferred the hard compound, a temperature drop had pushed him on to the medium. Now the rare sight of the 27-year-old saving front-end slides followed. Martin took advantage to pass for the lead entering Turn Three on lap 12. After his costly Saturday crash, Bagnaia wasn't inclined to resist.

Martin was also having moments, missing his braking marker at Turn Three the following lap. Then Bagnaia saved a near crash at Turn Seven on lap 14. Bastianini was second now, just eight-tenths down.

Martin defended stoutly, but was powerless to resist as

Above: Ducati dominance. Martin heads Bagnaia and Bastianini.

Top right: Jake Dixon pounced on Aron Canet to give the home crowd a victory to cheer.

Above right: And that's his happy face…
Photos: Gold & Goose

Right: Moto3 went to the wire. Ortola leads Alonso, Veijer, Holgado, Nepa (82), Yamanaka (6) and Kelso in the race to the line.
Photo: Clive Challinor Motorsport Photography

Bastianini closed by tenths. Then, as the race edged toward a thrilling late fight, Martin's challenge was up. Starting the penultimate lap, he was wide again at Turn Three, Bastianini accepting the open space to the Spaniard's right. Seeing that the new leader was still capable of running laps inside two minutes, Martin accepted second, 1.9 seconds down. "Enea was much stronger today," he conceded. "The pace was outstanding."

The tenth different Silverstone winner in as many years, Bastianini's summer break had helped him understand "where it was possible to do something more. I was always fast enough to be on the podium, but I was always starting from behind. Not today."

Bagnaia's pace completely deserted him with three laps to go, while Marquez had passed the fading Espargaro on lap 16. He closed to within just over a second, but the race wasn't quite long enough to snatch the podium.

Di Giannantonio also passed Espargaro with two laps to go for a strong fifth – a third five-strong clean sweep for Ducati in 2024.

Alex Marquez and Bezzecchi, through in the closing laps, were ahead of Acosta on the top KTM; Morbidelli was some way back in tenth after two long-laps, gaining three places in the last four laps. His final victim was Quartararo; while Miller, in 12th, was clear of a downbeat Vinales.

The Hondas of Zarco, Marini and Nakagami were next, but Marini was docked 16 seconds and dropped three places for a tyre-pressure infringement, promoting Augusto Fernandez to the last point.

Raul Fernandez had slipped off and his bike had knocked down team-mate Oliveira on the first lap, a bad day for Trackhouse Aprilia; Mir crashed out unhurt after half-distance.

MOTO2 RACE – 17 laps

The lap record fell to Canet on Friday afternoon and again on Saturday morning, and finally for a third time to Ogura in qualifying, for his first pole of the season. Canet was alongside, then rookie Moreira, continuing to gain strength through his first season.

Vietti, Dixon and Arenas were behind. Roberts was ninth, Aldeguer 11th and Garcia an unexpected 16th, albeit barely seven-tenths down.

Surprises continued on Sunday, when Ogura fell back through the field and almost out of the points, with a rear tyre problem.

It was left to Canet to make the running, with a new race record on lap two, doggedly pursued by Dixon, shrugging off the effects of a stomach bug earlier in the weekend, as well as the memories of 2023, when he had been knocked off on the first lap.

It seemed that Roberts might make it a three-way fight. He passed Vietti on lap two and Ogura on the fifth, and was closing when he tucked the front at Turn Two on lap seven, a second no-score in three races denting his title hopes.

From there, Canet and Dixon pulled clear of a hectic fight for third by an eventual seven seconds. Canet led throughout, but Dixon was never far away, feeling that he had an edge in the track's numerous heavy braking zones. Clearly, it would come down to the final lap – often Canet's downfall.

Right on cue, about to start the final lap, Moto2's perennial bridesmaid fluffed the exit on to the start/finish straight, giving Dixon the perfect chance to pass into Turn One. Then the Spaniard missed a gear through Turn Two. He closed again through the Maggots/Becketts complex, but Dixon defend-

ed ably, if somewhat nervously, into Vale for a season's first victory by 0.17 of a second, only the fourth Briton to win on home soil since the event had moved from the Isle of Man to the mainland in 1977.

The scrap for third was wild and unpredictable. Initially, the Gresini Kalexes of Arenas and Gonzalez led a group that included Binder and Lopez. Then an inspired charge by Garcia – through from 20th after being punted off-track at the first turn – put him third with two laps to go. But a late attack by Vietti denied him the podium while earning the Italian's first of the season. He was a full second faster than anyone on the final lap.

Gonzalez was more than a second away by the end, fending off Binder, sixth equalling his career best. Alcoba took seventh from Arenas with two laps to go.

Lopez was a subdued ninth, three places clear of title hopeful Aldeguer, never comfortable at the track where he had been irresistible a year before. In between, Agius and van den Goorbergh. Bendsneyder was close, Ogura more than two seconds down, and pressured by Ramirez for the last points.

Arbolino, Chantra and Salac joined Maria and Aji on the crash list.

Garcia extended his points lead over Ogura and Roberts.

MOTO3 RACE – 15 laps

The all-time record was smashed again in practice and qualifying – three times, by Alonso, Veijer and then Ortola, with his second pole of the season. Veijer and Kelso were alongside, the Australian's second front row of the season; Alonso led the second row.

Given Alonso's 58-point lead, Ortola's title chances were all but written off, but a crucial victory on an epic last lap showed that he was still in the hunt.

Eleven riders made up the fight, with Ortola, Alonso and Veijer muscling past early leaders Kelso and Holgado with three laps to go.

Veijer had waited patiently near the back of the group before his closing moves, and the Dutchman's penultimate-lap pass on Alonso at Stowe appeared to be decisive. Then the Colombian was shuffled back behind Ortola and Holgado.

Veijer started the last lap four-tenths to the good. But halfway around, Ortola had closed up and elbowed him out of the way through Becketts. Alonso followed him past in the confusion and attacked for the lead into Stowe at the end of the straight. Ortola resisted brilliantly and stayed ahead of a seven-strong gang covered by less than six-tenths.

Alonso and Veijer were on the podium, then Holgado, Nepa, Yamanaka and Kelso.

Fernandez led the next gaggle, first and only Honda in the points, from Rueda and Suzuki. Munoz survived a first-lap tangle with rookie Roulstone for 12th, behind Bertelle. Roulstone was hit with a long-lap, spoiling his impressive second-row qualifying position.

Ogden, Piqueras and Perez tangled on the second lap, the last named remounting only to retire; Zurutuza fell out later in the race.

FIM WORLD CHAMPIONSHIP: ROUND 10
MONSTER ENERGY BRITISH GRAND PRIX
2–4 AUGUST, 2024

SILVERSTONE GRAND PRIX CIRCUIT
20 laps
Length: 5.900km / 3.670 miles
Width: 17m

MOTOGP: RACE DISTANCE: 20 laps, 73.322 miles/118.000km

WEATHER: Dry (air 18°, humidity 55%, track 30°)

Pos.	Rider	Nat.	No.	Entrant	Machine	Race tyre choice	Laps	Time & speed
1	Enea Bastianini	ITA	23	Ducati Lenovo Team	Ducati Desmosedici GP24	F: Medium/R: Medium	20	39m 51.879s 110.4mph/177.6km/h
2	Jorge Martin	SPA	89	Prima Pramac Racing	Ducati Desmosedici GP24	F: Medium/R: Medium	20	39m 53.810s
3	Francesco Bagnaia	ITA	1	Ducati Lenovo Team	Ducati Desmosedici GP24	F: Medium/R: Medium	20	39m 57.745s
4	Marc Marquez	SPA	93	Gresini Racing MotoGP	Ducati Desmosedici GP23	F: Medium/R: Medium	20	39m 58.785s
5	Fabio Di Giannantonio	ITA	49	Pertamina Enduro VR46 Racing	Ducati Desmosedici GP23	F: Medium/R: Medium	20	39m 59.615s
6	Aleix Espargaro	SPA	41	Aprilia Racing	Aprilia RS-GP24	F: Hard/R: Medium	20	40m 01.393s
7	Alex Marquez	SPA	73	Gresini Racing MotoGP	Ducati Desmosedici GP23	F: Medium/R: Medium	20	40m 01.620s
8	Marco Bezzecchi	ITA	72	Pertamina Enduro VR46 Racing	Ducati Desmosedici GP23	F: Medium/R: Medium	20	40m 05.895s
9	Pedro Acosta	SPA	31	Red Bull GASGAS Tech3	KTM RC16	F: Medium/R: Medium	20	40m 08.265s
10	Franco Morbidelli	ITA	21	Prima Pramac Racing	Ducati Desmosedici GP24	F: Medium/R: Medium	20	40m 15.488s
11	Fabio Quartararo	FRA	20	Monster Energy Yamaha MotoGP	Yamaha YZR-M1	F: Medium/R: Medium	20	40m 16.081s
12	Jack Miller	AUS	43	Red Bull KTM Factory Racing	KTM RC16	F: Medium/R: Medium	20	40m 17.646s
13	Maverick Vinales	SPA	12	Aprilia Racing	Aprilia RS-GP24	F: Medium/R: Medium	20	40m 18.630s
14	Johann Zarco	FRA	5	CASTROL Honda LCR	Honda RC213V	F: Medium/R: Medium	20	40m 18.832s
15	Takaaki Nakagami	ITA	10	Repsol Honda Team	Honda RC213V	F: Medium/R: Medium	20	40m 29.157s
16	Augusto Fernandez	JPN	30	IDEMITSU Honda LCR	KTM RC16	F: Medium/R: Medium	20	40m 29.484s
17	Luca Marini*	SPA	37	Red Bull GASGAS Tech3	Honda RC213V	F: Medium/R: Medium	20	40m 39.386s
18	Remy Gardner	AUS	87	Monster Energy Yamaha MotoGP	Yamaha YZR-M1	F: Medium/R: Medium	20	40m 51.016s
	Joan Mir	SPA	36	Repsol Honda Team	Honda RC213V	F: Medium/R: Medium	11	DNF-technical
	Brad Binder	RSA	33	Red Bull KTM Factory Racing	KTM RC16	F: Medium/R: Medium	0	DNF-technical
	Raul Fernandez	SPA	25	Trackhouse Racing	Aprilia RS-GP24	F: Hard/R: Medium	0	DNF-crash
	Miguel Oliveira	POR	88	Trackhouse Racing	Aprilia RS-GP24	F: Medium/R: Medium	0	DNF-crash

*Luca Marini 16s penalty – technical infringement.

Fastest lap: Aleix Espargaro, on lap 3, 1m 58.895s, 111.0mph/178.6km/h.
Lap record: Alex Rins, 1m 59.346s, 110.5mph/177.9km/h (2022).
Event maximum speed: Brad Binder, 211.0mph/339.6km/h (qualifying).

Qualifying: Weather: Dry **Air:** 19° **Humidity:** 73% **Track:** 30°
1 A. Espargaro 1m 57.309s, 2 Bagnaia 1m 57.517s, 3 Bastianini 1m 57.693s, 4 Martin 1m 57.734s, 5 A. Marquez 1m 57.817s, 6 Binder 1m 57.950s, 7 M. Marquez 1m 58.098s, 8 Vinales 1m 58.137s, 9 Acosta 1m 58.312s, 10 Di Giannantonio 1m 58.371s, 11 Miller 1m 58.736s, 12 Bezzecchi 1m 59.671s.
Q1: 13 Morbidelli 1m 58.599s, 14 R. Fernandez 1m 58.608s, 15 Oliveira 1m 58.655s, 16 Zarco 1m 58.730s, 17 A. Fernandez 1m 59.012s, 18 Quartararo 1m 59.092s, 19 Marini 1m 59.097s, 20 Mir 1m 59.468s, 21 Nakagami 1m 59.822s, 22 Gardner 1m 59.887s.

SPRINT RACE: 10 laps, 36.661 miles/59.000km

WEATHER: Dry (air 20°, humidity 48%, track 37°)

Pos.	Rider	Race tyre choice	Laps	Time & speed
1	Enea Bastianini	F: Medium/R: Soft	10	19m 49.929s 110.9mph/178.4km/h
2	Jorge Martin	F: Medium/R: Soft	10	19m 51.023s
3	Aleix Espargaro	F: Hard/R: Soft	10	19m 51.952s
4	Brad Binder	F: Medium/R: Soft	10	19m 58.573s
5	Pedro Acosta	F: Medium/R: Soft	10	19m 58.706s
6	Alex Marquez	F: Medium/R: Soft	10	19m 58.972s
7	Jack Miller	F: Medium/R: Medium	10	20m 01.433s
8	Maverick Vinales	F: Hard/R: Soft	10	20m 01.618s
9	Fabio Di Giannantonio	F: Medium/R: Soft	10	20m 01.757s
10	Miguel Oliveira	F: Hard/R: Soft	10	20m 03.257s
11	Fabio Quartararo	F: Medium/R: Soft	10	20m 05.302s
12	Raul Fernandez	F: Soft/R: Soft	10	20m 08.163s
13	Augusto Fernandez	F: Medium/R: Soft	10	20m 08.255s
14	Johann Zarco	F: Medium/R: Soft	10	20m 08.421s
15	Luca Marini	F: Medium/R: Soft	10	20m 08.979s
16	Joan Mir	F: Medium/R: Soft	10	20m 09.603s
17	Takaaki Nakagami	F: Soft/R: Soft	10	20m 19.231s
18	Remy Gardner	F: Medium/R: Soft	10	20m 20.999s
	Marc Marquez	F: Hard/R: Soft	9	DNF-crash
	Francesco Bagnaia	F: Medium/R: Soft	4	DNF-crash
	Marco Bezzecchi	F: Medium/R: Soft	0	DNF-crash
	Franco Morbidelli	F: Medium/R: Soft	0	DNF-crash

Fastest race lap: Francesco Bagnaia, on lap 4, 1m 58.260s.

Fastest race laps
1 A. Espargaro 1m 58.895s, 2 Bastianini 1m 59.010s, 3 Martin 1m 59.025s, 4 M. Marquez 1m 59.046s, 5 Bagnaia 1m 59.049s, 6 Di Giannantonio 1m 59.180s, 7 A. Marquez 1m 59.253s, 8 Acosta 1m 59.278s, 9 Bezzecchi 1m 59.409s, 10 Vinales 1m 59.692s, 11 Miller 1m 59.845s, 12 Morbidelli 1m 59.908s, 13 Zarco 2m 00.063s, 14 Quartararo 2m 00.065s, 15 Mir 2m 00.306s, 16 Marini 2m 00.420s, 17 A. Fernandez 2m 00.549s, 18 Nakagami 2m 00.825s, 19 Gardner 2m 01.194s.

Lap chart

Grid order	1	2	3	4	5	6	7	8	9	10	11	12	13	14	15	16	17	18	19	20	
41 A. ESPARGARO	1	1	1	1	1	1	1	1	1	1	1	89	89	89	89	89	89	89	23	23	1
1 BAGNAIA	23	89	89	89	89	89	89	89	89	89	89	1	23	23	23	23	23	23	89	89	2
23 BASTIANINI	89	23	41	41	41	41	41	41	41	23	23	23	1	1	1	1	1	1	1	1	3
89 MARTIN	41	41	23	23	23	23	23	23	23	41	41	41	41	93	93	93	93	93	93	93	4
73 A. MARQUEZ	93	93	93	93	93	93	93	93	93	93	93	93	93	41	41	41	49	49	49	49	5
33 BINDER	73	73	73	73	73	73	49	49	49	49	49	49	49	49	49	49	41	41	41	41	6
93 M. MARQUEZ	49	31	31	31	31	49	73	73	73	73	73	73	73	73	73	73	73	73	73	73	7
12 VINALES	31	49	49	49	49	31	31	31	31	31	31	31	31	31	31	31	31	72	72	72	8
31 ACOSTA	43	43	43	43	43	43	72	72	72	72	72	72	72	72	72	72	72	31	31	31	9
49 DI GIANNANTONIO	12	12	12	72	72	72	43	43	43	43	43	43	43	43	43	43	43	20	21	21	10
43 MILLER	21	21	72	20	20	12	12	12	12	12	12	12	12	20	20	20	20	21	20	20	11
72 BEZZECCHI	20	72	20	12	12	20	20	20	20	20	20	20	20	20	12	12	21	43	43	43	12
21 MORBIDELLI	72	20	21	21	10	10	10	10	10	21	21	21	21	21	21	21	12	12	12	12	13
25 R. FERNANDEZ	10	5	10	10	36	36	36	36	36	10	10	10	10	10	10	10	5	5	5	5	14
88 OLIVEIRA	5	10	36	36	37	21	21	21	21	5	5	5	5	5	5	5	10	10	10	10	15
5 ZARCO	36	36	37	37	21	5	5	5	5	37	37	37	37	37	37	37	37	37	37	30	
37 A. FERNANDEZ	37	37	5	5	5	37	37	37	30	30	30	30	30	30	30	30	30	30	30	37	
20 QUARTARARO	87	87	87	87	87	87	87	87	87	87	87	87	87	87	87	87	87	87	87	87	
10 MARINI	30	30	30	30	87	30	30	30	87	87	87	87	87	87	87	87	87	87	87	87	
36 MIR							87	87	36												
30 NAKAGAMI																					
87 GARDNER																					

Championship Points

1	Martin	155	(86)	241
2	Bagnaia	193	(45)	238
3	Bastianini	145	(47)	192
4	M. Marquez	121	(58)	179
5	Vinales	79	(51)	130
6	Acosta	79	(43)	122
7	Binder	89	(25)	114
8	Di Giannantonio	88	(16)	104
9	A. Espargaro	60	(39)	99
10	A. Marquez	80	(12)	92
11	Bezzecchi	60	(1)	61
12	Morbidelli	43	(18)	61
13	Oliveira	40	(11)	51
14	Quartararo	40	(9)	49
15	R. Fernandez	44	(2)	46
16	Miller	26	(16)	42
17	A. Fernandez	12	(3)	15
18	Zarco	14	(0)	14
19	Mir	12	(1)	13
20	Nakagami	11	(0)	11
21	Rins	8	(0)	8
22	Pedrosa	0	(7)	7
23	Marini	1	(0)	1

Constructor Points

1	Ducati	241	(111)	352
2	Aprilia	112	(80)	192
3	KTM	119	(59)	178
4	Yamaha	44	(9)	53
5	Honda	24	(2)	26

MOTO2: RACE DISTANCE: 17 laps, 62.324 miles/100.300km
RACE WEATHER: Dry (air 18°, humidity 73%, track 29°)

Pos.	Rider	Nat.	No.	Entrant	Machine	Laps	Time & Speed
1	Jake Dixon	GBR	96	CFMOTO Inde Aspar Team	Kalex	17	35m 25.147s
							105.6mph/169.9km/h
2	Aron Canet	SPA	44	Fantic Racing	Kalex	17	35m 25.324s
3	Celestino Vietti	ITA	13	Red Bull KTM Ajo	Kalex	17	35m 32.201s
4	Sergio Garcia	SPA	3	MT Helmets - MSI	Boscoscuro	17	35m 33.623s
5	Manuel Gonzalez	SPA	18	QJMOTOR Gresini Moto2	Kalex	17	35m 33.865s
6	Darryn Binder	RSA	15	Liqui Moly Husqvarna Intact GP	Kalex	17	35m 34.048s
7	Jeremy Alcoba	SPA	52	Yamaha VR46 Master Camp Team	Kalex	17	35m 35.652s
8	Albert Arenas	SPA	75	QJMOTOR Gresini Moto2	Kalex	17	35m 36.836s
9	Alonso Lopez	SPA	21	GT Trevisan SpeedUp	Boscoscuro	17	35m 37.537s
10	Senna Agius	AUS	81	Liqui Moly Husqvarna Intact GP	Kalex	17	35m 39.082s
11	Zonta van den Goorbergh	NED	84	RW-Idrofoglia Racing GP	Kalex	17	35m 39.262s
12	Fermin Aldeguer	SPA	54	GT Trevisan SpeedUp	Boscoscuro	17	35m 39.455s
13	Bo Bendsneyder	NED	64	Preicanos Racing Team	Kalex	17	35m 40.089s
14	Ai Ogura	JPN	79	MT Helmets - MSI	Boscoscuro	17	35m 42.688s
15	Marcos Ramirez	SPA	24	OnlyFans American Racing Team	Kalex	17	35m 42.914s
16	Barry Baltus	BEL	7	RW-Idrofoglia Racing GP	Kalex	17	35m 47.375s
17	Marcel Schrotter	GER	32	Red Bull KTM Ajo	Kalex	17	35m 47.449s
18	Jorge Navarro	SPA	9	KLINT Forward Factory Team	Forward	17	35m 50.149s
19	Dennis Foggia	ITA	71	Italtrans Racing Team	Kalex	17	35m 54.392s
20	Izan Guevara	SPA	28	CFMOTO Inde Aspar Team	Kalex	17	35m 54.522s
21	Ayumu Sasaki	JPN	22	Yamaha VR46 Master Camp Team	Kalex	17	35m 57.849s
22	Alex Escrig	SPA	11	KLINT Forward Factory Team	Forward	17	36m 15.323s
23	Xavier Artigas	SPA	43	KLINT Forward Factory Team	Forward	17	36m 36.651s
	Mario Aji	INA	34	IDEMITSU Honda Team Asia	Kalex	9	DNF-crash
	Joe Roberts	USA	16	OnlyFans American Racing Team	Kalex	6	DNF-crash
	Tony Arbolino	ITA	14	Elf Marc VDS Racing Team	Kalex	6	DNF-crash
	Filip Salac	CZE	12	Elf Marc VDS Racing Team	Kalex	6	DNF-crash
	Diogo Moreira	BRA	10	Italtrans Racing Team	Kalex	5	DNF-crash
	Somkiat Chantra	THA	35	IDEMITSU Honda Team Asia	Kalex	4	DNF-crash
	Xavi Cardelus	AND	20	Fantic Racing	Kalex	4	DNF-crash
	Jaume Masia	SPA	5	Preicanos Racing Team	Kalex	1	DNF-crash

Fastest lap: Aron Canet, on lap 2, 2m 3.984s, 106.4mph/171.3km/h.
Lap record: Jorge Navarro, 2m 4.312s, 106.1mph/170.8km/h (2021).
Event maximum speed: Celestino Vietti, 176.6mph/284.2km/h (race).

Qualifying
Weather: Dry
Air: 21° Humidity: 52% Track: 36°

1	Ogura	2m 02.940s
2	Canet	2m 02.992s
3	Moreira	2m 03.123s
4	Vietti	2m 03.149s
5	Dixon	2m 03.169s
6	Arenas	2m 03.205s
7	Gonzalez	2m 03.206s
8	Bendsneyder	2m 03.276s
9	Roberts	2m 03.289s
10	Lopez	2m 03.378s
11	Aldeguer	2m 03.463s
12	Arbolino	2m 03.521s
13	Chantra	2m 03.531s
14	Ramirez	2m 03.593s
15	V d Goorbergh	2m 03.639s
16	Garcia	2m 03.659s
17	Alcoba	2m 03.747s
18	Binder	2m 03.925s
Q1		
19	Baltus	2m 04.316s
20	Agius	2m 04.327s
21	Aji	2m 04.342s
22	Salac	2m 04.449s
23	Masia	2m 04.503s
24	Guevara	2m 04.713s
25	Foggia	2m 04.727s
26	Schrotter	2m 04.869s
27	Escrig	2m 04.884s
28	Sasaki	2m 05.067s
29	Navarro	2m 05.181s
30	Cardelus	2m 05.444s
31	Artigas	2m 08.371s

Fastest race laps

1	Canet	2m 03.984s
2	Dixon	2m 04.021s
3	Roberts	2m 04.271s
4	Arbolino	2m 04.305s
5	Moreira	2m 04.352s
6	Ogura	2m 04.410s
7	Gonzalez	2m 04.427s
8	Chantra	2m 04.463s
9	Arenas	2m 04.474s
10	Binder	2m 04.482s
11	Lopez	2m 04.518s
12	Vietti	2m 04.569s
13	Garcia	2m 04.598s
14	Bendsneyder	2m 04.606s
15	Aji	2m 04.793s
16	V d Goorbergh	2m 04.853s
17	Aldeguer	2m 04.858s
18	Alcoba	2m 04.863s
19	Agius	2m 04.870s
20	Navarro	2m 05.074s
21	Salac	2m 05.245s
22	Ramirez	2m 05.254s
23	Baltus	2m 05.263s
24	Schrotter	2m 05.386s
25	Sasaki	2m 05.462s
26	Foggia	2m 05.595s
27	Guevara	2m 05.618s
28	Cardelus	2m 05.902s
29	Escrig	2m 06.018s
30	Artigas	2m 07.538s

Championship Points

1	Garcia	160
2	Ogura	142
3	Roberts	123
4	Aldeguer	112
5	Lopez	100
6	Gonzalez	88
7	Dixon	78
8	Canet	78
9	Vietti	71
10	Alcoba	57
11	Chantra	56
12	Arenas	56
13	Arbolino	50
14	Ramirez	45
15	Agius	32
16	Baltus	23
17	Guevara	21
18	Moreira	20
19	Van den Goorbergh	18
20	Binder	16
21	Foggia	14
22	Salac	14
23	Bendsneyder	7
24	Navarro	6
25	Oncu	6
26	Masia	4
27	Aji	2
28	Ferrari	1

Constructor Points
1	Boscoscuro	217
2	Kalex	197
3	Forward	6

MOTO3: RACE DISTANCE: 15 laps, 54.991 miles/88.500km
RACE WEATHER: Dry (air 17°, humidity 65%, track 26°)

Pos.	Rider	Nat.	No.	Entrant	Machine	Laps	Time & Speed
1	Ivan Ortola	SPA	48	MT Helmets - MSI	KTM	15	32m 42.328s
							100.8mph/162.3km/h
2	David Alonso	COL	80	CFMOTO Valresa Aspar Team	CFMOTO	15	32m 42.451s
3	Collin Veijer	NED	95	Liqui Moly Husqvarna Intact GP	Husqvarna	15	32m 42.554s
4	Daniel Holgado	SPA	96	Red Bull GASGAS Tech3	GASGAS	15	32m 42.661s
5	Stefano Nepa	ITA	82	LEVELUP - MTA	KTM	15	32m 42.725s
6	Ryusei Yamanaka	JPN	6	MT Helmets - MSI	KTM	15	32m 42.791s
7	Joel Kelso	AUS	66	BOE Motorsports	KTM	15	32m 42.876s
8	Adrian Fernandez	SPA	31	Leopard Racing	Honda	15	32m 43.649s
9	Jose Antonio Rueda	SPA	99	Red Bull KTM Ajo	KTM	15	32m 43.759s
10	Tatsuki Suzuki	JPN	24	Liqui Moly Husqvarna Intact GP	Husqvarna	15	32m 43.865s
11	Matteo Bertelle	ITA	18	Kopron Rivacold Snipers Team	Honda	15	32m 43.942s
12	David Munoz	SPA	64	BOE Motorsports	KTM	15	32m 54.870s
13	Joel Esteban	SPA	78	CFMOTO Valresa Aspar Team	CFMOTO	15	32m 54.970s
14	Riccardo Rossi	ITA	54	CIP Green Power	KTM	15	32m 55.075s
15	Nicola Carraro	ITA	10	LEVELUP - MTA	KTM	15	32m 55.340s
16	Filippo Farioli	ITA	7	SIC58 Squadra Corse	Honda	15	32m 56.036s
17	Jacob Roulstone	AUS	12	Red Bull GASGAS Tech3	GASGAS	15	33m 05.387s
18	David Almansa	SPA	22	Kopron Rivacold Snipers Team	Honda	15	33m 05.894s
19	Tatchakorn Buasri	THA	5	Honda Team Asia	Honda	15	33m 14.913s
20	Noah Dettwiler	SWI	55	CIP Green Power	KTM	15	33m 30.159s
21	Danial Shahril	MAL	57	SIC58 Squadra Corse	Honda	15	33m 34.677s
	Vicente Perez	SPA	21	Fibre Tec Honda - MLav Racing	Honda	6	DNF-crash
	Xabi Zurutuza	SPA	85	Red Bull KTM Ajo	KTM	4	DNF-crash
	Angel Piqueras	SPA	36	Leopard Racing	Honda	1	DNF-crash
	Scott Ogden	GBR	19	Fibre Tec Honda - MLav Racing	Honda	1	DNF-crash

Fastest lap: Adrian Fernandez, on lap 4, 2m 9.727s, 101.7mph/163.7km/h.
Lap record: Deniz Oncu, 2m 11.011s, 100.7mph/162.1km/h (2022).
Event maximum speed: Collin Veijer, 148.1mph/238.4km/h (race).

Qualifying:
Weather: Dry
Air: 20° Humidity: 60% Track: 35°

1	Ortola	2m 09.270s
2	Veijer	2m 09.311s
3	Kelso	2m 09.753s
4	Alonso	2m 09.898s
5	Yamanaka	2m 09.931s
6	Roulstone	2m 10.040s
7	Nepa	2m 10.119s
8	Holgado	2m 10.128s
9	Suzuki	2m 10.454s
10	Rueda	2m 10.786s
11	Piqueras	2m 10.804s
12	Fernandez	2m 10.906s
13	Bertelle	2m 10.929s
14	Zurutuza	2m 11.097s
15	Carraro	2m 11.104s
16	Farioli	2m 11.171s
17	Ogden	No Time
18	Rossi	No Time
Q1		
19	Buasri	2m 11.514s
20	Perez	2m 11.594s
21	Munoz	2m 11.953s
22	Esteban	2m 11.978s
23	Almansa	2m 12.035s
24	Dettwiler	2m 12.464s
25	Shahril	2m 13.260s

Fastest race laps

1	Fernandez	2m 09.727s
2	Nepa	2m 09.773s
3	Holgado	2m 09.879s
4	Veijer	2m 09.918s
5	Alonso	2m 09.931s
6	Suzuki	2m 09.945s
7	Bertelle	2m 09.948s
8	Munoz	2m 09.955s
9	Rueda	2m 09.964s
10	Yamanaka	2m 10.117s
11	Ortola	2m 10.185s
12	Roulstone	2m 10.304s
13	Kelso	2m 10.325s
14	Esteban	2m 10.453s
15	Rossi	2m 10.526s
16	Carraro	2m 10.601s
17	Farioli	2m 10.623s
18	Zurutuza	2m 10.781s
19	Almansa	2m 10.783s
20	Buasri	2m 11.018s
21	Dettwiler	2m 11.360s
22	Shahril	2m 12.544s
23	Perez	2m 13.486s

Championship Points

1	Alonso	199
2	Ortola	146
3	Holgado	133
4	Veijer	131
5	Munoz	88
6	Yamanaka	82
7	Fernandez	75
8	Rueda	65
9	Kelso	64
10	Piqueras	60
11	Furusato	54
12	Nepa	51
13	Suzuki	44
14	Roulstone	44
15	Esteban	41
16	Lunetta	34
17	Bertelle	20
18	Rossi	18
19	Carraro	16
20	Farioli	14
21	Ogden	11
22	Zurutuza	3
23	Perez	3
24	Dettwiler	2
25	Almansa	2

Constructor Points
1	CFMOTO	199
2	KTM	179
3	Husqvarna	148
4	GASGAS	138
5	Honda	118

Above: First-lap fight in the sprint, but no points in sight for Raul Fernandez, Zarco, Nakagami and Rins.

Top right: Double or quits. Pol Espargaro and Oliveira play the numbers game in the sprint.
Photos: Gold & Goose

Above right: Aleix Espargaro's podium in the sprint gave him something to shout about.
Photo: Bernd Fischer

Right: Martin chases Bagnaia on Sunday. A hopeless quest.
Photo: Ducati Corse

Opening spread: …on a lazy Sunday afternoon. At a quiet race in Spielberg, Bagnaia, Martin and Bastianini were firmly in control.
Photo: Gold & Goose

THE Red Bull Ring is accustomed to thrilling close races and last-corner battles. In 2017, Dovizioso beat Marquez by 0.176 of a second; in 2018, Lorenzo beat Marc by 0.130. The next year, two-tenths (Dovi and Marc again), and in 2020, Oliviera beat Miller by 0.316, the top four inside seven-tenths. Nor does Bagnaia always win by miles – less than half a second over Quartararo in 2022.

Since then, the gaps had stretched – five seconds in 2023, and 3.2 seconds in 2024 for Bagnaia's third straight win, after a rather processional afternoon.

Was Bagnaia just too good? The race time was an impressive 12 seconds faster than the previous year. But this was no explanation. That year, the race had been rather surprisingly slow, almost nine seconds slower than in 2022.

The blame had shifted to the technical. Duller racing had coincided with burgeoning aerodynamics and ride-height adjustments – the very things that riders accuse of making overtaking difficult, and tyre supplier Michelin blames for having to introduce swingeing minimum tyre-pressure rules.

This was underlined by Marquez's singular experience. Walking into his pit pre-race, he was almost knocked over by two mechanics sprinting the other way, carrying his front wheel. A failed tyre valve required a new rim. He started the sighting lap with his front Michelin at a dangerously low temperature. As others crept around to save fuel at a notoriously greedy track, he made repeated attempts to heat the rubber, accelerating and braking sharply. Before he lined up on the grid, he braked hard again to engage the start device, but then "I braked again and disengaged it. Then I didn't have enough speed [to engage it again]."

It ruined his race. Boxed in off the start, then pushed out at the first corner, he dropped to mid-pack, robbing the front group of potential interference.

Another spoiler was even more oblique. Martin had slashed his left thumb in his motorhome shower on Friday night, badly enough to need stitches. It remained painful and something of a hindrance, since it was involved in such modern-bike functions as engaging and disengaging the ride-height device, switching electronic maps and operating the rear-brake thumb lever – most important at a track where slow corners link short, but fast straights, making braking and acceleration paramount.

Aero and on-track ride-height adjustment would be limited from the following season, and ride-height devices banned altogether from 2027, but there were calls after this weekend for the ban to be brought forward.

Meanwhile, home manufacturer KTM ran a prototype for wild-carding test rider Pol Espargaro that took aero to new levels – 'batwings' arching up and back from the swing-arm, with a zig-zag trailing edge. The bizarre appearance suggested that it might even have been a heavy-handed attempt at humour, but the revised engine configuration was certainly no joke. Pol was third fastest on Friday morning (track familiarity helped, of course), but hopes of staying in the top ten were thwarted with an engine failure in the afternoon, which cost him a chance to get into Q2. The advantage, according to factory rider Binder, was improved corner exit, "which is where we're looking for a lot of time."

Initially, aero interference was suspected as the cause of a terrifying accident on Friday, when Pedro Acosta fell at some 185mph. He was very lucky not to strike the barrier as he slid past on the grass, and lucky also that there were no other riders about as he slid back across the track at the next corner. He had fallen earlier that lap at the chicane, breaking the top left wing. He had remounted and was completing the lap when he lost the front over the brow towards Turn Four. It wasn't the wing's fault, he said, nor because of brake-pad knock-off, but because the left side of the tyre had cooled.

The rest of the news was mainly about contracts.

Firstly, redemption was confirmed for Jack Miller, a step closer to formalising a return to Pramac, now on a Yamaha. Dorna, anxious to retain Australian interest, had been influential. However, the same influence failed at Trackhouse Aprilia, which now confirmed British GP rumours that they'd ignored pressure to enlist American Joe Roberts in favour of Ai Ogura. The Japanese rider said, "It looks like the team

and the bike are really competitive, so I think I am in the right place for next year." But he retained a personal contract with HRC, and his heart clearly still belonged there: "I've grown up with Honda. Maybe I can finish my career with them. Let's see, because it is not only in my hands."

Meanwhile, Trackhouse team principal Davide Brivio said of rejecting Roberts, "We considered him, then made some evaluations, more from the performance point of view … and decided that Ai was a better choice, regardless of the passport." Team owner Justin Marks cited "the big vision and big strategy as a company … MotoGP is the international expansion of the Trackhouse brand." None of which was any comfort to the depressed Roberts.

Morbidelli's future was saved, signed to VR46 alongside Di Giannantonio, albeit not on a GP25 Ducati; displaced KTM rider Raul Fernandez also had a lifeline, to join Cal Crutchlow as a Yamaha test rider. He would leave the paddock, but he thought it offered a better chance of returning than switching to WorldSBK. There were strong rumours that Moto2's Somkiat Chantra would be replacing Nakagami at Honda, while impressive Australian Moto3 rookie Jacob Roulstone had signed up with the KTM factory, to stay with his Tech3 team in 2025.

Di Giannantonio's use of a factory bike the following season was also confirmed, before his weekend came to an abrupt end on Friday afternoon, when he fell and dislocated his left shoulder.

MOTOGP SPRINT RACE – 14 laps

As usual, records tumbled in practice, to Bagnaia on Friday, then Martin on Saturday with his fifth pole of the year. Bagnaia was alongside, then Marc Marquez, also under the previous all-time record.

So, too, Aleix Espargaro, leading row two after a dire start with two Friday crashes. Miller was next, then Vinales; Bastianini led row three. Pol Espargaro was tenth after a more promising Friday start, a downbeat Acosta 14th.

Bagnaia led away, Martin's launch hampered by his thumb, but he forced to the front at Turn Three. Marquez was third, then Aleix Espargaro and Miller. Bastianini, wide at the first chicane, finished lap one ninth.

Martin was forceful, Bagnaia was more so, seizing the lead briefly at the end of lap one. On lap two, his pressure caused Martin take to the escape road at the chicane. He rejoined second, but the stewards judged that he'd failed to lose the required second (he disagreed) and on lap five issued him a long-lap.

He took it on the eighth, rejoining just ahead of Espargaro, but more than 2.5 seconds behind Marquez.

The next turning point came on lap ten, when Marquez, with faint hopes of closing the 1.3-second gap to Bagnaia, instead lost the front at Turn Three, putting Martin back in a serendipitous second, and promoting Espargaro to an unexpected podium.

Bastianini got the better first of Morbidelli and then Miller to lead them over the line in fourth; Binder completed the quartet. Bezzecchi was a lone eighth, with Pol taking the last point, comfortably clear of Acosta.

MOTOGP RACE – 28 laps

This was vintage Bagnaia. Aggressive in the opening laps, the Italian appeared to have an extra gear when out front in a race where the order of the top three changed only once – when Martin lost his early lead at the start of lap two.

Impressive in execution, the race was low on spectacle, Bagnaia easing clear by two- or three-tenths a lap, while Ducati's GP24 contingent once again made the race depressing viewing for the four other factories. By half-distance, Bagnaia, Martin and Bastianini were a massive ten seconds clear.

As often, most excitement came from Marquez, recover-

Above: Miller took a fighting fifth on Saturday, but suffered a familiar slump on Sunday.
Photo: Gold & Goose

Above right: Thumb's up (what's left of it). Stitches notwithstanding, Martin managed to keep Bagnaia's points lead within reach.
Photo: Bernd Fischer

Above far right: Celestino Vietti finally came good for Red Bull Ajo in the Moto2 race.

Right: Win number seven for Alonso earned respect from Holgado.

Below right: Chasing David. Moto3 superstar Alonso leads Munoz (64), Piqueras (36), Holgado, Veijer and Fernandez.
Photos: Gold & Goose

ing from his start-line disturbance. Swamped off the line, he was forced off-track into Turn One by contact with Morbidelli, the unfortunate Italian following. Rejoining 14th, Marc's chances of an unlikely victory challenge lay in tatters.

There were initial signs that Martin might threaten Bagnaia. He'd started with gusto, beyond the kerbs at Turn One to assume early control, Bastianini third behind Bagnaia. Miller and Binder – a sensational fifth by Turn Three from 12th on the grid, Espargaro, Vinales and Bezzecchi followed.

With temperatures in the high 30s and the track's brake-heavy nature leading to rocketing front-tyre pressures, gaining clean air out front was imperative. Bagnaia acted immediately, passing Martin as lap two began. Martin pressed his rival into Turn Nine, regaining the lead for a few fleeting seconds, only to run wide.

Soon, the lead trio were pulled apart. Bastianini was out of the victory fight by lap seven. And Bagnaia's devastating run of times from laps 12 to 16 stretched his lead from six-tenths to a full two seconds by lap 23. The Pramac rider attempted to harry the leader into making a mistake, skimming half a second off the deficit by lap 26; Bagnaia responded to win by 3.2 seconds.

The top three settled, attention turned to Marquez's comeback. He made fast work of Quartararo, Acosta and Pol Espargaro to sit tenth on lap four, before quick-fire moves on Alex Marquez, Vinales and Aleix Espargaro on laps six, seven and eight. Now he was in the fight for fourth, with Binder gradually stretching out on Bezzecchi and Miller. The Australian saved the Catalan some trouble by tucking the front at Turn Two the 11th time around, a lap after Marquez had almost run into the rear of the KTM, elbowing Miller's rear tyre as he braked late for the chicane.

By lap 17, Marquez had disposed of Bezzecchi. Next lap, he cut inside Binder into Turn Six. Fourth concluded his run, as 8.5 seconds lay between him and Bastianini. Not even he could close that, even though he ran at almost Bagnaia's pace in the final 12 laps.

There was little else of incident in one of MotoGP's less memorable encounters of the year. As Oliveira explained, "Aerodynamics allow us to go faster, but you can only brake so hard. Brake temperature and front tyre pressure increase and overtaking is harder."

Binder was fifth, top KTM; Bezzecchi's sixth was his best since Jerez in June. Vinales was a lone seventh, after a gutsy move on team-mate Espargaro at Turn Nine on lap 20. Morbidelli recovered to eighth, while Espargaro dropped to ninth, with overheating front discs, barely a second clear of a close trio: Alex Marquez, Pol Espargaro and Oliveira. Three seconds away, Acosta was clear of the trio disputing the final points – Nakagami, Augusto Fernandez and Rins. Marini and Raul Fernandez retired; Quartararo dropped to 18th after a long-lap for exceeding track limits.

Two victories put Bagnaia back on top on points, five clear of Martin.

MOTO2 RACE – 23 laps

Absentees caught the interest in Moto2. Most notable, Ai Ogura, who dominated on Friday only to suffer an innocuous-looking crash at the chicane on Saturday morning. It was his first of the season, and cruelly, it broke three bones in his right hand. He was out for the rest of the weekend.

Secondly, absent from the front group, was pre-season favourite Aldeguer. He had to go through Q1 to end up 17th on the grid, then made negative progress to finish 20th.

Celestino Vietti took advantage, turning his second pole of the season, and second in three races, to his first win since this race a year before, and by a commanding 1.8 seconds.

Canet and Garcia were alongside the Italian on the front row; Arbolino, Lopez and Dixon behind. Downcast MotoGP reject Roberts was 11th.

Canet led away, but Vietti made light work of him on the second lap. Fastest lap on lap six put real daylight between him and the pursuit, and he was untroubled to the flag.

The fight was for second. Lopez passed Canet on lap three, but was unable to shake him off. A little way back, Dixon caught Garcia and was ahead of him on lap six, and starting to whittle away at a 1.5-second gap to Canet. He joined the podium fight with three laps to go.

The race had dragged a little at mid-distance. Now it came to life. On the last lap, Dixon replicated his Silverstone heroics, passing Canet at Turn One for third only to touch the green on corner exit. A one-place penalty was incoming, which the Spaniard surely would have known.

Then Canet himself inexplicably exceeded track limits at the final turn, also incurring the same penalty – preserving Dixon's third podium in four races. As at the previous race, Canet fluffed his lines just when it really mattered.

It wasn't all gloom for Ogura. It was a terrible day for the championship front-runners. Garcia had dropped to sixth behind Arbolino, then plummeted to 14th after a track-limits long-lap penalty. With Ramirez, and on-form Darryn Binder and Chantra chasing Arbolino, Roberts was ninth, relieved to see Garcia drop behind him.

The American was narrowly ahead of Salac and Deniz Oncu, in the points after returning from his long absence, and half a second clear of Guevara and a downbeat Gonza-

FIM WORLD CHAMPIONSHIP 11

lez. Agius claimed the last point, a couple of seconds adrift of Garcia.

Wild-card Mattia Pasini was 23rd after his long-lap – one of five riders to suffer for exceeding track limits; second wild-card Navarro crashed out, so too Escrig, Aji and Foggia.

Garcia still increased his advantage over Ogura to 20 points, with Roberts closer in third.

MOTO3 RACE – 20 laps

Finally, it was business usual for David Alonso, with win number seven in perhaps his finest ride to date. After the usual new record on Friday morning, he had missed the front row for only the fifth time, and been hit with a long-lap for dawdling in Q2.

He was one of four sanctioned thus, with Furusato, Piqueras and Suzuki; while Lunetta and Farioli were given double long-laps for the same offence. Three more followed in the race: for Carraro, Zurutuza and Furusato again.

Alonso's comeback was helped by pole-sitter Ortola's misfortune. He stalled on the grid and was hastily removed, to start from the pit lane.

An on-form Kelso and Collin Veijer completed the front row; Holgado, Rueda and only then Alonso made the second. And it was Kelso who led from the start, pursued at first by a very aggressive Munoz and Holgado.

Alonso had been third, but took his penalty (along with fast rookie Piqueras) on lap three, which dropped them to tenth and 11th.

With Rueda and Veijer closing for a lead group of five, Alonso was at the back of the next gang – but heading it by lap five, albeit 3.5 seconds off the lead. Victory hopes weren't over, however. Both he and Piqueras had joined the front gang by lap ten.

The Columbian hit the front for the first time on lap 15, before narrowly avoiding contact with Munoz into Turn One on the last lap, to win by 0.1 of a second.

Munoz had made an eye-catching recovery on the last lap, passing Veijer and Piqueras in quick succession, before out-dragging Holgado for second to the line. Three-tenths covered the top five.

Fernandez led the next trio, from Rueda and Kelso, who had lost places, complaining of rear grip. Another five seconds away, Ortola had come through from the back to lead the next group from Furusato, Rossi, Bertelle and Suzuki (who set a new lap record). Yamanaka and Roulstone were next. But Furusato's second long-lap, too late to serve, resulted in him being demoted from tenth to 15th

FIM WORLD CHAMPIONSHIP • ROUND 12
ARAGON GRAND PRIX
MOTORLAND ARAGON

Above: "You'll be hearing from my lawyer." Bagnaia accused Alex Marquez of sabotage after crashing out on Sunday.
Photos: Gold & Goose

Top right: All on his own. Alex Rins and his Yamaha were at the back of the grid.
Photo: Monster Yamaha

Right: The fight for fourth. Oliveira chases Alex Marquez in the sprint.
Photo: Gold & Goose

Opening spread: Napoleon returns! Marquez celebrates his first win in nearly three years.
Photo: Gresini Racing MotoGP

IT took a new surface and a bit of rain to upset the order of 2024. It was still a Ducati win, but not by one of the dominant pair. And the first podium in eight races not to be a Ducati lockout.

Acosta and KTM's return was one upset. So, too, an unpleasant accusation by Bagnaia, that Alex Marquez had deliberately crashed into him.

But this was not the big news.

Aragon marked the return of Napoleon, after more than a thousand days of exile. Otherwise known as Marc Marquez.

It was actually 1,043 days since his previous win, for those who'd been counting. It was achieved in emphatic style, and not only because he was almost five seconds ahead of the championship leader. Marc led, indeed dominated, every session except race-morning warm-up. It was wet, so he didn't bother.

Nor just because, as a left-handed, anti-clockwise track, it suited his predilections. It was the surface. That overnight rain not only had washed away any rubber laid down, but also had replaced it with a layer of dirt from the arid surroundings. "My conditions," he called them.

Ducati's fleet was left to admire Marquez's riding from afar. "I saw a bit of his data, and he's leaning a lot ... crazy compared to the rest of the Ducatis. For sure, he's taking some risk," said Jorge Martin.

Marquez ranked this triumph alongside his 2021 Sachsenring comeback win: "When you have a lot of injuries, the value of victory is different. It's true that I won 60 times, but these two victories, together with the first in MotoGP, are the most important.

"This weekend," he continued, "the laps were short. It was easy. Just flowing, and I was extra concentrated, to don't make any mistakes." But he'd known it was only a matter of time since he first rode a Ducati: "In the Valencia test [the previous November], I realised we would arrive ... we would have our opportunities."

The strange conditions meant that no teams had effective reference from previous years – everyone starting afresh. This worked in favour of Pedro Acosta, who in addition had taken "a step back to go forward" with his settings.

In particular, they also worked against Bagnaia. Despite the cleaning effort, the left-hand side of the grid was visibly dirtier than the right. He'd qualified third, and that's where he would start. In both sprint and the grand prix, his rear wheel spun, he slewed sideways and was left by the pack.

This was at least partly why he clashed with Alex Marquez on Sunday. He'd finished the first lap sixth, but by lap 11 he was fourth, almost 2.5 seconds adrift of the younger brother. As the race wore on, he was obviously faster while Alex was slowing. It was only a matter of time. But instead of waiting for one of the clear overtaking places, Bagnaia snatched a random opportunity after the Spaniard ran wide into the left/right Turn 12/13 complex, under Aragon's famous stone wall. In a move reminiscent of his ill-fated attack on Marc in Portugal, Bagnaia seized the moment, then swung right to the next apex.

They collided, and the aftermath was ugly, with the Italian trapped under Marquez's bike in a tangle of arms, legs and machinery. Surprisingly, he escaped serious injury. But then it became uglier...

It looked as though Bagnaia simply hadn't left enough room. The collision was inevitable. The stewards attached no blame to either rider. A racing incident.

Bagnaia saw it differently. He insisted that he had heard

174   GRAN PREMIO GOPRO DE ARAGÓN

– and that the data proved – Marquez opening the throttle: "I was in front, leaving space, knowing that he was there, but with much more speed. Then I heard him opening the throttle. Even worse is that he remained from 40 to 60 per cent of throttle until he crashed. Very dangerous … normally you try to avoid contact."

A week later, he apologised, admitting that "my words were a bit strong". But for Alex, the damage had been done, the accusation remained. Obviously, he'd denied it at the time: "If you decide to make a move from the outside, you cannot close the line completely to the kerb. He closed too much and I was there. Nothing more."

Events rather overshadowed other news.

For the calendar, it was announced that 2025 would start not as usual in Qatar, but in Thailand. Of more import was news of the return of majestic Brno, abandoned after 2020 because of the deterioration of the surface. Now it was under new ownership and would be fit for racing in 2025.

The pleasure at the return of a favourite fast and technical track, which Marc likened to Mugello, was somewhat reduced by talk that in 2025, Hungary's Balatonring might replace the Portuguese GP at the well-liked Algarve circuit.

Rider news finally confirmed that Aldeguer would replace Marc at Gresini, while Moto2 rider Somkiat Chantra would become the first Thai in the premier class, replacing Nakagami at LCR Honda – the Japanese veteran set to remain with HRC as a test rider in Japan.

MOTOGP SPRINT RACE – 11 laps

The new surface was crucial for qualifying and the race. Marc Marquez rose imperiously above it, with a new record on Friday afternoon and an assured pole on Saturday. A revived Acosta was alongside, with Bagnaia snitching the final front-row slot from Martin at the last gasp.

Alex Marquez and Morbidelli completed row two; Binder – through from a hectic Q1 – led the third. Zarco was a best-so-far tenth, his first time in Q1, straight in, by far the best Honda rider.

As Marquez took the perfect launch, chased by Martin and Acosta, Bagnaia slewed sideways and was swamped, lucky not to be clobbered. Ironically, considering what would follow, he congratulated Alex Marquez for his "quick reflexes". He finished lap one fifth, between Alex and Oliveira. Morbidelli crashed out on the first lap.

Marquez Senior immediately pulled away, almost a second ahead after three laps and 3.9 on the tenth, slacking off on the last.

This stretched the pursuing pair, themselves comfortably clear of the rest.

Bagnaia held fourth until lap four, when he ran wide at Turn Five, letting Alex Marquez and Oliveira through into positions they held to the end.

The champion was in trouble and continued to drop back, finally losing eighth to Quartararo's Yamaha on the final lap. Although he didn't say the word "tyre", he made it clear that the problems were nothing to do with bike, rider or team, and angrily gestured 'second time' to his Michelin technician after the race.

Team-mate Bastianini was moving in the opposite direction. Qualified a shocking 14th, he spent the race cutting through to seventh, less than two-tenths away from adding Binder to his hit list.

With Quartararo eighth, Bezzecchi was close to taking ninth and the last point off the fading Bagnaia.

Espargaro and Zarco joined Morbidelli on the crash list.

MOTOGP RACE – 23 laps

"When I crossed the finish line, I felt I lost two or three kilos," Marc Marquez said of the relief that followed his 60th triumph in MotoGP. Not that there had been much room for doubt by anybody witnessing the race. He had called the shots from the first lap. His lead over the pursuing Martin was already two seconds on the second lap, and it would stretch steadily to more than five seconds.

The consolation for his pursuing countryman was that if

Above: On the gas and untouchable, Marquez simply owned Aragon.
Photo: Gold & Goose

Inset, above: A red wall of fans greets the comeback kid.
Photo: Ducati Corse

Top right: Dixon saw off Arbolino for his second win of the season.

Above right: Moto2 rookie Deniz Oncu made light of injury delays for a maiden class podium.

Above far right: Moto3's Luca Lunetta was another rookie to make the top three.

Right: Jose Antonio Rueda's tyre gamble paid off, as he outpaced Collin Veijer.
Photos: Gold & Goose

he couldn't match Marquez, neither could anyone match him. And with Bagnaia crashing out, two second places were a welcome boost to his championship lead.

Despite a clean-up operation before the start, the inside of the track was still filthy. As on Saturday, Bagnaia's starting spot on that side was badly affected. As Marquez, Acosta and Martin filed into Turn One, Bagnaia was stuck behind Alex Marquez, Morbidelli and Oliveira in seventh until promoted one place when Oliveira crashed out.

Having optimistically insisted on Saturday night that he could go with Marquez, Martin was desperate to get by Acosta and give chase. A rather reckless move at Turn Nine pushed both men wide, off-track, and allowed the rookie back through on the inside. By the time Martin drafted by the KTM on the back straight, Marquez was beyond reach.

Martin had a go anyway. A fastest lap on the third allowed him to quickly gap Acosta, the rookie now acting as a rolling roadblock to a horde of Ducatis. However, any hopes of reining in the leader went with Marquez's new fastest lap on the ninth.

The dirty track meant that straying off-line was treacherous. Overtaking was both tricky and risky. Alex Marquez made it work on Acosta for third on lap four, quickly establishing a one-second gap. Bagnaia took some time to get going, but when Morbidelli ran wide at Turn Five on lap nine, he, Binder and Bezzecchi all got by. A tight line through the final turn was enough to pass Acosta on lap 11. Seven laps later, the 2.4-second gap to Alex Marquez was gone, and he prepared to attack.

With disastrous results.

That handed Acosta third, while Binder was fourth, after a lonely race.

Miller had pushed through to eighth from 15th on the grid, ahead of Bezzecchi and Di Giannantonio. The Australian's strong start wouldn't last, however, as he ran into worsening grip problems in the changes of direction.

Bastianini, behind this group, was left to count the cost of another poor qualifying, failure to escape Q1 having left him on the fifth row. Eleventh on lap one, he found himself to and fro in a lively battle with Di Giannantonio, Bezzecchi and Morbidelli, who had run wide on lap nine after running fifth until then. Miller was losing places and had lost touch by half-distance.

Soon afterwards, Bastianini's late-race pace allowed him to pick off Di Giannantono, then Morbidelli. He had the speed for a podium place, but not the opportunity, climbing to fifth, still two seconds adrift of Binder.

With four laps to go, Diggia got the better of Bezzecchi for seventh. But after the race, the stewards became involved and he was hit with a 16-second tyre-pressure penalty. With the pursuit so far behind, he lost only one position.

That pursuit was led by Alex Rins, a welcome top-ten for the injury victim. But Miller, tenth over the line, also suffered a 16-second penalty and was demoted to 15th, behind a close group – Espargaro, Nakagami, Augusto Fernandez and Zarco, as well as Mir, another six seconds away.

Raul Fernandez suffered the same sanction, but it didn't affect his 16th position, still well ahead of a troubled Marini, who had started from the pit lane already well out of touch, after problems on the start line.

Quartararo crashed out of 12th on lap six; Vinales from 19th on lap 11, after another puzzling weekend – qualified 12th, he dropped to the back after an awful start and never got over it.

Martin extended his lead to 23 points ahead of Bagnaia, while Marquez displaced Bastianini from third, the Italian's slim title hopes fading fast.

MOTO2 RACE – 19 laps

It was an affirmative day for Dixon, with a second win in three races, fourth podium in four – a purple patch during which he had scored more points in eight successive races even than the fast-rising Ogura, 119 to 107. It gave a touch of hope for a title challenge, after his injury-hit start to the season.

The race raised many questions. How long could Garcia, who had dislocated his shoulder in a training accident, still lead the championship? Was Aldeguer ready for MotoGP, with another no-score? How could Lopez, dominant early on, be so meek on Sunday? And how could Deniz Oncu, a rookie

back after missing three races and three months with a serious wrist injury, make the podium?

Dixon took his first pole of the year, from rookie Moreira and Canet. Oncu led row two, Arbolino and Arenas alongside. Lopez was seventh, Roberts eighth, Aldeguer a lacklustre 11th. Ogura was ruled fit and came through Q2 to 16th. Points leader Garcia was 28th after crashing in Q1.

Dixon led away, from Moreira, who had given way to Arbolino by the end of the lap. By then, Canet had crashed out. Next time around, Aldeguer was also ahead of the Brazilian rookie. Oncu was in contention as well, plus Lopez, Vietti and Roberts. Dixon, although overtaken on laps four and five by Arbolino, otherwise headed an eight-rider gang on a track still far from perfect after the overnight rain.

Soon, the challengers began falling by the wayside. Aldeguer ruled himself out with a rash crash while trying to pass Oncu on lap seven; then Vietti was pushed off-track by Roberts on lap eight, which dropped the Italian to 13th and earned the American a long-lap. By half-distance, Moreira was also dropping back, having used too much rear tyre too early in the race.

Only Arbolino could stay with Dixon from mid-race, until four laps from home the Englishman's fastest lap broke the challenge. The Italian was content with a first podium of a so-far troubled campaign.

Oncu got the better of Lopez on lap 14 and left him behind. A couple of seconds further back, Gonzalez came through to fifth, while Chantra fought through from 14th on the grid to place sixth. He'd been promoted when Roberts took his long-lap; meanwhile, the American had found himself in a battle with team-mate Marcos Ramirez. Trying to prevail on the last lap, he high-sided for a third no-score in six races.

This put a gutsy Ogura 17th, reviving his title hopes, in contrast to Garcia, who suffered a long-lap while lying a dismal 25th, then pitted without any technical defect, walked straight out of the garage and left.

Close behind, Binder held off Vietti for another top-ten in his improving season; likewise, Salac held off Sasaki, with Baltus, van den Goorbergh and Aji together. Agius missed the final point by half a second after passing the fading Arenas and then also Moreira on the last lap.

MOTO3 RACE – 17 laps

Alonso led every session for a new record and pole number five, Rueda and Munoz alongside, and Piqueras fourth for an all-Spanish top four. Kelso was next, then rookie Lunetta.

The class suffered the worst of the conditions. Although the track, soaking at 9am, was dry for the first race two hours later, grip was very poor and erratic, especially off-line. Early laps were some six seconds off those of the previous day.

Alonso claimed a 1.6-second advantage on the first lap while the pursuers gradually discovered the track limits.

The Hondas of Fernandez and Furusato took turns in leading the chase towards the KTM, before Veijer's Husqvarna took over on lap seven. Another five laps allowed him to demolish Alonso's two-second lead and take over. But even as the Dutchman hacked chunks from the gap, a bigger threat loomed behind.

Both Rueda and rookie Lunetta had gambled on Pirelli's hard rear slick; the other front-runners were on the rapidly shredding medium. The young Spaniard dived under Veijer at Turn Ten on lap 13 and never looked back, becoming the 400th different rider to win a GP.

Veijer was second, his rear Pirelli destroyed, with Lunetta taking a maiden podium in third.

Alonso hung on to fourth, with earlier front-runner Kelso dropping more than three seconds behind at the end. Furusato was another five seconds away, with Munoz leading rookie Zurutuza and Holgado next, and Bertelle completing the top ten close behind. Piqueras was an early faller.

Alonso still managed to extend his massive championship lead; Veijer moved into second ahead of Ortola, 12th on this particular day.

FIM WORLD CHAMPIONSHIP: ROUND 12
GRAN PREMIO DE ARAGON

30 AUGUST–1 SEPTEMBER, 2024

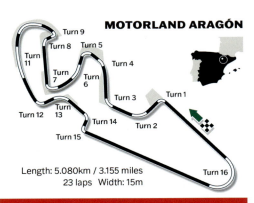

MOTORLAND ARAGÓN

Length: 5.080km / 3.155 miles
23 laps   Width: 15m

MOTOGP: RACE DISTANCE: 23 laps, 72.558 miles/116.771km
WEATHER: Dry (air 25°, humidity 57%, track 39°)

Pos.	Rider	Nat. No.	Entrant	Machine	Race tyre choice	Laps	Time & speed
1	Marc Marquez	SPA 93	Gresini Racing MotoGP	Ducati Desmosedici GP23	F: Medium/R: Medium	23	41m 47.082s 104.1mph/167.6km/h
2	Jorge Martin	SPA 89	Prima Pramac Racing	Ducati Desmosedici GP24	F: Medium/R: Medium	23	41m 51.871s
3	Pedro Acosta	SPA 31	Red Bull GASGAS Tech3	KTM RC16	F: Medium/R: Medium	23	42m 01.986s
4	Brad Binder	RSA 33	Red Bull KTM Factory Racing	KTM RC16	F: Medium/R: Medium	23	42m 03.541s
5	Enea Bastianini	ITA 23	Ducati Lenovo Team	Ducati Desmosedici GP24	F: Medium/R: Medium	23	42m 05.858s
6	Franco Morbidelli	ITA 21	Prima Pramac Racing	Ducati Desmosedici GP24	F: Medium/R: Medium	23	42m 07.631s
7	Marco Bezzecchi	ITA 72	Pertamina Enduro VR46 Racing	Ducati Desmosedici GP23	F: Medium/R: Medium	23	42m 11.841s
8	Fabio Di Giannantonio*	ITA 49	Pertamina Enduro VR46 Racing	Ducati Desmosedici GP23	F: Medium/R: Medium	23	42m 24.241s
9	Alex Rins	SPA 42	Monster Energy Yamaha MotoGP	Yamaha YZR-M1	F: Medium/R: Medium	23	42m 26.502s
10	Aleix Espargaro	SPA 41	Aprilia Racing	Aprilia RS-GP24	F: Medium/R: Medium	23	42m 27.684s
11	Takaaki Nakagami	JPN 30	IDEMITSU Honda LCR	Honda RC213V	F: Medium/R: Medium	23	42m 28.864s
12	Augusto Fernandez	SPA 37	Red Bull GASGAS Tech3	KTM RC16	F: Medium/R: Medium	23	42m 29.165s
13	Johann Zarco	FRA 5	CASTROL Honda LCR	Honda RC213V	F: Medium/R: Medium	23	42m 30.346s
14	Joan Mir	SPA 36	Repsol Honda Team	Honda RC213V	F: Medium/R: Medium	23	42m 36.817s
15	Jack Miller*	AUS 43	Red Bull KTM Factory Racing	KTM RC16	F: Medium/R: Medium	23	42m 43.048s
16	Raul Fernandez*	SPA 25	Trackhouse Racing	Aprilia RS-GP24	F: Medium/R: Medium	23	43m 00.404s
17	Luca Marini	ITA 10	Repsol Honda Team	Honda RC213V	F: Medium/R: Medium	23	43m 39.468s
	Alex Marquez	SPA 73	Gresini Racing MotoGP	Ducati Desmosedici GP23	F: Medium/R: Medium	17	DNF-crash
	Francesco Bagnaia	ITA 1	Ducati Lenovo Team	Ducati Desmosedici GP24	F: Medium/R: Medium	17	DNF-crash
	Maverick Vinales	SPA 12	Aprilia Racing	Aprilia RS-GP24	F: Medium/R: Medium	10	DNF-ret in pit
	Fabio Quartararo	FRA 20	Monster Energy Yamaha MotoGP	Yamaha YZR-M1	F: Medium/R: Medium	5	DNF-crash
	Miguel Oliveira	POR 88	Trackhouse Racing	Aprilia RS-GP24	F: Medium/R: Medium	0	DNF-crash

Fabio Di Giannantonio, Jack Miller and Raul Fernandez 16s penalty – technical infringement.

Fastest lap: Marc Marquez, on lap 9, 1m 48.186s, 104.9mph/168.9km/h.
Lap record: Luca Marini, 1m 47.795s, 105.3mph/169.5km/h (2022).
Event maximum speed: Marco Bezzecchi, 217.9mph/350.6km/h (sprint).

Qualifying: Weather: Dry **Air:** 24° **Humidity:** 36% **Track:** 31°
1 M. Marquez 1m 46.766s, 2 Acosta 1m 47.606s, 3 Bagnaia 1m 47.608s, 4 Martin 1m 47.642s,
5 A. Marquez 1m 47.807s, 6 Morbidelli 1m 48.114s, 7 Binder 1m 48.492s, 8 Oliveira 1m 48.550s,
9 R. Fernandez 1m 48.923s, 10 Zarco 1m 49.080s, 11 A. Espargaro 1m 49.707s, 12 Vinales 1m 50.526s.
Q1:13 Bezzecchi 1m 48.086s, 14 Bastianini 1m 48.542s, 15 Miller 1m 48.649s, 15 Miller 1m 48.649s,
16 Di Giannantonio 1m 48.687s, 17 Quartararo 1m 48.775s, 18 Nakagami 1m 49.081s, 19 A. Fernandez
1m 49.238s, 20 Marini 1m 49.802s, 21 Rins 1m 49.872s, 22 Mir 1m 50.120s.

SPRINT RACE: 11 laps, 34.702 miles/55.847km
WEATHER: Dry (air 31°, humidity 40%, track 49°)

Pos.	Rider	Race tyre choice	Laps	Time & speed
1	Marc Marquez	F: Medium/R: Soft	11	19m 50.034s 104.9mph/168.9km/h
2	Jorge Martin	F: Medium/R: Soft	11	19m 52.995s
3	Pedro Acosta	F: Medium/R: Soft	11	19m 56.728s
4	Alex Marquez	F: Medium/R: Soft	11	19m 59.984s
5	Miguel Oliveira	F: Medium/R: Soft	11	20m 01.783s
6	Brad Binder	F: Medium/R: Soft	11	20m 04.178s
7	Enea Bastianini	F: Medium/R: Soft	11	20m 04.325s
8	Fabio Quartararo	F: Medium/R: Soft	11	20m 08.870s
9	Francesco Bagnaia	F: Medium/R: Soft	11	20m 10.332s
10	Marco Bezzecchi	F: Medium/R: Soft	11	20m 10.482s
11	Raul Fernandez	F: Medium/R: Soft	11	20m 10.712s
12	Augusto Fernandez	F: Medium/R: Soft	11	20m 11.463s
13	Jack Miller	F: Medium/R: Soft	11	20m 12.144s
14	Takaaki Nakagami	F: Medium/R: Soft	11	20m 12.474s
15	Fabio Di Giannantonio	F: Medium/R: Soft	11	20m 13.502s
16	Luca Marini	F: Medium/R: Soft	11	20m 16.856s
17	Alex Rins	F: Medium/R: Soft	11	20m 16.944s
18	Joan Mir	F: Medium/R: Soft	11	20m 21.181s
19	Maverick Vinales	F: Medium/R: Soft	11	20m 27.676s
	Franco Morbidelli	F: Medium/R: Soft	11	DNF-crash
	Johann Zarco	F: Medium/R: Soft	4	DNF-crash
	Aleix Espargaro	F: Medium/R: Soft	0	DNF-crash

Fastest race lap: Marc Marquez, on lap 3, 1m 47.284s.

Fastest race laps
1 M. Marquez 1m 48.186s, 2 Martin 1m 48.359s, 3 Bastianini 1m 48.603s, 4 Bagnaia 1m 48.673s,
5 A. Marquez 1m 48.797s, 6 Morbidelli 1m 48.877s, 7 Binder 1m 48.921s, 8 Acosta 1m 48.931s,
9 Bezzecchi 1m 48.951s, 10 Di Giannantonio 1m 49.163s, 11 Rins 1m 49.512s, 12 Miller 1m 49.562s,
13 Quartararo 1m 49.598s, 14 Zarco 1m 49.705s, 15 A. Fernandez 1m 49.723s, 16 A. Espargaro
1m 49.914s, 17 Nakagami 1m 49.932s, 18 R. Fernandez 1m 50.115s, 19 Marini 1m 50.198s,
20 Mir 1m 50.312s, 21 Vinales 1m 50.925s.

Lap Chart

Grid order	1	2	3	4	5	6	7	8	9	10	11	12	13	14	15	16	17	18	19	20	21	22	23
93 M. MARQUEZ	93	93	93	93	93	93	93	93	93	93	93	93	93	93	93	93	93	93	93	93	93	93	93
31 ACOSTA	31	89	89	89	89	89	89	89	89	89	89	89	89	89	89	89	89	89	89	89	89	89	89
1 BAGNAIA	89	31	73	73	73	73	73	73	73	73	73	73	73	73	73	73	31	31	31	31	31	31	31
89 MARTIN	73	73	31	31	31	31	31	31	31	1	1	1	1	1	1	1	33	33	33	33	33	33	33
73 A. MARQUEZ	21	21	21	21	21	21	21	21	1	1	31	31	31	31	31	31	72	23	23	23	23	23	23
21 MORBIDELLI	1	1	1	1	1	1	1	1	33	33	33	33	33	33	33	33	23	21	21	21	21	21	6
33 BINDER	33	33	33	33	33	33	33	33	72	72	72	72	72	72	72	72	21	72	49	49	49	49	49
88 OLIVEIRA	43	43	43	72	72	72	72	72	21	21	21	21	21	21	21	21	23	49	49	72	72	72	72
25 R. FERNANDEZ	72	72	72	43	43	43	49	49	49	49	49	49	23	23	23	23	21	43	43	43	43	43	42
5 ZARCO	49	23	23	23	23	23	23	23	23	23	23	23	49	49	49	49	30	30	30	42	42	42	43
41 A. ESPARGARO	23	49	49	49	49	49	43	43	43	43	43	43	43	43	43	43	41	41	42	41	41	41	41
12 VINALES	25	25	25	20	20	30	30	30	30	30	30	30	41	41	41	41	42	42	41	30	30	30	
72 BEZZECCHI	20	20	20	25	25	41	41	41	41	41	41	41	30	30	30	30	37	37	37	37	37	37	
23 BASTIANINI	5	30	30	30	30	25	25	25	37	42	42	42	42	42	42	42	5	5	5	5	5	5	
43 MILLER	30	5	5	5	5	37	37	37	42	37	37	37	5	37	37	37	36	36	36	36	36	36	
49 DI GIANNANTONIO	41	41	41	41	41	5	42	42	5	5	5	37	37	5	5	5	25	25	25	25	25		
20 QUARTARARO	37	37	37	37	37	42	36	5	5	36	36	36	36	36	36	36	10	10	10	10	10		
30 NAKAGAMI	36	36	36	36	42	36	5	25	25	25	25	25	25	25	25	25							
37 A. FERNANDEZ	42	42	42	42	36	12	12	12	10	10	10	10	10	10	10	10							
10 MARINI	12	12	12	12	12	10	10	10															
42 RINS	10	10	10	10	10																		
36 MIR																							

Championship Points

1	Martin	195(104)	299
2	Bagnaia	218 (58)	276
3	M. Marquez	159 (70)	229
4	Bastianini	172 (56)	228
5	Acosta	98 (50)	148
6	Binder	113 (32)	145
7	Vinales	88 (51)	139
8	A. Espargaro	73 (46)	119
9	Di Giannantonio	96 (16)	112
10	A. Marquez	86 (18)	104
11	Morbidelli	61 (22)	83
12	Bezzecchi	79 (3)	82
13	Oliveira	44 (16)	60
14	Quartararo	40 (11)	51
15	Miller	27 (21)	48
16	R. Fernandez	44 (2)	46
17	A. Fernandez	17 (3)	20
18	Nakagami	18 (0)	18
19	Zarco	17 (0)	17
20	Rins	15 (0)	15
21	Mir	14 (1)	15
22	Pedrosa	0 (7)	7
23	P. Espargaro	5 (1)	6
24	Marini	1 (0)	1

Constructor Points

1	Ducati	291 (135)	426
2	Aprilia	127 (92)	219
3	KTM	146 (71)	217
4	Yamaha	51 (11)	62
5	Honda	31 (2)	33

MOTO2: RACE DISTANCE: 19 laps, 59.939 miles/96.463km

RACE WEATHER: Dry (air 25°, humidity 62%, track 39°)

Pos.	Rider	Nat.	No.	Entrant	Machine	Laps	Time & Speed
1	Jake Dixon	GBR	96	CFMOTO Inde Aspar Team	Kalex	19	35m 54.402s / 100.1mph/161.1km/h
2	Tony Arbolino	ITA	14	Elf Marc VDS Racing Team	Kalex	19	35m 56.181s
3	Deniz Oncu	TUR	53	Red Bull KTM Ajo	Kalex	19	35m 59.881s
4	Alonso Lopez	SPA	21	Sync SpeedUp	Boscoscuro	19	36m 03.592s
5	Manuel Gonzalez	SPA	18	QJMOTOR Gresini Moto2	Kalex	19	36m 05.500s
6	Somkiat Chantra	THA	35	IDEMITSU Honda Team Asia	Kalex	19	36m 07.462s
7	Marcos Ramirez	SPA	24	OnlyFans American Racing Team	Kalex	19	36m 10.896s
8	Ai Ogura	JPN	79	MT Helmets - MSI	Boscoscuro	19	36m 13.074s
9	Darryn Binder	RSA	15	Liqui Moly Husqvarna Intact GP	Kalex	19	36m 14.159s
10	Celestino Vietti	ITA	13	Red Bull KTM Ajo	Kalex	19	36m 15.703s
11	Filip Salac	CZE	12	Elf Marc VDS Racing Team	Kalex	19	36m 19.139s
12	Ayumu Sasaki	JPN	22	Yamaha VR46 Master Camp	Kalex	19	36m 19.817s
13	Barry Baltus	BEL	7	RW-Idrofoglia Racing GP	Kalex	19	36m 22.196s
14	Zonta van den Goorbergh	NED	84	RW-Idrofoglia Racing GP	Kalex	19	36m 22.895s
15	Mario Aji	INA	34	IDEMITSU Honda Team Asia	Kalex	19	36m 24.086s
16	Senna Agius	AUS	81	Liqui Moly Husqvarna Intact GP	Kalex	19	36m 24.482s
17	Diogo Moreira	BRA	10	Italtrans Racing Team	Kalex	19	36m 25.690s
18	Albert Arenas	SPA	75	QJMOTOR Gresini Moto2	Kalex	19	36m 25.820s
19	Jaume Masia	SPA	5	Preicanos Racing Team	Kalex	19	36m 32.000s
20	Daniel Munoz	SPA	17	Preicanos Racing Team	Kalex	19	36m 32.171s
21	Jeremy Alcoba	SPA	52	Yamaha VR46 Master Camp	Kalex	19	36m 38.203s
22	Xavi Cardelus	AND	20	Fantic Racing	Kalex	19	36m 38.713s
23	Jorge Navarro	SPA	9	KLINT Forward Factory Team	Forward	19	36m 57.003s
24	Alex Escrig	SPA	11	KLINT Forward Factory Team	Forward	19	37m 10.818s
	Joe Roberts	USA	16	OnlyFans American Racing Team	Kalex	18	DNF-crash
	Dennis Foggia	ITA	71	Italtrans Racing Team	Kalex	13	DNF-ret in pit
	Sergio Garcia	SPA	3	MT Helmets - MSI	Boscoscuro	11	DNF-ret in pit
	Fermin Aldeguer	SPA	54	Sync SpeedUp	Boscoscuro	6	DNF-crash
	Aron Canet	SPA	44	Fantic Racing	Kalex	0	DNF-crash
	Bo Bendsneyder	NED	64	Preicanos Racing Team	Kalex	0	DNF-crash
	Izan Guevara	SPA	28	CFMOTO Inde Aspar Team	Kalex	0	DNF-crash
	Xavier Artigas	SPA	43	KLINT Forward Factory Team	Forward	0	DNF-technical

Fastest lap: Jake Dixon, on lap 16, 1m 52.597s, 100.8mph/162.3km/h.
Lap record: Sam Lowes, 1m 51.730s, 101.6mph/163.5km/h (2020).
Event maximum speed: Deniz Oncu, 180.9mph/291.2km/h (qualifying).

Qualifying
Weather: Dry
Air: 29° Humidity: 52% Track: 47°

1	Dixon	1m 51.636s
2	Moreira	1m 51.770s
3	Canet	1m 51.784s
4	Oncu	1m 51.923s
5	Arbolino	1m 51.938s
6	Arenas	1m 51.965s
7	Lopez	1m 51.968s
8	Roberts	1m 52.044s
9	Vietti	1m 52.111s
10	Gonzalez	1m 52.141s
11	Aldeguer	1m 52.358s
12	Ramirez	1m 52.374s
13	Bendsneyder	1m 52.750s
14	Chantra	1m 52.778s
15	Guevara	1m 52.887s
16	Ogura	1m 53.011s
17	Salac	1m 53.506s
18	V d Goorbergh	1m 53.548s
Q1		
19	Sasaki	1m 53.007s
20	Binder	1m 53.090s
21	Aji	1m 53.223s
22	Baltus	1m 53.348s
23	Masia	1m 53.349s
24	Agius	1m 53.558s
25	Alcoba	1m 53.759s
26	Foggia	1m 53.818s
27	Cardelus	1m 53.887s
28	Munoz	1m 53.911s
29	Garcia	1m 54.611s
30	Artigas	1m 55.361s
31	Escrig	1m 57.418s
32	Navarro	1m 52.367s

Fastest race laps

1	Dixon	1m 52.597s
2	Arbolino	1m 52.796s
3	Aldeguer	1m 52.887s
4	Oncu	1m 52.894s
5	Lopez	1m 52.947s
6	Vietti	1m 52.989s
7	Gonzalez	1m 53.048s
8	Chantra	1m 53.072s
9	Ogura	1m 53.183s
10	Moreira	1m 53.187s
11	Roberts	1m 53.261s
12	Ramirez	1m 53.429s
13	Munoz	1m 53.456s
14	Binder	1m 53.474s
15	Arenas	1m 53.629s
16	Aji	1m 53.649s
17	V d Goorbergh	1m 53.661s
18	Agius	1m 53.686s
19	Sasaki	1m 53.718s
20	Baltus	1m 53.782s
21	Salac	1m 53.942s
22	Masia	1m 53.989s
23	Alcoba	1m 54.260s
24	Cardelus	1m 54.538s
25	Garcia	1m 54.797s
26	Foggia	1m 55.048s
27	Navarro	1m 55.109s
28	Escrig	1m 55.681s

Championship Points

1	Garcia	162
2	Ogura	150
3	Lopez	133
4	Roberts	130
5	Dixon	119
6	Aldeguer	112
7	Vietti	102
8	Gonzalez	102
9	Canet	91
10	Arbolino	81
11	Chantra	74
12	Ramirez	64
13	Alcoba	57
14	Arenas	56
15	Agius	33
16	Binder	32
17	Oncu	27
18	Baltus	26
19	Guevara	25
20	Salac	25
21	Moreira	20
22	Van den Goorbergh	20
23	Foggia	14
24	Bendsneyder	7
25	Navarro	6
26	Sasaki	4
27	Masia	4
28	Aji	3
29	Ferrari	1

Constructor Points

1	Boscoscuro	250
2	Kalex	247
3	Forward	6

MOTO3: RACE DISTANCE: 17 laps, 53.630 miles/86.309km

RACE WEATHER: Dry (air 23°, humidity 72%, track 43°)

Pos.	Rider	Nat.	No.	Entrant	Machine	Laps	Time & Speed
1	Jose Antonio Rueda	SPA	99	Red Bull KTM Ajo	KTM	17	34m 51.635s / 92.3mph/148.5km/h
2	Collin Veijer	NED	95	Liqui Moly Husqvarna Intact GP	Husqvarna	17	34m 53.620s
3	Luca Lunetta	ITA	58	SIC58 Squadra Corse	Honda	17	34m 55.191s
4	David Alonso	COL	80	CFMOTO Gaviota Aspar Team	CFMOTO	17	34m 56.577s
5	Joel Kelso	AUS	66	BOE Motorsports	KTM	17	35m 00.138s
6	Taiyo Furusato	JPN	72	Honda Team Asia	Honda	17	35m 05.263s
7	David Munoz	SPA	64	BOE Motorsports	KTM	17	35m 08.597s
8	Xabi Zurutuza	SPA	85	Red Bull KTM Ajo	KTM	17	35m 08.664s
9	Daniel Holgado	SPA	96	Red Bull GASGAS Tech3	GASGAS	17	35m 08.800s
10	Matteo Bertelle	ITA	18	Kopron Rivacold Snipers Team	Honda	17	35m 09.213s
11	Adrian Fernandez	SPA	31	Leopard Racing	Honda	17	35m 10.661s
12	Ivan Ortola	SPA	48	MT Helmets - MSI	KTM	17	35m 12.057s
13	Stefano Nepa	ITA	82	LEVELUP - MTA	KTM	17	35m 15.052s
14	Tatsuki Suzuki	JPN	24	Liqui Moly Husqvarna Intact GP	Husqvarna	17	35m 15.167s
15	Joel Esteban	SPA	78	CFMOTO Gaviota Aspar Team	CFMOTO	17	35m 15.229s
16	Scott Ogden	GBR	19	Fibre Tec Honda - MLav Racing	Honda	17	35m 22.785s
17	Noah Dettwiler	SWI	55	CIP Green Power	KTM	17	35m 29.329s
18	David Almansa	SPA	22	Kopron Rivacold Snipers Team	Honda	17	35m 29.434s
19	Ryusei Yamanaka	JPN	6	MT Helmets - MSI	KTM	17	35m 36.092s
20	Riccardo Rossi	ITA	54	CIP Green Power	KTM	17	35m 43.169s
21	Jacob Roulstone	AUS	12	Red Bull GASGAS Tech3	GASGAS	17	35m 43.228s
22	Arbi Aditama	INA	93	Honda Team Asia	Honda	17	35m 47.217s
	Tatchakorn Buasri	THA	5	Honda Team Asia	Honda	7	DNF-crash
	Filippo Farioli	ITA	7	SIC58 Squadra Corse	Honda	7	DNF-technical
	Angel Piqueras	SPA	36	Leopard Racing	Honda	6	DNF-crash

Fastest lap: Jose Antonio Rueda, on lap 10, 2m 1.193s, 93.7mph/150.8km/h.
Lap record: Deniz Oncu, 1m 57.896s, 96.3mph/155.0km/h (2022).
Event maximum speed: Angel Piqueras, 150.9mph/242.9km/h (race).

Qualifying
Weather: Dry
Air: 27° Humidity: 60% Track: 40°

1	Alonso	1m 58.059s
2	Rueda	1m 58.492s
3	Munoz	1m 59.064s
4	Piqueras	1m 59.090s
5	Kelso	1m 59.099s
6	Lunetta	1m 59.308s
7	Holgado	1m 59.414s
8	Bertelle	1m 59.463s
9	Veijer	1m 59.717s
10	Ortola	1m 59.755s
11	Nepa	2m 00.053s
12	Ogden	2m 00.058s
13	Esteban	2m 00.239s
14	Almansa	2m 00.249s
15	Furusato	2m 00.274s
16	Farioli	2m 00.590s
17	Fernandez	2m 01.251s
18	Roulstone	No Time
Q1		
19	Suzuki	2m 02.322s
20	Dettwiler	2m 02.550s
21	Zurutuza	2m 03.093s
22	Aditama	2m 04.298s
23	Rossi	2m 04.582s
24	Carraro	1m 58.656s
25	Yamanaka	1m 58.779s
26	Perez	1m 59.301s
27	Buasri	1m 59.811s

Fastest race laps

1	Rueda	2m 01.193s
2	Veijer	2m 01.292s
3	Lunetta	2m 01.558s
4	Alonso	2m 01.604s
5	Kelso	2m 01.686s
6	Furusato	2m 01.829s
7	Munoz	2m 01.874s
8	Zurutuza	2m 02.302s
9	Bertelle	2m 02.340s
10	Ortola	2m 02.361s
11	Ogden	2m 02.446s
12	Nepa	2m 02.586s
13	Piqueras	2m 02.612s
14	Fernandez	2m 02.883s
15	Holgado	2m 02.908s
16	Suzuki	2m 02.936s
17	Esteban	2m 02.963s
18	Almansa	2m 02.977s
19	Buasri	2m 03.140s
20	Dettwiler	2m 03.204s
21	Roulstone	2m 03.314s
22	Yamanaka	2m 03.574s
23	Farioli	2m 03.648s
24	Rossi	2m 04.264s
25	Aditama	2m 04.811s

Championship Points

1	Alonso	237
2	Veijer	162
3	Ortola	157
4	Holgado	156
5	Munoz	117
6	Rueda	99
7	Fernandez	90
8	Yamanaka	85
9	Kelso	83
10	Piqueras	73
11	Furusato	65
12	Nepa	54
13	Lunetta	50
14	Suzuki	50
15	Roulstone	46
16	Esteban	42
17	Bertelle	31
18	Rossi	24
19	Carraro	16
20	Farioli	14
21	Zurutuza	11
22	Ogden	11
23	Perez	3
24	Dettwiler	2
25	Almansa	2

Constructor Points

1	CFMOTO	237
2	KTM	224
3	Husqvarna	179
4	GASGAS	161
5	Honda	147

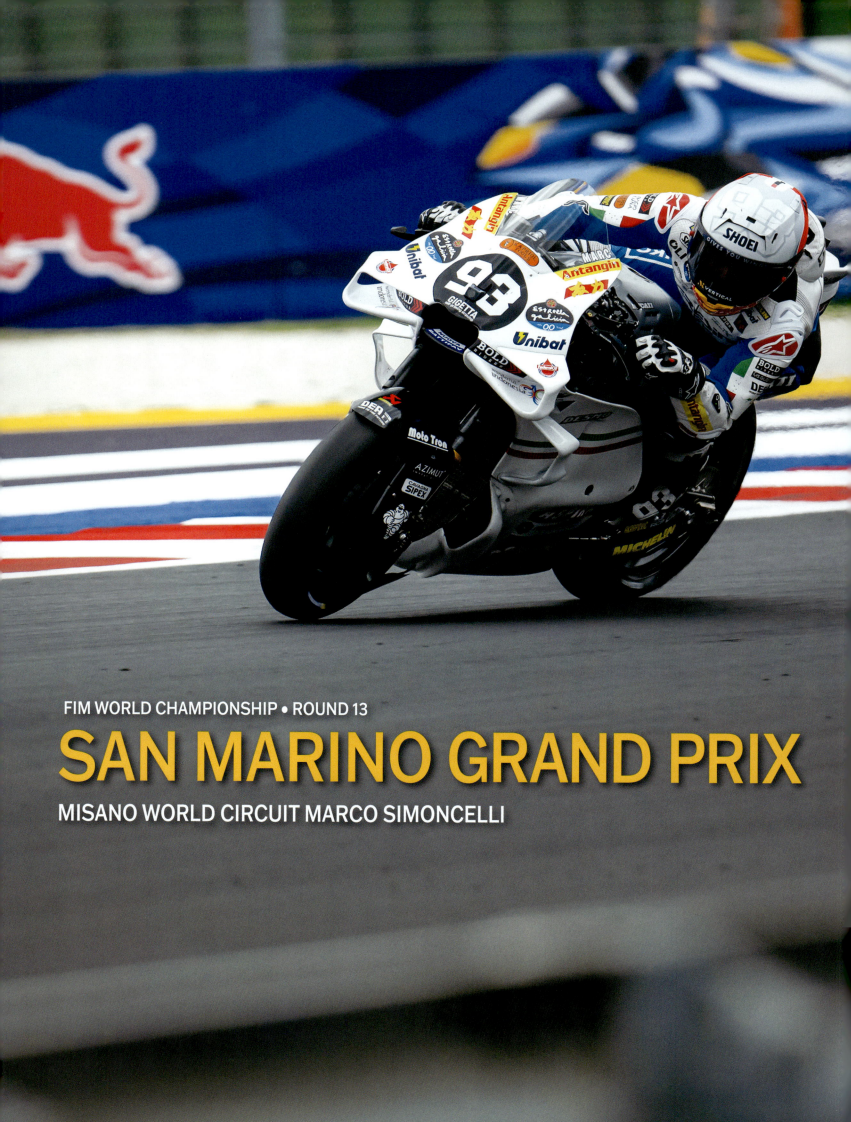

FIM WORLD CHAMPIONSHIP • ROUND 13
SAN MARINO GRAND PRIX
MISANO WORLD CIRCUIT MARCO SIMONCELLI

Above: When the going gets tough… Marquez, racing in late team founder Fausto Gresini's old livery, revelled in the difficult conditions.

Inset: Marc and the Gresini gang celebrate a second win in consecutive weekends.
Photos: Gresini Racing MotoGP

Above: Martin grabs the sprint lead from Bagnaia and Morbidelli in the first-corners fumble.

Top: Pol Espargaro's KTM displays the 'Wacky Racers' swing-arm aero.

Top right: Stefan Bradl was a wild-card for Honda. Factory livery could be a foretaste of a Repsol-free works team for 2025.

Top far right: Martin's Saturday win compensated for Sunday's blunder.

Above right: Rimini boy Marco Bezzecchi acknowledges the support of Bologna's Kimi Antonelli, the young F1 driver due to debut for Mercedes in 2025.

Centre right: Trackhouse Racing's Miguel Oliveira contemplates his move from Aprilia to Pramac Yamaha.

Right: Jack Miller was still in limbo.
Photos: Gold & Goose

RACES, even championships, often come down to split-second decisions. As rain peppered the track seven laps into the grand prix, Martin fluffed his lines, while Marquez sniffed his chance. He rose from seventh to first in a single lap. In conditions that rewarded quick reflexes and even quicker decisions, he excelled.

Marquez winning in Aragon, on an anti-clockwise layout in oddly demanding conditions, was one thing. Defeating Bagnaia in a straight duel was another, even if the Italian had a stiff neck and painful ribs from his spill seven days before.

His second straight win and Martin's no-score moved Marquez to within 53 points of the leader. It elevated his championship challenge from faint hope to intriguing possibility. The more so because this and the previous two races, when he had been as fast or faster than anybody, marked his maturity as a Ducati rider: "I've started to play more with the bike. Still some points to discover, but every time when you have more confidence, you are able to be faster." A setting change during August's British GP had been key, he said. "It's my first year with this bike, with the technicians and with the team. Sometimes, it takes time to find the direction." But there was an inevitability. He'd always believed that he could make the Ducati into "my bike". In Austria, he had been as fast as anyone. It was time: "For that reason, I was calm and not over-riding too much."

Spots of rain fell before the start. When it arrived in earnest, around the first corners, Acosta had already fallen, and then Morbidelli – lying third – also went down. It was decision time. Marc said that he had chosen to rely on local knowledge, which meant doing the same as Bagnaia. There was another serendipitous reason: he didn't have a 'wet' bike available, after a mechanical failure in morning warm-up.

Martin was left to rue his headlong dive into the pits. Had the rain continued, it would have been a masterstroke, but it stopped directly. His explanation was simple: "It was raining. A lot. Morbidelli crashed, so it was wet. If it kept the same, I would have won." It revealed poor team planning and flawed tactics. "We didn't speak about it. Maybe this time we missed a bit of understanding, but it was 100 per cent my fault. I took the chance. I was thinking more about the race than the championship. Next time, I will wait behind Pecco and do the same as him."

In post-race tests, Dorna trialled previously banned live radio communication with riders – not ship-to-shore, but vice versa. Race Direction and teams already had a limited selection of pre-set dashboard text messages; speech was a new dimension, however, adding another facet to Dorna's multi-layered TV coverage, as in F1. Unsurprisingly, most riders were opposed. For example, as in the rain-hit race, Marc Marquez said, "It must be the rider to decide. It's impossible for the team to know how the racetrack is. But for the show, it would be interesting for the people at home." Bezzecchi was also unsure: "Difficult to listen properly. With a bike, you are moving your body a lot. In a car, you are sitting there. I tried the earplugs, but I wasn't able to hear anything because of the noise."

Sunday brought news of the parting of Honda and Repsol – the end of a 30-year era that had yielded 15 championships and 183 race wins. With Marlboro-Yamaha, this was an iconic livery of the two-stroke years. The loss of Marc Marquez and Honda's worst ever run of results were factors in Repsol's unhappiness with the partnership, and reduced sponsorship for 2024 was apparent when the trademark orange was less prevalent on the fairings. The sponsor's de-

MOTOGP SPRINT RACE – 13 laps

Qualifying favoured riders from the nearby VR46 stable, for whom the track is very much 'their' circuit, after thousands of laps. The front row comprised Bagnaia, his second pole of the year, an increasingly feisty Morbidelli and a now-and-then revived Bezzecchi. Martin led row two from Acosta and Binder, through from Q1; the Marquez brothers straddled Bastianini on row three, Alex seventh and Marc ninth, after a tumble in Q2.

The top three were settled early, after Martin took a flying start off the second row to seize a lead that he would never relinquish. Bagnaia chased, but hadn't the speed to attack; Morbidelli gradually fell back and three laps from the end was under attack by Alex Marquez. The Spaniard got ahead briefly on the penultimate lap, but Morbidelli had redressed the balance by the flag.

As usual, brother Marc was making the moves. Ninth for the first two laps, he picked off Bezzecchi – slow away and soon to crash – on the third; on lap seven, Di Giannantnio; and two laps later, also Binder.

Now he was sixth and some 1.5 seconds behind Acosta. He quickly closed the gap and pounced on the last lap, but was still too far from Bastianini, four seconds away.

Miller was less than half a second behind Binder, and three-tenths ahead of Quartararo, who took the last point narrowly from Alex Marquez; the Aprilias of Vinales and Espargaro close behind.

Fourteen of 23 riders received track-limits warnings: of the top 15, only Marc Marquez, Aleix Espargaro, Zarco and Oliveira escaped; while Raul Fernandez erred once more and was given a long-lap, in the course of which he strayed again to be docked three seconds and three positions (to 17th).

Di Giannantonio crashed out early; wild-card Bradl retired.

MOTOGP RACE – 27 laps

Bagnaia's start was perfect this time, with Morbidelli second, ahead of Martin as they muddled into the first tight corners. In Turn Three, a brilliant cut-back on his team-mate put Martin second; and by the end of the lap, Acosta had got ahead of fast-away Binder.

Acosta now turned his attention to third place and got ahead of Morbidelli briefly – only to tumble on lap four. Now Bastianini was fourth; Marquez mired in a multi-rider fight for fifth, the podium contenders well clear. But as raindrops fell across the track's first sector at the start of lap six, both Bagnaia and Martin slowed, while Morbidelli crashed at the start of lap seven, Augusto Fernandez also at the end of it.

That was the trigger, along with a scary run-off at Turn 13 that sent Martin into the pits, followed by the Aprilias of Espargaro, Raul Fernandez and Vinales, plus Rins and the re-mounted Acosta. All changed to 'wet' bikes, just as the rain stopped. Martin knew immediately that he had blundered: "as soon as I left pit lane."

All pitted again within two laps to change back, and Espargaro once more a bit later to retire. Martin soldiered on, suffering the ignominy of rejoining behind the lead group, a lap down.

Up front, Bagnaia was testing the conditions, which allowed the pursuers to close in. Quickly, the top nine formed a group.

Marquez pounced with characteristic verve, and in the resulting chaos, grabbed the lead from Bagnaia at the final turn on lap eight, a spectacular rise from sixth on the previous lap. Miller, also strong in iffy conditions, was third.

Now, as conditions improved, Bagnaia began harrying Marquez. On lap 12, it appeared only a matter of time before another change of the lead. And when Bastianini passed Miller for third at Turn Eight on the following lap and began edging towards the lead pair, a three-way Ducati shootout appeared possible.

The heavyweight fight never materialised. By lap 18, Mar-

mands had proved tiring to some at Honda and there was no dismay, with a replacement already lined up. In any case, Mick Doohan's first title, in 1994, had been won in factory colours, in the year between Rothmans and Repsol sponsorship.

Headline contract news came from Dorna and the FIM, their partnership renewed until an astonishing 2060. At the opposite end of the time scale, the recruitment of Miguel Oliveira to 2025's Pramac Yamaha squad was confirmed, but expected partner Miller was still in limbo; while Aprilia MotoGP reject Joe Roberts had signed up for another Moto2 year with American Racing.

By immense good fortune, a freak pit-lane accident caused no serious injury. A marshal crossing the lane was struck by injured Escrig's Moto2 replacement Unai Orradre during final practice. Both went flying, unhurt, but the bike continued, swerving into the Aprilia garage, where, as Aleix Espargaro explained, "it hit my engineer's table. Luckily, one minute before, Antonio and my data guy had gone out to take a coffee." Another mechanic suffered a minor hand injury, "but the bike completely destroyed the garage."

Misano has very slow corners almost immediately after the start, which played a trick on Alex Marquez and Bezzecchi. Unable to brake as hard as usual as the field funnelled in, their hole-shot devices failed to disengage until later in the lap.

With an official IRTA test the following day, both Honda tester Bradl and KTM's Pol Espargaro had wild-card rides, the latter again sporting the extraordinary 'Wacky Racer' batwing swing-arm aerodynamics. However, with no concessions, Ducati were unable to field their usual entry for their tester, Michele Pirro.

Above: One lap down, chased by fellow tyre misadventurer Vinales, Martin rescued a point for 15th.

Above right: Ogura took a timely Moto2 win and the championship points lead. Canet, Arbolino and Vietti give chase.

Right: Moto2 is tough. Foggia, van den Goorbergh, Aji and Masia fight for 22nd place.

Far right: Luca Boscoscuro. The chassis bearing his name took another step forward in breaking the Kalex stranglehold.

Below right: Brilliant rookie Angel Piqueras overcame Holgado, Ortola and Furusato – and two long-lap penalties – for his first Moto3 victory. It was Honda's first of the season.

Photos: Gold & Goose

quez had edged his lead to half a second, while Bastianini began losing chunks, his corner speed failing. The front pair had medium/medium tyres; he was left to rue his choice of a soft rear.

Marquez set a new lap record on the 20th, stretching his lead beyond one second. He was safe for a second successive win, by better than three seconds. Later, he succumbed to whimsy, saying, "Someone in the sky said, 'Drop some rain, lead the race and win it for the Gresini family.'" He and Alex were celebrating the team's home race in the livery made famous by the late founder, Fausto Gresini.

Bagnaia decided to settle for a safe second. "I saw Jorge entering the box and I said, 'I don't have to take any risks,'" he explained. Plus, still somewhat battered, "in the last four laps, I was starting to lose my physical edge."

Bastianini was another two seconds back at the flag.

Behind the leaders, Alex Marquez had got ahead of Binder, then closed on Miller, going past on lap 14. The Australian would start losing positions gradually, with fading rear grip. Once ahead of him, Binder closed again on Marquez, taking fourth with five laps to go – his second-best result of the year.

Bezzecchi also recovered well, claiming fifth from Alex Marquez at Turn 14 on the second-last lap and finishing almost a second clear.

That left Marquez with his hands full fending off Quartararo after a strong ride, having passed Miller with two laps to go.

The remainder were well spread out, Di Giannantonio quite alone, then wild-card Pol Espargaro ten seconds clear of Oliveira. Nakagami, Bradl and Martin – still one lap down – who wrapped up the points, Vinales missing out by less than a second.

Martin's points advantage was nearly wiped out – Bagnaia just seven down, and Marquez a potential challenger after waiting 12 races for a first Ducati win and taking another a week later. For the first time in three years, for three races, he'd been capable of fighting with the best.

MOTO2 RACE – 22 laps

Arbolino's improving performance netted his first pole of the year. Vietti was alongside, then Ogura. Canet had led on Friday afternoon and Saturday morning, and headed row two from rookie Moreira and Arenas. Dixon lost a lap time to a yellow flag and was 14th; points leader Garcia failed to escape from Q1 and was 24th.

Arbolino led away from Ogura and Vietti, but by lap two, Canet had moved into third, and the trio broke clear. But Arbolino was one of several in the paddock to suffer from sickness during a sleepless Saturday night, and he began to tire. Meanwhile, Canet had taken over from Ogura. Both were past Arbolino on lap ten.

Vietti's early pace at his home track was a surprise. He lost touch with the leaders and was left to contend with Gresini Kalex team-mates Gonzalez and Arenas. After half-distance, he was almost 2.5 seconds off the front, but he found his groove and started to close. With four laps to go, it had become a lead quartet. Next time around, he crashed out at the penultimate corner, relieving Arbolino of a growing threat.

Up front, Ogura ran wide after his first attack on Canet at Turn 14 on lap 18. He made it stick at Turn Ten next time around. A third win gave him the overall lead for the first time. A tiring Arbolino was four seconds behind Canet, Gonzalez a lonely fourth, after a weekend that had promised more.

Behind, Arenas followed a familiar path backwards, Aldeguer the first to take over on lap eight. Meanwhile, Dixon was on a charge. "I don't think I made many friends in that race," he said, after a number of spicy moves as he rose from 14th on the grid. Aldeguer was his final victim with two laps to go.

It was Aldeguer's first top-six since the Sachsenring. By contrast, team-mate Lopez's first-lap crash at the final corner undermined his claim as a major Moto2 player. He remounted, setting a new lap record on his way to 29th.

Filip Salac was a season-best seventh, with Diogo Moreira, Arenas and Darryn Binder completing the top ten; Agius was six-tenths down in 11th.

Sergio Garcia, leading the championship when they arrived at Misano, endured another troubled weekend. Still suffering a painful shoulder from Aragon, he injured the other in a vicious Friday-morning high-side. He fought valiantly to 12th from 24th on the grid, but ended the race in tears of pain and frustration.

It was a disappointing race also for Roberts, who dropped from seventh on the grid to 13th, heading a close trio, from Chantra (qualified 22nd) and Ramirez.

MOTO3 RACE – 20 laps

Angel Piqueras produced Honda's first win of the year with a rookie ride to rank with Acosta's win from a pit-lane start in Qatar in 2021. The reigning Red Bull Rookies champion came back to trounce the established stars after a double long-lap, earned for a collision with Scott Ogden in practice, had dropped him to 17th.

Alonso claimed pole and a new all-time record, from fellow rookie Luca Lunetta and Ortola. Piqueras led row two from Veijer and Kelso.

Piqueras led lap one, while Rossi, Rueda and Munoz crashed out together in Turn Two, earning the last named a double long-lap for the next race.

Ortola took over on lap two, chased by Holgado, the pair opening up a gap of better than a second over Lunetta, Kelso, Furusato and Alonso, before Lunetta dropped back for his own long-lap, for a (disputed) jumped start.

Alonso took over the pursuit and they had closed up by half-distance.

Piqueras had served his penalty laps promptly, finishing lap four 17th, five seconds down. He scythed through the midfield, and by lap ten, he was seventh, right behind Veijer, leading the second group, two-and-a-half seconds off the front five.

Now the pair started to close, and at the end of lap 17 – by which point Holgado led a constantly swapping quintet – they had caught up. Now the 17-year-old cut through with devastating precision, past Ortola and Furusato on lap 19 with quick-fire moves at Turn 14 before taking Alonso and Holgado on the final lap.

Unusually, Alonso was beaten up in the final scramble, finishing sixth, behind Furusato and Veijer, before losing an additional place to Kelso for exceeding track limits on the final lap.

Suzuki was three seconds adrift in eighth; Lunetta recovered for ninth, ahead of team-mate Farioli at the SIC58 squad's home track.

FIM WORLD CHAMPIONSHIP: ROUND 13
GRAN PREMIO RED BULL DI SAN MARINO E DELLA RIVIERA DI RIMINI
6–8 SEPTEMBER, 2024

MISANO WORLD CIRCUIT
27 laps
Length: 4.230 km / 2.63 miles
Width: 14m

MOTOGP: RACE DISTANCE: 27 laps, 70.900 miles/114.102km
WEATHER: Dry (air 30°, humidity 51%, track 30°)

Pos.	Rider	Nat.	No.	Entrant	Machine	Race tyre choice	Laps	Time & speed
1	Marc Marquez	SPA	93	Gresini Racing MotoGP	Ducati Desmosedici GP23	F: Medium/R: Medium	27	41m 52.083s 101.6mph/163.5km/h
2	Francesco Bagnaia	ITA	1	Ducati Lenovo Team	Ducati Desmosedici GP24	F: Medium/R: Medium	27	41m 55.185s
3	Enea Bastianini	ITA	23	Ducati Lenovo Team	Ducati Desmosedici GP24	F: Medium/R: Soft	27	41m 57.511s
4	Brad Binder	RSA	33	Red Bull KTM Factory Racing	KTM RC16	F: Medium/R: Medium	27	42m 06.268s
5	Marco Bezzecchi	ITA	72	Pertamina Enduro VR46 Racing	Ducati Desmosedici GP23	F: Medium/R: Soft	27	42m 08.808s
6	Alex Marquez	SPA	73	Gresini Racing MotoGP	Ducati Desmosedici GP23	F: Medium/R: Soft	27	42m 09.665s
7	Fabio Quartararo	FRA	20	Monster Energy Yamaha MotoGP	Yamaha YZR-M1	F: Medium/R: Medium	27	42m 09.725s
8	Jack Miller	AUS	43	Red Bull KTM Factory Racing	KTM RC16	F: Medium/R: Soft	27	42m 11.410s
9	Fabio Di Giannantonio	ITA	49	Pertamina Enduro VR46 Racing	Ducati Desmosedici GP23	F: Medium/R: Soft	27	42m 20.029s
10	Pol Espargaro	SPA	44	Red Bull KTM Factory Racing	KTM RC16	F: Medium/R: Soft	27	42m 30.864s
11	Miguel Oliveira	POR	88	Trackhouse Racing	Aprilia RS-GP24	F: Medium/R: Medium	27	42m 38.469s
12	Johann Zarco	FRA	5	CASTROL Honda LCR	Honda RC213V	F: Medium/R: Soft	27	42m 54.720s
13	Takaaki Nakagami	JPN	30	IDEMITSU Honda LCR	Honda RC213V	F: Medium/R: Soft	27	43m 02.800s
14	Stefan Bradl	GER	6	HRC Test Team	Honda RC213V	F: Medium/R: Soft	27	43m 09.630s
15	Jorge Martin	SPA	89	Prima Pramac Racing	Ducati Desmosedici GP24	F: Medium/R: Medium	26	42m 10.721s
16	Maverick Vinales	SPA	12	Aprilia Racing	Aprilia RS-GP24	F: Medium/R: Medium	26	42m 11.570s
17	Pedro Acosta	SPA	31	Red Bull GASGAS Tech3	KTM RC16	F: Medium/R: Soft	26	42m 24.712s
18	Raul Fernandez	SPA	25	Trackhouse Racing	Aprilia RS-GP24	F: Medium/R: Soft	26	42m 41.158s
19	Alex Rins	SPA	42	Monster Energy Yamaha MotoGP	Yamaha YZR-M1	F: Medium/R: Medium	26	42m 50.509s
	Aleix Espargaro	SPA	41	Aprilia Racing	Aprilia RS-GP24	F: Medium/R: Soft	14	DNF-ret in pit
	Franco Morbidelli	ITA	21	Prima Pramac Racing	Ducati Desmosedici GP24	F: Medium/R: Soft	6	DNF-crash
	Augusto Fernandez	SPA	37	Red Bull GASGAS Tech3	KTM RC16	F: Medium/R: Medium	6	DNF-crash
	Luca Marini	SPA	10	Repsol Honda Team	Honda RC213V	–	–	DNS

Fastest lap: Marc Marquez, on lap 20, 1m 31.564s, 103.2mph/166.1km/h.
Lap record: Francesco Bagnaia, 1m 31.791s, 103.0mph/165.7km/h (2023).
Event maximum speed: Jorge Martin, 188.5mph/303.3km/h (race).

Qualifying: Weather: Dry **Air:** 27° **Humidity:** 67% **Track:** 35°
1 Bagnaia 1m 30.304s, 2 Morbidelli 1m 30.589s, 3 Bezzecchi 1m 30.609s, 4 Martin 1m 30.645s, 5 Acosta 1m 30.656s, 6 Binder 1m 30.748s, 7 A. Marquez 1m 30.878s, 8 Bastianini 1m 30.900s, 9 M. Marquez 1m 30.929s, 10 Quartararo 1m 31.054s, 11 Vinales 1m 31.155s, 12 Miller 1m 31.202s.
Q1: 13 A. Espargaro 1m 31.101s, 14 Di Giannantonio 1m 31.260s, 15 P. Espargaro 1m 31.471s, 19 R. Fernandez 1m 31.591s, 20 Rins 1m 31.721s, 21 Marini 1m 31.923s, 22 Nakagami 1m 32.071s, 23 Bradl 1m 32.972s.

SPRINT RACE: 13 laps, 34.137 miles/54.938km
WEATHER: Dry (air 29°, humidity 63%, track 42°)

Pos.	Rider	Race tyre choice	Laps	Time & speed
1	Jorge Martin	F: Medium/R: Soft	13	19m 56.502s 102.7mph/165.2km/h
2	Francesco Bagnaia	F: Medium/R: Soft	13	19m 57.997s
3	Franco Morbidelli	F: Medium/R: Soft	13	19m 58.334s
4	Enea Bastianini	F: Medium/R: Soft	13	19m 58.543s
5	Marc Marquez	F: Medium/R: Soft	13	20m 02.971s
6	Pedro Acosta	F: Medium/R: Soft	13	20m 03.298s
7	Brad Binder	F: Medium/R: Soft	13	20m 06.481s
8	Jack Miller	F: Medium/R: Soft	13	20m 07.228s
9	Fabio Quartararo	F: Medium/R: Soft	13	20m 07.517s
10	Alex Marquez	F: Medium/R: Soft	13	20m 07.854s
11	Maverick Vinales	F: Medium/R: Soft	13	20m 08.160s
12	Aleix Espargaro	F: Medium/R: Soft	13	20m 08.585s
13	Johann Zarco	F: Medium/R: Soft	13	20m 17.621s
14	Pol Espargaro	F: Medium/R: Soft	13	20m 18.044s
15	Miguel Oliveira	F: Medium/R: Soft	13	20m 18.497s
16	Augusto Fernandez	F: Medium/R: Soft	13	20m 19.944s
17	Raul Fernandez	F: Medium/R: Soft	13	20m 20.782s
18	Luca Marini	F: Medium/R: Soft	13	20m 21.249s
19	Alex Rins	F: Medium/R: Soft	13	20m 21.375s
20	Takaaki Nakagami	F: Medium/R: Soft	13	20m 21.656s
	Fabio Di Giannantonio	F: Medium/R: Soft	6	DNF-crash
	Marco Bezzecchi	F: Medium/R: Soft	4	DNF-crash
	Stefan Bradl	F: Medium/R: Soft	2	DNF-crash

Fastest race lap: Francesco Bagnaia, on lap 2, 1m 31.236s.

Fastest race laps
1 M. Marquez 1m 31.564s, 2 Morbidelli 1m 31.646s, 3 Martin 1m 31.650s, 4 Bagnaia 1m 31.714s, 5 Bastianini 1m 31.750s, 6 Acosta 1m 31.827s, 7 Bezzecchi 1m 32.145s, 8 A. Marquez 1m 32.162s, 9 Binder 1m 32.191s, 10 Vinales 1m 32.218s, 11 Miller 1m 32.228s, 12 Quartararo 1m 32.273s, 13 Di Giannantonio 1m 32.411s, 14 A. Fernandez 1m 32.634s, 15 Rins 1m 32.754s, 16 Oliveira 1m 32.868s, 17 A. Fernandez 1m 32.951s, 18 R. Fernandez 1m 32.996s, 19 P. Espargaro 1m 33.018s, 20 Zarco 1m 33.411s, 21 Nakagami 1m 33.545s, 22 Bradl 1m 34.247s.

Lap chart

Grid order	1	2	3	4	5	6	7	8	9	10	11	12	13	14	15	16	17	18	19	20	21	22	23	24	25	26	27
1 BAGNAIA	1	1	1	1	1	1	93	93	93	93	93	93	93	93	93	93	93	93	93	93	93	93	93	93	93	93	93
21 MORBIDELLI	89	89	89	89	89	89	23	1	1	1	1	1	1	1	1	1	1	1	1	1	1	1	1	1	1	1	1
72 BEZZECCHI	21	21	21	21	21	21	33	43	43	43	23	23	23	23	23	23	23	23	23	23	23	23	23	23	23	23	23
89 MARTIN	31	31	31	33	23	23	43	33	23	23	43	43	73	73	73	73	73	73	73	73	73	33	33	33	33	33	33
31 ACOSTA	33	33	33	23	33	33	23	23	33	73	73	73	43	43	43	33	33	33	33	33	33	73	73	73	73	73	73
33 BINDER	23	23	23	93	93	93	73	72	73	73	33	33	33	33	33	43	43	43	43	43	43	72	72	72	72	72	72
73 A. MARQUEZ	93	93	93	43	72	43	72	73	72	72	72	72	72	72	72	72	72	72	72	72	72	43	43	43	43	20	20
23 BASTIANINI	43	43	43	72	43	73	20	20	20	20	20	20	20	20	20	20	20	20	20	20	20	20	20	20	20	43	43
93 M. MARQUEZ	72	72	72	73	73	72	49	49	49	49	49	49	49	49	49	49	49	49	49	49	49	49	49	49	49	49	49
20 QUARTARARO	20	73	73	20	20	20	44	44	44	44	44	44	44	44	44	44	44	44	44	44	44	44	44	44	44	44	44
12 VINALES	73	20	20	49	49	49	88	88	88	88	88	88	88	88	88	88	88	88	88	88	88	88	88	88	88	88	88
43 MILLER	41	49	49	41	41	41	5	5	5	5	5	5	5	5	5	5	5	5	5	5	5	5	5	5	5	5	5
41 A. ESPARGARO	49	41	41	37	37	37	30	30	30	30	30	30	30	30	30	30	30	30	30	30	30	30	30	30	30	30	30
49 DI GIANNANTONIO	44	37	37	44	44	44	6	6	6	6	6	6	6	6	6	6	6	6	6	6	6	6	6	6	6	6	6
44 P. ESPARGARO	37	44	44	12	12	25	89	89	42	89	89	89	89	89	89	89	89	89	89	89	89	89	89	89	89		
5 ZARCO	12	12	12	25	25	12	41	25	89	12	12	12	12	12	12	12	12	12	12	12	12	12	12	12			
37 A. FERNANDEZ	5	25	25	5	88	88	25	41	12	41	41	41	31	31	31	31	31	31	31	31	31	31	31	31			
88 OLIVEIRA	25	5	5	88	5	5	12	12	41	42	25	31	41	25	25	25	25	25	25	25	25	25	25	25			
25 R. FERNANDEZ	88	88	88	30	30	30	42	31	25	31	31	25	25	42	42	42	42	42	42	42	42	42	42				
42 RINS	30	30	30	42	42	42	31	42	31	25	42	42	42	41	41	41	41	41	41								
30 NAKAGAMI	42	42	42	6	6	6																					
6 BRADL	6	6	6	31	31	31																					

89 Pit stop – bike swap   89, 12, 41, 42, 31 and 25 – lapped riders

Championship Points

1	Martin	196 (116)	312
2	Bagnaia	238 (67)	305
3	M. Marquez	184 (75)	259
4	Bastianini	188 (62)	250
5	Binder	126 (35)	161
6	Acosta	98 (54)	152
7	Vinales	88 (51)	139
8	Di Giannantonio	103 (16)	119
9	A. Espargaro	73 (46)	119
10	A. Marquez	96 (18)	114
11	Bezzecchi	90 (3)	93
12	Morbidelli	61 (29)	90
13	Oliveira	49 (16)	65
14	Quartararo	49 (12)	61
15	Miller	35 (23)	58
16	R. Fernandez	44 (2)	46
17	Nakagami	21 (0)	21
18	Zarco	21 (0)	21
19	A. Fernandez	17 (3)	20
20	Rins	15 (0)	15
21	Marini	14 (1)	15
22	P. Espargaro	11 (1)	12
23	Pedrosa	0 (7)	7
24	Bradl	2 (0)	2
25	Marini	1 (0)	1

Constructor Points

1	Ducati	316 (147)	463
2	KTM	159 (75)	234
3	Aprilia	132 (92)	224
4	Yamaha	60 (12)	72
5	Honda	35 (2)	37

MOTO2: RACE DISTANCE: 22 laps, 57.770 miles/92.972km
RACE WEATHER: Dry (air 31°, humidity 49%, track 31°)

Pos.	Rider	Nat.	No.	Entrant	Machine	Laps	Time & Speed
1	Ai Ogura	JPN	79	MT Helmets - MSI	Boscoscuro	22	35m 26.583s
							97.7mph/157.3km/h
2	Aron Canet	SPA	44	Fantic Racing	Kalex	22	35m 27.192s
3	Tony Arbolino	ITA	14	Elf Marc VDS Racing Team	Kalex	22	35m 31.222s
4	Manuel Gonzalez	SPA	18	QJMOTOR Gresini Moto2	Kalex	22	35m 33.531s
5	Jake Dixon	GBR	96	CFMOTO Inde Aspar Team	Kalex	22	35m 37.446s
6	Fermin Aldeguer	SPA	54	Beta Tools SpeedUp	Boscoscuro	22	35m 39.225s
7	Filip Salac	CZE	12	Elf Marc VDS Racing Team	Kalex	22	35m 40.107s
8	Diogo Moreira	BRA	10	Italtrans Racing Team	Kalex	22	35m 41.585s
9	Albert Arenas	SPA	75	QJMOTOR Gresini Moto2	Kalex	22	35m 42.553s
10	Darryn Binder	RSA	15	Liqui Moly Husqvarna Intact GP	Kalex	22	35m 42.615s
11	Senna Agius	AUS	81	Liqui Moly Husqvarna Intact GP	Kalex	22	35m 43.217s
12	Sergio Garcia	SPA	3	MT Helmets - MSI	Boscoscuro	22	35m 44.522s
13	Joe Roberts	USA	16	OnlyFans American Racing Team	Kalex	22	35m 47.143s
14	Somkiat Chantra	THA	35	IDEMITSU Honda Team Asia	Kalex	22	35m 47.526s
15	Marcos Ramirez	SPA	24	OnlyFans American Racing Team	Kalex	22	35m 47.891s
16	Ayumu Sasaki	JPN	22	Yamaha VR46 Master Camp Team	Kalex	22	35m 51.291s
17	Jeremy Alcoba	SPA	52	Yamaha VR46 Master Camp Team	Kalex	22	35m 51.370s
18	Barry Baltus	BEL	7	RW-Idrofoglia Racing GP	Kalex	22	35m 52.519s
19	Deniz Oncu	TUR	53	Red Bull KTM Ajo	Kalex	22	35m 53.390s
20	Bo Bendsneyder	NED	64	Preicanos Racing Team	Kalex	22	35m 53.706s
21	Izan Guevara	SPA	28	CFMOTO Inde Aspar Team	Kalex	22	35m 56.754s
22	Dennis Foggia	ITA	71	Italtrans Racing Team	Kalex	22	36m 02.935s
23	Zonta van den Goorbergh	NED	84	RW-Idrofoglia Racing GP	Kalex	22	36m 03.109s
24	Jaume Masia	SPA	5	Preicanos Racing Team	Kalex	22	36m 03.629s
25	Mario Aji	INA	34	IDEMITSU Honda Team Asia	Kalex	22	36m 04.808s
26	Xavier Artigas	SPA	43	KLINT Forward Factory Team	Forward	22	36m 21.678s
27	Xavi Cardelus	AND	20	Fantic Racing	Kalex	22	36m 22.790s
28	Unai Orradre	SPA	40	KLINT Forward Factory Team	Forward	22	36m 31.665s
29	Alonso Lopez	SPA	21	Beta Tools SpeedUp	Boscoscuro	20	35m 58.320s
	Celestino Vietti	ITA	13	Red Bull KTM Ajo	Kalex	19	DNF-crash
	Mattia Pasini	ITA	19	Team Ciatti Boscoscuro	Boscoscuro	14	DNF-ret

Fastest lap: Alonso Lopez, on lap 8, 1m 36.003s, 98.4mph/158.4km/h.
Lap record: Celestino Vietti, 1m 36.173s, 98.2mph/158.1km/h (2023).
Event maximum speed: Deniz Oncu, 157.1mph/252.9km/h (free practice).

Qualifying:
Weather: Dry
Air: 29° Humidity: 63% Track: 41°

1	Arbolino	1m 35.229s
2	Vietti	1m 35.240s
3	Ogura	1m 35.419s
4	Canet	1m 35.466s
5	Moreira	1m 35.521s
6	Arenas	1m 35.538s
7	Roberts	1m 35.650s
8	Lopez	1m 35.650s
9	Gonzalez	1m 35.805s
10	Aldeguer	1m 35.810s
11	Salac	1m 35.841s
12	Ramirez	1m 35.922s
13	Oncu	1m 35.967s
14	Dixon	1m 35.999s
15	Bendsneyder	1m 36.014s
16	Agius	1m 36.073s
17	Sasaki	1m 36.275s
18	Foggia	No Time

Q1

19	V d Goorbergh	1m 36.001s
20	Baltus	1m 36.045s
21	Alcoba	1m 36.056s
22	Chantra	1m 36.103s
23	Pasini	1m 36.122s
24	Garcia	1m 36.168s
25	Binder	1m 36.176s
26	Guevara	1m 36.388s
27	Masia	1m 36.542s
28	Aji	1m 36.977s
29	Cardelus	1m 37.478s
30	Orradre	1m 37.818s
31	Artigas	1m 38.242s

Fastest race laps

1	Lopez	1m 36.003s
2	Canet	1m 36.025s
3	Vietti	1m 36.063s
4	Ogura	1m 36.093s
5	Arbolino	1m 36.095s
6	Gonzalez	1m 36.114s
7	Garcia	1m 36.349s
8	Aldeguer	1m 36.373s
9	Dixon	1m 36.405s
10	Arenas	1m 36.438s
11	Moreira	1m 36.466s
12	Salac	1m 36.550s
13	Binder	1m 36.589s
14	Chantra	1m 36.590s
15	Sasaki	1m 36.654s
16	Ramirez	1m 36.733s
17	Roberts	1m 36.735s
18	Agius	1m 36.742s
19	Oncu	1m 36.834s
20	Baltus	1m 36.843s
21	Bendsneyder	1m 36.843s
22	Alcoba	1m 36.874s
23	Guevara	1m 36.954s
24	Pasini	1m 37.200s
25	V d Goorbergh	1m 37.211s
26	Aji	1m 37.327s
27	Masia	1m 37.353s
28	Foggia	1m 37.358s
29	Orradre	1m 38.052s
30	Artigas	1m 38.126s
31	Cardelus	1m 38.219s

Championship Points

1	Ogura	175
2	Garcia	166
3	Roberts	133
4	Lopez	133
5	Dixon	130
6	Aldeguer	122
7	Gonzalez	115
8	Canet	111
9	Vietti	102
10	Arbolino	97
11	Chantra	76
12	Ramirez	65
13	Arenas	63
14	Alcoba	57
15	Agius	38
16	Binder	38
17	Salac	34
18	Moreira	28
19	Oncu	27
20	Baltus	26
21	Guevara	25
22	Van den Goorbergh	20
23	Foggia	14
24	Bendsneyder	7
25	Navarro	6
26	Sasaki	4
27	Masia	4
28	Aji	3
29	Ferrari	1

Constructor Points
1	Boscoscuro	275
2	Kalex	267
3	Forward	6

MOTO3: RACE DISTANCE: 20 laps, 52.518 miles/84.520km
RACE WEATHER: Dry (air 31°, humidity 49%, track 33°)

Pos.	Rider	Nat.	No.	Entrant	Machine	Laps	Time & Speed
1	Angel Piqueras	SPA	36	Leopard Racing	Honda	20	34m 02.766s
							92.5mph/148.9km/h
2	Daniel Holgado	SPA	96	Red Bull GASGAS Tech3	GASGAS	20	34m 02.801s
3	Ivan Ortola	SPA	48	MT Helmets - MSI	KTM	20	34m 02.992s
4	Taiyo Furusato	JPN	72	Honda Team Asia	Honda	20	34m 03.025s
5	Collin Veijer	NED	95	Liqui Moly Husqvarna Intact GP	Husqvarna	20	34m 03.257s
6	Joel Kelso	AUS	66	BOE Motorsports	KTM	20	34m 03.743s
7	David Alonso	COL	80	CFMOTO Gaviota Aspar Team	CFMOTO	20	34m 03.362s
8	Tatsuki Suzuki	JPN	24	Liqui Moly Husqvarna Intact GP	Husqvarna	20	34m 06.522s
9	Luca Lunetta	ITA	58	SIC58 Squadra Corse	Honda	20	34m 09.555s
10	Filippo Farioli	ITA	7	SIC58 Squadra Corse	Honda	20	34m 10.854s
11	David Almansa	SPA	22	Kopron Rivacold Snipers Team	Honda	20	34m 10.888s
12	Jacob Roulstone	AUS	12	Red Bull GASGAS Tech3	GASGAS	20	34m 11.166s
13	Adrian Fernandez	SPA	31	Leopard Racing	Honda	20	34m 12.132s
14	Stefano Nepa	ITA	82	LEVELUP - MTA	KTM	20	34m 12.677s
15	Scott Ogden	GBR	19	FleetSafe Honda - MLav Racing	Honda	20	34m 13.833s
16	Nicola Carraro	ITA	10	LEVELUP - MTA	KTM	20	34m 19.888s
17	Ryusei Yamanaka	JPN	6	MT Helmets - MSI	KTM	20	34m 33.250s
18	Xabi Zurutuza	SPA	85	Red Bull KTM Ajo	KTM	20	34m 34.807s
19	Jakob Rosenthaler	AUT	34	Liqui Moly Husqvarna Intact GP	Husqvarna	20	34m 34.904s
20	Noah Dettwiler	SWI	55	CIP Green Power	KTM	20	34m 40.846s
21	Tatchakorn Buasri	THA	5	Honda Team Asia	Honda	20	34m 40.914s
22	Joel Esteban	SPA	78	CFMOTO Gaviota Aspar Team	CFMOTO	20	34m 46.726s
	Matteo Bertelle	ITA	18	Kopron Rivacold Snipers Team	Honda	16	DNF-crash
	Vicente Perez	SPA	21	FleetSafe Honda - MLav Racing	Honda	16	DNF-crash
	Jose Antonio Rueda	SPA	99	Red Bull KTM Ajo	KTM	0	DNF-crash
	David Munoz	SPA	64	BOE Motorsports	KTM	0	DNF-crash
	Riccardo Rossi	ITA	54	CIP Green Power	KTM	0	DNF-crash

Fastest lap: Angel Piqueras, on lap 7, 1m 40.856s, 93.7mph/150.8km/h.
Lap record: David Alonso, 1m 41.297s, 93.3mph/150.1km/h (2023).
Event maximum speed: Daniel Holgado, 133.7mph/215.1km/h (race).

Qualifying:
Weather: Dry
Air: 29° Humidity: 61% Track: 40°

1	Alonso	1m 40.505s
2	Lunetta	1m 40.922s
3	Ortola	1m 40.940s
4	Piqueras	1m 40.950s
5	Veijer	1m 40.959s
6	Kelso	1m 41.012s
7	Holgado	1m 41.028s
8	Fernandez	1m 41.106s
9	Furusato	1m 41.204s
10	Nepa	1m 41.211s
11	Farioli	1m 41.235s
12	Rueda	1m 41.293s
13	Yamanaka	1m 41.307s
14	Munoz	1m 41.331s
15	Rossi	1m 41.331s
16	Bertelle	1m 41.345s
17	Roulstone	1m 41.390s
18	Perez	1m 42.454s

Q1

19	Almansa	1m 42.030s
20	Ogden	1m 42.075s
21	Carraro	1m 42.220s
22	Zurutuza	1m 42.243s
23	Suzuki	1m 42.274s
24	Esteban	1m 42.692s
25	Dettwiler	1m 43.318s
26	Buasri	1m 43.325s
27	Rosenthaler	1m 43.686s

Fastest race laps

1	Piqueras	1m 40.856s
2	Furusato	1m 41.062s
3	Alonso	1m 41.125s
4	Kelso	1m 41.157s
5	Bertelle	1m 41.275s
6	Ortola	1m 41.320s
7	Suzuki	1m 41.344s
8	Lunetta	1m 41.350s
9	Holgado	1m 41.377s
10	Veijer	1m 41.407s
11	Almansa	1m 41.477s
12	Farioli	1m 41.478s
13	Fernandez	1m 41.640s
14	Nepa	1m 41.658s
15	Perez	1m 41.685s
16	Ogden	1m 41.693s
17	Roulstone	1m 41.736s
18	Carraro	1m 41.747s
19	Yamanaka	1m 42.058s
20	Rosenthaler	1m 42.439s
21	Dettwiler	1m 42.454s
22	Zurutuza	1m 42.465s
23	Buasri	1m 42.699s
24	Esteban	1m 42.717s

Championship Points

1	Alonso	246
2	Holgado	176
3	Ortola	173
4	Veijer	173
5	Munoz	117
6	Rueda	99
7	Piqueras	98
8	Fernandez	93
9	Kelso	93
10	Yamanaka	85
11	Furusato	78
12	Suzuki	58
13	Lunetta	57
14	Nepa	56
15	Roulstone	50
16	Esteban	42
17	Bertelle	31
18	Rossi	24
19	Farioli	20
20	Carraro	16
21	Ogden	12
22	Zurutuza	11
23	Almansa	7
24	Perez	3
25	Dettwiler	2

Constructor Points
1	CFMOTO	246
2	KTM	240
3	Husqvarna	190
4	GASGAS	181
5	Honda	172

Inset, right: "I hit a bump that wasn't there." Martin and Bastianini disappear as Bagnaia takes his turn for a race-day blunder.
Photo: Gold & Goose

Inset, centre right: Close combat for Martin and Bastianini.
Photo: Ducati Corse

Inset, far right: Martin sportingly accepted his fate.
Photo: Gold & Goose

Main: Bastianini aviates over the 'Misano kerb', now the approved method of preventing any advantage from running wide.
Photo: Ducati Corse

FIM WORLD CHAMPIONSHIP • ROUND 14

EMILIA-ROMAGNA GRAND PRIX

MISANO WORLD CIRCUIT MARCO SIMONCELLI

Above: "Oh, yeah?" Martin and Marquez react to Bastianini's explanations at the post-race press conference.

Top right: A better weekend for Yamaha and Quartararo, able to trade blows with Binder's KTM and Morbidelli's Ducati in the sprint.

Above right: Gloves off for Zarco and Miller, disputing the last point.

Right: Martin checks for potential penalties at the finish.
Photos: Gold & Goose

BACK to Misano after a weekend off, where threatening weather had melted away by Friday lunchtime, but the results continued with elements of the unexpected. Particularly on Sunday, with another fluff for Bagnaia.

He won the sprint, but his bid to win Ducati's 100th MotoGP in his own 100th premier-class outing caused puzzlement the next day. He started fast, then became slow, then fast again, with a new lap record as he closed on the leaders again. Then he fell off, early in the braking phase for Turn Eight. All quite inexplicable.

"Very strange," he said. "Normally, you cannot crash at 32 degrees. I didn't brake hard, but lost the front like I touched a bump that isn't there. But everything was strange from the start."

He'd lost the rear on the warm-up lap and again on lap one, then the front, but he still led away. Then, dropping back, he was "pushing a lot, then in a moment, one lap to another, without doing anything, I dropped lap time by six- or seven-tenths. Really strange. I never heard of a tyre starting to work after 15 laps."

Michelin's Piero Taramasso concurred: "It's not usual to see good performance at the beginning, then a hole, then good performance again." They would analyse the data, but he questioned whether the tyre was the issue.

That left long-time leader Martin and late assailant Bastianini to provide more controversy. Martin was an innocent victim, though the pair had opposing views.

Bastianini had closed on Martin, but passing was another matter. Until a desperate last-lap inside dive into Turn Nine ended in the pair colliding. Martin cannoned off way wide on to hard paving, shaking his head; Bastianini also ran over the outside kerb, but quickly regained the track, well ahead. He went on to win; Martin gesturing his anger as he crossed the line.

Unsurprisingly, Martin said that the move had been "over the limit"; Bastianini said it had been his only opportunity to try to win. And the race stewards, so often criticised for inconsistent decisions, effectively agreed. It was two title contenders fighting on the last lap. They didn't even announce an investigation.

Marc Marquez saw the point: "It's the only way to overtake with these bikes. But Enea jumped over the kerb ... that's when the question arrives. If he doesn't stay on the track, maybe it's time to drop one position. But if he does the same overtake, but stays on the track, then it's okay for me." Aleix Espargaro couldn't hide his disgust: "I don't understand what the stewards' panel is doing. One rider touched the other one, and both riders went out of the track, and they didn't even put it under investigation. The message to riders is that you can do whatever you want. It's very dangerous."

In any case, had they applied a long-lap penalty, adding three seconds because there was no chance to serve it, Bastianini would still have won, because Martin had slowed to just over five seconds behind. Meanwhile, the 'drop one position' applies not for just going over the kerb, but on to one of the prohibited areas delineated by green paint – not the situation here.

In the end, Martin's last-lap anger dissipated directly. He shook Bastianini's hand on the slow-down lap, earning kudos for his sporting attitude while still netting 20 points for a valuable lead over no-score Bagnaia.

Small signs of Japanese recovery came following tests after the previous race. For Honda, a relatively modest repeat of best-yet Aragon, where three riders had garnered ten points. For Yamaha, much more from much less – with Rins

FIM WORLD CHAMPIONSHIP | 14

lighter, it's new material, when you brake you squash more the tyre, you get a bigger contact patch, the grip is better. So it's quite different."

Also at the test was a KTM engine with revised firing intervals, welcomed by riders. "Everything's a lot calmer … it feels like it's not going anywhere, but when you look at lap times, it is," commented Binder.

Fast Moto2 rookie Diogo Moreira pulled out on Saturday with abdominal pain. It was acute appendicitis, and after surgery, he would also miss the next race.

MOTOGP SPRINT RACE – 13 laps

Familiarity bred a new all-time record for Bagnaia on Friday afternoon and another on Saturday, for his second pole in a row, third of the year. Martin was alongside, then Bastianini, only his fourth front-row of 2024.

Binder led row two from Acosta and Bezzecchi; Marc Marquez was on row three again after another Q2 slip-off, just two-tenths faster than the on-form Quartararo, ninth. Alex Marquez was last on the grid after a fall in Q1.

Martin seized the first corners from Binder, Bagnaia, Bastianini and Marc Marquez. By the end of the lap, he was seven-tenths clear, while Bagnaia was second ahead of Bastianini and Marquez. Binder, his hole-shot device having failed to disengage, was behind Acosta.

Bagnaia gradually closed and by lap seven was on Martin. The Spaniard was undone when distracted by a dashboard track-limits warning. He ran wide at Turn 13, giving Bagnaia an easy pass and a second straight sprint.

The pursuit gradually spread out, Bastianini just a second down, Marquez another four seconds away, though clear of Acosta. Binder was still sixth, but under pressure from an inspired Quartararo, who had regained seventh after a brief to-and-fro with Bezzecchi on the penultimate lap.

Morbidelli secured the last point, three-tenths adrift and a little less ahead of Vinales; Alex Marquez (essaying a medium rear against the universal softs, to prepare for the main race) had a good run to 13th from 17th.

There were 14 track-limits warnings, and of the points scorers, only Bagnaia, Marquez, Binder and Bezzecchi escaped. Mir transgressed again and suffered a long-lap, Raul Fernandez also for taking a short cut, docked three seconds because he failed to complete it.

Di Giannantonio suffered an eight-second (rear!) tyre-pressure penalty, dropping from 13th to 18th.

MOTOGP RACE – 27 laps

The first Emilia-Romagna Grand Prix since 2021 was the best race so far in the season since Le Mans, thanks to Bagnaia's slow-fast-crash performance, the tense final three laps and Bastianini's ruthless finish.

The contest had a different complexion at the start. As if anticipating Martin's superior starting capabilities, pole-sitter Bagnaia managed the first corner to perfection, holding a tight line to squeeze by the Spaniard, who was deep, on the way to Turn Two. Bastianini, Binder, Acosta and Marquez followed, with Bezzecchi, Quartararo and Morbidelli in tow.

As Binder crashed out of fourth on the second lap, it became clear that Bagnaia's rhythm wasn't what it should have been. Martin first made a play to pass on lap three, before decisively barging by at Turn Eight on the next lap. Then it was Bastianini's turn on lap five, this time at Turn Ten. Acosta's hopes of further pressuring the defending champion had been shaken by a massive front-end slide through the third of the four fast rights, followed by a fast crash at Turn 15, but there were fears that the fading factory Ducati might yet fall into Marquez's clutches by lap 11.

Bagnaia was struggling with a lack of rear grip early on. Then came a puzzling recovery. As the gap between Martin and Bastianini fluctuated between two- and six-tenths, Bagnaia set personal-best times on laps 12 and 13, before aston-

sidelined by a dose of flu, Quartararo made 12 points in his best weekend of the season so far. It would have been 14, had he not run low of fuel just short of the flag, dropping from fifth to seventh.

"To see the first guys not super-far away makes me happy," he said, noting three successive races where he had scored in the sprints. Engine work had returned some Yamaha character, sacrificing power for better manoeuvrability. "At the beginning of the year, I was able to stay with the KTM on the straights," he explained. "Step by step, we went with less power, but more agility. Now we have to get back the power, but keep the agility."

More radical reforms were afoot, with MD Lin Jarvis confirming that a V4 was already undergoing bench tests, with the possibility of it being ready to race as soon as 2025. It was 'Plan B' rather than a decision to switch from the company's now unique inline engine, exploring possibilities for the 2027 850cc rules. "The inline four still has plenty of capacity to be developed, but when all of your competitors use V4s, it's important to fully understand its potential." More than ten years previously, Valentino Rossi had already been urging Yamaha to develop a V4.

Riders had tested Michelin's new front tyre after the previous race, to a generally favourable response. Now came news that its introduction would be delayed for a year, to 2026. The current front profile needed changing to deal with the greater aerodynamic forces and combat sensitivity to temperature changes, and the delay would mean that the much-derided tyre-pressure penalties would remain. Taramasso explained: "After analysing the data, we decided to push back the introduction, because we need the time to make a few changes, then test again. This tyre is almost 1kg

GRAN PREMIO PRAMAC DELL'EMILIA-ROMAGNA

Above: All smiles. No Pecco, but Michele Pirro was on hand to celebrate Ducati's 100th GP win, along with clinching the 2024 constructors' title.

Top right: Moto3 title favourite Alonso tightened his grip on the championship with another win, ahead of Holgado, Piqueras and Veijer.

Top far right: A second win in four races for home boy Vietti.

Above right: Too much of a good thing? A second Misano race in a fortnight attracted fewer spectators.

Right: How to define a hair's breadth. Vietti pipped Canet at the death.
Photos: Gold & Goose

ishing fastest laps on the 15th and 16th. He began recovering three-tenths per lap to go from 3.3 seconds off the leader to 1.6s by lap 21. Then his afternoon took another bizarre turn.

Braking for Turn Eight, his front unexpectedly tucked.

Now there were two. Three laps from home, Bastianini began to climb all over Martin's rear, almost taking them both down through Turns Four and Five. The Spaniard had an edge exiting Turn Ten on to the back straight, making a pass into the following series of slowing rights risky. The Italian knew he had to pounce in sector one.

Bastianini couldn't have been closer as they started the final lap. And even though Martin braked as late as possible entering Turn Four, his rival moved to the inside anyway. There was contact, which forced Martin to lift. And though Bastianini ran just over the kerb, it was deemed fair. Martin furiously coasted to second, with Marquez a further 2.8s in arrears in third.

Behind, Bezzecchi rode to fourth, his best result since Jerez, despite struggling in the early laps with a full fuel tank and a new rear tyre pushing the front.

Quartararo had gradually lost time behind him, but heroically was fending off Morbidelli. By the end, Vinales – who had disposed of team-mate Espargaro shortly before half-distance – had joined the pair. But the Frenchman's efforts came to naught almost within sight of the flag as he ran out of fuel, dropping from fifth to seventh.

Two seconds behind, Espargaro was a muted eighth, five seconds clear of Alex Marquez, who had another good ride through from his last-on-the-grid start. All the same, in a processional race, his last overtake had been on lap seven on Jack Miller, who had finished lap two tenth after a stirring getaway from 19th, only to drop back to an eventual 16th, with familiar chatter and grip issues.

Oliveira had led the next group for most of the way, with Mir finishing top Honda (his season's best so far), clear of Marini, who had passed Raul Fernandez on the last lap. A pained Di Giannantonio was 14th, dropped from 11th in the closing laps by a track-limits long-lap; Zarco wrapped up the final point, from Miller, Nakagami and Fernandez, with the remounted Binder last.

After his championship lead had been trimmed to just four points in the sprint, circumstances gave Martin 24 points of breathing space before the fly-aways.

MOTO2 RACE – 22 laps

Canet claimed a first pole since round four, with Roberts also displacing Friday leader Arbolino. Vietti and Dixon led Aldeguer on row two; Ogura was seventh, while title rival Garcia was 13th.

For 18 laps, this contest was low on action. But the final four laps made up for it as Vietti made amends for a costly crash a fortnight before, outfoxing and outdragging a hapless Aron Canet to the finish line.

The pair had chased down Arbolino after the Italian enjoyed a flawless first lap, building an early buffer of seven-tenths. They had closed by lap eight, and despite a few close calls – Vietti almost tailgating Arbolino at Turn Two on lap 17 – the pair were biding their time.

On lap 19, Arbolino ran wide midway through the fast rights, dropping to third. Vietti almost collided with Canet into the final corner. Arbolino stayed close, then regained control at Turn Eight on the penultimate lap. He looked set for a first victory of a difficult year.

But a missed downshift into Turn 14 for the final time sent him wide again, giving Canet the lead. Even then, he couldn't win it. He was too defensive into the last corner. Vietti took a sweeping line and a faster exit, and was ahead over the line by a minuscule, but distinct 0.029-second margin.

Heartbroken in third, Arbolino knelt in penitence in front of a grandstand full of his fans, but he could content himself with having set a red-hot pace: The race time was close to 12 seconds faster than the fortnight before.

Ogura, Aldeguer and (a little way back) Roberts were never in contention, in the same order all race long. The results were valuable for their championship challenges, not least because of crashes for Garcia and Dixon, both of whom fell prey to Turn Two on the sixth lap. Garcia was 12th, Dixon seventh at the time. Roberts had rekindled some verve after a ten-day break back home in LA, finally casting off the disappointment of his MotoGP rejection.

Rookie Senna Agius was an excellent seventh, overtaking Ramirez in the early laps, then keeping him at bay. Lopez was ninth after gaining five places on the first lap from his 17th-placed grid position. Salac came through steadily to tenth in a race with minimal overtaking, past Foggia and on the last lap also Gonzalez.

Guevara was close; three seconds back, Chantra eventually made it to 14th from 18th on lap one, after a second poor qualifying position; while Alcoba snitched the last point from Binder on the last lap, Arenas close behind.

Van den Goorbergh, Oncu and Masia were early fallers.

Ogura now had a 22-point buffer over his no-score teammate, Garcia.

MOTO3 RACE – 23 laps

Taiyo Furusato came through Q1 for a career-first pole, putting Alonso second. Piqueras was third, only a second front-row start for the previous fortnight's winner, putting two Hondas up front. Ortola, Nepa and Veijer were behind; Friday leader Fernandez (another Honda) was seventh.

Alonso seized the lead from Furusato at Turn 13, with Veijer third at the end of the first lap, from Piqueras, Holgado, Fernandez and Ortola. By then, Munoz had already clashed with Nepa in the first corners, repeating the misadventure of the previous Misano race that had earned him a double long-lap, but evading the punishment by crashing out.

Holgado took over up front on lap four, but the lead was only notional. On lap seven, Piqueras was in front over the line, and at half-distance, there were still 11 riders within two seconds, Furusato at the back of the group after a collision with Fernandez while disputing fifth on lap nine.

Veijer set a new record on the 13th as he closed on a breakaway quartet, led from lap ten by Alonso, who was intent on revenge after being roughed up on the final lap two weeks before.

Few riders could live with his late-race pace, though Holgado got ahead on the penultimate lap, Piqueras following him through.

As Piqueras shaped to pass Holgado into Turn Eight, Alonso outbraked both of them before defending admirably into Turn 14 for his eighth win of the year.

Piqueras was an excellent second, while Holgado found himself demoted to fourth behind Veijer after exceeding track limits on the final lap. Ortola was a costly fifth, almost three seconds back; Lunetta led the next rider pack from Kelso, Fernandez, Bertelle, Rueda and Suzuki, with 12th-placed Farioli out of touch and Furusato fading to 13th behind him.

FIM WORLD CHAMPIONSHIP: ROUND 14
GRAN PREMIO PRAMAC DELL'EMILIA-ROMAGNA
20–22 SEPTEMBER, 2024

MISANO WORLD CIRCUIT
27 laps
Length: 4.230 km / 2.63 miles
Width: 14m

MOTOGP: RACE DISTANCE: 27 laps, 70.900 miles/114.102km
WEATHER: Dry (air 21°, humidity 69%, track 28°)

Pos.	Rider	Nat.	No.	Entrant	Machine	Race tyre choice	Laps	Time & speed
1	Enea Bastianini	ITA	23	Ducati Lenovo Team	Ducati Desmosedici GP24	F: Medium/R: Medium	27	41m 14.653s 103.1ph/165.9km/h
2	Jorge Martin	SPA	89	Prima Pramac Racing	Ducati Desmosedici GP24	F: Medium/R: Medium	27	41m 19.655s
3	Marc Marquez	SPA	93	Gresini Racing MotoGP	Ducati Desmosedici GP23	F: Medium/R: Medium	27	41m 22.501s
4	Marco Bezzecchi	ITA	72	Pertamina Enduro VR46 Racing	Ducati Desmosedici GP23	F: Medium/R: Soft	27	41m 23.853s
5	Franco Morbidelli	ITA	21	Prima Pramac Racing	Ducati Desmosedici GP23	F: Medium/R: Medium	27	41m 28.254s
6	Maverick Vinales	SPA	12	Aprilia Racing	Aprilia RS-GP24	F: Medium/R: Medium	27	41m 30.137s
7	Fabio Quartararo	FRA	20	Monster Energy Yamaha MotoGP	Yamaha YZR-M1	F: Medium/R: Medium	27	41m 35.575s
8	Aleix Espargaro	SPA	41	Aprilia Racing	Aprilia RS-GP24	F: Medium/R: Medium	27	41m 37.448s
9	Alex Marquez	SPA	73	Gresini Racing MotoGP	Ducati Desmosedici GP23	F: Medium/R: Medium	27	41m 42.357s
10	Miguel Oliveira	POR	88	Trackhouse Racing	Aprilia RS-GP24	F: Medium/R: Medium	27	41m 46.544s
11	Joan Mir	SPA	36	Repsol Honda Team	Honda RC213V	F: Medium/R: Medium	27	41m 47.715s
12	Luca Marini	ITA	10	Repsol Honda Team	Honda RC213V	F: Medium/R: Medium	27	41m 50.064s
13	Raul Fernandez	SPA	25	Trackhouse Racing	Aprilia RS-GP24	F: Medium/R: Medium	27	41m 50.988s
14	Fabio Di Giannantonio	ITA	49	Pertamina Enduro VR46 Racing	Ducati Desmosedici GP23	F: Medium/R: Medium	27	41m 52.048s
15	Johann Zarco	FRA	5	CASTROL Honda LCR	Honda RC213V	F: Medium/R: Medium	27	41m 53.562s
16	Jack Miller	AUS	43	Red Bull KTM Factory Racing	KTM RC16	F: Medium/R: Medium	27	41m 55.107s
17	Takaaki Nakagami	JPN	30	IDEMITSU Honda LCR	Honda RC213V	F: Medium/R: Medium	27	42m 01.047s
18	Augusto Fernandez	SPA	37	Red Bull GASGAS Tech3	KTM RC16	F: Medium/R: Medium	27	42m 02.408s
19	Brad Binder	RSA	33	Red Bull KTM Factory Racing	KTM RC16	F: Medium/R: Medium	27	42m 40.571s
	Francesco Bagnaia	ITA	1	Ducati Lenovo Team	Ducati Desmosedici GP24	F: Medium/R: Medium	20	DNF-crash
	Pedro Acosta	SPA	31	Red Bull GASGAS Tech3	KTM RC16	F: Medium/R: Medium	8	DNF-crash

Fastest lap: Francesco Bagnaia, on lap 16, 1m 30.877s, 104.0mph/167.4km/h.
Lap record: Marc Marquez, 1m 31.564s, 103.2mph/166.1km/h (2024).
Event maximum speed: Jorge Martin, 190.1mph/305.9km/h (warm-up).

Qualifying: Weather: Dry **Air:** 22° **Humidity:** 67% **Track:** 30°
1 Bagnaia 1m 30.031s, 2 Martin 1m 30.245s, 3 Bastianini 1m 30.564s, 4 Binder 1m 30.636s,
5 Acosta 1m 30.731s, 6 Bezzecchi 1m 30.837s, 7 M. Marquez 1m 30.880s, 8 Vinales 1m 30.909s,
9 Quartararo 1m 30.921s, 10 Morbidelli 1m 30.932s, 11 A. Espargaro 1m 31.037s, 12 Oliveira 1m 31.114s.
Q1: 13 Di Giannantonio 1m 31.285s, 14 R. Fernandez 1m 31.402s, 15 Marini 1m 31.428s, 16 Mir 1m 31.450s,
17 Zarco 1m 31.501s, 18 A. Fernandez 1m 31.554s, 19 Miller 1m 31.695s, 20 Nakagami 1m 32.061s,
21 A. Marquez 1m 32.332s, 22 Rins No Time.

SPRINT RACE: 13 laps, 34.137 miles/54.938km
WEATHER: Dry (air 24°, humidity 61%, track 36°)

Pos.	Rider	Race tyre choice	Laps	Time & speed
1	Francesco Bagnaia	F: Medium/R: Soft	13	19m 50.237s 103.2mph/166.1km/h
2	Jorge Martin	F: Medium/R: Soft	13	19m 50.522s
3	Enea Bastianini	F: Medium/R: Soft	13	19m 51.556s
4	Marc Marquez	F: Medium/R: Soft	13	19m 55.623s
5	Pedro Acosta	F: Medium/R: Soft	13	19m 56.817s
6	Brad Binder	F: Medium/R: Soft	13	19m 58.380s
7	Fabio Quartararo	F: Medium/R: Soft	13	19m 58.642s
8	Marco Bezzecchi	F: Medium/R: Soft	13	19m 59.202s
9	Franco Morbidelli	F: Medium/R: Soft	13	19m 59.508s
10	Maverick Vinales	F: Medium/R: Soft	13	19m 59.775s
11	Miguel Oliveira	F: Medium/R: Soft	13	20m 01.779s
12	Aleix Espargaro	F: Medium/R: Soft	13	20m 02.286s
13	Alex Marquez	F: Medium/R: Medium	13	20m 06.803s
14	Jack Miller	F: Medium/R: Soft	13	20m 09.648s
15	Luca Marini	F: Medium/R: Soft	13	20m 10.338s
16	Johann Zarco	F: Medium/R: Soft	13	20m 10.835s
17	Raul Fernandez	F: Medium/R: Soft	13	20m 10.979s
18	Fabio Di Giannantonio	F: Medium/R: Soft	13	20m 13.056s*
19	Takaaki Nakagami	F: Medium/R: Soft	13	20m 15.631s
20	Augusto Fernandez	F: Medium/R: Soft	13	20m 15.668s
21	Joan Mir	F: Medium/R: Soft	13	20m 17.445s

* Fabio di Giannantonio: 8s penalty – technical infringement.

Fastest race lap: Francesco Bagnaia, on lap 5, 1m 30.792s.

Fastest race laps
1 Bagnaia 1m 30.877s, 2 Bastianini 1m 31.057s, 3 Martin 1m 31.150s, 4 Vinales 1m 31.411s,
5 Morbidelli 1m 31.435s, 6 Bezzecchi 1m 31.435s, 7 A. Espargaro 1m 31.437s, 8 M. Marquez 1m 31.481s,
9 Acosta 1m 31.585s, 10 Quartararo 1m 31.623s, 11 Zarco 1m 31.905s, 12 Mir 1m 31.972s,
13 A. Marquez 1m 32.003s, 14 Marini 1m 32.018s, 15 Oliveira 1m 32.079s, 16 R. Fernandez 1m 32.132s,
17 Di Giannantonio 1m 32.164s, 18 Binder 1m 32.228s, 19 Miller 1m 32.278s, 20 Nakagami 1m 32.582s, 21 A. Fernandez 1m 32.646s.

Grid order	1	2	3	4	5	6	7	8	9	10	11	12	13	14	15	16	17	18	19	20	21	22	23	24	25	26	27
1 BAGNAIA	1	1	1	89	89	89	89	89	89	89	89	89	89	89	89	89	89	89	89	89	89	89	89	89	89	89	23
89 MARTIN	89	89	89	1	23	23	23	23	23	23	23	23	23	23	23	23	23	23	23	23	23	23	23	23	23	23	89
23 BASTIANINI	23	23	23	23	1	1	1	1	1	1	1	1	1	1	1	1	1	93	93	93	93	93	93	93	93	93	93
33 BINDER	33	31	31	31	31	31	31	31	93	93	93	93	93	93	93	93	93	72	72	72	72	72	72	72	72	72	72
31 ACOSTA	31	93	93	93	93	93	93	93	72	72	72	72	72	72	72	72	72	20	20	20	20	20	20	20	20	21	
72 BEZZECCHI	93	72	72	72	72	72	72	72	20	20	20	20	20	20	20	20	20	21	21	21	21	21	21	21	21	12	
93 M. MARQUEZ	72	20	20	20	20	20	20	20	21	21	21	21	21	21	21	21	21	12	12	12	12	12	12	12	12	20	
12 VINALES	20	21	21	21	21	21	21	21	41	41	41	12	12	12	12	12	12	41	41	41	41	41	41	41			
20 QUARTARARO	12	41	41	41	41	41	41	41	12	12	12	41	41	41	41	41	41	73	73	73	73	73	73	73			
21 MORBIDELLI	21	43	43	43	12	12	12	12	73	73	73	73	73	73	73	73	73	88	88	88	88	88	88	88			
41 A. ESPARGARO	41	12	12	12	43	43	73	73	43	43	43	43	88	88	88	88	88	49	49	49	49	36	36	36	11		
88 OLIVEIRA	43	88	88	88	73	73	43	43	88	88	88	88	49	49	49	49	49	25	25	25	36	25	25	10	12		
49 DI GIANNANTONIO	88	49	73	49	49	49	88	88	49	49	49	49	25	25	25	25	25	36	36	36	25	10	10	25	13		
25 R. FERNANDEZ	49	73	49	88	88	88	49	49	25	25	25	25	43	43	43	43	43	10	10	10	49	49	49	49	14		
10 MARINI	37	37	37	37	25	25	25	25	5	5	5	5	5	10	10	10	10	43	43	43	43	43	43	5	15		
36 MIR	73	5	5	25	37	37	37	5	36	36	36	36	36	5	5	5	5	5	5	5	5	5	5	43			
5 ZARCO	10	10	25	5	5	5	5	37	36	36	10	10	10	10	30	30	30	5	30	30	30	30	30	30			
37 A. FERNANDEZ	5	25	36	36	36	36	36	36	10	10	37	37	37	30	5	5	30	30	37	37	37	37	37	37			
43 MILLER	30	36	10	10	10	10	10	10	30	30	30	30	30	37	37	37	37	37	33	33	33	33	33	33			
30 NAKAGAMI	25	30	30	30	30	30	30	30	37	37	33	33	33	33	33	33	33	33									
73 A. MARQUEZ	36	33	33	33	33	33	33																				

Championship Points

1	Martin	216	(125)	341
2	Bagnaia	238	(79)	317
3	Bastianini	213	(69)	282
5	Binder	126	(39)	165
6	Acosta	98	(59)	157
7	Vinales	98	(51)	149
8	A. Espargaro	81	(46)	127
9	A. Marquez	103	(18)	121
10	Di Giannantonio	105	(16)	121
11	Bezzecchi	103	(5)	108
12	Morbidelli	72	(30)	102
13	Quartararo	58	(15)	73
14	Oliveira	55	(16)	71
15	Miller	35	(23)	58
16	R. Fernandez	47	(2)	49
17	Zarco	22	(0)	22
18	Nakagami	21	(0)	21
19	Mir	19	(1)	20
20	A. Fernandez	17	(3)	20
21	Rins	15	(0)	15
22	P. Espargaro	11	(1)	12
23	Pedrosa	0	(7)	7
24	Marini	5	(0)	5
25	Bradl	2	(0)	2

Constructor Points

1	Ducati	341	(159)	500
2	KTM	159	(80)	239
3	Aprilia	142	(92)	234
4	Yamaha	69	(15)	84
5	Honda	40	(2)	42

MOTO2: RACE DISTANCE: 22 laps, 57.770 miles/92.972km
RACE WEATHER: Dry (air 21°, humidity 67%, track 28°)

Pos.	Rider	Nat.	No.	Entrant	Machine	Laps	Time & Speed
1	**Celestino Vietti**	ITA	13	Red Bull KTM Ajo	Kalex	22	35m 14.240s
							98.4mph/158.3km/h
2	**Aron Canet**	SPA	44	Fantic Racing	Kalex	22	35m 14.269s
3	**Tony Arbolino**	ITA	14	Elf Marc VDS Racing Team	Kalex	22	35m 16.161s
4	**Ai Ogura**	JPN	79	MT Helmets – MSI	Boscoscuro	22	35m 17.230s
5	**Fermin Aldeguer**	SPA	54	MB Conveyors SpeedUp	Boscoscuro	22	35m 18.731s
6	**Joe Roberts**	USA	16	OnlyFans American Racing Team	Kalex	22	35m 24.047s
7	**Senna Agius**	AUS	81	Liqui Moly Husqvarna Intact GP	Kalex	22	35m 26.749s
8	**Marcos Ramirez**	SPA	24	OnlyFans American Racing Team	Kalex	22	35m 27.174s
9	**Alonso Lopez**	SPA	21	MB Conveyors SpeedUp	Boscoscuro	22	35m 28.326s
10	**Filip Salac**	CZE	12	Elf Marc VDS Racing Team	Kalex	22	35m 30.295s
11	**Manuel Gonzalez**	SPA	18	QJMOTOR Gresini Moto2	Kalex	22	35m 30.705s
12	**Dennis Foggia**	ITA	71	Italtrans Racing Team	Kalex	22	35m 32.891s
13	**Izan Guevara**	SPA	28	CFMOTO Inde Aspar Team	Kalex	22	35m 33.730s
14	**Somkiat Chantra**	THA	35	IDEMITSU Honda Team Asia	Kalex	22	35m 36.641s
15	**Jeremy Alcoba**	SPA	52	Yamaha VR46 Master Camp	Kalex	22	35m 37.282s
16	Darryn Binder	RSA	15	Liqui Moly Husqvarna Intact GP	Kalex	22	35m 37.681s
17	Albert Arenas	SPA	75	QJMOTOR Gresini Moto2	Kalex	22	35m 37.788s
18	Barry Baltus	BEL	7	RW-Idrofoglia Racing GP	Kalex	22	35m 38.633s
19	Ayumu Sasaki	JPN	22	Yamaha VR46 Master Camp	Kalex	22	35m 51.805s
20	Daniel Munoz	SPA	17	Preicanos Racing Team	Kalex	22	35m 53.519s
21	Mario Aji	INA	34	IDEMITSU Honda Team Asia	Kalex	22	35m 54.586s
22	Xavier Artigas	SPA	43	KLINT Forward Factory Team	Forward	22	36m 04.393s
23	Xavi Cardelus	AND	20	Fantic Racing	Kalex	22	36m 06.727s
24	Alex Escrig	SPA	11	KLINT Forward Factory Team	Forward	22	36m 06.968s
	Matteo Ferrari	ITA	23	QJMOTOR Gresini Moto2	Kalex	16	DNF-ret in pit
	Zonta van den Goorbergh	NED	84	RW-Idrofoglia Racing GP	Kalex	8	DNF-crash
	Jake Dixon	GBR	96	CFMOTO Inde Aspar Team	Kalex	5	DNF-crash
	Sergio Garcia	SPA	3	MT Helmets – MSI	Boscoscuro	5	DNF-crash
	Jaume Masia	SPA	5	Preicanos Racing Team	Kalex	4	DNF-crash
	Deniz Oncu	TUR	53	Red Bull KTM Ajo	Kalex	3	DNF-crash
	Diogo Moreira	BRA	10	Italtrans Racing Team	Kalex	–	DNS

Fastest lap: Celestino Vietti, on lap 4, 1m 35.468s, 99.0mph/159.3km/h.
Lap record: Alonso Lopez, 1m 36.003s, 98.4mph/158.4km/h (2024).
Event maximum speed: Izan Guevara, 158.3mph/254.7km/h (race).

Qualifying
Weather: Dry
Air: 24° Humidity: 61% Track: 36°

1	Canet	1m 34.935s
2	Roberts	1m 34.939s
3	Arbolino	1m 34.945s
4	Vietti	1m 34.972s
5	Dixon	1m 35.230s
6	Aldeguer	1m 35.279s
7	Ogura	1m 35.307s
8	V d Goorbergh	1m 35.380s
9	Foggia	1m 35.403s
10	Ramirez	1m 35.410s
11	Agius	1m 35.427s
12	Salac	1m 35.439s
13	Garcia	1m 35.443s
14	Arenas	1m 35.463s
15	Gonzalez	1m 35.464s
16	Baltus	1m 35.491s
17	Lopez	1m 35.540s
18	Chantra	1m 35.805s
Q1		
19	Moreira	1m 35.518s
20	Binder	1m 35.701s
21	Masia	1m 35.725s
22	Sasaki	1m 35.888s
23	Alcoba	1m 35.929s
24	Guevara	1m 35.989s
25	Ferrari	1m 36.259s
26	Aji	1m 36.457s
27	Oncu	1m 36.474s
28	Escrig	1m 36.639s
29	Munoz	1m 36.758s
30	Cardelus	1m 36.904s
31	Artigas	1m 37.188s

Fastest race laps

1	Vietti	1m 35.468s
2	Canet	1m 35.474s
3	Arbolino	1m 35.476s
4	Ogura	1m 35.610s
5	Aldeguer	1m 35.625s
6	Roberts	1m 35.852s
7	Dixon	1m 35.856s
8	Agius	1m 35.905s
9	Ramirez	1m 35.966s
10	Gonzalez	1m 36.003s
11	Garcia	1m 36.061s
12	Salac	1m 36.102s
13	Lopez	1m 36.105s
14	Foggia	1m 36.168s
15	Binder	1m 36.192s
16	Guevara	1m 36.278s
17	Alcoba	1m 36.300s
18	Baltus	1m 36.307s
19	Arenas	1m 36.308s
20	Chantra	1m 36.381s
21	Sasaki	1m 36.555s
22	Aji	1m 36.571s
23	V d Goorbergh	1m 36.971s
24	Masia	1m 37.009s
25	Oncu	1m 37.010s
26	Munoz	1m 37.027s
27	Cardelus	1m 37.079s
28	Ferrari	1m 37.084s
29	Artigas	1m 37.363s
30	Escrig	1m 37.553s

Championship Points

1	Ogura	188
2	Garcia	166
3	Roberts	143
4	Lopez	140
5	Aldeguer	133
6	Canet	131
7	Dixon	130
8	Vietti	127
9	Gonzalez	120
10	Arbolino	113
11	Chantra	78
12	Ramirez	73
13	Arenas	63
14	Alcoba	58
15	Agius	47
16	Salac	40
17	Binder	38
18	Moreira	28
19	Guevara	28
20	Oncu	27
21	Baltus	26
22	Van den Goorbergh	20
23	Foggia	18
24	Bendsneyder	7
25	Navarro	6
26	Sasaki	4
27	Masia	4
28	Aji	3
29	Ferrari	1

Constructor Points

1	Kalex	292
2	Boscoscuro	288
3	Forward	6

MOTO3: RACE DISTANCE: 20 laps, 52.518 miles/84.520km
RACE WEATHER: Dry (air 19°, humidity 73%, track 20°)

Pos.	Rider	Nat.	No.	Entrant	Machine	Laps	Time & Speed
1	**David Alonso**	COL	80	CFMOTO Gaviota Aspar Team	CFMOTO	20	33m 53.212s
							93.0mph/149.6km/h
2	**Angel Piqueras**	SPA	36	Leopard Racing	Honda	20	33m 53.387s
3	**Collin Veijer**	NED	95	Liqui Moly Husqvarna Intact GP	Husqvarna	20	33m 53.579s
4	**Daniel Holgado**	SPA	96	Red Bull GASGAS Tech3	GASGAS	20	33m 53.507s
5	**Ivan Ortola**	SPA	48	MT Helmets – MSI	KTM	20	33m 56.175s
6	**Luca Lunetta**	ITA	58	SIC58 Squadra Corse	Honda	20	33m 57.762s
7	**Joel Kelso**	AUS	66	BOE Motorsports	KTM	20	33m 57.934s
8	**Adrian Fernandez**	SPA	31	Leopard Racing	Honda	20	33m 58.786s
9	**Matteo Bertelle**	ITA	18	Kopron Rivacold Snipers Team	Honda	20	33m 59.180s
10	**Jose Antonio Rueda**	SPA	99	Red Bull KTM Ajo	KTM	20	33m 59.224s
11	**Tatsuki Suzuki**	JPN	24	Liqui Moly Husqvarna Intact GP	Husqvarna	20	33m 59.255s
12	**Filippo Farioli**	ITA	7	SIC58 Squadra Corse	Honda	20	34m 02.470s
13	**Taiyo Furusato**	JPN	72	Honda Team Asia	Honda	20	34m 04.766s
14	**Stefano Nepa**	ITA	82	LEVELUP – MTA	KTM	20	34m 06.210s
15	**Ryusei Yamanaka**	JPN	6	MT Helmets – MSI	KTM	20	34m 08.691s
16	Nicola Carraro	ITA	10	LEVELUP – MTA	KTM	20	34m 10.487s
17	David Almansa	SPA	22	Kopron Rivacold Snipers Team	Honda	20	34m 12.179s
18	Scott Ogden	GBR	19	FleetSafe Honda – MLav Racing	Honda	20	34m 12.508s
19	Xabi Zurutuza	SPA	85	Red Bull KTM Ajo	KTM	20	34m 24.008s
20	Joel Esteban	SPA	78	CFMOTO Gaviota Aspar Team	CFMOTO	20	34m 24.023s
21	Jacob Roulstone	AUS	12	Red Bull GASGAS Tech3	GASGAS	20	34m 24.425s
22	Noah Dettwiler	SWI	55	CIP Green Power	KTM	20	34m 27.934s
23	Riccardo Rossi	ITA	54	CIP Green Power	KTM	20	34m 52.073s
	David Munoz	SPA	64	BOE Motorsports	KTM	9	DNF-crash
	Tatchakorn Buasri	THA	5	Honda Team Asia	Honda	2	DNF-crash
	Vicente Perez	SPA	21	FleetSafe Honda – MLav Racing	Honda	–	DNS

Fastest lap: Collin Veijer, on lap 13, 1m 40.629s, 93.9mph/151.1km/h.
Lap record: Angel Piqueras, 1m 40.856s, 93.7mph/150.8km/h (2024).
Event maximum speed: Tatsuki Suzuki, 133.7mph/215.1km/h (race).

Qualifying:
Weather: Dry
Air: 23° Humidity: 62% Track: 36°

1	Furusato	1m 40.394s
2	Alonso	1m 40.453s
3	Piqueras	1m 40.460s
4	Ortola	1m 40.461s
5	Nepa	1m 40.510s
6	Veijer	1m 40.614s
7	Fernandez	1m 40.677s
8	Munoz	1m 40.713s
9	Rueda	1m 40.744s
10	Kelso	1m 40.772s
11	Holgado	1m 40.791s
12	Lunetta	1m 40.820s
13	Farioli	1m 41.228s
14	Bertelle	1m 41.256s
15	Yamanaka	1m 41.556s
16	Ogden	1m 41.704s
17	Suzuki	1m 41.894s
18	Almansa	1m 42.678s
Q1		
19	Roulstone	1m 41.658s
20	Rossi	1m 41.832s
21	Carraro	1m 41.861s
22	Esteban	1m 41.903s
23	Zurutuza	1m 41.986s
24	Perez	1m 42.127s
25	Dettwiler	1m 42.200s
26	Buasri	1m 42.725s

Fastest race laps

1	Veijer	1m 40.629s
2	Piqueras	1m 40.641s
3	Ortola	1m 40.646s
4	Holgado	1m 40.659s
5	Alonso	1m 40.710s
6	Lunetta	1m 40.817s
7	Suzuki	1m 40.885s
8	Kelso	1m 40.891s
9	Furusato	1m 41.038s
10	Rueda	1m 41.048s
11	Farioli	1m 41.092s
12	Fernandez	1m 41.157s
13	Bertelle	1m 41.166s
14	Yamanaka	1m 41.190s
15	Nepa	1m 41.345s
16	Almansa	1m 41.545s
17	Ogden	1m 41.590s
18	Munoz	1m 41.699s
19	Esteban	1m 41.753s
20	Carraro	1m 41.793s
21	Rossi	1m 41.802s
22	Roulstone	1m 41.822s
23	Zurutuza	1m 41.888s
24	Dettwiler	1m 42.290s

Championship Points

1	Alonso	271
2	Holgado	189
3	Veijer	189
4	Ortola	184
5	Piqueras	118
6	Munoz	117
7	Rueda	105
8	Kelso	102
9	Fernandez	101
10	Yamanaka	86
11	Furusato	81
12	Lunetta	67
13	Suzuki	63
14	Nepa	58
15	Roulstone	50
16	Esteban	42
17	Bertelle	38
18	Rossi	24
19	Farioli	24
20	Carraro	16
21	Ogden	12
22	Zurutuza	11
23	Almansa	7
24	Perez	3
25	Dettwiler	2

Constructor Points

1	CFMOTO	271
2	KTM	251
3	Husqvarna	206
4	GASGAS	194
5	Honda	192

Above: Rostrum or not? Acosta looks subdued as he awaits the verdict.

Right: Big-boy bromance. Bagnaia congratulates Martin on his win.

Main: Martin leaves Acosta and the rest in a shimmering heat haze.
Photos: Gold & Goose

FIM WORLD CHAMPIONSHIP • ROUND 15
INDONESIAN GRAND PRIX
MANDALIKA CIRCUIT

ANOTHER race, another blunder. This time, it was Martin who suffered the unforced crash, on the first lap of the sprint, after a trademark blazing start had gained him a handy early lead. As sprint winner Bagnaia had it, this was becoming "a championship of mistakes."

Between them, Martin and Bagnaia had crashed out of ten races – four for the Spaniard, six for the Italian. In each of the last four rounds, one or other of them had fallen in either sprint or GP.

Bagnaia was not alone in blaming Michelin's rear tyre compound, new for this season. Marc Marquez also spoke of how "the rear is pushing the front." Confusingly, Aprilia's Espargaro complained of a lack of rear grip: "It looks like we are not making the rear tyre work."

For Bagnaia, "The rear made an enormous step forward, but we are braking so hard because the rear is also helping with braking … entering corners much, much faster. At all circuits, we have improved the pace a lot. At this limit, it is easy also to have a crash."

Michelin made headlines for another more oblique reason, a different order of blunder, after Sunday's race. It was that frequent bugbear, the minimum-tyre-pressure regulation, and once again, it provoked the stewards into frankly laughable shenanigans.

Martin redeemed himself by winning on Sunday, pushed hard by an inspired Pedro Acosta. Yet the 20-year-old was glum in the post-race ceremonials, for a Damoclean sword hung over him – an investigation to confirm live data that he'd been below the required 8.5 bar for more than 40 per cent of the race. The mandatory 16-second penalty would have kicked him off the podium, to ninth.

He was guilty, it transpired, but absolved. A leaking valve seal was the culprit. The right decision, obviously. But it took too long, and to many, the rule itself was in the wrong.

Adding to the muddle, stewards announced that Binder and Nakagami were also under investigation, flagged up by the real-time onboard monitoring equipment – but (obviously because of the pressure of time on travel arrangements from offshore Lombok to Japan) the decision would be announced "at the next event". Since this would drop Binder from fifth to tenth (Nakagami one place to 12th), the delay was reprehensible. Then, suddenly all change: they'd reached a decision after all. Binder, innocent; Nakagami, guilty.

Being stewards, no explanation was required.

This attracted widespread criticism, of the process and of the rule, which obliged teams to make an educated guess at the correct pressure without knowing whether the rider would be alone or in a group, and exacted a swingeing penalty if they erred.

The focus was on Michelin again, who wanted the rule because modern aero and ride-height devices were over-stressing their existing front tyre. The French company, when in competition with Dunlop and Bridgestone, had produced special track-specific tyres virtually overnight for Rossi. This was a matter of special compound rather than actual construction, but now – as uncontested control-tyre suppliers – they had failed to solve the problem for more than two years.

The criticism was more acute because a new front promised for 2025 had been tested after the first Misano race, to riders' general approval – only to be told that pending further development, the tyre would not be available now until 2026.

Until then, the problem of post-race changes to results would likely remain, to the detriment of riders, teams, fans and the reputation of the sport. It was hard to see MotoGP's commercially minded new owners, Liberty, tolerating it.

Tyres, and not only Michelins, offer riders many other opportunities to fall off, and there were a number of crashes in all classes at a circuit where, in spite of major cleaning efforts, it remained slippery off-line. But tyres were innocent in another unpleasant incident, when Miguel Oliveira suffered a major high-side exiting Turn Four on Friday morning. He was flown to hospital in nearby Mataram, where scans confirmed multiple fractures to his right radius bone, and thence back to Europe for surgery. The culprit was his Aprilia's unruly electronics, confirmed in his social media as a traction-control failure.

Di Giannantonio, suffering pain, weakness and problems with training from the shoulder dislocated in Austria, was also contemplating a return to Europe for surgery, sacrificing the end of his season to be in top condition for his works-Ducati role in 2025.

There were more green shoots from Honda, as Zarco made it directly into Q2 for a second time in four races, and for the first time finished in the top ten in both sprint and grand prix. A new aero package used in the Emilia-Romagna GP, plus a new swing-arm, had paid off, he said – plus "more of a random situation" at a track that was unfamiliar to all.

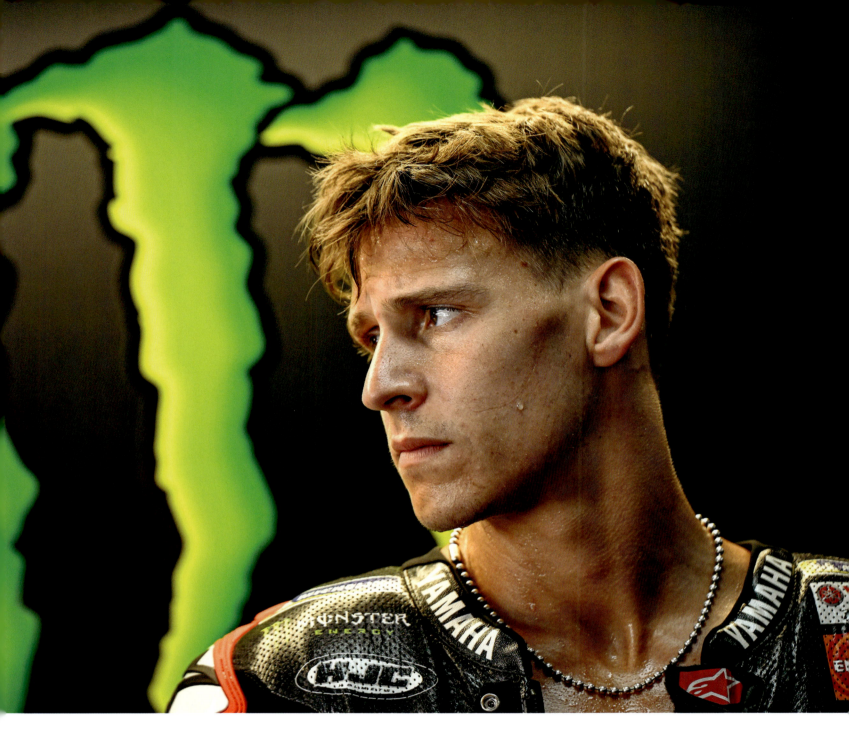

He'd made "a huge step" also with braking, but an excess of wheelie was still hurting acceleration.

After months of speculation, a provisional 22-race 2025 MotoGP calendar was released, starting for the first time in Thailand in March and running for eight-and-a-half months to Valencia in November. Round two in Argentina was considered vulnerable, however, while Brno made a welcome return, and likewise Hungary, at the Balaton Park circuit, pending homologation. A hoped-for return to India was postponed until 2026.

Continuing turmoil in the KTM team, following the earlier departure of technical director Fabiano Sterlacchini, led to confirmation of the departure of team manager Francesco Guidotti, as well as several from Miller's side of the garage, including crew chief Cristhian Pupulin. On the positive side, came the confirmation that Guidotti's replacement would be serially successful Moto2 and Moto3 team chief Aki Ajo.

Moto2 numbers were depleted by the absence of both Italtrans riders, Moreira recovering from an appendectomy after Misano, and Foggia suffering from a wisdom-tooth abscess. They would return the following week.

MOTOGP SPRINT RACE – 13 laps

Records fell again, first to Bastianini on Friday afternoon, then again to Martin as he took his sixth pole. The unfamiliar track shuffled the names a bit: Bezzecchi was second, Acosta alongside – a third front row of the year for each. Bagnaia led row two from Bastianini, with Quartararo sixth and Zarco seventh, a 2024 best for both Frenchmen. Meanwhile, Binder was 19th, for him a worst.

Marc Marquez continued his unfortunate habit of falling in Q2, twice, so he set no time and was 12th at the far end of row four.

Martin took his usual flier off the line, from Bagnaia, Acosta and Bezzecchi, with Marc pushing through to fifth. Martin would not finish the lap, sliding off harmlessly at the penultimate corner, hastily scrambling back to finish the first lap last.

Bagnaia led to the flag, while Bezzecchi took second after Acosta ran wide at Turn Ten, holding it until half-distance. Then it was his turn to run wide, dropping behind both Marc and Bastianini.

Marquez never got quite close enough to attack the leader, while Bastianini was in familiar mode, becoming faster as others slowed – with another lap, he might have won, but he was a tenth behind his team-mate over the line.

Bezzecchi was a lone fourth; more than five seconds behind, Morbidelli triumphed in a close quartet, passing Vinales and Acosta in the penultimate and last laps. The inspired Zarco was right with them.

Di Giannantonio was ninth; Martin's last victim in his charge through was Miller, but he missed the final point by 1.3 seconds.

Above: Quartararo pensive after a heartening seventh for Yamaha.
Photo: Monster Yamaha

Left: A first-lap melee in the main race eliminated Espargaro, Alex Marquez, Marini and Miller.
Photo: Gold & Goose

Above: Acosta at full risk earned – and kept – a superb second.

Top right: Canet made up for Misano's narrow defeat with an overwhelming win.

Above right: Adrian Fernandez, now a regular Moto3 front-runner, took a first podium.

Right: Eddie O'Shea had a tough grand prix baptism, with three crashes ruling him out.

Above far right: Sergio Garcia's end-of-season slump continued, while team-mate Ogura consolidated his championship lead.

Below right: Fernandez leads Lunetta, Munoz, a lurking Alonso, Piqueras, Suzuki, Holgado and Kelso.
Photos: Gold & Goose

MOTOGP RACE – 27 laps

In blazing heat, there was one burning question: could Martin keep his head? The opening lap allayed any fears on that issue, as he led Bastianini, Acosta, Bagnaia, Bezzecchi, Morbidelli and Marquez through the first chicane. The field was quickly reduced by four when Miller wiped out Espargaro at Turn Four, with Alex Marquez and Marini also brought down in the melee.

It soon became better for Martin. As he was extending his lead to 1.2 seconds in the first three laps, his rivals were faltering: Bastianini couldn't repeat his searing Friday pace and dropped behind Acosta on lap three. And Bagnaia had been relegated to sixth at the close of lap one when Bezzecchi and Morbidelli – both on Michelin's soft front – ganged up on him at Turn 14.

Soon the race for victory was effectively between Martin and himself. A fastest lap fourth time around extended his lead to better than 1.5 seconds. The chasing Acosta was something of a roadblock, with Morbidelli pinching third from Bastianini at Turn One on lap five, before Bezzecchi relegated him a further place on the next lap. A little behind, Di Giannantonio – risking it all with Michelin's soft front and rear – was proving a real nuisance to Bagnaia and Marquez in the fight for sixth.

Acosta, a lone KTM in a sea of Ducatis, came alive on the fifth lap. He broke clear of the chasing pack, and fastest laps on the tenth and 13th closed him to within seven-tenths of the leader. A lap-17 mistake by Martin reduced the gap further. Suddenly, it was a half-second, and a maiden victory for the rookie was a real possibility.

Martin was reliving Saturday's (and 2023's) nightmare, fearing a fall at every turn. In reality, by lap 17, Acosta was no longer his main threat. Bastianini had finally got going after struggling to get his rear tyre working. Moves on Bezzecchi (Turn 14, lap 13) and Morbidelli (Turn 12, lap 17) gave him 2.8 seconds of clear tarmac to attack. He set about his task with vigour, taking three-tenths out of the gap on lap 18 and a full half-second next time around. A fastest lap on lap 20 put him within 1.4s of Acosta. But he was right on the limit, proved when he tucked the front as he braked for the first corner moments later.

From there, the contest was run, as Martin eased away for a much-needed, if nervy win. It was Ducati's 12th victory in succession, a new record for the brand and a first for a MotoGP manufacturer since Honda's run in 2014.

Acosta was unable to celebrate an impressive second fully as he awaited the outcome of the tyre-pressure investigation, but in the end, he held on to the points.

Fully four seconds down, by lap 23, Bagnaia had been able to take advantage of Bezzecchi and Morbidelli's fading soft front tyres, for a satisfactory, if not brilliant third.

He'd been freed from Di Giannantonio's pressure when he crashed out on lap nine. Four laps later, Marquez's threat ended dramatically when his Ducati's engine blew up and the bike caught fire. He stopped and leapt off. The fire was quickly extinguished, but the bike badly damaged in the process.

These absences promoted Vinales to sixth; Quartararo recovered to seventh after an error on lap two had dropped him from ninth to 13th. As well as benefiting from the attrition, the Yamaha rider had passed Raul Fernandez, Zarco and Binder to get there.

By the finish, Binder had regained eighth from Zarco by a few tenths. Fernandez, Rins and Nakagami trailed in, and there were points for all with only 12 finishers. Mir was another to crash out; Augusto Fernandez retired.

Martin's survival minimised the damage of Saturday, his lead now down to 21 points.

MOTO2 RACE – 22 laps

Criticised the weekend before at Misano, Canet had faced the ignominy of snatching defeat from the jaws of victory at the final corner. Indonesia was about putting that right. The Spaniard boldly proclaimed that he had his sights set on victory after securing pole position on Saturday, and with the most dominant performance so far in the season, he came home 6.2 seconds clear.

His pole, fifth of the year and second in a row, came after the usual new all-time record on Friday. Dixon had taken time

to find the speed to come up to second, while points leader Ogura completed the front row. Gonzales led the second from Aldeguer and Lopez; seventh-fastest Arbolino – another Misano last-lap loser – had been in the top three until Q2; Garcia was still struggling, through from Q1 to 15th.

Arbolino ran off-track on lap one to finish it 22nd. Canet's rapid escape, four seconds ahead on lap eight, was further assisted as Lopez, Aldeguer, Ogura and Dixon (a lone Kalex among the Boscoscuros) squabbled among themselves.

Dixon didn't last, slipping off on lap three. Lopez was acting as the cork in the bottle, resisting every attempt at passing by Ogura and then Aldeguer, which allowed Gonzalez and an inspired Darryn Binder to tag on behind.

Then Aldeguer's desperation to pass his team-mate got the better of him, and he ran way wide on lap eight, dropping to ninth.

Ogura finally made it past late-braking Lopez on lap 12 and was able to escape, leaving the Spaniard to fend off Rodriguez and Binder. At the same time, Aldeguer was recovering, first past Guevara, then following Roberts past a fading Oncu before going by the American on lap 18. He quickly closed a gap of some two seconds to the group ahead, and with two laps to go, he set about them, passing all except the persistent Lopez.

His last-lap attack on Gonzalez pushed him wide, leaving Binder to a season (and career) best fifth, ahead of Roberts, Guevara and the recovered Arbolino. Gonzalez was next, three seconds ahead of Oncu, then a close quintet of Ramirez, Baltus, Vietti, Alcoba and Arenas. Salac was 15th over the line, then Sasaki, promoted into the points when erstwhile seventh-placed Guevara was disqualified for being narrowly under the minimum weight limit.

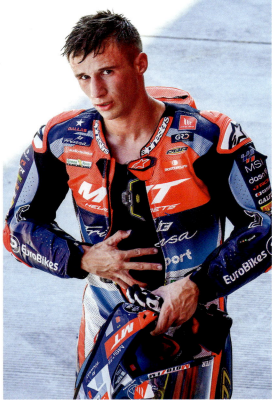

Masia and Agius were early fallers; Chantra retired at the end of the first lap, in agony after Aldeguer had hit his dangling right leg under braking. At first, a knee injury and possible foot fractures were feared, and the ever-smiling Thai rider was out of the next two GPs.

In another pivotal day for the championship, Garcia had climbed to tenth, only to crash out on lap 16, boosting Ogura's lead to 42 points. In a potential fight for second, Canet and Lopez were just ten points behind the early championship leader.

MOTO3 RACE – 20 laps

Alonso's weekend began badly with a Friday-morning highside, followed by a rather unusual second-row start. It would get better, while pole qualifier Ortola's became worse – a double long-lap incurred for dawdling in practice was followed by a third for a mid-race short cut without losing the requisite time.

It was a tough weekend also for second and third qualifiers Veijer and Furusato. The Dutchman had led until after half-distance, but then crashed out violently; Furusato had been third with four laps to go when he dropped back before also falling.

Veijer's abrupt departure left Fernandez with the lead, but title designate Alonso had been lurking in the big front group. He led over the line on the 17th, only to be pushed back to fourth next time around by Fernandez, fast rookie Lunetta and Munoz.

But his last-lap tactics proved invincible once again, as he repassed them for his ninth win of the year and a 97-point title lead.

At one point, his last numerical rival Holgado had been contesting the lead, but he was shuffled back to sixth behind Piqueras and Lunetta over the line. Suzuki and Kelso were still close; Ortola recovered to ninth at the head of a tight sextet from Carraro, Rueda (another with a double long-lap), Bertelle, Ogden and Esteban.

Nepa took the last point, after his own double long-lap.

It was a brief debut for Ogden's new MLav Racing team-mate, Eddie O'Shea – replacing Josh Whatley, after his third crash, in qualifying, ruled him out of this race and the next.

FIM WORLD CHAMPIONSHIP: ROUND 15
PERTAMINA GRAND PRIX OF INDONESIA
27–29 SEPTEMBER, 2024

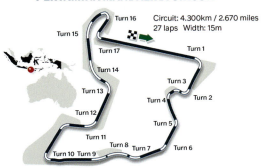

PERTAMINA MANDALIKA CIRCUIT
Circuit: 4.300km / 2.670 miles
27 laps Width: 15m

MOTOGP: 27 laps, 72.158 miles/116.127km
WEATHER: Dry (air 29°, humidity 76%, track 56°)

Pos.	Rider	Nat.	No.	Entrant	Machine	Race tyre choice	Laps	Time & speed
1	Jorge Martin	SPA	89	Prima Pramac Racing	Ducati Desmosedici GP24	F: Hard/R: Medium	27	41m 04.389s
								105.4mph/169.6km/h
2	Pedro Acosta	SPA	31	Red Bull GASGAS Tech3	KTM RC16	F: Hard/R: Medium	27	41m 05.793s
3	Francesco Bagnaia	ITA	1	Ducati Lenovo Team	Ducati Desmosedici GP24	F: Hard/R: Medium	27	41m 09.984s
4	Franco Morbidelli	ITA	21	Prima Pramac Racing	Ducati Desmosedici GP24	F: Soft/R: Medium	27	41m 10.896s
5	Marco Bezzecchi	ITA	72	Pertamina Enduro VR46 Racing	Ducati Desmosedici GP23	F: Soft/R: Medium	27	41m 11.161s
6	Maverick Vinales	SPA	12	Aprilia Racing	Aprilia RS-GP24	F: Hard/R: Medium	27	41m 15.719s
7	Fabio Quartararo	FRA	20	Monster Energy Yamaha MotoGP	Yamaha YZR-M1	F: Hard/R: Medium	27	41m 17.592s
8	Brad Binder	RSA	33	Red Bull KTM Factory Racing	KTM RC16	F: Hard/R: Medium	27	41m 19.251s
9	Johann Zarco	FRA	5	CASTROL Honda LCR	Honda RC213V	F: Hard/R: Medium	27	41m 19.540s
10	Raul Fernandez	SPA	25	Trackhouse Racing	Aprilia RS-GP24	F: Hard/R: Medium	27	41m 25.468s
11	Alex Rins	SPA	42	Monster Energy Yamaha MotoGP	Yamaha YZR-M1	F: Soft/R: Medium	27	41m 38.022s
12	Takaaki Nakagami*	JPN	30	IDEMITSU Honda LCR	Honda RC213V	F: Hard/R: Medium	27	41m 48.085s
	Enea Bastianini	ITA	23	Ducati Lenovo Team	Ducati Desmosedici GP24	F: Hard/R: Medium	20	DNF-technical
	Augusto Fernandez	SPA	37	Red Bull GASGAS Tech3	KTM RC16	F: Hard/R: Medium	19	DNF-technical
	Joan Mir	SPA	36	Repsol Honda Team	Honda RC213V	F: Hard/R: Medium	12	DNF-crash
	Marc Marquez	SPA	93	Gresini Racing MotoGP	Ducati Desmosedici GP23	F: Hard/R: Medium	11	DNF-technical
	Fabio Di Giannantonio	ITA	49	Pertamina Enduro VR46 Racing	Ducati Desmosedici GP23	F: Soft/R: Soft	8	DNF-crash
	Aleix Espargaro	SPA	41	Aprilia Racing	Aprilia RS-GP24	F: Soft/R: Medium	0	DNF-crash
	Alex Marquez	SPA	73	Gresini Racing MotoGP	Ducati Desmosedici GP23	F: Soft/R: Medium	0	DNF-crash
	Jack Miller	AUS	43	Red Bull KTM Factory Racing	KTM RC16	F: Hard/R: Medium	0	DNF-crash
	Luca Marini	ITA	10	Repsol Honda Team	Honda RC213V	F: Hard/R: Medium	0	DNF-crash

Takaaki Nakagami: 16s penalty – technical infringement.

Fastest lap: Enea Bastianini, on lap 20, 1m 30.539s, 106.3mph/171.0km/h.
Lap record: Enea Bastianini, 1m 30.906s, 105.8mph/170.3km/h (2023).
Event maximum speed: Pedro Acosta, 198.5mph/319.5km/h (qualifying).

Qualifying: Weather: Dry Air: 29° Humidity: 78% Track: 56°
1 Martin 1m 29.088s, 2 Bezzecchi 1m 29.623s, 3 Acosta 1m 29.671s, 4 Bagnaia 1m 29.745s, 5 Bastianini 1m 29.792s, 6 Quartararo 1m 29.848s, 7 Zarco 1m 29.942s, 8 Di Giannantonio 1m 29.963s, 9 Morbidelli 1m 30.107s, 10 Vinales 1m 30.418s, 11 R. Fernandez 1m 30.524s, 12 M. Marquez 0m 00.000s.
Q1: 13 A. Espargaro 1m 30.110s, 14 A. Marquez 1m 30.243s, 15 Rins 1m 30.293s, 16 Miller 1m 30.385s, 17 Marini 1m 30.395s, 18 Nakagami 1m 30.430s, 19 Binder 1m 30.582s, 20 Mir 1m 30.698s, 21 A. Fernandez 1m 31.086s.

SPRINT RACE: 13 laps, 34.743 miles/55.913km
WEATHER: Dry (air 29°, humidity 73%, track 60°)

Pos.	Rider	Race tyre choice	Laps	Time & speed
1	Francesco Bagnaia	F: Hard/R: Soft	13	19m 41.354s
				105.8mph/170.3km/h
2	Enea Bastianini	F: Hard/R: Soft	13	19m 41.461s
3	Marc Marquez	F: Hard/R: Soft	13	19m 43.055s
4	Marco Bezzecchi	F: Soft/R: Soft	13	19m 44.426s
5	Franco Morbidelli	F: Soft/R: Soft	13	19m 47.321s
6	Pedro Acosta	F: Hard/R: Soft	13	19m 47.564s
7	Maverick Vinales	F: Hard/R: Soft	13	19m 48.018s
8	Johann Zarco	F: Hard/R: Soft	13	19m 48.292s
9	Fabio Di Giannantonio	F: Soft/R: Soft	13	19m 49.060s
10	Jorge Martin	F: Hard/R: Soft	13	19m 50.458s
11	Jack Miller	F: Hard/R: Soft	13	19m 50.972s
12	Fabio Quartararo	F: Soft/R: Soft	13	19m 51.197s
13	Brad Binder	F: Hard/R: Soft	13	19m 52.472s
14	Alex Marquez	F: Hard/R: Soft	13	19m 53.772s
15	Alex Rins	F: Soft/R: Soft	13	19m 53.933s
16	Aleix Espargaro	F: Hard/R: Soft	13	19m 54.306s
17	Takaaki Nakagami	F: Hard/R: Soft	13	19m 54.705s
18	Luca Marini	F: Soft/R: Soft	13	19m 56.850s
19	Raul Fernandez*	F: Hard/R: Soft	13	20m 11.249s
	Augusto Fernandez	F: Hard/R: Soft	11	DNF-crash
	Joan Mir	F: Hard/R: Soft	1	DNF-crash

Raul Fernandez: 8s penalty – technical infringement.

Fastest race lap: Enea Bastianini, on lap 8, 1m 30.189s.

Fastest race laps
1 Bastianini 1m 30.906s, 2 Martin 1m 31.035s, 3 Quartararo 1m 31.116s, 4 Binder 1m 31.159s, 5 Di Giannantonio 1m 31.197s, 6 Morbidelli 1m 31.280s, 7 Vinales 1m 31.314s, 8 Bagnaia 1m 31.324s, 9 Bezzecchi 1m 31.351s, 10 A. Fernandez 1m 31.436s, 11 Miller 1m 31.463s, 12 A. Espargaro 1m 31.467s, 13 Mir 1m 31.577s, 14 Nakagami 1m 31.675s, 15 R. Fernandez 1m 31.712s, 16 Rins 1m 31.791s, 17 Oliveira 1m 31.823s, 18 M. Marquez 1m 31.909s, 19 Zarco 1m 32.596s, 20 Marini 1m 48.616s.

Grid order / Lap-by-lap

Grid order	1	2	3	4	5	6	7	8	9	10	11	12	13	14	15	16	17	18	19	20	21	22	23	24	25	26	27
89 MARTIN	89	89	89	89	89	89	89	89	89	89	89	89	89	89	89	89	89	89	89	89	89	89	89	89	89	89	89
72 BEZZECCHI	23	23	31	31	31	31	31	31	31	31	31	31	31	31	31	31	31	31	31	31	31	31	31	31	31	31	31
31 ACOSTA	31	31	23	21	21	21	21	21	21	21	21	21	21	21	21	23	23	23	23	21	21	1	1	1	1	1	1
1 BAGNAIA	72	72	21	23	23	72	72	72	72	72	72	72	23	23	23	23	21	21	21	72	1	21	21	21	21	21	21
23 BASTIANINI	21	21	72	72	72	23	23	23	23	23	23	23	72	72	72	72	1	72	72	72	72	72	72	72	72	72	72
20 QUARTARARO	1	1	1	1	1	1	1	1	1	1	1	1	1	1	1	1	72	12	12	12	12	12	12	12	12	12	12
5 ZARCO	93	93	93	93	93	93	93	93	49	93	93	93	33	33	33	12	12	12	12	20	20	20	20	20	20	20	20
49 DI GIANNANTONIO	49	49	49	49	49	49	49	93	33	33	33	12	12	12	33	33	33	33	20	5	5	5	5	5	5	33	33
21 MORBIDELLI	20	5	5	33	33	33	33	5	5	12	5	5	5	5	5	20	33	33	33	33	33	33	33	33	33	5	5
12 VINALES	12	12	33	5	5	5	5	12	12	5	12	33	20	20	20	5	5	5	5	25	25	25	25	25	25	25	25
25 R. FERNANDEZ	5	33	12	12	12	12	12	33	25	25	25	20	25	25	25	25	25	25	25	30	30	30	30	30	30	30	30
93 M. MARQUEZ	33	25	25	25	25	25	25	20	20	20	20	25	30	30	30	30	30	30	30	42	42	42	42	42	42	42	42
41 A. ESPARGARO	25	20	20	20	20	20	20	25	30	30	30	30	37	37	37	37	37	37	37								
73 A. MARQUEZ	37	37	37	37	37	37	30	30	37	37	37	42	42	42	42	42	42	42	42								
42 RINS	30	30	30	30	30	30	37	37	36	42	42	42	42	42	42												
43 MILLER	42	42	42	42	42	36	36	36	42	42	42																
10 MARINI	36	36	36	36	36	42	42	42																			
30 NAKAGAMI*																											
33 BINDER																											
36 MIR																											
37 A. FERNANDEZ																											

Championship Points

	Rider			
1	Martin	241	(125)	366
2	Bagnaia	254	(91)	345
3	Bastianini	216	(78)	294
4	M. Marquez	200	(88)	288
5	Acosta	118	(63)	181
6	Binder	134	(39)	173
7	Vinales	108	(54)	162
8	A. Espargaro	81	(46)	127
9	Bezzecchi	114	(11)	125
10	Di Giannantonio	105	(17)	122
11	A. Marquez	103	(18)	121
12	Morbidelli	85	(35)	120
13	Quartararo	67	(15)	82
14	Oliveira	55	(16)	71
15	Miller	35	(23)	58
16	R. Fernandez	53	(2)	55
17	Zarco	29	(2)	31
18	Nakagami	25	(0)	25
19	Mir	19	(3)	22
20	A. Fernandez	20	(1)	21
21	Rins	20	(0)	20
22	P. Espargaro	11	(1)	12
23	Pedrosa	0	(7)	7
24	Marini	5	(0)	5
25	Bradl	2	(0)	2

Constructor Points

1	Ducati	366	(171)	537
2	KTM	179	(84)	263
3	Aprilia	152	(95)	247
4	Yamaha	78	(15)	93
5	Honda	47	(4)	51

MOTO2: RACE DISTANCE: 22 laps, 58.795 miles/94.622km

RACE WEATHER: Dry (air 29°, humidity 76%, track 59°)

Pos.	Rider	Nat.	No.	Entrant	Machine	Laps	Time & Speed
1	Aron Canet	SPA	44	Fantic Racing	Kalex	22	34m 41.557s
							101.7mph/163.6km/h
2	Ai Ogura	JPN	79	MT Helmets - MSI	Boscoscuro	22	34m 47.775s
3	Alonso Lopez	SPA	21	Beta Tools SpeedUp	Boscoscuro	22	34m 49.170s
4	Fermin Aldeguer	SPA	54	Beta Tools SpeedUp	Boscoscuro	22	34m 49.354s
5	Darryn Binder	RSA	15	Liqui Moly Husqvarna Intact GP	Kalex	22	34m 49.654s
6	Joe Roberts	USA	16	OnlyFans American Racing Team	Kalex	22	34m 51.380s
7	Tony Arbolino	ITA	14	Elf Marc VDS Racing Team	Kalex	22	34m 51.951s
8	Manuel Gonzalez	SPA	18	QJMOTOR Gresini Moto2	Kalex	22	34m 52.557s
9	Deniz Oncu	TUR	53	Red Bull KTM Ajo	Kalex	22	34m 55.993s
10	Marcos Ramirez	SPA	24	OnlyFans American Racing Team	Kalex	22	34m 58.452s
11	Barry Baltus	BEL	7	RW-Idrofoglia Racing GP	Kalex	22	34m 58.635s
12	Celestino Vietti	ITA	13	Red Bull KTM Ajo	Kalex	22	34m 59.576s
13	Jeremy Alcoba	SPA	52	Yamaha VR46 Master Camp Team	Kalex	22	34m 59.758s
14	Albert Arenas	SPA	75	QJMOTOR Gresini Moto2	Kalex	22	35m 00.173s
15	Filip Salac	CZE	12	Elf Marc VDS Racing Team	Kalex	22	35m 08.999s
16	Ayumu Sasaki	JPN	22	Yamaha VR46 Master Camp Team	Kalex	22	35m 11.608s
17	Zonta van den Goorbergh	NED	84	RW-Idrofoglia Racing GP	Kalex	22	35m 15.535s
18	Mario Aji	INA	34	IDEMITSU Honda Team Asia	Kalex	22	35m 16.430s
19	Alex Escrig	SPA	11	KLINT Forward Factory Team	Forward	22	35m 20.113s
20	Xavier Artigas	SPA	43	KLINT Forward Factory Team	Forward	22	35m 22.149s
21	Daniel Munoz	SPA	17	Preicanos Racing Team	Kalex	22	35m 28.642s
22	Jake Dixon	GBR	96	CFMOTO Inde Aspar Team	Kalex	22	35m 41.399s
	Sergio Garcia	SPA	3	MT Helmets - MSI	Boscoscuro	15	DNF-crash
	Xavi Cardelus	AND	20	Fantic Racing	Kalex	2	DNF-crash
	Somkiat Chantra	THA	35	IDEMITSU Honda Team Asia	Kalex	1	DNF-injured
	Senna Agius	AUS	81	Liqui Moly Husqvarna Intact GP	Kalex	0	DNF-crash
	Jaume Masia	SPA	5	Preicanos Racing Team	Kalex	0	DNF-crash
	Izan Guevara	SPA	28	CFMOTO Inde Aspar Team	Kalex	-	DSQ

Fastest lap: Aron Canet, on lap 4, 1m 33.840s, 102.5mph/165.0km/h.
Lap record: Pedro Acosta, 1m 34.420s, 101.8mph/163.9km/h (2023).
Event maximum speed: Somkiat Chantra, 163.7mph/263.4km/h (practice).

Qualifying
Weather: Dry
Air: 29° **Humidity:** 74% **Track:** 61°

1	Canet	1m 33.434s
2	Dixon	1m 33.503s
3	Ogura	1m 33.504s
4	Gonzalez	1m 33.628s
5	Aldeguer	1m 33.662s
6	Lopez	1m 33.667s
7	Arbolino	1m 33.696s
8	Roberts	1m 33.752s
9	Chantra	1m 33.825s
10	Alcoba	1m 33.838s
11	Oncu	1m 33.839s
12	Baltus	1m 33.841s
13	Binder	1m 33.846s
14	Arenas	1m 33.888s
15	Garcia	1m 33.913s
16	Agius	1m 33.975s
17	Masia	1m 34.060s
18	Vietti	No Time

Q1
19	Guevara	1m 34.168s
20	V d Goorbergh	1m 34.190s
21	Ramirez	1m 34.232s
22	Sasaki	1m 34.394s
23	Salac	1m 34.450s
24	Aji	1m 34.461s
25	Escrig	1m 34.573s
26	Cardelus	1m 34.649s
27	Munoz	1m 34.695s
28	Artigas	1m 35.050s

Fastest race laps

1	Canet	1m 33.840s
2	Aldeguer	1m 34.088s
3	Guevara	1m 34.197s
4	Ogura	1m 34.300s
5	Garcia	1m 34.329s
6	Lopez	1m 34.348s
7	Binder	1m 34.367s
8	Arbolino	1m 34.369s
9	Roberts	1m 34.377s
10	Gonzalez	1m 34.411s
11	Oncu	1m 34.429s
12	Arenas	1m 34.594s
13	Baltus	1m 34.608s
14	Alcoba	1m 34.621s
15	Ramirez	1m 34.776s
16	Sasaki	1m 34.871s
17	Vietti	1m 34.873s
18	Salac	1m 34.991s
19	Dixon	1m 34.997s
20	V d Goorbergh	1m 35.002s
21	Escrig	1m 35.052s
22	Aji	1m 35.083s
23	Munoz	1m 35.286s
24	Artigas	1m 35.525s
25	Cardelus	1m 35.957s

Championship Points

Pos	Rider	Pts
1	Ogura	208
2	Garcia	166
3	Canet	156
4	Lopez	156
5	Roberts	153
6	Aldeguer	146
7	Vietti	131
8	Dixon	130
9	Gonzalez	128
10	Arbolino	122
11	Ramirez	79
12	Chantra	78
13	Arenas	65
14	Alcoba	61
15	Binder	49
16	Agius	47
17	Salac	41
18	Oncu	34
19	Baltus	31
20	Moreira	28
21	Guevara	28
22	Van den Goorbergh	20
23	Foggia	18
24	Bendsneyder	7
25	Navarro	6
26	Sasaki	4
27	Masia	4
28	Aji	3
29	Ferrari	1

Constructor Points
1	Kalex	317
2	Boscoscuro	308
3	Forward	6

MOTO3: RACE DISTANCE: 20 laps, 53.450 miles/86.020km

RACE WEATHER: Dry (air 29°, humidity 78%, track 58°)

Pos.	Rider	Nat.	No.	Entrant	Machine	Laps	Time & Speed
1	David Alonso	COL	80	CFMOTO Gaviota Aspar Team	CFMOTO	20	32m 57.410s
							97.3mph/156.6km/h
2	Adrian Fernandez	SPA	31	Leopard Racing	Honda	20	32m 57.495s
3	David Munoz	SPA	64	BOE Motorsports	KTM	20	32m 57.635s
4	Angel Piqueras	SPA	36	Leopard Racing	Honda	20	32m 58.074s
5	Luca Lunetta	ITA	58	SIC58 Squadra Corse	Honda	20	32m 58.245s
6	Daniel Holgado	SPA	96	Red Bull GASGAS Tech3	GASGAS	20	32m 58.272s
7	Tatsuki Suzuki	JPN	24	Liqui Moly Husqvarna Intact GP	Husqvarna	20	32m 58.710s
8	Joel Kelso	AUS	66	BOE Motorsports	KTM	20	32m 59.245s
9	Ivan Ortola	SPA	48	MT Helmets - MSI	KTM	20	33m 14.074s
10	Nicola Carraro	ITA	10	LEVELUP - MTA	KTM	20	33m 14.084s
11	Jose Antonio Rueda	SPA	99	Red Bull KTM Ajo	KTM	20	33m 14.180s
12	Matteo Bertelle	ITA	18	Kopron Rivacold Snipers Team	Honda	20	33m 14.217s
13	Scott Ogden	GBR	19	FleetSafe Honda - MLav Racing	Honda	20	33m 14.415s
14	Joel Esteban	SPA	78	CFMOTO Gaviota Aspar Team	CFMOTO	20	33m 14.654s
15	Stefano Nepa	ITA	82	LEVELUP - MTA	KTM	20	33m 21.214s
16	Jacob Roulstone	AUS	12	Red Bull GASGAS Tech3	GASGAS	20	33m 23.534s
17	Ryusei Yamanaka	JPN	6	MT Helmets - MSI	KTM	20	33m 36.722s
18	Noah Dettwiler	SWI	55	CIP Green Power	KTM	20	33m 54.750s
	Taiyo Furusato	JPN	72	Honda Team Asia	Honda	17	DNF-crash
	Collin Veijer	NED	95	Liqui Moly Husqvarna Intact GP	Husqvarna	11	DNF-crash
	Riccardo Rossi	ITA	54	CIP Green Power	KTM	10	DNF-ret in pit
	Xabi Zurutuza	SPA	85	Red Bull KTM Ajo	KTM	10	DNF-crash
	Tatchakorn Buasri	THA	5	Honda Team Asia	Honda	4	DNF-crash
	Arbi Aditama	INA	93	Honda Team Asia	Honda	4	DNF-crash
	Filippo Farioli	ITA	7	SIC58 Squadra Corse	Honda	2	DNF-crash
	David Almansa	SPA	22	Kopron Rivacold Snipers Team	Honda	2	DNF-crash

Fastest lap: Daniel Holgado, on lap 3, 1m 37.936s, 98.2mph/158.0km/h.
Lap record: Ivan Ortola, 1m 38.936s, 97.2mph/156.5km/h (2023).
Event maximum speed: Jose Antonio Rueda, 139.5mph/224.5km/h (race).

Qualifying:
Weather: Dry
Air: 29° **Humidity:** 78% **Track:** 62°

1	Ortola	1m 37.332s
2	Veijer	1m 37.589s
3	Furusato	1m 37.701s
4	Fernandez	1m 37.726s
5	Alonso	1m 37.845s
6	Lunetta	1m 37.976s
7	Suzuki	1m 38.078s
8	Kelso	1m 38.110s
9	Piqueras	1m 38.120s
10	Rueda	1m 38.190s
11	Nepa	1m 38.210s
12	Ogden	1m 38.302s
13	Munoz	1m 38.372s
14	Holgado	1m 38.399s
15	Almansa	1m 38.414s
16	Farioli	1m 38.465s
17	Yamanaka	1m 38.539s
18	Rossi	1m 39.630s

Q1
19	Roulstone	1m 38.766s
20	O'Shea	1m 38.770s
21	Carraro	1m 38.863s
22	Aditama	1m 38.987s
23	Esteban	1m 39.165s
24	Bertelle	1m 39.184s
25	Buasri	1m 39.488s
26	Dettwiler	1m 39.732s
27	Zurutuza	1m 39.854s

Fastest race laps

1	Holgado	1m 37.936s
2	Suzuki	1m 37.971s
3	Lunetta	1m 37.998s
4	Piqueras	1m 38.033s
5	Munoz	1m 38.038s
6	Kelso	1m 38.137s
7	Alonso	1m 38.216s
8	Fernandez	1m 38.263s
9	Veijer	1m 38.275s
10	Furusato	1m 38.303s
11	Ortola	1m 38.320s
12	Esteban	1m 38.610s
13	Rueda	1m 38.617s
14	Rossi	1m 38.675s
15	Nepa	1m 38.758s
16	Bertelle	1m 38.891s
17	Yamanaka	1m 38.939s
18	Carraro	1m 38.957s
19	Ogden	1m 39.002s
20	Roulstone	1m 39.029s
21	Almansa	1m 39.159s
22	Farioli	1m 39.378s
23	Zurutuza	1m 39.426s
24	Aditama	1m 39.600s
25	Dettwiler	1m 39.738s
26	Buasri	1m 39.819s

Championship Points

Pos	Rider	Pts
1	Alonso	296
2	Holgado	199
3	Ortola	191
4	Veijer	189
5	Munoz	133
6	Piqueras	131
7	Fernandez	121
8	Rueda	110
9	Kelso	110
10	Yamanaka	86
11	Furusato	81
12	Lunetta	78
13	Suzuki	72
14	Nepa	59
15	Roulstone	50
16	Esteban	44
17	Bertelle	42
18	Rossi	24
19	Farioli	24
20	Carraro	22
21	Ogden	15
22	Zurutuza	11
23	Almansa	7
24	Perez	3
25	Dettwiler	2

Constructor Points
1	CFMOTO	296
2	KTM	267
3	Husqvarna	215
4	Honda	212
5	GASGAS	204

FIM WORLD CHAMPIONSHIP • ROUND 16
JAPANESE GRAND PRIX
MOTEGI CIRCUIT

Above: Acosta, chasing Pecco, goes down for a second time in "the saddest weekend of my life."
Photo: Ducati Corse

Inset, above: Manual Gonzalez dons the controversial headband before his maiden Moto2 win.
Photo: Motosport 101.com

Inset, above right: Pedro stares into the future from his pole position.

Right: In his last home race as a full-time rider, Nakagami gambled on a soft rear tyre for a spirited 13th.

Opening spread: The pursuing pack, led by Binder, couldn't keep pace with Acosta as he chased Bagnaia. The young Spaniard's race wouldn't last much longer.
Photos: Gold & Goose

THE year began with speculation that Pedro Acosta might oust Marc Marquez from some 'youngest-ever' achievements. Now the 20-year-old – using a new KTM chassis (rejected by Binder) fitted with the swing-arm 'batwings' – claimed a first pole, with a new track record.

Could the apprentice finally usurp the current masters?

The races showed that he still had much to learn. He was having to ride on the ragged edge, and occasionally over it to live with the best the class had to offer. Twenty-six hours after becoming the third youngest premier-class pole-sitter, he was pondering how two victory challenges had fallen apart in as many days.

On Saturday, he was leading the sprint with four laps to go when he crashed out. On Sunday, his fall from second on the fourth lap arguably deprived KTM – competitive for the previous two visits to the brake-heavy circuit – of its final chance of victory in 2024.

In fact, his pole had an element of luck. Marquez had actually been faster, only for the lap to be disallowed for exceeding track limits. That left the veteran fuming that he hadn't been told until too late to respond. He suspected that he might have touched the green, but "when I saw they didn't cancel the lap, I decided to not take risks, because there were some drops." Race director Mike Webb explained that while "the track-limits sensor was triggered immediately," unfortunately, a software glitch had interrupted the usual automatic instant reaction. "The lap had to be cancelled manually, causing a delay." This had never happened before.

Honda chose their home track for a bombshell announcement: they had poached Aprilia's Romano Albesiano. The Italian would become its first ever non-Japanese technical director, a significant departure in HRC's quest to regain competitive status. Albesiano had significant experience, especially in aerodynamics, and had overseen Aprilia's rise from back-markers to race winners.

One significant fan was the marque's first race winner, Aleix Espargaro, as significantly also recently recruited for Honda's test team. "What Romano was able to do these last six or seven years in Aprilia has been amazing," Espargaro said. "We've grown these last two or three seasons, but the first ones were very difficult. He never gave up, he had a lot of ideas, he made the bike better year by year. HRC doesn't have to change everything, but obviously today the Italian engineers are on top of the world, so to mix this will make Honda really, really strong."

Ken Kawauchi, ex-Suzuki and current technical manager, would move to Honda's test team in 2025, while the retiring Nakagami would carry out testing duties at home in Japan.

Aprilia had a riposte, confirming directly that his replacement would be Fabiano Sterlacchini, ex-Ducati and (until ear-

lier in 2024) also KTM. Current riders Vinales and Fernandez were downcast. Said the latter, "Romano most improved this project, so for me it's really disappointing." Yet 2025 recruit Jorge Martin remained positive, contemplating "a big change and a good change. Fabiano has a lot of experience so will give a lot of know-how to Aprilia."

After Quartararo's good run at Misano, Yamaha were back to struggling for grip in spite of trying four different chassis over the previous five races. Disappointment for home fans was underlined when their star rider ran short of fuel yet again on the run to the line, losing a place – although this time, it was merely 11th to 12th, rather than Misano's fifth to seventh.

Remy Gardner was back on the YZR for another wild-card outing. He revealed that he was due to go under the surgeon's knife to correct spine problems caused by crashes and a wake-boarding mishap. Similar news from Di Giannantonio, contemplating an early end to his season for surgery to repair the troublesome shoulder initially dislocated at the Red Bull Ring.

After Marquez's Indonesian blow-up, for complex rev-control reasons, Ducati had equipped all of the GP23s with lighter flywheels.

Spaniard Manuel Gonzalez's long-awaited first Moto2 win was overshadowed when inadvertently he triggered an embarrassing international incident for the Gresini team, sponsored by Chinese motorcycle factory QJMotor. The 22-year-old was pictured wearing a *hachimaki* – a Japanese headband given to him by a fan – on the grid. QJMotor took umbrage because the *hachimaki* had been worn by Japanese soldiers during the Second Sino-Japanese War, between 1937 and 1945.

The Chinese company issued an official statement, urging the sacking of Gonzalez after "a very discordant incident… Although it was unintentional due to his lack of knowledge of Chinese history, such behaviour offended the national sentiments of motorcyclists and citizens of China. Qianjiang Motorcycle immediately initiated a serious discussion with the Gresini team, and demanded that the team cease all collaboration with the involved rider." Gonzalez responded by expressing deep regret and apologies for "a thoughtless and involuntary gesture." Discussions rumbled on, but while Gonzalez stayed on board, QJMotor's branding disappeared from the fairings for the rest of the season.

On a happier note, Spanish-born David Alonso – racing as a Colombian in honour of his Colombian-born mother – tied up the first title of 2024 after a dominant Moto3 season.

MOTOGP SPRINT RACE – 12 laps

Changeable conditions made practice and qualifying difficult, but Marc Marquez showed his mastery with a new all-time record – only to have it snatched away. He ended up ninth. Martin was even worse off, falling on his fast lap and placing 11th.

That left Acosta to celebrate a first pole (KTM's first in four years), with Bagnaia and an on-form Vinales alongside; Bastianini, Binder and Morbidelli on row two.

Bagnaia led away, while Acosta came out better in a first-lap skirmish with Bastianini. Binder was next, but he would not last beyond the end of lap two, slowing suddenly to retire with a power-sapping electronic glitch.

Acosta, fully aggressive, took the lead at Turn Five on the second lap, and he, Bagnaia and Bastianini opened up a slight gap on Marquez, who led Martin in pursuit. A first victory beckoned for the GasGas rider as Bagnaia chased in vain, now six-tenths down.

The omens flattered to deceive, and at Turn Seven, Acosta crashed out.

That left Bagnaia just four-tenths clear of Bastianini, but the latter had his hands full with an attacking Marquez, and over the 10th and 11th laps, he ably repulsed the older rider's aggression, in several changes of position, to retain second.

Martin was alone in fourth, regretting his bad qualifying, but comfortably clear of Morbidelli and Di Giannantonio. Alex Marquez won a lively tussle for seventh from Miller and Vinales, with Bezzecchi dropping to the back of the gang and out of the points in the last lap.

MOTOGP RACE – 24 laps

Acosta's premature departure at the end of lap three deprived the Motegi crowd of drama that would have enlivened the event no end. To say the 21 laps that followed fell well below the billing is an understatement.

For once, Bagnaia had clear air behind him, and he was left to do what he does with such ruthless regularity: control his lead down to the tenth of a second. Martin gave it his best, recovering expertly from row four to second by lap three. Yet even when he pushed for one late attack, closing to within a second, the tension fizzled out.

Bagnaia was simply calling the tune for his eighth win of the year, a personal record and the fifth to reach that number in the four-stroke era. And Italy's 900th. Amazingly skilled? Impressively executed? Yes. But not exciting.

Above: A determined ride to sixth made KTM's Brad Binder the only non-Ducati rider in the top eight.
Photo: Gold & Goose

Above right: On tip-toe, Bagnaia was untouchable in Japan.
Photo: Ducati Corse

Top far right: Gonzalez slips his Kalex past Ogura's Boscoscuro en route to his first win.

Above far right: Filip Salac copied Ogura's choice of slicks for the Moto2 restart, and was rewarded with a podium.

Right: Celebration time. David Alonso clinched the Moto3 title with four rounds to spare.
Photos: Gold & Goose

Most thrills came in the first four laps, after Bagnaia had led Acosta, Binder and Bastianini out of Turn Two. Marquez was quickly on the move, pushing past Morbidelli for fifth at Turn Three, while Martin followed his compatriot.

Then it became even more lively: Bastianini's Turn Nine move on Binder triggered a rapid reaction from the South African, who barged the factory Ducati wide at the following turn, allowing Martin through. With Marquez also pushed off line, Miller took advantage, passing the pair on the following downhill straight to sit an opportunistic fifth behind Binder and Martin, from 14th on the grid.

Clear of the madness, Bagnaia settled into a fearsome rhythm. Two-tenths clear at the close of lap one, he extended his lead over Acosta to three-tenths on the following lap. The Spaniard had designs on taking the lead at Turn One on lap four, but tucking the front as he completed the previous lap made it "the saddest weekend of my life."

Bagnaia now had 1.2 seconds over Martin, past Binder at the close of lap three. Then the title rivals engaged in a well-worn routine as Martin threatened to reel in Bagnaia. The lead was down to six-tenths on lap nine, only for the Italian's steady run of fast laps to reduce it to 1.8 seconds by lap 17. For Martin, "when I closed the gap to Pecco, I started to get chatter with the front."

He pushed again in the final five laps. "I was so, so close, but I had a big moment in Turn Three," he said, after saving it with his knee. "So, I said, 'It's time to stop. I did a great job, so I have to be happy with second.'"

One fleeting moment of jeopardy occurred on lap ten, when it began to spit with rain, bringing out white flags to indicate that riders could swap bikes. Yet lap times never wavered. Marquez's lap-five pass on Binder put him third, with Bastianini doing the same four laps on. The podium looked set until an error by Marquez into the first corner brought the factory Ducati to within a second.

Marquez's luck was in on the final lap. Despite touching the green exiting Turn Four, he crossed the line 0.536 of a second clear of Bastianini. Had the gap been half a second or less, he'd have had to drop a place. "Super-boring race," Marquez lamented afterwards as Bastianini and his team manager, Davide Tardozzi, lodged a protest about the decision in Race Control.

Morbidelli came home 17 seconds behind Bagnaia in fifth, with Binder a close, but despondent sixth, having succumbed with three laps to go, his KTM having little to offer the red bikes. VR46 Ducati duo Bezzecchi and Di Giannantonio were close together in seventh and eighth, well ahead of Espargaro, who had taken the fading Miller on lap 20 and held him at bay.

Zarco took 11th off Quartararo on the run to the line, the fuel-starved Yamaha stuttering to the finish for a second race in a row. Nakagami was less than a second behind, grabbing 13th from Marini on the last lap, with Raul Fernandez claiming the final point, clear of the other two Yamahas.

Vinales had another bad start from the front row and had dropped from ninth to 11th when he crashed out on lap 12. Augusto Fernandez also fell, Savadori retired, while Alex Marquez collided with Mir on the first lap, taking both down and earning a long-lap at the next race for his indiscretion.

Bagnaia's maximum score took 11 points out of Martin's lead, the gap down to ten.

MOTO2 RACE – 12 laps (shortened)

Saturday showers turned qualifying topsy-turvy, with Dixon striking lucky and setting a pole time running just two laps before the rain hit. Van den Goorbergh (through from Q1) and Canet were alongside, Roberts, Guevara and Moreira next. Title favourite Ogura was ninth, Aldeguer 15th, Garcia 17th and Salac – fastest on the first day – 18th.

More rain turned the race upside down, a sudden shower hitting the far side of the circuit during the first of 19 scheduled laps and bringing out the flags.

It carried on raining before the 12-lap restart, 20 minutes later, but nine riders gambled on the drizzle stopping and the track drying. To everyone's surprise, championship leader Ogura was one of them.

It was a bold call. Even, for Tony Arbolino, "crazy". So tricky were the conditions on the warm-up lap that Arenas pitted to switch back to wets – a decision he came to regret.

FIM WORLD CHAMPIONSHIP | 16

Dixon made the early running, but Ogura – 16th on lap one – was soon making rapid progress. With the rain relenting and the track still nowhere approaching fully wet, by only the second lap, the decision to go with slicks appeared inspired, as the home hero cut through the field. By lap three, he had taken the lead.

With other title contenders Lopez, Garcia and Canet floundering on wets in ninth, 14th and 16th respectively, the Japanese rider saw no sense in scrapping with Manuel Gonzalez – also on slicks – once the Spaniard had taken control of the contest with four laps to go.

Gonzalez became the ninth different Moto2 winner of the year in the process, comfortably 2.5 seconds clear of Ogura. Sadly, the joy of his maiden win would be dulled by controversy because of his start-line headgear.

Ogura spoke of thinking of "the bigger picture. This result was huge. The team really pushed me to make this decision, which was correct."

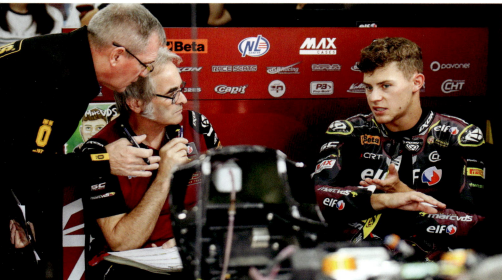

Salac, 24th on lap one, was another to benefit from slicks, fighting through to third by half-distance. "We had nothing to lose," he said of his decision. "On the warm-up lap, I waited under the bridge [exiting Turn 11] for Ogura to see if he'd enter the pits [to change tyres]. When he didn't, I thought the guy leading the championship must know what he's doing." It was the Czech rider's third podium.

Jeremy Alcoba pressed him to the flag, narrowly missing his own first podium, while van den Goorbergh (his career best) and a distant Artigas made it six slick-shod runners in the top six.

Vietti was the best of the riders on wets, in seventh, albeit a massive 53 seconds back from the victor. Diogo Moreira was close in ninth; then Guevara led a quartet from Arbolino, Aldeguer and Dixon, all within one second. The last named had led the gang on the penultimate lap, only to lose four places on the last.

Garcia was 14th, ahead of Binder, who took the final point. Canet was another five seconds down, promoted ahead of Oncu, who had exceeded track limits on the final lap.

Joe Roberts retired; amazingly there were no crashes.

Ogura's masterstroke put him 60 points ahead of Garcia, and another five from Lopez.

MOTO3 RACE – 17 laps

Ortola took a fifth pole, with Alonso third, Veijer between them. Piqueras, Yamanaka and Kelso were behind, with Fernandez heading row three.

This was the first match point for Alonso, and second place would be good enough. On race eve, he decided not to play it safe. And fittingly, the 18-year-old wrapped up the title in trademark style, duelling with rivals early on before making a decisive push in the closing laps.

Ortola led away, with Holgado, Alonso and Fernandez in pursuit, and it was Fernandez who took over from laps three to 13. At one stage, Alonso was as low as seventh, but by lap 11, he was challenging for the lead, now and then ahead during the lap, and over the line on lap 14, after Fernandez had run slightly wide.

Fernandez was left to fight with Ortola, who appeared to have the speed to reel in Alonso once he was through to second on the penultimate lap, but he crashed out at Turn Ten in the attempt.

Veijer, as low as ninth in the early stages, played a familiar waiting game, and his late push was enough to pass Fernandez, but Alonso was cruising to his tenth win of the year by then – and Colombia's first GP championship.

Holgado was a close fourth, then Rueda and Yamanaka, the top six within just over a second of the lead. Suzuki was a lone seventh; Munoz led Furusao for eighth.

Six riders crashed, including Lunetta, Piqueras (twice) and Kelso, who remounted to finish a lap down in last.

Championship decided, now the battle was for second, with Holgado three points clear of Veijer and Ortola 18 adrift.

FIM WORLD CHAMPIONSHIP: ROUND 16
MOTUL GRAND PRIX OF JAPAN
4–6 OCTOBER, 2024

TWIN RING MOTEGI
Length: 4.800km / 2.980 miles
24 laps   Width: 15m

MOTOGP: RACE DISTANCE: 24 laps, 71.597 miles/115.224km
WEATHER: Dry (air 21°, humidity 91%, track 26°)

Pos.	Rider	Nat.No.	Entrant	Machine	Race tyre choice	Laps	Time & speed
1	Francesco Bagnaia	ITA 1	Ducati Lenovo Team	Ducati Desmosedici GP24	F: Hard/R: Medium	24	42m 09.790s 101.8mph/163.9km/h
2	Jorge Martin	SPA 89	Prima Pramac Racing	Ducati Desmosedici GP24	F: Hard/R: Medium	24	42m 10.979s
3	Marc Marquez	SPA 93	Gresini Racing MotoGP	Ducati Desmosedici GP23	F: Hard/R: Medium	24	42m 13.612s
4	Enea Bastianini	ITA 23	Ducati Lenovo Team	Ducati Desmosedici GP24	F: Hard/R: Medium	24	42m 14.148s
5	Franco Morbidelli	ITA 21	Prima Pramac Racing	Ducati Desmosedici GP24	F: Hard/R: Medium	24	42m 27.730s
6	Brad Binder	RSA 33	Red Bull KTM Factory Racing	KTM RC16	F: Hard/R: Medium	24	42m 28.292s
7	Marco Bezzecchi	ITA 72	Pertamina Enduro VR46 Racing	Ducati Desmosedici GP23	F: Hard/R: Medium	24	42m 29.161s
8	Fabio Di Giannantonio	ITA 49	Pertamina Enduro àVR46 Racing	Ducati Desmosedici GP23	F: Hard/R: Medium	24	42m 29.989s
9	Aleix Espargaro	SPA 41	Aprilia Racing	Aprilia RS-GP24	F: Hard/R: Medium	24	42m 40.232s
10	Jack Miller	AUS 43	Red Bull KTM Factory Racing	KTM RC16	F: Hard/R: Medium	24	42m 40.974s
11	Johann Zarco	FRA 5	CASTROL Honda LCR	Honda RC213V	F: Hard/R: Medium	24	42m 41.357s
12	Fabio Quartararo	FRA 20	Monster Energy Yamaha MotoGP	Yamaha YZR-M1	F: Hard/R: Medium	24	42m 42.089s
13	Takaaki Nakagami	JPN 30	IDEMITSU Honda LCR	Honda RC213V	F: Hard/R: Soft	24	42m 42.793s
14	Luca Marini	ITA 10	Repsol Honda Team	Honda RC213V	F: Hard/R: Medium	24	42m 45.764s
15	Raul Fernandez	SPA 25	Trackhouse Racing	Aprilia RS-GP24	F: Hard/R: Medium	24	42m 49.111s
16	Alex Rins	SPA 42	Monster Energy Yamaha MotoGP	Yamaha YZR-M1	F: Hard/R: Medium	24	42m 50.629s
17	Remy Gardner	AUS 87	Yamaha Factory Racing Team	Yamaha YZR-M1	F: Hard/R: Medium	24	43m 09.337s
	Pedro Acosta	SPA 31	Red Bull GASGAS Tech3	KTM RC16	F: Hard/R: Medium	12	DNF-crash
	Maverick Vinales	SPA 12	Aprilia Racing	Aprilia RS-GP24	F: Hard/R: Medium	11	DNF-crash
	Augusto Fernandez	SPA 37	Red Bull GASGAS Tech3	KTM RC16	F: Hard/R: Medium	6	DNF-crash
	Lorenzo Savadori	ITA 32	Trackhouse Racing	Aprilia RS-GP24	F: Hard/R: Medium	1	DNF-technical
	Alex Marquez	SPA 73	Gresini Racing MotoGP	Ducati Desmosedici GP23	F: Hard/R: Medium	0	DNF-crash
	Joan Mir	SPA 36	Repsol Honda Team	Honda RC213V	F: Hard/R: Medium	0	DNF-crash

Fastest lap: Jorge Martin, on lap 5, 1m 44.461s, 102.8mph/165.4km/h.
Lap record: Jack Miller, 1m 45.198s, 102.0mph/164.2km/h (2022).
Event maximum speed: Pedro Acosta, 198.5mph/319.5km/h (practice).

Qualfying: Weather: Dry Air: 21° Humidity: 84% Track: 23°
1 Acosta 1m 43.018s, 2 Bagnaia 1m 43.264s, 3 Vinales 1m 43.441s, 4 Bastianini 1m 43.539s, 5 Binder 1m 43.661s, 6 Morbidelli 1m 43.828s, 7 Di Giannantonio 1m 43.998s, 8 Bezzecchi 1m 44.073s, 9 M. Marquez 1m 44.136s, 10 A. Marquez 1m 44.263s, 11 Martin 1m 44.303s, 12 Quartararo 1m 44.497s.
Q1: 13 R. Fernandez 1m 44.122s, 14 Miller 1m 44.193s, 15 A. Espargaro 1m 44.202s, 16 Zarco 1m 44.302s, 17 Mir 1m 44.498s, 18 A. Fernandez 1m 44.547s, 19 Rins 1m 44.552s, 20 Marini 1m 44.648s, 21 Nakagami 1m 44.886s, 22 Savadori 1m 45.422s, 23 Gardner 1m 45.594s.

SPRINT RACE: 12 laps, 35.796 miles/57.612km
WEATHER: Dry (air 29°, humidity 73°, track 60°)

Pos.	Rider	Race tyre choice	Laps	Time & speed
1	Francesco Bagnaia	F: Hard/R: Soft	12	21m 01.074s 102.2mph/164.4km/h
2	Enea Bastianini	F: Hard/R: Soft	12	21m 01.255s
3	Marc Marquez	F: Hard/R: Soft	12	21m 01.423s
4	Jorge Martin	F: Hard/R: Soft	12	21m 03.572s
5	Franco Morbidelli	F: Hard/R: Soft	12	21m 05.400s
6	Fabio Di Giannantonio	F: Hard/R: Soft	12	21m 05.520s
7	Alex Marquez	F: Hard/R: Soft	12	21m 12.518s
8	Jack Miller	F: Soft/R: Soft	12	21m 12.949s
9	Maverick Vinales	F: Hard/R: Soft	12	21m 13.021s
10	Marco Bezzecchi	F: Hard/R: Soft	12	21m 13.373s
11	Raul Fernandez	F: Hard/R: Soft	12	21m 15.633s
12	Fabio Quartararo	F: Hard/R: Soft	12	21m 15.719s
13	Luca Marini	F: Hard/R: Soft	12	21m 16.960s
14	Johann Zarco	F: Hard/R: Soft	12	21m 17.244s
15	Augusto Fernandez	F: Medium/R: Soft	12	21m 21.596s
16	Alex Rins	F: Soft/R: Soft	12	21m 25.489s
17	Lorenzo Savadori	F: Hard/R: Soft	12	21m 26.556s
18	Remy Gardner	F: Hard/R: Soft	12	21m 33.694s
	Joan Mir	F: Hard/R: Soft	11	DNF-ret in pit
	Aleix Espargaro	F: Hard/R: Soft	9	DNF-crash
	Pedro Acosta	F: Hard/R: Soft	8	DNF-crash
	Takaaki Nakagami	F: Hard/R: Soft	4	DNF-crash
	Brad Binder	F: Hard/R: Soft	2	DNF-technical

Fastest race lap: Pedro Acosta, on lap 2, 1m 43.825s.

Fastest race laps
1 Martin 1m 44.461s, 2 Bagnaia 1m 44.519s, 3 Bastianini 1m 44.707s, 4 Acosta 1m 44.850s, 5 M. Marquez 1m 44.860s, 6 Binder 1m 45.037s, 7 Bezzecchi 1m 45.081s, 8 Di Giannantonio 1m 45.172s, 9 Miller 1m 45.208s, 10 Vinales 1m 45.376s, 11 Morbidelli 1m 45.406s, 12 A. Espargaro 1m 45.568s, 13 Zarco 1m 45.701s, 14 Quartararo 1m 45.710s, 15 R. Fernandez 1m 45.814s, 16 A. Fernandez 1m 45.908s, 17 Nakagami 1m 45.918s, 18 Rins 1m 45.940s, 19 Marini 1m 46.195s, 20 Gardner 1m 47.044s.

Grid order / Lap chart

Grid order	1	2	3	4	5	6	7	8	9	10	11	12	13	14	15	16	17	18	19	20	21	22	23	24
31 ACOSTA	1	1	1	1	1	1	1	1	1	1	1	1	1	1	1	1	1	1	1	1	1	1	1	1
1 BAGNAIA	31	31	89	89	89	89	89	89	89	89	89	89	89	89	89	89	89	89	89	89	89	89	89	2
12 VINALES	33	33	33	33	93	93	93	93	93	93	93	93	93	93	93	93	93	93	93	93	93	93	93	3
23 BASTIANINI	89	89	93	93	33	33	33	33	23	23	23	23	23	23	23	23	23	23	23	23	23	23	21	4
33 BINDER	43	43	43	23	23	23	23	23	33	33	33	33	33	33	33	33	33	33	33	33	33	21	33	5
21 MORBIDELLI	93	93	23	43	43	43	43	21	21	21	21	21	21	21	21	21	21	21	21	21	33	33	33	6
49 DI GIANNANTONIO	23	23	21	21	21	21	43	72	72	72	72	72	72	72	72	72	72	72	72	72	72	72	72	7
72 BEZZECCHI	21	21	41	41	72	72	72	43	43	43	49	49	49	49	49	49	49	49	49	49	49	49	49	8
93 M. MARQUEZ	12	41	72	72	41	41	41	41	49	49	43	43	43	43	43	43	41	41	41	41	41	41	41	9
73 A. MARQUEZ	41	12	12	12	12	49	49	49	41	41	41	41	41	41	41	41	43	43	43	43	43	43	43	10
89 MARTIN	20	72	20	49	49	12	12	12	12	20	20	20	20	20	20	20	20	20	20	20	20	5	5	11
20 QUARTARARO	72	20	49	20	20	20	20	20	20	5	5	5	5	5	5	5	5	5	5	5	5	20		12
25 R. FERNANDEZ	5	5	5	5	5	5	5	5	5	25	25	25	30	30	30	30	30	30	30	30	30			13
43 MILLER	49	49	25	25	25	25	25	25	25	30	30	30	25	25	25	25	10	10	10	10	10			14
41 A. ESPARGARO	25	25	37	37	37	37	30	30	30	42	42	42	10	10	10	10	25	25	25	25	25			15
5 ZARCO	37	37	30	30	30	30	42	42	42	10	10	10	42	42	42	42	42	42	42	42	42			
36 MIR	30	30	42	42	42	42	10	10	10	87	87	87	87	87	87	87	87	87	87	87	87			
37 A. FERNANDEZ	42	42	10	10	10	10	87	87	87	31														
42 RINS	10	10	87	87	87	31	31	31	31															
10 MARINI	87	87	31	31	31																			
30 NAKAGAMI	32																							
32 SAVADORI																								
87 GARDNER																								

31 – lapped rider

Championship Points

	Rider			
1	Martin	261	(131)	392
2	Bagnaia	279	(103)	382
3	Bastianini	226	(87)	313
4	M. Marquez	216	(95)	311
5	Binder	144	(39)	183
6	Acosta	118	(63)	181
7	Vinales	108	(55)	163
8	Morbidelli	96	(40)	136
9	A. Espargaro	88	(46)	134
10	Bezzecchi	123	(11)	134
11	Di Giannantonio	113	(21)	134
12	A. Marquez	103	(21)	124
13	Quartararo	71	(15)	86
14	Oliveira	55	(16)	71
15	Miller	41	(25)	66
16	R. Fernandez	54	(2)	56
17	Zarco	34	(2)	36
18	Nakagami	28	(0)	28
19	A. Fernandez	17	(3)	20
20	Mir	19	(1)	20
21	Rins	20	(0)	20
22	P. Espargaro	11	(1)	12
23	Pedrosa	0	(7)	7
24	Marini	7	(0)	7
25	Bradl	2	(0)	2

Constructor Points

1	Ducati	391	(183)	574
2	KTM	189	(86)	275
3	Aprilia	159	(96)	255
4	Yamaha	82	(15)	97
5	Honda	52	(4)	56

MOTO2: RACE DISTANCE: 12 laps, 35.798 miles/57.612km

RACE WEATHER: Wet (air 21°, humidity 90%, track 26°)

Pos.	Rider	Nat.	No.	Entrant	Machine	Laps	Time & Speed
1	Manuel Gonzalez	SPA	18	QJMOTOR Gresini Moto2	Kalex	12	22m 52.521s
							93.9mph/151.1km/h
2	Ai Ogura	JPN	79	MT Helmets - MSI	Boscoscuro	12	22m 55.056s
3	Filip Salac	CZE	12	Elf Marc VDS Racing Team	Kalex	12	23m 01.624s
4	Jeremy Alcoba	SPA	52	Yamaha VR46 Master Camp Team	Kalex	12	23m 01.761s
5	Zonta van den Goorbergh	NED	84	RW-Idrofoglia Racing GP	Kalex	12	23m 07.279s
6	Xavier Artigas	SPA	43	KLINT Forward Factory Team	Forward	12	23m 28.333s
7	Celestino Vietti	ITA	13	Red Bull KTM Ajo	Kalex	12	23m 46.368s
8	Diogo Moreira	BRA	10	Italtrans Racing Team	Kalex	12	23m 46.880s
9	Alonso Lopez	SPA	21	Beta Tools SpeedUp	Boscoscuro	12	23m 49.404s
10	Izan Guevara	SPA	28	CFMOTO Inde Aspar Team	Kalex	12	23m 51.454s
11	Tony Arbolino	ITA	14	Elf Marc VDS Racing Team	Kalex	12	23m 51.811s
12	Fermin Aldeguer	SPA	54	Beta Tools SpeedUp	Boscoscuro	12	23m 52.213s
13	Jake Dixon	GBR	96	CFMOTO Inde Aspar Team	Kalex	12	23m 52.473s
14	Sergio Garcia	SPA	3	MT Helmets - MSI	Boscoscuro	12	23m 55.736s
15	Darryn Binder	RSA	15	Liqui Moly Husqvarna Intact GP	Kalex	12	23m 56.016s
16	Aron Canet	SPA	44	Fantic Racing	Kalex	12	24m 01.701s
17	Deniz Oncu	TUR	53	Red Bull KTM Ajo	Kalex	12	24m 01.384s
18	Barry Baltus	BEL	7	RW-Idrofoglia Racing GP	Kalex	12	24m 01.967s
19	Marcos Ramirez	SPA	24	OnlyFans American Racing Team	Kalex	12	24m 02.674s
20	Senna Agius	AUS	81	Liqui Moly Husqvarna Intact GP	Kalex	12	24m 02.817s
21	Ayumu Sasaki	JPN	22	Yamaha VR46 Master Camp Team	Kalex	12	24m 12.028s
22	Albert Arenas	SPA	75	QJMOTOR Gresini Moto2	Kalex	12	24m 17.979s
23	Alex Escrig	SPA	11	KLINT Forward Factory Team	Forward	12	24m 18.724s
24	Jaume Masia	SPA	5	Preicanos Racing Team	Kalex	12	24m 21.309s
25	Xavi Cardelus	AND	20	Fantic Racing	Kalex	12	24m 38.230s
26	Dennis Foggia	ITA	71	Italtrans Racing Team	Kalex	12	24m 40.924s
27	Joe Roberts	USA	16	OnlyFans American Racing Team	Kalex	11	23m 47.235s
	Mario Aji	INA	34	IDEMITSU Honda Team Asia	Kalex	8	DNF-ret in pit

Fastest lap: Manuel Gonzalez, on lap 7, 1m 50.783s, 96.9mph/156.0km/h.
Lap record: Somkiat Chantra, 1m 50.679s, 97.0mph/156.1km/h (2023).
Event maximum speed: Celestino Vietti, 164.8mph/265.3km/h (qualifying).

Qualifying:
Weather: Dry
Air: 20° **Humidity:** 84% **Track:** 23°

1	Dixon	1m 52.693s
2	V d Goorbergh	1m 52.699s
3	Canet	1m 53.000s
4	Roberts	1m 53.002s
5	Guevara	1m 53.116s
6	Moreira	1m 53.126s
7	Baltus	1m 53.174s
8	Lopez	1m 53.385s
9	Ogura	1m 53.894s
10	Arbolino	1m 54.056s
11	Vietti	1m 54.233s
12	Ramirez	1m 54.293s
13	Oncu	1m 54.451s
14	Gonzalez	1m 54.629s
15	Aldeguer	1m 54.750s
16	Arenas	1m 54.763s
17	Garcia	1m 55.820s
18	Salac	1m 56.762s
Q1		
19	Foggia	1m 50.135s
20	Agius	1m 50.147s
21	Binder	1m 50.158s
22	Alcoba	1m 50.235s
23	Masia	1m 50.245s
24	Sasaki	1m 50.397s
25	Escrig	1m 50.419s
26	Aji	1m 50.719s
27	Artigas	1m 50.871s
28	Cardelus	1m 51.155s
29	Munoz	1m 51.161s

Fastest race laps

1	Gonzalez	1m 50.783s
2	Salac	1m 51.175s
3	Alcoba	1m 51.269s
4	Ogura	1m 51.457s
5	Roberts	1m 51.642s
6	V d Goorbergh	1m 51.782s
7	Artigas	1m 53.853s
8	Vietti	1m 56.784s
9	Moreira	1m 56.984s
10	Aldeguer	1m 56.996s
11	Guevara	1m 57.794s
12	Lopez	1m 57.801s
13	Arbolino	1m 57.815s
14	Dixon	1m 58.107s
15	Garcia	1m 58.228s
16	Binder	1m 58.278s
17	Oncu	1m 58.344s
18	Agius	1m 58.744s
19	Baltus	1m 58.773s
20	Canet	1m 58.810s
21	Ramirez	1m 58.817s
22	Arenas	1m 59.168s
23	Sasaki	1m 59.443s
24	Aji	1m 59.784s
25	Escrig	1m 59.807s
26	Masia	2m 00.385s
27	Cardelus	2m 00.883s
28	Foggia	2m 01.547s

Championship Points

1	Ogura	228
2	Garcia	168
3	Lopez	163
4	Canet	156
5	Roberts	153
6	Gonzalez	153
7	Aldeguer	150
8	Vietti	140
9	Dixon	133
10	Arbolino	127
11	Ramirez	79
12	Chantra	78
13	Alcoba	74
14	Arenas	65
15	Salac	57
16	Binder	50
17	Agius	47
18	Moreira	36
19	Oncu	34
20	Guevara	34
21	Baltus	31
22	Van den Goorbergh	31
23	Foggia	18
24	Artigas	10
25	Bendsneyder	7
26	Navarro	6
27	Sasaki	4
28	Masia	4
29	Aji	3
30	Ferrari	1

Constructor Points

1	Kalex	342
2	Boscoscuro	328
3	Forward	16

MOTO3: RACE DISTANCE: 17 laps, 50.714 miles/81.617km

RACE WEATHER: Dry (air 23°, humidity 82%, track 29°)

Pos.	Rider	Nat.	No.	Entrant	Machine	Laps	Time & Speed
1	David Alonso	COL	80	CFMOTO Gaviota Aspar Team	CFMOTO	17	33m 03.606s
							92.0mph/148.1km/h
2	Collin Veijer	NED	95	Liqui Moly Husqvarna Intact GP	Husqvarna	17	33m 04.130s
3	Adrian Fernandez	SPA	31	Leopard Racing	Honda	17	33m 04.372s
4	Daniel Holgado	SPA	96	Red Bull GASGAS Tech3	GASGAS	17	33m 04.774s
5	Jose Antonio Rueda	SPA	99	Red Bull KTM Ajo	KTM	17	33m 04.815s
6	Ryusei Yamanaka	JPN	6	MT Helmets - MSI	KTM	17	33m 04.995s
7	Tatsuki Suzuki	JPN	24	Liqui Moly Husqvarna Intact GP	Husqvarna	17	33m 05.942s
8	David Munoz	SPA	64	BOE Motorsports	KTM	17	33m 07.496s
9	Taiyo Furusato	JPN	72	Honda Team Asia	Honda	17	33m 07.559s
10	Stefano Nepa	ITA	82	LEVELUP - MTA	KTM	17	33m 11.599s
11	Matteo Bertelle	ITA	18	Kopron Rivacold Snipers Team	Honda	17	33m 11.648s
12	David Almansa	SPA	22	Kopron Rivacold Snipers Team	Honda	17	33m 13.844s
13	Filippo Farioli	ITA	7	SIC58 Squadra Corse	Honda	17	33m 15.403s
14	Riccardo Rossi	ITA	54	CIP Green Power	KTM	17	33m 16.858s
15	Joel Esteban	SPA	78	CFMOTO Gaviota Aspar Team	CFMOTO	17	33m 16.900s
16	Ivan Ortola	SPA	48	MT Helmets - MSI	KTM	17	33m 26.001s
17	Jacob Roulstone	AUS	12	Red Bull GASGAS Tech3	GASGAS	17	33m 26.058s
18	Xabi Zurutuza	SPA	85	Red Bull KTM Ajo	KTM	17	33m 26.145s
19	Scott Ogden	GBR	19	FleetSafe Honda - MLav Racing	Honda	17	33m 28.434s
20	Rei Wakamatsu	JPN	32	FleetSafe Honda - MLav Racing	Honda	17	33m 49.368s
21	Joel Kelso	AUS	66	BOE Motorsports	KTM	16	33m 51.294s
	Angel Piqueras	SPA	36	Leopard Racing	Honda	12	DNF-crash
	Nicola Carraro	ITA	10	LEVELUP - MTA	KTM	6	DNF-crash
	Luca Lunetta	ITA	58	SIC58 Squadra Corse	Honda	2	DNF-crash
	Tatchakorn Buasri	THA	5	Honda Team Asia	Honda	2	DNF-crash
	Noah Dettwiler	SWI	55	CIP Green Power	KTM	0	DNF-crash

Fastest lap: David Alonso, on lap 9, 1m 55.675s, 92.8mph/149.4km/h.
Lap record: Ayumu Sasaki, 1m 57.064s, 91.7mph/147.6km/h (2023).
Event maximum speed: Ivan Ortola, 139.5mph/224.5km/h (qualifying).

Qualifying:
Weather: Dry
Air: 20° **Humidity:** 85% **Track:** 23°

1	Ortola	1m 54.761s
2	Veijer	1m 55.117s
3	Alonso	1m 55.170s
4	Piqueras	1m 55.485s
5	Yamanaka	1m 55.494s
6	Kelso	1m 55.679s
7	Fernandez	1m 55.928s
8	Munoz	1m 55.931s
9	Holgado	1m 56.165s
10	Almansa	1m 56.234s
11	Nepa	1m 56.331s
12	Lunetta	1m 56.360s
13	Furusato	1m 56.418s
14	Rueda	1m 56.420s
15	Bertelle	1m 56.436s
16	Rossi	1m 56.784s
17	Suzuki	1m 56.952s
18	Farioli	1m 57.220s
Q1		
19	Esteban	1m 57.057s
20	Ogden	1m 57.136s
21	Roulstone	1m 57.282s
22	Zurutuza	1m 57.295s
23	Carraro	1m 57.346s
24	Dettwiler	1m 57.761s
25	Buasri	1m 57.829s
26	Wakamatsu	1m 58.599s

Fastest race laps

1	Alonso	1m 55.675s
2	Veijer	1m 55.798s
3	Holgado	1m 55.803s
4	Piqueras	1m 55.836s
5	Suzuki	1m 55.844s
6	Rueda	1m 55.856s
7	Ortola	1m 55.910s
8	Fernandez	1m 55.943s
9	Yamanaka	1m 55.991s
10	Munoz	1m 56.029s
11	Nepa	1m 56.047s
12	Furusato	1m 56.057s
13	Bertelle	1m 56.070s
14	Almansa	1m 56.254s
15	Kelso	1m 56.421s
16	Esteban	1m 56.461s
17	Farioli	1m 56.507s
18	Rossi	1m 56.550s
19	Carraro	1m 56.725s
20	Ogden	1m 57.003s
21	Zurutuza	1m 57.020s
22	Roulstone	1m 57.128s
23	Lunetta	1m 57.196s
24	Buasri	1m 57.434s
25	Wakamatsu	1m 58.513s

Championship Points

1	Alonso	321
2	Holgado	212
3	Veijer	209
4	Ortola	191
5	Munoz	141
6	Fernandez	137
7	Piqueras	131
8	Rueda	121
9	Kelso	110
10	Yamanaka	96
11	Furusato	88
12	Suzuki	81
13	Lunetta	78
14	Nepa	65
15	Roulstone	50
16	Bertelle	47
17	Esteban	45
18	Farioli	27
19	Rossi	26
20	Carraro	22
21	Ogden	15
22	Zurutuza	11
23	Almansa	11
24	Perez	3
25	Dettwiler	2

Constructor Points

1	CFMOTO	321
2	KTM	278
3	Husqvarna	235
4	Honda	228
5	GASGAS	217

Above: No smoke without fire. Marquez struggles with his self-sabotaged start.

Top right: Pecco Bagnaia had to settle for damage limitation. Twice.

Above right: Aprilia's Romano Albesiano in conversation with future Honda colleague Alberto Puig.

Right: Raul Fernandez took sixth in the sprint, then stripped the wings for tenth on Sunday.
Photos: Gold & Goose

Opening spread: Once, twice, three times a winner. Marquez added another chapter to his Phillip Island legend.
Photo: Gresini Racing

WILDLIFE was much to the fore at Phillip Island. There were the grazing Cape Barren Geese that twice brought out red flags in practice. The rabbit that just managed to evade a charging Jorge Martin. The seagull that lodged itself in Jack Miller's handlebar, behind the brake lever, in the sprint. And Marc Marquez's mosquito.

Actually more than a mosquito, as he explained: "Some of the bugs in Australia are quite big." One of them splattered itself on his visor as he approached the start line on Sunday, while engaging the launch-control system. The smear was bad enough to spoil his view of the lights, and with little chance between start and first corner, he elected to break with convention and remove a tear-off on the grid. Something the riders had agreed not to do, after one had lodged in Miller's intake, choking his Ducati at Misano in 2020.

The consequences were extraordinary.

Instead of it being blown away safely, one of the seaside circuit's unpredictable gusts deposited it right under his back wheel. Seconds later, the race started. Marc released the clutch, his back wheel spun and as the pack flashed past on either side, he fought the fishtailing Ducati in a cloud of blue smoke.

That put him 13th into the first corner. Before the end of the first lap, he was up to sixth. Abandoning all thoughts of the usually crucial tyre tactics, he'd decided just to go for it. All the way to a most spectacular victory.

In previous Australian masterstrokes, he had pipped Lorenzo on the final lap in 2015, Vinales in 2019 and fought off seven others in 2017. This latest was one of his finest rides. Martin and Bagnaia might have been gunning for 2024's title, but Marquez left both in little doubt that even bigger challenges lay in wait in 2025. The manner in which he reeled in Martin, before striking decisively with three laps to go, showcased the very best of his talent.

It was another high point at Australia's circuit for the ages, scene of much drama over the years. Marc became the latest multiple PI winner to make history, alongside such as Wayne Gardner, Mick Doohan, Valentino Rossi and especially Casey Stoner. A fitting climax to a dramatic weekend.

The weather had played its usual role: rain so heavy on Friday that MotoGP's first free practice didn't even take place, being replaced by a slightly extended FP2 on Saturday. It meant that Friday afternoon's timed practice was the first outing on a completely new surface, so riders had to gather information while also going for a top-ten lap time to avoid the Q2 jungle.

Those on GP23 Ducatis at least had 2023's data as a base, but that was not the only reason why Marc Marquez was so dominant. As would become increasingly obvious.

Riders enjoy Phillip Island because its nature – fast corners, no stop-and-go, and no acceleration from low speed make it more than just a horsepower contest. The rider can make the difference – notably, winner Marquez was only seventh fastest down the straight, at 217.2mph, and while a Ducati (Bastianini's) was fastest at 220.7mph, Miller's KTM and Vinales's Aprilia were also ahead of Marc.

The speed has its own risks, especially in the notoriously gusty conditions: Raul Fernandez elected to race without wings on Sunday, which made the bike "feel like it was flying". But aero played its part in an ugly 140mph collision between Vinales and Bezzecchi in the sprint. The Spaniard had passed the Italian apparently cleanly, but as he braked for the first turn, Bezzecchi locked his front wheel and slammed into the back of the Aprilia, sending both cartwheeling sickeningly through the gravel. It was a repeat of a similar crash between Marquez and Zarco in 2018, blamed on the latter having been sucked past his braking point by the high-speed slipstream, and stewards accepted that this was probably part of the reason this time. The other part was Bezzecchi's fault, they decided, but because of "mitigating circumstances", he only suffered a single, rather than double long-lap.

Vinales also pointed the finger at Bezzecchi's error, while the Italian took a different view, blaming Vinales for braking early and criticising him also for hurling abuse in the gravel rather than checking the still prone Bezzecchi's condition (he was flown to Melbourne for a check-up afterwards) – "but the important thing is we are both not hurt," he concluded.

Both bikes had effectively disintegrated, and while a nervy Di Giannantonio, who was right behind, escaped unharmed, Aprilia substitute Savadori was struck by some debris, suffering nerve damage to his arm. He finished this race, but retired from the full race on Sunday.

After his difficult Japanese GP, things became worse for Acosta, starting with the upset of missing a chance for Q2 in Friday's first-time-out practice – a disappointment he shared with Miller and Bastianini, as well as Quartararo, who really would have benefited from a wet session. Having started from a season's worst 15th, he was only up to 11th when he fell with three laps to go, landing heavily and suffering painful ligament damage to his left shoulder that ruled him out on Sunday, potentially affecting the upcoming races as well. It was his 24th crash of the season, the most of any rider.

Injuries disrupted Moto2 somewhat, with 2024 race winners Vietti and Roberts both out of action by Sunday. Vietti had fallen on Friday, breaking his collarbone; the American had fractured his right scaphoid after high-siding on his out-lap on a cold, wet Saturday morning. Meanwhile, Di Giannantonio confirmed that he would miss the last two rounds for shoulder surgery.

MOTOGP SPRINT RACE – 13 laps

Attenuated practice favoured the bold, Martin and Marquez leading from Vinales; Bezzecchi, Bagnaia and Raul Fernandez next, the last through from Q1. So, too, Bastianini, who languished on row four. Ahead of him, Alex Rins, unusually top Yamaha.

Martin led Marquez away, but the latter was boxed into Turn One and ran wide, finishing lap one seventh. Bezzecchi was second, ahead of Bagnaia, Binder, fast-starting Bastianini and Vinales.

Martin soon began drawing away, better than a second clear on lap four; 2.6 on lap seven. By now, Bagnaia was leading the pursuit, but suffering front grip issues that would haunt his weekend, with Marquez and Bastianini both past Binder and closing rapidly.

Marquez sliced inside at Turn Four, Bastianini following. The top three were fixed, with Marquez halving a three-second gap to Martin by the finish.

By lap ten, Bagnaia's fourth was under threat from Bezzecchi, Vinales and Di Giannantonio. Two laps later, the pressure was relieved dramatically after Vinales passed Bezzecchi into the first corner, only for the Italian to go barrelling into the back of the Aprilia in a move that earned growing condemnation, taking both out in spectacular fashion.

Di Giannantonio lost touch with Bagnaia as a result, but was clear of Morbidelli, in turn relieved of Binder's pressure when the South African crashed out on the penultimate lap. Then Diggia suffered an eight-second tyre-pressure penalty, promoting Morbidelli to fifth and Raul Fernandez to sixth. Espargaro and Augusto Fernandez closed the points, the latter hotly pursued by Marini, Quartararo and Rins, all within less than four-tenths.

Acosta, Miller, Alex Marquez and Zarco all swelled the crash list.

Above: "Something more to risk." Marquez shoves past Martin to seize the lead.

Top right: Racing as a contact sport. Aldeguer shoulder-barged Canet in a last-lap showdown. The loser approved.

Above right: Third place at home for class rookie Senna Agius.

Above far right: Hanging on for dear life – a hairy moment in wet practice for local Moto2 replacement Harrison Voight.

Right: Alonso finished well clear of the pack for his 11th win – equalling Rossi's 1997 record.

Photos: Gold & Goose

MOTOGP RACE – 27 laps

With sunny (if breezy) conditions at last, the stage was set for a confrontation between the two fastest riders of the weekend, and Marquez's sprint fight-back from seventh to second indicated that this would be a straight shootout. Events on the start-line seemed to have cancelled that, as Marquez spun up and was swamped.

While Martin led into the first turn from Bezzecchi, Bagnaia, Morbidelli and Binder, the light-blue Gresini Ducati was nowhere.

Then a flash of fortune. Alex Marquez's lunge on Miller pushed both riders off-track and caused several others to lift. The seas parted, and Marc Marquez found himself eighth, just behind Bastianini and Vinales entering the Southern Loop. Exiting Siberia, he had passed both, a seven-place rise in under a minute.

As Bezzecchi served his long-lap, Martin had an eight-tenths margin over Bagnaia. Yet his lead never exceeded a full second. And with Marquez passing Binder for fourth at Turn Four and then Morbidelli for third two laps later, he was free to really find his groove as he sought to cut the 1.6-second deficit to the leader. Plans of tyre preservation had been abandoned on the first lap. Now, fastest laps on the fifth, seventh and ninth put him within touching distance of Bagnaia.

The pair were given unexpected encouragement by a Martin moment at Turn One on lap ten, a first sign that he wasn't entirely comfortable on Michelin's hard-compound front. The title protagonists traded the lead through Turns Three and Four, Marquez joining Martin in passing Bagnaia into the latter. Now we had the contest everyone was expecting.

A combination of Phillip Island's new track surface and pleasant weather led to a red-hot pace, Martin setting the tone, repeatedly in the low 1m 28s. By lap 16, it was clear that Bagnaia's challenge was faltering as he began losing around a second per lap. For the following seven laps, Marquez was a constant menace, hovering just over a tenth of a second behind Martin. An attack was inevitable.

The first came at Turn Four, with Martin wide on lap 24. The championship leader responded swiftly, showing off his Ducati GP24's awesome speed advantage over the GP23 to reclaim the lead on the run to Turn One the next time around.

Marquez knew he had to muster an immediate response; it came with a daring late lunge into Turn Four, which pushed his rival to the edge of the track. With one eye on his championship lead, Martin couldn't live with the new leader's pace in the final two laps. "He had something else in terms of the risk he could take," he conceded, leaving Marquez clear to claim a third win of the year by nine-tenths, with Bagnaia a colossal ten seconds back in third.

Behind, Di Giannantonio mounted a fine comeback from 12th on the grid, warding off Bastianini, who was frustrated by what he felt was a dodgy Michelin front tyre, and three others. Morbidelli was sixth, making it an all-Ducati top six – the first in history, and a first for any manufacturer in the premier class since Honda in the French Grand Prix of 1997.

With Acosta out hurt, Binder led the KTM charge just behind, Vinales in tow. Quartararo finally escaped from Raul Fernandez (who had ditched his wings pre-race to improve agility), Miller and Zarco in a tight fight for ninth. The Australian had recovered well from the Turn One punt, which had dropped him to the back, regaining the top ten, before familiar chatter problems struck and he was left unable to resist the Yamaha.

Rins was a couple of seconds down, followed by Marini, fending off Alex Marquez for the last points. Another six seconds away, Espargaro got back ahead of Augusto Fernandez at the end. Nakagami was close behind. Bezzecchi was last, falling at the hairpin after his long-lap, then remounting. Savadori retired in pain, Mir suffered another race crash.

Martin's haul of 32 points doubled his lead over Bagnaia to 20, while Marc Marquez moved 14 ahead of Bastianini in the fight for third.

MOTO2 RACE – 23 laps

The conditions were no kinder to Moto2, but it dried up for qualifying, when Aldeguer set a new circuit record for his third pole, but first in nine races. Canet and Lopez were alongside, Ramirez, Baltus and Gonzalez next. Ogura was ninth. Home rider Agius had been fastest in the wet in the morning, and also in Q1, but now was 13th on the grid. That would prove no obstacle.

The first two qualifiers made the race their own, breaking

clear of early leader Lopez on the fifth lap after some initial skirmishes and fighting to the end. In the aftermath of a wild contest, with plenty of barging, Canet insisted that motorcycle racing shouldn't be averse to the odd coming-together, even if he had come off worse.

He had led marginally fewer laps, but appeared to have gained a vital edge with a fine last-lap pass at Turn Four, only for Aldeguer to respond into Turn Ten. Yet his compatriot didn't relent, leading the pair to rub as they edged out toward the kerb. Having picked up his bike on his knee, Aldeguer recovered to win by 0.194 of a second.

It begged the question: where had the pre-season favourite been for the past three months? Phillip Island was a sparkling return to form. "After the summer break, I didn't feel good with the bike," he explained. "The pace and speed were missing. But after Aragon, I started to work in the same way as last year and the start of this season – going on track and giving my 100 per cent each lap, trying to find the limit on the bike earlier than before. If I didn't make the mistake in Indonesia, I could've easily finished on the podium."

Lopez crashed out of third with three laps to go. This to the delight of the hardy crowd, for it left home hero Agius in third, seven seconds down, but claiming a well-deserved podium after a fine fight through from 13th on the grid.

Agius had even passed championship leader Ogura, and he finished a second clear. Had Aldeguer and Canet fallen in their last-lap clash, as might easily have happened, he would have won.

Although marginally short of sealing the championship, fourth was a solid result at one of the Japanese rider's less favoured tracks, where his previous best had been 11th. On Saturday, he was lucky to walk away from a brutally fast high-side at Turn One, but he calmly held off Moreira for fourth, with Gonzalez claiming sixth, just ahead of Baltus, after taking a long-lap.

Arbolino was a disappointed eighth, after suffering with vibration from his front tyre, with Garcia ninth and Ramirez tenth. Alcoba led Binder, Arenas, Salac and Aji over the line for the last points.

There were a number of crashes, starting on lap one when a bump from Sasaki knocked both Dixon and Foggia off at the second corner. Sasaki himself fell late in the race; van den Goorbergh, Masia and Oncu also went down.

With 75 points left, Ogura sat 65 clear of Canet, who was just one ahead of Aldeguer and early leader Garcia.

MOTO3 RACE – 21 laps

Moto3 didn't enjoy a dry surface until qualifying, when Ortola took this third pole in a row, ahead of Veijer and Fernandez. With Scott Ogden on row two, between Munoz and Nepa, Alonso was an unusual tenth, on row four, his second worst of the year.

Not that it made any difference, as the new champion made history by moving clear of a typically huge and volatile Phillip Island lead group in the closing laps, to equal Valentino Rossi's tally of 11 wins in a lightweight-class season.

Alonso, the only rider to risk Pirelli's harder-option rear tyre, bided his time before launching a devastating late attack, which pulled the lead group apart and helped him win by a stunning 2.9 seconds.

It had been chaotic until the moment Alonso hit the front for a second time, with 16 riders locked in combat. Piqueras was a constant pest as he pushed home hero Kelso wide, dropping him from third to 17th, before tangling with Veijer at Turn Four, causing the Dutchman to crash into Ortola.

Alonso took decisive control on lap 17, leaving Holgado to claim a close second from Fernandez, Nepa (after two long-laps!) and Munoz on the run to the flag.

Ogden was an early faller, but he remounted and was one lap behind for last.

Now the fight was for second, with Holgado (232), Veijer (209) and Ortola (191) in the mix.

FIM WORLD CHAMPIONSHIP: ROUND 17
QATAR AIRWAYS AUSTRALIAN MOTORCYCLE GRAND PRIX
18–20 OCTOBER, 2024

PHILLIP ISLAND
27 laps
Length: 4.450km / 2.760 miles
Width: 13m

MOTOGP: RACE DISTANCE: 27 laps, 74.624 miles/120.096km
WEATHER: Dry (air 15°, humidity 80%, track 38°)

Pos.	Rider	Nat. No.	Entrant	Machine	Race tyre choice	Laps	Time & speed
1	Marc Marquez	SPA 93	Gresini Racing MotoGP	Ducati Desmosedici GP23	F: Hard/R: Soft	27	39m 47.702s
							112.5mph/181.0km/h
2	Jorge Martin	SPA 89	Prima Pramac Racing	Ducati Desmosedici GP24	F: Hard/R: Soft	27	39m 48.699s
3	Francesco Bagnaia	ITA 1	Ducati Lenovo Team	Ducati Desmosedici GP24	F: Hard/R: Soft	27	39m 57.802s
4	Fabio Di Giannantonio	ITA 49	Pertamina Enduro VR46 Racing	Ducati Desmosedici GP23	F: Hard/R: Soft	27	40m 00.699s
5	Enea Bastianini	ITA 23	Ducati Lenovo Team	Ducati Desmosedici GP24	F: Hard/R: Soft	27	40m 01.012s
6	Franco Morbidelli	ITA 21	Prima Pramac Racing	Ducati Desmosedici GP24	F: Hard/R: Soft	27	40m 03.136s
7	Brad Binder	RSA 33	Red Bull KTM Factory Racing	KTM RC16	F: Hard/R: Soft	27	40m 03.152s
8	Maverick Vinales	SPA 12	Aprilia Racing	Aprilia RS-GP24	F: Hard/R: Soft	27	40m 04.338s
9	Fabio Quartararo	FRA 20	Monster Energy Yamaha MotoGP	Yamaha YZR-M1	F: Hard/R: Soft	27	40m 06.459s
10	Raul Fernandez	SPA 25	Trackhouse Racing	Aprilia RS-GP24	F: Hard/R: Soft	27	40m 07.047s
11	Jack Miller	AUS 43	Red Bull KTM Factory Racing	KTM RC16	F: Hard/R: Soft	27	40m 07.634s
12	Johann Zarco	FRA 5	CASTROL Honda LCR	Honda RC213V	F: Hard/R: Soft	27	40m 07.997s
13	Alex Rins	SPA 42	Monster Energy Yamaha MotoGP	Yamaha YZR-M1	F: Hard/R: Soft	27	40m 09.912s
14	Luca Marini	ITA 10	Repsol Honda Team	Honda RC213V	F: Hard/R: Soft	27	40m 11.941s
15	Alex Marquez	SPA 73	Gresini Racing MotoGP	Ducati Desmosedici GP23	F: Hard/R: Soft	27	40m 12.293s
16	Aleix Espargaro	SPA 41	Aprilia Racing	Aprilia RS-GP24	F: Hard/R: Soft	27	40m 18.201s
17	Augusto Fernandez	SPA 37	Red Bull GASGAS Tech3	KTM RC16	F: Hard/R: Soft	27	40m 18.235s
18	Takaaki Nakagami	JPN 30	IDEMITSU Honda LCR	Honda RC213V	F: Hard/R: Soft	27	40m 18.467s
19	Marco Bezzecchi	ITA 72	Pertamina Enduro VR46 Racing	Ducati Desmosedici GP23	F: Hard/R: Soft	27	40m 33.095s
	Joan Mir	SPA 36	Repsol Honda Team	Honda RC213V	F: Hard/R: Soft	25	DNF-crash
	Lorenzo Savadori	ITA 32	Trackhouse Racing	Aprilia RS-GP24	F: Hard/R: Soft	17	DNF-physical
	Pedro Acosta	SPA 31	Red Bull GASGAS Tech3	KTM RC16	–	–	DNS-injured

Fastest lap: Marc Marquez, on lap 9, 1m 27.765s, 113.3mph/182.4km.
Lap record: Marc Marquez, 1m 28.108s, 112.9mph/181.7km/h (2013).
Event maximum speed: Enea Bastianini, 220.7mph/355.2km/h (race).

Qualfying: Weather: Dry **Air:** 14° **Humidity:** 80% **Track:** 22°
1 Martin 1m 27.296s, 2 M. Marquez 1m 27.890s, 3 Vinales 1m 27.991s, 4 Bezzecchi 1m 28.375s, 5 Bagnaia 1m 28.478s, 6 R. Fernandez 1m 28.498s, 7 Morbidelli 1m 28.622s, 8 A. Marquez 1m 29.009s, Rins 1m 29.059s, 10 Bastianini 1m 29.996s, 11 Binder 1m 30.290s, 12 Di Giannantonio 1m 30.336s.
Q1: 13 Marini 1m 29.727s, 14 Zarco 1m 29.786s, 15 Acosta 1m 29.817s, 16 Miller 1m 29.909s, 17 A. Fernandez 1m 30.149s, 18 Mir 1m 30.448s, 19 Quartararo 1m 30.635s, 20 A. Espargaro 1m 31.808s, 21 Nakagami* 1m 31.835s, 22 Savadori 1m 32.213s.
* Takaaki Nakagami: 3-place grid penalty.

SPRINT RACE: 13 laps, 35.930 miles/57.824km
WEATHER: Dry (air 14°, humidity 81%, track 26°)

Pos.	Rider	Race tyre choice	Laps	Time & speed
1	Jorge Martin	F: Hard/R: Soft	13	19m 13.301s
				112.1mph/180.4km/h
2	Marc Marquez	F: Hard/R: Soft	13	19m 14.821s
3	Enea Bastianini	F: Hard/R: Soft	13	19m 17.669s
4	Francesco Bagnaia	F: Hard/R: Soft	13	19m 20.180s
5	Franco Morbidelli	F: Hard/R: Soft	13	19m 22.924s
6	Raul Fernandez	F: Hard/R: Soft	13	19m 28.550s
7	Fabio Di Giannantonio*	F: Hard/R: Soft	13	19m 29.206s
8	Aleix Espargaro	F: Hard/R: Soft	13	19m 32.581s
9	Augusto Fernandez	F: Hard/R: Soft	13	19m 34.427s
10	Luca Marini	F: Hard/R: Soft	13	19m 34.495s
11	Fabio Quartararo	F: Hard/R: Soft	13	19m 34.680s
12	Alex Rins	F: Medium/R: Soft	13	19m 34.784s
13	Joan Mir	F: Medium/R: Soft	13	19m 36.829s
14	Takaaki Nakagami	F: Hard/R: Soft	13	19m 47.356s
15	Lorenzo Savadori	F: Hard/R: Medium	13	19m 51.625s
	Marco Bezzecchi	F: Hard/R: Medium	11	DNF-crash
	Maverick Vinales	F: Hard/R: Soft	11	DNF-crash
	Brad Binder	F: Hard/R: Soft	11	DNF-crash
	Pedro Acosta	F: Hard/R: Soft	10	DNF-crash
	Jack Miller	F: Hard/R: Soft	7	DNF-crash
	Alex Marquez	F: Hard/R: Soft	5	DNF-crash
	Johann Zarco	F: Hard/R: Soft	4	DNF-crash

* Fabio Di Giannantonio: 8s penalty – technical infringement.

Fastest race lap: Jorge Martin, on lap 7, 1m 27.831s.

Fastest race laps
1 M. Marquez 1m 27.765s, 2 Martin 1m 27.859s, 3 Di Giannantonio 1m 27.918s, 4 Bagnaia 1m 27.941s, 5 Bastianini 1m 27.961s, 6 Morbidelli 1m 28.054s, 7 Bezzecchi 1m 28.111s, 8 Binder 1m 28.253s, 9 Rins 1m 28.266s, 10 Quartararo 1m 28.313s, 11 A. Espargaro 1m 28.320s, 12 Vinales 1m 28.371s, 13 A. Marquez 1m 28.380s, 14 Marini 1m 28.411s, 15 Nakagami 1m 28.443s, 16 Miller 1m 28.472s, 17 R. Fernandez 1m 28.537s, 18 Zarco 1m 28.584s, 19 A. Fernandez 1m 28.649s, 20 Mir 1m 28.803s, 21 Savadori 1m 29.960s.

Grid order	1	2	3	4	5	6	7	8	9	10	11	12	13	14	15	16	17	18	19	20	21	22	23	24	25	26	27
89 MARTIN	89	89	89	89	89	89	89	89	89	89	89	89	89	89	89	89	89	89	89	89	89	89	89	93	93	93	93
93 M. MARQUEZ	72	72	72	1	1	1	1	1	1	1	93	93	93	93	93	93	93	93	93	93	93	93	93	89	89	89	89
12 VINALES	1	1	1	21	21	93	93	93	93	93	1	1	1	1	1	1	1	1	1	1	1	1	1	1	1	1	1
72 BEZZECCHI	21	33	33	93	93	21	21	21	21	21	21	21	21	21	21	21	21	21	23	23	23	23	23	49	49	49	49
1 BAGNAIA	33	21	21	33	33	33	33	33	33	33	33	33	33	33	33	33	33	33	21	21	21	21	21	23	23	23	23
25 R. FERNANDEZ	93	93	93	23	23	23	23	23	49	49	49	49	49	49	49	49	49	23	33	33	33	33	33	21	21	21	21
21 MORBIDELLI	23	23	23	72	49	49	49	49	23	23	23	23	23	23	49	49	49	49	12	12	12	12	12	21	21	21	33
73 A. MARQUEZ	12	12	12	49	12	12	12	12	12	12	12	12	12	12	12	12	12	12	49	49	49	49	49	12	12	12	12
42 RINS	49	49	49	12	20	25	25	25	25	25	25	25	25	25	25	25	25	25	25	25	25	25	25	20	20	20	20
23 BASTIANINI	20	20	20	25	25	20	20	20	20	20	20	43	43	43	43	43	43	43	43	43	20	25	25	25	25	25	10
33 BINDER	5	5	25	25	5	5	5	5	43	43	43	20	20	20	20	20	20	20	5	5	43	43	43	43	43	43	11
49 DI GIANNANTONIO	42	25	5	43	43	43	43	43	5	5	5	5	5	5	5	5	5	5	20	20	5	5	5	5	5	5	12
10 MARINI	25	42	42	5	42	42	42	42	42	42	42	42	42	42	42	42	42	42	42	42	42	42	42	42	42	42	13
5 ZARCO	10	10	43	42	10	10	37	37	41	41	41	41	41	10	10	10	10	10	10	10	10	10	10	10	10	10	14
43 MILLER	43	43	10	10	37	37	41	41	37	10	10	10	10	73	73	73	73	73	73	73	73	73	73	73	73	73	15
37 A. FERNANDEZ	36	37	37	37	41	41	10	10	10	73	73	73	73	41	41	41	41	41	41	41	41	41	41	41	37	37	41
36 MIR	37	41	41	41	36	36	36	36	73	37	37	37	37	37	37	37	37	37	37	37	37	37	41	37	41	41	37
20 QUARTARARO	32	36	36	36	73	73	73	73	36	36	36	36	36	36	36	36	36	36	36	36	36	36	36	36	36	30	30
41 A. ESPARGARO	41	32	32	73	32	30	30	30	30	30	30	30	30	30	30	30	30	30	30	30	30	30	30	30	30	72	72
30 NAKAGAMI	73	30	30	32	30	32	32	32	32	32	72	72	72	72	72	72	72	72	72	72	72	72	72	72	72		
32 SAVADORI	30	73	73	30	72	72	72	72	72	72	32	32	32	32	32	32											

Championship Points

1	Martin	281 (143)	424
2	Bagnaia	295 (109)	404
3	M. Marquez	241 (104)	345
4	Bastianini	237 (94)	331
5	Binder	153 (39)	192
6	Acosta	118 (63)	181
7	Vinales	116 (55)	171
8	Morbidelli	106 (45)	151
9	Di Giannantonio	126 (24)	150
10	A. Espargaro	88 (48)	136
11	Bezzecchi	123 (11)	134
12	A. Marquez	104 (21)	125
13	Quartararo	78 (15)	93
14	Oliveira	55 (16)	71
15	Miller	46 (25)	71
16	R. Fernandez	60 (6)	66
17	Zarco	38 (2)	40
18	Nakagami	28 (0)	28
19	Rins	23 (0)	23
20	A. Fernandez	17 (4)	21
21	Mir	19 (1)	20
22	P. Espargaro	11 (1)	12
23	Marini	9 (0)	9
24	Pedrosa	0 (7)	7
25	Bradl	2 (0)	2

Constructor Points

1	Ducati	416 (195)	611
2	KTM	198 (87)	285
3	Aprilia	167 (100)	267
4	Yamaha	89 (15)	104
5	Honda	56 (4)	60

MOTO2: RACE DISTANCE: 23 laps, 63.569 miles/102.304km
RACE WEATHER: Dry (air 16°, humidity 80%, track 35°)

Pos.	Rider	Nat.	No.	Entrant	Machine	Laps	Time & Speed
1	Fermin Aldeguer	SPA	54	Beta Tools SpeedUp	Boscoscuro	23	35m 08.816s
							108.5mph/174.6km/h
2	Aron Canet	SPA	44	Fantic Racing	Kalex	23	35m 09.010s
3	Senna Agius	AUS	81	Liqui Moly Husqvarna Intact GP	Kalex	23	35m 16.044s
4	Ai Ogura	JPN	79	MT Helmets - MSI	Boscoscuro	23	35m 17.201s
5	Diogo Moreira	BRA	10	Italtrans Racing Team	Kalex	23	35m 17.213s
6	Manuel Gonzalez	SPA	18	Gresini Moto2	Kalex	23	35m 19.558s
7	Barry Baltus	BEL	7	RW-Idrofoglia Racing GP	Kalex	23	35m 19.591s
8	Tony Arbolino	ITA	14	Elf Marc VDS Racing Team	Kalex	23	35m 26.159s
9	Sergio Garcia	SPA	3	MT Helmets - MSI	Boscoscuro	23	35m 26.407s
10	Marcos Ramirez	SPA	24	OnlyFans American Racing Team	Kalex	23	35m 26.537s
11	Jeremy Alcoba	SPA	52	Yamaha VR46 Master Camp Team	Kalex	23	35m 38.176s
12	Darryn Binder	RSA	15	Liqui Moly Husqvarna Intact GP	Kalex	23	35m 38.203s
13	Albert Arenas	SPA	75	Gresini Moto2	Kalex	23	35m 38.680s
14	Filip Salac	CZE	12	Elf Marc VDS Racing Team	Kalex	23	35m 38.893s
15	Mario Aji	INA	34	IDEMITSU Honda Team Asia	Kalex	23	35m 39.281s
16	Izan Guevara	SPA	28	CFMOTO Inde Aspar Team	Kalex	23	35m 52.750s
17	Alex Escrig	SPA	11	KLINT Forward Factory Team	Forward	23	35m 52.756s
18	Harrison Voight	AUS	29	Preicanos Racing Team	Kalex	23	36m 00.048s
19	Xavier Artigas	SPA	43	KLINT Forward Factory Team	Forward	23	36m 24.346s
20	Xavi Cardelus	AND	20	Fantic Racing	Kalex	23	36m 31.677s
21	Deniz Oncu	TUR	53	Red Bull KTM Ajo	Kalex	22	35m 23.983s
	Alonso Lopez	SPA	21	Beta Tools SpeedUp	Boscoscuro	20	DNF-crash
	Ayumu Sasaki	JPN	22	Yamaha VR46 Master Camp Team	Kalex	17	DNF-crash
	Jaume Masia	SPA	5	Preicanos Racing Team	Kalex	10	DNF-crash
	Zonta van den Goorbergh	NED	84	RW-Idrofoglia Racing GP	Kalex	4	DNF-crash
	Jake Dixon	GBR	96	CFMOTO Inde Aspar Team	Kalex	0	DNF-crash
	Dennis Foggia	ITA	71	Italtrans Racing Team	Kalex	0	DNF-crash

Fastest lap: Aron Canet, on lap 14, 1m 30.816s, 109.5mph/176.3km/h.
Lap record: Thomas Luthi, 1m 32.609s, 107.4mph/172.9km/h (2019).
Event maximum speed: Ayumu Sasaki, 187.0mph/301.0km/h (race).

Qualifying
Weather: Dry
Air: 14° **Humidity:** 81% **Track:** 28°

1	Aldeguer	1m 30.876s
2	Canet	1m 31.072s
3	Lopez	1m 31.144s
4	Ramirez	1m 31.168s
5	Baltus	1m 31.413s
6	Gonzalez	1m 31.420s
7	Moreira	1m 31.426s
8	Arenas	1m 31.452s
9	Ogura	1m 31.455s
10	Dixon	1m 31.576s
11	Arbolino	1m 31.652s
12	Foggia	1m 31.661s
13	Agius	1m 31.661s
14	Sasaki	1m 31.769s
15	Binder	1m 32.036s
16	Garcia	1m 32.049s
17	Oncu	1m 32.165s
18	Guevara	1m 32.512s
Q1		
19	V d Goorbergh	1m 32.588s
20	Aji	1m 32.644s
21	Alcoba	1m 32.694s
22	Salac	1m 32.737s
23	Escrig	1m 33.283s
24	Voight	1m 33.673s
25	Masia	1m 33.676s
26	Cardelus	1m 34.089s
27	Artigas	1m 34.429s

Fastest race laps

1	Canet	1m 30.816s
2	Aldeguer	1m 30.859s
3	Moreira	1m 31.089s
4	Baltus	1m 31.293s
5	Lopez	1m 31.295s
6	Agius	1m 31.318s
7	Gonzalez	1m 31.320s
8	Arbolino	1m 31.325s
9	Ogura	1m 31.349s
10	Oncu	1m 31.513s
11	Sasaki	1m 31.693s
12	Garcia	1m 31.698s
13	Ramirez	1m 31.713s
14	Binder	1m 31.808s
15	Aji	1m 31.990s
16	Salac	1m 32.129s
17	Arenas	1m 32.147s
18	Alcoba	1m 32.190s
19	Guevara	1m 32.224s
20	V d Goorbergh	1m 32.527s
21	Masia	1m 32.721s
22	Voight	1m 32.790s
23	Escrig	1m 32.855s
24	Artigas	1m 33.199s
25	Cardelus	1m 33.928s

Championship Points

	Rider	Pts
1	Ogura	241
2	Canet	176
3	Aldeguer	175
4	Garcia	175
5	Lopez	163
6	Gonzalez	163
7	Roberts	153
8	Vietti	140
9	Arbolino	135
10	Dixon	133
11	Ramirez	85
12	Alcoba	79
13	Chantra	78
14	Arenas	68
15	Agius	63
16	Salac	59
17	Binder	54
18	Moreira	47
19	Baltus	40
20	Oncu	34
21	Guevara	34
22	Van den Goorbergh	31
23	Foggia	18
24	Artigas	10
25	Bendsneyder	7
26	Navarro	6
27	Sasaki	4
28	Masia	4
29	Aji	4
30	Ferrari	1

Constructor Points

1	Kalex	362
2	Boscoscuro	353
3	Forward	16

MOTO3: RACE DISTANCE: 21 laps, 58.041 miles/93.408km
RACE WEATHER: Dry (air 15°, humidity 79%, track 29°)

Pos.	Rider	Nat.	No.	Entrant	Machine	Laps	Time & Speed
1	David Alonso	COL	80	CFMOTO Gaviota Aspar Team	CFMOTO	21	33m 49.557s
							102.9mph/165.6km/h
2	Daniel Holgado	SPA	96	Red Bull GASGAS Tech3	GASGAS	21	33m 52.493s
3	Adrian Fernandez	SPA	31	Leopard Racing	Honda	21	33m 52.496s
4	Stefano Nepa	ITA	82	LEVELUP - MTA	KTM	21	33m 52.514s
5	David Munoz	SPA	64	BOE Motorsports	KTM	21	33m 52.529s
6	Ryusei Yamanaka	JPN	6	MT Helmets - MSI	KTM	21	33m 52.934s
7	Taiyo Furusato	JPN	72	Honda Team Asia	Honda	21	33m 52.960s
8	Luca Lunetta	ITA	58	SIC58 Squadra Corse	Honda	21	33m 53.443s
9	Jose Antonio Rueda	SPA	99	Red Bull KTM Ajo	KTM	21	33m 53.465s
10	Angel Piqueras	SPA	36	Leopard Racing	Honda	21	33m 53.500s
11	Joel Kelso	AUS	66	BOE Motorsports	KTM	21	33m 54.006s
12	Riccardo Rossi	ITA	54	CIP Green Power	KTM	21	33m 54.031s
13	Jacob Roulstone	AUS	12	Red Bull GASGAS Tech3	GASGAS	21	33m 54.035s
14	Matteo Bertelle	ITA	18	Kopron Rivacold Snipers Team	Honda	21	33m 54.621s
15	Tatsuki Suzuki	JPN	24	Liqui Moly Husqvarna Intact GP	Husqvarna	21	34m 02.003s
16	Joel Esteban	SPA	78	CFMOTO Gaviota Aspar Team	CFMOTO	21	34m 20.135s
17	Xabi Zurutuza	SPA	85	Red Bull KTM Ajo	KTM	21	34m 20.168s
18	Collin Veijer	NED	95	Liqui Moly Husqvarna Intact GP	Husqvarna	21	34m 28.867s
19	Eddie O'Shea	GBR	8	FleetSafe Honda - MLav Racing	Honda	21	34m 29.482s
20	Tatchakorn Buasri	THA	5	Honda Team Asia	Honda	21	34m 40.452s
21	Noah Dettwiler	SWI	55	CIP Green Power	KTM	21	34m 40.464s
22	Scott Ogden	GBR	19	FleetSafe Honda - MLav Racing	Honda	20	34m 28.148s
	Ivan Ortola	SPA	48	MT Helmets - MSI	KTM	11	DNF-crash
	David Almansa	SPA	22	Kopron Rivacold Snipers Team	Honda	11	DNF-crash
	Nicola Carraro	ITA	10	LEVELUP - MTA	KTM	6	DNF-crash
	Filippo Farioli	ITA	7	SIC58 Squadra Corse	Honda	3	DNF-crash

Fastest lap: Stefano Nepa, on lap 3, 1m 35.370s, 104.3mph/167.9km/h.
Lap record: Jack Miller, 1m 36.302s, 103.3mph/166.2km/h (2014).
Event maximum speed: Jose Antonio Rueda, 158.4mph/254.9km/h (race).

Qualifying:
Weather: Dry
Air: 14° **Humidity:** 76% **Track:** 29°

1	Ortola	1m 35.872s
2	Veijer	1m 35.996s
3	Fernandez	1m 36.023s
4	Munoz	1m 36.201s
5	Ogden	1m 36.275s
6	Nepa	1m 36.360s
7	Kelso	1m 36.366s
8	Piqueras	1m 36.423s
9	Furusato	1m 36.487s
10	Alonso	1m 36.602s
11	Yamanaka	1m 36.630s
12	Lunetta	1m 36.831s
13	Roulstone	1m 36.974s
14	Holgado	1m 37.101s
15	Rueda	1m 37.293s
16	Farioli	1m 37.326s
17	Suzuki	1m 37.451s
18	Bertelle	1m 38.203s
Q1		
19	Carraro	1m 37.716s
20	Almansa	1m 37.860s
21	Esteban	1m 37.971s
22	Zurutuza	1m 38.531s
23	Rossi	1m 39.079s
24	Dettwiler	1m 39.426s
25	O'Shea	1m 39.645s
26	Buasri	1m 39.987s

Fastest race laps

1	Nepa	1m 35.370s
2	Alonso	1m 35.465s
3	Piqueras	1m 35.482s
4	Suzuki	1m 35.500s
5	Holgado	1m 35.524s
6	Veijer	1m 35.555s
7	Furusato	1m 35.576s
8	Rueda	1m 35.697s
9	Carraro	1m 35.722s
10	Lunetta	1m 35.767s
11	Yamanaka	1m 35.784s
12	Kelso	1m 35.796s
13	Rossi	1m 35.805s
14	Roulstone	1m 35.814s
15	Fernandez	1m 35.900s
16	Bertelle	1m 35.925s
17	Ortola	1m 35.932s
18	Munoz	1m 35.980s
19	Ogden	1m 36.214s
20	Farioli	1m 36.286s
21	Zurutuza	1m 36.616s
22	Esteban	1m 36.621s
23	O'Shea	1m 36.881s
24	Buasri	1m 37.463s
25	Almansa	1m 37.691s
26	Dettwiler	1m 37.963s

Championship Points

	Rider	Pts
1	Alonso	346
2	Holgado	232
3	Veijer	209
4	Ortola	191
5	Fernandez	153
6	Munoz	152
7	Piqueras	137
8	Rueda	128
9	Kelso	115
10	Yamanaka	106
11	Furusato	97
12	Lunetta	86
13	Suzuki	82
14	Nepa	78
15	Roulstone	53
16	Bertelle	49
17	Esteban	45
18	Rossi	30
19	Farioli	27
20	Carraro	22
21	Ogden	15
22	Zurutuza	11
23	Almansa	11
24	Perez	3
25	Dettwiler	2

Constructor Points

1	CFMOTO	346
2	KTM	291
3	Honda	244
4	GASGAS	237
5	Husqvarna	236

Main: Bagnaia mastered Martin and the conditions to keep his championship chances alive.

Inset, right: Complete. A measured Ai Ogura clinched the Moto2 championship.

Inset, above right: Pedro Acosta shrugged off his injury to claim a fighting podium.
Photos: Gold & Goose

Inset, above far right: Double delight. Congratulations for Pecco from wife Domizia and team boss Tardozzi.
Photo: Ducati Corse

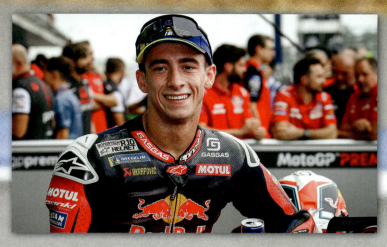

FIM WORLD CHAMPIONSHIP • ROUND 18

GRAND PRIX OF THAILAND
BURIRAM CIRCUIT

Above: A wet track helped KTM/Gas-Gas riders Miller, Binder and Acosta to escape from Bastianini's Ducati.

Top right: A welcome top-ten for LCR Honda's Johann Zarco.

Top far right: Aron Canet's third Moto2 win reinforced his claim to second overall.

Above right: Somkat Chiantra's brave ride almost brought him a podium and thrilled the home crowd.

Right: Scott Ogden took a season-best eighth in Moto3.

Far right: Ogura sported the No.1 plate (but the 79 flag) to celebrate his championship.

Below right: Last-lap action in Moto3 – Alonso heads for victory, followed by the squabbling Ortola (48), Furusato (72), Lunetta (58) and Veijer.
Photos: Gold & Goose

crashed on the sighting lap, and he started from the back of the grid after starting the warm-up from the pit lane.

Bezzecchi crashed out at the first corner starting lap four, shortly before Morbidelli knocked Quartararo down, attempting an optimistic overtake at Turn Eight. Then the Italian binned it at the same spot four laps later, after serving a long-lap penance and subsequently setting an erstwhile fastest lap. And Martin's nervousness became apparent on lap five as again he ran on at Turn Three, allowing both Bagnaia and Marquez through.

By lap seven, Jack Miller had recovered from a starting berth of 15th, jumped ten places and joined team-mate Binder in the fight for fourth. Yet the KTM pair were unable to live with the top three as the gaps between the protagonists yo-yoed back and forth. It was very much a three-way fight on lap nine, when Marquez launched his first attack at Turn 12, passing Bagnaia, only to run wide and cede the place. The reigning world champ immediately dropped the pace and began dropping Martin to boot.

Short of acceleration compared with the GP24s through the track's horsepower-heavy first half, Marquez could only get close enough for an attack at the final turn. Again, he tried to work on Bagnaia there on lap 13, only for the Italian to fight straight back. And, bizarrely, the eight-times champ became flustered. Feeling the need to attempt the same move on the very next lap, he tucked the front at Turn Eight, crashing out on the kerb, despite nearly saving it with his right knee. And Martin almost followed him, briefly running off-track. It showed just how hard Bagnaia was pushing.

With Bagnaia left to control a gap to Martin in second, he was clear to win by almost three seconds. None of his previous eight wins of the season had been as important or as impressive.

With Martin left to watch the gap to the KTMs, attention turned to two coming men: Acosta and Di Giannantonio. The rookie caught and passed Binder for fourth at Turn Five with just four laps to go, before launching a sensational around-the-outside pass on Miller into Turn Three on the penultimate lap. Miller wasn't going to relinquish his podium hopes easily, however. They traded blows in the subsequent turns before Acosta emerged ahead by Turn Seven after three cor-

ners taken side by side. By this point, Miller's front tyre was ruined, giving Di Giannantonio fourth on the final lap.

Behind Binder, Vinales rescued an otherwise disastrous weekend for Aprilia in seventh, with Zarco eighth after a minor epic, having dropped to 17th on lap three. He passed Espargaro on the last lap. Alex Marquez recovered from his back-row start for tenth, one place ahead of elder brother Marc, who had remounted in 16th without a rear brake, yet still managed to pass four riders, in spite of being instructed to drop one place for running Joan Mir off track at Turn Three.

Marini was his last victim, six-tenths behind. Nakagami, Bastianini (remounted after his own crash) and Mir claimed the last points, the remounted and fuming Quartararo out of luck.

Rins, Augusto Fernandez and Savadori also crashed, the last named twice before retiring.

Now it was a two-horse race, with Martin's lead cut to 17 points, but Marquez and Bastianini disputing third.

MOTO2 RACE – 20 laps (shortened)

As usual, records fell, to Canet and then Ogura, who claimed only his second pole of the year, fifth in his career. Canet and rookie Moreira were alongside; Arbolino was fourth, but demoted three places, leaving the second row to Ramirez, Salac and Arenas. Aldeguer was eighth, Dixon 11th.

Home star Chantra – returned, but still not fully fit – qualified 13th.

With 22 laps scheduled, light showers peppered the track, but the field started on slicks as the rain eased off. Understandably, the championship leader was cautious during the early laps as Canet broke clear with Ramirez. He was left to field attacks from Dixon, Lopez and Moreira,

Arbolino and Aldeguer were already out, after the Spaniard had taken down Arbolino with a wild first-lap move, which also pushed Salac wide. Aldeguer blamed a false neutral, and the data bore him out, so the stewards applied only a single rather than double long-lap punishment. Far worse, he broke bones in his hand, which seriously jeopardised the pre-season favourite's hopes in a close fight for third in the championship.

By lap ten, Ogura, who could seal the title with fifth, had made his way to third. After passing Ramirez for second on lap 14, he was chasing Canet, one second ahead. A classic showdown between the championship's two standout names was in the offing. But the elements intervened, with spits of rain falling on lap 16, causing the Japanese rider to back off. Second would do. Meanwhile, Canet signalled that nothing would hold him back, posting a remarkable personal-best lap the 17th time around, moments after the rain had stopped again.

But it was only fleeting. With two laps to go, the red flags came out as the rain intensified and Alcoba suffered a massive crash through Turn 11. That handed Canet a third win of the year, and Ogura Japan's first grand prix title since Hiroshi Aoyama had won the 250cc class in 2009.

Home fans were disappointed as Chantra's brilliant recovery from 13th on the grid almost resulted in a podium – through to fourth and catching Ramirez. He'd passed Guevara on lap 17, then Moreira two laps on, closing the gap to third from almost 3.5 seconds to a tenth over one second in the two laps prior to the stoppage.

Dixon was seventh, behind Moreira and Guevara, with Gresini team-mates Arenas and Gonzalez eighth and ninth. Deniz Oncu was tenth. Lopez led the next trio from Garcia and Sasaki; Salac recovered to 14th, while Navarro, in place of Roberts, took the last point.

Agius, Baltus, Binder and Escrig added to the crash toll.

Ogura was confirmed champion; Canet took a big step towards second, with Aldeguer sidelined and Garcia continuing to lose ground.

MOTO3 RACE – 12 laps (shortened)

Kelso took a long-awaited career-first pole, ahead of Veijer, rookie Piqueras's Honda joining the KTM and Husqvarna. Furusato led Alonso on row two, with Ogden alongside, his second successive second-row start.

The second row would be no drawback to Alonso, already with the most Moto3 wins, as he added a 12th to beat Rossi's 27-year-old lightweight-class record.

After a wet start to the morning, inevitably, the weather played a hand, with a wet race called, the distance shortened from 19 laps, and the start delayed slightly. Yet it was marginally dry enough for slicks, with O'Shea the only rider to gamble on wets.

The lead group of ten was tentative at first, before a double crash for Leopard Honda team-mates Piqueras and Fernandez split the pack with two laps to go.

That left Alonso battling with Ortola, and after passing him at Turn Four on the final lap, he successfully defended into the final turn. Ortola's failed attack sent him wide, letting Lunetta into a sneaky second, while Veijer tagged mid-race leader Furusato on the run to the line. The Dutchman took third, Furusata crashed. Despite bike and rider sliding separately across the line, he was classified fifth, behind Ortola.

O'Shea retired with two laps to go after dropping miles behind. His beginner's gamble on wet tyres might have gone the other way had the weather turned.

Early leader Kelso was pushed back to finish seventh behind Munoz; Ogden was a season-best eighth. Early title leader Holgado had an off-day in 12th, allowing Veijer to close to within 11 points in the battle for second overall.

FIM WORLD CHAMPIONSHIP: ROUND 18
PT GRAND PRIX OF THAILAND
25–27 OCTOBER, 2024

CHANG INTERNATIONAL CIRCUIT
26 laps
Length: 4.550km / 2.830 miles
Width: 12m

MOTOGP: RACE DISTANCE: 26 laps, 73.573 miles/118.404km
WEATHER: Wet (air 25°, humidity 93%, track 28°)

Pos.	Rider	Nat.	No.	Entrant	Machine	Race tyre choice	Laps	Time & speed
1	Francesco Bagnaia	ITA	1	Ducati Lenovo Team	Ducati Desmosedici GP24	F: Med Wet/R: Med Wet	26	43m 38.108s
								101.2mph/162.8km/h
2	Jorge Martin	SPA	89	Prima Pramac Racing	Ducati Desmosedici GP24	F: Med Wet/R: Med Wet	26	43m 41.013s
3	Pedro Acosta	SPA	31	Red Bull GASGAS Tech3	KTM RC16	F: Med Wet/R: Med Wet	26	43m 41.908s
4	Fabio Di Giannantonio	ITA	49	Pertamina Enduro VR46 Racing	Ducati Desmosedici GP23	F: Med Wet/R: Med Wet	26	43m 42.744s
5	Jack Miller	AUS	43	Red Bull KTM Factory Racing	KTM RC16	F: Med Wet/R: Med Wet	26	43m 43.640s
6	Brad Binder	RSA	33	Red Bull KTM Factory Racing	KTM RC16	F: Med Wet/R: Med Wet	26	43m 44.006s
7	Maverick Vinales	SPA	12	Aprilia Racing	Aprilia RS-GP24	F: Med Wet/R: Med Wet	26	43m 46.606s
8	Johann Zarco	FRA	5	CASTROL Honda LCR	Honda RC213V	F: Med Wet/R: Med Wet	26	43m 55.780s
9	Aleix Espargaro	SPA	41	Aprilia Racing	Aprilia RS-GP24	F: Med Wet/R: Med Wet	26	43m 56.696s
10	Alex Marquez	SPA	73	Gresini Racing MotoGP	Ducati Desmosedici GP23	F: Med Wet/R: Med Wet	26	43m 59.271s
11	Marc Marquez	SPA	93	Gresini Racing MotoGP	Ducati Desmosedici GP23	F: Med Wet/R: Med Wet	26	44m 00.359s
12	Luca Marini	ITA	10	Repsol Honda Team	Honda RC213V	F: Med Wet/R: Med Wet	26	44m 00.967s
13	Takaaki Nakagami	JPN	30	IDEMITSU Honda LCR	Honda RC213V	F: Med Wet/R: Med Wet	26	44m 02.639s
14	Enea Bastianini	ITA	23	Ducati Lenovo Team	Ducati Desmosedici GP24	F: Med Wet/R: Med Wet	26	44m 05.198s
15	Joan Mir	SPA	36	Repsol Honda Team	Honda RC213V	F: Med Wet/R: Med Wet	26	44m 08.978s
16	Fabio Quartararo	FRA	20	Monster Energy Yamaha MotoGP	Yamaha YZR-M1	F: Med Wet/R: Med Wet	26	44m 28.129s
	Augusto Fernandez	SPA	37	Red Bull GASGAS Tech3	KTM RC16	F: Med Wet/R: Med Wet	23	DNF-crash
	Alex Rins	SPA	42	Monster Energy Yamaha MotoGP	Yamaha YZR-M1	F: Med Wet/R: Med Wet	22	DNF-crash
	Lorenzo Savadori	ITA	32	Trackhouse Racing	Aprilia RS-GP24	F: Med Wet/R: Med Wet	16	DNF-crash
	Franco Morbidelli	ITA	21	Prima Pramac Racing	Ducati Desmosedici GP24	F: Med Wet/R: Med Wet	7	DNF-crash
	Raul Fernandez	SPA	25	Trackhouse Racing	Aprilia RS-GP24	F: Med Wet/R: Med Wet	6	DNF-crash
	Marco Bezzecchi	ITA	72	Pertamina Enduro VR46 Racing	Ducati Desmosedici GP23	F: Med Wet/R: Med Wet	3	DNF-crash

Fastest lap: Fabio Giannantonio, on lap 17, 1m 39.576s, 102.3mph/164.6km/h.
Lap record: Marco Bezzecchi, 1m 30.896s, 112.0mph/180.3km/h (2023).
Event maximum speed: Pedro Acosta, 211.6mph/340.6km/h (qualifying).

Qualifying: Weather: Dry Air: 33° Humidity: 71% Track: 44°
1 Bagnaia 1m 28.700s, 2 Bastianini 1m 28.932s, 3 Martin 1m 29.130s, 4 Bezzecchi 1m 29.324s,
5 M. Marquez 1m 29.386s, 6 Quartararo 1m 29.408s, 7 Acosta 1m 29.419s, 8 Di Giannantonio 1m 29.435s,
9 A. Marquez 1m 29.527s, 10 Vinales 1m 29.628s, 11 Morbidelli 1m 29.736s, 12 Zarco 1m 29.797s.
Q1: 13 Binder 1m 29.535s, 14 A. Espargaro 1m 29.568s, 15 Miller 1m 29.773s, 16 A. Fernandez 1m 29.828s,
17 Rins 1m 29.835s, 18 Nakagami 1m 29.903s, 19 Mir 1m 30.045s, 20 R. Fernandez 1m 30.102s,
21 Marini 1m 30.137s, 22 Savadori 1m 30.592s.

SPRINT RACE: 13 laps, 36.786 miles/59.202km
WEATHER: Dry (air 30°, humidity 67%, track 46°)

Pos.	Rider	Race tyre choice	Laps	Time & speed
1	Enea Bastianini	F: Hard/R: Medium	13	19m 31.131s
				113.0mph/181.9km/h
2	Jorge Martin	F: Hard/R: Medium	13	19m 32.488s
3	Francesco Bagnaia	F: Hard/R: Medium	13	19m 33.503s
4	Marc Marquez	F: Hard/R: Medium	13	19m 36.533s
5	Alex Marquez	F: Soft/R: Medium	13	19m 41.271s
6	Franco Morbidelli	F: Hard/R: Medium	13	19m 42.218s
7	Marco Bezzecchi	F: Soft/R: Medium	13	19m 42.669s
8	Fabio Di Giannantonio	F: Soft/R: Medium	13	19m 42.811s
9	Brad Binder	F: Hard/R: Medium	13	19m 44.823s
10	Fabio Quartararo	F: Hard/R: Medium	13	19m 45.614s
11	Jack Miller	F: Hard/R: Medium	13	19m 49.528s
12	Johann Zarco	F: Hard/R: Medium	13	19m 49.675s
13	Joan Mir	F: Hard/R: Hard	13	19m 50.396s
14	Raul Fernandez	F: Hard/R: Medium	13	19m 50.819s
15	Aleix Espargaro	F: Soft/R: Medium	13	19m 51.119s
16	Augusto Fernandez	F: Hard/R: Medium	13	19m 52.429s
17	Alex Rins	F: Hard/R: Medium	13	19m 52.544s
18	Takaaki Nakagami	F: Hard/R: Medium	13	19m 54.531s
19	Luca Marini	F: Hard/R: Medium	13	19m 55.110s
20	Maverick Vinales	F: Hard/R: Medium	13	20m 00.605s
21	Lorenzo Savadori	F: Hard/R: Medium	13	20m 10.520s
	Pedro Acosta	F: Hard/R: Medium	10	DNF-crash

Fastest lap: Jorge Martin, on lap 5, 1m 29.554s.

Fastest race laps
1 Di Giannantonio 1m 39.576s, 2 M. Marquez 1m 39.720s, 3 Bagnaia 1m 39.794s, 4 Martin 1m 39.841s,
5 Bastianini 1m 39.883s, 6 Morbidelli 1m 39.979s, 7 Acosta 1m 40.081s, 8 Binder 1m 40.114s,
9 Miller 1m 40.155s, 10 Vinales 1m 40.283s, 11 Zarco 1m 40.329s, 12 Nakagami 1m 40.347s,
13 Rins 1m 40.395s, 14 Marini 1m 40.439s, 15 A. Marquez 1m 40.501s, 16 Mir 1m 40.511s,
17 A. Fernandez 1m 40.547s, 18 A. Espargaro 1m 40.557s, 19 Quartararo 1m 40.561s,
20 Savadori 1m 41.043s, 21 R. Fernandez 1m 41.178s, 22 Bezzecchi 1m 41.376s.

Grid order	1	2	3	4	5	6	7	8	9	10	11	12	13	14	15	16	17	18	19	20	21	22	23	24	25	26
1 BAGNAIA	89	89	89	89	1	1	1	1	1	1	1	1	1	1	1	1	1	1	1	1	1	1	1	1	1	1
23 BASTIANINI	1	1	1	1	93	93	93	93	93	93	93	93	89	89	89	89	89	89	89	89	89	89	89	89	89	2
89 MARTIN	93	93	93	93	89	89	89	89	89	89	89	89	43	43	43	43	43	43	43	43	43	43	43	43	31	3
72 BEZZECCHI	20	20	20	33	33	33	33	43	43	43	43	43	33	33	33	33	33	33	33	31	31	31	31	49	4	
93 M. MARQUEZ	31	33	33	43	43	43	43	33	33	33	33	33	31	31	31	31	31	31	31	33	33	33	49	43	5	
20 QUARTARARO	33	21	21	21	21	31	31	31	31	31	31	31	12	12	49	49	49	49	49	49	49	49	33	33	6	
31 ACOSTA	21	31	43	31	31	23	23	23	12	12	12	12	49	49	12	12	12	12	12	12	12	12	12	12	7	
49 DI GIANNANTONIO	49	43	31	23	23	21	21	12	49	49	49	49	37	37	37	37	37	37	37	41	41	41	41	5	8	
73 A. MARQUEZ	5	49	41	12	12	12	12	41	41	37	37	37	41	41	41	41	41	41	41	5	5	5	5	41	9	
12 VINALES	41	41	23	41	41	41	41	49	37	41	41	41	36	36	73	73	73	73	5	5	73	73	73	73	10	
21 MORBIDELLI	43	23	12	49	49	49	49	37	36	36	36	36	73	73	5	5	5	5	73	37	37	10	10	93	11	
5 ZARCO	12	12	72	37	37	37	37	36	73	73	5	73	10	10	36	10	36	36	10	10	10	30	93	10	12	
33 BINDER	23	5	49	73	73	73	73	5	5	5	73	10	5	5	10	36	10	10	36	42	30	93	30	30	13	
41 A. ESPARGARO	72	72	37	36	36	36	36	5	10	10	10	10	42	42	42	42	42	42	42	30	93	23	23	23	14	
43 MILLER	73	73	73	5	5	5	5	10	42	42	42	42	30	30	30	30	30	30	30	36	36	36	36	36	15	
37 A. FERNANDEZ	37	37	36	10	25	10	42	30	30	30	30	30	93	93	93	93	93	93	93	23	20	20	20			
42 RINS	36	36	5	25	10	10	42	30	23	23	23	23	23	23	23	23	23	23	23	20						
30 NAKAGAMI	42	10	10	42	42	42	30	20	20	20	20	20	20	20	20	20	20	20	20							
36 MIR	10	25	25	32	32	30	20	32	32	32	32	32	32	32												
25 R. FERNANDEZ	25	42	42	30	30	20	32																			
10 MARINI	32	32	32	20	20	32																				
32 SAVADORI	30	30	30																							

32 – Lapped rider

Championship Points

1	Martin	301 (152)	453
2	Bagnaia	320 (116)	436
3	M. Marquez	246 (110)	356
4	Bastianini	239 (106)	345
5	Binder	163 (40)	203
6	Acosta	134 (63)	197
7	Vinales	125 (55)	180
8	Di Giannantonio	139 (26)	165
9	Morbidelli	106 (49)	155
10	A. Espargaro	95 (48)	143
11	Bezzecchi	123 (14)	137
12	A. Marquez	110 (26)	136
13	Quartararo	78 (15)	93
14	Miller	57 (25)	82
15	Oliveira	55 (16)	71
16	R. Fernandez	60 (6)	66
17	Zarco	46 (2)	48
18	Nakagami	31 (0)	31
19	Rins	23 (0)	23
20	A. Fernandez	17 (4)	21
21	Mir	20 (1)	21
22	Marini	13 (0)	13
23	P. Espargaro	11 (1)	12
24	Pedrosa	0 (7)	7
25	Bradl	2 (0)	2

Constructor Points

1	Ducati	441 (207)	648
2	KTM	214 (88)	302
3	Aprilia	176 (100)	276
4	Yamaha	89 (15)	104
5	Honda	64 (4)	68

MOTO2: RACE DISTANCE: 20 laps, 56.594 miles/91.080km
RACE WEATHER: Dry (air 25°, humidity 89%, track 28°)

Pos.	Rider	Nat.	No.	Entrant	Machine	Laps	Time & Speed
1	Aron Canet	SPA	44	Fantic Racing	Kalex	20	32m 02.751s
							105.9mph/170.5km/h
2	Ai Ogura	JPN	79	MT Helmets - MSI	Boscoscuro	20	32m 06.435s
3	Marcos Ramirez	SPA	24	OnlyFans American Racing Team	Kalex	20	32m 07.434s
4	Somkiat Chantra	THA	35	IDEMITSU Honda Team Asia	Kalex	20	32m 08.550s
5	Diogo Moreira	BRA	10	Italtrans Racing Team	Kalex	20	32m 08.923s
6	Izan Guevara	SPA	28	CFMOTO Inde Aspar Team	Kalex	20	32m 09.156s
7	Jake Dixon	GBR	96	CFMOTO Inde Aspar Team	Kalex	20	32m 09.660s
8	Albert Arenas	SPA	75	Gresini Moto2	Kalex	20	32m 10.155s
9	Manuel Gonzalez	SPA	18	Gresini Moto2	Kalex	19	30m 34.327s
10	Deniz Oncu	TUR	53	Red Bull KTM Ajo	Kalex	19	30m 37.509s
11	Alonso Lopez	SPA	21	Beta Tools SpeedUp	Boscoscuro	19	30m 39.016s
12	Sergio Garcia	SPA	3	MT Helmets - MSI	Boscoscuro	19	30m 39.399s
13	Ayumu Sasaki	JPN	22	Yamaha VR46 Master Camp	Kalex	19	30m 40.731s
14	Filip Salac	CZE	12	Elf Marc VDS Racing Team	Kalex	19	30m 44.039s
15	Jorge Navarro	SPA	9	OnlyFans American Racing Team	Kalex	19	30m 47.446s
16	Mario Aji	INA	34	IDEMITSU Honda Team Asia	Kalex	19	30m 48.061s
17	Jaume Masia	SPA	5	Preicanos Racing Team	Kalex	19	30m 53.198s
18	Dennis Foggia	ITA	71	Italtrans Racing Team	Kalex	19	30m 54.017s
19	Zonta van den Goorbergh	NED	84	RW-Idrofoglia Racing GP	Kalex	19	30m 57.148s
20	Xavi Cardelus	AND	20	Fantic Racing	Kalex	19	30m 57.554s
21	Xavier Artigas	SPA	43	KLINT Forward Factory Team	Forward	19	31m 18.450s
22	Harrison Voight	AUS	29	Preicanos Racing Team	Kalex	19	31m 23.458s
	Jeremy Alcoba	SPA	52	Yamaha VR46 Master Camp	Kalex	19	DNF-crash
	Alex Escrig	SPA	11	KLINT Forward Factory Team	Forward	16	DNF-crash
	Darryn Binder	RSA	15	Liqui Moly Husqvarna Intact GP	Kalex	7	DNF-crash
	Barry Baltus	BEL	7	RW-Idrofoglia Racing GP	Kalex	7	DNF-crash
	Senna Agius	AUS	81	Liqui Moly Husqvarna Intact GP	Kalex	6	DNF-crash
	Tony Arbolino	ITA	14	Elf Marc VDS Racing Team	Kalex	0	DNF-crash
	Fermin Aldeguer	SPA	54	Beta Tools SpeedUp	Boscoscuro	0	DNF-crash

Fastest lap: Ai Ogura, on lap 12, 1m 35.597s, 106.5mph/171.4km/h.
Lap record: Fermin Aldeguer, 1m 35.778s, 106.3mph/171.1km/h (2023).
Event maximum speed: Deniz Oncu, 176.1mph/283.4km/h (race).

Qualifying
Weather: Dry
Air: 32° **Humidity:** 66% **Track:** 46°

1	Ogura	1m 34.728s
2	Canet	1m 34.779s
3	Moreira	1m 34.802s
4	Arbolino	1m 34.866s
5	Ramirez	1m 34.871s
6	Salac	1m 34.871s
7	Arenas	1m 34.918s
8	Aldeguer	1m 34.936s
9	Garcia	1m 35.012s
10	Gonzalez	1m 35.033s
11	Dixon	1m 35.121s
12	Sasaki	1m 35.174s
13	Chantra	1m 35.189s
14	Lopez	1m 35.234s
15	V d Goorbergh	1m 35.303s
16	Oncu	1m 35.346s
17	Binder	1m 35.601s
18	Foggia	1m 35.658s
Q1		
19	Guevara	1m 35.314s
20	Navarro	1m 35.350s
21	Agius	1m 35.355s
22	Alcoba	1m 35.412s
23	Aji	1m 35.469s
24	Masia	1m 35.625s
25	Cardelus	1m 35.681s
26	Baltus	1m 35.690s
27	Escrig	1m 36.067s
28	Voight	1m 36.819s
29	Artigas	1m 38.137s

Fastest race laps

1	Ogura	1m 35.597s
2	Chantra	1m 35.751s
3	Canet	1m 35.759s
4	Gonzalez	1m 35.763s
5	Moreira	1m 35.778s
6	Arenas	1m 35.795s
7	Ramirez	1m 35.813s
8	Dixon	1m 35.837s
9	Binder	1m 35.855s
10	Guevara	1m 35.894s
11	Salac	1m 36.041s
12	Oncu	1m 36.111s
13	V d Goorbergh	1m 36.113s
14	Garcia	1m 36.115s
15	Alcoba	1m 36.210s
16	Sasaki	1m 36.211s
17	Lopez	1m 36.227s
18	Aji	1m 36.314s
19	Navarro	1m 36.400s
20	Agius	1m 36.439s
21	Baltus	1m 36.612s
22	Masia	1m 36.700s
23	Escrig	1m 36.712s
24	Foggia	1m 36.742s
25	Cardelus	1m 36.909s
26	Voight	1m 37.847s
27	Artigas	1m 37.997s

Championship Points

1	Ogura	261
2	Canet	201
3	Garcia	179
4	Aldeguer	175
5	Gonzalez	170
6	Lopez	168
7	Roberts	153
8	Dixon	142
9	Vietti	140
10	Arbolino	135
11	Ramirez	101
12	Chantra	91
13	Alcoba	79
14	Arenas	76
15	Agius	63
16	Salac	61
17	Moreira	58
18	Binder	54
19	Guevara	44
20	Baltus	40
21	Oncu	40
22	Van den Goorbergh	31
23	Foggia	18
24	Artigas	10
25	Navarro	7
26	Sasaki	7
27	Bendsneyder	7
28	Masia	4
29	Aji	4
30	Ferrari	1

Constructor Points

1	Kalex	387
2	Boscoscuro	373
3	Forward	16

MOTO3: RACE DISTANCE: 12 laps, 33.957 miles/54.648km
RACE WEATHER: Wet (air 24°, humidity 92%, track 27°)

Pos.	Rider	Nat.	No.	Entrant	Machine	Laps	Time & Speed
1	David Alonso	COL	80	CFMOTO Gaviota Aspar Team	CFMOTO	12	20m 29.345s
							99.4mph/160.0km/h
2	Luca Lunetta	ITA	58	SIC58 Squadra Corse	Honda	12	20m 29.698s
3	Collin Veijer	NED	95	Liqui Moly Husqvarna Intact GP	Husqvarna	12	20m 29.867s
4	Ivan Ortola	SPA	48	MT Helmets - MSI	KTM	12	20m 30.281s
5	Taiyo Furusato	JPN	72	Honda Team Asia	Honda	12	20m 31.028s
6	David Munoz	SPA	64	BOE Motorsports	KTM	12	20m 31.837s
7	Joel Kelso	AUS	66	BOE Motorsports	KTM	12	20m 32.151s
8	Scott Ogden	GBR	19	FleetSafe Honda - MLav Racing	Honda	12	20m 34.367s
9	Stefano Nepa	ITA	82	LEVELUP - MTA	KTM	12	20m 36.986s
10	Tatsuki Suzuki	JPN	24	Liqui Moly Husqvarna Intact GP	Husqvarna	12	20m 37.653s
11	Ryusei Yamanaka	JPN	6	MT Helmets - MSI	KTM	12	20m 38.385s
12	Daniel Holgado	SPA	96	Red Bull GASGAS Tech3	GASGAS	12	20m 40.985s
13	Riccardo Rossi	ITA	54	CIP Green Power	KTM	12	20m 41.042s
14	Filippo Farioli	ITA	7	SIC58 Squadra Corse	Honda	12	20m 44.334s
15	Jacob Roulstone	AUS	12	Red Bull GASGAS Tech3	GASGAS	12	20m 46.435s
16	Jose Antonio Rueda	SPA	99	Red Bull KTM Ajo	KTM	12	20m 46.290s
17	Tatchakorn Buasri	THA	5	Honda Team Asia	Honda	12	20m 46.971s
18	Xabi Zurutuza	SPA	85	Red Bull KTM Ajo	KTM	12	20m 48.784s
19	Nicola Carraro	ITA	10	LEVELUP - MTA	KTM	12	20m 48.536s
20	David Almansa	SPA	22	Kopron Rivacold Snipers Team	Honda	12	20m 48.589s
21	Matteo Bertelle	ITA	18	Kopron Rivacold Snipers Team	Honda	12	20m 49.012s
22	Adrian Fernandez	SPA	31	Leopard Racing	Honda	12	21m 12.951s
23	Noah Dettwiler	SWI	55	CIP Green Power	KTM	12	21m 13.017s
	Angel Piqueras	SPA	36	Leopard Racing	Honda	10	DNF-crash
	Joel Esteban	SPA	78	CFMOTO Gaviota Aspar Team	CFMOTO	9	DNF-crash
	Eddie O'Shea	GBR	8	FleetSafe Honda - MLav Racing	Honda	9	DNF-ret in pit

Fastest lap: Luca Lunetta, on lap 10, 1m 41.231s, 100.6mph/161.9km/h.
Lap record: Deniz Oncu, 1m 42.346s, 99.5mph/160.1km/h (2023).
Event maximum speed: Tatsuki Suzuki, 149.1mph/240.0km/h (race)..

Qualifying
Weather: Dry
Air: 30° **Humidity:** 73% **Track:** 40°

1	Kelso	1m 40.603s
2	Veijer	1m 40.676s
3	Piqueras	1m 40.727s
4	Furusato	1m 40.865s
5	Alonso	1m 40.959s
6	Ogden	1m 41.019s
7	Holgado	1m 41.117s
8	Almansa	1m 41.174s
9	Ortola	1m 41.186s
10	Lunetta	1m 41.223s
11	Fernandez	1m 41.258s
12	Yamanaka	1m 41.390s
13	Bertelle	1m 41.415s
14	Nepa	1m 41.578s
15	Farioli	1m 41.696s
16	Rueda	1m 41.713s
17	Munoz	1m 41.851s
18	Esteban	1m 42.669s
Q1		
19	Roulstone	1m 41.494s
20	Suzuki	1m 41.562s
21	Zurutuza	1m 41.622s
22	O'Shea	1m 41.643s
23	Carraro	1m 41.762s
24	Rossi	1m 42.172s
25	Buasri	1m 42.547s
26	Dettwiler	1m 43.486s

Fastest race laps

1	Lunetta	1m 41.231s
2	Ortola	1m 41.254s
3	Kelso	1m 41.298s
4	Fernandez	1m 41.385s
5	Piqueras	1m 41.423s
6	Munoz	1m 41.425s
7	Veijer	1m 41.443s
8	Alonso	1m 41.449s
9	Furusato	1m 41.518s
10	Nepa	1m 41.734s
11	Ogden	1m 41.858s
12	Suzuki	1m 41.936s
13	Yamanaka	1m 42.002s
14	Rossi	1m 42.089s
15	Esteban	1m 42.145s
16	Roulstone	1m 42.161s
17	Holgado	1m 42.218s
18	Rueda	1m 42.326s
19	Zurutuza	1m 42.343s
20	Farioli	1m 42.427s
21	Carraro	1m 42.460s
22	Buasri	1m 42.478s
23	Almansa	1m 42.931s
24	Bertelle	1m 43.107s
25	Dettwiler	1m 44.433s
26	O'Shea	1m 52.311s

Championship Points

1	Alonso	371
2	Holgado	236
3	Veijer	225
4	Ortola	204
5	Munoz	162
6	Fernandez	153
7	Piqueras	137
8	Rueda	128
9	Kelso	124
10	Yamanaka	111
11	Furusato	108
12	Lunetta	106
13	Suzuki	88
14	Nepa	85
15	Roulstone	54
16	Bertelle	49
17	Esteban	45
18	Rossi	33
19	Farioli	29
20	Ogden	23
21	Carraro	22
22	Zurutuza	11
23	Almansa	11
24	Perez	3
25	Dettwiler	2

Constructor Points

1	CFMOTO	371
2	KTM	304
3	Honda	264
4	Husqvarna	252
5	GASGAS	241

MALAYSIAN GRAND PRIX
SEPANG CIRCUIT

FIM WORLD CHAMPIONSHIP • ROUND 19

Inset, left: After the flood. A minute's silence for Spanish flood victims.
Photo: Gold & Goose

Inset, far left: Martin waved the flag of Valencia as he shared Sunday's podium with winner Bagnaia.
Photo: Ducati Corse

Main: Marquez had a VIP seat for the brutal leading battle in the opening three laps.
Photo: Gold & Goose

Above: Martin went on alone to win his seventh sprint of the season.

Top right: A frightening first-lap crash took out Miller, Quartararo and Binder. Neither of the KTM riders was able to restart.
Photos: Gold & Goose

Above right: A costly slip for Bagnaia in the sprint.
Photo: MotoGP

Above far right: Back from banishment. Andrea Iannone had a one-off ride on friend Rossi's VR46 Ducati.

Right: Luckily unhurt, Quartararo took a best-so-far sixth in the re-started race.

Below right: A good weekend for Alex Marquez, twice fourth from a first front-row of the year.
Photos: Gold & Goose

TWO corners. That's how long it took, in the blazing heat of Sepang, for a MotoGP rider's front tyre to overheat if he was following another bike closely. "A disaster." That was the opinion of Luca Marini, who admittedly had been following a lot more than just one bike, stuck near the back on a Honda. But it concisely explained the opening three laps of a Malaysian GP of two very unequal halves.

During the first, throwing caution to the wind, the title protagonists laid on a fearsome display. The front-tyre syndrome, a defining factor in so many ways, made it imperative to be the one in front.

If they never actually collided, they came desperately close, and the quality of riding was evident from the fact that – far from slowing one another down – they were actually gaining marginally on the pursuing Marquez, and more than marginally on everybody else.

Given the risks, not only of crashing, but also of exhausting riders and tyres, it couldn't last. And it was a measure of Bagnaia's Sunday strength that he prevailed, going on for a spectacularly determined victory. A measure he needed, after all but handing the title on a plate to his Spanish rival the day before, with an early headlong crash in the sprint.

At least, Bagnaia's win preserved the contest to the final round. At best, it gave him a real, if slender, chance to join the pantheon of grand prix greats with three championships in a row at the next race. At worst, a career-best tenth of the season, which would put him in elite company.

The next race was a vexed question, only days after horrendous floods in Spain, with a particular focus on Valencia, where the finale was to have taken place. Access to the Ricardo Tormo circuit had been cut off, but this was the least of the catastrophic damage to property and tragic loss of life.

Dorna were determined that the championship would be completed, and at first even hoped that it might be at the same venue, with the date to be decided. A possibility that made many uncomfortable, considering the human and material cost to the region. "Unethical," said Marc Marquez. Bagnaia went further, stating, "Even at the cost of losing the title, I'm not willing to race in Valencia." Dorna were intent on making a commitment before racing began at Sepang, if only to clarify the championship situation for the riders. The decision to switch to the Barcelona-Catalunya circuit at Montmelo came on Friday. It was welcomed by almost all.

At the same time, there were both official and other pledges to raise aid money, and there was not a top-three rider on Sunday who did not dedicate his result to the victims.

Bagnaia had an explanation of sorts for his Saturday crash, his fifth sprint no-score compared with just one for his rival – a sharp contrast to his ten Sunday wins compared to only three for Martin. "All the mistakes I did were on Saturdays," he said. This time, "honestly, I just told myself I'd brake earlier, with more calm, to not risk. And I crashed. I entered a bit slower, but touched the bump at the apex and lost the front. I knew Jorge was in more trouble with used tyres, and I was just waiting. The pace wasn't that fast. I knew I'd have a chance to overtake in the next laps. We need to find out how to be more aggressive on Saturday, like I can be on Sunday."

Sunday was interrupted by a frightening crash on the second corner of the feature race, a frequent trouble spot when a crowd of bikes swarms into a tight left-hander. Brad Binder tagged the back of Alex Marquez, which pushed him into Quartararo and Miller, who went down with his head almost under the Yamaha's rear tyre. The race was stopped and Miller was treated on the spot for a worrying several minutes, but miraculously the Australian was unharmed.

As rumoured the weekend before, Di Giannantonio's place was taken by Andrea Iannone, his first time on a MotoGP bike since the final race of 2019, thanks to his licence suspension. It came after a personal call from VR46 team owner Rossi, and the one-time MotoGP winner was not unimpressive, qualifying less than two seconds off pole, ahead of three Hondas, as well as Augusto Fernandez and Savadori, and finishing both races in front of the latter. The eye-opener had been "entry, braking point and corner speed – this is the biggest difference," he said, compared with his 2019 bike. "It's unbelievable. It's really difficult to touch the limit. It's more easy to ride, less nervous, more stability, and so entering is more easy. It's turning really well. But on the braking point, with these brakes, pffff… It destroys [me]."

Yamaha had brought a new engine, at least the fifth of the season, but Quartararo managed fewer than two laps before "an issue" that meant he had to be pushed back to

the pits. Results were still positive, however, with a third-row start and a year's best sixth. It was down to improved electronic strategy, he believed. "From Thailand, I would say we have changed the way to handle the electronics." He was able to ride "in a completely different style. It's quite difficult to adapt."

MOTOGP SPRINT RACE – 10 laps

Bagnaia and Martin's qualifying face-off was memorable. The latter's second flying lap of 1m 56.552s was spectacular, as he put half a second into his pursuers. But Bagnaia's response – 1m 56.337s – was not only 1.1 seconds under his previous lap record, but also 0.9 of a second faster than third-placed Alex Marquez.

The top six were all inside the all-time record, with Morbidelli, Marc Marquez and Bastianini on row two, then Miller, and Yamaha riders Quartararo and Rins together on row three for the first time.

Spots of rain fell five minutes before start time and white flags signalled a wet race, but the rain stopped without wetting the baking-hot track.

Martin needed only to follow Bagnaia, but he was determined to take the initiative as he led Bagnaia and Marquez into the first corners.

Bagnaia had a stab at the final hairpin, but decided to wait, relying on his stronger rhythm – only to slip off on the notorious Turn Nine bump on lap three.

That left Martin in complete control for a seventh sprint win. Only Marquez was able to stay within a second, with 2023 GP winner Bastianini a similar distance behind him.

High temperatures meant a minimum of close riding and overtaking, with Alex Marquez continuing to enjoy his settings breakthrough to hold fourth to the end, better than a second ahead of Quartararo, each equalling his best of the year. Morbidelli was sixth, after losing three places in a lap-two moment. He had repassed Binder soon afterwards, the South African a close seventh, with Miller less than a second behind, having fended off a persistent Acosta.

Bezzecchi missed the points by less than a second, but was a couple clear of Rins. Zarco retired.

MOTOGP RACE – 19 laps (shortened)

Do you prefer racing to be short and scrappy? Or long and drawn out? Sunday offered both as Bagnaia and Martin put everything on the line to serve up a modern classic – for just three laps.

It had to wait 25 minutes, after the tangle in the second corner brought out instant red flags. Binder and Quartararo were able to walk away, but Miller was stretchered off. Shortly before the restart, however, he was seen walking unharmed back from the medical centre with his wife.

Martin maintained the cool facade he'd worn in recent weeks, but would have no truck with a tame following role. Meanwhile, defending match point spurred Bagnaia on and he dominated three-quarters of Sunday's restarted outing, turning the final 16 laps into a rather joyless procession.

With the distance cut by one lap, the pair laid on a dizzying opening exchange. Bagnaia got the jump into Turn One, Martin attacked soon after, only to run wide. The lead changed hands four times through Turns 14 and 15; five times on lap two, the pair nearly coming together exiting Turn 15; and six times on lap three. But Martin's lead was always short lived, and when Bagnaia led on to the start of lap four, it was by enough that the battle was over.

It had been a back-to-front GP, all the fighting at the beginning rather than the end.

Marc Marquez "was a VIP spectator. I didn't understand, because they were battling, but the lap times were superfast," he said. The trio edged clear of Morbidelli, Bastianini, Alex Marquez and Acosta, who had forced through from 13th on the grid.

Now the spectacle was over. In the 15 laps that remained, there was little overtaking of note as Michelin's front tyre became close to unrideable when in another bike's slipstream. Thus the field gradually spread out into one of those trying modern MotoGP affairs.

One question that had hung over the start was whether Bagnaia would attempt to bring Marquez and Bastianini into the events in a bid to upset Martin. But later he denied that the thought had even crossed his mind: "I'm a clean guy and a true sportsman. I don't like these kinds of things."

Above: Lap one of the feature race, and Quartararo leads team-mate Rins, Acosta, Vinales, Zarco and Bezzecchi.
Photo: Monster Yamaha

Top right: Two podiums still left 2023 winner Bastianini frustrated.
Photo: Ducati Corse

Top far right: Overheated substitute Moto2 rider Jorge Navarro claimed pole, finished second – and looked shattered.

Above right: Keeping his cool. Vinales with ice pack and cold towel on the grid.

Above far right: Vietti held off a determined Navarro in Moto2.

Right: Alonso scored his 13th win of the year, defending his lead from the challenge of Ortola (48), Furusato (72), Veijer and the rest. Behind, fast-charging Rueda will soon join the party for third.
Photos: Gold & Goose

He steadily built an advantage of more than two seconds. The only jeopardy arose when Martin – running Michelin's medium front as opposed to the rest on the soft – made a late push on lap 15, just as Bagnaia had switched to a lower power-delivery map. The gap came down to 1.6 seconds, but a near crash at Turn Nine ended Martin's charge, leaving Bagnaia to come home better than three seconds clear. Asked whether it had been a struggle in the blazing sunshine, he quipped, "The heat was the easiest thing to manage."

Any role Marquez might have played came to an end when he fell victim to the last hairpin on lap seven, hastily remounting down in 16th.

Bastianini was third, albeit a gargantuan ten seconds behind his team-mate, a fact that clearly irked the winner of 2023's race, who complained that problems in corner entry had robbed him of competitive pace.

Alex Marquez enjoyed his best Sunday of the year in fourth, having held Acosta at arm's length in the closing five laps, with Ducati once again demonstrating an almost absurd level of superiority. Quartararo was a stellar sixth, passed by Acosta on lap three, but then promoted when Morbidelli slipped off on lap seven.

It was a tough weekend for Aprilia, with both Espargaro and Raul Fernandez complaining that excessive heat coming off their RS-GPs had drained them of all energy. Yet Vinales saved some face with a solid seventh, ahead of Rins in a season-best eighth. Bezzecchi narrowly beat Augusto Fernandez to tenth.

Some way behind, a lone Zarco was saved by the flag from having to defend against the remounted Marc Marquez, who had passed Espargaro on the last lap. The similarly remounted Morbidelli failed to do the same by less than three-tenths, having dropped Marini to the bottom of the points, also on the last lap.

Raul Fernandez, Iannone and Savadori trailed in. Mir had crashed out, while Nakagami had retired. Miller did not start, while a battered Binder had retired after completing the warm-up lap.

Martin now had some clear breathing space, his lead up to 24 points. Marquez's bad afternoon meant that Bastianini was one point behind in the fight for third.

MOTO2 RACE – 17 laps

With the title decided, Canet was now close to securing second. Qualifying was not promising for the Spaniard, placed 13th, while the injured Roberts's replacement, Jorge Navarro, claimed a surprise record-speed pole, in his second race on the Only Fans American Racing Kalex. Ramirez was alongside, then Vietti; Arenas led row two from Oncu and Arbolino. New champion Ogura headed the third.

There was a surprise in the race, too, when Vietti took a comeback victory just two weeks on from cracking his left collarbone at Phillip Island. He controlled the race from start to finish, recovering from a moment at Turn One on lap six to hold off Navarro by 1.4 seconds.

There was a definite post-championship feeling, Ogura and Canet failing to find the intensity of previous weeks. That opened the door for a few less-fancied names. After he had spent two largely troubled years in World Supersport, it was a surprise to watch how Navarro was a match for the best from Friday. He recovered three places after a shaky start, and had passed Ogura, Guevara and Ramirez by lap nine. After Vietti's mistake, it appeared that an unlikely win was on the cards. Yet he didn't have enough to reel in the Italian.

Ogura's hopes were thwarted when he was forced to retire on lap 11 with a mechanical issue, slowing suddenly exiting Turn Nine, which forced Dixon into drastic avoiding action. Having already come through from 12th, he soon recovered to sit third, only to commit the cardinal sin of sitting up and celebrating a lap early, which handed team-mate Guevara a maiden Moto2 podium. A devastated Dixon later explained an issue with the lap count on his dashboard, which had led to the error.

Arbolino recovered from a ropey opening to fight through to fifth, ahead of Ramirez. Oncu was seventh, with an off-colour Canet eighth. Chantra and Moreira concluded the top ten, while Gonzalez, Lopez and Garcia – all contenders for third overall – were a disappointing 11th, 13th and 14th.

Agius, Surra and van den Goorbergh crashed within yards of one another at Turn Nine, Agius alone and the other two together, Surra being hit with a double long-lap for the next race. Voight, Binder and Alcoba also crashed out.

Canet had secured second overall; third was still up for grabs between Garcia, Aldeguer, Gonzalez, Lopez and Vietti, all within 16 points.

MOTO3 RACE – 15 laps

With this championship also very much decided, Alonso admitted that it was difficult to focus. He'd already broken all the records, and as a Valencian resident riding for a Valencian team, understandably the desperate events back home weighed heavily on his mind.

The attention was on Holgado, Veijer and Ortola for second overall. The other point of interest was a new engine for the Honda runners, after a season of playing second fiddle to KTM.

Ortola qualified second, between pole-sitter Fernandez and champion Alonso. With Suzuki leading row two, Veijer was eighth and Holgado a distant 11th, almost 1.3 seconds adrift of pole.

David Almansa got a flying start, and the Honda rider led the first three laps before giving way first to Kelso's KTM then Furusato's Honda.

Holgado also got off the line well and finished lap one third, only to high-side out next time around – which dropped Alonso to 13th, taking avoiding action.

That spurred him on. He'd picked off the entire lead group of seven by lap 12 to lead. Despite Furusato's persistent efforts, Alonso defended brilliantly on the last lap to score a 13th win of the year.

Rueda grabbed third on the final lap, ahead of Ortola and Veijer; Kelso and Yamanaka were next, the top seven covered by 1.4 seconds. Nepa followed, then Bertelle, Lunetta and Almansa, with rookie Roulstone a lone 12th.

Munoz was out of the points after a long-lap for causing a crash in practice; Rossi, Esteban, Carraro and Dettwiller crashed out.

The new Hondas brought mixed fortunes: Furusato was second, but front-runners Fernandez and Piqueras suffered engine failures, as did Ogden, who pitted, only to be sent out again to put some miles on the engine.

Holgado and Veijer left equal on points, Ortola 19 behind.

FIM WORLD CHAMPIONSHIP: ROUND 19
PETRONAS GRAND PRIX OF MALAYSIA

1-3 NOVEMBER, 2024

SEPANG INTERNATIONAL CIRCUIT
19 laps
Length: 5.540km / 3.440 miles
Width: 16m

MOTOGP: RACE DISTANCE: 19 laps, 65.441 miles/105.317km
WEATHER: Dry (air 34°, humidity 57%, track 54°)

Pos.	Rider	Nat.	No.	Entrant	Machine	Race tyre choice	Laps	Time & speed
1	Francesco Bagnaia	ITA	1	Ducati Lenovo Team	Ducati Desmosedici GP24	F: Soft/R: Medium	19	38m 04.563s 103.1mph/165.9km/h
2	Jorge Martin	SPA	89	Prima Pramac Racing	Ducati Desmosedici GP24	F: Medium/R: Medium	19	38m 07.704s
3	Enea Bastianini	ITA	23	Ducati Lenovo Team	Ducati Desmosedici GP24	F: Soft/R: Medium	19	38m 15.047s
4	Alex Marquez	SPA	73	Gresini Racing MotoGP	Ducati Desmosedici GP23	F: Soft/R: Medium	19	38m 16.793s
5	Pedro Acosta	SPA	31	Red Bull GASGAS Tech3	KTM RC16	F: Soft/R: Medium	19	38m 18.262s
6	Fabio Quartararo	FRA	20	Monster Energy Yamaha MotoGP	Yamaha YZR-M1	F: Medium/R: Medium	19	38m 20.808s
7	Maverick Vinales	SPA	12	Aprilia Racing	Aprilia RS-GP24	F: Soft/R: Medium	19	38m 24.010s
8	Alex Rins	SPA	42	Monster Energy Yamaha MotoGP	Yamaha YZR-M1	F: Soft/R: Medium	19	38m 25.174s
9	Marco Bezzecchi	ITA	72	Pertamina Enduro VR46 Racing	Ducati Desmosedici GP23	F: Soft/R: Medium	19	38m 26.557s
10	Augusto Fernandez	SPA	37	Red Bull GASGAS Tech3	KTM RC16	F: Soft/R: Medium	19	38m 26.737s
11	Johann Zarco	FRA	5	CASTROL Honda LCR	Honda RC213V	F: Soft/R: Medium	19	38m 30.188s
12	Marc Marquez	SPA	93	Gresini Racing MotoGP	Ducati Desmosedici GP23	F: Soft/R: Medium	19	38m 31.839s
13	Aleix Espargaro	SPA	41	Aprilia Racing	Aprilia RS-GP24	F: Soft/R: Medium	19	38m 32.167s
14	Franco Morbidelli	ITA	21	Prima Pramac Racing	Ducati Desmosedici GP24	F: Soft/R: Medium	19	38m 32.512s
15	Luca Marini	ITA	10	Repsol Honda Team	Honda RC213V	F: Medium/R: Medium	19	38m 33.401s
16	Raul Fernandez	SPA	25	Trackhouse Racing	Aprilia RS-GP24	F: Soft/R: Medium	19	38m 43.410s
17	Andrea Iannone	ITA	29	Pertamina Enduro VR46 Racing	Ducati Desmosedici GP23	F: Soft/R: Medium	19	38m 52.162s
18	Lorenzo Savadori	ITA	32	Trackhouse Racing	Aprilia RS-GP24	F: Soft/R: Medium	19	38m 53.519s
	Takaaki Nakagami	JPN	30	IDEMITSU Honda LCR	Honda RC213V	F: Soft/R: Medium	14	DNF-ret in pit
	Joan Mir	SPA	36	Repsol Honda Team	Honda RC213V	F: Soft/R: Medium	5	DNF-crash
	Jack Miller	AUS	43	Red Bull KTM Factory Racing	KTM RC16	-	-	DNS
	Brad Binder	RSA	33	Red Bull KTM Factory Racing	KTM RC16	-	-	DNS

Fastest lap: Francesco Bagnaia, on lap 5, 1m 59.118s, 104.1mph/167.5km/h.
Lap record: Alex Marquez, 1m 58.979s, 104.2mph/167.7km/h (2023).
Event maximum speed: Pedro Acosta, 209.7mph/337.5km/h (warm-up).

Qualifying: Weather: Dry Air: 29° Humidity: 69% Track: 36°
1 Bagnaia 1m 56.337s, 2 Martin 1m 56.553s, 3 A. Marquez 1m 57.275s, 4 Morbidelli 1m 57.279s, 5 M. Marquez 1m 57.301s, 6 Bastianini 1m 57.366s, 7 Miller 1m 57.558s, 8 Quartararo 1m 57.592s, 9 Rins 1m 57.726s, 10 Binder 1m 57.882s, 11 Zarco 1m 57.971s, 12 Vinales 1m 58.046s.
Q1: 13 Acosta 1m 57.839s, 14 Bezzecchi 1m 57.869s, 15 R. Fernandez 1m 58.023s, 15 R. Fernandez 1m 58.023s, 16 A. Espargaro 1m 58.107s, 17 Iannone 1m 58.183s, 18 Nakagami 1m 58.300s, 19 Marini 1m 58.520s, 20 Mir 1m 58.618s, 21 A. Fernandez 1m 59.006s, 22 Savadori 1m 59.263s.

SPRINT RACE: 10 laps, 34.443 miles/55.430km
WEATHER: Dry (air 30°, humidity 71%, track 40°)

Pos.	Rider	Race tyre choice	Laps	Time & speed
1	Jorge Martin	F: Soft/R: Medium	10	19m 49.230s 104.2mph/167.7km/h
2	Marc Marquez	F: Soft/R: Medium	10	19m 50.143s
3	Enea Bastianini	F: Soft/R: Medium	10	19m 51.240s
4	Alex Marquez	F: Soft/R: Medium	10	19m 55.805s
5	Fabio Quartararo	F: Soft/R: Medium	10	19m 57.147s
6	Franco Morbidelli	F: Soft/R: Medium	10	19m 58.187s
7	Brad Binder	F: Soft/R: Medium	10	20m 00.245s
8	Jack Miller	F: Soft/R: Medium	10	20m 01.064s
9	Pedro Acosta	F: Soft/R: Medium	10	20m 01.321s
10	Marco Bezzecchi	F: Soft/R: Medium	10	20m 02.070s
11	Alex Rins	F: Soft/R: Medium	10	20m 04.131s
12	Aleix Espargaro	F: Soft/R: Medium	10	20m 04.454s
13	Augusto Fernandez	F: Soft/R: Medium	10	20m 06.345s
14	Maverick Vinales	F: Soft/R: Medium	10	20m 07.833s
15	Luca Marini	F: Soft/R: Medium	10	20m 08.320s
16	Joan Mir	F: Soft/R: Medium	10	20m 09.434s
17	Takaaki Nakagami	F: Soft/R: Medium	10	20m 10.941s
18	Raul Fernandez	F: Soft/R: Medium	10	20m 13.044s
19	Andrea Iannone	F: Soft/R: Medium	10	20m 15.128s
20	Lorenzo Savadori	F: Soft/R: Medium	10	20m 19.008s
	Johann Zarco	F: Soft/R: Medium	7	DNF-technical
	Francesco Bagnaia	F: Soft/R: Medium	2	DNF-crash

Fastest lap: Jorge Martin, on lap 3, 1m 57.805s.

Fastest race laps
1 Bagnaia 1m 59.118s, 2 Martin 1m 59.338s, 3 M. Marquez 1m 59.397s, 4 Bastianini 1m 59.723s, 5 Acosta 1m 59.763s, 6 A. Marquez 1m 59.785s, 7 Morbidelli 1m 59.800s, 8 Quartararo 2m 00.125s, 9 Rins 2m 00.145s, 10 Vinales 2m 00.160s, 11 Bezzecchi 2m 00.305s, 12 A. Fernandez 2m 00.329s, 13 R. Fernandez 2m 00.334s, 14 Zarco 2m 00.400s, 15 A. Espargaro 2m 00.432s, 16 Mir 2m 00.438s, 17 Marini 2m 00.553s, 18 Nakagami 2m 00.632s, 19 Iannone 2m 01.001s, 20 Savadori 2m 01.502s.

Grid order	1	2	3	4	5	6	7	8	9	10	11	12	13	14	15	16	17	18	19	
1 BAGNAIA	89	1	1	1	1	1	1	1	1	1	1	1	1	1	1	1	1	1	1	1
89 MARTIN	1	89	89	89	89	89	89	89	89	89	89	89	89	89	89	89	89	89	89	2
73 A. MARQUEZ	93	93	93	93	93	93	23	23	23	23	23	23	23	23	23	23	23	23	23	3
21 MORBIDELLI	21	21	21	21	21	23	73	73	73	73	73	73	73	73	73	73	73	73	73	4
93 M. MARQUEZ	23	23	23	23	23	21	31	31	31	31	31	31	31	31	31	31	31	31	31	5
23 BASTIANINI	73	73	73	73	73	73	20	20	20	20	20	20	20	20	20	20	20	20	20	6
43 MILLER	20	20	31	31	31	31	12	12	42	12	12	12	12	12	12	12	12	12	12	7
20 QUARTARARO	42	31	20	20	20	20	42	42	12	42	42	42	42	42	42	42	42	42	42	8
42 RINS	31	42	42	12	12	12	72	5	5	5	5	72	72	72	72	72	72	72	72	9
33 BINDER	12	12	12	42	42	42	5	72	72	72	72	37	37	37	37	37	37	37	37	10
5 ZARCO	5	5	5	72	72	72	37	37	37	37	37	5	5	5	5	5	5	5	5	11
12 VINALES	72	72	72	5	5	5	41	41	41	41	41	41	41	41	41	41	41	93	12
31 ACOSTA	25	25	25	25	37	37	25	25	25	25	25	25	25	25	25	10	93	41	41	13
72 BEZZECCHI	37	37	37	37	25	25	10	10	10	10	10	10	10	10	10	93	10	21	14
25 R. FERNANDEZ	41	41	41	41	41	41	30	30	30	30	30	21	21	21	21	21	21	10	15
41 A. ESPARGARO	36	36	36	36	36	10	93	21	21	93	21	93	93	93	93	25	25	25	
29 IANNONE	10	10	10	10	10	30	21	93	93	93	21	93	30	29	29	29	29	29	
30 NAKAGAMI	30	30	30	30	30	29	29	29	29	29	29	29	29	32	32	32	32	32	
10 MARINI	29	29	29	29	29	32	32	32	32	32	32	32	32							
36 MIR	32	32	32	32	32															
37 A. FERNANDEZ																				
32 SAVADORI																				

Championship Points

1	Martin	321	(164)	485
2	Bagnaia	345	(116)	461
3	M. Marquez	250	(119)	369
4	Bastianini	255	(113)	368
5	Acosta	145	(64)	209
6	Binder	163	(43)	206
7	Vinales	134	(55)	189
8	Di Giannantonio	139	(26)	165
9	Morbidelli	108	(53)	161
10	A. Marquez	123	(32)	155
11	A. Espargaro	98	(48)	146
12	Bezzecchi	130	(14)	144
13	Quartararo	88	(20)	108
14	Miller	57	(27)	84
15	Oliveira	55	(16)	71
16	R. Fernandez	60	(6)	66
17	Zarco	51	(2)	53
18	Nakagami	31	(0)	31
19	Rins	31	(0)	31
20	A. Fernandez	23	(4)	27
21	Mir	20	(1)	21
22	Marini	14	(0)	14
23	P. Espargaro	11	(1)	12
24	Pedrosa	0	(7)	7
25	Bradl	2	(0)	2

Constructor Points

1	Ducati	466	(219)	685
2	KTM	225	(91)	316
3	Aprilia	185	(100)	285
4	Yamaha	99	(20)	119
5	Honda	69	(4)	73

MOTO2: RACE DISTANCE: 17 laps, 58.552 miles/94.231km

RACE WEATHER: Dry (air 35°, humidity 45%, track 58°)

Pos.	Rider	Nat.	No.	Entrant	Machine	Laps	Time & Speed
1	Celestino Vietti	ITA	13	Red Bull KTM Ajo	Kalex	17	36m 06.629s
							97.2mph/156.5km/h
2	Jorge Navarro	SPA	9	OnlyFans American Racing Team	Kalex	17	36m 08.115s
3	Izan Guevara	SPA	28	CFMOTO RCB Aspar Team	Kalex	17	36m 09.894s
4	Jake Dixon	GBR	96	CFMOTO RCB Aspar Team	Kalex	17	36m 11.131s
5	Tony Arbolino	ITA	14	Elf Marc VDS Racing Team	Kalex	17	36m 11.462s
6	Marcos Ramirez	SPA	24	OnlyFans American Racing Team	Kalex	17	36m 12.313s
7	Deniz Oncu	TUR	53	Red Bull KTM Ajo	Kalex	17	36m 14.349s
8	Aron Canet	SPA	44	Fantic Racing	Kalex	17	36m 15.986s
9	Somkiat Chantra	THA	35	IDEMITSU Honda Team Asia	Kalex	17	36m 17.058s
10	Diogo Moreira	BRA	10	Italtrans Racing Team	Kalex	17	36m 17.465s
11	Manuel Gonzalez	SPA	18	Gresini Moto2	Kalex	17	36m 18.684s
12	Albert Arenas	SPA	75	Gresini Moto2	Kalex	17	36m 19.923s
13	Alonso Lopez	SPA	21	Sync SpeedUp	Boscoscuro	17	36m 21.015s
14	Sergio Garcia	SPA	3	MT Helmets - MSI	Boscoscuro	17	36m 24.742s
15	Filip Salac	CZE	12	Elf Marc VDS Racing Team	Kalex	17	36m 27.574s
16	Jaume Masia	SPA	5	Preicanos Racing Team	Kalex	17	36m 31.563s
17	Mario Aji	INA	34	IDEMITSU Honda Team Asia	Kalex	17	36m 32.557s
18	Barry Baltus	BEL	7	RW-Idrofoglia Racing GP	Kalex	17	36m 33.894s
19	Dennis Foggia	ITA	71	Italtrans Racing Team	Kalex	17	36m 45.031s
20	Alex Escrig	SPA	11	KLINT Forward Factory Team	Forward	17	36m 45.586s
21	Xavi Cardelus	AND	20	Fantic Racing	Kalex	17	36m 46.868s
22	Xavier Artigas	SPA	43	KLINT Forward Factory Team	Forward	17	36m 47.020s
23	Helmi Azman	MAL	55	PETRONAS MIE Racing RW	Kalex	17	36m 55.868s
	Zonta van den Goorbergh	NED	84	RW-Idrofoglia Racing GP	Kalex	10	DNF-crash
	Jeremy Alcoba	SPA	52	Yamaha VR46 Master Camp Team	Kalex	16	DNF-crash
	Ai Ogura	JPN	79	MT Helmets - MSI	Boscoscuro	10	DNF-technical
	Darryn Binder	RSA	15	Liqui Moly Husqvarna Intact GP	Kalex	7	DNF-crash
	Senna Agius	AUS	81	Liqui Moly Husqvarna Intact GP	Kalex	0	DNF-crash
	Alberto Surra	ITA	67	Sync SpeedUp	Boscoscuro	0	DNF-crash
	Harrison Voight	AUS	29	Preicanos Racing Team	Kalex	0	DNF-crash

Fastest lap: Celestino Vietti, on lap 2, 2m 5.898s, 98.4mph/158.4km/h.
Lap record: Alex Marquez, 2m 5.860s, 98.5mph/158.5km/h (2019).
Event maximum speed: Jake Dixon, 172.5mph/277.6km/h (practice).

Qualifying

Weather: Dry
Air: 31° **Humidity:** 69% **Track:** 43°

1	Navarro	2m 04.412s
2	Ramirez	2m 04.475s
3	Vietti	2m 04.559s
4	Arenas	2m 04.643s
5	Oncu	2m 04.697s
6	Arbolino	2m 04.756s
7	Ogura	2m 04.759s
8	Gonzalez	2m 04.802s
9	Moreira	2m 04.919s
10	Salac	2m 04.937s
11	Guevara	2m 04.944s
12	Dixon	2m 05.004s
13	Canet	2m 05.035s
14	V d Goorbergh	2m 05.246s
15	Chantra	2m 05.339s
16	Baltus	2m 05.443s
17	Alcoba	2m 05.513s
18	Agius	2m 05.860s
Q1		
19	Garcia	2m 05.544s
20	Lopez	2m 05.624s
21	Aji	2m 05.795s
22	Binder	2m 05.885s
23	Foggia	2m 05.918s
24	Masia	2m 06.262s
25	Surra	2m 06.483s
26	Cardelus	2m 06.755s
27	Escrig	2m 07.067s
28	Artigas	2m 07.336s
29	Azman	2m 07.554s
30	Pawi	2m 07.570s
31	Voight	2m 08.085s

Fastest race laps

1	Vietti	2m 05.898s
2	Ramirez	2m 05.904s
3	Guevara	2m 06.067s
4	Ogura	2m 06.203s
5	Arbolino	2m 06.310s
6	Navarro	2m 06.371s
7	Oncu	2m 06.411s
8	Arenas	2m 06.613s
9	Dixon	2m 06.645s
10	Moreira	2m 06.683s
11	Gonzalez	2m 06.688s
12	Canet	2m 06.786s
13	Aji	2m 06.877s
14	Lopez	2m 06.944s
15	Salac	2m 06.983s
16	Chantra	2m 07.005s
17	Binder	2m 07.064s
18	Garcia	2m 07.158s
19	Alcoba	2m 07.181s
20	V d Goorbergh	2m 07.300s
21	Baltus	2m 07.576s
22	Foggia	2m 07.602s
23	Masia	2m 07.823s
24	Cardelus	2m 07.973s
25	Artigas	2m 08.391s
26	Escrig	2m 08.445s
27	Azman	2m 08.670s

Championship Points

1	Ogura	261
2	Canet	209
3	Garcia	181
4	Aldeguer	175
5	Gonzalez	175
6	Lopez	171
7	Vietti	165
8	Dixon	155
9	Roberts	153
10	Arbolino	146
11	Ramirez	111
12	Chantra	98
13	Arenas	80
14	Alcoba	79
15	Moreira	64
16	Agius	63
17	Salac	62
18	Guevara	60
19	Binder	54
20	Oncu	49
21	Baltus	40
22	Van den Goorbergh	31
23	Navarro	27
24	Foggia	18
25	Artigas	10
26	Sasaki	7
27	Bendsneyder	7
28	Masia	4
29	Aji	4
30	Ferrari	1

Constructor Points

1	Kalex	412
2	Boscoscuro	376
3	Forward	16

MOTO3: RACE DISTANCE: 15 laps, 51.664 miles/83.145km

RACE WEATHER: Dry (air 33°, humidity 56%, track 50°)

Pos.	Rider	Nat.	No.	Entrant	Machine	Laps	Time & Speed
1	David Alonso	COL	80	CFMOTO Gaviota Aspar Team	CFMOTO	15	33m 03.671s
							93.7mph/150.8km/h
2	Taiyo Furusato	JPN	72	Honda Team Asia	Honda	15	33m 03.759s
3	Jose Antonio Rueda	SPA	99	Red Bull KTM Ajo	KTM	15	33m 04.082s
4	Ivan Ortola	SPA	48	MT Helmets - MSI	KTM	15	33m 04.667s
5	Collin Veijer	NED	95	Liqui Moly Husqvarna Intact GP	Husqvarna	15	33m 04.762s
6	Joel Kelso	AUS	66	BOE Motorsports	KTM	15	33m 04.896s
7	Ryusei Yamanaka	JPN	6	MT Helmets - MSI	KTM	15	33m 05.167s
8	Stefano Nepa	ITA	82	LEVELUP - MTA	KTM	15	33m 10.915s
9	Matteo Bertelle	ITA	18	Kopron Rivacold Snipers Team	Honda	15	33m 11.017s
10	Luca Lunetta	ITA	58	SIC58 Squadra Corse	Honda	15	33m 14.477s
11	David Almansa	SPA	22	Kopron Rivacold Snipers Team	Honda	15	33m 14.575s
12	Jacob Roulstone	AUS	12	Red Bull GASGAS Tech3	GASGAS	15	33m 19.690s
13	Filippo Farioli	ITA	7	SIC58 Squadra Corse	Honda	15	33m 24.216s
14	Xabi Zurutuza	SPA	85	Red Bull KTM Ajo	KTM	15	33m 24.464s
15	Tatchakorn Buasri	THA	5	Honda Team Asia	Honda	15	33m 24.672s
16	Eddie O'Shea	GBR	8	FleetSafe Honda - MLav Racing	Honda	15	33m 24.902s
17	David Munoz	SPA	64	BOE Motorsports	KTM	15	33m 47.376s
18	Noah Dettwiler	SWI	55	CIP Green Power	KTM	15	33m 48.830s
	Nicola Carraro	ITA	10	LEVELUP - MTA	KTM	10	DNF-ret in pit
	Tatsuki Suzuki	JPN	24	Liqui Moly Husqvarna Intact GP	Husqvarna	8	DNF-technical
	Scott Ogden	GBR	19	FleetSafe Honda - MLav Racing	Honda	8	DNF-ret in pit
	Angel Piqueras	SPA	36	Leopard Racing	Honda	5	DNF-ret in pit
	Adrian Fernandez	SPA	31	Leopard Racing	Honda	2	DNF-technical
	Daniel Holgado	SPA	96	Red Bull GASGAS Tech3	GASGAS	1	DNF-crash
	Riccardo Rossi	ITA	54	CIP Green Power	KTM	0	DNF-crash
	Joel Esteban	SPA	78	CFMOTO Gaviota Aspar Team	CFMOTO	0	DNF-crash

Fastest lap: David Alonso, on lap 4, 2m 11.047s, 94.6mph/152.2km/h.
Lap record: Ayumu Sasaki, 2m 12.268s, 93.7mph/150.8km/h (2023).
Event maximum speed: Ryusei Yamanaka, 146.1mph/235.2km/h (race).

Qualifying:

Weather: Dry
Air: 30° **Humidity:** 69% **Track:** 42°

1	Fernandez	2m 09.542s
2	Ortola	2m 09.895s
3	Alonso	2m 10.015s
4	Suzuki	2m 10.128s
5	Kelso	2m 10.278s
6	Lunetta	2m 10.289s
7	Piqueras	2m 10.512s
8	Veijer	2m 10.518s
9	Almansa	2m 10.579s
10	Rueda	2m 10.747s
11	Holgado	2m 10.814s
12	Yamanaka	2m 10.835s
13	Nepa	2m 10.868s
14	Carraro	2m 10.970s
15	Munoz	2m 11.055s
16	Rossi	2m 11.084s
17	Furusato	2m 11.198s
18	Ogden	2m 11.314s
Q1		
19	Bertelle	2m 11.357s
20	Roulstone	2m 11.449s
21	Esteban	2m 11.509s
22	O'Shea	2m 11.576s
23	Farioli	2m 11.847s
24	Buasri	2m 11.948s
25	Zurutuza	2m 12.069s
26	Dettwiler	2m 12.803s

Fastest race laps

1	Alonso	2m 11.047s
2	Munoz	2m 11.139s
3	Furusato	2m 11.245s
4	Yamanaka	2m 11.313s
5	Rueda	2m 11.338s
6	Bertelle	2m 11.369s
7	Suzuki	2m 11.376s
8	Veijer	2m 11.398s
9	Ortola	2m 11.437s
10	Kelso	2m 11.454s
11	Nepa	2m 11.516s
12	Piqueras	2m 11.614s
13	Carraro	2m 11.817s
14	Almansa	2m 11.817s
15	Farioli	2m 11.821s
16	Roulstone	2m 11.821s
17	Lunetta	2m 11.844s
18	Ogden	2m 12.015s
19	Fernandez	2m 12.067s
20	O'Shea	2m 12.197s
21	Buasri	2m 12.199s
22	Zurutuza	2m 12.245s
23	Dettwiler	2m 12.369s

Championship Points

1	Alonso	396
2	Holgado	236
3	Veijer	236
4	Ortola	217
5	Munoz	162
6	Fernandez	153
7	Rueda	144
8	Piqueras	137
9	Kelso	134
10	Furusato	128
11	Yamanaka	120
12	Lunetta	112
13	Nepa	93
14	Suzuki	88
15	Roulstone	58
16	Bertelle	56
17	Esteban	45
18	Rossi	33
19	Farioli	32
20	Ogden	23
21	Carraro	22
22	Almansa	16
23	Zurutuza	13
24	Perez	3
25	Dettwiler	2
26	Buasri	1

Constructor Points

1	CFMOTO	396
2	KTM	320
3	Honda	284
4	Husqvarna	263
5	GASGAS	245

Above: Showdown, lap one. Bagnaia fends off Martin, with Marquez and Bastianini behind.

Above right: The Marquez brothers celebrate their Gresini partnership.

Right: Bastianini harried – then passed – Martin in the sprint.

Below right: Adios Aleix – 339 races later, Espargaro called time on his MotoGP career.
Photos: Gold & Goose

Opening spread: Martin celebrates that world champion feeling.
Photo: Andrea Wilson

AROUND rescheduled at the last minute. The coldest temperatures of the season. A hugely expanded Michelin tyre allocation to deal with the perils of riding in mid-November. And a host of names fired up to sign off in style. The final round of 2024 offered banana skins aplenty for Jorge Martin. Yet the Spaniard held his nerve in a tense finale to claim motorcycle racing's biggest prize.

Holding a 24-point advantage with 37 still left in play, he had to manage the season's final round. It was far from easy. Defending champion and two-year rival Bagnaia exerted maximum pressure throughout the weekend. He qualified on pole, won the sprint convincingly, leading from first lap to last, and did the same on Sunday. By then, Martin needed only ninth place to become the first independent-team champion in the four-stroke era. But he had to stay clear of any other rider's trouble, and be sure that he couldn't put a foot wrong.

The Martin of 12 months earlier might well have cracked under such pressure. As Bagnaia and Marc Marquez pulled clear, at one point, seven bikes were biting at his heels, threatening to relegate him to tenth. He remained as mistake-free on Sunday as on Saturday, however, and benefited from the defensive riding of mentor and close friend Aleix Espargaro just behind. Eventually, he was able to ease into a comfortable zone that meant the title was a mere formality.

He had shone so brightly in 2023, only to regret a litany of mistakes, but a cool head prevailed this time. Now it was Bagnaia who was left to reflect on seven race crashes, after becoming just the third rider in history to score 11 premier-class wins in a single season. His resigned air in *parc fermé* as he watched his rival celebrate spoke of his crushing disappointment.

There was nothing more he could have done. Having helped Marquez with a tow in qualifying, ensuring that there was at least one rider between himself and his title rival, he also tried to play mind games on the grid. A late switch to Michelin's soft rear tire briefly threw Martin, who stuck to his guns by selecting the medium.

After the dust had settled, Martin spoke frankly for the first time of having to exorcise some demons before the start of the season, having sought professional help that taught him to build his mental strength: "In January, I started to have a lot of fears, like 'I will never be MotoGP champion.' Thanks to my coach, I improved a lot … to focus on the hope of winning rather than the fear of losing. This helped me a lot."

There were other scores to be settled on Sunday – Marc Marquez versus Enea Bastianini for third overall. It went the way of the veteran by six points, Bastianini being miffed after coming off second best in a mid-race joust with Espargaro, which bumped him back into the chasing pack. Marquez had already said that the result didn't interest him, because "in a few years, nobody remembers who was third." He also spoke of how riding for the first time with an independent team had helped him rediscover the pleasure in racing: "It reminded me of the passion of motorbikes … everything a bit more casual and familiar. The perfect atmosphere to be reborn."

Then the question of top KTM rider, where GasGas-mounted rookie Acosta arrived three points clear of factory number-one Brad Binder. On Saturday, it was the rookie's turn for another no-score, while Binder recovered one point, but it was settled only on the last lap on Sunday. Binder gained a place by passing Bastianini; Acosta, suffering brake trouble, lost a place to Bezzecchi – and fifth overall went to the older rider by three points.

There were significant departures. Aleix Espargaro left Aprilia with a final top-five flourish, admitting that his accomplishments (among other things, 255 premier-class starts and Aprilia's first MotoGP win) had come not from natural ability, but dedication. "I always said hard work beats talent," he said. Two days later, he was in Honda livery, as HRC's new top test rider.

Miller also said goodbye to KTM, expressing disappointment in his second season, when difficulties in coming to terms with the new rear tyre meant that he couldn't repeat his promising first year with the factory team. He, too, was in different clothes for the test for Yamaha, leaving Aprilia as the only MotoGP make that he had yet to ride.

Oliveira was back, after having a plate and seven screws inserted in the right wrist he had broken in Indonesia, for a final run on an Aprilia, finishing in the points before also moving to Yamaha. Vinales was closing his Aprilia account as well, off to KTM

Michelin made special efforts for the low-grip track in the low temperatures, with an astonishing 1,400 tyres, offering four instead of three front tyre choices, and three instead of two rear.

In Moto3, Honda had withdrawn the new engine launched to serial disappointment at Sepang. The problem there had been overheating, which would hardly have been an issue in the weak November sunshine of Europe – but better safe than sorry.

The weekend was heavily dedicated to Valencia, the usual season-end venue, with moving musical tributes on the starting grid and an online auction to raise funds. One notable item donated was Maverick Vinales's 2013 Moto3 title-winning KTM. "I thought it was the right thing to do," he said.

FIM WORLD CHAMPIONSHIP

MOTOGP SPRINT RACE – 12 laps

Bagnaia closed his qualifying account as he needed to close his weekend – fastest for his sixth pole, third in a row. Home-track specialist Espargaro was alongside and Marc Marquez third, having followed Bagnaia throughout Q2, benefiting from his stated aim of helping anyone to get between him and his rival.

Martin had had an earlier stab at pole, but ended up fourth. The main protagonists would start the races effectively in line astern. Alongside him, team-mate Morbidelli and Acosta; Bagnaia's team-mate, Bastianini, was in the middle of row three. Would they be able, or inclined, to help either?

Bastianini got the jump into the first turn; Bagnaia seized the advantage up the hill. Martin skirmished for second, but Bastianini was obstinate, holding the place for two laps as his team-mate gained a four-tenths advantage.

Martin pounced at the end of the straight at the start of lap three, and the first three positions seemed set. Bagnaia was almost 1.5 seconds clear by half-distance and unfaltering to the end.

Likewise, Martin, but Bastianini was never more than a few tenths away, although busy holding Alex Marquez and Espargaro at bay, the latter having recovered from eighth on lap one.

Bastianini's usual late pace told, and into the first-gear Turn Five, he launched a desperate inside attack on Martin, who had little choice but to lift and cede second.

Espargaro passed Alex Marquez with two laps to go and narrowly held on; likewise, Morbidelli kept Marc at bay, Bezzecchi and Binder glued on behind, then Quartararo, who missed the last point by two-tenths.

Marc's race was spoiled after a first-lap collision with Acosta, which put the rookie off-track and out of the race, minus most of his GasGas's bodywork.

Bagnaia's recovery of five points cut Martin's lead to 19. The fight was not over.

MOTOGP RACE – 24 laps

Again, Bagnaia grabbed the initiative on the run to Turn One, with Martin rising from fourth to second, ahead of Marc Marquez, Bastianini, Espargaro and Acosta. Despite protestations to the contrary, Marquez soon showed that beating Bastianini to third in the championship was a priority, and that he wasn't there to help either of the main protagonists, taking a fully committed second off Martin at the start of lap two, and tagging on to the back of Bagnaia's rear wheel.

Soon, the lead pair began breaking clear of Martin. The Pramac rider wasn't looking entirely comfortable, at least until close ally Espargaro became his closest rival starting lap three, thanks to a clean pass on Bastianini at the Turn Five hairpin. Keen to catch Marquez, Bastianini displayed an air of desperation in his riding. His immediate attempts to get back into fourth were thwarted as the Aprilia rider responded aggressively, and at the start of lap eight, he ran wide and lost three places into the first corner.

Espargaro was determined to lend Martin a helping hand, after towing him around to a fast lap in qualifying, and his tactics to thwart the second factory Ducati later drew criticism. "I don't think it was correct for him to ride like this in his final race," bemoaned Bastianini. Aprilia's 'Captain' had an immediate retort: "In the last laps, I was waiting for him to fight, but he was three seconds behind me. With a factory Ducati!"

As Alex Marquez, Acosta, Morbidelli, Binder and Bezzecchi all sat closely behind the fight for third in the first seven laps, there was a real air of tension. One significant mistake, and Martin would no longer be in a championship winning position. Yet that tension was alleviated after Bastianini's run-off, which dropped him to seventh. His subsequent fighting with Morbidelli splintered the group, leaving Martin, Espargaro and Alex Marquez clear in the fight for third.

Above: Coach Fonsi Nieto (*top left*), Pramac team manager Gino Borsoi (*alongside Martin*) and Martin's father, Angel (*below Borsoi*), lead the victory cheers.

Top right: Espargaro plays blocker to Bastianini and Acosta.

Above right: Rookie of the year Diogo Moreira secured a brilliant maiden podium.

Above far right: An impassive Bagnaia in *parc fermé*.

Right: Last-lap battle. Canet leads Gonzalez, Ogura and Moreira in the Moto2 finale.

Below right: Holgado and Piqueras flank Alonso on the Moto3 podium.

Below far right: Alonso heads the pack on his way to a record 14th win of the season.

Photos: Gold & Goose

As the season edged toward its end, Marc Marquez made several threats to Bagnaia's supremacy. He shaved three-tenths off the lead on lap 20, getting to within half a second. Yet this was textbook Bagnaia, saving himself before a final push. That inevitable late rally left him clear to win an 18th race of the season, including sprints, by 1.4 seconds.

His 11th Sunday win meant that he joined Marquez (13), Doohan (12) and Rossi (11) with more than ten in one season, outranking Stoner by one as the most successful Ducati rider – although in a season with 20, rather than 18 races.

Ultimately, however, it would count for little. By lap 16, it was clear that Martin could breathe, as he pulled clear in third, with Espargaro fending off Alex Marquez behind. "With seven laps to go was a difficult moment," he said. "I started to remember a lot of moments in all my career. But then I said, 'Jorge, you need to finish the job. Nothing is done until you go on the finish line!'" It wasn't a thrilling finale to live long in the memory. Yet Martin stuck to his habit of the previous months, holding it together to become the first satellite-team rider since Rossi in 2001, in the pre-MotoGP two-stroke era, to win a premier-class crown.

While far from happy, Bagnaia was predictably gracious in defeat. "I don't want to talk too much. This is Jorge's moment," he said from behind a grimace in *parc fermé*.

Not even losing fourth to Alex Marquez two laps from the flag could deflate Espargaro, who enjoyed a fitting finale. As Acosta faded late on with brake issues, Binder rescued an impressive sixth, coming home ahead of an incandescent Bastianini and Morbidelli. Bezzecchi was ninth, in his final race for VR46, just ahead of a disappointed Acosta and Fabio Quartararo, encouraged by the fact that he was just over ten seconds behind the winner, the closest all year.

Oliveira and Miller chased behind; Zarco, in 14th, was top Honda rider once more, while Vinales finally passed a fading Raul Fernandez for 15th and the last point after another anonymous outing in his Aprilia farewell. Marini missed the points by less than two seconds; Pirro, riding Di Giannantonio's VR46 Ducati, was a distant 20th; the unfortunate Joan Mir the only faller, for his tenth Sunday non-finish of the year.

MOTO2 RACE – 21 laps

After 68 races without a Moto2 win, Canet was finally making a habit of it. He dominated every practice session for his sixth pole of the season, ahead of Gonzalez and front-row second-timer van den Goorbergh.

Ogura, with nothing to prove, was in the middle of row two, between Dixon and Moreira, each with championship business in hand – Dixon within 20 points of a top-five in his last ride for the Aspar team, Moreira one point clear of Agius in the rookie battle.

Gonzalez led away, chased by Ogura, Moreira and a charging Salac, up to second on lap two. Canet had muffed the start, 11th out of the first chicane, ninth by the end of lap one, but recovering quickly.

His climb was aided by a first-lap collision between Lopez, Navarro and Dixon, the latter two crashing out. The lead group was cut further when van den Goorbergh torpedoed Vietti at the start of the second lap at Turn One when avoiding Oncu in the braking zone. The first two fell, Oncu ran off as well.

Suddenly, Canet was fourth. He made swift progress past Salac and Ogura before pouncing on Gonzalez with a daring last-turn move at the close of lap four.

From there, he gradually stretched away, while Moreira passed Salac to sit seemingly powerless inches behind Ogura, thanks to the champion's braking prowess.

At the end, Gonzalez attempted to make a fight of it, slashing tenths out of Canet's 1.1-second lead, to begin the final lap just two-tenths behind. And Ogura and Moreira's late rhythm was such that they were less than a second down in a tense finale.

Gonzalez was never quite close enough to pounce, Canet standing firm to win by just 0.09 of a second. Moreira set about Ogura at the start of the penultimate lap, only to be slapped back to fourth at Turn Ten. The rookie attacked again, however, finally securing a thrilling debut podium thanks to a brilliant pass at the final corner. He was confirmed as Rookie of the Year, after Agius dropped from sixth to

12th, suffering from sudden numbness in his right arm.

Salac took his best dry result of the year in fifth, while Garcia finally regained some of his early-season form with sixth, his best since Silverstone. That wasn't enough to retain third overall, however, Gonzalez's second vaulting him past his countryman.

Izan Guevara was a second adrift, followed by Lopez, who was narrowly ahead of the returned Aldeguer, in a strong last Moto2 outing. In spite of qualifying 18th and serving a long-lap for his Thai GP misdemeanour, he had even threatened to catch the podium runners until tyre wear slowed him. Chantra was tenth. Ramirez, Agius, a downbeat Arbolino, rookie Masia and Binder tussled to the end over the final points, with Aji missing out, less than a tenth behind.

MOTO3 RACE – 18 laps

Alonso claimed his seventh pole, his first for seven races, before another of those perfect race finishes. His seventh successive win was his 14th of the year, the most in GP history across all classes.

The fight for second was still alive, with Holgado and Veijer equal on points, Ortola a more daunting 19 behind. The last two lined up alongside Alonso on the front row; Holgado was in the middle of the second, between fast rookies Piqueras and Lunetta.

Alonso led away for a typical Catalunya Moto3 race, a big lead pack swapping places over and over under braking after slipstreaming down the long straight. Holgado was next up front over the line, then Fernandez's Honda for a spell, then Holgado again.

There was still an air of inevitability about this contest once the 18-year old posted fastest lap with four to go and moved back to the front of a 12-rider lead group. There were a few nervy moments, not least when he was elbowed wide and back to fifth by Holgado on lap 16 at Turn Four. But he regained the lead on the penultimate lap and successfully defended from Holgado on the last, even though the latter posted a faster final lap.

Piqueras inherited third after Fernandez was given a three-second penalty for cutting across the first chicane on the final lap, which dropped him to 11th. Rueda came through to fourth, from Yamanaka. Munoz, Furusato, Roulstone, Ortola and Veijer completed the top ten, Veijer being 2.7 seconds down, unable to produce his usual late-race speed and ceding second overall to Holgado.

Ogden was 17th, a tenth out of the points; Red Bull Rookie champion Alvaro Carpe was 19th, just behind Lunetta, who had run a double long-lap for dangerous riding. Nepa crashed out; Rossi also was given a double long-lap penalty, for dawdling in practice.

WORLD CHAMPIONSHIP POINTS 2024

MotoGP – Riders

Position	Rider	Nationality	Machine	QATAR Sprint	QATAR MotoGP	PORTUGAL Sprint	PORTUGAL MotoGP	USA Sprint	USA MotoGP	SPAIN Sprint	SPAIN MotoGP	FRANCE Sprint	FRANCE MotoGP	CATALUNYA Sprint	CATALUNYA MotoGP	ITALY Sprint	ITALY MotoGP	NETHERLANDS Sprint	NETHERLANDS MotoGP	GERMANY Sprint	GERMANY MotoGP
1	Jorge Martin	SPA	Ducati	12	16	7	25	7	13	12	R	12	25	6	20	R	16	9	20	12	R
2	Francesco Bagnaia	ITA	Ducati	6	25	6	R	2	11	R	25	R	16	R	25	12	25	12	25	7	25
3	Marc Marquez	SPA	Ducati	5	13	9	0	9	R	4	20	9	20	9	16	9	13	R	6	4	20
4	Enea Bastianini	ITA	Ducati	4	11	4	20	4	16	R	11	6	13	5	0	R	20	6	16	6	13
5	Brad Binder	RSA	KTM	9	20	R	13	0	7	R	10	0	8	R	8	4	6	4	10	2	7
6	Pedro Acosta	SPA	KTM	2	7	3	16	6	20	9	6	4	R	7	3	7	11	0	R	0	9
7	Maverick Vinales	SPA	Aprilia	1	6	12	R	12	25	R	7	7	11	2	4	5	8	7	11	3	4
8	Alex Marquez	SPA	Ducati	3	10	0	R	0	1	R	13	0	6	0	9	2	7	2	9	1	16
9	Franco Morbidelli	ITA	Ducati	0	0	0	0	0	R	6	R	0	9	0	R	6	10	1	7	5	11
10	Fabio Di Giannantonio	ITA	Ducati	R	9	R	6	R	10	0	9	3	10	4	11	3	9	5	13	0	R
11	Aleix Espargaro	SPA	Aprilia	7	8	2	8	5	9	R	R	5	7	12	13	1	5	R	-	-	-
12	Marco Bezzecchi	ITA	Ducati	0	2	0	10	0	8	R	16	R	R	1	5	0	3	0	R	0	8
13	Fabio Quartararo	FRA	Yamaha	0	5	1	9	0	4	5	1	0	R	0	7	R	0	3	4	0	5
14	Jack Miller	AUS	KTM	0	0	5	11	3	3	0	R	2	R	3	R	0	0	0	5	0	3
15	Miguel Oliveira	POR	Aprilia	0	1	0	7	0	5	2	0	0	R	R	6	R	2	0	1	9	10
16	Raul Fernandez	SPA	Aprilia	0	R	0	R	1	6	0	5	1	5	R	10	0	4	0	8	0	6
17	Johann Zarco	FRA	Honda	0	4	R	1	R	R	0	R	0	4	R	0	0	0	0	3	0	0
18	Alex Rins	SPA	Yamaha	0	0	R	3	0	R	0	3	R	1	0	0	0	1	0	R	-	-
19	Takaaki Nakagami	JPN	Honda	0	0	0	2	R	R	0	2	0	2	0	2	0	R	0	0	0	2
20	Augusto Fernandez	SPA	KTM	0	0	0	5	R	2	3	R	0	3	0	R	0	R	0	2	0	0
21	Joan Mir	SPA	Honda	0	3	0	4	R	R	1	4	R	R	0	1	R	R	0	R	0	0
22	Luca Marini	ITA	Honda	0	0	0	0	0	0	R	0	0	0	0	0	0	0	R	0	0	1
23	Pol Espargaro	SPA	KTM	-	-	-	-	-	-	-	-	-	-	-	-	1	0	-	-	-	-
24	Dani Pedrosa	SPA	KTM	-	-	-	-	-	-	7	R	-	-	-	-	-	-	-	-	-	-
25	Stefan Bradl	GER	Honda	-	-	-	-	-	-	R	0	-	-	-	-	0	0	-	-	0	0
26	Remy Gardner	AUS	Yamaha	-	-	-	-	-	-	-	-	-	-	-	-	-	-	-	-	0	0
27	Andrea Iannone	ITA	Ducati	-	-	-	-	-	-	-	-	-	-	-	-	-	-	-	-	-	-
28	Lorenzo Savadori	ITA	Aprilia	-	-	-	-	-	-	0	R	-	-	-	-	0	0	R	-	-	-
29	Michele Pirro	ITA	Ducati	-	-	-	-	-	-	-	-	-	-	-	-	-	-	-	-	-	-

R - Did Not Finish DNS - Did Not Start DSQ - Disqualified

MotoGP - Teams

Position	Team	QATAR Sprint	QATAR MotoGP	PORTUGAL Sprint	PORTUGAL MotoGP	USA Sprint	USA MotoGP	SPAIN Sprint	SPAIN MotoGP	FRANCE Sprint	FRANCE MotoGP	CATALUNYA Sprint	CATALUNYA MotoGP	ITALY Sprint	ITALY MotoGP	NETHERLANDS Sprint	NETHERLANDS MotoGP	GERMANY Sprint	GERMANY MotoGP
1	Ducati Lenovo Team	10	36	10	20	6	27	0	36	6	29	5	25	12	45	18	41	13	38
2	Prima Pramac Racing	12	16	7	25	7	13	18	0	12	34	6	20	6	26	10	27	17	11
3	Gresini Racing MotoGP	8	23	9	0	9	1	4	33	9	26	9	25	11	20	2	15	5	36
4	Aprilia Racing	8	14	14	8	17	34	0	7	12	18	14	17	6	13	7	11	3	4
5	Pertamina Enduro VR46 Racing	0	11	0	16	0	18	0	25	3	10	5	16	3	12	5	13	0	8
6	Red Bull KTM Factory Racing	9	20	5	24	3	10	0	10	2	8	3	8	4	6	4	15	2	10
7	Red Bull GASGAS Tech3	2	7	3	21	6	22	12	6	4	3	7	3	7	11	0	2	0	9
8	Monster Energy Yamaha MotoGP	0	5	1	12	0	4	5	4	0	1	0	7	0	1	3	4	0	5
9	Trackhouse Racing	0	1	0	7	1	11	2	13	1	5	0	16	0	6	0	9	9	16
10	LCR Honda	0	4	0	3	0	0	0	2	0	6	0	2	0	0	0	3	0	2
11	Repsol Honda Team	0	3	0	4	0	0	1	4	0	0	0	1	0	0	0	0	0	1

Compiled by PETER McLAREN

GREAT BRITAIN Sprint	GREAT BRITAIN MotoGP	AUSTRIA Sprint	AUSTRIA MotoGP	ARAGON Sprint	ARAGON MotoGP	SAN MARINO Sprint	SAN MARINO MotoGP	EMILIA-ROMAGNA Sprint	EMILIA-ROMAGNA MotoGP	INDONESIA Sprint	INDONESIA MotoGP	JAPAN Sprint	JAPAN MotoGP	AUSTRALIA Sprint	AUSTRALIA MotoGP	THAILAND Sprint	THAILAND MotoGP	MALAYSIA Sprint	MALAYSIA MotoGP	SOLIDARITY Sprint	SOLIDARITY MotoGP	Points total	Position
9	20	9	20	9	20	12	1	9	20	0	25	6	20	12	20	9	20	12	20	7	16	**508**	1
R	16	12	25	1	R	9	20	12	R	12	16	12	25	6	16	7	25	R	25	12	25	**498**	2
R	13	R	13	12	25	5	25	6	16	7	R	7	16	9	25	6	5	9	4	3	20	**392**	3
12	25	6	16	3	11	6	16	7	25	9	R	9	13	7	11	12	2	7	16	9	9	**386**	4
6	R	3	11	4	13	3	13	4	0	0	8	R	10	R	9	1	10	3	R	1	10	**217**	5
5	7	0	3	7	16	4	0	5	R	4	20	R	R	R	-	R	16	1	11	R	6	**215**	6
2	3	0	9	0	R	0	0	0	10	3	10	1	R	R	8	0	9	0	9	0	1	**190**	7
4	9	0	6	6	R	0	10	0	7	0	R	3	R	R	1	5	6	6	13	5	13	**173**	8
R	6	4	8	R	10	7	R	1	11	5	13	5	11	5	10	4	R	4	2	4	8	**173**	9
1	11	-	-	0	8	R	7	0	2	1	R	4	8	3	13	2	13	-	-	-	-	**165**	10
7	10	7	7	R	6	0	R	0	8	0	R	R	7	2	0	0	7	0	3	6	11	**163**	11
R	8	2	10	0	9	R	11	2	13	6	11	0	9	R	0	3	R	0	7	2	7	**153**	12
0	5	0	0	2	R	1	9	3	9	0	9	0	4	0	7	0	0	5	10	0	5	**113**	13
3	4	5	0	0	1	2	8	0	0	0	R	2	6	R	5	0	11	2	-	0	3	**87**	14
0	R	0	4	5	R	0	5	0	6	-	-	-	-	-	-	-	-	-	-	0	4	**75**	15
0	R	0	R	0	0	0	0	0	3	0	6	0	1	4	6	0	R	0	0	0	0	**66**	16
0	2	0	0	R	3	0	4	0	1	2	7	0	5	R	4	0	8	R	5	0	2	**55**	17
-	-	R	0	0	7	0	0	-	-	0	5	0	0	0	3	0	R	0	8	0	0	**31**	18
0	1	0	2	0	5	0	3	0	0	0	4	R	3	0	0	0	3	0	-	0	0	**31**	19
0	0	R	1	0	4	0	R	0	0	R	R	0	R	1	0	0	R	0	6	0	0	**27**	20
0	R	0	0	0	2	-	-	0	5	R	R	R	R	0	R	0	1	0	R	0	R	**21**	21
0	0	0	R	0	0	0	R	0	4	0	R	0	2	0	2	0	4	0	1	0	0	**14**	22
-	-	1	5	-	-	0	6	-	-	-	-	-	-	-	-	-	-	-	-	-	-	**12**	23
-	-	-	-	-	-	-	-	-	-	-	-	-	-	-	-	-	-	-	-	-	-	**7**	24
-	-	R	0	-	-	R	2	-	-	-	-	-	-	-	-	-	-	-	-	0	0	**2**	25
0	0	-	-	-	-	-	-	-	-	-	-	0	0	-	-	-	-	-	-	-	-	**0**	26
-	-	-	-	-	-	-	-	-	-	-	-	-	-	-	-	-	-	0	0	-	-	**0**	27
-	-	0	0	-	-	-	-	-	-	-	-	0	R	0	R	0	R	0	0	-	-	**0**	28
-	-	-	-	-	-	-	-	-	-	-	-	-	-	-	-	-	-	-	-	0	0	**0**	29

GREAT BRITAIN Sprint	GREAT BRITAIN MotoGP	AUSTRIA Sprint	AUSTRIA MotoGP	ARAGON Sprint	ARAGON MotoGP	SAN MARINO Sprint	SAN MARINO MotoGP	EMILIA-ROMAGNA Sprint	EMILIA-ROMAGNA MotoGP	INDONESIA Sprint	INDONESIA MotoGP	JAPAN Sprint	JAPAN MotoGP	AUSTRALIA Sprint	AUSTRALIA MotoGP	THAILAND Sprint	THAILAND MotoGP	MALAYSIA Sprint	MALAYSIA MotoGP	CATALUNYA Sprint	CATALUNYA MotoGP	Points total	Position
12	41	18	41	4	11	15	36	19	25	21	16	21	38	13	27	19	27	7	41	21	34	**884**	1
9	26	13	28	9	30	19	1	10	31	5	38	11	31	17	30	13	20	16	22	11	24	**681**	2
4	22	0	19	18	25	5	35	6	23	7	0	10	16	9	26	11	11	15	17	8	33	**565**	3
9	13	7	16	0	6	0	0	0	18	3	10	1	7	2	8	0	16	0	12	6	12	**353**	4
1	19	2	10	0	17	0	18	2	15	7	11	4	17	3	13	5	13	0	7	2	7	**318**	5
9	4	8	11	4	14	5	21	4	0	0	8	2	16	0	14	1	21	5	-	1	13	**304**	6
5	7	0	4	7	20	4	0	5	0	4	20	0	0	1	0	0	16	1	17	0	6	**242**	7
0	5	0	0	2	7	1	9	3	9	0	14	0	4	0	10	0	0	5	18	0	5	**144**	8
0	0	0	4	5	0	0	5	0	9	0	6	0	1	4	6	0	0	0	0	0	4	**141**	9
0	3	0	2	0	8	0	7	0	1	2	11	0	8	0	4	0	11	0	5	0	2	**86**	10
0	0	0	0	0	2	-	0	0	9	0	0	0	2	0	2	0	5	0	1	0	0	**35**	11

Moto2

Position	Rider	Nationality	Machine	Qatar	Portugal	United States	Spain	France	Catalunya	Italy	Netherlands	Germany	Great Britain	Austria	Aragon	San Marino	Emilia-Romagna	Indonesia	Japan	Australia	Thailand	Malaysia	Catalunya	Points total
1	Ai Ogura	JPN	Boscoscuro	13	11	9	10	20	25	11	25	16	2	-	8	25	13	20	20	13	20	R	13	274
2	Aron Canet	SPA	Kalex	6	25	7	-	10	R	10	R	R	20	13	R	20	20	25	0	20	25	8	25	234
3	Manuel Gonzalez	SPA	Kalex	11	16	3	16	0	0	20	7	4	11	3	11	13	5	8	25	10	7	5	20	195
4	Sergio Garcia	SPA	Boscoscuro	16	10	25	13	25	20	13	16	9	13	2	R	4	R	R	2	7	4	2	10	191
5	Fermin Aldeguer	SPA	Boscoscuro	0	13	16	25	9	R	R	20	25	4	0	R	10	11	13	4	25	R	-	7	182
6	Alonso Lopez	SPA	Boscoscuro	25	0	13	R	16	9	16	8	6	7	20	13	0	7	16	7	R	5	3	8	179
7	Celestino Vietti	ITA	Kalex	7	9	6	7	-	R	9	6	11	16	25	6	R	25	4	9	-	-	25	R	165
8	Jake Dixon	GBR	Kalex	-	-	0	R	16	4	13	20	25	16	25	11	R	0	3	R	9	13	R	-	155
9	Joe Roberts	USA	Kalex	9	20	20	20	13	8	25	-	8	R	7	R	3	10	10	0	-	-	-	-	153
10	Tony Arbolino	ITA	Kalex	0	4	5	9	8	7	0	10	7	R	11	20	16	16	9	5	8	R	11	3	149
11	Marcos Ramirez	SPA	Kalex	10	7	11	R	1	DSQ	6	9	0	1	10	9	1	8	6	0	6	16	10	5	116
12	Somkiat Chantra	THA	Kalex	5	6	0	6	11	R	7	11	10	R	8	10	2	2	R	-	-	13	7	6	104
13	Diogo Moreira	BRA	Kalex	0	0	2	R	0	R	5	0	13	R	0	0	8	R	-	8	11	11	6	16	80
14	Albert Arenas	SPA	Kalex	8	8	4	11	7	10	0	R	0	8	0	0	7	0	2	0	3	8	4	DSQ	80
15	Jeremy Alcoba	SPA	Kalex	4	5	8	8	5	13	R	3	2	9	0	0	0	1	3	13	5	R	R	-	79
16	Filip Salac	CZE	Kalex	0	-	1	5	4	4	R	-	R	6	5	9	6	1	16	2	2	1	11	-	73
17	Izan Guevara	SPA	Kalex	R	0	0	4	6	-	8	0	3	0	4	R	0	3	DSQ	6	0	10	16	9	69
18	Senna Agius	AUS	Kalex	0	2	0	R	3	11	0	5	5	6	1	0	5	9	R	0	16	R	R	4	67
19	Darryn Binder	RSA	Kalex	0	1	0	0	2	2	R	1	0	10	9	7	6	0	11	1	4	R	R	1	55
20	Deniz Oncu	TUR	Kalex	1	0	0	2	0	0	3	-	-	5	16	0	R	7	0	0	6	9	0	-	49
21	Barry Baltus	BEL	Kalex	20	3	0	R	R	0	0	0	0	R	3	0	0	5	0	9	R	0	0	-	40
22	Zonta van den Goorbergh	NED	Kalex	3	0	R	3	0	5	2	R	R	5	0	2	0	R	0	11	R	0	R	R	31
23	Jorge Navarro	SPA	Forward/Kalex	-	-	0	0	R	6	-	-	-	-	R	0	-	-	-	-	1	20	R	-	27
24	Dennis Foggia	ITA	Kalex	0	0	10	R	R	R	0	4	0	0	R	R	0	4	-	0	R	0	0	0	18
25	Xavier Artigas	SPA	Forward	0	-	0	R	0	0	0	0	0	0	R	0	0	0	10	0	0	0	0	-	10
26	Ayumu Sasaki	JPN	Kalex	R	R	-	-	0	R	R	R	0	0	0	4	0	0	0	0	3	-	-	-	7
27	Bo Bendsneyder	NED	Kalex	2	0	0	R	-	-	-	2	R	3	0	R	0	-	-	-	-	-	-	-	7
28	Jaume Masia	SPA	Kalex	0	0	0	R	0	3	0	0	1	R	0	0	0	R	R	0	R	0	0	2	6
29	Mario Aji	INA	Kalex	0	0	R	0	-	1	1	0	R	R	1	0	0	0	R	1	0	0	0	0	4
30	Matteo Ferrari	ITA	Kalex	-	-	-	1	-	-	-	-	-	-	-	-	R	-	-	-	-	-	-	-	1
31	Xavi Cardelus	AND	Kalex	0	R	0	0	0	0	-	-	R	0	0	0	0	R	0	0	0	0	0	0	0
32	Marcel Schrotter	GER	Kalex	-	-	-	-	-	-	-	-	-	-	-	-	-	-	-	-	-	-	-	-	0
33	Alex Escrig	SPA	Forward	0	0	-	-	-	0	0	0	-	-	R	0	-	0	R	0	0	-	-	-	0
34	Mattia Pasini	ITA	Boscoscuro	-	-	-	-	-	-	0	0	-	-	-	0	-	R	-	-	-	-	-	-	0
35	Daniel Muñoz	SPA	Kalex	-	-	-	-	-	-	0	R	0	0	-	-	-	-	0	-	-	-	-	0	0
36	Roberto Garcia	SPA	Kalex	-	-	-	-	-	-	-	-	R	-	-	-	-	-	-	-	-	-	-	R	0
37	Harrison Voight	AUS	Kalex	-	-	-	-	-	-	-	-	-	-	-	-	-	-	-	-	-	0	0	R	-	0
38	Stefano Manzi	ITA	Kalex	-	-	-	-	-	-	-	-	-	-	-	-	-	-	-	-	-	-	-	0	0
39	Helmi Azman	MAL	Kalex	-	-	-	-	-	-	-	-	-	-	-	-	-	-	-	-	-	-	0	-	0
40	Andrea Migno	ITA	Kalex	-	-	-	-	-	-	-	-	-	-	-	-	-	-	-	-	-	-	0	-	0
41	Alberto Surra	ITA	Boscoscuro	-	-	-	-	-	-	-	-	-	-	-	-	-	-	-	-	-	-	R	-	0
42	Khairul Idham Pawi	MAL	Kalex	-	-	-	-	-	-	-	-	-	-	-	-	-	-	-	-	-	-	DNS	-	0
43	Simone Corsi	ITA	Forward	-	-	-	-	-	-	-	-	-	-	-	-	-	-	-	-	-	-	0	-	0
44	Unai Orradre	SPA	Forward	-	-	-	-	-	-	-	-	-	-	-	0	-	-	-	-	-	-	-	-	0

R - Did Not Finish DNS - Did Not Start DSQ - Disqualified

Moto3

Position	Rider	Nationality	Machine	Qatar	Portugal	United States	Spain	France	Catalunya	Italy	Netherlands	Germany	Great Britain	Austria	Aragon	San Marino	Emilia-Romagna	Indonesia	Japan	Australia	Thailand	Malaysia	Catalunya	Points total
1	David Alonso	COL	CFMOTO	25	13	25	5	25	25	25	11	25	20	25	13	9	25	25	25	25	25	25	25	421
2	Daniel Holgado	SPA	GASGAS	20	25	20	9	20	10	2	5	9	13	16	7	20	13	10	13	20	4	R	20	256
3	Collin Veijer	NED	Husqvarna	11	10	R	25	16	13	20	20	0	16	11	20	11	16	R	20	0	16	11	6	242
4	Ivan Ortola	SPA	KTM	7	16	R	16	11	20	10	25	16	25	7	4	16	11	7	0	R	13	13	7	224
5	David Munoz	SPA	KTM	0	7	11	20	R	11	11	16	8	4	20	9	R	R	16	8	11	10	0	10	172
6	Adrian Fernandez	SPA	Honda	R	6	5	10	10	6	8	9	13	8	10	5	3	8	20	16	16	0	R	5	158
7	Jose Antonio Rueda	SPA	KTM	R	20	-	-	8	16	1	13	R	7	9	25	R	6	5	11	7	0	16	13	157
8	Angel Piqueras	SPA	Honda	4	R	16	6	6	4	5	8	11	R	13	R	25	20	13	R	6	R	R	16	153
9	Joel Kelso	AUS	KTM	8	11	9	11	3	R	4	4	5	9	8	11	10	9	8	0	5	9	10	4	138
10	Taiyo Furusato	JPN	Honda	16	0	R	0	2	R	13	3	20	-	1	10	13	3	R	7	9	11	20	9	137
11	Ryusei Yamanaka	JPN	KTM	R	R	13	13	9	5	16	6	10	10	3	0	0	1	0	10	10	5	9	11	131
12	Luca Lunetta	ITA	Honda	1	0	0	0	5	9	9	10	R	-	0	16	7	10	11	R	8	20	6	0	112
13	Stefano Nepa	ITA	KTM	10	9	0	7	0	3	R	7	4	11	R	3	2	2	1	6	13	7	8	R	93
14	Tatsuki Suzuki	JPN	Husqvarna	9	4	10	0	7	1	R	R	7	6	4	2	8	5	9	9	1	6	R-	3	91
15	Jacob Roulstone	AUS	GASGAS	6	5	8	4	4	8	7	2	R	0	2	0	4	0	0	0	3	1	4	8	66
16	Matteo Bertelle	ITA	Honda	R	DSQ	6	2	R	0	6	0	1	5	5	6	R	7	4	5	2	0	7	1	57
17	Joel Esteban	SPA	CFMOTO	5	8	7	R	13	2	0	1	2	3	0	1	0	0	2	1	0	R	R	-	45
18	Riccardo Rossi	ITA	KTM	13	R	0	0	R	R	3	0	0	2	6	0	R	0	R	2	4	3	R	R	33
19	Filippo Farioli	ITA	Honda	R	0	1	3	R	7	0	0	3	0	0	R	6	4	R	3	R	2	3	0	32
20	Scott Ogden	GBR	Honda	3	2	DSQ	0	R	0	0	0	6	R	0	0	1	0	3	0	0	8	R	0	23
21	Nicola Carraro	ITA	KTM	2	1	4	8	0	0	0	0	0	1	0	-	0	0	6	R	R	0	R	0	22
22	David Almansa	SPA	Honda	-	-	-	1	1	R	0	R	0	0	0	0	0	5	0	R	4	R	0	5	2	18
23	Xabi Zurutuza	SPA	KTM	-	-	3	0	0	0	R	0	0	R	0	8	0	R	0	0	0	0	2	0	13
24	Vicente Perez	SPA	KTM/Honda	R	3	-	0	-	-	-	-	-	R	0	-	R	-	-	-	-	-	-	-	3
25	Noah Dettwiler	SWI	KTM	0	0	2	0	0	0	0	0	0	0	0	0	0	0	R	0	0	0	0	0	2
26	Tatchakorn Buasri	THA	Honda	0	0	-	0	0	0	0	0	0	0	R	0	R	R	R	0	0	1	0	-	1
27	Eddie O'Shea	GBR	Honda	-	-	-	-	-	-	-	-	-	-	-	-	-	-	-	-	0	R	0	0	0
28	Joshua Whatley	GBR	Honda	0	0	0	0	0	0	0	0	-	-	-	-	-	-	-	-	-	-	-	-	0
29	Jakob Rosenthaler	AUT	Husqvarna	-	-	-	-	-	-	-	-	-	-	-	0	-	0	-	-	-	-	-	-	0
30	Alvaro Carpe	SPA	KTM	-	-	-	-	-	-	-	-	-	-	-	-	-	-	-	-	-	-	-	0	0
31	Rei Wakamatsu	JPN	Honda	-	-	-	-	-	-	-	-	-	-	-	-	-	-	-	0	-	-	-	-	0
32	Danial Shahril	MAL	Honda	-	-	-	-	-	-	-	-	0	-	-	-	-	-	-	-	-	-	-	-	0
33	Hamad Al Sahouti	QAT	Honda	-	0	-	-	-	-	-	-	-	-	-	-	-	-	-	-	-	-	-	-	0
34	Arbi Aditama	INA	Honda	-	-	-	-	-	0	-	-	-	-	-	0	-	R	-	-	-	-	-	-	0
35	Marcos Uriarte	SPA	CFMOTO	-	-	-	-	-	-	-	-	-	-	-	-	-	-	-	-	-	-	0	-	0

R - Did Not Finish DNS - Did Not Start DSQ - Disqualified

MotoE WORLD CHAMPIONSHIP
GREAT RACING, POOR RESPONSE

The sixth season of MotoE was electrically exciting on track, but left fans underwhelmed. NEIL MORRISON charts the season and assesses its importance...

Above: Close racing guaranteed. Garzo leads Casadei, Gutierrez, Torres, Granado, Zannone and the gang.

Top right: Kevin Zannone took two wins for the Aspar Team.

Above right: Four-times winner Garzo triumphed twice in Germany.

Above far right: Consistent Casadei just failed to retain the title.

Right: Impressive rookie Oscar Gutierrez, heading seasoned campaigner Jordi Torres at a wet Sachsenring. The veteran would deny him a podium, however.

Photos: Gold & Goose

HOLDING station or fading from the radar? That was the question hanging over MotoE in 2024, the second year in which the series enjoyed full world championship status. As often in its six-year history, the racing delivered across eight rounds and 16 races. But its impact on the racing world remained muted at best, forgotten at worst.

Perhaps a freeze in technical development was partly to blame. As 2023 was a year of great change, the technical novelties were limited in 2024. Eyeing substantial changes for the near future, Ducati's stunning V21L, first raced in 2023, remained largely unchanged. Innovation was left to Michelin, whose new tyre compounds were largely responsible for the class becoming faster, with new lap and race records at all eight tracks.

Even if the racing world remained largely indifferent, MotoE continued to offer consistently close racing. Hector Garzo won out in a close and, at times, chaotic year, a mid-season run of six straight podiums enough to give him his maiden world title with a race to spare. But usually it was a close-run thing. The average winning gap in dry races was 0.408 of a second, and a second covered the podium on seven of 16 occasions. There was a total of six winners, five pole-sitters and eight podium finishers. Simply put, 2023's variety hadn't been a one-off.

Four different names topped the title charts, indicating an unpredictable championship fight that only calmed a bit after its summer hiatus. The reason for such variety was the forgiving nature of Ducati's V21L. Electronic controls took away something from a rider's right hand, a point the Italian factory aimed to address for 2025.

"We made sure the riders had more testing days during the winter," MotoE executive director Nicolas Goubert told MOTOCOURSE. "Previously, we also organised tests for replacement riders. Now we know after two sessions, the rider will be at ease. There are two factors: the weight has been reduced quite a lot, so there isn't such a big difference with a combustion-engine bike. Then, because of all the electronics, it's easier to ride. So you don't see highsides anymore.

"That's positive from one side, but on the other, some riders are complaining that the electronics are too intrusive and they cannot show their real potential because the bikes are too easy to ride. The riders were asked [at Misano] what should be the next step. I'd say 70 per cent asked for more freedom with the electronics, traction control mainly, and the anti-wheelie. So Ducati is working on this."

The format was largely unchanged from 2023: eight rounds of Saturday double-headers. The previous season's calendar was "too condensed" across four months; thus the championship began two months earlier in Portugal, before stops at Le Mans, Barcelona-Catalunya (replacing Silverstone), Mugello, Assen, the Sachsenring, Red Bull Ring and Misano.

As before, nine teams fielded two entries apiece. Dynavolt Intact GP, Felo Gresini, Openbank Aspar, Tech3 E-Racing, Ongetta SIC58 Squadra Corse and LCR E-Team returned; Axxis-MSI ably replaced HP Pons Los40, as they had done in Moto2. KLINT Forward Factory Team and Aruba Cloud MotoE – entering unsuccessfully with World Superbike legend Chaz Davies – came in for RNF MotoE and Prettl Pramac.

Defending champion Mattia Casadei was back, in LCR colours, after a triumphant year with HP Pons Los40. He would be pushed hardest by Garzo, with IntactGP for a second straight season, impressive rookie Oscar Gutierrez (Axxis-MSI), Kevin Zannoni – now with Openbank Aspar instead of Ongetta SIC58 – along with team-mate Jordi Torres, and Tech3 E-Racing duo Alessandro Zaccone and Nicholas Spinelli, who had switched from HP Pons Los40.

The tone was set from the first, after rain had played havoc with pre-season testing, leaving question marks over

who would start strongest. The podium from the final race of 2023 was repeated, as Spinelli took control, winning a close duel with Garzo and Casadei. Yet the Italian's mercurial nature soon became clear: having jumped the start in race two, he crashed out of the lead on the third lap after being told that he had a penalty to serve. That left Casadei free to edge Garzo and the impressive Gutierrez, with Eric Granado (LCR E-Team) and Torres ensuring one second covered the top five. Casadei left one point clear of Garzo in the standings.

The series resumed in France two months later, where Spinelli appeared to be a more complete contender after his Portuguese misdemeanour, claiming a convincing double victory. He broke clear of Zannoni and Casadei by 1.3 seconds in race one, edging Casadei in a fine late fight in race two. Again, Gutierrez showed strongly, third in race two, while compatriot Garzo fell from both after qualifying on pole. "I felt so bad, even that my career was ending," he recalled later. "It was a really good point for reflection on the work we needed to do. I made a change of mentality – to be clever and not make mistakes." Casadei (77 points) still led overall, but Spinelli (75) had closed right in.

Then the rounds came thick and fast. The title fight had an entirely different complexion after Barcelona, where Spinelli crashed out of both races and Casadei collected a lone sixth in race one, before falling from second later that afternoon. Gutierrez took an epic race-one win from Granado and Zannoni, who claimed his maiden victory in the second. Gutierrez was second, then Zaccone, on the podium for the first time in 2024. Now Zannoni (88 points) led Casadei (87), with Gutierrez (86) right in the mix.

The topsy-turvy results continued at Mugello, where Lukas Tulovic (Dynavolt Intact GP) high-sided out of the final turn, leading to a red flag in race one. It was restarted in the evening, after race two. Casadei won that, mugging long-time leader Zaccone on the last lap; Garzo was third.

Above: Defender Casadei heads Spinelli and the rest in a sunny season-opener in Portugal. They claimed a win apiece.

Top right: Eric Granado's season was interrupted by injury, but he bounced back with podiums at Misano.

Above centre right: Gresini's Matteo Ferrari was consistent, but winless.

Above right: Alessandro Zaccone – always a threat.
Photos: Gold & Goose

Inset, top: The futuristic Swedish Stark Varg costs more than £10,000. The name means 'Strong Wolf'.
Photo: Starc

Inset, below: Honda's CR-E Proto first raced in Japan in 2023.
Photo: HRC

Meanwhile, Zannoni had won race two, beating Casadei by two-tenths, while Granado was third. With Gutierrez eleventh and tenth, Casadei (132 points) and Zannoni (126) were breaking clear.

As it transpired, Garzo's podium was crucial to an upcoming charge. "Things really changed after Mugello," he said. "[From there,] I didn't doubt myself. Mugello was difficult for me every year, but third really started my rhythm."

Viewed one way, Assen was Garzo's round. He claimed a first MotoE victory in race one, backing it up with another podium. Yet Gutierrez was the standout star, recovering from a poor qualifying in 11th to fight through to second on each occasion. The first was slightly fortuitous, as Zaccone was disqualified from second for a front tyre pressure below the limit (he had led five out of the seven laps), allowing Torres into third. The second race was anything but, as he beat Garzo and Tulovic into second, a massive 1.9s back from Zaccone, who finally claimed a deserved win. Casadei was taken out of race one by Spinelli and struggled to eighth in race two, cutting his lead to two points from Zannoni (138) and Gutierrez (137).

Despite being the most chaotic weekend of the season, the German Grand Prix finally established some order in the title fight. Race one was red-flagged after a first-lap collision between Gutierrez and Granado, the restart running over five laps. And heavy rain plus lightning meant that there was a near interminable 90-minute wait for race two to get under way.

Challenging conditions resulted in several contenders coming apart. Gutierrez was handed a double long-lap for running into Granado from a wide line at Turn One. He jumped the start in the restart, which added a further two long-laps – four, in a race cut to five laps. His crash out in the long-lap lane added to the sense of slapstick. Both Casadei and Zannoni crashed in qualifying, starting from eighth and tenth respectively. And it became worse: the reigning champion had a penalty to serve after falling under yellow flags, while Zannoni was suffering from stretched ligaments in his left knee and a battered right wrist.

Garzo rose above the chaos. He beat Zaccone to victory in race one by a handsome four-tenths, Spinelli 1.5 seconds back. And the Spaniard produced the most dominant showing of the entire year in the wet race two, 3.4s clear of Spinelli. Torres was a colossal 6.2 seconds behind. As Garzo took home 50 points ahead of the summer break, the meagre tallies of Casadei, Gutierrez and Zannoni put the Spaniard in charge in the championship race by 25 points from Casadei.

Austria proved decisive. Garzo held his head brilliantly to beat Gutierrez, Casadei (third after Zannoni was dropped a place post-race due to track limits) and Torres in a tense race one. But he had no answer for Gutierrez, trailing his compatriot on the final circuit. Yet for once Gutierrez's inexperience showed when he fell two corners from the flag, handing Garzo victory and a healthy 38-point championship lead going into the final double-header.

A single fourth at the traditional Misano season-ender would be enough to seal the title. But Misano didn't go completely to plan. Garzo's team sensed major nervousness from their contender early in the weekend, which wasn't helped by a crash on the first lap of a Michelin tyre test on Thursday. Anxiety accelerated further when the Spaniard found himself in Q1 for the first time all season. Qualifying eighth, seven places and two rows behind pole-sitter Casadei did little to aid Garzo's sleep on the eve of the decider.

"I suffered a lot," he admitted later. "I was super-nervous.

WHAT DOES MOTOE MEAN FOR ELECTRIC BIKES?

I slept two hours." Despite that, he came out swinging in race one in the victory fight from the second lap, sitting behind Zannoni, Casadei, Zaccone and Granado. And luck was on his side: Zannoni's fall on the penultimate lap handed him the fourth he craved. The title was his.

Race two had the potential to be something of an anticlimax. Yet another wild fight ensued as Gutierrez jumped three places on lap one to sit third, before going toe to toe with Casadei for victory. Not even the Italian had an answer on the final lap as the rookie rounded out his year in style, winning by 0.109 of a second. Granado was third, while Garzo's seventh place was enough to cement Dynavolt Intact GP's position at the head of the teams' championship.

There could be no doubting the excitement generated from the racing. But there was an impression from within the MotoE community that Dorna needed to provide greater visibility. At a media presentation in March, Tech3 E-Racing team owner Herve Poncharal had openly pushed Goubert and Cane. "We are very proud to be part of it," he said, "but we need to show it more to our bosses, our sponsors. We need to attract more charismatic riders. Top job, but let's make it more 'seen'." Goubert's counter? "It takes time to convince people of new technology. And a lot of people aren't convinced by electrification. But what's happening in the car field is going to help show it's something valid."

At least, Ducati is pushing ahead with further innovations. Plans to bring down the V21L's weight from 225kg to a potential 217kg should reduce the difference between the class and internal-combustion machines. But there is a feeling that the current grid – ten Italians and five Spaniards – needs greater variety and more star quality to attract budding fans.

NICHOLAS GOUBERT found much to celebrate in MotoE's sixth season: "The main difference is we had more riders capable of the podium. We've improved lap times. Okay, the tyres have improved a little bit. But the bike hasn't changed, so it's basically been the riders and teams understanding the bike better, and pushing each other, to around eight-tenths [per lap] improvement."

But what does MotoE mean away from racing?

"Short-term, the market is on a plateau," explained Goubert. "The bad news was what happened in Germany last December, stopping all subsidies for electric cars. Holland is still growing fast, France is slightly increasing. With Germany, the market is [decreasing] slightly. The German carmakers are very influential in the European Commission. The petrol lobby is working very hard to keep the electrification down. I think we're going through a phase of uncertainty. It won't last too long in my opinion. It will depend as well on what happens in the US election [in November].

"The UK has postponed the ban on IC cars from 2030 until 2035. In Europe, it was 2035 to start with. They might postpone it. They will allow e-fuel to be used. To what extent, I don't know. Everybody knows we can't make enough. I don't see any other solution than going electric.

"For the bike on the street, we'll see. It was the same when the regulation was applied to the four-stroke engine on mopeds early on. It killed some bikes, the 125s. They might take the same kind of decision in a few years. What I expect is that electric bikes will really start off-road. Now you have very powerful bikes like the HRC one, the Spanish one, Stark. They're a bit expensive, but that will change in time. You have so many places where you cannot make noise. So, it's a question of time.

"The day people realise you can build a very powerful motocross bike that can be faster, they will maybe think it's not that stupid to put them on a track. It's more difficult for sure, because we need more power, because of the speed. The maximum speed in motocross is 100km/h."

Another negative is battery development, which has been slower than anticipated in 2023. "At the moment, improvements with batteries are linear. Everyone's waiting to see a big step with solid-state batteries. It's not going to happen as rapidly as what we thought. They'll need a few more years."

RED BULL ROOKIES CUP
DOWN TO THE WIRE

Red Bull's important learner series, launch pad for champions, had a thrilling season, decided at the final corner. PETER CLIFFORD reports...

Above: Friends and foes. Spaniards Alvaro Carpe (83) and Brian Uriate (51) went wheel to wheel to the last corner of the last race.

Top right: Carpe took the title in his second season.

Above right: Uriate celebrates his race-one win in Misano. It wasn't quite enough.

Right: Typical Cup action – a ten-bike train at Misano.

Photos: Red Bull Content Pool/Gold & Goose

THE final incredible corner of the 2024 Red Bull MotoGP Rookies season decided the Cup when Alvaro Carpe held off a last attack from season-long rival Brian Uriarte. Then the Spanish pair charged across the Misano finish line behind Argentina's Valentin Perrone.

"Even after the disappointment of yesterday, I was planning to be sitting here as Cup champion today," said perspiring 17-year-old Carpe following the podium ceremony. "It was a difficult final lap. With three to go, I went wide, but I told myself to stay calm, there was time to get back to the front.

"In the last lap, I was looking at the TV screens to see where Brian was, and I saw he was third. I knew this would be difficult because I knew that he would try. He is a very good rider."

A very good rider, indeed, Uriarte completed a superb Rookies Cup debut season with third in the final race and second in the points table. "I did all I could. More would have been to crash," said the slightly subdued 16-year-old.

Perrone was also completing his first year. "It's an amazing way to finish the season," enthused the 16-year-old Argentine. "It's been a fantastic first year. To get six podiums, two victories is incredible. The Rookies Cup was a big step up for me. Knowing what a high level it is, I was hoping to be in the top ten."

It was the perfect end to a fabulous race and another wonderful season, which had started in Jerez in late April. The Argentine national anthem rang out after the first drama-packed race, but it was for 17-year-old Marco Morelli, who finished just ahead of compatriot Perrone.

It had all changed at that final corner in Jerez, where it so often does. Sixteen-year-old Finn Rico Salmela had led the pack of six into the tight left-hander, but was outbraked up the inside by Uriarte, who then slid off. Forced wide, Salmela finished fifth, Uriarte having remounted for sixth.

Morelli knew that it would be decided there. Ruche Moodley and Hakim Danish had gone down there a lap earlier, while Giulio Pugliese fell halfway around the last lap, cutting the lead battle from nine to six: "I braked, later, later, but…the other guys braked so, so late. I thought, for sure they go wide, and I went inside."

Race two was equally intense, with 0.242 of a second covering the top five at the end of 14 laps. Danish made the perfect last-corner move for the win, but Carpe picked up the 16-year-old Malaysian's slipstream and timed a masterful pass right on the line; fellow Spaniard Uriarte was third.

Carpe began the year as a 16-year-old favourite after finishing second in 2023 with two victories – the only one who had taken the battle to that year's dominant winner, Angel Piqueras. He left Jerez leading Morelli 38 points to 35, with Perrone on 29, tied for third with Max Quiles, another pre-season favourite in his third year.

At round two at Le Mans, Quiles was congratulated by Marc Marquez in race-one *parc fermé* after a brilliantly executed last-lap pass had stolen victory from Salmela after 15 thrilling laps. The podium was completed by Carpe. The 16-year-old Spaniards shared the points lead; Salmela was tied for third with Perrone, but fellow Argentine Morelli did his chances no favours by falling on lap one.

Quiles had needed to expunge the memory of his disastrous 2023 Le Mans error, when he had taken out two fellow Rookies in a last-lap crash. He recounted race one: "A great race, we could see a big crowd watching us and that also made me happy. I tried to open a gap, but then one guy overtook me and the group closed up again. Then Rico tried to push again. I kept behind him, then overtook him on the last lap. It wasn't easy. Rico's style is really different – carrying more mid-corner speed and a bit softer in braking."

Riders talking of having to save the front prompted a discussion about the Pirelli tyres, which had replaced the

Dunlops for 2024, the only change since the inception of the Rookies Cup in 2007. Pirelli had taken over the Moto3 and Moto2 classes for 2024, so as a training ground, the Cup followed.

There had been concerns that Pirellis might suffer from troublesome fade, but that unfounded reputation was soon discarded. While performance did drop, as with Dunlops and, indeed, all tyres, their excellent feel encouraged the Rookies to flirt with the limits all the way to the flag. Perrone set a new lap record on the penultimate lap of race one, almost a second quicker than the record from 2023.

Lap records continued to tumble throughout the season, and the confidence-inspiring feel of the Pirelli tyres probably encouraged first-year Rookies like Uriarte and Perrone to run so hard from the beginning. And that is how race two played out. A perfect and dramatic down-the-inside outbraking lunge into the Le Mans final first-gear double right gave victory to Uriarte. Quiles survived the shock and a nasty front-wheel slide to retain second place ahead of Danish.

Perrone, one of the race's many leaders, and Carpe were right on their tail, with 0.617 of a second covering the top five riders.

Said Uriarte, a calm, well-spoken 15-year-old, after his first Cup win, "I worked a lot this weekend, the track is new for me."

Quiles left Le Mans leading on 74 points – a warning to second-placed Carpe that his 'take as few risks as possible' attitude might not be enough. He'd finished third and fifth.

Mugello produced one of those nasty shocks that put racing into perspective, but that was on Sunday. Saturday provided a glorious example of what makes Rookies Cup so special. A superb 13-KTM lead battle blessed the beautiful Tuscan curves, and it was points leader Quiles who flashed across the line just 0.004 of a second ahead of Uriarte. Carpe grabbed third, 0.044 off the win.

Ruche Moodley, Veda Pratama, Perrone and Danish

Above: The identical KTM machines are serviced under canvas at Jerez.

Top right: Hakim Danish took a win in the wet at Aragon.

Above right: Double winner Argentinian Valentin Perrone was third overall in his first season.

Right: Max Quiles won at Le Mans, but later was banned for two races.

Far right: Finn Rico Salmela was an Assen winner, and fourth overall.

Below right: Marco Morelli's race of the year was at Assen.

Below far right: Indonesian Veda Patrama showed pace in his first year, with a podium in Austria.

Photos: Red Bull Content Pool/Gold & Goose

completed the drama, all seven covered by just 0.518 of a second. South African Moodley (17) was in his third season and had made steady progress. So far, though, the year had not been kind, but now he was on the pace. Pratama, in his first season, had already shown pace, but this time raced at the front throughout.

With the same determination to hold the lead on Sunday morning, Quiles went a significant step too far and triggered a frightening crash that might easily have resulted in multiple serious injuries. That it was only Moodley who went sliding across the tarmac and grass was miraculous.

It was a troubling end to an otherwise brilliant race. Moodley had executed a perfect last corner and might have won, but Quiles swung from the right-hand kerbing back across to almost mid-track, smacking into him. Moodley fought for control in the midst of the 12-rider pack, lost it and might have taken six with him. But he slid off alone and without serious injury.

Perrone flashed across the line for his first win, the fifth different rider in six races, ahead of Uriarte, Carpe, Salmela and Quiles. Danish was sixth ahead of Leonardo Zanni, Pratama, Dodo Boggio, Giulio Pugliese and Morelli, the top 11 inside eight-tenths. Only a second behind, another tight pack: Evan Belford, Guillem Planques, Leo Rammerstorfer and Kgopotso Mononyane.

Racing at its best and worst, catastrophic consequences ducked. But Quiles did face the stewards, and he was disqualified from the next two races. He still had the points lead on Sunday evening in Mugello, but that was bound to change. It was little consolation for battered Moodley, who had lost a possible win and languished tenth overall.

After Mugello's swooping elevation changes, Assen provided a very different challenge: flat with many of the corners linked.

Uriarte scored a sensational victory with a sixth-to-fifth-gear masterstroke on the final, incredible, pass-rich lap. The Spaniard led Salmela and Perrone in a flash across the line, with a second covering the top eight.

Carpe had fought to hold on to the lead for much of the race, but he had shown his cards and was trumped on the final lap.

After a first-lap crash on Saturday, Marco Morelli was virtually unpassable around Assen on Sunday. Dutch clouds had cooled the surface, and perhaps that helped him to a record pace and a superb second 2024 win – a demonstration of skill and consistency over 15 laps, almost 14 seconds quicker than Saturday's race. Carpe chased Morelli home, with Salmela third after six KTMs had broken away from the field, towed by Morelli at a pace faster than qualifying. At the finish, the rest were 15 seconds behind the leading six. On the final lap, both Uriarte and Perrone almost crashed.

"I knew that I could do it," exclaimed Morelli, who had remounted on Saturday and fought through from last to 14th. "I feel that at all the tracks I am fast, alone or with a group."

To Austria for round five. Uriarte led on 140 points; Carpe stood second on 127, ten ahead of Perrone. Absent from Assen, Quiles had slipped to fourth ahead of Salmela, Danish and Morelli.

Non-stop action for 16 laps of Spielberg ended with Carpe wringing the perfect drive from his KTM out of the final corner, crossing the line just 0.024 of a second ahead of Morelli.

Quiles was as awesome. He'd rejoined 11th after a long-lap, with just four laps to go, and blasted back into contention for a very close third.

Carpe's second victory of the year gave the Spaniard a two-point advantage, after arch-rival Uriarte finished sixth. Things became even better for him in race two, and worse for Uriarte. Carpe put on a perfect demonstration of race-craft and pace to win after another race-long battle, while closest challenger Uriarte slid off on the last lap.

Quiles was next; Pratama an excellent third for his first Cup podium.

"Fifty points this weekend," grinned Carpe, who extended his lead to 24 over Uriarte. His breakthrough win of 2023 had occurred at the Red Bull Ring; in 2024, his double victory began a streak that would take him to the Cup. A third win in Aragon's race one extended his points lead to 33. It was incredibly close, though, as Perrone almost passed him on the line, missing out by just 0.026 of a second after a thrilling battle. Third was Uriarte, just 0.052 behind.

Uriarte was still second in the points table and, crucially, Perrone moved up to third after double faller Quiles scored zero points.

The race was run in two parts following a red flag after four laps, due to a fallen rider on the track, luckily uninjured. Part two ran for five laps and determined the overall result.

Carpe didn't plan to stop winning: "Tomorrow is my first possible match point. I am not going to play just for points, I want to win because that is what I enjoy." He would need Uriarte and Perrone to roll over for him, while even Quiles still had a mathematical chance of the title.

But if Carpe had begun writing his name in the record books, it was washed off by overnight rain. Bouncing back from an awful weekend in Austria and 14th on Saturday, Hakim Danish was simply brilliant on the soaking wet Motorland circuit. He dominated, scoring his and Malaysia's first Rookies Cup victory. A fall and no points for Carpe re-opened the title chase. Uriarte finished second, closing the points gap to just 13 with two races remaining.

Third-placed Salmela had fought through the field to swap places several times with Uriarte at the final corner, losing out on the drive for the line.

"I'd prepared myself for a wet race," said Danish (17). "I made two sighting laps and I already got confidence in the bike, I had grip and a good feeling. So on the starting grid, I said to my mechanic, 'Okay, maybe this is my time.'"

So the battle for the Cup came down to the last two races on the Adriatic coast. Uriarte snatched victory in race one and seized the points lead. Pole-man Perrone was second, just 0.26 of a second ahead of Danish. Points leader Carpe had led down the back straight on the final lap, but after Quiles crashed in front of him, he dropped back to sixth, losing the points lead.

That set the scene for a Hollywood-style finish that couldn't have been scripted better. Pulsating tension built all the way to that final corner and Uriarte's great lunge down the inside of Carpe that could give him the Cup. Carpe's perfect defence, and Uriarte's intelligence and respect gave the title to his friend and rival as they crossed the line behind Perrone.

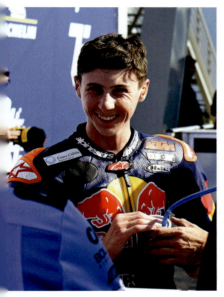 

That victory earned Perrone third overall behind Uriarte and Cup winner Carpe. Perrone would turn 17 in December, so both benefited from the FIM regulation that gives a year's dispensation to the first three in the Cup and allows them to start in the Moto3 World Championship, otherwise restricted to 18-year-olds. Both would receive offers from GP teams.

Uriarte would only turn 17 in August, 2025, so he looked set to chase the Rookies Cup for a second season. That made him a firm favourite, but as 2024 demonstrated, form books count for very little.

The 18th Rookies Cup season ended with ex-Rookies leading all three world championships: Jorge Martín in MotoGP, Ai Ogura in Moto2 and David Alonso in Moto3, while Toprak Razgatlıoğlu took the Superbike World Championship, and Kyle Ryde British Superbike.

SUPERBIKE WORLD CHAMPIONSHIP
HITTING THE HIGHEST PEAKS
By GORDON RITCHIE

IT'S always dangerous to predict the future in WorldSBK. In 2023, the idea that Toprak Razgatlioglu and BMW could deliver an astonishing championship win in 2024 would have been thought delusional to the point of hallucination for even the most optimistic of pundits. Even more so when examined in the cold light of day.

A title challenge of any heft or consistency was impossible on a BMW. Even for Razgatlioglu. Surely, shock Yamaha signing Jonathan Rea had a better shot, after his own move to the more proven YZF-R1.

Such 'logical' thoughts were completely valid – until Toprak went out and won the biggest production prize of all, seemingly with one hand tied behind his back and despite a punctured lung. It was Rea's big move that proved close to disaster.

A few extra Ducati kilos, which varied from week to week, caused Alvaro Bautista to alternate between glorious Jekyll on the podiums and wearing out hides on the asphalt.

Taking a dispassionate view, especially after Ducati were given back the extra 500rpm they had lost in two stages through 2023 (under the previous balancing rule), the V4-R was still the bike to be on for everyone of medium-to-large build. Even Toprak said so, after he had beaten around half a dozen Ducati efforts from truly top riders old and new.

A proven Ducati WorldSSP star, Nicolo Bulega, went supernova inside the established WorldSBK order.

After a whole slew of new rules, sporting and technical, WorldSBK will be subject to the full implementation of fuel-flow controls in 2025, for all five competing manufacturers – BMW, Ducati, Honda, Kawasaki and Yamaha.

Fuel-flow monitoring was introduced in 2024, anticipating regulations for 2025. Fuel-flow control is both the way forward and a way to trim things back, with regard to top-end engine performance.

Even without fuel-flow control, some subtle and not-so-subtle concessions and super-concessions, plus a new homologation (then another, mid-season, no less!) ensured that podiums were there for all in 2024, even in such a dominant season for BMW (i.e., Toprak) and Ducati.

Racing on a different suite of tracks is the other way to slow things down. In 2024, WorldSBK went to just one new circuit, Cremona, but it was a track with only one long back straight and masses of slow, stadium-style corners everywhere else. That led to limited cornering speeds and thus slower crash velocities.

Some potential new WorldSBK tracks seem conceived in the same 'slower' vein – Balatonring Park, Slovakia Ring, etc.

In a championship that is very much still the second string on the Dorna bow, the future of WorldSBK will be dictated by the needs of the MotoGP class. Which, as we know, will drop capacity and, therefore, its absolute top-end performance in 2027.

There are elements within MotoGP, and always have been, who want WorldSBK simply to go away. But WorldSBK (in any kind of potential format you care to mention) has one really big hand still to play that hyper-expensive prototype

MotoGP racing can never have. That was as true in 2024 as any previous year.

The bikes being raced are actually based on real machines, from the biggest, most established Superbike producers to the newest, smallest-capacity WorldSSP300 hopefuls. In short, almost everything being raced in the post-two-stroke FIM world is not a MotoGP bike. Almost all are production-derived motorcycles, no matter how humble or exotic.

Completely new manufacturers have, indeed, been joining the WorldSBK paddock. Sophomore participants Kove won their first race in WorldSSP300 in 2024, with a bike of their own design and manufacture. New entrants QJ somehow topped a 'wet' timesheet in WorldSSP, and made so much progress in year one with their Italian engineering support that anything might be possible. Superbike is QJ's ultimate goal, and soon.

The 'Next Generation' WorldSSP rules have been such a hit that there are seven competing manufacturers already. And more on the sidelines, liking what they see.

Finally, is it significant that so many in the MotoGP establishment said that the new-for-2024 WorldWCR women's championship would inevitably race inside MotoGP in 2025, only for it to be reconfirmed inside WorldSBK?

Across all four permanent classes, the WorldSBK stage looks brightly lit, if still an 'off-Broadway' production.

The 2024 season will be long brought to mind for Toprak's second and BMW's first title wins, but there was much more going on behind the most memorable of scenes.

Main: Chasing the unexpected. Rookie runner-up Bulega pursues champion Razgatlioglu.

Inset: Champion Toprak was BMW's Golden Boy.

Photos: Gold & Goose

CHAMPION PROFILE: TOPRAK RAZGATLIOGLU

THE UNDISPUTED CHAMPION

By GORDON RITCHIE

AFTER he secured 27 podiums, of which 18 were wins, there can be no doubt that Toprak Razgatlioglu was the strongest and fastest force across all 36 races of the 2024 season. Conversely, he was also the most unexpected champion, for many reasons.

In reality, Razgatlioglu's personal 2024 season was only 30 races long, after a sickening crash that could have done a lot more physical harm than puncturing his lung. That horrible millisecond of impact could very easily have ended a simply astounding first BMW season for rider, SMR team and BMW as a manufacturer.

It could have ended everything in the most tragic way possible. Those words should be taken literally. And very seriously by the powers that be. Never have so many people been so grateful for the invention and mandatory implementation of airbags inside racing suits.

The person most adversely affected by all this jeopardy was the one who complained least about it. The same person who literally walked away from the crash, despite his punctured lung.

The same person who shook it all off to win races as soon as he returned at Motorland Aragon, just two weeks later.

Even an only slightly more severe injury for Toprak, one that would have prevented him from completing a season that was heavily weighted to the autumnal months, would have been a tragedy in a sporting sense. With four whole rounds and 12 points-scoring races within a six-week period after Magny-Cours, that crash could easily have robbed the most deserving package of what, finally, became an *annus mirabilis* for all in BMW colours.

There is no hyperbole here. Toprak was well on his way to making an assumed impossibility an increasing certainty before that crash.

Assumed impossibility?

Yes, even he and his mentor/manager, Kenan Sofuoglu, didn't think that winning the title in year one of his BMW contract was realistic. Their joint decision starting out was 'win races this year, fight for the title next year'.

Most also thought that once again BMW would follow the data from their dynos rather than the comments from their riders and crew chief trackside. That once again, they would create super-fast machines that were simply too difficult to ride for 20-odd laps against a sea of more compliant Ducatis, Kawasakis and Yamahas.

However, BMW had finally learned its lesson from several well-resourced, but unsuccessful seasons. Munich's finest were more than ready for Toprak's high-stakes arrival.

In 2023, BMW Motorrad had a full-on test team – Sylvain Guintoli and Bradley Smith (plus others) – running interference on too much interference from the megawatt-obsessed minds in Munich. It seems that the test team's job was only presenting Razgatlioglu, Michael van der Mark and the two other Bonovo BMW riders with the truly usable and suitable new components and software bytes.

Taking on Chris Gonschor as technical director was another entirely positive move that resulted in them looking at the whole bike and the whole gamut of rider feedback, before making suitable changes that produced a machine that worked from front to back and side to side. Finally, crew chief Phil Marron was responsible for the vital 'Toprak whispering' in the pit box.

When we speak about the final on-track achievement of Razgatlioglu's race winning ambitions, we have to acknowledge that he had more than just the missing engine power he had needed while being beaten by Ducati and Bautista in 2022 and 2023. He had a receptive and co-operative BMW industrial behemoth behind him, trusting his feedback and the evidence of the stopwatches. And just the right humans to help him at every stage.

What makes Razgatlioglu a gold-plated phenomenon in WorldSBK, with his record 13 victories in succession the most obvious recent example, is partly his personal approach to winning. It's a mixture of sheer joy in victory, and absolute personal and cultural expectation that he should win every single time. Like a rainbow Doohan; a Rossi-on-Bosphorus.

Any rider who can win all those races in a single season and not induce boredom or even hostility in the global fanbase is clearly a special kind of human. His rivals struggle to say anything bad about him, even when he beats them over and over again on a bike that nobody else could get to work very well. Maybe it's because he and only he could.

Toprak Razgatlioglu was the clear 2024 WordSBK champion and the people's champion to boot, with performance and personality forming a remarkable golden amalgam within the tall Turk.

Photo: Gold & Goose

SUPERBIKE WORLD CHAMPIONSHIP
2024 TEAMS & RIDERS

By GORDON RITCHIE

BMW

ROKiT BMW Motorrad WorldSBK Team
Toprak Razgatlioglu (28) turned Shaun Muir's UK-based SMR effort and Marc Bongers's BMW Motorrad cohorts into all they could be in 2024.

In reality, BMW had made enough positive backroom and organisational changes to react very quickly to the sudden whirlwind of new technical demands from Razgatlioglu's particular style of riding.

Michael van der Mark (30) made enough of a recovery from his many previous injuries to win again in 2024. **Markus Reiterberger** (30) stood in for Toprak at Cremona and took some engine penalties to help the overall championship cause.

Bonovo Action BMW
Garrett Gerloff (28) stayed for year two on a BMW and returned to the podium status he craved. His positive late-season form happened just as the team was about to be wound up, as a BMW effort at least. **Scott Redding** (31) was an unwilling refugee from the official squad; he still had a factory bike, but didn't use it to return to his very best. This was not classed as an Independent team in 2024.

DUCATI

Aruba.it Racing – Ducati World Superbike Team
Defender **Alvaro Bautista** (39) was gloriously effective in some races, but a terrible (and sometimes plain unlucky) qualifier in too many others. The qualifying issues required his very best performances just to get to within touching distance of the podium at times. When he qualified well – sometimes via a strong Superpole race finish on Sunday mornings – occasionally he won.

The still-young **Nicolo Bulega** (24) blew in from WorldSSP success and made his hybrid riding style good enough to become a rookie race winner and the biggest threat to Razgatliolgu over the whole season. An amazing WorldSBK start for yet another MotoGP paddock refugee, who initially had found career redemption in WorldSSP.

Michele Pirro (38) wild-carded and scored points at Misano, a reward for being Ducati's human answer to the Swiss Army knife for bike development and testing.

Barni Spark Racing Team Ducati
Danilo Petrucci (33) was Marco Barnabo's choice again, and together they made history, with the first three wins for the rider, and at their local brand-new Cremona track.

Somewhat bizarrely, the Bergamo boys and girls had already made their own first ever WorldSBK race winning history at Assen with **Nicholas Spinelli** (23), standing in for the injured 'Petrux'. He won a wet and red-flagged race. Spinelli's win was both brave (and a little fortunate), but in general, 2024 was an amazing overall effort from what proved to be the top Independent team and top Independent rider – officially so in their respective championship rankings.

Team GO Eleven Ducati
Andrea Iannone (35) arrived in WorldSBK both cocky and unsure whether his absence in FIM-mandated purgatory had been too long. Rider and team jumped in feet first anyway and scored podiums, then a highly charged and fully deserved win at Motorland. Team manager Denis Sacchetti and team owner Giovanni Romello had rolled the dice almost perfectly, even in such a tough season as this.

Motocorsa Racing Ducati
Michael Ruben Rinaldi (27) had a torrid time when he took over Axel Bassani's bike, especially after he had lost his factory Ducati team ride at the end of 2023. It was a tough season from first to last.

ELF Marc VDS Racing Team Ducati
An initial shot in the arm for the whole WorldSBK paddock, the combination of **Sam Lowes** (34), and some of his high-profile MotoGP new boys and girls moving into the WorldSBK paddock never quite lived up to the billing.

JDT Racing Team Ducati
Hafizh Syahrin (30) showed up for a single round, at Portimao, with a smartly presented Ducati effort.

HONDA

Team HRC Honda
Iker Lecuona (24) and **Xavi Vierge** (27) were back again, and with a new homologation of Fireblade to boot. This time, the team was under the Barcelona-based control of Jose Manuel Escamez, following the exit of Leon Camier at the end of 2023.

Initial results were highly disappointing, considering that so much was new and supposedly fixed, but better results came as the season edged towards its big finish in Iberia. **Tetsuta Nagashima** (32) turned up to race at the season finale in Jerez, with the Honda test team for his pit crew.

PETRONAS MIE Racing Honda Team
Tarran Mackenzie (28) had a very tough introduction to full-time WorldSBK racing. He was still battling away, like team-mate **Adam Norrodin** (26), on a private version of the Honda that even HRC could not make competitive.

Even with the force of racing nature that is Midori Moriwaki behind it, and the experienced Mick Shanley looking after the technical side, it was tough going.

Injuries for the regular riders meant that Portuguese **Ivo Lopes** (28), American **Hayden Gillim** (29) and Argentinian **Leandro Mercado** (32) made guest appearances.

HONDA RACING UK
Tommy Bridewell (36), 2023 BSB champion, came to the races at Cremona and Jerez, along with his UK team.

KAWASAKI

Kawasaki Racing Team
Guim and Biel Roda, plus their cousin, Alvar Gar-riga, faced up to the post-Rea KRT era, with **Alex Lowes** (32) scoring two race wins and more than ten podiums. Better than expected? Probably.

Axel Bassani (25) had abandoned Motocorsa Ducati for a factory ride and learned a lot, as he had planned to do.

Kawasaki Puccetti Racing
Tito Rabat (34) received a full-on KRT-supplied Ninja ZX-10RR for 2024, but still had to work hard to put points on the board. Manuel Puccetti's experienced squad will run the only official ZX-10RR in WorldSBK in 2025.

YAMAHA

Pata Yamaha Prometeon WorldSBK Team
Faced with the loss of Toprak Razgatlioglu for 2024, Paul Denning from Crescent Racing and Andrea Dosoli from HQ thought they had sealed the sudden hole in the waterline with a sufficiently large talent to carry on their hopes of victory. **Jonathan Rea** (37) struggled in most races, however, with only a couple of bright spots. Not a single person thought that it would be like this for the team, manufacturer or rider.

Even **Andrea Locatelli** (28) found podiums hard to come by in 2024, so there was a bit of a Yamaha issue in general.

Niccolo Canepa (36) stood in for Rea for the Cremona round, after the six-times champion had suffered a badly injured thumb at the previous Magny-Cours outing.

GYTR GRT Yamaha WorldSBK
Remy Gardner (26) claimed his first podium finish after quite a few near misses, in a year when suddenly it was not easy to be a Yamaha rider.

Dominique Aegerter (34) was injured in a training accident before Magny-Cours and missed some races. **Alessandro Delbianco** (27) stood in not once, but twice, while **Marvin Fritz** (31) rode at Cremona and Motorland.

Filippo Conti continued in his role as manager of an outfit that was no longer classed as an Independent team.

Yamaha Motoxracing WorldSBK Team
Bradley Ray (26) had a second, largely reward-free season with the Italian-based team, which took on all but the opening flyaway round in 2024. **Luca Bernardi** (23) joined Ray at the end of the season for two rounds, while **Alessandro Delbianco** rode at Cremona.

GMT94 Yamaha
Moving from a fast privateer Ducati to a slightly breathless privateer Yamaha proved to be a step too far for the dedicated **Philipp Oettl** (27). A pity for both the popular German rider and Christophe Guyot's popular French team.

OMG Racing Yamaha
Kyle Ryde (27) came to Jerez to race just one week after winning the BSB championship.

THE SUPERBIKES OF 2024

By GORDON RITCHIE

BMW M1000RR

NOT a new homologation, but the inline-four BMW was the most transformed unit in terms of results. A holistic approach to development contributed to race and ultimately also championship wins.

The main chassis was actually a super-concession part, adjusted in terms of stiffness – softer in some areas and planes. Balancing stiffness against flex was the Holy Grail, which required a 'total machine' approach to the design. The chassis was of a different weight and stiffness to previous versions. BMW said that the post-winter testing result was consistent from Phillip Island to the end.

Forged alloy PVM wheels were fitted, while brakes were standard Brembo WorldSBK-approved units. Counterintuitively, Razgatlioglu did not use the biggest and thickest steel discs for every race, preferring the smaller units, which helped during the turning-in phase of cornering.

Ohlins asymmetric front forks were used, requiring a change of other front-end chassis parts, including both triple clamps. The top yoke was thinned considerably, to obtain the important neutral-braking-phase feel that Toprak really needed. This extra stability and feel even allowed him to make use of the harder front tyres at times.

There were two swing-arm options, though only one design could be used on any given weekend.

The seat of the BMW came under scrutiny, to a bizarre degree at times. One change asked for by Toprak was protested as not being within allowable limits. In height, not width, as was first assumed.

There were minor changes other than the aerodynamic package, within strict regulations, to the front and rear of the bike. They began with advances in pure top speed, and then BMW worked on making it agile enough in the corners. The 2024 bike was narrower than the previous one.

BMW differed greatly from its rivals in its continued use of a Bosch ECU and electronics system, with a Motec display and data-logging system. They tried to reduce the mapping options available to the riders, with two and very occasionally three settings, just to avoid potential confusion.

Razgatlioglu's style of riding caused significant early ramping up in the depth and accuracy of engine braking (reverse-torque limiting) and electronics strategies.

The engine itself was retuned, via the intake and cylinder head, not only to create a little more power, but also to make the whole bike more rideable. BMW said that it was more linear and less peaky in every respect. The new Akrapovic exhaust was the result of work to maintain a high horsepower figure while producing even smoother power delivery.

DUCATI PANIGALE V4-R

THERE were some changes to the most potent and deliberately race-focused creation of them all, but the two biggest alterations were regulatory. For every V4-R rider, Ducati was given back the extra 500rpm peak (raised to 16,100rpm again) that had been removed by two balancing interventions in 2023.

The price for that liberalisation was a similar combined bike and rider weight limit approach as in Supersport. Naturally, that only really affected the very lightest riders, like Bautista. From first to last in 2024, he and his crew were playing with where to put the ballast weight, and what to do when he was adjudged to be heavier or lighter (with all his riding kit) than at the previous weigh-in.

Technically, it also meant that Bautista did not opt to use the latest underslung Akrapovic exhaust system, as that was a kilo or so lighter than the older one, and thus more problematic for his relative bike/rider weight-balance figures.

For 2024, with the mandatory adoption of fuel that featured a 40-per cent bio content, Ducati had to significantly retune and remap to suit the fuel's different characteristics. The bike was still fast.

The 90-degree V4 engine, with 81 x 48.5mm internal dimensions, was fed by elliptical throttle bodies equivalent to 54mm in diameter.

If you accept the 'team Bautista' point of view that the combined weight rule was introduced to target him deliberately as a too-dominant recent double champion, the supposed aim of slowing him down on the straights didn't work at all.

What it did do was make his bike less consistent in feel and more reluctant to change direction. Even only 4-6kg of extra bike weight for the quite tiny Bautista to push and pull around proved tricky.

On the chassis side, the official V4-R used cost-capped Ohlins suspension: 46mm RVP25/30 front forks and an RSP50 rear shock.

A longer new rear link needed some work to make it fit the existing swing-arms.

Brakes were cost-capped Brembo radial calipers and discs, with the same options as all.

Rider ergonomics in general was an area of real effort, mostly to help Bulega fit the bike and Bautista to move around it, and allow for the extra – and variable – weight he had to add.

HONDA CBR1000RR-R SP

A NEW homologation that looked much like the previous version, the 2024 CBR1000RR-R SP came out of the box with the chassis 'softening' and geometry adjustments allowed by regulation at the end of 2022 and through 2023. This time, the chassis of a stock bike was redesigned to be more flexible in some planes and stiffer in others.

The idea was to provide more feel and rider confidence in all areas of corner entry, full lean and exit. It was not an instantaneous improvement, but the bike gained better results during the busy autumnal run of races, once it was understood as a complete package.

Another main design change on the new road-bike was a lighter stock crankshaft than before, which meant that Honda did not need to be concerned about new crank rules for all manufacturers in 2024.

FUEL FLOW TO BALANCE POWER

DURING 2024, each manufacturer was required to have two machines fitted with fuel-flow monitoring equipment – an exercise to gather data. In 2025, fuel-flow controls will be introduced as the primary balancing intervention in respect of ultimate peak horsepower.

More than that, it is also the main method by which the FIM and Dorna can control (read 'reduce') the peak performance of all WorldSBK machines. In part, this initiative is a reaction to the reduction of MotoGP engine capacity to 850cc in 2027, to avoid the threat of 1000cc Superbikes becoming faster than the prototypes. It is also a method of stopping ever more powerful WorldSBK bikes outgrowing many of the B-grade circuits on which they are obliged to race.

The 'silver bullet' effect of fuel-flow control is simple to understand – and should be simple to enforce. No matter how powerful an engine design, and no matter how high it can rev in theory, it can only produce peak power with a enough fuel flowing into the combustion chamber. (Flow is the correct term, as all gases, vapours and liquids are termed fluids.)

The energy for every power stroke of any engine is provided by the chemical energy stored in the fuel. Air is necessary for combustion, but only fuel provides energy.

The higher an engine revs, the greater the amount of fuel it needs, and – vitally – within an ever-reducing time frame. If you limit the fuel flow rate artificially, that restricts power.

Less fuel, less power. Simple.

When you are the controller of the power that any WorldSBK engine can make simply by manipulating fuel flow to the combustion chamber, you can limit ultimate top-end performance to any level you please.

Anyone could lighten or beef-up their crank and balancer mass by a very generous 20-per cent tolerance on either side.

What Honda did have, again from the new roadbike, was a split throttle system. This idea is proven to have benefits in both corner-exit engine control under acceleration, and more subtle interventions under corner-entry and negative engine torque conditions. A gentle 'virtual twin', but a full-on four-cylinder screamer when needed.

The inline engine had the same 81mm engine bore as before, with its 54mm-diameter split throttle bodies mounted very close to the cylinder head.

Honda's permitted maximum was 15,600rpm, unchanged from 2023.

The bike was very fast, but it seemed that the Ducati and now BMW in the right hands were better around a lap.

Back to the chassis. After all those built-in flex changes, the future appeared to be the past, as the preferred 2024 swing-arm was the same as that used in the early stages of the whole new generation of Fireblade of five years ago. It seemed to match the character of the new chassis best and was reintroduced from round two in Catalunya.

Again, Honda joined Kawasaki in employing Showa suspension.

HRC was a factory team outlier in its use of Nissin brakes, which according to the FIM approved list of parts meant that both 335 and 340mm-diameter front disc rotors were available, as were the latest cost-capped vented Nissin calipers.

KAWASAKI NINJA ZX-10RR

ONCE, the Kawasaki Ninja ZX-10R and ZX-10RR models were the most dominant in the WorldSBK paddock, even after some of their rivals had maximised the permitted engine bores, and created far more expensive and race-orientated street-bikes.

WorldSBK's most venerable overall design featured positively archaic 76 x 55mm bore-and-stroke figures for the inline four. But the 2024 official KRT riders found themselves on a bike with several upgrades, even in some ways in top-end performance.

Enough concessions had been earned in a tough 2023 to allow for a 500rpm uplift in peak revs, to a possible 15,100. Without a final concession step to incorporate a package of potential top-end and gearbox changes, the Kawasaki's extra revs would have been merely a theoretical improvement.

New intake-port shaping helped the engine to breathe better at the top, while a lighter crank (under the new plus-or-minus 20-per cent rules) reduced inertia. Kawasaki said that they were not near the maximum crank weight reduction, but did not give any particular figure.

The result of these cumulative upgrades was a higher-revving 2024 engine, with perhaps 5 or 6bhp more than before. There was also a close-ratio gearset from third to sixth that allowed the extra power to be used more effectively, and a handy over-rev facility between corners.

Given the Kawasaki's longer stroke compared to the most recent models in the class, the lighter crank was mostly designed to help with reverse-torque characteristics entering corners, but it was naturally more free-revving under acceleration.

Reverse-torque limiting via electronics was another particular point of study and improvement, with a greater input from Kawasaki Heavy Industries R&D to create what Kawasaki called TFC – Tyre Force Control – which worked even when the bike was leaned over entering a corner.

Showa front forks with a new internal design, which had no through-rod, allowed softer spring rates for the same level of overall support, providing greater finesse in operation.

The forks' lower design allowed more cooling air to reach the brake calipers and featured 'fluted' sections at points down their length. These gave more suppleness when reacting to side forces created during cornering, but kept the required strength from front to back under heavy braking.

YAMAHA YZF-R1

THERE was no new Yamaha homologation for 2024, until suddenly there was. In September, Yamaha declared a new homologation, the D45, but in reality, it seemed like the existing B3L bike with some quite large aero winglets.

The 79 x 50.9mm, forward-slanted inline engine continued the cross-plane-crankshaft philosophy, but even with the freedom for some extra revs, the bike needed a lot of work to maximise that potential without compromising engine life.

There was a great deal of focus on reverse-torque characteristics and electronics in 2024. Like the others, Yamaha had a suite of electronics and programming for their Magneti Marelli MLE ECUs that could control the machine on a corner-by-corner basis.

There were no great changes on the chassis side, but a new rear suspension link was used – actually a 2023 design that couldn't be used during the previous season. After winter testing, it was added to a modified 2023 swing-arm.

The front forks were the longer of the cost-capped Ohlins choices, at 770mm from top to bottom. They were also of asymmetric design, referred to as 'ovalised', but that was not quite correct. They began life as round fork stanchions, but had flat sections machined into their sides so that they offered more sideways 'give' and feedback on full lean, yet retained strength under direct heavy braking loads. The triple clamps were the same as those used in 2023.

Braking was by Brembo, using their heavily-finned, four-piston front calipers, the pistons being of equal diameter. Anti-drag elements were also added to some calipers. There was a choice of 338.5 or 336mm-diameter discs, which also had small cooling fins or tangs on the inner edge. There were three thickness options for the larger discs, and two for the smaller size. For a machine that had been fighting Alvaro Bautista's Ducati hardest of all in 2023, because of Razgatlioglu at least, 2024 was a tough year with no race wins and a remarkably low podium count.

SUPERBIKE WORLD CHAMPIONSHIP
PHILLIP ISLAND
ROUND 1 · AUSTRALIA

Above: New tyres for elevated champion Bautista during Friday practice.
Photo: Ducati Corse

Top: Kawasaki's Alex Lowes took the race-two win over Bautista.
Photo Gold & Goose

Above right: Class rookie Bulega won the season's opening race.
Photo: Ducati Corse

Right: Iannone leads Lowes, Bulega, Razgatlioglu and Locatelli in the aborted first attempt at race two.
Photo: Gold & Goose

Above: Locatelli made two podiums for Yamaha...

Left: ...but it was an unhappy start for new team-mate, six-times champion Rea.

Below: Danilo Petrucci claimed a podium in race two.

Bottom: Two wins for Alex Lowes.

Below right: Dorna's Gregorio Lavilla and Pirelli's Giorgio Barbier talk about tyres.

Photos: Gold & Goose

THE new kids on the starting blocks were reigning WorldSSP champion Nicolo Bulega (Aruba.it Racing – Ducati) and freshly unbanned MotoGP race winner Andrea Iannone (Team GoEleven Ducati) – a real pair of Duke cats going one-two among the pigeons of the establishment – even after the usual pre-season official testing shortly before race weekend itself.

Which was highly unusual.

Two days indicated that both new Ducati factory riders could be very fast, but also demonstrated that the post-Covid world still has some issues with logistics. The bulk of the WorldSBK tyres turned up too late to complete day one. A sole second day on the new track surface also showed that it was too abrasive on any race tyre option intended to go full race distance.

So the 'long' races were shortened and had a mandatory pit stop jammed into the middle. The Superpole race remained unchanged at ten laps.

For Toprak Razgatlioglu (ROKiT BMW Motorrad WorldSBK Team), his once mystifying gamble to join BMW in 2024 paid off almost instantly, as he led the final testing time sheets on Tuesday. Then he was fifth in Superpole, qualifying for real.

From the front row of race one, Alex Lowes (KRT) would prove his and his slightly changed Ninja ZX-10RR's much-refreshed prowess. Reigning world champion Alvaro Bautista (Aruba.it Racing – Ducati) was only ninth fastest, while first-time Yamaha man Jonathan Rea (Pata Yamaha Prometeon WorldSBK Team) was 11th.

Race one was partly determined by pit stops, but a debut win for Bulega was an amazing start in this company. Especially as he was fully 2.280 seconds clear of his nearest challenger. That was second Pata Yamaha rider Andrea Locatelli, an established Superbike-class runner, with the yellow flash of Iannone only just missing the runner-up spot first time out.

Lowes was fourth and Razgatlioglu a penalised fifth (too fast out of the pit lane after his tyre stop). Bautista was 15th, after a clash and crash with local hero Remy Gardner (GYTR GRT Yamaha), while Rea missed out on the points in 17th.

Some furrowed brows were visible as the old world order was firmly usurped.

The Superpole race was claimed by rejuvenated and *de facto* lead Kawasaki rider Lowes. He crossed the line 1.157 seconds up on Locatelli. In only the second race of his BMW career, Razgatlioglu took his first podium on the M1000RR. Bautista recovered well enough from his first-race troubles to take fourth in the Superpole sprint. Rea was tenth.

The climax of the weekend, appropriately given the earlier antipodean upsets and uncertainties, was a messy, but exciting race two.

The first running was red-flagged after a tech issue for Razgatlioglu's bike at Turn Nine, followed by Rea crashing out at Turn Ten and Gardner subsequently running into the gravel.

The restarted finale ran to 11 laps and was won once again by Lowes. Not only did he manage back-to-back race wins on a hyper-challenging day for all, but also he took the often unfancied Kawasaki to victory in a race with no pit stops. He was just 0.048 of a second ahead of Bautista. Danilo Petrucci (Barni Spark Racing Ducati) was a popular third. Neither Razgatlioglu nor Rea made the restart.

With a new crew chief and a slightly better 2024 bike, Lowes actually managed to hold off an unbroken line of six Ducati riders, all with potentially faster engines in 2024 after the V4-R had regained 500rpm following some changes in the technical rules.

Almost nothing about the look, feel and all-important results of round one could have been predicted. By anyone, not even the main protagonists.

From early logistical embarrassment, through a rookie race-one victory and all the way to the oldest bike in the championship leading the rest home twice, Phillip Island felt as though some kind of altered state of consciousness had jolted our brimming hearts and blown minds.

ROUND 1 • PHILLIP ISLAND 265

SUPERBIKE WORLD CHAMPIONSHIP
CATALUNYA
ROUND 2 · SPAIN

ONE full month after the first round, battle was rejoined. This time, it was in Europe, but again it was preceded by a virtual 'all-out' test session. The Circuit de Barcelona-Catalunya is a legendary MotoGP track, which WorldSBK might never have visited had the pandemic not struck. It has become a popular venue, but we might not get back to it in 2025, which made the 2024 version even more special. Furthermore, two of the five official WorldSBK teams' home bases (KRT and HRC) are located nearby.

After all the wild first-round happenings, things would get back on track, in more senses than the literal one, surely?

Almost everyone expected Razgatlioglu to make a play for race wins around the half-season mark. Too many other strong riders ranged against him and too many well-sorted machines appeared to form a blockade to BMW's top-step ambitions. Especially over 20 laps or so. History was also against him. The last BMW race win – in a ten-lap wet sprint – had been way back in 2021.

He made a startling start in Barcelona, with a record-setting Superpole lap of 1m 39.489s, heading off Bulega and Iannone. Then, astoundingly, he took his first BMW victory in a 20-lap race one, held in dry springtime conditions. He beat Bulega across the line by 0.868 of a second, with Bautista a solid third and Iannone fourth.

Long-time leader Bulega's pace had collapsed as Razgatlioglu's soared, and a four-second advantage was overturned. Quiet man Bulega smashed his bike's screen in rage during the slowdown lap.

Rookie WorldSBK rider Sam Lowes (ELF Marc VDS Ducati) wanted to make an early break in race one, but fell while leading. Rea suffered a clutch-related DNF as his new Yamaha era hit the buffers again.

The Superpole race, over the usual ten laps, was a classic of its kind.

With Bautista leading after passing the No.54 BMW on the final lap, Toprak waited until the very last corner to make a Rossi-replica 'undertake' on his rival's inside right. It was an inspired manoeuvre, which Bautista had not suspected. It was judged hard, but fair, if not fully so by Bautista.

That last-corner calamity even allowed the rapidly skulking Iannone to swoop past and take second. 'The Maniac' only missed out on the win by 0.075 of a second.

Bautista was finally 0.260 of a second back, and even Bulega almost nabbed him. The top four finished within 0.411 of a second of each other. Alex Lowes was just 1.611 seconds back, in fifth.

It was one of the best WorldSBK races of this or any era.

Toprak's wins were a massive vindication of the progress going on within BMW. Another major Bavarian plus was earned by the often-injured Michael van der Mark, in sixth, just over 2.5 seconds behind his team-mate.

There would be no winning triple in Toprak's second Beemer weekend, however, thanks to the official Panigale pairing of Bautista and Bulega. Their one-two was doubly significant. First, the return of Bautista to winning ways. Second, both the true factory Panigales beating all the others by a relatively vast margin.

Razgatlioglu simply could not compete for pace and was just over seven seconds behind the win, although still on the podium. Van der Mark was fourth in race two, proving that his Superpole race was no flash in the pan for man and machine.

Rea finally scored a first Yamaha point, eighth place in race two.

BMW left Barcelona with two wins from three races – and a Superpole trophy. The revamped project was clearly ahead of schedule now that the most talented Superbike rider imaginable was wrestling their bike's handlebars.

Above: Razgatlioglu's first win for BMW. Bulega had no reply.

Left: 'Quiet man' Bulega smashed his screen in rage after race one.

Far left: Blanket finish – Razgatlioglu shades Iannone, Bautista and Bulega at the end of a breathless Superpole race.
Photos: Gold & Goose

Below far left: Early-laps shuffle. Rinaldi and Gerloff lead the pack from Rea (65), Vierge (97) and Redding (obscured), chased by Bassani (behind Redding), Lecuona (7), Oettl (5), Rabat (53) and Ray (28).
Photo: HRC

Below left: Sam Lowes was finding WorldSBK tough.

Bottom: Bautista had the upper hand over team-mate Bulega during race two.

Below right: Tears of joy for BMW's Marc Bongers after Toprak's race-one win.
Photos: Gold & Goose

ROUND 2 • CATALUNYA   267

SUPERBIKE WORLD CHAMPIONSHIP
ASSEN
ROUND 3 · NETHERLANDS

Above: Anxious moments on the wet race-one grid for Nicolo Bulega.
Photo: Ducati Corse

Top: Razgatlioglu leads Bautista and Gardner in race two.

Above right: Team boss Marco Barnabo and rookie replacement Nicholas Spinelli of the Barni team were surprise winners in race one.

Right: Spinelli, on intermediate tyres, just held off the late charge of Razgatlioglu and Bautista in the wet/dry race one.
Photos: Gold & Goose

Above: Win number two in the seventh outing for defending champion Bautista.
Photo: Ducati Corse

Left: Something to smile about. Jonathan Rea was fastest qualifier.

Below: Tarran Mackenzie scored some welcome points for Petronas MIE Honda.

Bottom: Denied in the morning, Remy Gardner took a coveted first podium in race two.

Below right: No home-race joy for Dutchman Michael van der Mark.
Photos: Gold & Goose

WE know that the current Assen layout, no longer forming a capital 'Q', poses fewer questions to the riders than its many previous formats. The perennial question remains, however. What kind of April weather will we have to face at a circuit that is located so close to the North Sea?

However, not all the regulars would face any Assen weather in 2024.

Danilo Petrucci had come close to ending his career in a motocross crash after the Catalunya round. He was ruled out due to multiple fractures. His place was taken by 2023-season, Phillip Island WorldSSP podium runner Nicholas Spinelli. A complete WorldSBK rookie.

In Superpole qualifying, held in wet-then-drying conditions, Jonathan Rea took his first Yamaha pole 'win' to bring some light into the surprisingly dark corners of the manufacturer's effort in 2024.

Spinelli started race one 11th after that damp Superpole qualifying, on a wet track and with rain starting to fall again in a few places. With front and rear intermediate tyres, Spinelli was into the lead long before the start of the second lap, passing both Rea and Iannone in audacious fashion.

The rookie's inters worked well enough on both the really wet and drying areas of asphalt. His pace put him more than four seconds ahead on lap one, and more than 24 with 15 laps to go.

Razgatlioglu and Bautista were already fighting for the final two podium places with half the race still to run.

When Toprak and Alvaro had finally reeled in Spinelli, with seven laps still to go, a red flag was thrown due to a serious fluid leak from Locatelli's Yamaha. Thus Spinelli took his maiden race win, from Razgatlioglu and Bautista.

The first WorldSBK race victory for the Barni Spark team was bitter sweet, Petrucci watching history being made by his stand-in from his hospital bed.

Sunday's Superpole race brought a second win of the year for Bautista, through from seventh in one of his most imperious performances.

His last five laps were remarkable, his last two even more so, as he caught then escaped from long-time leader Bulega with polished ease.

Alex Lowes used his well-conserved tyres to jump Remy Gardner right at the end to snatch third, depriving the Australian of his first WorldSBK podium.

The final race of the weekend was dry, but with a slab of grey infiltrating the low-level cloud cover.

Bautista, having started from pole, was the early leader, but with Locatelli right behind him.

Razgatlioglu, only ninth in the Superpole race, was third after just two laps. He took the lead with 14 to go.

Drops of rain in sector two were reported on lap nine, which closed up the motorised peloton again, as some of the front-running riders chose caution while the chasers took greater risks. Then Bautista reclaimed the lead.

Rea and Lowes, closing in on the leading bunch, collided and crashed, Lowes losing the front and then accepting the blame for wiping out his rival.

Heavier rain began to affect the track surface. Gardner took the lead in the changing conditions; Locatelli joined him in second as a seven-rider leading group formed.

Once the rain had stopped again, Razgatlioglu started passing for fun, eventually reaching the very front in his usual confident fashion. He kept his head, his pace and his lead as more spots of rain affected the circuit with two laps to go.

Full commitment gave Razgatlioglu his first win at Assen on a BMW and a first ever Assen win for the marque. With Bautista second, Gardner took his coveted first WorldSBK podium.

Three different winners demonstrated three very different ways of winning.

SUPERBIKE WORLD CHAMPIONSHIP
MISANO
ROUND 4 · ITALY

Above: One-wheel wonder – Razgatlioglu took the third of three wins in race two.

Right: Bassani collected points for Kawasaki in all three races.
Photos: Gold & Goose

Below: A rare outing for Ducati test rider Michele Pirro.
Photo: Ducati Corse

Below right: Battle-scarred, but back in action, Petrucci made a racing return.
Photo: Gold & Goose

Above: No wins for Ducati Corse boss Gigi Dall'Igna, taking a break from MotoGP.
Photo: Ducati Corse

Left: Yamaha privateer Phillip Oettl.
Photo: Gold & Goose

Below: Sun-baked conditions were a marked contrast to the previous outing at Assen.
Photo: Ducati Corse

FROM the rain and wind-blasted north to the sun-kissed beaches of the Italian Adriatic, WorldSBK had to endure fully two months of inaction between rounds three and four.

According to the always reliable internet, the paddock personnel could have walked the considerable 1,334km distance between these two beloved tracks in 13 days. If we all had the proper shoes, of course.

Such a big gap in the race action, just after we had really started the season proper, was simply a reality of contemporary WorldSBK life. After two of the contracted long-haul races, at Manadalika and Villicum, had severed ties, there were no obvious or immediate replacements.

One new Italian venue would appear ahead of schedule, but this first venture over the Alps would cross the Rubicon in a literal sense, as we headed back to an old friend, the Misano World Circuit Marco Simoncelli. Constant updates and investments in the entire facility have made it even more of a nailed-on WorldSBK favourite.

The almost totally flat circuit layout is 'enlivened' by the wildly long succession of right-handers, from the top-gear/full-commitment of the Curvone to the more obvious passing spot at the Curva del Carro.

In 2024, heat and dust were our Misano bedfellows again (after all, it was mid-June), but the hot tarmac could not stop Toprak Razgatlioglu from turning one of his 'Okay' circuits into a personal asphalt fiefdom. Superpole qualifying glory was placed at his feet with his 1m 32.320s new track best, with Nicolo Bulega and Remy Gardner also on the front row.

Gardner, riding in his GYTR GRT Yamaha team's first home round, led for three laps, but once Razgatlioglu got ahead, it was all over bar the sliding and cheering. The win gave him the championship lead.

Bulega finished second and Alvaro Bautista third. Andrea Locatelli took a fine fourth, having held off the consistent and determined Alex Lowes.

The Superpole race on Sunday morning was aced by the combination of Razgatlioglu and BMW, again from Bulega, although on this occasion, Lowes came home third.

Bautista fell from podium contention, at the Tramonto corner on lap five, and eventually was ranked 17th. That's well out of the half-points that the ten-lap races score for the top nine finishers.

Local riders Locatelli, Iannone and Axel Bassani (KRT) finished fourth to sixth, with new factory Ninja rider Bassani having his best race so far in the world of official team expectations.

The final Sunday face-off, held in hot conditions once again, produced the same Razgatlioglu, Bulega and Bautista podium order of race one, but this time, it was all very different.

For seven laps, at least.

Bulega pushed as hard as he could in the early stages and appeared likely to add another race win to his portfolio. Razgatlioglu's inline four was performing miracles under the racing force of nature that is Toprak, however, and Bulega ended up almost three seconds down at the flag after 21 laps. BMW's first ever weekend hat trick.

Bautista's third was disappointing for him, but a great recovery from his Superpole race calamity earlier in the day.

Fourth was Alex Lowes, fifth Locatelli, but by some miracle, the returning Danilo Petrucci, with a smashed jaw just one of his evident injuries, took sixth. He said it felt like a win, and for the power of the human spirit to overcome pain and setback, it certainly was a full-points score.

With Imola no longer on the calendar, Misano is the closest Ducati gets to race in its own backyard. Normally, there is a win somewhere for them, often more. The fact that Razgatlioglu and BMW mopped up every measurable success in 2024 (including a new lap record of 1m 32.687s set in the Superpole race) had a few people in red visibly concerned.

SUPERBIKE WORLD CHAMPIONSHIP
DONINGTON
ROUND 5 · GREAT BRITAIN

Above: Family and friends join Jonathan Rea and the Pata Yamaha gang for a first (and last) podium celebration of the year.

Left: Swooping and undulating, Donington's parkland circuit is a WorldSBK classic.

Below far left: Scott Redding used local knowledge to good effect.
Photos: Gold & Goose

Below left: The Mackenzie brothers.

Bottom left: Alex Lowes was twice on the podium at home.
Photos: Clive Challinor Motorsport Photography

Below: With new lap records every outing, Razgatlioglu demonstrated total control for a second triple in succession.
Photo: Gold & Goose

DONINGTON can be an inland version of Assen as far as the weather is concerned, but the birthplace of WorldSBK racing way back in 1988 is also a regular stop for the production-derived travelling circus. The 4.023km track layout offers literally a bit of everything.

It really is a 21st-century schizoid track, despite an ancient motorsport provenance going back to 1931. The opening part of the frequently off-camber tarmac is fast, flowing and endlessly undulating. The last sector is all hard braking and acceleration – first for a chicane, then for a very slow right hairpin and a final tight left hairpin.

Thus a perfect bike set-up is an impossibility, but in 2024, the perfect overall weekend was easily located inside the official BMW garage.

Razgatlioglu simply loves Donington, which is strange, as he says he doesn't like long corners as much as stop-start tracks. But the first 70 per cent of Donington is sweeping and flowing in extremis.

Nonetheless, Toprak said he was aiming for a triple winning weekend, and he achieved it, with some ease in the end.

He set himself up for the races with the fastest time on Friday and another Superpole 'win' on Saturday. Bulega was his closest competitor again, while the previously struggling Scott Redding (Bonovo Action BMW) took third on the grid.

A barnstorming 1m 24.629s Superpole lap time was a track best for Razgatlioglu. He was the only one under 1m 25s and a whopping 0.573 of a second faster than Bulega.

Track-limits infractions on his fastest lap dropped Alex Lowes to ninth. Struggling 2024 qualifier Bautista was 11th.

The opening race was so dominated by Razgatlioglu that second-place rider Lowes finished over 11 seconds back. Bautista was third, just over 13 seconds behind the fleeing M1000RR.

And flee he truly did, with a new lap record of 1m 25.786s, set on lap three.

Redding was on course for a good finish, but after a second escape-road venture at the chicane, he retired with a technical issue.

Bulega, also off-track at one stage, was fourth.

The Superpole race was led initially by Bulega, but as soon as Razgatlioglu hit the front on lap three, and managed to make a gap, the race one-two was set. Razgatlioglu, naturally if only just, reduced the lap record to 1m 25.733s.

The most remarkable thing about the Superpole race was a return to the podium by Jonathan Rea. He made an amazing start from row three, getting away from the pack and settling into a fast-paced third. He even kept this place until the end to score an entirely unlikely podium, even for a six-times champion. The surprise, and delight, from many was a measure of how tough things had been until this result.

The final Donington race was memorable even before the start. Bautista fell on the sighting lap, and mechanics had to make hurried repairs on the grid for him to make the warm-up lap.

Another race, another front-running shift put in by Razgatlioglu, and a final new lap record at 1m 25.597s.

Bulega, still not quite happy with his bike set-up, was the runner-up, but over eight seconds down on Razgatlioglu.

Redding could have taken third had it not been for the final home flourish of Alex Lowes, who added a bronze to his race-one silver medal.

Another fourth for Redding was definite progress; Bautista could only finish fifth, however.

The season was hardening into some form of top-four battle, with Razgatlioglu, Bulega, Bautista and Lowes all forming a kind of loose breakaway group. Somebody was going to have to find a way to stop the victory-harvesting unit that was Toprak to prevent it from becoming a one-man winning show, now suffixed by home-baked trackside comedy skits on the slow-down laps.

SUPERBIKE WORLD CHAMPIONSHIP
MOST
ROUND 6 · CZECH REPUBLIC

Above: Another race, another triple for Toprak.

Right: Petrucci managed to keep Iannone at bay on Saturday.

Top right: Michael Rinaldi, now reduced to privateer, was seventh in race two.

Above right: Rabat and Ray battle over the final points in race two.

Far right: With Mackenzie and Norrodin having been injured at Donington, Petronas MIE Honda ran the experienced Argentine Leandro Mercado (*left*), and rookie from MotoAmerica Hayden Gillim.

Below right: Yamaha-mounted Gardner and Locatelli disputed the last podium spot in race two. By the flag, the order had been reversed.

Photos: Gold & Goose

DESPITE needing some extra safety measures, the Autodrom Most has settled nicely into the canon of WorldSBK's post-pandemic work. Brno was a great loss from the calendar, but Most and its enthusiastic management make this race weekend worthwhile, despite the limitations of space and facilities.

The media grouse, quite rightly, about still having to work inside a noisy tent in 2024. And the pit garages are perhaps even more Lilliputian than Donington's. That said, the unique ribbon of asphalt and the former Communist-era grandeur of the track's overall design offer a true one-off challenge and spectacle. More than 20 corners (depending on how you count them) wrap around a semi-conical hillside, the paddock being dominated by two angular grandstands.

Castles to the right of us, satanic industry behind us; the bikes fairly volley and thunder within panoramic sight around every kind of curve, kink and frequent change of direction imaginable.

There had been some real issues with tyres in 2023, and to a lesser extent in 2024, but once again, Toprak found a potential banana-skin venue that would provide a small barrel of golden apples. Would anyone be surprised to hear that he secured the Superpole win, then three race wins, at yet another kind of unique track design?

Superpole was not so much a win as an exercise in domination, with a new track best of 1m 30.064s. That was 0.6 of a second faster than the next best qualifier, Iannone. Razgatlioglu was even a little disappointed not to get into the 1:29s.

This winning monoculture might have become wearying by this stage but for the fact that he is so deservedly popular, genuine and unique in his riding style. Watching him in isolation is a form of entertainment.

His closest rivals had been watching him ride on his own far too often for their liking, but they couldn't do anything about him again in race one, as he simply cleared off in the 22-lap race.

The independent Ducati battle going on behind was intense. Miraculously, Petrucci was riding like he had never been away, and he secured second, more than five seconds adrift of Razgatlioglu, and only 0.141 of a second ahead of Iannone. Second, however, after having lost at least a couple of his nine lives in that fateful motocross crash, was almost transcendental.

Iannone's first podium place since the second round was also remarkable, especially as official Ducati riders Bautista and Bulega crossed the line in fourth and sixth respectively.

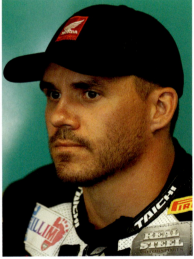

In the Superpole race on Sunday morning, Bulega and Bautista led Razgatlioglu for a time, with some genuine fights in the first few laps. Sam Lowes crashed early, taking out Scott Redding; then eventually Bautista ran Bulega wide at the infamous T1/2 chicane and crashed himself as he tried to regain the track.

Bulega finally took second, with Alex Lowes pressing hard on the last lap after passing Petrucci.

The third and final Most race was another Razgatlioglu benefit, as he crushed all attempts at 22-lap parity.

In a multi-rider T1, lap-one incident, Petrucci felt that he had been eased to the left, only to clatter into Bautista. Both Ducati riders fell – neither getting back on – and Iannone was also pushed wide to spoil his podium chances.

Bulega had escaped, but he finished second again, having led Razgatlioglu for the first four laps. Andrea Locatelli claimed a rare podium for Yamaha. Gardner was fourth, for a season-best weekend finishing record of 5-5-4.

Even with only half of the races now complete, Bautista's points losses, Bulega's regularly rebuffed assaults and Razgatlioglu's untouchable pace around the snaking Czech asphalt had people heralding a championship win for BMW well before October. Perhaps wisely, BMW staff held their counsel on that.

SUPERBIKE WORLD CHAMPIONSHIP
PORTIMAO
ROUND 7 · PORTUGAL

Above: Did they jump or were they pushed? The BMW squad celebrated another triple by taking a fully-clothed dip.

Right: Danilo Petrucci was twice on the podium.

Below: Bautista was close to Razgatlioglu when he tumbled in race two.

Photos: Gold & Goose

Above: On-the-gas Gerloff was fourth in race one.

Left: Thirteen straight wins for BMW.
Photos: Gold & Goose

Below: Bulega found his muse to challenge for a win in race two.

Bottom: A kiss for m'lady. Bautista cuddles up to his Duke after taking second in race one.
Photos: Ducati Corse

Below right: Progress for Honda's Xavi Vierge, who collected points in all three races.
Photo: Gold & Goose

THE early sadness in the air at Portimao was due to the untimely loss of the man without whom the entire Autodromo Internacional do Algarve facility would not have existed. The late Paulo Pinheiro was missed by all who had ever known him. The greatest testimony was that, once again, we had three typically dramatic and tense WorldSBK races at this truly unique hillside roller coaster of tarmac.

The 4.592km circuit is a real rider's track, where bravery and skill count for a lot in the infield sections. In fairness, enough engine power is also required to take on the lengthy uphill/downhill front straight and remain in contention for the lead.

In 2023, Razgatlioglu did not quite have that top-end power. But now he was so fast on the straight that he clipped Alex Lowes' Kawasaki tailpiece while slipstreaming and lost an entire aero winglet.

As was becoming the norm, Razgatlioglu secured the Superpole qualifying 'win', making it five pre-race successes in a row. However, he was only 0.104 of a second ahead of second-placed Alex Lowes and 0.188 of a second up on Danilo Petrucci's Ducati.

If Donington had been demolition and Most merely supremacy, would Portimao allow at least one rider with an equally fast engine (Ducati or even Honda) the chance to beat the champion-elect in a real race?

Razgatlioglu's amazing form ensured that the answer would be three times nay by Sunday evening. And we do mean evening. Portimao experimented with running the feature WorldSBK races much later than normal, starting at 18:00. They still ended in daylight, but not long before twilight, encouraging people to make it a night at the races as well as a day.

Feared delays, red flags, heavy oil spills and a subsequent possibility of a cancellation due to bad light were all averted.

The action on track was as breathtaking as ever, as Toprak won race one from Bautista and Petrucci. Alex Lowes led for four laps, then Petrucci for eight, but Razgatlioglu triumphed after all. Only by 0.780 of a second this time around, however, and from an inspired Bautista, who had been only 13th after lap one of 20. An amazing podium recovery from the reigning champ.

Race one gave Razgatlioglu 11 race wins in succession, equalling the record held by Rea and Bautista. He won the Superpole race, too, and became the most repeatable race winner that the class had ever seen: 12 wins in 12 successive races.

He had to beat a determined Petrucci by almost three seconds to ensure that record-breaking status in the sprint race, with Alex Lowes' Kawasaki close behind the privateer Ducati rider in third.

In the final, with the pressure of history suddenly released for Razgatlioglu and BMW, the self-generated on-track pressure remained. No problem for the Turk? After all, he did secure win number three of the weekend, his 15th for the season.

The reality was that Bulega was only just behind, by 0.035 of a second, as Razgatlioglu slowed up a little over the line.

Lowes was third again, and with Bautista a faller and then 19th, the KRT man really was closing in on a potential overall third place.

It was one of those remarkable WorldSBK weekends, with the extremely hilly circuit – and in particular its tricky first-turn downhill passing opportunity – adding a certain something extra to a spectacle that more fans really should come to see first hand.

After the on-track expectation, it seemed that the entire official BMW squad had congregated at the side of the swimming pool, located just outside the circuit restaurant. One by one, the bosses jumped in (or were pushed) to join the jubilant Razgatliolgu who, by this stage, was bathing in as much glory as he was chlorinated water.

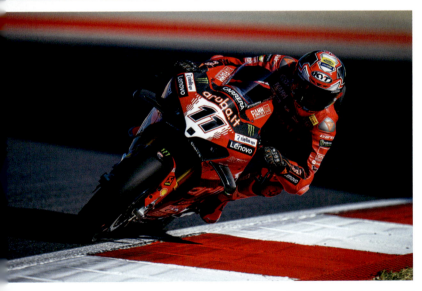

SUPERBIKE WORLD CHAMPIONSHIP
MAGNY-COURS
ROUND 8 · FRANCE

Above: Razgatlioglu meets the tyre barrier at speed. The next day, protective foam was in place.
Photo: WorldSBK

Top: With his team leader hurt, Michael van der Mark took a long-awaited win.

Above right: Toprak was on hand to congratulate fellow BMW rider van der Mark.

Right: Redding held Iannone at bay for fourth in race one.
Photos: Gold & Goose

Above: Lowes narrowly lost out to Bulega in the Superpole race.

Left: With Aegerter hurt in a training crash, Italian Alessandro Delbianco stood in on the GYRT Yamaha, scoring points in both feature races.

Below: Lecuona was a season's-best fourth for Honda.

Bottom: Gerloff enjoyed his first podium of the year for third in race two.

Below right: Petrucci was twice third and once second in France.

Photos: Gold & Goose

IN the absence of car racing's steel roll cages and carbon-fibre bathtubs, motorcycle racers rely on primary safety protocols, like run-off areas and gravel traps (so realistically they cannot hit anything hard, no matter how fast they fall). If that's impossible, secondary safety precautions are adopted. That means any barrier that cannot be removed is heavily shrouded in the appropriate foam layers or air-fence. Or both.

At Magny-Cours – between the drop from Chateaux d'Eau to the final Complexe du Lycee corners – there is a safety barrier designed to stop bikes and riders from sliding back on-track if they fall at the apex of the fast downhill left. Just as Toprak Razgatlioglu did during the FP2 session. With no appropriate foam or inflatable barriers for that aforesaid 'protective' wall (or even a correctly sited gravel trap to slow him down before impact), the championship leader took a horrifying blow to his midriff as he caught the end of the tyre wall.

He was spun back towards the track, like an earthbound rag doll, and ended up back on the track itself.

It looked bad, like a crash from another racing era.

He had a miraculous escape from a much more serious injury than a mild pneumothorax (punctured lung). The fact that he walked away came down to the mandatory airbag system inside his racing suit.

Foam protection appeared on the offending tyre barrier the next day, but their original omission had been an unacceptable lapse in the safety protocols that can never be allowed to happen anywhere ever again.

When action got under way on Saturday, a Superpole qualifying win for Alex Lowes was only the second of his long career and his first for Kawasaki.

With Toprak ruled out, it was a painful and disturbed weekend for two other recent world champions. Rea fell in a lap-one accident in race one, entering the chicane when Niccolo Bulega discovered that his intermediate tyres had not enough grip on the wet track. Bulega high-sided off, while Rea, right behind him, appeared to have his own crash, injuring his right thumb. He was declared unfit.

Alvaro Bautista fell hard after crashing in the Superpole race on Sunday morning and was also ruled out, having cracked his eighth rib.

The first race, run in damp, then wet conditions, was a flag-to-flag maelstrom of pit-lane action and snap decisions, finally won by Michael van der Mark. It was a tremendous result for a rider who had been so plagued by injuries in recent times. He had also been fastest on a dry Friday, so wet-weather Saturday win or not, his personal best pace was clearly returning.

Alex Lowes had fallen from a leading position during race one, simply by being too eager.

Bautista was second in that first race, after another miraculous run from 17th on the grid. Third was the podium-bound Lazarus, Danilo Petrucci.

Most riders had started on slicks or inters, the podium players changing to wets as the rain became heavier.

The Superpole scrap on Sunday was headed up by Bulega, from the closely following and combative Lowes. He was finally only 0.115 of a second behind. Petrucci was third again, but only after a tough fight between several ambitious riders, including Scott Redding, eventually fourth.

In the final full Magny-Cours race, Bulega doubled his French total. Petrucci completed a superb triple-podium weekend with second place. America's lone WorldSBK star, Garrett Gerloff (Bonovo Action BMW), made good on his occasional podium promises. Lowes was one place behind in fourth, having dropped to 19th at one stage.

Even with no Toprak, the racing was far from flat, but the mood definitely was, with introspection reigning more heavily than the physical rain ever did.

SUPERBIKE WORLD CHAMPIONSHIP
CREMONA
ROUND 9 · ITALY

Above: Petrucci again – leading the pack on Sunday morning.

Right: The wet conditions left seas of mud.

Centre right: Last-minute work to get the new track into shape.
Photos: Gold & Goose

Below: Lecuona leads Locatelli, Bautista and Honda team-mate Vierge during race one.
Photo: HRC

CHAMPIONSHIP leader Toprak Razgatlioglu might have lost his points lead altogether had things gone differently for his closest championship challenger at an all-new WorldSBK venue, the Cremona Circuit in northern Italy.

With Razgatlioglu absent, the facility was a blank canvas for any aspiring rider, just as it had been for a mid-season test in May. Many of the buildings, rumble strips and facilities that were present on race weekend had not been visible then.

Cremona had never hosted so much as a national championship round before, operating essentially as a test and track-day venue.

WorldSBK longs for a second Italian round every year, as Italy is the bedrock on which half its teams stand. They all need more home rounds to find more sponsors. After the enforced cancellation of the expected Mandalika and Villicum flyaway rounds, WorldSBK needed a new circuit, and Cremona dived into the fray a year ahead of schedule.

At just 3.768km, the circuit is short, with a lot of small, tight corners and one massive back straight – possibly with not enough run-off at the end. Heavy rains before the event turned the 'car parks' in nearby fields into muddy skating rinks.

More importantly, an unexpected power overload in one part of the new facility caused a temporary outage of some vital track safety systems during race one. That meant it was red-flagged, not restarted and called a result on lap 17.

And what a result.

After Bulega had taken pole, with an automatic new track best time, of course, race one was being led by sixth-place qualifier Danilo Petrucci when the red flag was thrown. He was more than worth his advantage, thankfully, having ridden with aplomb to lead the official V4-Rs of Bulega and Bautista. The latter had been 13th off the grid after yet another horrorific Superpole.

Petrucci's fully deserved win, and the sheer noise made by the local fans (despite limited numbers being allowed in each day at this early stage of the venue's development), overshadowed another significant happening. Iker Lecuona (HRC Honda) was fourth and his team-mate, Xavi Vierge, sixth. Honda had been making some improvements to their latest homologation of Fireblade and it was finally starting to show.

Axel Bassani also had his best ride in Kawasaki colours, in fifth place despite the relatively warm track temperature.

In the Superpole race on Sunday, Petrucci won again, but on this occasion from first-race no-scorer Alex Lowes and Petrucci's Ducati privateer compatriot, Andrea Iannone.

Bulega was fourth, Lecuona fifth and Bautista sixth.

The almost perfect weekend for Petrucci soon became just that with a close win over Bautista in the final race, which made it to the planned 23 laps this time around. Bautista was just over a second behind, Bulega almost two seconds further back.

Gerloff was fourth, winning a final man-to-man fight with Alex Lowes.

No Razgatlioglu, of course, but the redemptive powers of WorldSBK had worked their magic on another rider's career. Petrucci's victory floodgates (an appropriate term given the pre-race precipitation) had their bloody doors blown off in the self-penned reworking of his own Italian job.

He not only joined the list of WorldSBK race winners, but also became the 18th winner of at least one WorldSBK and one MotoGP race. In addition, he carved out a niche for himself in being the only rider to have won a stage of the Dakar rally. These three triumphs were Barni Spark Racing's first hat trick of wins at this level.

Petrucci's personal success was no help to the leading Ducati rider in the title fight, as Bulega left Cremona still behind Razgatlioglu in the championship, but by only 13 points.

Above: Marvin Fritz *(left)* and Nicolo Canepa were in as Yamaha replacements – Canepa subbing for Rea, injured in France.

Top: Xavi Vierge took eighth for Honda in race two.

Left: Markus Reiterberger stood in for Razgatlioglu.

Below: Three wins made a little history for Petrucci.

Below right: Iannone made a podium return in the Superpole race.

Photos: Gold & Goose

SUPERBIKE WORLD CHAMPIONSHIP
ARAGON
ROUND 10 · SPAIN

Above: Sam Lowes clashed with Rea on the opening lap of race one, coming off worse.

Top: Iannone leads Gerloff, Razgatlioglu and Bautista during race one.

Above right: Bautista and Razgatlioglu fought for first in Superpole.

Right: Line astern, the field stretches out on Aragon's baked track.
Photos: Gold & Goose

Above: Bautista and Ducati celebrated two wins.
Photo: Ducati Corse

Left: Good enough. Toprak returned to action with three seconds.
Photo: Gold & Goose

Bottom: Chasing the leaders. Lecuona leads Locatelli, Rinaldi, Vierge and Gardner.
Photo: HRC

Below right: Iannone joined the select ranks of winners in grand prix and superbike racing.
Photo: Gold & Goose

THE first and most significant question asked at Motorland Aragon was whether Toprak Razgatlioglu would be declared fit to ride. Having been ruled out just one week before in Cremona, he was literally driven from a recuperation facility in Austria to potential competition in Spain by his manager and mentor, Kenan Sofuoglu.

Toprak was declared free of any lung puncture, passed a further review after FP1 and was declared fit to race.

Sighs of relief all round, because the championship fight needed to carry on without the crash in France being the ultimate determining factor.

As it turned out, almost the entire post-Superpole qualifying action at Motorland would be a series of surprises and freakish scenarios.

In Superpole, four Ducati riders – Bulega, Iannone, Bautista and Petrucci – dominated the windy conditions, but Razgatlioglu was clearly already on form in fifth. He had come straight back to be fastest in Friday's FP1, naturally.

The first race would be another Latin love poem dedicated to the spirit of pure competition, just as it had been for Petrucci a few days before. But only after some wicked Pandoras had been unboxed.

Sam Lowes was ruled out of the first start when a piece of Yamaha's newly homologated winglets, from Rea's bike, became lodged in his back wheel, eventually throwing him off. It looked like oil at first, with all that blue smoke from the tyre, so a red flag was thrown and we started all over again, the race being cut from 18 to 17 laps.

Then, suddenly, Bulega stopped by the trackside on his way to the restart. A problem with his engine, he said later.

Iannone, everybody's favourite bad boy, duly took his hyper-yellow Ducati to the race-one win after leading every single lap bar one. Only Petrucci briefly broke his stride across the stripe.

Many had expected long-time second-placed Razgatlioglu to catch Iannone and then pounce with a trademark outbraking manoeuvre. Iannone had plotted and ridden just perfectly, however, and had enough tyre left for a first Superbike race win. His bike had spluttered on the long back straight, short of fuel, but he had just enough left to coax it to the line, 0.845 of a second ahead of runner-up Razgatlioglu.

On the podium, Iannone cried, then laughed, all while his team members in the pit lane bounced off each other in happy hysteria; two of them even knocking each other over with their uncontrolled expressions of joy. Team and rider had taken a risk on each other pre-season and now the payoff was being celebrated by the delirious Italians.

Iannone became the 19th rider to have won both a MotoGP and a WorldSBK race, and the fourth first-time race winner in 2024.

Razgatlioglu, on an abused front tyre, held off a very strong fight from Gerloff for second, with Bautista just 0.066 of a second from the podium. Truly superb stuff for the disappointingly small crowd to enjoy as WorldSBK racing revelled at Toprak being back.

Sunday would be a return to funday for Bautista, as he won both races. He was too crafty in a late ding-dong with Razgatlioglu in the Superpole race, edging him out by just 0.088 of a second. Bulega, in a battling third, was only 0.172 of a second from the win himself.

Bautista's assertion that he was back to his best from 2023 proved true again in race two, as eventually he took a 3.366-second advantage over Razgatlioglu after 18 laps.

A third Motorland runner-up spot for Razgatlioglu proved that he was back at almost full pace, but he remained winless at Motorland, one of his least favourite tracks. Bulega was third in race two, 10.8 seconds behind his team-mate, but now an elongated 39 points adrift of Razgatlioglu.

SUPERBIKE WORLD CHAMPIONSHIP
ESTORIL
ROUND 11 · PORTUGAL

Above: Three unimaginable thousandths – Bulega beat Razgatlioglu in the sprint, in the closest ever WorldSBK finish.
Photo: Ducati Corse

Right: Redding was facing an uncertain future in the class.

Centre right: Luca Bernardi was Yamaha's latest substitute rider.

Below: Bulega was shadowed, but not challenged, by team-mate Bautista on Sunday afternoon.
Photos: Gold & Goose

Above: Jonathan Rea set third-fastest time in Superpole.

Left: A welcome point for Portuguese Petronas Honda replacement Ivo Lopes.

Below: Razgatlioglu took race-two victory to make it two out of three.

Bottom: From 14th on lap one, Lecuona made it to the race-one podium.

Below right: Lecuona's improved Honda leads Iannone, team-mate Vierge and Gerloff in race one.

Photos: Gold & Goose

WITH the full force of the Atlantic Ocean just a few kilometres to the west, the Circuito do Estoril can be a wet and windy place in October. The early weekend weather was unusually dreadful, however, affecting every WorldSBK session in some way or other, right until the start of the first 21-lap race on Saturday.

A wet Superpole was finally headed by 2024's great man/machine package, Toprak Razgatlioglu and the M1000RR. He only just saw off a late charge from Petrucci, by 0.082 of a second, but it was the sight of Jonathan Rea in third that echoed previously better times for both rider and his new partners, Yamaha.

Petrucci ran out of luck and road in race one, falling and no-scoring, like another aggressive early force, Andrea Locatelli. Crashes, too, for Axel Bassani and Remy Gardner, the latter breaking the hamate bone in his left hand.

Up front and out front from lap five onwards, Toprak Razgatlioglu gave another masterclass in how to transcend all conventions, taking the previously too-tricky BMW to not just another race win, but also a margin of victory of over nine seconds. He had set a race fastest lap on the ninth go-around. After opting for a regular 'cooking' SC0 rear tyre, not an SCX of some kind like the rest, his patient start and consistently high pace made this one of his more dominant wins.

Bautista was third after four laps, having started in 11th, but he fell from second place with 11 laps to go.

Bulega took over second after Bautista slid off and finished runner-up.

Crashes by other riders just behind the top two resulted in Lecuona taking third place. Not bad for a rider who had crossed the finish line on lap one in a lowly 14th.

This was Lecuona's first podium since Assen in 2022, and Honda's first since Xavi Vierge's third place at Mandalika in 2023. Recent improvements had made a difference.

The Superpole race was held on a sunny Sunday and was shaping up to be yet another Razgatlioglu ten-lap victory roll until Bulega began to dig, and dig deeply into the vast resources of his machine and his own self-belief.

A new lap record of 1m 36.178s on lap eight kept him close enough to the otherwise imperious Razgatlioglu to slip into his wake around the final complex of corners. Exiting the last long right, which had witnessed so many dramas over the years, he and Toprak were fixed on two different racing lines. Bulega's inside trajectory was squeezed even tighter to the pit wall as Razgatlioglu gradually moved across in an attempt to defend.

As the riders flashed across the line, neither knew who had won – until a Ducati team member handed a *tricolore* banner to Bulega, and he celebrated win number four. He and his Turkish rival had just made history with the closest ever WorldSBK race finish. A minuscule 0.003 of a second had separated 2024's big two.

Bautista crossed the line third, having literally powered past Locatelli on the straight on lap eight. His modified street-bike was clocked at nearly 204mph in the Superpole race…

The penultimate round's mini-finale was not quite a flop, but it was a flip from the closest ever margin of victory to a 3.866-second advantage for Razgatlioglu over Bulega. A dutiful, but mischievous Bautista harried and hustled behind bike No.11, but didn't pass him at the end. A personal decision, not team orders, it seems. With the podium set, Rea had his personal-best long-race finish of the year, and his best weekend yet.

No title decided quite yet, but 46 points gave Razgatlioglu a handy advantage as WorldSBK crossed the Iberian border into Spain for a true championship finale.

ROUND 11 • ESTORIL

SUPERBIKE WORLD CHAMPIONSHIP
JEREZ
ROUND 12 · SPAIN

Above: The 'alien' emerges from his makeshift spacecraft.

Top: Golden boy Razgatlioglu clinched the title in race one and celebrated in style.

Above right: Gilded helmet and BMW – the 2024 WorldSBK champion.

Right: Michael van der Mark leads Iannone and Lowes in race two, on his way to the podium.

Photos: Gold & Goose

BECAUSE of that unforgettably awful crash for Toprak Razgatlioglu at Magny-Cours, we had to wait until mid-October for the greatest showman in modern WorldSBK history to make his indelible mark in the history books with his BMW.

The arithmetic was on Razgatlioglu's side. He had left the penultimate round in Estoril with a 46-point lead over the quiet upstart, 2023 WorldSSP champ Nicolo Bulega. The new lead Ducati rider's final mission to overhaul the Turkish rider was beginning to look impossible.

Alvaro Bautista? He was a nailed-on third overall before we had even started the final three races of the season in Andalusia.

Bulega clearly approached the last weekend with fire in his belly. His Superpole qualifying win laid down a marker for Razgatlioglu, and his opening-race winning pace was a reality that the BMW rider could not overcome.

Even when Toprak had been right behind Bulega for most of the 20 laps, his rival maintained a strong pace, then upped it in truly dominant fashion.

Razgatlioglu's slightly imperfect full-race set-up left him with a dilemma. Naturally, he wanted to win the race to claim the title, but it wasn't really necessary. For perhaps the first time in his recent life, discretion proved the better part of valour, much to the relief of his team.

Above: Rookie runner-up Bulega claimed the race-one win.

Left: The vastly experienced Tetsu Nagashima made a wild-card appearance, scoring a point.

Below: Locatelli took the final race-one podium place after a close battle with Lecuona and Alex Lowes.

Bottom: BMW's Razgatlioglu and van der Mark finally shared a podium.

Below right: BSB champion Kyle Ryde made a wild-card appearance.
Photos: Gold & Goose

Bulega's superb win – by more than six seconds – spoiled only one element of Toprak's championship-winning effort, however. First, the Turk's rivals stopped one by one out on track to congratulate him. Then the latest celebratory comedy caper unfolded – Razgatlioglu, WorldSBK's very own alien, entered a makeshift 'flying saucer' out by the T12 grandstand. He emerged through the green haze created by distress flares wearing a golden race suit and gilded crash helmet.

Then he performed a massive rolling stoppie down the pit lane, so enthusiastically executed that he literally killed his rear tyre. It went pop long before he reached the podium *parc fermé*. It was paradoxical to watch his bike's rear end juddering and lolloping towards the red-carpet celebrations with a self-imposed puncture after such a sure-footed season.

Not quite lost in the smoke from an abused rear tyre and bright green flares was the fact that Andrea Locatelli had given a slightly desperate Yamaha season a welcome podium sheen, having held off Alex Lowes and Iker Lecuona for third in race one.

With the points pressure off, Razgatlioglu was keen to win the ten-lap Superpole race on Sunday morning. He didn't – couldn't – as Bulega still had enough tyre, personal grit and sheer go to ease away from him and score his sixth win of the year.

Razgatlioglu had taken the lead from Bulega early on, at T5, but with five to go, the Ducati rider repaid the compliment at the same corner and set about stretching the gap to the end.

With Razgatlioglu second, Lowes took his final podium place of 2024. Alex's rival for fourth overall, Danilo Petrucci, finished one place behind.

In the season finale, Razgatlioglu attained his desired race win to give him 18 in all across the 12 rounds. Bulega had to settle for an enforced second this time, but the end of the year came prematurely, due to a blown Yamaha engine and subsequent red flag, which ended the fun on lap 17, not 20.

Razgatlioglu looked like he had the beating of Bulega – finally.

There was another fairy-tale BMW ending, for Michael van der Mark this time, who finally shared the podium with his team-mate and real-life mate, Razgatlioglu.

Lowes' fifth place meant that he was classified fourth overall in the championship on the slightly ancient Ninja ZX-10RR.

2024 WORLD SUPERBIKE CHAMPIONSHIP RESULTS

COMPILED by PETER McLAREN

Round 1 — PHILLIP ISLAND, Australia · 24–26 February, 2024 · 2.762-mile/4.445km circuit

Race 1: 20 laps, 55.240 miles/88.900km
Weather: Dry · Track 35°C · Air 18°C
Time of race: 30m 55.801s
Average speed: 107.158mph/172.454km/h

Pos.	Rider	Nat.	No.	Entrant	Machine	Time & Gap	Laps
1	Nicolo Bulega	ITA	11	Aruba.it Racing - Ducati	Ducati Panigale V4R		20
2	Andrea Locatelli	ITA	55	Pata Prometeon Yamaha	Yamaha YZF R1	2.280s	20
3	Andrea Iannone	ITA	29	Team GoEleven	Ducati Panigale V4R	2.630s	20
4	Alex Lowes	GBR	22	Kawasaki Racing Team WorldSBK	Kawasaki ZX-10RR	4.728s	20
5	Toprak Razgatlioglu	TUR	54	ROKiT BMW Motorrad WorldSBK Team	BMW M 1000 RR	5.706s	20
6	Dominique Aegerter	SUI	77	GYTR GRT Yamaha WorldSBK Team	Yamaha YZF R1	8.333s	20
7	Michael van der Mark	NED	60	ROKiT BMW Motorrad WorldSBK Team	BMW M 1000 RR	8.647s	20
8	Danilo Petrucci	ITA	9	Barni Spark Racing Team	Ducati Panigale V4R	9.965s	20
9	Garrett Gerloff	USA	31	Bonovo Action BMW	BMW M 1000 RR	11.699s	20
10	Xavi Vierge	ESP	97	Team HRC	Honda CBR1000 RR-R	12.423s	20
11	Scott Redding	GBR	45	Bonovo Action BMW	BMW M 1000 RR	14.413s	20
12	Alex Bassani	ITA	47	Kawasaki Racing Team WorldSBK	Kawasaki ZX-10RR	16.668s	20
13	Sam Lowes	GBR	14	ELF Marc VDS Racing Team	Ducati Panigale V4R	18.388s	20
14	Michael Rinaldi	ITA	21	Team Motocorsa Racing	Ducati Panigale V4R	23.560s	20
15	Alvaro Bautista	ESP	1	Aruba.it Racing - Ducati	Ducati Panigale V4R	32.471s	20
16	Philipp Oettl	GER	5	GMT94 Yamaha	Yamaha YZF R1	35.580s	20
17	Jonathan Rea	GBR	65	Pata Prometeon Yamaha	Yamaha YZF R1	37.949s	20
18	Tito Rabat	ESP	53	Kawasaki Puccetti Racing	Kawasaki ZX-10RR	39.427s	20
19	Tarran Mackenzie	GBR	95	PETRONAS MIE Racing Honda	Honda CBR1000 RR-R	54.890s	20
20	Adam Norrodin	MAS	27	PETRONAS MIE Racing Honda	Honda CBR1000 RR-R	57.202s	20
21	Bradley Ray	GBR	28	Yamaha Motoxracing WorldSBK Team	Yamaha YZF R1	58.642s	20
	Remy Gardner	AUS	87	GYTR GRT Yamaha WorldSBK Team	Yamaha YZF R1	DNF	2

Fastest race lap: Bulega on lap 11, 1m 28.564s, 112.271mph/180.683km/h.
Lap record: Rea, 1m 30.075s, 110.388mph/177.652km/h (2019).

Superpole: 10 laps, 27.620 miles/44.450km
Weather: Dry · Track 40°C · Air 20°C
Time of race: 15m 0.995s
Average speed: 110.358mph/177.604km/h

Pos.	Rider	Time & Gap	Laps
1	Alex Lowes		10
2	Andrea Locatelli	1.157s	10
3	Toprak Razgatlioglu	1.738s	10
4	Alvaro Bautista	1.812s	10
5	Nicolo Bulega	2.838s	10
6	Remy Gardner	2.853s	10
7	Dominique Aegerter	3.051s	10
8	Sam Lowes	3.341s	10
9	Michael Rinaldi	5.140s	10
10	Jonathan Rea	5.535s	10
11	Axel Bassani	6.064s	10
12	Xavi Vierge	6.958s	10
13	Garrett Gerloff	7.017s	10
14	Andrea Iannone	7.814s	10
15	Danilo Petrucci	8.580s	10
16	Michael van der Mark	9.158s	10
17	Scott Redding	11.070s	10
18	Philipp Oettl	13.228s	10
19	Tito Rabat	16.843s	10
20	Adam Norrodin	28.706s	10
21	Bradley Ray	49.720s	10
	Tarran Mackenzie	DNF	0

Fastest race lap: Bautista on lap 9, 111.380mph/179.248km/h.

Race 2: 11 laps, 30.382 miles/48.895km
Weather: Dry · Track 36°C · Air 22°C
Time of race: 16m 27.565s
Average speed: 110.752mph/178.238km/h

Pos.	Rider	Time & Gap	Laps
1	Alex Lowes		11
2	Alvaro Bautista	0.048s	11
3	Danilo Petrucci	1.178s	11
4	Andrea Iannone	1.275s	11
5	Nicolo Bulega	2.346s	11
6	Michael Rinaldi	2.913s	11
7	Sam Lowes	3.480s	11
8	Garrett Gerloff	4.119s	11
9	Michael van der Mark	5.159s	11
10	Dominique Aegerter	5.165s	11
11	Axel Bassani	5.183s	11
12	Remy Gardner	7.652s	11
13	Xavi Vierge	9.082s	11
14	Philipp Oettl	10.729s	11
15	Bradley Ray	11.806s	11
16	Tito Rabat	17.416s	11
17	Scott Redding	21.815s	11
18	Tarran Mackenzie	25.481s	11
19	Adam Norrodin	32.107s	11
	Andrea Locatelli	DNF	10
	Toprak Razgatlioglu	DNS	-
	Jonathan Rea	DNS	-

Fastest race lap: Bulega on lap 9, 1m 28.639s, 112.176mph/180.53km/h.

Superpole
1, Bulega 1m 27.916s; 2, Iannone 1m 28.154s; 3, A. Lowes 1m 28.239s; 4, Aegerter 1m 28.403s; 5, Razgatlioglu 1m 28.520s; 6, Locatelli 1m 28.540s; 7, Gardner 1m 28.604s; 8, S. Lowes 1m 28.676s; 9, Bautista 1m 28.700s; 10, Rinaldi 1m 28.784s; 11, Rea 1m 28.890s; 12, Petrucci 1m 28.903s; 13, Vierge 1m 29.000s; 14, Gerloff 1m 29.045s; 15, Bassani 1m 29.118s; 16, Van der Mark 1m 29.127s; 17, Ray 1m 29.242s; 18, Oettl 1m 29.263s; 19, Redding 1m 29.726s; 20, Rabat 1m 29.809s; 21, Mackenzie 1m 31.133s; 22, Norrodin 1m 31.888s.

Points
1, A. Lowes 50; 2, Bulega 41; 3, Locatelli 29; 4, Iannone 29; 5, Bautista 27; 6, Petrucci 24; 7, Aegerter 19; 5, Razgatlioglu 18; 9, Van der Mark 16; 10, Gerloff 15; 11, S. Lowes 14; 12, Rinaldi 13; 13, Vierge 9; 14, Bassani 9; 15, Gardner 8; 16, Redding 5; 17, Oettl 2; 18, Ray 1.

Round 2 — CATALUNYA, Spain · 22–24 March, 2024 · 2.875-mile/4.627km circuit

Race 1: 20 laps, 57.875 miles/93.140km
Weather: Dry · Track 36°C · Air 30°C
Time of race: 34m 19.817s
Average speed: 101.149mph/162.783km/h

Pos.	Rider	Nat.	No.	Entrant	Machine	Time & Gap	Laps
1	Toprak Razgatlioglu	TUR	54	ROKiT BMW Motorrad WorldSBK Team	BMW M 1000 RR		20
2	Nicolo Bulega	ITA	11	Aruba.it Racing - Ducati	Ducati Panigale V4R	0.868s	20
3	Alvaro Bautista	ESP	1	Aruba.it Racing - Ducati	Ducati Panigale V4R	5.338s	20
4	Andrea Iannone	ITA	29	Team GoEleven	Ducati Panigale V4R	8.543s	20
5	Andrea Locatelli	ITA	55	Pata Prometeon Yamaha	Yamaha YZF R1	9.818s	20
6	Alex Lowes	GBR	22	Kawasaki Racing Team WorldSBK	Kawasaki ZX-10RR	11.190s	20
7	Danilo Petrucci	ITA	9	Barni Spark Racing Team	Ducati Panigale V4R	12.020s	20
8	Dominique Aegerter	SUI	77	GYTR GRT Yamaha WorldSBK Team	Yamaha YZF R1	12.329s	20
9	Michael van der Mark	NED	60	ROKiT BMW Motorrad WorldSBK Team	BMW M 1000 RR	16.677s	20
10	Alex Bassani	ITA	47	Kawasaki Racing Team WorldSBK	Kawasaki ZX-10RR	17.144s	20
11	Michael Rinaldi	ITA	21	Team Motocorsa Racing	Ducati Panigale V4R	18.895s	20
12	Garrett Gerloff	USA	31	Bonovo Action BMW	BMW M 1000 RR	19.447s	20
13	Iker Lecuona	ESP	7	Team HRC	Honda CBR1000 RR-R	22.194s	20
14	Xavi Vierge	ESP	97	Team HRC	Honda CBR1000 RR-R	22.233s	20
15	Remy Gardner	AUS	87	GYTR GRT Yamaha WorldSBK Team	Yamaha YZF R1	32.087s	20
16	Tarran Mackenzie	GBR	95	PETRONAS MIE Racing Honda	Honda CBR1000 RR-R	34.181s	20
17	Scott Redding	GBR	45	Bonovo Action BMW	BMW M 1000 RR	37.540s	20
18	Bradley Ray	GBR	28	Yamaha Motoxracing WorldSBK Team	Yamaha YZF R1	38.241s	20
19	Philipp Oettl	GER	5	GMT94 Yamaha	Yamaha YZF R1	38.752s	20
20	Adam Norrodin	MAS	27	PETRONAS MIE Racing Honda	Honda CBR1000 RR-R	59.422s	20
21	Tito Rabat	ESP	53	Kawasaki Puccetti Racing	Kawasaki ZX-10RR	1 Lap	19
	Sam Lowes	GBR	14	ELF Marc VDS Racing Team	Ducati Panigale V4R	DNF	4
	Jonathan Rea	GBR	65	Pata Prometeon Yamaha	Yamaha YZF R1	DNF	1

Fastest race lap: S. Lowes on lap 3, 1m 41.440s, 102.695mph/165.272km/h.
Lap record: Bautista, 1m 41.135s, 103.005mph/165.771km/h (2022).

Superpole: 10 laps, 28.937 miles/46.570km
Weather: Dry · Track 22°C · Air 14°C
Time of race: 16m 58.029s
Average speed: 102.329mph/164.683km/h

Pos.	Rider	Time & Gap	Laps
1	Toprak Razgatlioglu		10
2	Andrea Iannone	0.075s	10
3	Alvaro Bautista	0.260s	10
4	Nicolo Bulega	0.411s	10
5	Alex Lowes	1.611s	10
6	Michael van der Mark	2.634s	10
7	Danilo Petrucci	4.249s	10
8	Andrea Locatelli	4.354s	10
9	Remy Gardner	5.196s	10
10	Dominique Aegerter	5.269s	10
11	Sam Lowes	6.831s	10
12	Scott Redding	7.338s	10
13	Jonathan Rea	7.435s	10
14	Axel Bassani	7.891s	10
15	Xavi Vierge	10.288s	10
16	Tito Rabat	11.060s	10
17	Garrett Gerloff	11.864s	10
18	Michael Rinaldi	11.937s	10
19	Philipp Oettl	16.125s	10
20	Tarran Mackenzie	16.300s	10
21	Iker Lecuona	16.901s	10
22	Bradley Ray	19.389s	10
	Adam Norrodin	DNF	9

Fastest race lap: Bulega on lap 4, 1m 40.955s, 103.189mph/166.066km/h.

Race 2: 20 laps, 57.875 miles/93.140km
Weather: Dry · Track 28°C · Air 15°C
Time of race: 34m 12.160s
Average speed: 101.526mph/163.391km/h

Pos.	Rider	Time & Gap	Laps
1	Alvaro Bautista		20
2	Nicolo Bulega	2.041s	20
3	Toprak Razgatlioglu	7.005s	20
4	Michael van der Mark	12.452s	20
5	Danilo Petrucci	15.076s	20
6	Alex Lowes	15.285s	20
7	Remy Gardner	16.000s	20
8	Jonathan Rea	16.963s	20
9	Dominique Aegerter	19.849s	20
10	Garrett Gerloff	21.644s	20
11	Scott Redding	22.108s	20
12	Sam Lowes	24.985s	20
13	Andrea Locatelli	26.329s	20
14	Xavi Vierge	26.452s	20
15	Tito Rabat	34.445s	20
16	Philipp Oettl	36.522s	20
17	Tarran Mackenzie	46.934s	20
18	Adam Norrodin	1m 07.842s	20
	Andrea Iannone	DNF	12
	Iker Lecuona	DNF	2
	Bradley Ray	DNF	2
	Axel Bassani	DNF	0
	Michael Rinaldi	DNF	0

Fastest race lap: Bulega on lap 5, 1m 41.578s, 102.556mph/165.048km/h.

Superpole
1, Razgatlioglu 1m 39.489s; 2, Bulega 1m 39.591s; 3, Iannone 1m 39.799s; 4, Van der Mark 1m 39.947s; 5, S. Lowes 1m 39.988s; 6, Aegerter 1m 40.100s; 7, A. Lowes 1m 40.116s; 8, Gardner 1m 40.131s; 9, Locatelli 1m 40.227s; 10, Petrucci 1m 40.240s; 11, Bautista 1m 40.297s; 12, Redding 1m 40.534s; 13, Rea 1m 40.537s; 14, Gerloff 1m 40.705s; 15, Bassani 1m 40.858s; 16, Rinaldi 1m 40.921s; 17, Rabat 1m 41.145s; 18, Lecuona 1m 41.177s; 19, Vierge 1m 41.197s; 20, Oettl 1m 41.337s; 21, Ray 1m 41.422s; 22, Mackenzie 1m 41.643s; 23, Norrodin 1m 42.793s.

Points
1, Bulega 87; 2, Bautista 75; 3, A. Lowes 75; 4, Razgatlioglu 71; 5, Iannone 51; 6, Petrucci 47; 7, Locatelli 45; 8, Van der Mark 40; 9, Aegerter 34; 10, Gerloff 25; 11, Gardner 19; 12, Rinaldi 18; 13, S. Lowes 18; 14, Bassani 15; 15, Vierge 13; 16, Redding 10; 17, Rea 8; 18, Lecuona 3; 19, Oettl 2; 20, Rabat 1; 21, Ray 1.

Round 3	ASSEN, The Netherlands · 19–21 April, 2024 · 2.822-mile/4.542km circuit

Race 1: 14 laps, 40.863 miles/65.762km
Weather: Wet · Track 28°C · Air 9°C
Time of race: 25m 8.898s
Average speed: 97.492mph/156.898km/h

Pos.	Rider	Nat.	No.	Entrant	Machine	Time & Gap	Laps
1	Nicholas Spinelli	ITA	24	Barni Spark Racing Team	Ducati Panigale V4R		14
2	Toprak Razgatlioglu	TUR	54	ROKiT BMW Motorrad WorldSBK Team	BMW M 1000 RR	1.979s	14
3	Alvaro Bautista	ESP	1	Aruba.it Racing - Ducati	Ducati Panigale V4R	2.089s	14
4	Remy Gardner	AUS	87	GYTR GRT Yamaha WorldSBK Team	Yamaha YZF R1	4.851s	14
5	Alex Lowes	GBR	22	Kawasaki Racing Team WorldSBK	Kawasaki ZX-10RR	5.147s	14
6	Jonathan Rea	GBR	65	Pata Prometeon Yamaha	Yamaha YZF R1	5.376s	14
7	Michael van der Mark	NED	60	ROKiT BMW Motorrad WorldSBK Team	BMW M 1000 RR	5.545s	14
8	Scott Redding	GBR	45	Bonovo Action BMW	BMW M 1000 RR	11.271s	14
9	Alex Bassani	ITA	47	Kawasaki Racing Team WorldSBK	Kawasaki ZX-10RR	11.476s	14
10	Xavi Vierge	ESP	97	Team HRC	Honda CBR1000 RR-R	17.034s	14
11	Nicolo Bulega	ITA	11	Aruba.it Racing - Ducati	Ducati Panigale V4R	1 Sector	14
12	Andrea Locatelli	ITA	55	Pata Prometeon Yamaha	Yamaha YZF R1	4 Sectors	14
13	Dominique Aegerter	SUI	77	GYTR GRT Yamaha WorldSBK Team	Yamaha YZF R1	4 Sectors	14
14	Tarran Mackenzie	GBR	95	PETRONAS MIE Racing Honda	Honda CBR1000 RR-R	4 Sectors	14
15	Bradley Ray	GBR	28	Yamaha Motoxracing WorldSBK Team	Yamaha YZF R1	1 Lap	13
16	Garrett Gerloff	USA	31	Bonovo Action BMW	BMW M 1000 RR	1 Lap	13
17	Adam Norrodin	MAS	27	PETRONAS MIE Racing Honda	Honda CBR1000 RR-R	1 Lap	13
18	Philipp Oettl	GER	5	GMT94 Yamaha	Yamaha YZF R1	2 Laps	12
19	Sam Lowes	GBR	14	ELF Marc VDS Racing Team	Ducati Panigale V4R	3 Laps	11
	Michael Rinaldi	ITA	21	Team Motocorsa Racing	Ducati Panigale V4R	DNF	11
	Tito Rabat	ESP	53	Kawasaki Puccetti Racing	Kawasaki ZX-10RR	DNF	11
	Andrea Iannone	ITA	29	Team GoEleven	Ducati Panigale V4R	DNF	4

Fastest race lap: Razgatlioglu on lap 14, 1m 35.777s, 106.082mph/170.722km/h.
Lap record: Bautista, 1m 33.620s, 108.526mph/174.655km/h (2022).

Superpole: 10 laps, 28.223 miles/45.420km
Weather: Dry · Track 14°C · Air 8°C
Time of race: 15m 53.996s
Average speed: 106.501mph/171.397km/h

Pos.	Rider	Time & Gap	Laps
1	Alvaro Bautista		10
2	Nicolo Bulega	2.686s	10
3	Alex Lowes	7.403s	10
4	Remy Gardner	7.551s	10
5	Jonathan Rea	8.177s	10
6	Andrea Locatelli	9.114s	10
7	Sam Lowes	9.702s	10
8	Michael van der Mark	9.824s	10
9	Toprak Razgatlioglu	10.034s	10
10	Scott Redding	11.981s	10
11	Garrett Gerloff	14.886s	10
12	Xavi Vierge	15.148s	10
13	Axel Bassani	15.922s	10
14	Dominique Aegerter	16.927s	10
15	Andrea Iannone	21.202s	10
16	Michael Rinaldi	22.384s	10
17	Tarran Mackenzie	25.887s	10
18	Nicholas Spinelli	26.597s	10
19	Philipp Oettl	29.518s	10
20	Bradley Ray	29.851s	10
	Adam Norrodin	DNF	5
	Tito Rabat	DNF	3

Fastest race lap: Bulega on lap 3, 1m 33.882s, 108.223mph/174.168km/h.

Race 2: 21 laps, 59.268 miles/95.382km
Weather: Dry · Track 17°C · Air 9°C
Time of race: 33m 29.448s
Average speed: 106.180mph/170.880km/h

Pos.	Rider	Time & Gap	Laps
1	Toprak Razgatlioglu		21
2	Alvaro Bautista	0.625s	21
3	Remy Gardner	1.022s	21
4	Andrea Iannone	3.120s	21
5	Andrea Locatelli	3.217s	21
6	Sam Lowes	5.174s	21
7	Dominique Aegerter	5.538s	21
8	Nicolo Bulega	6.337s	21
9	Michael van der Mark	8.059s	21
10	Xavi Vierge	19.453s	21
11	Tarran Mackenzie	19.556s	21
12	Garrett Gerloff	21.771s	21
13	Michael Rinaldi	22.322s	21
14	Philipp Oettl	31.822s	21
15	Tito Rabat	35.305s	21
16	Nicholas Spinelli	35.392s	21
17	Bradley Ray	37.947s	21
18	Axel Bassani	43.360s	21
19	Jonathan Rea	1m 18.925s	21
20	Adam Norrodin	1m 34.526s	21
	Alex Lowes	DNF	9
	Scott Redding	DNF	1

Fastest race lap: Gardner on lap 2, 1m 34.295s, 107.749mph/173.405km/h.

Superpole
1, Rea 1m 42.650s; 2, Bulega 1m 42.744s; 3, Razgatlioglu 1m 43.003s; 4, S. Lowes 1m 43.190s; 5, A. Lowes 1m 43.442s; 6, Gardner 1m 43.633s; 7, Bautista 1m 43.730s; 8, Rinaldi 1m 43.744s; 9, Iannone 1m 43.769s; 10, Locatelli 1m 43.950s; 11, Spinelli 1m 44.049s; 12, Vierge 1m 44.095s; 13, Van der Mark 1m 44.111s; 14, Mackenzie 1m 44.112s; 15, Redding 1m 44.216s; 16, Bassani 1m 44.231s; 17, Gerloff 1m 44.582s; 18, Oettl 1m 45.075s; 19, Aegerter 1m 45.420s; 20, Ray 1m 46.093s; 21, Norrodin 1m 47.083s; 22, Rabat 1m 48.996s.

Points
1, Bautista 123; 2, Razgatlioglu 117; 3, Bulega 109; 4, A. Lowes 93; 5, Locatelli 64; 6, Iannone 64; 7, Van der Mark 58; 8, Gardner 54; 9, Petrucci 47; 10, Aegerter 46; 11, S. Lowes 31; 12, Gerloff 29; 13, Spinelli 25; 14, Vierge 25; 15, Rea 23; 16, Bassani 22; 17, Rinaldi 21; 18, Redding 18; 19, Mackenzie 7; 20, Oettl 4; 21, Lecuona 3; 22, Rabat 2; 23, Ray 2.

Round 4	MISANO, Italy · 14–16 June, 2024 · 2.626-mile/4.226km circuit

Race 1: 21 laps, 55.144 miles/88.746km
Weather: Dry · Track 44°C · Air 29°C
Time of race: 33m 7.016s
Average speed: 99.908mph/160.787km/h

Pos.	Rider	Nat.	No.	Entrant	Machine	Time & Gap	Laps
1	Toprak Razgatlioglu	TUR	54	ROKiT BMW Motorrad WorldSBK Team	BMW M 1000 RR		21
2	Nicolo Bulega	ITA	11	Aruba.it Racing - Ducati	Ducati Panigale V4R	1.782s	21
3	Alvaro Bautista	ESP	1	Aruba.it Racing - Ducati	Ducati Panigale V4R	3.176s	21
4	Andrea Locatelli	ITA	55	Pata Prometeon Yamaha	Yamaha YZF R1	10.337s	21
5	Alex Lowes	GBR	22	Kawasaki Racing Team WorldSBK	Kawasaki ZX-10RR	11.671s	21
6	Remy Gardner	AUS	87	GYTR GRT Yamaha WorldSBK Team	Yamaha YZF R1	14.822s	21
7	Andrea Iannone	ITA	29	Team GoEleven	Ducati Panigale V4R	16.637s	21
8	Michael van der Mark	NED	60	ROKiT BMW Motorrad WorldSBK Team	BMW M 1000 RR	19.044s	21
9	Danilo Petrucci	ITA	9	Barni Spark Racing Team	Ducati Panigale V4R	20.686s	21
10	Iker Lecuona	ESP	7	Team HRC	Honda CBR1000 RR-R	24.041s	21
11	Alex Bassani	ITA	47	Kawasaki Racing Team WorldSBK	Kawasaki ZX-10RR	26.233s	21
12	Garrett Gerloff	USA	31	Bonovo Action BMW	BMW M 1000 RR	30.303s	21
13	Michele Pirro	ITA	51	Aruba.it Racing - Ducati	Ducati Panigale V4R	32.536s	21
14	Michael Rinaldi	ITA	21	Team Motocorsa Racing	Ducati Panigale V4R	35.186s	21
15	Scott Redding	GBR	45	Bonovo Action BMW	BMW M 1000 RR	35.566s	21
16	Xavi Vierge	ESP	97	Team HRC	Honda CBR1000 RR-R	45.895s	21
17	Philipp Oettl	GER	5	GMT94 Yamaha	Yamaha YZF R1	46.811s	21
18	Bradley Ray	GBR	28	Yamaha Motoxracing WorldSBK Team	Yamaha YZF R1	54.387s	21
19	Tito Rabat	ESP	53	Kawasaki Puccetti Racing	Kawasaki ZX-10RR	1m 04.508s	21
20	Adam Norrodin	MAS	27	PETRONAS MIE Racing Honda	Honda CBR1000 RR-R	1m 10.077s	21
	Sam Lowes	GBR	14	ELF Marc VDS Racing Team	Ducati Panigale V4R	DNF	15
	Dominique Aegerter	SUI	77	GYTR GRT Yamaha WorldSBK Team	Yamaha YZF R1	DNF	10
	Tarran Mackenzie	GBR	95	PETRONAS MIE Racing Honda	Honda CBR1000 RR-R	DNF	8
	Jonathan Rea	GBR	65	Pata Prometeon Yamaha	Yamaha YZF R1	DNF	0

Fastest race lap: Bulega on lap 6, 1m 33.920s, 100.653mph/161.985km/h.
Lap record: Razgatlioglu 1m 33.174s, 101.459mph/163.282km/h (2023).

Superpole: 10 laps, 26.259 miles/42.260km
Weather: Dry · Track 37°C · Air 26°C
Time of race: 15m 36.088s
Average speed: 100.987mph/162.523km/h

Pos.	Rider	Time & Gap	Laps
1	Toprak Razgatlioglu		10
2	Nicolo Bulega	1.651s	10
3	Alex Lowes	4.779s	10
4	Andrea Locatelli	8.061s	10
5	Andrea Iannone	10.913s	10
6	Axel Bassani	12.013s	10
7	Iker Lecuona	12.436s	10
8	Jonathan Rea	14.981s	10
9	Danilo Petrucci	15.255s	10
10	Dominique Aegerter	16.071s	10
11	Michael Rinaldi	17.038s	10
12	Michael van der Mark	19.858s	10
13	Xavi Vierge	20.227s	10
14	Scott Redding	20.317s	10
15	Tito Rabat	23.507s	10
16	Michele Pirro	24.417s	10
17	Alvaro Bautista	26.037s	10
18	Tarran Mackenzie	26.969s	10
19	Philipp Oettl	27.588s	10
20	Bradley Ray	27.798s	10
21	Adam Norrodin	34.941s	10
	Remy Gardner	DNF	5
	Garrett Gerloff	DNF	3
	Sam Lowes	DNF	1

Fastest race lap: Razgatlioglu on lap 5, 1m 32.687s, 101.992mph/164.14km/h.

Race 2: 21 laps, 55.144mi/88.746km
Weather: Dry · Track 45°C · Air 28°C
Time of race: 33m 6.338s
Average speed: 99.943mph/160.842km/h

Pos.	Rider	Time & Gap	Laps
1	Toprak Razgatlioglu		21
2	Nicolo Bulega	2.980s	21
3	Alvaro Bautista	6.920s	21
4	Alex Lowes	9.951s	21
5	Andrea Locatelli	11.974s	21
6	Danilo Petrucci	15.900s	21
7	Axel Bassani	16.055s	21
8	Remy Gardner	19.125s	21
9	Iker Lecuona	22.535s	21
10	Jonathan Rea	27.237s	21
11	Andrea Iannone	27.292s	21
12	Scott Redding	29.948s	21
13	Sam Lowes	31.044s	21
14	Tito Rabat	38.090s	21
15	Philipp Oettl	43.840s	21
16	Michael Rinaldi	43.852s	21
17	Bradley Ray	44.363s	21
18	Garrett Gerloff	45.078s	21
19	Tarran Mackenzie	48.580s	21
	Michele Pirro	DNF	20
	Xavi Vierge	DNF	8
	Michael van der Mark	DNF	6
	Dominique Aegerter	DNF	5
	Adam Norrodin	DNF	1

Fastest race lap: Razgatlioglu on lap 6, 1m 33.307s, 101.314mph/163.049km/h.

Superpole
1, Razgatlioglu 1m 32.320s; 2, Bulega 1m 32.556s; 3, Gardner 1m 32.906s; 4, A. Lowes 1m 33.075s; 5, Bautista 1m 33.111s; 6, Locatelli 1m 33.129s; 7, Iannone 1m 33.188s; 8, S. Lowes 1m 33.196s; 9, Aegerter 1m 33.234s; 10, Rabat 1m 33.544s; 11, Bassani 1m 33.608s; 12, Petrucci 1m 33.632s; 13, Gerloff 1m 33.634s; 14, Lecuona 1m 33.644s; 15, Rea 1m 33.682s; 16, Van der Mark 1m 33.774s; 17, Vierge 1m 33.834s; 18, Rinaldi 1m 33.935s; 19, Pirro 1m 33.942s; 20, Redding 1m 34.104s; 21, Mackenzie 1m 34.733s; 22, Oettl 1m 35.032s; 23, Ray 1m 35.538s; 24, Norrodin 1m 36.082s.

Points
1, Razgatlioglu 179; 2, Bulega 158; 3, Bautista 155; 4, A. Lowes 124; 5, Locatelli 94; 6, Iannone 83; 7, Gardner 72; 8, Van der Mark 66; 9, Petrucci 65; 10, Aegerter 46; 11, Bassani 40; 12, S. Lowes 34; 13, Gerloff 33; 14, Rea 31; 15, Spinelli 25; 16, Vierge 25; 17, Rinaldi 23; 18, Redding 23; 19, Lecuona 19; 20, Mackenzie 7; 21, Oettl 5; 22, Rabat 4; 23, Pirro 3; 24, Ray 2.

Round 5 — DONINGTON PARK, UK · 12–14 July, 2024 · 2.500-mile/4.023km circuit

Race 1: 23 laps, 57.495 miles/92.529km
Weather: Dry · Track 30°C · Air 21°C
Time of race: 33m 16.535s
Average speed: 103.670mph/166.841km/h

Pos.	Rider	Nat.	No.	Entrant	Machine	Time & Gap	Laps
1	Toprak Razgatlioglu	TUR	54	ROKiT BMW Motorrad WorldSBK Team	BMW M 1000 RR		23
2	Alex Lowes	GBR	22	Kawasaki Racing Team WorldSBK	Kawasaki ZX-10RR	11.384s	23
3	Alvaro Bautista	ESP	1	Aruba.it Racing - Ducati	Ducati Panigale V4R	13.167s	23
4	Nicolo Bulega	ITA	11	Aruba.it Racing - Ducati	Ducati Panigale V4R	14.913s	23
5	Jonathan Rea	GBR	65	Pata Prometeon Yamaha	Yamaha YZF R1	16.349s	23
6	Andrea Locatelli	ITA	55	Pata Prometeon Yamaha	Yamaha YZF R1	16.611s	23
7	Danilo Petrucci	ITA	9	Barni Spark Racing Team	Ducati Panigale V4R	17.634s	23
8	Dominique Aegerter	SUI	77	GYTR GRT Yamaha WorldSBK Team	Yamaha YZF R1	24.648s	23
9	Michael van der Mark	NED	60	ROKiT BMW Motorrad WorldSBK Team	BMW M 1000 RR	25.099s	23
10	Remy Gardner	AUS	87	GYTR GRT Yamaha WorldSBK Team	Yamaha YZF R1	25.563s	23
11	Andrea Iannone	ITA	29	Team GoEleven	Ducati Panigale V4R	27.272s	23
12	Alex Bassani	ITA	47	Kawasaki Racing Team WorldSBK	Kawasaki ZX-10RR	28.838s	23
13	Iker Lecuona	ESP	7	Team HRC	Honda CBR1000 RR-R	30.210s	23
14	Garrett Gerloff	USA	31	Bonovo Action BMW	BMW M 1000 RR	30.467s	23
15	Michael Rinaldi	ITA	21	Team Motocorsa Racing	Ducati Panigale V4R	33.306s	23
16	Bradley Ray	GBR	28	Yamaha Motoxracing WorldSBK Team	Yamaha YZF R1	44.244s	23
17	Tito Rabat	ESP	53	Kawasaki Puccetti Racing	Kawasaki ZX-10RR	44.785s	23
18	Philipp Oettl	GER	5	GMT94 Yamaha	Yamaha YZF R1	45.309s	23
19	Sam Lowes	GBR	14	ELF Marc VDS Racing Team	Ducati Panigale V4R	58.529s	23
20	Adam Norrodin	MAS	27	PETRONAS MIE Racing Honda	Honda CBR1000 RR-R	1m 24.454s	23
	Scott Redding	GBR	45	Bonovo Action BMW	BMW M 1000 RR	DNF	18
	Xavi Vierge	ESP	97	Team HRC	Honda CBR1000 RR-R	DNF	1
	Tarran Mackenzie	GBR	95	PETRONAS MIE Racing Honda	Honda CBR1000 RR-R	DNF	0

Fastest race lap: Razgatlioglu on lap 3, 1m 25.786s, 104.903mph/168.825km/h.
Lap record: Bautista, 1m 25.896s, 104.769mph/168.609km/h (2023).

Superpole: 10 laps, 24.998 miles/40.230km
Weather: Dry · Track 21°C · Air 18°C
Time of race: 14m 23.681s
Average speed: 104.196mph/167.687km/h

Pos.	Rider	Time & Gap	Laps
1	Toprak Razgatlioglu		10
2	Nicolo Bulega	4.826s	10
3	Jonathan Rea	6.526s	10
4	Scott Redding	8.375s	10
5	Alex Lowes	8.576s	10
6	Alvaro Bautista	9.188s	10
7	Andrea Locatelli	10.037s	10
8	Sam Lowes	11.760s	10
9	Danilo Petrucci	12.229s	10
10	Andrea Iannone	12.828s	10
11	Dominique Aegerter	12.906s	10
12	Michael van der Mark	13.108s	10
13	Remy Gardner	13.766s	10
14	Garrett Gerloff	14.022s	10
15	Xavi Vierge	15.010s	10
16	Michael Rinaldi	15.646s	10
17	Iker Lecuona	18.023s	10
18	Tito Rabat	18.408s	10
19	Bradley Ray	18.916s	10
20	Philipp Oettl	20.914s	10
21	Adam Norrodin	34.700s	10
	Axel Bassani	DNF	1

Fastest race lap: Razgatlioglu on lap 4, 1m 25.733s, 104.968mph/168.929km/h.

Race 2: 23 laps, 57.495 miles/92.529km
Weather: Dry · Track 26°C · Air 21°C
Time of race: 33m 11.699s
Average speed: 103.922mph/167.246km/h

Pos.	Rider	Time & Gap	Laps
1	Toprak Razgatlioglu		23
2	Nicolo Bulega	8.062s	23
3	Alex Lowes	10.026s	23
4	Scott Redding	12.275s	23
5	Alvaro Bautista	13.476s	23
6	Danilo Petrucci	15.562s	23
7	Andrea Locatelli	16.343s	23
8	Jonathan Rea	16.742s	23
9	Dominique Aegerter	18.919s	23
10	Axel Bassani	23.306s	23
11	Remy Gardner	25.980s	23
12	Michael van der Mark	26.107s	23
13	Garrett Gerloff	27.579s	23
14	Iker Lecuona	29.658s	23
15	Xavi Vierge	30.026s	23
16	Sam Lowes	30.158s	23
17	Michael Rinaldi	30.673s	23
18	Bradley Ray	31.449s	23
19	Tito Rabat	40.357s	23
20	Philipp Oettl	48.929s	23
	Andrea Iannone	DNF	17
	Adam Norrodin	DNF	2

Fastest race lap: Razgatlioglu on lap 3, 1m 25.597s, 105.135mph/169.198km/h.

Superpole
1, Razgatlioglu 1m 24.629s; 2, Bulega 1m 25.202s; 3, Redding 1m 25.406s; 4, S. Lowes 1m 25.492s; 5, Aegerter 1m 25.528s; 6, Van der Mark 1m 25.621s; 7, Locatelli 1m 25.630s; 8, Rea 1m 25.638s; 9, A. Lowes 1m 25.644s; 10, Gardner 1m 25.764s; 11, Bautista 1m 25.839s; 12, Gerloff 1m 25.845s; 13, Petrucci 1m 25.895s; 14, Vierge 1m 26.156s; 15, Rinaldi 1m 26.167s; 16, Bassani 1m 26.197s; 17, Ray 1m 26.242s; 18, Lecuona 1m 26.393s; 19, Iannone 1m 26.529s; 20, Rabat 1m 26.607s; 21, Oettl 1m 26.692s; 22, Mackenzie 1m 26.815s; 23, Norrodin 1m 28.488s.

Points
1, Razgatlioglu 241; 2, Bulega 200; 3, Bautista 186; 4, A. Lowes 165; 5, Locatelli 116; 6, Iannone 88; 7, Petrucci 85; 8, Gardner 83; 9, Van der Mark 77; 10, Aegerter 61; 11, Rea 57; 12, Bassani 50; 13, Redding 42; 14, Gerloff 38; 15, S. Lowes 36; 16, Vierge 26; 17, Spinelli 25; 18, Rinaldi 24; 19, Lecuona 24; 20, Mackenzie 7; 21, Oettl 5; 22, Rabat 4; 23, Pirro 3; 24, Ray 2.

Round 6 — MOST, Czech Republic · 19–21 July, 2024 · 2.617-mile/4.212km circuit

Race 1: 22 laps, 57.579 miles/92.664km
Weather: Dry · Track 43°C · Air 29°C
Time of race: 33m 53.537s
Average speed: 101.932mph/164.044km/h

Pos.	Rider	Nat.	No.	Entrant	Machine	Time & Gap	Laps
1	Toprak Razgatlioglu	TUR	54	ROKiT BMW Motorrad WorldSBK Team	BMW M 1000 RR		22
2	Danilo Petrucci	ITA	9	Barni Spark Racing Team	Ducati Panigale V4R	5.740s	22
3	Andrea Iannone	ITA	29	Team GoEleven	Ducati Panigale V4R	5.881s	22
4	Alvaro Bautista	ESP	1	Aruba.it Racing - Ducati	Ducati Panigale V4R	9.217s	22
5	Remy Gardner	AUS	87	GYTR GRT Yamaha WorldSBK Team	Yamaha YZF R1	11.622s	22
6	Nicolo Bulega	ITA	11	Aruba.it Racing - Ducati	Ducati Panigale V4R	13.841s	22
7	Andrea Locatelli	ITA	55	Pata Prometeon Yamaha	Yamaha YZF R1	14.186s	22
8	Garrett Gerloff	USA	31	Bonovo Action BMW	BMW M 1000 RR	14.596s	22
9	Michael van der Mark	NED	60	ROKiT BMW Motorrad WorldSBK Team	BMW M 1000 RR	19.520s	22
10	Jonathan Rea	GBR	65	Pata Prometeon Yamaha	Yamaha YZF R1	23.579s	22
11	Michael Rinaldi	ITA	21	Team Motocorsa Racing	Ducati Panigale V4R	25.370s	22
12	Sam Lowes	GBR	14	ELF Marc VDS Racing Team	Ducati Panigale V4R	25.993s	22
13	Dominique Aegerter	SUI	77	GYTR GRT Yamaha WorldSBK Team	Yamaha YZF R1	28.213s	22
14	Xavi Vierge	ESP	97	Team HRC	Honda CBR1000 RR-R	29.628s	22
15	Scott Redding	GBR	45	Bonovo Action BMW	BMW M 1000 RR	32.972s	22
16	Alex Bassani	ITA	47	Kawasaki Racing Team WorldSBK	Kawasaki ZX-10RR	35.666s	22
17	Tito Rabat	ESP	53	Kawasaki Puccetti Racing	Kawasaki ZX-10RR	36.979s	22
18	Philipp Oettl	GER	5	GMT94 Yamaha	Yamaha YZF R1	39.711s	22
19	Bradley Ray	GBR	28	Yamaha Motoxracing WorldSBK Team	Yamaha YZF R1	39.850s	22
20	Leandro Mercado	ARG	36	PETRONAS MIE Racing Honda	Honda CBR1000 RR-R	56.310s	22
21	Hayden Gillim	USA	79	PETRONAS MIE Racing Honda	Honda CBR1000 RR-R	1m 02.692s	22
	Alex Lowes	GBR	22	Kawasaki Racing Team WorldSBK	Kawasaki ZX-10RR	DNF	17
	Iker Lecuona	ESP	7	Team HRC	Honda CBR1000 RR-R	DNF	9

Fastest race lap: Razgatlioglu on lap 3, 1m 31.540s, 102.928mph/165.646km/h.
Lap record: Razgatlioglu, 1m 31.180s, 103.334mph/166.300km/h (2022).

Superpole: 10 laps, 26.172 miles/42.120km
Weather: Dry · Track 40°C · Air 27°C
Time of race: 15m 20.668s
Average speed: 102.339mph/164.698km/h

Pos.	Rider	Time & Gap	Laps
1	Toprak Razgatlioglu		10
2	Nicolo Bulega	3.812s	10
3	Alex Lowes	4.251s	10
4	Danilo Petrucci	6.534s	10
5	Remy Gardner	6.673s	10
6	Andrea Locatelli	7.510s	10
7	Andrea Iannone	7.556s	10
8	Jonathan Rea	10.044s	10
9	Michael van der Mark	10.100s	10
10	Michael Rinaldi	10.928s	10
11	Xavi Vierge	11.291s	10
12	Garrett Gerloff	12.532s	10
13	Axel Bassani	14.128s	10
14	Iker Lecuona	14.133s	10
15	Tito Rabat	17.553s	10
16	Bradley Ray	17.899s	10
17	Philipp Oettl	19.060s	10
18	Dominique Aegerter	25.346s	10
19	Leandro Mercado	27.054s	10
20	Hayden Gillim	29.199s	10
	Alvaro Bautista	NC	10
	Scott Redding	DNF	2
	Sam Lowes	DNF	2

Fastest race lap: Razgatlioglu on lap 6, 1m 31.180s, 103.334mph/166.3km/h.

Race 2: 22 laps, 57.579 miles/92.664km
Weather: Dry · Track 51°C · Air 32°C
Time of race: 34m 4.044s
Average speed: 101.408mph/163.201km/h

Pos.	Rider	Time & Gap	Laps
1	Toprak Razgatlioglu		22
2	Nicolo Bulega	3.239s	22
3	Andrea Locatelli	5.462s	22
4	Remy Gardner	6.569s	22
5	Michael van der Mark	8.529s	22
6	Jonathan Rea	12.577s	22
7	Michael Rinaldi	13.808s	22
8	Andrea Iannone	16.507s	22
9	Alex Lowes	16.715s	22
10	Iker Lecuona	19.250s	22
11	Xavi Vierge	20.389s	22
12	Garrett Gerloff	21.132s	22
13	Scott Redding	24.596s	22
14	Tito Rabat	26.330s	22
15	Bradley Ray	28.227s	22
16	Dominique Aegerter	43.343s	22
17	Leandro Mercado	50.770s	22
18	Hayden Gillim	53.367s	22
	Axel Bassani	DNF	21
	Philipp Oettl	DNF	10
	Danilo Petrucci	DNF	0
	Alvaro Bautista	DNF	0

Fastest race lap: van der Mark on lap 2, 1m 32.100s, 102.301mph/164.638km/h.

Superpole
1, Razgatlioglu 1m 30.064s; 2, Iannone 1m 30.729s; 3, A. Lowes 1m 30.758s; 4, Bulega 1m 30.857s; 5, Gardner 1m 30.889s; 6, Petrucci 1m 30.997s; 7, Bautista 1m 31.017s; 8, Gerloff 1m 31.082s; 9, Locatelli 1m 31.110s; 10, Rinaldi 1m 31.170s; 11, Redding 1m 31.229s; 12, S. Lowes 1m 31.345s; 13, Lecuona 1m 31.390s; 14, Vierge 1m 31.465s; 15, Rea 1m 31.467s; 16, Van der Mark 1m 31.493s; 17, Aegerter 1m 31.533s; 18, Bassani 1m 31.618s; 19, Rabat 1m 32.113s; 20, Oettl 1m 32.123s; 21, Ray 1m 32.216s; 22, Mercado 1m 32.961s; 23, Gillim 1m 33.756s.

Points
1, Razgatlioglu 303; 2, Bulega 239; 3, Bautista 199; 4, A. Lowes 179; 5, Locatelli 145; 6, Iannone 115; 7, Gardner 112; 8, Petrucci 111; 9, Van der Mark 96; 10, Rea 75; 11, Aegerter 64; 12, Bassani 50; 13, Gerloff 50; 14, Redding 46; 15, S. Lowes 40; 16, Rinaldi 38; 17, Vierge 33; 18, Lecuona 30; 19, Spinelli 25; 20, Mackenzie 7; 21, Rabat 6; 22, Oettl 5; 23, Pirro 3; 24, Ray 3.

Round 7 — PORTIMAO, Portugal · 9–11 August, 2024 · 2.853-mile/4.592km circuit

Race 1: 20 laps, 57.067 miles/91.840km
Weather: Dry · Track 38°C · Air 30°C
Time of race: 33m 44.531s
Average speed: 101.476mph/163.309km/h

Pos.	Rider	Nat.	No.	Entrant	Machine	Time & Gap	Laps
1	Toprak Razgatlioglu	TUR	54	ROKiT BMW Motorrad WorldSBK Team	BMW M 1000 RR		20
2	Alvaro Bautista	ESP	1	Aruba.it Racing - Ducati	Ducati Panigale V4R	0.780s	20
3	Danilo Petrucci	ITA	9	Barni Spark Racing Team	Ducati Panigale V4R	1.450s	20
4	Garrett Gerloff	USA	31	Bonovo Action BMW	BMW M 1000 RR	4.313s	20
5	Alex Lowes	GBR	22	Kawasaki Racing Team WorldSBK	Kawasaki ZX-10RR	4.690s	20
6	Michael van der Mark	NED	60	ROKiT BMW Motorrad WorldSBK Team	BMW M 1000 RR	4.963s	20
7	Nicolo Bulega	ITA	11	Aruba.it Racing - Ducati	Ducati Panigale V4R	5.496s	20
8	Alex Bassani	ITA	47	Kawasaki Racing Team WorldSBK	Kawasaki ZX-10RR	11.782s	20
9	Dominique Aegerter	SUI	77	GYTR GRT Yamaha WorldSBK Team	Yamaha YZF R1	13.108s	20
10	Remy Gardner	AUS	87	GYTR GRT Yamaha WorldSBK Team	Yamaha YZF R1	13.740s	20
11	Andrea Locatelli	ITA	55	Pata Prometeon Yamaha	Yamaha YZF R1	14.137s	20
12	Iker Lecuona	ESP	7	Team HRC	Honda CBR1000 RR-R	15.424s	20
13	Xavi Vierge	ESP	97	Team HRC	Honda CBR1000 RR-R	16.007s	20
14	Tito Rabat	ESP	53	Kawasaki Puccetti Racing	Kawasaki ZX-10RR	17.886s	20
15	Jonathan Rea	GBR	65	Pata Prometeon Yamaha	Yamaha YZF R1	18.459s	20
16	Michael Rinaldi	ITA	21	Team Motocorsa Racing	Ducati Panigale V4R	18.491s	20
17	Bradley Ray	GBR	28	Yamaha Motoxracing WorldSBK Team	Yamaha YZF R1	19.191s	20
18	Hafizh Syahrin	MAS	10	JDT Racing Team	Ducati Panigale V4R	40.761s	20
19	Ivo Lopes	POR	75	PETRONAS MIE Racing Honda	Honda CBR1000 RR-R	49.967s	20
20	Adam Norrodin	MAS	27	PETRONAS MIE Racing Honda	Honda CBR1000 RR-R	59.791s	20
	Scott Redding	GBR	45	Bonovo Action BMW	BMW M 1000 RR	DNF	16
	Andrea Iannone	ITA	29	Team GoEleven	Ducati Panigale V4R	DNF	11
	Philipp Oettl	GER	5	GMT94 Yamaha	Yamaha YZF R1	DNF	5

Fastest race lap: Bautista on lap 7, 1m 40.612s, 102.095mph/164.306km/h.
Lap record: Razgatlioglu, 1m 39.826s, 102.899mph/165.600km/h (2023).

Superpole: 10 laps, 28.533 miles/45.920km
Weather: Dry · Track 46°C · Air 31°C
Time of race: 16m 46.626s
Average speed: 102.044mph/164.224km/h

Pos.	Rider	Time & Gap	Laps
1	Toprak Razgatlioglu		10
2	Danilo Petrucci	2.980s	10
3	Alex Lowes	3.251s	10
4	Michael van der Mark	3.272s	10
5	Nicolo Bulega	3.563s	10
6	Alvaro Bautista	3.729s	10
7	Xavi Vierge	8.025s	10
8	Dominique Aegerter	9.769s	10
9	Andrea Iannone	9.823s	10
10	Jonathan Rea	9.942s	10
11	Garrett Gerloff	10.081s	10
12	Axel Bassani	10.944s	10
13	Andrea Locatelli	12.835s	10
14	Iker Lecuona	12.902s	10
15	Remy Gardner	15.281s	10
16	Tito Rabat	15.470s	10
17	Scott Redding	15.599s	10
18	Bradley Ray	15.939s	10
19	Michael Rinaldi	18.419s	10
20	Hafizh Syahrin	21.380s	10
21	Philipp Oettl	21.643s	10
22	Ivo Lopes	32.605s	10

Fastest race lap: Razgatlioglu on lap 2, 1m 40.069s, 102.649mph/165.198km/h.

Race 2: 20 laps, 57.067 miles/91.840km
Weather: Dry · Track 34°C · Air 26°C
Time of race: 33m 49.138s
Average speed: 101.245mph/162.938km/h

Pos.	Rider	Time & Gap	Laps
1	Toprak Razgatlioglu		20
2	Nicolo Bulega	0.035s	20
3	Alex Lowes	6.299s	20
4	Andrea Iannone	9.715s	20
5	Danilo Petrucci	11.318s	20
6	Jonathan Rea	11.428s	20
7	Michael van der Mark	11.518s	20
8	Garrett Gerloff	16.231s	20
9	Xavi Vierge	16.909s	20
10	Dominique Aegerter	16.966s	20
11	Andrea Locatelli	18.138s	20
12	Remy Gardner	18.251s	20
13	Iker Lecuona	18.959s	20
14	Scott Redding	20.579s	20
15	Axel Bassani	20.934s	20
16	Michael Rinaldi	21.020s	20
17	Tito Rabat	23.318s	20
18	Bradley Ray	23.418s	20
19	Alvaro Bautista	24.551s	20
20	Ivo Lopes	58.505s	20
21	Philipp Oettl	1m 02.896s	20
22	Hafizh Syahrin	3 Laps	17

Fastest race lap: Bautista on lap 12, 1m 40.753s, 101.953mph/164.077km/h.

Superpole
1, Razgatlioglu 1m 39.783s; 2, A. Lowes 1m 39.887s; 3, Petrucci 1m 39.971s; 4, Bulega 1m 40.127s; 5, Van der Mark 1m 40.246s; 6, Bautista 1m 40.361s; 7, Locatelli 1m 40.386s; 8, Rea 1m 40.398s; 9, Gerloff 1m 40.471s; 10, Aegerter 1m 40.505s; 11, Rabat 1m 40.518s; 12, Bassani 1m 40.538s; 13, Vierge 1m 40.592s; 14, Gardner 1m 40.608s; 15, Iannone 1m 40.775s; 16, Redding 1m 40.813s; 17, Rinaldi 1m 40.849s; 18, Ray 1m 40.983s; 19, Syahrin 1m 41.512s; 20, Oettl 1m 41.621s; 21, Norrodin 1m 42.769s; 22, Lopes 1m 43.181s; 23, Lecuona 1m 43.308s.

Points
1, Razgatlioglu 365; 2, Bulega 273; 3, Bautista 223; 4, A. Lowes 213; 5, Locatelli 155; 6, Petrucci 147; 7, Iannone 129; 8, Gardner 122; 9, Van der Mark 121; 10, Rea 86; 11, Aegerter 79; 12, Gerloff 71; 13, Bassani 59; 14, Redding 48; 15, Vierge 46; 16, S. Lowes 40; 17, Rinaldi 38; 18, Lecuona 37; 19, Spinelli 25; 20, Rabat 8; 21, Mackenzie 7; 22, Oettl 5; 23, Pirro 3; 24, Ray 3; 25.

Round 8 — MAGNY-COURS, France · 6–8 September, 2024 · 2.741-mile/4.411km circuit

Race 1: 21 laps, 57.558 miles/92.631km
Weather: Wet · Track 21°C · Air 19°C
Time of race: 40m 27.006s
Average speed: 85.376mph/137.400km/h

Pos.	Rider	Nat.	No.	Entrant	Machine	Time & Gap	Laps
1	Michael van der Mark	NED	60	ROKiT BMW Motorrad WorldSBK Team	BMW M 1000 RR		21
2	Alvaro Bautista	ESP	1	Aruba.it Racing - Ducati	Ducati Panigale V4R	8.288s	21
3	Danilo Petrucci	ITA	9	Barni Spark Racing Team	Ducati Panigale V4R	24.285s	21
4	Scott Redding	GBR	45	Bonovo Action BMW	BMW M 1000 RR	34.037s	21
5	Andrea Iannone	ITA	29	Team GoEleven	Ducati Panigale V4R	42.108s	21
6	Iker Lecuona	ESP	7	Team HRC	Honda CBR1000 RR-R	50.799s	21
7	Xavi Vierge	ESP	97	Team HRC	Honda CBR1000 RR-R	52.361s	21
8	Andrea Locatelli	ITA	55	Pata Prometeon Yamaha	Yamaha YZF R1	52.369s	21
9	Michael Rinaldi	ITA	21	Team Motocorsa Racing	Ducati Panigale V4R	1m 11.573s	21
10	Alessandro Delbianco	ITA	52	GYTR GRT Yamaha WorldSBK Team	Yamaha YZF R1	1m 18.169s	21
11	Alex Bassani	ITA	47	Kawasaki Racing Team WorldSBK	Kawasaki ZX-10RR	1m 25.369s	21
12	Garrett Gerloff	USA	31	Bonovo Action BMW	BMW M 1000 RR	2m 06.163s	21
	Sam Lowes	GBR	14	ELF Marc VDS Racing Team	Ducati Panigale V4R	DNF	17
	Remy Gardner	AUS	87	GYTR GRT Yamaha WorldSBK Team	Yamaha YZF R1	DNF	16
	Alex Lowes	GBR	22	Kawasaki Racing Team WorldSBK	Kawasaki ZX-10RR	DNF	14
	Bradley Ray	GBR	28	Yamaha Motoxracing WorldSBK Team	Yamaha YZF R1	DNF	12
	Tarran Mackenzie	GBR	95	PETRONAS MIE Racing Honda	Honda CBR1000 RR-R	DNF	10
	Philipp Oettl	GER	5	GMT94 Yamaha	Yamaha YZF R1	DNF	9
	Tito Rabat	ESP	53	Kawasaki Puccetti Racing	Kawasaki ZX-10RR	DNF	3
	Ivo Lopes	POR	75	PETRONAS MIE Racing Honda	Honda CBR1000 RR-R	DNF	1
	Jonathan Rea	GBR	65	Pata Prometeon Yamaha	Yamaha YZF R1	DNF	0
	Nicolo Bulega	ITA	11	Aruba.it Racing - Ducati	Ducati Panigale V4R	DNF	0
	Toprak Razgatlioglu	TUR	54	ROKiT BMW Motorrad WorldSBK Team	BMW M 1000 RR	DNS	-

Fastest race lap: Locatelli on lap 2, 1m 42.753s, 96.027mph/154.541km/h.
Lap record: Bautista, 1m 36.084s, 102.693mph/165.268km/h (2023).

Superpole: 10 laps, 27.409 miles/44.110km
Weather: Dry · Track 24°C · Air 20°C
Time of race: 16m 15.040s
Average speed: 101.197mph/162.861km/h

Pos.	Rider	Time & Gap	Laps
1	Nicolo Bulega		10
2	Alex Lowes	0.115s	10
3	Danilo Petrucci	3.677s	10
4	Scott Redding	3.903s	10
5	Xavi Vierge	5.710s	10
6	Garrett Gerloff	5.854s	10
7	Iker Lecuona	6.613s	10
8	Michael van der Mark	7.788s	10
9	Remy Gardner	8.397s	10
10	Axel Bassani	10.270s	10
11	Andrea Iannone	17.510s	10
12	Michael Rinaldi	18.040s	10
13	Alessandro Delbianco	18.907s	10
14	Philipp Oettl	19.130s	10
15	Bradley Ray	19.288s	10
16	Sam Lowes	20.436s	10
17	Tito Rabat	25.603s	10
18	Tarran Mackenzie	25.910s	10
19	Ivo Lopes	27.319s	10
	Andrea Locatelli	DNF	5
	Alvaro Bautista	DNF	0
	Jonathan Rea	DNS	-
	Toprak Razgatlioglu	DNS	-

Fastest race lap: A. Lowes on lap 5, 1m 36.873s, 101.856mph/163.922km/h.

Race 2: 21 laps, 57.558 miles/92.631km
Weather: Dry · Track 28°C · Air 21°C
Time of race: 34m 3.028s
Average speed: 101.423mph/163.224km/h

Pos.	Rider	Time & Gap	Laps
1	Nicolo Bulega		21
2	Danilo Petrucci	2.303s	21
3	Garrett Gerloff	4.300s	21
4	Alex Lowes	6.576s	21
5	Michael van der Mark	7.521s	21
6	Remy Gardner	11.620s	21
7	Xavi Vierge	12.155s	21
8	Scott Redding	12.200s	21
9	Andrea Locatelli	13.821s	21
10	Iker Lecuona	15.219s	21
11	Axel Bassani	17.918s	21
12	Andrea Iannone	26.852s	21
13	Alessandro Delbianco	28.630s	21
14	Tito Rabat	28.646s	21
15	Michael Rinaldi	29.418s	21
16	Philipp Oettl	35.166s	21
17	Bradley Ray	36.438s	21
18	Tarran Mackenzie	49.190s	21
19	Ivo Lopes	49.535s	21
	Sam Lowes	DNF	12
	Alvaro Bautista	DNS	-
	Jonathan Rea	DNS	-
	Toprak Razgatlioglu	DNS	-

Fastest race lap: Bulega on lap 5, 1m 36.717s, 102.020mph/164.186km/h.

Superpole
1, Razgatlioglu 1m 30.801s; 2, Petrucci 1m 31.261s; 3, Gardner 1m 31.419s; 4, Bassani 1m 31.430s; 5, Rea 1m 31.458s; 6, Gerloff 1m 31.659s; 7, Locatelli 1m 31.680s; 8, Rinaldi 1m 31.715s; 9, Vierge 1m 31.813s; 10, Aegerter 1m 31.822s; 11, Lecuona 1m 31.931s; 12, Lowes 1m 31.951s; 13, Baz 1m 32.037s; 14, Bautista 1m 32.177s; 15, Redding 1m 32.253s; 16, Baldassarri 1m 32.713s; 17, Granado 1m 32.953s; 18, Van der Mark 1m 33.175s; 19, Vinales 1m 33.297s; 20, Rabat 1m 33.440s; 21, Tamburini 1m 33.575s; 22, Soomer 1m 33.662s; 23, Konig 1m 34.939s; 24, Oettl No Time.

Points
1, Bautista 427; 2, Razgatlioglu 353; 3, Rea 251; 4, Locatelli 227; 5, Bassani 207; 6, Petrucci 155; 7, Rinaldi 147; 8, Lowes 121; 9, Aegerter 114; 10, Vierge 105; 11, Redding 99; 12, Gardner 98; 13, Lecuona 87; 14, Gerloff 68; 15, Oettl 56; 16, Baz 42; 17, Van der Mark 23; 18, Ray 19; 19, Sykes 11; 20, Baldassarri 9; 21, Syahrin 8; 22, Haslam 2; 23, Rabat 1; 24, Vinales 1; 25, Lopes 1.

Round 9 — CREMONA, Italy · 20–22 September, 2024 · 2.341-mile/3.768km circuit

Race 1: 17 laps, 41.719 miles/67.141km
Weather: Dry · Track 34°C · Air 24°C
Time of race: 26m 49.788s
Average speed: 93.298mph/150.149km/h

Pos.	Rider	Nat.	No.	Entrant	Machine	Time & Gap	Laps
1	Danilo Petrucci	ITA	9	Barni Spark Racing Team	Ducati Panigale V4R		17
2	Nicolo Bulega	ITA	11	Aruba.it Racing - Ducati	Ducati Panigale V4R	2.590s	17
3	Alvaro Bautista	ESP	1	Aruba.it Racing - Ducati	Ducati Panigale V4R	6.383s	17
4	Iker Lecuona	ESP	7	Team HRC	Honda CBR1000 RR-R	7.583s	17
5	Alex Bassani	ITA	47	Kawasaki Racing Team WorldSBK	Kawasaki ZX-10RR	10.125s	17
6	Xavi Vierge	ESP	97	Team HRC	Honda CBR1000 RR-R	10.211s	17
7	Michael van der Mark	NED	60	ROKiT BMW Motorrad WorldSBK Team	BMW M 1000 RR	1 Sector	17
8	Garrett Gerloff	USA	31	Bonovo Action BMW	BMW M 1000 RR	1 Sector	17
9	Michael Rinaldi	ITA	21	Team Motocorsa Racing	Ducati Panigale V4R	2 Sectors	17
10	Remy Gardner	AUS	87	GYTR GRT Yamaha WorldSBK Team	Yamaha YZF R1	2 Sectors	17
11	Bradley Ray	GBR	28	Yamaha Motoxracing WorldSBK Team	Yamaha YZF R1	2 Sectors	17
12	Andrea Locatelli	ITA	55	Pata Prometeon Yamaha	Yamaha YZF R1	2 Sectors	17
13	Scott Redding	GBR	45	Bonovo Action BMW	BMW M 1000 RR	2 Sectors	17
14	Markus Reiterberger	GER	37	ROKiT BMW Motorrad WorldSBK Team	BMW M 1000 RR	2 Sectors	17
15	Alessandro Delbianco	ITA	52	Yamaha Motoxracing WorldSBK Team	Yamaha YZF R1	2 Sectors	17
16	Philipp Oettl	GER	5	GMT94 Yamaha	Yamaha YZF R1	3 Sectors	17
17	Marvin Fritz	GER	17	GYTR GRT Yamaha WorldSBK Team	Yamaha YZF R1	3 Sectors	17
18	Tommy Bridewell	GBR	46	Honda Racing UK	Honda CBR1000 RR-R	3 Sectors	17
19	Ivo Lopes	POR	75	PETRONAS MIE Racing Honda	Honda CBR1000 RR-R	3 Sectors	17
20	Alex Lowes	GBR	22	Kawasaki Racing Team WorldSBK	Kawasaki ZX-10RR	1 Lap	16
	Tarran Mackenzie	GBR	95	PETRONAS MIE Racing Honda	Honda CBR1000 RR-R	DNF	16
	Niccolo Canepa	ITA	59	Pata Prometeon Yamaha	Yamaha YZF R1	DNF	13
	Andrea Iannone	ITA	29	Team GoEleven	Ducati Panigale V4R	DNF	7
	Sam Lowes	GBR	14	ELF Marc VDS Racing Team	Ducati Panigale V4R	DNF	5
	Tito Rabat	ESP	53	Kawasaki Puccetti Racing	Kawasaki ZX-10RR	DNF	0

Fastest race lap: Iannone on lap 2, 1m 29.397s, 94.285mph/151.737km/h.
Lap record: New circuit.

Superpole: 10 laps, 23.413 miles/37.680km
Weather: Dry · Track 24°C · Air 20°C
Time of race: 14m 56.130s
Average speed: 94.058mph/151.371km/h

Pos.	Rider	Time & Gap	Laps
1	Danilo Petrucci		10
2	Alex Lowes	1.797s	10
3	Andrea Iannone	2.572s	10
4	Nicolo Bulega	3.431s	10
5	Iker Lecuona	4.729s	10
6	Alvaro Bautista	5.578s	10
7	Andrea Locatelli	5.909s	10
8	Xavi Vierge	6.650s	10
9	Garrett Gerloff	6.815s	10
10	Tito Rabat	7.149s	10
11	Axel Bassani	7.273s	10
12	Michael van der Mark	7.600s	10
13	Scott Redding	11.088s	10
14	Sam Lowes	11.244s	10
15	Bradley Ray	11.506s	10
16	Markus Reiterberger	14.251s	10
17	Michael Rinaldi	16.335s	10
18	Niccolo Canepa	19.679s	10
19	Philipp Oettl	20.380s	10
20	Alessandro Delbianco	20.533s	10
21	Tommy Bridewell	24.960s	10
22	Ivo Lopes	31.813s	10
23	Tarran Mackenzie	1 Lap	9
	Remy Gardner	DNF	7
	Marvin Fritz	DNF	1

Fastest race lap: Petrucci on lap 2, 1m 28.289s, 95.468mph/153.641km/h.

Race 2: 23 laps, 53.851 miles/86.664km
Weather: Dry · Track 35°C · Air 28°C
Time of race: 34m 33.263s
Average speed: 93.506mph/150.483km/h

Pos.	Rider	Time & Gap	Laps
1	Danilo Petrucci		23
2	Alvaro Bautista	1.023s	23
3	Nicolo Bulega	2.910s	23
4	Garrett Gerloff	8.452s	23
5	Alex Lowes	8.761s	23
6	Iker Lecuona	13.397s	23
7	Michael van der Mark	15.873s	23
8	Xavi Vierge	19.228s	23
9	Andrea Locatelli	19.523s	23
10	Tito Rabat	24.368s	23
11	Sam Lowes	24.691s	23
12	Scott Redding	25.664s	23
13	Michael Rinaldi	26.726s	23
14	Bradley Ray	27.167s	23
15	Markus Reiterberger	39.566s	23
16	Alessandro Delbianco	44.483s	23
17	Philipp Oettl	50.786s	23
18	Marvin Fritz	52.608s	23
19	Niccolo Canepa	59.505s	23
20	Ivo Lopes	1m 00.237s	23
	Remy Gardner	DNF	21
	Andrea Iannone	DNF	16
	Tarran Mackenzie	DNF	9
	Axel Bassani	DNF	2

Fastest race lap: Bulega on lap 2, 1m 29.438s, 94.242mph/151.667km/h.

Superpole
1, Bulega 1m 27.953s; 2, Iannone 1m 28.068s; 3, Petrucci 1m 28.285s; 4, A. Lowes 1m 28.310s; 5, Locatelli 1m 28.602s; 6, S. Lowes 1m 28.615s; 7, Vierge 1m 28.752s; 8, Lecuona 1m 28.845s; 9, Ray 1m 28.883s; 10, Rabat 1m 28.921s; 11, Gerloff 1m 28.959s; 12, Bassani 1m 29.018s; 13, Bautista 1m 29.115s; 14, Reiterberger 1m 29.116s; 15, Redding 1m 29.120s; 16, Gardner 1m 29.310s; 17, Van der Mark 1m 29.435s; 18, Rinaldi 1m 29.516s; 19, Canepa 1m 30.174s; 20, Fritz 1m 30.195s; 21, Oettl 1m 30.227s; 22, Mackenzie 1m 30.243s; 23, Delbianco 1m 30.295s; 24, Bridewell 1m 30.615s; 25, Lopes 1m 30.853s.

Points
1, Razgatlioglu 365; 2, Bulega 352; 3, Bautista 283; 4, A. Lowes 255; 5, Petrucci 252; 6, Locatelli 184; 7, Van der Mark 177; 8, Iannone 151; 9, Gardner 139; 10, Gerloff 117; 11, Vierge 89; 12, Rea 86; 13, Lecuona 84; 14, Redding 82; 15, Bassani 80; 16, Aegerter 79; 17, Rinaldi 56; 18, S. Lowes 45; 19, Spinelli 25; 20, Rabat 16; 21, Delbianco 10; 22, Ray 10; 23, Mackenzie 7; 24, Oettl 5; 25, Pirro 3; 26, Reiterberger 3.

Round 10 — ARAGON, Spain · 27–29 September, 2024 · 3.155-mile/5.077km circuit

Race 1: 17 laps, 53.630 miles/86.309km
Weather: Dry · Track 34°C · Air 23°C
Time of race: 31m 9.154s
Average speed: 103.292mph/166.232km/h

Pos.	Rider	Nat.	No.	Entrant	Machine	Time & Gap	Laps
1	Andrea Iannone	ITA	29	Team GoEleven	Ducati Panigale V4R		17
2	Toprak Razgatlioglu	TUR	54	ROKiT BMW Motorrad WorldSBK Team	BMW M 1000 RR	0.845s	17
3	Garrett Gerloff	USA	31	Bonovo Action BMW	BMW M 1000 RR	1.124s	17
4	Alvaro Bautista	ESP	1	Aruba.it Racing - Ducati	Ducati Panigale V4R	1.190s	17
5	Danilo Petrucci	ITA	9	Barni Spark Racing Team	Ducati Panigale V4R	2.528s	17
6	Iker Lecuona	ESP	7	Team HRC	Honda CBR1000 RR-R	4.758s	17
7	Alex Lowes	GBR	22	Kawasaki Racing Team WorldSBK	Kawasaki ZX-10RR	5.352s	17
8	Xavi Vierge	ESP	97	Team HRC	Honda CBR1000 RR-R	6.477s	17
9	Michael van der Mark	NED	60	ROKiT BMW Motorrad WorldSBK Team	BMW M 1000 RR	8.749s	17
10	Andrea Locatelli	ITA	55	Pata Prometeon Yamaha	Yamaha YZF R1	8.926s	17
11	Scott Redding	GBR	45	Bonovo Action BMW	BMW M 1000 RR	9.003s	17
12	Alex Bassani	ITA	47	Kawasaki Racing Team WorldSBK	Kawasaki ZX-10RR	10.660s	17
13	Michael Rinaldi	ITA	21	Team Motocorsa Racing	Ducati Panigale V4R	11.976s	17
14	Jonathan Rea	GBR	65	Pata Prometeon Yamaha	Yamaha YZF R1	14.901s	17
15	Bradley Ray	GBR	28	Yamaha Motoxracing WorldSBK Team	Yamaha YZF R1	16.291s	17
16	Remy Gardner	AUS	87	GYTR GRT Yamaha WorldSBK Team	Yamaha YZF R1	21.047s	17
17	Philipp Oettl	GER	5	GMT94 Yamaha	Yamaha YZF R1	30.353s	17
18	Tarran Mackenzie	GBR	95	PETRONAS MIE Racing Honda	Honda CBR1000 RR-R	31.777s	17
	Tito Rabat	ESP	53	Kawasaki Puccetti Racing	Kawasaki ZX-10RR	DNF	10
	Marvin Fritz	GER	17	GYTR GRT Yamaha WorldSBK Team	Yamaha YZF R1	DNF	5
	Sam Lowes	GBR	14	ELF Marc VDS Racing Team	Ducati Panigale V4R	DNS	-
	Nicolo Bulega	ITA	11	Aruba.it Racing - Ducati	Ducati Panigale V4R	DNS	-

Fastest race lap: Iannone on lap 16, 1m 49.040s, 104.154mph/167.619km/h.
Lap record: Rea, 1m 49.028s, 104.165mph/167.638km/h (2023).

Superpole: 10 laps, 31.547 miles/50.770km
Weather: Dry · Track 25°C · Air 17°C
Time of race: 18m 7.997s
Average speed: 104.384mph/167.989km/h

Pos.	Rider	Time & Gap	Laps
1	Alvaro Bautista		10
2	Toprak Razgatlioglu	0.088s	10
3	Nicolo Bulega	0.172s	10
4	Andrea Iannone	4.691s	10
5	Garrett Gerloff	5.317s	10
6	Danilo Petrucci	6.940s	10
7	Iker Lecuona	7.988s	10
8	Michael van der Mark	10.170s	10
9	Xavi Vierge	10.894s	10
10	Scott Redding	11.112s	10
11	Andrea Locatelli	11.509s	10
12	Jonathan Rea	11.590s	10
13	Remy Gardner	12.151s	10
14	Michael Rinaldi	12.927s	10
15	Axel Bassani	14.134s	10
16	Bradley Ray	14.676s	10
17	Tito Rabat	15.918s	10
18	Philipp Oettl	28.650s	10
19	Tarran Mackenzie	28.716s	10
	Alex Lowes	DNF	2
	Marvin Fritz	DNF	2
	Sam Lowes	DNS	-

Fastest race lap: Razgatlioglu on lap 7, 1m 47.935s, 105.220mph/169.335km/h.

Race 2: 18 laps, 56.785 miles/91.386km
Weather: Dry · Track 38°C · Air 25°C
Time of race: 32m 39.243s
Average speed: 104.339mph/167.917km/h

Pos.	Rider	Time & Gap	Laps
1	Alvaro Bautista		18
2	Toprak Razgatlioglu	3.366s	18
3	Nicolo Bulega	10.800s	18
4	Andrea Iannone	12.338s	18
5	Garrett Gerloff	13.903s	18
6	Danilo Petrucci	14.647s	18
7	Michael van der Mark	16.427s	18
8	Iker Lecuona	17.072s	18
9	Andrea Locatelli	18.631s	18
10	Xavi Vierge	20.291s	18
11	Scott Redding	22.674s	18
12	Axel Bassani	24.710s	18
13	Jonathan Rea	26.707s	18
14	Michael Rinaldi	28.126s	18
15	Remy Gardner	31.144s	18
16	Bradley Ray	31.193s	18
17	Tito Rabat	40.961s	18
18	Tarran Mackenzie	52.330s	18
19	Philipp Oettl	52.713s	18
	Marvin Fritz	DNF	4
	Alex Lowes	DNS	-
	Sam Lowes	DNS	-

Fastest race lap: Bautista on lap 17, 1m 48.121s, 105.039mph/169.044km/h.

Superpole
1, Bulega 1m 47.840s; 2, Iannone 1m 48.208s; 3, Bautista 1m 48.258s; 4, Petrucci 1m 48.314s; 5, Razgatlioglu 1m 48.331s; 6, A. Lowes 1m 48.348s; 7, Locatelli 1m 48.357s; 8, S. Lowes 1m 48.382s; 9, Lecuona 1m 48.408s; 10, Gerloff 1m 48.655s; 11, Van der Mark 1m 48.699s; 12, Vierge 1m 48.747s; 13, Rea 1m 48.900s; 14, Redding 1m 48.951s; 15, Gardner 1m 49.038s; 16, Bassani 1m 49.053s; 17, Ray 1m 49.095s; 18, Rinaldi 1m 49.102s; 19, Rabat 1m 49.201s; 20, Oettl 1m 49.975s; 21, Mackenzie 1m 50.591s; 22, Fritz 1m 51.794s.

Points
1, Razgatlioglu 414; 2, Bulega 375; 3, Bautista 333; 4, Petrucci 277; 5, A. Lowes 264; 6, Locatelli 197; 7, Iannone 195; 8, Van der Mark 195; 9, Gerloff 149; 10, Gardner 140; 11, Lecuona 105; 12, Vierge 104; 13, Redding 92; 14, Rea 91; 15, Bassani 88; 16, Aegerter 79; 17, Rinaldi 61; 18, S. Lowes 45; 19, Spinelli 25; 20, Rabat 16; 21, Ray 11; 22, Delbianco 10; 23, Mackenzie 7; 24, Oettl 5; 25, Pirro 3; 26, Reiterberger 3.

Round 11 — ESTORIL, Portugal · 11–13 October, 2024 · 2.598-mile/4.182km circuit

Race 1: 21 laps, 54.570 miles/87.822km
Weather: Dry · Track 29°C · Air 21°C
Time of race: 34m 15.509s
Average speed: 95.574mph/153.811km/h

Pos.	Rider	Nat.	No.	Entrant	Machine	Time & Gap	Laps
1	Toprak Razgatlioglu	TUR	54	ROKiT BMW Motorrad WorldSBK Team	BMW M 1000 RR		21
2	Nicolo Bulega	ITA	11	Aruba.it Racing - Ducati	Ducati Panigale V4R	9.221s	21
3	Iker Lecuona	ESP	7	Team HRC	Honda CBR1000 RR-R	11.020s	21
4	Alex Lowes	GBR	22	Kawasaki Racing Team WorldSBK	Kawasaki ZX-10RR	11.973s	21
5	Jonathan Rea	GBR	65	Pata Prometeon Yamaha	Yamaha YZF R1	14.018s	21
6	Garrett Gerloff	USA	31	Bonovo Action BMW	BMW M 1000 RR	17.727s	21
7	Michael van der Mark	NED	60	ROKiT BMW Motorrad WorldSBK Team	BMW M 1000 RR	19.250s	21
8	Xavi Vierge	ESP	97	Team HRC	Honda CBR1000 RR-R	23.589s	21
9	Andrea Iannone	ITA	29	Team GoEleven	Ducati Panigale V4R	24.239s	21
10	Tito Rabat	ESP	53	Kawasaki Puccetti Racing	Kawasaki ZX-10RR	30.893s	21
11	Michael Rinaldi	ITA	21	Team Motocorsa Racing	Ducati Panigale V4R	30.943s	21
12	Scott Redding	GBR	45	Bonovo Action BMW	BMW M 1000 RR	31.476s	21
13	Sam Lowes	GBR	14	ELF Marc VDS Racing Team	Ducati Panigale V4R	31.702s	21
14	Dominique Aegerter	SUI	77	GYTR GRT Yamaha WorldSBK Team	Yamaha YZF R1	34.886s	21
15	Ivo Lopes	POR	75	PETRONAS MIE Racing Honda	Honda CBR1000 RR-R	47.016s	21
16	Bradley Ray	GBR	28	Yamaha Motoxracing WorldSBK Team	Yamaha YZF R1	48.226s	21
17	Philipp Oettl	GER	5	GMT94 Yamaha	Yamaha YZF R1	51.000s	21
18	Tarran Mackenzie	GBR	95	PETRONAS MIE Racing Honda	Honda CBR1000 RR-R	55.393s	21
19	Alvaro Bautista	ESP	1	Aruba.it Racing - Ducati	Ducati Panigale V4R	2 Laps	19
20	Luca Bernardi	SMR	91	Yamaha Motoxracing WorldSBK Team	Yamaha YZF R1	3 Laps	18
	Andrea Locatelli	ITA	55	Pata Prometeon Yamaha	Yamaha YZF R1	DNF	14
	Danilo Petrucci	ITA	9	Barni Spark Racing Team	Ducati Panigale V4R	DNF	6
	Alex Bassani	ITA	47	Kawasaki Racing Team WorldSBK	Kawasaki ZX-10RR	DNF	6
	Remy Gardner	AUS	87	GYTR GRT Yamaha WorldSBK Team	Yamaha YZF R1	DNF	1

Fastest race lap: Razgatlioglu on lap 9, 1m 37.149s, 96.294mph/154.970km/h.
Lap record: Rea, 1m 36.204s, 97.240mph/156.492km/h (2022).

Superpole: 10 laps, 25.986 miles/41.820km
Weather: Dry · Track 26°C · Air 21°C
Time of race: 16m 10.735s
Average speed: 96.369mph/155.091km/h

Pos.	Rider	Time & Gap	Laps
1	Nicolo Bulega		10
2	Toprak Razgatlioglu	0.003s	10
3	Alvaro Bautista	4.253s	10
4	Andrea Locatelli	5.623s	10
5	Danilo Petrucci	7.161s	10
6	Alex Lowes	7.192s	10
7	Xavi Vierge	8.157s	10
8	Iker Lecuona	9.672s	10
9	Andrea Iannone	11.822s	10
10	Scott Redding	12.345s	10
11	Garrett Gerloff	12.613s	10
12	Axel Bassani	13.575s	10
13	Michael van der Mark	13.772s	10
14	Michael Rinaldi	14.264s	10
15	Sam Lowes	15.051s	10
16	Dominique Aegerter	15.432s	10
17	Tito Rabat	15.542s	10
18	Bradley Ray	18.018s	10
19	Tarran Mackenzie	21.003s	10
20	Ivo Lopes	24.271s	10
21	Philipp Oettl	24.714s	10
22	Jonathan Rea	27.011s	10
23	Luca Bernardi	39.701s	10
	Remy Gardner	DNS	-

Fastest race lap: Bulega on lap 8, 1m 36.178s, 97.266mph/156.535km/h.

Race 2: 21 laps, 54.570 miles/87.822km
Weather: Dry · Track 33°C · Air 24°C
Time of race: 34m 9.897s
Average speed: 95.835mph/154.232km/h

Pos.	Rider	Time & Gap	Laps
1	Toprak Razgatlioglu		21
2	Nicolo Bulega	3.866s	21
3	Alvaro Bautista	3.998s	21
4	Jonathan Rea	12.005s	21
5	Michael van der Mark	15.209s	21
6	Xavi Vierge	15.792s	21
7	Danilo Petrucci	16.914s	21
8	Andrea Iannone	17.371s	21
9	Michael Rinaldi	19.129s	21
10	Axel Bassani	19.966s	21
11	Scott Redding	22.007s	21
12	Alex Lowes	22.067s	21
13	Dominique Aegerter	31.487s	21
14	Bradley Ray	31.882s	21
15	Ivo Lopes	41.552s	21
16	Philipp Oettl	42.305s	21
17	Luca Bernardi	1m 06.825s	21
	Tito Rabat	DNF	12
	Iker Lecuona	DNF	9
	Andrea Locatelli	DNF	8
	Garrett Gerloff	DNF	4
	Sam Lowes	DNF	2
	Tarran Mackenzie	DNF	2
	Remy Gardner	DNS	-

Fastest race lap: Razgatlioglu on lap 7, 1m 36.802s, 96.639mph/155.526km/h.

Superpole
1, Razgatlioglu 1m 52.430s; 2, Petrucci 1m 52.512s; 3, Rea 1m 52.939s; 4, Locatelli 1m 53.357s; 5, Bulega 1m 53.429s; 6, Van der Mark 1m 53.628s; 7, S. Lowes 1m 53.673s; 8, Mackenzie 1m 53.796s; 9, A. Lowes 1m 53.937s; 10, Bassani 1m 54.049s; 11, Bautista 1m 54.239s; 12, Iannone 1m 54.516s; 13, Vierge 1m 54.575s; 14, Lecuona 1m 54.678s; 15, Rinaldi 1m 55.252s; 16, Gardner 1m 55.262s; 17, Gerloff 1m 55.887s; 18, Aegerter 1m 56.346s; 19, Redding 1m 56.764s; 20, Bernardi 1m 57.623s; 21, Ray 1m 57.941s; 22, Lopes 1m 58.107s; 23, Rabat 1m 58.407s; 24, Oettl 2m 00.479s.

Points
1, Razgatlioglu 473; 2, Bulega 427; 3, Bautista 356; 4, Petrucci 291; 5, A. Lowes 285; 6, Van der Mark 215; 7, Iannone 211; 8, Locatelli 203; 9, Gerloff 159; 10, Gardner 140; 11, Vierge 125; 12, Lecuona 123; 13, Rea 115; 14, Redding 101; 15, Bassani 94; 16, Aegerter 84; 17, Rinaldi 73; 18, S. Lowes 48; 19, Spinelli 25; 20, Rabat 22; 21, Ray 13; 22, Delbianco 10; 23, Mackenzie 7; 24, Oettl 5; 25, Pirro 3; 26, Reiterberger 3; 27, Lopes 2.

Round 12 — JEREZ, Spain · 18–20 October, 2024 · 2.748-mile/4.423km circuit

Race 1: 20 laps, 54.966 miles/88.460km
Weather: Dry · Track 30°C · Air 24°C
Time of race: 33m 32.738s
Average speed: 98.313mph/158.220km/h

Pos.	Rider	Nat.	No.	Entrant	Machine	Time & Gap	Laps
1	Nicolo Bulega	ITA	11	Aruba.it Racing - Ducati	Ducati Panigale V4R		20
2	Toprak Razgatlioglu	TUR	54	ROKiT BMW Motorrad WorldSBK Team	BMW M 1000 RR	6.067s	20
3	Andrea Locatelli	ITA	55	Pata Prometeon Yamaha	Yamaha YZF R1	9.361s	20
4	Alex Lowes	GBR	22	Kawasaki Racing Team WorldSBK	Kawasaki ZX-10RR	11.249s	20
5	Iker Lecuona	ESP	7	Team HRC	Honda CBR1000 RR-R	13.597s	20
6	Michael van der Mark	NED	60	ROKiT BMW Motorrad WorldSBK Team	BMW M 1000 RR	14.976s	20
7	Xavi Vierge	ESP	97	Team HRC	Honda CBR1000 RR-R	15.762s	20
8	Alex Bassani	ITA	47	Kawasaki Racing Team WorldSBK	Kawasaki ZX-10RR	16.285s	20
9	Dominique Aegerter	SUI	77	GYTR GRT Yamaha WorldSBK Team	Yamaha YZF R1	16.715s	20
10	Garrett Gerloff	USA	31	Bonovo Action BMW	BMW M 1000 RR	16.854s	20
11	Jonathan Rea	GBR	65	Pata Prometeon Yamaha	Yamaha YZF R1	19.768s	20
12	Andrea Iannone	ITA	29	Team GoEleven	Ducati Panigale V4R	19.773s	20
13	Sam Lowes	GBR	14	ELF Marc VDS Racing Team	Ducati Panigale V4R	27.133s	20
14	Scott Redding	GBR	45	Bonovo Action BMW	BMW M 1000 RR	30.105s	20
15	Tetsuta Nagashima	JPN	49	Team HRC	Honda CBR1000 RR-R	33.520s	20
16	Tito Rabat	ESP	53	Kawasaki Puccetti Racing	Kawasaki ZX-10RR	34.316s	20
17	Bradley Ray	GBR	28	Yamaha Motoxracing WorldSBK Team	Yamaha YZF R1	37.431s	20
18	Philipp Oettl	GER	5	GMT94 Yamaha	Yamaha YZF R1	40.497s	20
19	Alessandro Delbianco	ITA	52	GYTR GRT Yamaha WorldSBK Team	Yamaha YZF R1	43.443s	20
20	Ivo Lopes	POR	75	PETRONAS MIE Racing Honda	Honda CBR1000 RR-R	52.599s	20
21	Luca Bernardi	SMR	91	Yamaha Motoxracing WorldSBK Team	Yamaha YZF R1	54.917s	20
22	Kyle Ryde	GBR	33	OMG Racing	Yamaha YZF R1	1m 01.629s	20
23	Alvaro Bautista	ESP	1	Aruba.it Racing - Ducati	Ducati Panigale V4R	1m 02.084s	20
24	Tarran Mackenzie	GBR	95	PETRONAS MIE Racing Honda	Honda CBR1000 RR-R	1m 23.414s	20
	Michael Rinaldi	ITA	21	Team Motocorsa Racing	Ducati Panigale V4R	DNF	5
	Tommy Bridewell	GBR	46	Honda Racing UK	Honda CBR1000 RR-R	DNF	0
	Danilo Petrucci	ITA	9	Barni Spark Racing Team	Ducati Panigale V4R	DNF	0

Fastest race lap: Bulega on lap 2, 1m 39.371s, 99.566mph/160.236km/h.
Lap record: Bautista, 1m 39.004s, 99.935mph/160.830km/h (2019)..

Superpole: 10 laps, 27.483 miles/44.230km
Weather: Dry · Track 18°C · Air 21°C
Time of race: 16m 34.501s
Average speed: 99.486mph/160.108km/h

Pos.	Rider	Time & Gap	Laps
1	Nicolo Bulega		10
2	Toprak Razgatlioglu	2.375s	10
3	Alex Lowes	4.182s	10
4	Danilo Petrucci	5.511s	10
5	Andrea Locatelli	6.202s	10
6	Michael van der Mark	6.540s	10
7	Andrea Iannone	7.306s	10
8	Garrett Gerloff	7.500s	10
9	Alvaro Bautista	8.306s	10
10	Dominique Aegerter	8.697s	10
11	Jonathan Rea	9.702s	10
12	Scott Redding	11.312s	10
13	Michael Rinaldi	12.862s	10
14	Axel Bassani	14.283s	10
15	Tito Rabat	14.848s	10
16	Bradley Ray	15.271s	10
17	Sam Lowes	15.946s	10
18	Alessandro Delbianco	23.467s	10
19	Tetsuta Nagashima	23.753s	10
20	Tommy Bridewell	24.883s	10
21	Tarran Mackenzie	24.917s	10
22	Philipp Oettl	25.772s	10
23	Ivo Lopes	27.208s	10
24	Luca Bernardi	29.780s	10
	Iker Lecuona	DNF	1
	Xavi Vierge	DNF	1

Fastest race lap: Bulega on lap 6, 1m 38.528s, 100.418mph/161.607km/h.

Race 2: 16 laps, 45.353 miles/72.988km
Weather: Dry · Track 30°C · Air 25°C
Time of race: 27m 36.726s
Average speed: 98.549mph/158.600km/h

Pos.	Rider	Time & Gap	Laps
1	Toprak Razgatlioglu		16
2	Nicolo Bulega	0.812s	16
3	Michael van der Mark	11.356s	16
4	Andrea Iannone	12.634s	16
5	Alex Lowes	13.979s	16
6	Danilo Petrucci	14.545s	16
7	Garrett Gerloff	14.835s	16
8	Andrea Locatelli	1 Sectors	16
9	Jonathan Rea	1 Sectors	16
10	Axel Bassani	1 Sectors	16
11	Michael Rinaldi	1 Sectors	16
12	Scott Redding	1 Sectors	16
13	Xavi Vierge	1 Sectors	16
14	Sam Lowes	1 Sectors	16
15	Bradley Ray	2 Sectors	16
16	Tetsuta Nagashima	2 Sectors	16
17	Alessandro Delbianco	2 Sectors	16
18	Ivo Lopes	3 Sectors	16
19	Luca Bernardi	3 Sectors	16
	Tito Rabat	DNF	16
	Philipp Oettl	DNF	16
	Dominique Aegerter	DNF	14
	Alvaro Bautista	DNF	10
	Tarran Mackenzie	DNF	3
	Tommy Bridewell	DNF	2

Fastest race lap: Razgatlioglu on lap 2, 1m 39.246s, 99.692mph/160.438km/h.

Superpole
1, Bulega 1m 37.596s; 2, Razgatlioglu 1m 38.202s; 3, A. Lowes 1m 38.302s; 4, Petrucci 1m 38.354s; 5, Lecuona 1m 38.591s; 6, Locatelli 1m 38.665s; 7, Vierge 1m 38.677s; 8, Van der Mark 1m 38.680s; 9, Rinaldi 1m 38.750s; 10, Gerloff 1m 38.774s; 11, Iannone 1m 38.822s; 12, Redding 1m 38.858s; 13, Aegerter 1m 38.868s; 14, Bassani 1m 38.917s; 15, Bautista 1m 38.938s; 16, Rea 1m 38.953s; 17, S. Lowes 1m 39.019s; 18, Rabat 1m 39.248s; 19, Ray 1m 39.273s; 20, Nagashima 1m 39.792s; 21, Delbianco 1m 39.945s; 22, Oettl 1m 40.154s; 23, Mackenzie 1m 40.488s; 24, Bridewell 1m 40.643s; 25, Ryde 1m 41.008s; 26, Lopes 1m 41.164s; 27, Bernardi 1m 41.230s.

Points
1, Razgatlioglu 527; 2, Bulega 484; 3, Bautista 357; 4, A. Lowes 316; 5, Petrucci 307; 6, Van der Mark 245; 7, Locatelli 232; 8, Iannone 231; 9, Gerloff 176; 10, Gardner 140; 11, Vierge 137; 12, Lecuona 134; 13, Rea 127; 14, Bassani 108; 15, Redding 107; 16, Aegerter 91; 17, Rinaldi 78; 18, S. Lowes 53; 19, Spinelli 25; 20, Rabat 22; 21, Ray 14; 22, Delbianco 10; 23, Mackenzie 7; 24, Oettl 5; 25, Pirro 3; 26, Reiterberger 3; 27, Lopes 2; 28, Nagashima 1.

2024 FINAL WORLD SUPERBIKE POINTS TABLE

Position	Rider	Nationality	Machine	Phillip Island/1	Phillip Island/SPole	Phillip Island/2	Catalunya/1	Catalunya/SPole	Catalunya/2	Assen/1	Assen/SPole	Assen/2	Misano/1	Misano/SPole	Misano/2	Donington/1	Donington/SPole	Donington/2	Most/1	Most/SPole	Most/2	Portimao/1	Portimao/SPole	Portimao/2	Magny-Cours/1	Magny-Cours/SPole	Magny-Cours/2	Cremona/1	Cremona/SPole	Cremona/2	Aragon/1	Aragon/SPole	Aragon/2	Estoril/1	Estoril/SPole	Estoril/2	Jerez/1	Jerez/SPole	Jerez/2	Total Points
1	Toprak Razgatlioglu	TUR	BMW	11	7	-	25	12	16	20	1	25	25	12	25	25	12	25	25	12	25	25	12	25	-	-	-	-	-	-	20	9	20	25	9	25	20	9	25	**527**
2	Nicolo Bulega	ITA	Ducati	25	5	11	20	6	20	5	9	8	20	9	20	13	9	20	10	9	20	9	5	20	-	12	25	20	6	16	-	7	16	20	12	20	25	12	20	**484**
3	Alvaro Bautista	ESP	Ducati	1	6	20	16	7	25	16	12	20	16	-	16	16	4	11	13	-	-	20	4	-	20	-	-	16	4	20	13	12	25	-	7	16	-	1	-	**357**
4	Alex Lowes	GBR	Kawasaki	13	12	25	10	5	10	11	7	-	11	7	13	20	5	16	-	7	7	11	7	16	-	9	13	-	9	11	9	-	-	13	4	4	13	7	11	**316**
5	Danilo Petrucci	ITA	Ducati	8	-	16	9	3	11	-	-	-	7	1	10	9	1	10	20	6	-	16	9	11	16	7	20	25	12	25	11	4	10	-	5	9	-	6	10	**307**
6	Michael van der Mark	NED	BMW	9	-	7	7	4	13	9	2	7	8	-	-	7	-	4	7	1	11	10	6	9	25	2	11	9	-	9	7	2	9	9	-	11	10	4	16	**245**
7	Andrea Locatelli	ITA	Yamaha	20	9	-	11	2	3	4	4	11	13	6	11	10	3	9	9	4	16	5	-	5	8	-	7	4	3	7	6	-	7	-	6	-	16	5	8	**232**
8	Andrea Iannone	ITA	Ducati	16	-	13	13	9	-	-	-	13	9	5	5	5	-	-	16	3	8	-	1	13	11	-	4	-	7	-	25	6	13	7	1	8	4	3	13	**231**
9	Garrett Gerloff	USA	BMW	7	-	8	4	-	6	-	-	4	4	-	-	2	-	3	8	-	4	13	-	8	4	4	16	8	1	13	16	5	11	10	-	-	-	6	2	9	**176**
10	Remy Gardner	AUS	Yamaha	-	4	4	1	1	9	13	6	16	10	-	8	6	-	5	11	5	13	6	-	4	-	1	10	6	-	-	-	-	1	-	-	-	-	-	-	**140**
11	Xavi Vierge	ESP	Honda	6	-	3	2	-	2	6	-	6	-	-	-	-	-	1	2	-	5	3	3	7	9	5	9	10	2	8	8	1	6	8	3	10	9	-	3	**137**
12	Iker Lecuona	ESP	Honda	-	-	-	3	-	-	-	-	-	6	3	7	3	-	2	-	-	6	4	-	3	10	3	6	13	5	10	10	3	8	16	2	-	11	-	-	**134**
13	Jonathan Rea	GBR	Yamaha	-	-	-	-	-	8	10	5	-	-	2	6	11	7	8	6	2	10	1	-	10	-	-	-	-	-	-	2	-	3	11	-	13	5	-	7	**127**
14	Axel Bassani	ITA	Kawasaki	4	-	5	6	-	7	-	-	-	5	4	9	4	-	6	-	-	-	8	-	1	5	-	5	11	-	-	4	-	4	-	6	8	-	6	**108**
15	Scott Redding	GBR	BMW	5	-	-	-	-	5	8	-	1	-	4	-	-	6	13	1	-	3	-	-	-	2	-	-	13	6	8	3	-	4	5	-	4	-	5	2	-	4	**107**
16	Dominique Aegerter	SUI	Yamaha	10	3	6	8	-	7	3	-	9	-	-	-	8	-	7	3	-	-	7	2	6	-	-	-	-	-	-	-	-	-	2	-	3	7	-	-	**91**
17	Michael Ruben Rinaldi	ITA	Ducati	2	1	10	5	-	-	-	-	3	2	-	-	-	-	1	-	-	5	-	9	-	-	7	-	1	-	7	-	3	3	2	5	-	7	-	-	5	**78**
18	Sam Lowes	GBR	Ducati	3	2	9	-	-	4	-	-	3	10	-	-	3	-	-	2	-	4	-	-	-	-	-	-	-	-	5	-	-	-	3	-	-	3	-	2	**53**
19	Nicholas Spinelli	ITA	Ducati	-	-	-	-	-	-	-	-	25	-	-	-	-	-	-	-	-	-	-	-	-	-	-	-	-	-	-	-	-	-	-	-	-	-	-	-	**25**
20	Tito Rabat	ESP	Kawasaki	-	-	-	-	-	1	-	-	1	-	-	-	-	-	-	-	-	2	2	-	-	-	-	2	-	-	6	-	-	-	-	-	-	-	-	-	**22**
21	Bradley Ray	GBR	Yamaha	-	-	1	-	-	-	-	-	1	-	-	-	-	-	-	-	-	1	-	-	-	-	-	-	-	-	-	5	-	2	1	-	-	-	2	-	-	1	**14**
22	Alessandro Delbianco	ITA	Yamaha	-	-	-	-	-	-	-	-	-	-	-	-	-	-	-	-	-	-	-	-	-	6	-	3	1	-	-	-	-	-	-	-	-	-	-	-	**10**
23	Tarran Mackenzie	GBR	Honda	-	-	-	-	-	-	2	-	5	-	-	-	-	-	-	-	-	-	-	-	-	-	-	-	-	-	-	-	-	-	-	-	-	-	-	-	**7**
24	Philipp Oettl	GER	Yamaha	-	-	2	-	-	-	-	-	-	-	-	-	-	-	-	-	-	-	-	-	-	-	-	-	-	-	-	-	-	-	-	-	-	-	-	-	-	**5**
25	Michele Pirro	ITA	Ducati	-	-	-	-	-	-	-	-	-	-	-	-	3	-	-	-	-	-	-	-	-	-	-	-	-	-	-	-	-	-	-	-	-	-	-	-	**3**
26	Markus Reiterberger	GER	BMW	-	-	-	-	-	-	-	-	-	-	-	-	-	-	-	-	-	-	-	-	-	-	-	-	-	-	-	2	-	1	-	-	-	-	-	-	**3**
27	Ivo Lopes	POR	Honda	-	-	-	-	-	-	-	-	-	-	-	-	-	-	-	-	-	-	-	-	-	-	-	-	-	-	-	-	-	-	-	-	-	1	-	1	-	**2**
28	Tetsuta Nagashima	JPN	Honda	-	-	-	-	-	-	-	-	-	-	-	-	-	-	-	-	-	-	-	-	-	-	-	-	-	-	-	-	-	-	-	-	-	-	1	-	-	**1**

WORLD SUPERSPORT REVIEW
TWIN PEAKS, ONE CONQUERER

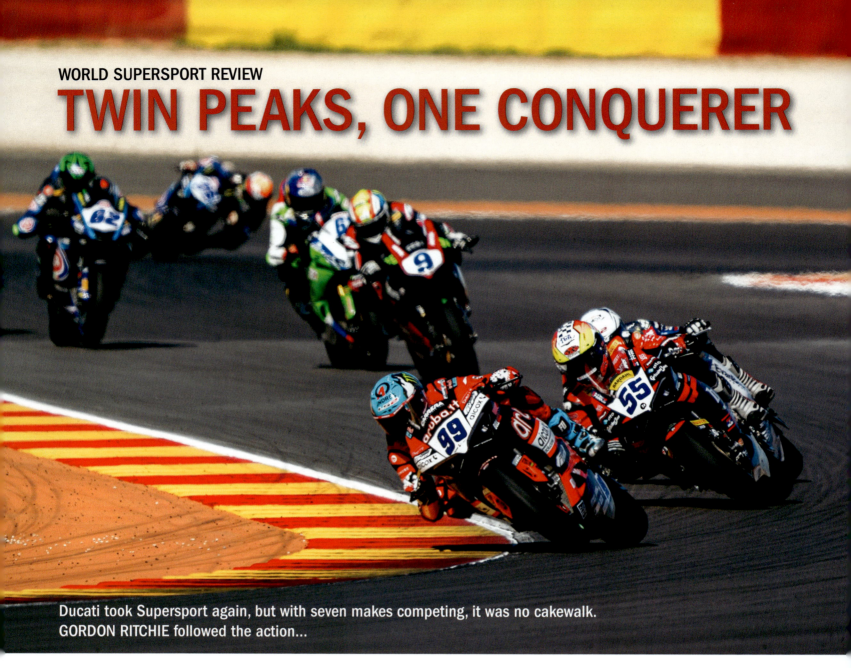

Ducati took Supersport again, but with seven makes competing, it was no cakewalk.
GORDON RITCHIE followed the action...

Above: Adrian Huertas, on the factory Ducati, leads Barni Racing's Yari Montella and the Yamaha of Valentin Debise. Jorge Navarro heads the pursuing pack.

Top right: Huertas clocked up ten wins to take the title.

Above right: Stefano Manzi (*left*) and Montella took the fight to Huertas.

Right: Orange accents celebrated Glenn van Straalen's home victory at Assen.

Far right, top: Marcel Schrotter was a podium visitor on the MV Agusta.

Far right, bottom: A work in progress. Raffaele De Rosa raced the Chinese QJ Motor.

Photos: Gold & Goose

THE 'Next Generation' era of the FIM Supersport World Championship clicked over into year three in 2024. In the first year, the thumping 955cc displacement of the Ducati Panigale V2 might have been over-neutered. In 2023, perhaps it was a little too potent. In 2024, once again, the Aruba.it Racing Ducati squad won the title, but with Spain's Adrian Huertas this time. Ducati also won the manufacturers' crown, one round early.

Seven manufacturers entered the championship in 2024, which says a lot about its popularity with the companies that actually make the bikes to be raced. While there were other race winners on non-Ducati machines, it really did seem that the Panigale was the beast of least burden for any ambitious WorldSSP rider.

Bulega's astounding 2023 season was not repeated, although Adrian Huertas did win ten races from a possible 24. He was beaten by similarly-mounted riders at times, and even by those 'old' Yamaha R6 four-cylinder 600cc screamers, especially after they received a rev uplift near the end of the year.

Balancing changes, done quietly inside the paddock for the most part, went on all year and certainly seemed to make the Yamaha a refreshed option by season's end.

Other cosmopolitan entries came from MV Agusta (800cc triple), Honda (600cc four), Kawasaki (600cc four), Triumph (765cc triple) and Chinese manufacturer QJ (with a unique 800cc four). Amazingly, given its excess weight at the beginning of the season and lack of power, the QJ topped one wet session in Estoril, thanks to Raffaele De Rosa, eventually becoming a mid-pack bike in his experienced hands.

As usual, there were some regulatory changes. Superpole qualifying was on day one of each weekend. The top nine grid positions for race two would go to the riders with the fastest race-one lap times, not the best finishes.

After the now infamous delayed-tyre drama at the opening round in Australia, and the usual hard time Phillip Island gives to the tyres, reality proved so unforgiving that race one was split into two halves, with riders mandated to come in for tyre changes.

With 2023 mega-champion Bulega having moved to WorldSBK, the field was open, but it appeared that Huertas was most people's favourite, even if he hadn't won a single race before this season. Yari Montella, on the Barni Spark Racing Ducati, was always going to be a challenger, as was Stefano Manzi, riding a Ten Kate Yamaha entry.

Valentin Debise (Evan Bros Yamaha) was on a strong R6 and was still improving as a rider.

Huertas was on pole for the opener, but he no-scored after his bike developed troubles that forced him to retire. He had suffered a fast, but low-trajectory high-side in Superpole earlier in the day.

Montella won race one, Manzi was second and Marcel Schrotter (MV Agusta Reparto Corse) placed third. Debise had crashed out of a podium place.

After the delays that had afflicted the WorldSBK race, race two only went to nine laps – an unplanned form of short flag-to-flag event.

Manzi crashed at T4 and again at T10, finally retiring. Montella won again to take his first double; Schrotter was a close second and Huertas a shadowing third.

All that madness and just one round gone.

Catalunya's race weekend was marginally less dramatic,

as Huertas took his first class win from pole. Manzi was second, Schrotter third and Montella fourth, after making hard contact with another rider.

The second Catalan race gave Manzi his first win of the year, but in a six-lap mini-sprint race, not the planned 18-lap version, after a red flag had negated the first start.

Schrotter was second and former champ Lucas Mahias (GMT94) was third, after Huertas had run wide and then toppled over, finishing 32nd. After a great last lap, the top three were 0.201 of a second apart, and the top five covered by only 0.714 of a second.

At Assen, surprise, surprise, the riders met a wet and dry surface in race one, with pole-sitter Manzi soaring out ahead, but slowing on the wet bits. Aussies Tom Edwards and Luke Power led for a time, but Debise was looking like the runaway winner, until Adrian Huertas found enough dry line to rampage forward and pass. At the last chicane, Manzi also barged past the Frenchman to take second, with home rider Glenn van Straalen (Ten Kate Yamaha) agonisingly close in fourth. Montella no-scored.

Things improved for van Straalen on Sunday, but the weather did not. There was a deluge at the start of race two, but Huertas poured forward over the glass-like surface on lap one.

Some came in to change tyres straight away, as the conditions changed, but others remained out for a time.

Van Straalen, running a special orange paint job at his and the Ten Kate team's home round, cut through on a drying line with great pace and bravado, taking Huertas's second place and finally Niki Tuuli's lead.

It was a delirious first win for van Straalen and yet another for WorldSSP emperors Ten Kate, a truly special victory at home. Huertas snatched second from Tuuli, but another Dutch-based team, EAB Ducati, achieved a podium thanks to their Finnish rider.

At his home Emilia-Romagna round at Misano, Montella eventually was on pole, but only after Huertas had been demoted for exceeding track limits. The first race was a two-rider fight between them, and a minor classic, over 18 laps. Montella lost his last-lap, last-corner advantage to Huertas's superior final-corner line and greater traction. Montella had used too much throttle, and his spinning rear allowed Huertas to win by just 0.021 of a second. Manzi was third, but more than five seconds back.

A second hot Misano race only lasted for 15 laps. Huertas was leading, but then he dropped back before losing time in what appeared to be terminal fashion as he exited on to the back straight. He got going again, upped his pace and clipped the back of Montella at Curva del Carro before regaining the lead.

When red flags appeared due to an incident at the fast Curvone, the race was declared finished. Thus Huertas was declared the winner, with Montella a close second and Debise a deserving third.

The swoops and hard braking of Donington Park were next, with Huertas claiming pole. He secured an early Saturday race lead and was never headed, with Manzi taking second place after a tough inside pass on Montella into the Foggy Esses.

An overcast race two was red-flagged with 17 laps to go, leaving a stand-alone 12-lap race. Montella won on track, Huertas was second and Manzi third – until a track-limits infringement for Montella changed the final order to Huertas, Montella and Jorge Navarra, his first podium since switching to Ducati (Orelac VerdNatura).

Autodrom Most marked the mid-point of the season, with double race-winning business as usual for Huertas, who recorded victories for the fifth and sixth time in succession. Manzi was third, then second; Montella, fourth, then third, while Debise claimed a career-best second in race one.

Portimao was pole territory for Huertas, but his luck deserted him as Montella secured the first race win, and then a second on Sunday. Huertas was second on day one, but fell

Above: Manzi and Debise head for a Yamaha one-two in the Jerez finale.

Top right: Five bikes, one corner. David Salvador (38), Marc Garcia (22), Loris Veneman (7), plus Julio Garcia Gonzalez and Aldi Mahendra dispute the same piece of tarmac.

Above right: One-time winner Mahendra's consistency made him Indonesia's first world champion.

Right: Ana Carrasco (left) and Maria Herrera monopolised the podiums in WorldWCR.

Below right: Experienced Spanish duo Carrasco (22) and Herrera (6) won ten of twelve races.
Photos: Gold & Goose

on Sunday, eventually finishing 12th. Manzi had third-, then second-place rides, with Debise third in race two.

Another full lunar cycle break in the season came before we congregated at Magny-Cours.

The rain made everything uncertain in race one, as riders chose between intermediates, slicks and wets. The early inter gamblers paid the price, and Niki Tuuli finally secured a win on his Ducati. Federico Caricasulo (MotoZoo ME Air MV Agusta) was second and van Straalen third. Race two returned 2024 racing life to almost normal, with Montella winning, from Manzi and Huertas.

Cremona, for round nine, looked like more of a compact WorldSSP track than a Superbike one. Huertas piled in a third Superpole win in succession, then took the first race win from Manzi and Montella.

Stung by being only third, and racing within less than an hour from his team's home base near Bergamo, Montella was out front of the second Cremona race – until he fell. Manzi batted on to the end for the win, with Huertas second and the remarkably quick Tom Booth-Amos (PTR Triumph) coming through for his first WorldSSP podium.

At Aragon, in race one, the high plains shifters proved to be Huertas (also in Superpole), Manzi in second and Debise third. Montella was a frustrated fourth.

He turned things around in race two, winning from Manzi, with Navarro third and Huertas only fifth.

On to Estoril and the penultimate round, Montella had to reapply the pressure on Huertas, and did so soundly with the Superpole trophy and then a race-one victory. Huertas secured second, and Manzi third.

Once more, a second race fall and no-score spelled disaster for Montella, with Manzi winning and taking overall second place from him with one round to go. Huertas placed second in the second race, and Debise third.

Amazingly, suddenly, Montella could no longer be champion. Manzi was still in with an arithmetical chance of championship success, but he was 45 points down with only 50 left for two race wins at Jerez.

The 2024 season finale could have been much more of a nail-biting finish had Montella not suffered his third big no-score of the year in Estoril.

In Spain, third in race one made Huertas the champion, and the youngest ever at 20. Fourth place in race two was a final '*Adios*', since he would move to Moto2 for 2025.

Manzi, with his extra Yamaha revs, won both Jerez races. Montella rounded out the season with seven wins in all, but second place in race one and an eighth place in race two.

The final podium places of the season went to the impressive Debise and recent replacement for Bahatthin Sofuoglu in the MV Agusta Reparto Corse Team, Bo Bendsneyder.

An amazing winning year for Huertas, manufacturers' champions Ducati and teams' champions Ten Kate Racing Yamaha. Simone Corsi (Renzi Corse Ducati) was the WorldSSP Challenge champion (for riders taking part in only European rounds) and 15th overall.

Supersport 300 World Championship

Mahendra Takes Title at Final Round

THREE riders arrived at the last round of the WorldSSP300 championship with the potential to win the title, after a season of the usual ridiculously close race finishes, frequent crashes, red flags and red mist.

Not one, but four manufacturers really fought it out for supremacy in the smallest world championship class, and Kawasaki came out on top of the manufacturers' championship with one round to spare. MTM Kawasaki were teams' champions, but they had to wait for the finale at Jerez to make sure of that status.

Kawasaki, KTM, Yamaha and a two-rider Chinese Kove effort fought for the wins, all of them taking at least one; famously, the Kove took its debut race win in the hands of Julio Garcia Gonzalez.

Nine riders won races in 2024, with Kawasaki riders Mirko Gennai and Inigo Iglesias Bravo winning three apiece. KTM star rider Jeffrey Buis won two, as did another Ninja 400 rider, Daniel Mogeda.

The 2024 season was a real coming of age for Loris Veneman (son of former GP rider Barry), who secured two wins on his Kawasaki. Only three Yamaha riders – Unai Calatayud, Aldi Satya Mahendra and David Salvador – won races, and only one apiece.

But the metronomic podium and points gathering regu-

larity of Mahendra in these uniquely close-fought and mistake-prone '300' races gave him the championship title. It took until the last of the 16 races for the big trophy to be awarded.

Veneman was runner-up and, after breaking his fibula and dislocating his foot in a pre-race crash at Jerez, Inigo Iglesias Bravo finished third overall. Garcia Gonzalez took the leading Kove to four overall.

One more season left in WorldSSP300 racing before the junior class switches to larger-engined twins in 2026.

Women's Circuit Racing World Championship

Carrasco Is First WorldWCR Champion

AN overdue new world championship was conducted on identical Yamaha R7 twins, with the variety of nationalities and experience on display only rivalled by the disparity of pace exhibited by the top riders compared to those towards the back.

Importantly, the action out front was simply glorious, with usually four Spanish riders battling consistently hard all the way to the flag.

It was edge-of-the-seat stuff and unmissable as a spectacle through the six weekends it featured as a new class within WorldSBK.

There were heavy and sometimes strange crashes and injuries very early in the year. 'Early' was a relative term, given that the six-round championship only started in June, at Misano.

Races thereafter at Donington, Portimao, Cremona, Estoril and Jerez provided the most dramatic and combative racing imaginable, but the Jerez deciders carried us all to another level.

Going into that final round, Maria Herrera had scored five race wins. Championship leader Ana Carrasco had four, and another Spanish rider, Sara Sanchez, one.

On the Saturday of the finale, and with Carrasco holding a strong 18-point lead, Herrera had to win – and she did. From Carrasco and Beatriz Neila. That left 13 points in it for the final race.

Race two was one of those events that had hearts in mouths and the form books in tatters.

Carrasco was in dire danger of losing 'her' championship on the last lap, down in sixth place for a time, while Herrera was leading.

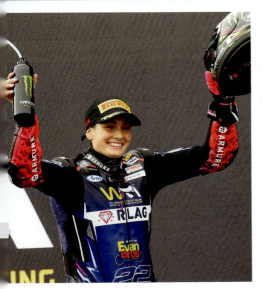

A late inside pass from Sanchez on Herrera at the final hairpin – scene of so many dramas over the decades – resulted in Maria cutting back to the apex and then touching her front tyre on her rival's rear.

Herrera was down and out.

Carrasco exploited the chaos to finish third, behind Sanchez and Neila. She became champion by an eventually generous 29 points – a truly fitting end to a wild season up front. Having won the 2018 SSP 300 World Championship in an unsegregated class, she became the first champion of an entire brave new world of racing, open to only half of the human population.

All four of the top riders – Carrasco, Herrera, Sanchez and Neila – were Spanish. The next best was an Italian, Roberta Ponziani, and then came another Spaniard, Pakita Ruiz, sixth overall.

The vast majority of the podium places were taken by the 'big three' of Carrasco, Herrera and Sanchez, and only those three won races. But that's not the whole story, on track or off. Neila (four), and single-time riders Ponziani and Australian Tayla Relph secured podium finishes.

The races provided the reliably closest finishes of all classes, almost all year. On balance, the choice of competing bikes was right, with enough power from the R7s to let the best riders leave the rest behind, but not so much that less experienced riders were overmatched.

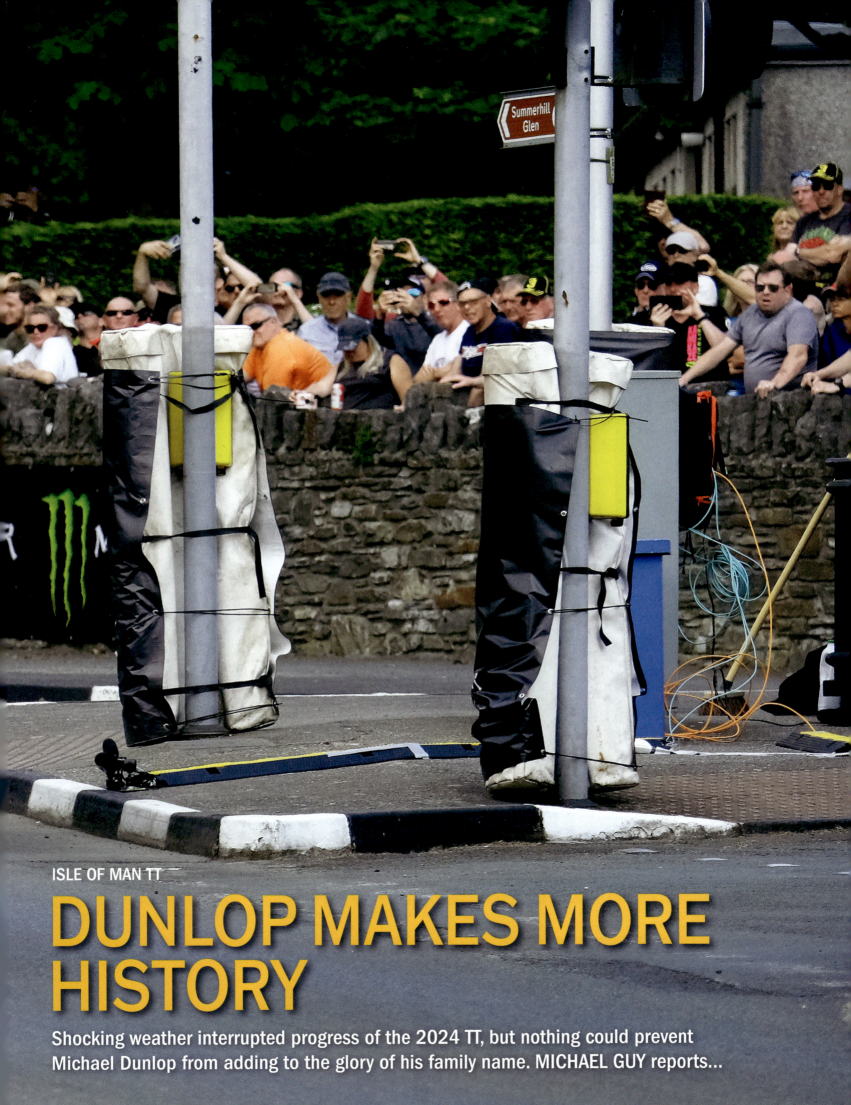

ISLE OF MAN TT

DUNLOP MAKES MORE HISTORY

Shocking weather interrupted progress of the 2024 TT, but nothing could prevent Michael Dunlop from adding to the glory of his family name. MICHAEL GUY reports...

Above: Dean Harrison, switched from Kawasaki to Honda Fireblade, thrills the crowd on his way to third in the sole Superbike race.

Top right: Unstoppable. At 52, John McGuinness gave his all, with a best of fifth in the Senior.
Photos: Dave Purves

Above right: Former winner James Hillier, here on the WTF Honda, was a reliable front-runner.
Photo: David Collister Photography

Above far right: Davey Todd, on the Supersport Powertoolmate Ducati, was third and second in the class. He went one better in the Senior.

Right: Dunlop doffs his cap to his late uncle Joey, after equalling his record. It was just the start...
Photos: Bernd Fischer - motoarchive.com

Opening spread: Lamp-posts, loudspeakers and fans almost close enough to touch. TT paraphernalia provides the backdrop to Michael Dunlop as he heads to the first of a record-breaking 29 TT wins on his Yamaha R6.
Photo: Gavan Caldwell

MICHAEL DUNLOP arrived on the Isle of Man knowing that he could cement his place in history by becoming the greatest ever TT racer. With 25 wins to his name, just one shy of Uncle Joey Dunlop's landmark 26, there was a huge amount of expectation on the shoulders of the 35-year-old. But in true Dunlop style, he remained seemingly unfazed, even uninterested in the prospect, instead shutting down the conversation and hype in an effort to stop it from gaining momentum.

But records and history-making aside, Dunlop arrived on the back of a brilliant TT 2023, where he had taken four wins, yet under no illusion of the enormity of the task to increase his tally when up against the likes of TT's fastest ever Peter Hickman and serial podium man Dean Harrison.

In previous years, there had been a number of key changes to the event, ranging from the introduction of live television coverage to a revised schedule, meaning that there were ten races to be run. For the 2024 event, the biggest changes came in terms of riders, teams and manufacturers.

The biggest news was that 2019 Senior TT winner Dean Harrison had left the Dao Racing Kawasaki team after eight years to join John McGuinness and Nathan Harrison in the official Honda Superbike team, to ride a Fireblade.

Michael Dunlop was another rider with a change of machinery. While he continued with the proven Hawk Racing squad aboard a Honda Fireblade in the Senior and Superbike races, and ran his own Honda in Superstock, he had teased a switch from Yamaha to Triumph Supersport machinery.

Former Padgetts-Honda man Davey Todd also had parted company with Clive Padgett's squad to join the TAS Racing team. That meant a switch to BMW machinery in stunning Milwaukee livery for Superbike and Superstock, along with a beautiful Powertoolmate Ducati Panigale V2 at his disposal for the two Supersport races.

Former TT winner James Hillier was another to change. Staying with the OMG squad that ran a Yamaha R1 to great effect in the British Superbike championship, Hillier arrived in a newly branded WTF Racing team with two Honda Fireblades at his disposal. He also made a welcome return to the Bournemouth Kawasaki team, where he'd enjoyed podiums, to race their Kawasaki ZX-6R in the two Supersport races.

In Sidecars, it was the end of an era, passenger Tom Birchall retiring after a period of utter domination, during which he and older brother Ben had won 11 consecutive Sidecar TTs and 14 in total. Tom was replaced by proven Frenchman Kevin Rousseau. The 2024 race was also the TT debut of double world champions Todd Ellis and Emanuelle Clement.

Bad weather was a major disrupting factor over both practice and race weeks, delaying some races and culminating in a three-race final Saturday, with the blue-riband Senior TT cut from six laps to four – a truncation that was criticised by many fans.

TT business development manager Paul Phillips explained the decision, taken on a rain-hit race-week Thursday, in an extended social media message that described "massive disruption, especially by weather", and a desire to meet the target to run all ten races. Moving Friday's Supertwin 2 race to Saturday had pushed the feature-race Senior into the afternoon, and the length had been cut in the interests of rider safety, after three days of back-to-back solo races. "For some riders, that will be close to 600 high-intensity racing miles … a big load for riders and their teams," he wrote.

A day later, race two of the Superstock TT was cancelled, cutting the programme to nine races.

PRACTICE WEEK

TT 2024 kicked off with the news that there would be a new docuseries and feature film covering the event. A partnership between Channing Tatum's Free Association, Brad Pitt's Plan B Entertainment, Entertainment 360, Jason Keller and Box To Box Films was teaming up with European studio Mediawan to produce a series and feature film – *The Greatest Race on Earth* – expected to be released in 2025.

On track, Michael Dunlop was quickest out of the blocks, setting a 129.590mph best aboard his Hawk Racing Honda Superbike ahead of fast-starting Davey Todd on his Milwaukee BMW. Hickman was third on his Superbike, then actually faster on his Superstock bike to top that class.

In Supersport, Todd made the early running ahead of Hillier and Triumph-mounted Dunlop.

The second day of practice was cancelled due to poor

weather; it also transpired that both Hickman and Dunlop were riding with wrist injuries. Dunlop's had been sustained at Cookstown when he high-sided his Triumph, while Hickman had suffered three uncharacteristic crashes at the Donington round of BSB and was forced to ride with a support throughout the event.

The remainder of practice week was interrupted by more rain and storms, which meant cancelled and rescheduled sessions. While usual suspects Hickman and Dunlop were running consistently at the sharp end, new names emerged, with Davey Todd bringing his short-circuit pedigree, honed in the British Superstock series, to the Mountain course. By the end of practice week, it was Hickman who went into race week with the advantage, thanks to a 134.638mph lap set on his Superstock bike.

In Supersport, Todd showed his affinity with the beautiful Powertoolmate Ducati, prepared by engine guru Stuart Johnstone. He set a best of 127.062mph. Michael Dunlop headed up the Supertwins class with an impressively quick 121.882mph lap, while Manx brothers Ryan and Callum Crowe laid down the sidecar benchmark with a lap at 115.682mph.

Ben Birchall and new team-mate Kevin Rousseau sustained a high-speed off at the Mountain Box, due to a technical failure. Both walked away from a big crash, which caused substantial damage to their outfit.

SUPERSPORT 1 – Four Laps

Dunlop wasted no time in equalling Uncle Joey's 26-win record. After starting practice week on a Triumph, he'd reverted to his proven MD Racing Yamaha R6 to continue his ongoing domination of the Supersport class.

Despite his unprecedented Supersport pedigree, he was third on the opening lap, behind fast-starters Harrison (Honda) and Todd (Ducati), who swapped the lead over the course of the lap. Both were riding their first race laps aboard their respective machinery, and they made an impressive start. Dunlop soon got into his stride, however, moving into the lead by Ballaugh Bridge on the second lap.

With Harrison fighting on the road with the impressive Jamie Coward, Todd moved into second, while Dunlop increased his advantage methodically at the front, stretching his lead to 5.5 seconds.

Todd, who openly admitted that he loved riding a V-twin Ducati, responded, and on the third lap, he began closing the gap to Dunlop. But it was short lived, the Ulsterman responding on the final lap to increase his lead to a comfortable 8.5 seconds. His 26th win and 40th TT podium matched Joey's statistics.

Dunlop admitted that it had been a tough day, given the pain following his Cookstown crash, but there was clear satisfaction in matching the record.

"Obviously, I was one behind and now, technically, I am the equal most successful rider of all time at the TT alongside Joey – it's something special. It's different eras, I've always said that, but just to be in that same sentence … I don't class myself as being as good as Joey. It was a different time, but it's an honour to be on the same number of wins. Joey was massive for the Isle of Man TT.

"No matter what ever happens in life now, everybody has always wanted to get to Joey's record, and I've got to it. So, for me, that's something special."

It was Dunlop's fifth consecutive Supersport win and 12th of his career.

Todd secured second, while Harrison exceeded all expectation on the sweet-handling, but underpowered new Honda CBR600RR.

James Hillier's first ride back on the Bournemouth Kawasaki ZX-6RR netted an impressive fourth place, while James Hind secured his best ever TT finish in fifth. Australian Josh Brookes got his race week off to a positive start by claiming sixth aboard the BPE/Russell Racing Yamaha.

Above: Dean Harrison and Davey Todd flank winner Peter Hickman after the Superbike race.

Top: Ryan and Callum Crowe became the new three-wheel masters, winning both sidecar races.
Photos: Bernd Fischer - motoarchive.com

Above right: Peter Hickman inherited victory in the only Superbike race – it would be his only one of the year.
Photo: David Collister Photography

Right: Michael Dunlop won both Supertwin races on the factory Paton. This is the first.
Photo: Stephen McClements

SIDECAR 1 – Three laps

Manx brothers Ryan and Callum Crowe rode into the history books by securing their maiden TT win, 20 years after their five-times victorious father. It was an emotional victory for the popular pair, who enjoy a huge level of support on the Island. Aged just 28 and 25, they led from start to finish, incredibly having overtaken second-placed duo Pete Founds and Jevan Walmsley on the road by the time they reached Quarry Bends on the opening lap.

Founds and Walmsley fought back, repassing the Crowe brothers on the road before running wide and losing track position. The Crowes' first lap from a standing start was a stunning 118.525mph, which equated to a 12.2-second lead over Founds and Walmsley as they began lap two.

A personal-best second lap of 119.8mph put them tantalisingly close to 120mph and stretched their lead to more than 30 seconds ahead of Founds and Walmsley, after their 117.923mph second lap.

Lap three delivered more of the same, with the Crowes retaining control, despite losing a few seconds to Founds and Walmsley.

The battle for third raged throughout the three laps, and at the finish, three outfits were separated by under ten seconds. Alan Founds and Rhys Gibbons claimed the final podium position ahead of Lewis Blackstock and Patrick Rosney, and Lee Crawford and Scott Hardie.

TT rookies Ellis and Clement claimed seventh, setting their first ever 110mph lap in the process.

SUPERBIKE – Six laps

Michael Dunlop wanted to become the TT GOAT by securing win number 27 in the prestigious Superbike TT. Achieving the milestone in a big-bike race would undoubtedly make the achievement even more special, and two-thirds of the way through the six-lap encounter, that's exactly what seemed to be happening.

Having taken the lead from Davey Todd at Ballaugh on lap two, Dunlop was in a league of his own, stretching his advantage through every timing split, with the chasing Todd, Hickman and Harrison seemingly having no answer to the relentless pace of the Hawk Racing Honda rider.

By the time he came in for his second pit stop, at the end of lap four, Dunlop enjoyed a seemingly unassailable 25-second lead ahead of Todd. But as he left the pits and headed down Bray Hill, something wasn't right with the sidepod that held the visor in place on his Arai helmet, following the pit-stop visor change. The race leader was forced to stop by the side of the road, where at first he tried to put it in place, before having to take his helmet off completely, remove his gloves and reattach the sidepod, losing his lead in the process. By the time he reached Glen Helen, he was fourth, the resurgent Peter Hickman now leading.

On the final lap, Hickman, Harrison and Todd were battling for the lead, with Hickman using all his experience to stay ahead. After 1 hour, 42 minutes and 56.114 seconds of racing, the FHO BMW rider secured victory by 5.8 seconds, ahead of an impressive Todd, who had clinched the position from Harrison.

It was the aimiable Hickman's 14th TT win, which put him alongside Mike Hailwood, joint sixth in the all-time list of TT winners.

Michael Dunlop ended the day fourth, fuming at having missed out on what had appeared to be a nailed-on victory. His only consolation was a new Superbike lap record of 135.970mph as he attempted to claw back the deficit.

Arguably the most intense of on-track battles was for

304 ISLE OF MAN TT REVIEW

fifth, with three Honda riders – James Hillier, John McGuinness and Jamie Coward – locked in a fierce race-long fight. Honours ultimately went to Hillier, who pipped 52-year-old McGuinness by under three seconds, with Coward just 0.233 of a second further back.

Aprilia-mounted Mike Browne secured eighth, while former TT winner Michael Rutter was ninth, and Irishman Brian McCormack rounded out the top ten.

SUPERTWIN 1 – Three Laps

Motivated by the extreme disappointment of the Superbike race, Michael Dunlop demonstrated his resilience and determination to win the opening Supertwin race in style, his 27th making him the winningest TT racer of all time – 24 years after Joey had notched up his 26th victory at the age of 48.

He led from start to finish aboard the factory Paton, posting a 121.044mph lap from a standing start to lead by 10.2 seconds at the end of lap one. As the race progressed, so did Dunlop's lead, and his ability to maintain his clear advantage. With no mechanical issues, as he had experienced in 2023, Dunlop crossed the finish line at the end of lap three with a comfortable 20.4s advantage.

Second was Hickman aboard the stunning-looking PHR-prepared (Peter Hickman Racing) Swan Yamaha R7. Now in its second year, the bike had clearly improved dramatically, but it was still a step behind the dominant Patons in terms of outright performance.

Dominic Herbertson secured a breakthrough and popular podium finish, thanks to an impressive 121mph final lap on his Burrows Engineering by RK Racing Paton. He finished 5.4s ahead of Kawasaki-mounted Jamie Coward, while Aprilia rider Mike Browne secured fifth.

ISLE OF MAN TT REVIEW 305

Above: Davey Todd aviates his Milwaukee BMW to take a memorable win in the first Superstock race.
Photo: Gavan Caldwell

Top right: Even Peter Hickman, on another BMW, couldn't catch Todd.

Above right: Ryan and Callum Crowe celebrate their second sidecar win, flanked by second-placed Ben Birchall and Kevin Rousseau (*left*), and third-placed Dave Molyneux with young passenger Jake Roberts.

Right: Brushing the kerb. A sixth successive Supersport win for Michael Dunlop brought his overall tally of TT wins to 28, with another to follow.
Photos: Bernd Fischer - motoarchive.com

SUPERSTOCK 1 – Three Laps

Davey Todd brought an end to years of domination by Dunlop, Hickman and Harrison with a brilliant performance to secure his maiden TT victory. Riding the Milwaukee BMW run by the proven TAS Racing team, he arrived at the TT full of confidence, leading the British Superstock championship and with two Superstock wins under his belt at the North West 200.

Fast throughout practice week, Todd showed that he had the pace not only to run with, but also beat the three TT aliens. In one of the best races of TT 2024, the 28-year-old claimed victory by just 2.2 seconds ahead of Hickman on his FHO Racing BMW M1000RR.

Todd led from the start, but he was pushed relentlessly by Hickman, the two men showing their strengths through different sectors of the 37.75-mile circuit.

Hickman had become a habitual winner in the Superstock class in previous years and had always been able to count on his superior pace in the final part of the lap – up and over the mountain. Todd having increased his lead thanks to a better pit stop, Hickman closed the gap to half a second with half a lap to go, and the smart money would have been on the 14-times TT winner overhauling his new rival. But Todd did the unthinkable, not only holding off Hickman, but also extending his lead on the run down the mountain to win by 2.2 seconds.

Michael Dunlop notched up another podium with third on the MD Racing Fireblade, albeit only 3.6 seconds ahead of Dean Harrison on the official Honda Racing CBR1000 RR.

James Hillier continued his strong run of form in fifth, his decision to swap his 2023 Yamaha R1 for the Honda in 2024 fully vindicated. Jamie Coward, John McGuinness and Conor Cummins made it six Hondas in the top eight, with two BMWs leading the way.

It turned out to be the only one of two planned Superstock races to be run due to adverse and ever changing weather conditions, which necessitated revisions to the schedule.

At the end of the race, popular Manxman Conor Cummins announced his withdrawal, having scored uncharacteristically disappointing results aboard his Padgetts Honda. Despite his premature 2024 departure, the 38-year-old was adamant that he would continue to race and intended to be back on the TT grid in 2025.

SIDECAR 2 – Two Laps

Having claimed their maiden TT victory in the opening Sidecar race, Ryan and Callum Crowe doubled up by taking their second in race two. The Manx pairing dominated from the off with the fastest ever standing-start lap to build a solid lead. Then they posted their fastest ever flying lap of 120.335mph on the second to join a very exclusive club of sidecar teams to lap at over 120mph.

Initially, the scheduled three-lap race was red-flagged after world champions Todd Ellis and Emanuelle Clement crashed at Waterworks. They were uninjured, but their outfit was blocking the circuit. The restarted race was reduced to two laps.

After their heavy practice crash, which meant that they had had to sit out the opening race, Ben Birchall and Kevin Rousseau showed their undoubted class to finish second. Despite working flat out all week to repair their outfit, with help from local fabricators, and an acute lack of track time,

they posted a seriously competitive 119.125mph lap, giving a taste of their future potential.

The rapturous cheer for the winners was topped by TT legend Dave Molyneux and his young passenger, Jake Roberts, securing third, making it four Manxmen in *parc fermé* at the end of the race. Molyneux, who had an incredible 17 TT victories and 31 podiums to his name from a career that had spanned over 30 years, subsequently confirmed his retirement from TT racing..

SUPERSPORT 2 – Two Laps

With wins 26 and 27 in the bag, Michael Dunlop continued his domination of the Supersport class by securing his 28th in a race shortened to two laps due to the schedule being overcrowded because of weather delays. His victory marked his sixth consecutive Supersport win and the 13th of his history-making career.

But it was a seriously contested race, with strong and persistent challenges from Dean Harrison and Davey Todd. James Hillier was also up for a fight, running with the top three early on aboard the Bournemouth Kawasaki ZX-6R.

Again riding his proven MD Racing Yamaha R6, Dunlop was faultless, and despite being unable to replicate his 130mph lap from 2023, he retained control, albeit by only a few seconds. He crossed the line 3.889 seconds in front of Harrison, who had overhauled Todd on the final lap. It was a particularly impressive performance by Harrison, who clearly was down on top speed on the new-for-2024 Honda. The Bradford man, who had moved to the Isle of Man earlier in the year, showed both his and the Honda's pedigree.

For Todd, third was another strong result, which backed up his maiden Superstock win and very much kept the ball rolling in what was already by far his most successful ever TT.

Peter Hickman, who had claimed two seconds in 2023's two Supersport races, was unable to replicate the same pace. Citing new technical regulations that had been adopted from British and world championships to balance performance between the four-cylinder 600cc machines, 765cc Triumph triple and 959cc V-twin Ducati, he complained of a lack of speed and acceleration. He finished fifth behind Jamie Coward, who also raced a Triumph, while Hillier ended the day sixth.

SIDECAR WORLD CHAMPIONSHIP
BEATING THE ODDS

The classic three-wheelers survived an existential threat over the winter to bounce back for a thrilling season, decided in the final yards. JOHN McKENZIE charts the action...

CONFIRMATION of the championship calendar came uncomfortably late after the initial withdrawal of series organisers Moto Presse Stuttgart. The FIM stepped forward, took over organisation of the first round at Le Mans and, after further discussions, reached an agreement with the German company to run the series in conjunction with the IDM Championship. That meant a season of six two-race rounds in five countries.

Reigning double world champions Todd Ellis and Emmanuelle Clement (LCR Yamaha) were hoping for a hat trick after two dominant seasons, having taken 14 wins and 26 rostrums over 30 races.

Ben Birchall, 2023 runner-up, had stepped away to concentrate on the IoM TT, while sponsorship issues had sidelined sure-fire contender Stephen Kershaw, who had been third the previous season.

A significant returnee was 2021 world champion Markus Schlosser (Yamaha LCR), back on track some 30 years after his GP debut.

Consistent Yorkshire brothers Sam and Tom Christie (Team Hannafin LCR Yamaha), quintuple champion Pekka Paivarinta (now on an ARS Yamaha and partnered by another Christie brother, Adam), and the ever cheerful and ominously improving duo Harry Payne and Kevin Rousseau (Steinhausen Racing ARS Yamaha) would all do much more than make up the numbers.

After the withdrawal of Avon after decades of service, the FIM chose Hoosier as tyre supplier.

Round 1 – Le Mans, France

After spending a year off the calendar, Le Mans greeted the sidecars with glorious sunshine for qualifying.

Pole went to Schlosser and Schmidt, but just over a second covered the first six qualifiers as they lined up for the 11-lapper.

Second on the grid, Payne, with local lad Kevin Rousseau on board, scorched away and soon built a lead. After parrying with Ellis, Schlosser secured second, leaving the former to fend off Wyssen for third until the Swiss retired with two laps to go.

Payne won by almost five seconds, laying down the gauntlet in imperious fashion for what would prove to be a close-fought season.

In Saturday's 18-lap Gold race, Schlosser took an early lead from Payne and Ellis. By lap two, Payne had reclaimed it and tried to pull a gap, with Schlosser and Ellis striving to stay with the pace. With three laps remaining, Payne was forced to retire with an electrical fault, his only DNF of the year. That left Schlosser in control, and he took the flag with 1.2 seconds over Ellis, while Christie was third.

Schlosser, who returned home to Switzerland with a nine-point lead over Ellis, had initially entered Le Mans to test the new Hoosier tyres. When regular passenger Marc Fries stepped down following free practice, young German Luca Schmidt climbed aboard. The pair gelled immediately, and the decision was made to continue.

Round 2 – Sachsenring, Germany

A first ever pole, with a time of 1m 28.696s, for Sam and Adam Christie on the Hannafin LCR Yamaha 600, and a fastest race lap on the hilly left-handed 3.6km circuit weren't quite enough for a win. Payne led into the first corner, but was challenged all the way by the Christies, who finally forced ahead on lap ten. They couldn't shake off Payne, however, and two corners from home on the final lap, he managed to squeeze through, winning the sprint to the flag.

Schlosser held off Streuer for third, while Ellis, who had suffered from set-up struggles, could only manage eighth.

Prior to Sunday's race, a wet track and clouds permitted an extra ten minutes of wet-tyre practice and then prompted a flurry of grid tyre changes as the track seemed to be drying.

Again, Christie led away, but by lap two, Payne had forced to the front and quickly gained a three-second lead that he would hold to the end. The battle was for second, with Christie, Schlosser and Paivarinta all scrapping. By lap eight, Ellis, had caught up from seventh on the grid, while Schlosser had faded. By lap 14, Ellis had fought through to second. Two laps later, with Streuer and Archer in the gravel trap, red flags were raised and the result declared. Schlosser had dropped to fifth, his only non-podium of the year, and ultimately costly. Three wins from four races gave Payne a three-point lead in the championship. Ellis's hard-won second would be his last top-three of the 2024 season.

Round 3 – Most, Czech Republic

An extremely hard-fought weekend rewarded Schlosser with the season's only clean sweep of pole, two wins and two fastest laps.

In the ten-lap sprint, Payne had shot away, but Schlosser reeled him in steadily. With two laps to go, the Swiss driver nosed in front at Turn One, only for Payne to snatch it back. Next time around, he did it again and made it stick, winning by less than a second.

The Christie Brothers held off constant pressure from Ellis for third.

Sunday's Gold race was a carbon copy, the top eight places identical.

Once again, Payne started fast, and with three to go, Schlosser repeated the same move at Turn One. Again, Payne fought back, but Schlosser's top-end speed gave him the advantage into Turn One. They exited side by side, but Schlosser took the win by a mere 0.268 of a second in a superb race. Schlosser was now back on top of the table, by just seven points.

Round 4 – Assen, Netherlands

Schlosser, on pole, led the charge to the first corner, but Payne forced ahead exiting the second and led from then on, resisting huge pressure. He tried to escape, but Schlosser clawed back the gap. With two laps to go, the Swiss tried to pass, but he couldn't quite match Payne's determination. The Brit took the win by just three-tenths.

The Christie brothers had a race-long joust with

Left: Oschersleben, and Markus Schlosser and Luca Schmidt lead away from pole.

Below left: Prematurely pink. FIM president Jorge Viegas joins the fun with new champions Payne and Rousseau.

Below: Third in the championship, Christie brothers Sam and Tom narrowly lead defending champions Todd Ellis and Emmanuelle Clement.

Far left: Worthy winners. Harry Payne and Kevin Rousseau at work.

Photos: Mark Walters

Bennie Streuer, desperate to achieve on his home circuit. Christie held on for third, but the Dutchman's efforts rewarded him with the fastest race lap. Returning six-times world champion Tim Reeves just held off current champion Ellis for fifth.

In Sunday's 16-lap race, Schlosser was determined to regain superiority. By half-distance, he'd pulled out two-seconds, but Payne began to close. Going into the last lap, the gap was just 0.287 of a second, but Payne just couldn't get close enough. He was pipped by just by 0.095 of a second.

A very happy Streuer eventually took third. He'd been second until Payne went past on lap five. Thereafter, the 2015 world champion had a lonely race, but he posted another fastest lap for his first podium since 2022.

Christie kept Ellis back to take fourth, and after some early skirmishes, Reeves retired on lap nine with brake problems.

Round 5 – Oschersleben, Germany

Schlosser, on pole for the fourth time in five races, made good to take the early lead in the 12-lap sprint race, again chased closely by Payne. Reeves, fourth-fastest qualifier, dropped into third place, with Streuer, Paivarinta and Christie in pursuit.

By lap six, Reeves was suffering from gear-selection issues, but he managed to hold Streuer back. With five laps to go, back-markers held up Schlosser, allowing Payne to close the gap, get in front and quickly pull out an unassailable lead. He won by four seconds; Reeves was third, just beating Streuer.

In Sunday's 21-lap race, Schlosser made another great getaway, although Payne was climbing all over the back of him. Reeves slotted into third, but Streuer squeezed through when he ran wide.

Christie's race ended on lap two when, desperate to pass Paivarinta, he overdid it, throwing passenger Tom from the outfit, fortunately without harm, and forcing a retirement.

Meanwhile, Schlosser and Payne continued to duel. Behind them, the battle for third between Streuer and Reeves was more robust, until brake problems on lap eight caused the latter to retire after an excursion through the gravel and across the grass. Streuer's third place was short lived, however, as a damaged fairing slowed him, forcing him out after another five laps.

In the meantime, Payne had taken the lead and appeared to be in control, but perhaps Schlosser had been playing a game. On the last lap, he reclaimed the lead with a masterful move, taking the flag by half a second. Paivarinta was third, his first podium of the year. Reigning champion Ellis was a further three seconds down in fourth, and subsequently he decided to withdraw from the final round to concentrate on the set-up issues that had plagued him all year.

That gave Schlosser a narrow seven-point lead going into the final nail-biting round.

Round 6 – Estoril, Portugal

The final confrontation – and two races in four hours. Estoril had been the scene of Payne's first ever world championship race win in 2021, in the same race where Schlosser had won the title – but come Sunday evening, only one of them would still be smiling.

Payne knew that he had to beat Schlosser to claw back the Swiss rider's small points lead. Schlosser probably hoped to keep him in check and use his apparent straight-line top speed advantage to line up a slipstream move late in the race.

Payne had taken his only pole of the year. The tension was electric. The pair surged side by side into the first corner, but Payne emerged as the leader, with Christie in third and Reeves fourth.

Determined to pull out a defendable lead, Payne was almost two seconds in front at the end of the first lap. By lap six of the ten, he was almost seven seconds in front, with enough in hand to ease off to preserve his tyres. He took the win by 4.3 seconds, whittling Schlosser's points lead down to just two. Christie was third.

It all came down to the final 17-lap race – Schlosser had to finish in front of Payne to take the title.

At the lights, Payne, Schlosser, Reeves and Christie hurtled into the first bend. Payne managed to keep the rest at bay as he tried to make a break. This time, Schlosser couldn't afford to let him go.

Payne couldn't stretch the gap to more than a second as Schlosser stuck to his task. He would close, Payne would almost get away, for lap after lap. At the start of the ninth, Schlosser almost pulled level, but he couldn't make it stick. Payne almost got away again, but then back-markers allowed Schlosser to close back up again.

With five laps to go, Schlosser made another attempt, but Payne wouldn't yield. Again, using the slipstream, Schlosser nearly passed, and yet again, Payne held it. Going into the last lap, Schlosser was close enough and desperate enough to make the move. Heading on to the finishing straight for the final time, he was wringing every ounce from the Yamaha engine, pulling almost alongside, barely a bike length down as the two outfits howled over the line, giving the race win – and the 2024 World Championship – to Harry Payne and Kevin Rousseau. What a climax to the season!

Reeves crossed the line third, but later he was disqualified when it was discovered that he had inadvertently used a non-approved kit generator, which elevated Paivarinta to third.

Incredibly, eight of the twelve races had been determined by winning margins of less than one second, and after 164 laps of racing at six circuits, for the winning margin in the very last race to be barely a couple of metres and an infinitesimally small gap of 0.053 of a second gave quite a staggering finale.

Underlining the season-long knife-edge battle, Schlosser had four poles to Payne's one, and five fastest laps to Payne's four, with 11 podiums apiece. Payne had eventually scored seven wins to Schlosser's five, and had beaten his Swiss rival by over four seconds on three occasions.

Payne and Rousseau were worthy world champions, but commiserations must go to Markus Schlosser and Luca Schmidt, after falling short by such a tiny margin at the absolute last instant.

2024 BENNETTS BRITISH SUPERBIKE CHAMPIONSHIP
CLIFFHANGER KYLE
A season of breathlessly close racing came down to the final lap to decide the championship. Kyle Ryde and Tommy Bridewell were separated by just one point. JOSH CLOSE recounts the drama...

Over recent years, we have ended each season with an incredible finale and each year it almost seems impossible to surpass the previous - but again in 2024, the Bennetts British Superbike Championship decider did just that.

I have said it before, that title fights will go down in history as being some of the closest ever, and this year it happened again! Last year there was just half a point between Tommy Bridewell and Glenn Irwin, and this year, Kyle Ryde beat Tommy Bridewell by a single point. To put it simply, it is nothing short of sensational.

After 32 races featuring nine different race winners and a further seven podium finishers, it came down to red versus blue, youth versus experience, Yamaha versus Honda with Ryde versus Bridewell as they delivered a finale that really was one for the ages.

The final two laps of the Brands Hatch finale has been shared globally, not only amongst motorsport fans, but also a much wider audience and that is what makes me proud of the Bennetts BSB and what it means to so many people. As I have said so many times, keep sharing the clip on social media far and wide – let's really continue to spread the message on what a fantastic sport and spectacle we have to offer.

It all came down to that last nervy, edge-of-the-seat final race and what a performance from both Kyle Ryde and Tommy Bridewell – it went down to the last lap and the final corner and decided by only 0.296s at the final chequered flag of 2024.

The racing this season has delivered some intense and dramatic action; the level of competition is unparalleled with each of the manufacturers celebrated a podium finish, notably represented by twelve different teams, demonstrating the continued strength of the championship and the level of competition derived from the series technical regulations.

Nine different riders celebrated a race win in 2024, and for Rory Skinner, Storm Stacey and Danny Kent, it was for the first time in their careers, whilst a further seven riders took top three finishes. For Lewis Rollo on the BSB Pathway specification Aprilia and Max Cook, they also celebrated their first visit to a Bennetts BSB podium.

My congratulations to Kyle Ryde on his first Bennetts BSB title and to OMG Racing for taking the championship victory for a second time.

We now look ahead to the 2025 Championship, with an incredible line-up of teams and riders, kicking off at Oulton Park on the May Bank Holiday weekend. We are getting ready for another unbelievable season and I thank all of our teams, riders, champions and officials for their dedication. I also send my thanks and appreciation to our fans around the world for their continued support both trackside, on social media and across our TV broadcasts.

Stuart Higgs
Series Director,
Bennetts British Superbike Championship

www.britishsuperbike.com

BRANDS HATCH
OCTOBER 2024

Above: Big prize, narrow margin. BSB Superbike champion Kyle Ryde.

Opening spread: The whole season came down to this – Ryde holds off the sliding Tommy Bridewell out of Clearways, last corner of the series.
Photo: Bryn Williams

THE 2024 Bennetts British Superbike Championship was an enthralling campaign, which concluded with a race that many have labelled the greatest of all time. It was a year when season-long consistency allowed reigning champion Tommy Bridewell and Kyle Ryde to battle it out at the Brands Hatch finale for the right to become BSB champion. Others had their moments of greatness, but also they crashed or suffered machine problems.

Ultimately, Ryde was crowned champion for the first time after what can only be described as a breakthrough campaign. He rode to another level in the season's second half, proving plenty of people wrong by improving in key areas.

Ryde won at circuits he dislikes, including Oulton Park and Cadwell Park; he got his elbows out and made key overtakes by any means necessary, and, while still not perfect every time, he won in wet conditions. His was the perfect campaign. He won nine races and collected a total of 18 podiums aboard the OMG Grilla Racing Yamaha. He also claimed four podiums and four fastest laps, and led for a total of 98 laps.

Bridewell deserves plenty of credit, too. After joining Honda, many wrote him off, but he was the most consistent rider of all, losing his crown by one point, despite only winning three races.

Others also shone throughout the year. Ryan Vickers won seven races aboard the second OMG Yamaha, while Glenn Irwin scored eight on his way to third overall.

The competition was as fierce as ever, with nine different riders standing on the top step of the podium. Another seven secured podium finishes, while eight teams could call themselves 2024 BSB race winners.

Following the death of Paul Bird in 2023, his daughter Jordan and son Frank took control of Paul Bird Motorsport, which evolved into PBM Racing Team. Glenn Irwin remained, while Hager became title sponsor.

Andrew Irwin, Glen's brother, remained at Honda Racing UK for a second consecutive season, while Danny Kent jumped aboard an R1 with McAMS Racing Yamaha (MarTrain Racing).

Christian Iddon continued as Oxford Products Racing Ducati's sole rider, and Leon Haslam's ROKiT Racing BMW continued into its second campaign.

Following the departure of Steve Rodgers' Raceways Yamaha team, Jason O'Halloran joined Max Cook at Completely Motorbikes Kawasaki. Danny Buchan also returned to 'Team Green' at DAO Racing, alongside Aussie Brayden Elliot. Lee Jackson swapped Kawasaki power for a Fireblade after joining Charlie Nesbitt at MasterMac Honda.

Rory Skinner returned to the championship after a season in Moto2, joining the Cheshire Mouldings BMW outfit as its only rider. Established BMW team FHO Racing remained unchanged, with Josh Brookes and Peter Hickman.

Storm Stacey continued with LKQ Euro Car Parts Kawasaki and began the year with Tom Neave as his GR Motosport team-mate, running under the STAUFF Fluid Power Kawasaki banner. However, injuries led to Neave being replaced by Bradley Perie for the final four rounds.

Likewise, Franco Bourne began the year with Rapid Honda, but an injury at Thruxton resulted in Tom Ward completing the season aboard the Fireblade.

Billy McConnell returned to the fray with C&L Fairburn Properties/Look Forward Racing Honda, as did Fraser Rogers with TAG Honda.

Three teams used 'Pathway Spec' machines, introduced to help Superstock teams move into the blue-riband class. Bikes were built to National Superstock specifications, but were equipped with BSB's MoTeC ECU and wiring harness.

Lewis Rollo (In Competition Sencat Aprilia), Jaime van Sikkelerus (TAG Honda) and Alex Olsen (Team IWR Honda) rode Pathway bikes, Rollo being crowned Pathway champion. Subsequently, Olsen was replaced by Richard Kerr, and then James Westmoreland.

Luke Hedger rode for Whitecliffe CDH Racing Kawasaki, while Louis Valleley, Corey Tinker and Connor Rossi Thomson all represented NP Racing Kawasaki at different stages of the season.

Apart from the opening round in Spain, the weekend format comprised feature races on Saturday and Sunday, with a half-distance sprint run on Sunday morning, which carried full points.

Again, the new-for-2023 points system, rewarding season-long performance while keeping the emphasis on the closing Showdown events, meant lower points for the first eight meetings (18-16-14 for the top three), an increase for the Oulton and Donington Showdowns (25-22-20, with other points proportionately increased), and another boost for the Brands Hatch finale, at 35-30-27, etc. The success of the system is demonstrated by a single point deciding the 2024 title, and half a point in 2023.

Above: Yamahas up front in the opener at Navarra, with double winner Vickers ahead of OMG team-mate Ryde. Kent, Andrew Irwin and Skinner give chase.
Photo: Motor Sport Vision Racing

Top right: With four podiums in the first five races, Danny Kent made a strong start on the McAMS Yamaha.
Photo: McAMS Yamaha

Above right: Christian Iddon, triple winner Glenn Irwin and Ryde celebrate on the race-three podium at Oulton Park.

Right: Irwin leads Iddon, Vickers and Ryde in the second race at the Cheshire track.
Photos: Gavan Caldwell

ROUND 1 – NAVARRA

The year began with something different, as BSB visited northern Spain. Navarra had been purchased by BSB organisers MSV towards the end of 2022 and replaced Silverstone on the calendar.

Riders participated in a three-day test leading to the shortened two-day race weekend, comprising two rather than three races.

The nature of the 2.44-mile circuit suited the sweet-handling Yamaha R1, a bike that was super-strong through the corners and grippy on the edge of the tyre. Riders reach speeds of around 180mph as they tip into the first corner.

Vickers, Ryde and Kent locked out the podium in both races, Vickers becoming the star man with a double victory. The Norfolk-based rider overtook team-mate Ryde at the incredibly fast Turn One with three laps remaining in race one, crossing the line with an advantage of 1.364 seconds.

Vickers led for the majority of race two, but almost threw away victory when his R1 went sideways through the last corner. Luckily, the OMG rider was able to pull the bike back up, regain his balance and take the chequer.

Kent's double podium – third in race one, followed by second in race two – was the first rostrum success for the MarTrain Racing team.

Bridewell's Honda debut was hampered by multiple technical problems, the last of which – a broken quickshifter – forced him to retire from fourth in race two.

ROUND 2 – OULTON PARK

Glenn Irwin dominated as he and fellow Ducati rider Iddon showcased the strengths of the V4-R. Irwin won all three races, securing the treble for the first time for PBM and second time in his BSB career – he had claimed a treble at Silverstone for Honda in 2022.

In race one, Irwin passed Ryde and Vickers in the opening two laps, overtaking the latter for the lead at Hizzys. Despite late race pressure from Iddon, and a slight moment on the final lap, he held position. Ryde claimed his third podium of the year in third, while Bridewell and Vickers completed the top five.

The rider from Carrickfergus, Northern Ireland, showcased fantastic defensive riding and an ability to withstand immense pressure in race two – traits that would become crucial as the year progressed – to fend off Bridewell, Iddon and Kent. The quartet were covered by 0.687 of a second over the line. Ryde completed the top five, but Vickers limped home in ninth due to bike problems.

Iddon led the opening 12 laps of race three before finally succumbing to a move from Irwin into Hizzys. Vickers completed the podium ahead of Kent, who continued his best-ever start to a BSB campaign.

A scary crash suffered by Skinner during Sunday's warm-up, after his helmet came off, ruled him out of action. He was briefly unconscious and he missed the next round at Donington Park.

ROUND 3 – DONINGTON PARK

Vickers regained his form from Navarra in the early stages of the weekend by topping two free practice sessions and claiming pole position. However, he crashed out of the lead at the Melbourne Loop on the second lap of race one, allowing team-mate Ryde to claim his first win of 2024. The race had come to a premature end following a crash for Iddon on the exit of Turn Four.

Bridewell finished second, while Haslam secured his 115th BSB podium. The latter had been challenging for the victory, but he ran in too deep at the final corner, which allowed Bridewell through.

Glenn Irwin returned to the top step in the sprint race, having led from start to finish. Haslam followed him home in second, while Bridewell's consistent form continued in third. Kent was fourth after setting a new lap record; Ryde completed the top five.

Vickers crashed again at the Melbourne Loop and fractured his collarbone, an injury that required surgery.

The season burst into life in race three as O'Halloran, Bridewell, Irwin and Kent fought in the closing stages. The quartet completed 14 overtakes on each other during the final two laps, but O'Halloran secured his first win for Kawasaki, while Bridewell beat Kent and Irwin to the line. The victory gave O'Halloran BSB wins aboard Honda, Yamaha and Kawasaki machinery.

Despite losing out on the podium by 0.050 of a second, Ducati rider Irwin left Donington with a 13-point championship lead over Kent.

ROUND 4 – KNOCKHILL

It was a weekend of firsts in Scotland, but it was stereotypically wet. Not only did it rain, but also fans endured thunder and lightning.

Despite being declared a wet race, race one was run on a largely dry circuit and was dominated by Bridewell. The 2023 champion led from start to finish, setting fastest lap after fastest lap on his way to a maiden Honda win.

The lead, which had been around five seconds at one stage, eventually shrunk to 2.572 seconds over home hero Skinner, who claimed his first podium since Cadwell Park in 2022. Likewise, Andrew Irwin bagged his first podium since the 2022 season finale at Brands Hatch.

Glenn Irwin was shown the black-and-orange flag, which indicated a technical problem with his Ducati – smoke coming from the rear. He retired as a result. Vickers and Iddon came together at Turn Three and crashed.

Left: First win on a Kawasaki for Jason O'Halloran, ahead of Bridewell, Andrew Irwin and Kent in a dramatic Donington race three.
Photo: Bryn Williams

Right: Rain at Knockhill? It brought a sole win for the returned Rory Skinner and his BMW.
Photo: Motor Sport Vision Racing

Below: An even wetter Snetterton played into the hands of Storm Stacey (Kawasaki) for a maiden win.
Photo: Bennett's Superbike Championship

Below left: Glenn Irwin maintained his championship lead at Donington.

Bottom left: Former champion Leon Haslam took two podiums on his BMW at his home track.
Photos: Bryn Williams

Bottom: Christian Iddon was second behind Skinner at Knockhill.
Photo: Motor Sport Vision Racing

Race two was wet and dominated by Skinner, the rider with more experience around Knockhill than anybody else. It was his maiden victory and first since his title-winning Supersport campaign in 2020. It was also the TAS Racing squad's first success since Buchan had done the double at Cadwell in 2022.

Iddon and Bridewell completed the podium, while Stacey showcased his wet-weather credentials in fourth. Andrew Irwin, O'Halloran and Kent all crashed, while Vickers withdrew due to a stomach bug.

Iddon claimed his first BSB victory since 2021 in the shortened final race, which came to an end following a crash suffered by Haslam.

Bridewell secured his sixth consecutive podium in second, becoming the first Honda rider to achieve that feat since Alex Lowes in 2013. Kent recovered from his earlier crash to finish third.

With Glenn Irwin finishing ninth, Bridewell left Scotland with an 11-point championship lead.

ROUND 5 – SNETTERTON

The torrential rain continued in Norfolk, producing a topsy-turvy result in race one.

Stacey claimed his first ever BSB victory after dominating the initial race, before holding off Rollo in the five-lap restart. The original race had been stopped after Skinner had suffered a high-side, which left him with a fractured right tibia and fibula.

Stacey's victory was also his first podium, coming at the 128th attempt, while second for Rollo was his maiden rostrum and the first for a Pathway-spec bike. Ryde completed the podium.

Kent and Bridewell crashed out within seconds of each other, allowing Glenn Irwin to move level on points with Bridewell after finishing fifth.

Race two was also restarted due to rain. When it had cleared, another five-lap dash was declared, and Glenn Irwin led from start to finish, ahead of Bridewell, moving two points clear as a result. Iddon completed the podium, while Ryde was fourth.

Irwin did the double later in the day, following some expert defensive riding to prevent Bridewell from getting by. Victory marked his 25th in BSB and his sixth for the season, moving him four points clear. Iddon's timely brace of podiums kept him within striking distance in the championship, just 21 points adrift.

Kent and Ryde completed the top five and now were level on points, 30 behind Irwin.

ROUND 6 – BRANDS HATCH

Brands Hatch was the setting for arguably one of the best individual performances in BSB history as Vickers secured pole position and won all three races.

Saturday's race was the most impressive, the OMG rider leading every lap, setting a new fastest lap on six consecutive circulations and crossing the line with an advantage of 7.334 seconds. At one stage, he was just under nine seconds clear.

Bridewell fought his way through from fifth on the grid to take second, while team-mate Andrew Irwin crossed the line in third. Glenn Irwin was fourth, which meant that he was level on points with Bridewell. Ryde completed the top five, but Kent crashed out of second at Stirlings.

Disaster struck Glenn Irwin on the opening lap of race two when he was involved in a collision with Buchan and Kent heading down Paddock Hill Bend. He was stretchered away, but declared fit later.

Vickers led the five-lap restarted race from start to finish, being 1.188 seconds clear of Bridewell, who managed to keep Ryde behind him.

In race three, Vickers celebrated again and was crowned Monster Energy King of Brands. Iddon and Ryde had an entertaining battle for the final two podium spots, the former coming out on top.

Bridewell and Andrew Irwin completed the top five, while a battered and bruised Glenn Irwin valiantly fought his way through from 23rd to seventh. Bridewell left Brands with a 19-point lead over Irwin, with Ryde 32 adrift.

ROUND 7 – THRUXTON

Thruxton always creates chaotic racing, with a large leading group of riders all trying to manage their tyres.

A seven-rider battle ensued in race one, with Ryde beating Vickers to the line by just 0.168 of a second. Thruxton specialist O'Halloran was only 0.334 of a second further back. Bridewell was fourth, ahead of surprise package McConnell, who was leading on the run to the final chicane.

Andrew Irwin and Kent were also involved, only for the former to suffer a huge crash heading towards the final chicane. He hit the back of Kent, catapulting his Fireblade high into the sky.

Ducati's woes continued at Thruxton, with Iddon ninth and Glenn Irwin 14th.

In race two, Vickers became the first rider in 2024 to win, despite not having started from one of the first two rows, battling through from 15th. Cook led the majority, but a mistake on the penultimate lap allowed Vickers through. Cook claimed second to celebrate his maiden podium, while Kent completed the top three ahead of Brookes and McConnell.

The race was red-flagged on the opening lap due to Glenn Irwin suffering a massive high-side at Turn Three. The PBM rider was fortunate not to be hit by any following riders. Earlier in the day, O'Halloran had suffered a high-speed crash in warm up, incurring tendon damage to two fingers on his right hand.

Vickers completed the double in race three, extending his winning run to five in six races, while Kent and McConnell joined him on the podium. Ryde and Nesbitt completed the top five, with Bridewell recovering to sixth after suffering a quickshifter problem earlier in the race.

Ryde moved to within 25 points of Bridewell, with Iddon a further ten behind.

Left: Sliding in the summer sunshine – Billy McConnell shone at Thruxton on his Honda, third in race three.

Below left: No quarter given as Josh Brookes's BMW heads Lewis Rollo (on the lone Aprilia), Leon Haslam (BMW) and Andrew Irwin (Honda) at Brands Hatch.

Far left: Race two, and Vickers leads Andrew Irwin, Haslam, Ryde and the rest at Brands Hatch.

Below far left: On a roll. Ryan Vickers took five wins and one second from six races at Brands and Thruxton.

Below: Kawasaki rivals Max Cook (30) and Storm Stacey (79) lead away for race two at Thruxton.
Photos: Bryn Wiliams

Left: Too close for comfort. Ryde and Bridewell go wheel to wheel in the thrilling BSB title decider.

Right: Bridewell lost the No.1 plate to Ryde by a single point.

Below far left: Aprilia-mounted Lewis Rollo won the inaugural BSB Pathway title and the R&G Rising Stars Award as top rookie.

Below left: Danny Kent finally scored a win for McAMS Yamaha in race one at Brands Hatch.

Below: A better weekend for Hickman in a largely forgettable BSB season.
Photos: Bryn Williams

Bottom: Flashback to 2015. Aspiring young racers Bradley Ray, Tarran Mackenzie and Kyle Ryde, all of whom would win the BSB Superbike title aboard Yamahas.
Photo: Clive Challinor Motorsport Photography

ROUND 11 – BRANDS HATCH

The final round was a tense affair as Ryde and Bridewell put on a show that will live long in the memory. The drama had begun in qualifying, rain falling moments before the session. The first half of the track was dry, but the back of the circuit, sheltered by trees, was damp and greasy.

A high-side for Jackson at Stirlings brought out the red flags, before a blown oil cooler launched Glenn Irwin off his bike at Surtees. Andrew Irwin was following and crashed on the oil dropped by the Ducati. Glenn was checked over at the scene and hobbled to the medical centre.

Kent celebrated his maiden victory on his 100th start in a wet opening race. The win also marked Mar-Train Racing's first in the Superbike class.

Vickers and Bridewell completed the podium. Ryde was fourth, having battled his way past Cook and Hickman in the closing stages to retain a one-point lead.

Glenn Irwin's title hopes ended following a crash at Graham Hill Bend. He had fought valiantly from 15th on the grid to fourth and was the fastest rider on the circuit when he went down.

In the sprint race, Bridewell and Ryde forced through from the second and third rows respectively within a couple of laps and fought bar to bar for victory. Both men pushed hard, but Bridewell pulled the pin with a couple of laps remaining to take the championship lead.

With one race to go, Bridewell was four points clear, and the pair lined up first and second on the grid for the finale. In a fight for victory, whoever won would be crowned champion.

What followed has been described as the greatest BSB race of all time. Bridewell led the opening few laps, with team-mate Andrew Irwin serving as wingman, holding off the chasing pack.

Eventually, Ryde fought through to lead, and Bridewell lost crucial time while fighting former team-mate Glenn Irwin. Bridewell had a gap of over a second to claw back, and he did so by breaking the all-time circuit record with a lap of 1m 24.759s.

Ryde and Bridewell exchanged positions multiple times during the final nine laps of the season, with the former strong into Hawthorns, and the latter almost unstoppable into Stirlings. They touched down the Cooper Straight.

On the final lap, Ryde made the title-winning move at Hawthorns, and Bridewell was almost launched off his Honda as he pushed to keep hold of his crown through Clearways. They completed 13 overtaking moves on each other, but in the end, it was Ryde's time to celebrate after being crowned champion by a single point.

BSB SUPPORT CHAMPIONSHIPS

The **Quattro Plant British Supersport Championship** entertained fans with a three-way duel between reigning champion Ben Currie (Oxford Products Racing Ducati), 2015 champion Luke Stapleford (Macadam Triumph Racing) and four-times champion Jack Kennedy (Honda Racing UK). Between them, they celebrated 18 race wins and 46 podiums.

At the final round, following qualifying crashes for Stapleford and Currie, Kennedy claimed his fifth title with victory in a wet race one. The Irishman had won the class aboard Yamaha, Kawasaki and Honda machinery.

Stapleford finished 62 points behind Kennedy; Currie was a further 29 points back after scoring no points at the final round.

Eugene McManus finished fourth, while Harry Truelove completed the top five. Other race winners in the class included Luke Jones, Tom Booth-Amos and Can Oncu.

Within the same championship, Cameron Hall clinched the Supersport Cup, while Owen Jenner dominated the **British GP2** category with 18 victories.

The **Pirelli National Superstock Championship** title fight went all the way to the Brands Hatch finale, Davey Todd being crowned champion following a crash for Joe Talbot at Druids. That made two Superstock titles for Todd in three seasons. following his 2022 success with Padgett's Honda.

Talbot finished 38 points behind Todd, but due to his impressive campaign, he secured a ride with BSB champions OMG Racing Yamaha for 2025.

Scott Swann completed the top three after winning five races during the season, with Luke Mossey claiming more victories than anybody else (six) in fourth, despite having missed the opening three rounds.

Left: Ducati's reigning Supersport champion, Ben Currie (1), duels with Luke Stapleford on the Macadam Triumph.

Below left: Stapleford, Kennedy and Currie made it a three-way battle for the Supersport crown.

Far left: Jack Kennedy (Honda) took his fifth title.

Bottom left: Superstock heavyweight battle between Davey Todd and Joe Talbot at Donington.

Bottom: Owen Jenner dominated the British GP2 category with 18 wins.

Photos: Bryn Williams

The **Tracker Kawasaki British Superteen Championship** reintroduced the famous series to the BSB paddock, with riders aged 15–20 competing on ZX-4RRs built by MSS Performance.

Kalvin Kelly was crowned champion after beating fellow ROKiT Rookie Brodie Gawith by nine points. Lewis Smart finished third, ahead of Chloe Jones, while Carl Harris, son of the late Karl 'Bomber' Harris, celebrated more victories than anybody else (5).

In the **R&G British Talent Cup,** having secured three wins and 12 podiums throughout the year, Lucas Brown edged out rivals Amenuel Brinton and Ryan Frost in a thrilling finale at Donington.

In the inaugural **Pirelli National Sportbike Championship**, Aprilia protégé Edoardo Colombi pushed veteran Richard Cooper all the way, eventually losing out by 4.5 points. Colombi made an instant impact, despite never having raced in the UK before, winning at uniquely British circuits like Oulton Park and Cadwell Park.

In a well supported field, Thomas Strudwick won the **2024 ABK Beer 0% BMW Motorrad F900 R Cup**, finishing well ahead of Barry Burrell and Nikki Coates after the nine-round series

Sam and Jack Laidlow secured the **British Sidecar Championship** crown with three victories in 2024. Lewis Blackstock and Paddy Rosney finished as runners-up, 68 points clear of George Holden and Oscar Lawrence.

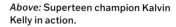

Above: Superteen champion Kalvin Kelly in action.

Above left: Lucas Brown was the R&G Talent Cup champion.

Top: The top three riders after a compelling Talent Cup title battle. Amanuel Brinton, Lucas Brown and Ryan Frost at Donington.

Left: Thomas Strudwick leads Nikki Coates and Barry Burrell in the Thruxton round of the BMW Motorrad F900 R Cup race.

Below left: Veteran Richard Cooper edged out impressive rookie Edoardo Colombi in the Pirelli National Sportbike championship.

Below: Sam and Jack Laidlow were victorious in the British sidecar championship.

Photos: Bryn Williams

2025 CALENDAR

OFFICIAL TESTS (PRE SEASON)

 **TEST 1** — 6/7 April — Circuito de Navarra (ESP)

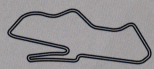 **TEST 2** — 18/19 April — Donington Park GP

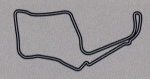 **TEST 3** — 23/24 April — Oulton Park

RACE EVENTS (11 ROUNDS/33 RACES)

MAIN SEASON

 **ROUND 1** — 3-5 May — Oulton Park

 **ROUND 2** — 16 - 18 May — Donington Park GP

 **ROUND 3** — 20 - 22 June — Snetterton

 **ROUND 4** — 4 - 6 July — Knockhill

 **ROUND 5** — 25 - 27 July — Brands Hatch GP

 **ROUND 6** — 8 - 10 August — Thruxton

 **ROUND 7** — 23 - 25 August — Cadwell Park

 **ROUND 8** — 5 - 7 September — Donington Park GP

SHOWDOWN

 **ROUND 9** — 19 - 21 September — TT Circuit Assen (NLD)

 **ROUND 10** — 3 - 5 October — Oulton Park

 **ROUND 11** — 17 - 19 October — Brands Hatch GP

- BRITISHSUPERBIKE
- @OFFICIALBSB
- OFFICIALBSB
- @BRITISHSUPERBIKE
- BRITISHSUPERBIKE

*All dates are provisional and subject to change

FOR EVENT AND TICKET INFORMATION **WWW.BRITISHSUPERBIKE.COM**

US RACING REVIEW

DUCATI TAKES HERRIN BACK TO THE TOP

More than a decade after his first Superbike title, Josh Herrin did it again. LARRY LAWRENCE reports on the action...

Inset: Ducati's Josh Herrin was crowned 2024 MotoAmerica Superbike champion.

Main: Herrin gave the Italian marque its first Superbike title since 1994.
Photos: MotoAmerica/Brian J. Nelson

THE 2024 MotoAmerica Superbike Championship was one of the closest in years. At mid-season, in fact, it was the closest title chase in the 48-year history of the series, the top four riders being separated by just nine points. Then Warhorse HSBK Racing Ducati's Josh Herrin got hot and claimed victory in five of the last nine rounds, pulled ahead and won by 55 points in the final standings over runner-up Cameron Beaubier of Tytlers BMW.

It marked the second MotoAmerica Superbike Championship for Herrin, who had won his first title in 2013. He started the year by winning the prestigious Supersport race at the stand-alone Daytona 200. Then he carried that momentum into the MotoAmerica Superbike season, run over 20 races across nine weekends.

In 2024, Herrin faced fierce competition from Beaubier, a five-times MotoAmerica Superbike champion and one of the most formidable racers in American road racing. Beaubier's return to MotoAmerica in 2023, after a stint in Moto2, elevated the level of competition, as his experience, speed and racecraft posed a significant challenge to Herrin. Across the season, there were intense battles between them, both riders pushing each other to the limit. Beaubier matched Herrin with six wins, but it was the latter's ability to remain consistent, avoid major mistakes and capitalise on key opportunities that proved crucial in his title run.

For Ducati, Herrin's title was just another in a long list of major achievements by the Italian marque in 2024, marking the first time Ducati had won the American Superbike title since Troy Corser's 1994 campaign.

It was a season of parity in respect of riders who were capable of winning. A total of seven claimed victories, equalling a record set in 1977. In addition to Herrin and Beaubier, other winners were Bobby Fong, Sean Dylan Kelly, Loris Baz, Cameron Petersen and Jake Gagne. Kelly and Baz were first-time series winners. Ducati and BMW took seven wins apiece, and Yamaha six.

Gagne, who had dominated MotoAmerica Superbike for the previous three seasons, was hampered by arm-pump problems and managed only a single victory in 2024. He left the series early to have the problem addressed and ended up seventh in the final standings.

In terms of series history, Beaubier moved past Josh Hayes to second in the all-time MotoAmerica/AMA Superbike wins list, ending the year with 65-career victories, second only to Mat Mladin's 82. Herrin's 16 career wins tied him with Wayne Rainey.

Ashton Yates (Honda), son of former multi-time AMA road racing champ Aaron Yates, won the MotoAmerica Superbike Cup title, for riders racing Superbike on Stock 1000 machines.

Yamaha claimed the 2024 Superbike Manufacturer's Championship, riders aboard R1s winning six races and reaching the podium 21 times.

This was the tenth season of MotoAmerica. Wayne Rainey and company seem to have stabilised road racing in America, and while not quite at the level of AMA Superbike racing's heyday, in the late 1990s and early 2000s, the championship had major successes in 2024, with large crowds at several rounds, most notably Road Atlanta, Road America and in its return to the Mid-Ohio Sports Car Course for the first time in ten years.

Road Atlanta – 20–21 April

In a titanic battle, as many as seven riders fought at the front of the season's opening race, but only three of them were in contention by the end. Of those, Beaubier came out on top with a pass on defender Gagne with two laps remaining in the thrilling Steel Commander Superbike race run at the Michelin Raceway.

It was Beaubier's 60th career win, and a close one. He, Gagne and third-placed Fong (Wrench Motorcycles Yamaha) were covered by less than four-tenths. Kelly (EasyHealth Plans.com/TopPro Racing BMW) was next, Herrin fifth, some five seconds down.

Gagne turned the tables on a wet track on Sunday, the three-times MotoAmerica Superbike champion withstanding the constant pressure applied by Tytlers BMW teammates Beaubier and JD Beach to take his first win of the season by just over a tenth. Ultimately, it proved to be the only one.

Beach dropped to fourth, with Petersen through to the last podium spot and Kelly a close fifth. Herrin was ninth.

After the opening two races in the championship, Gagne and Beaubier were tied with 45 points apiece.

Barber Motorsports Park – 11–12 May

South African Cameron Petersen never put a wheel wrong to top Attack Yamaha team-mate, Gagne by 0.438 of a second after 20 laps. Beaubier had led early on his BMW M1000RR, until lap four. Just when it was starting to look like the five-times champion would romp away to victory, he crashed out of the lead. That left Petersen in front, Gagne giving chase and piling on the pressure to see if Petersen would falter. He didn't. Instead, he was mostly perfect in earning his fourth MotoAmerica Superbike victory – three of them at Barber Motorsports Park.

On Sunday, Beaubier returned from the previous day's crash and won both races in the triple-header weekend – by better than three and four seconds respectively.

In race two, Kelly led Petersen, Baz and Fong in a close battle for second, while Gagne fell to eighth as arm-pump problems struck. Herrin, third on Saturday, no-scored.

In race three, Fong secured second from Kelly, while Herrin was fourth.

Beaubier had arrived trailing Gagne by 20 points: his two wins gave him a 13-point lead. At this stage of the championship, Sean Dylan Kelly was third and Herrin a distant sixth, 48 points adrift.

Above: Richie Escalante claimed one podium in an injury-hit season.
Photo: Vision Wheel M4 ECSTAR Suzuki

Top: Beaubier leads Gagne and the rest under sunny skies at Barber.

Right: In Road Atlanta's soggy second race, Jake Gagne's Yamaha beat the BMWs of Beaubier and JD Beach (95).
Photos: MotoAmerica/Brian J. Nelson

Championship points: **1** YART - Yamaha, 116; **2** Yoshimura SERT Motul, 110; **3** BMW Motorrad World Endurance Team, 72; **4** TATI Team Beringer Racing, 61; **5** Team Bolliger Switzerland #8, 43; **6** km 99, 41.

BOL D'OR, Paul Ricard Circuit, France, 14-15 September 2024.
FIM Endurance World Championship, Round 4.
737 laps of the 3.586-mile/5.771km circuit, 2,642.8 miles/4,253.2km
1 Yoshimura SERT Motul, 24h 1m 28.767s.
2 km 99, 730 laps; **3** YART - Yamaha, 721 laps; **4** Team18 Sapeurs Pompiers CMS Motostore, 720 laps; **5** BMW Motorrad World Endurance Team, 718 laps; **6** Chromeburner-RAC 41-Honda, 716 laps; **7** TRT27 AZ Moto, 713 laps; **8** Team 33 Louit April Moto, 712 laps; **9** 3ART Best Of Bike, 705 laps; **10** JMA Racing Action Bike, 703 laps; **11** Maco Racing Team, 702 laps; **12** Wójcik Racing Team 77, 700 laps; **13** Manau Competition, 698 laps; **14** Junior Team Le Mans Sud Suzuki, 697 laps; **15** Slider Endurance, 697 laps.
Fastest lap: BMW Motorrad World Endurance Team, 1m 52.517s, 114.7mph/184.6km/h, on lap 118.

FIM Teams' Endurance World Championship:

1	F.C.C. TSR Honda France	154
2	Yoshimura SERT Motul	130
3	Viltais Racing Igol	114
4	Tati Team Beringer Racing	107
5	Wójcik Racing Team EWC 77	97.5
6	YART - Yamaha Official Team EWC	97

7 Team Bolliger Switzerland #8, 88.5; **8** Webike SRC Kawasaki France, 78; **9** ERC Endurance Ducati, 74.5; **10** Team LRP Poland, 69.5; **11** BMW Motorrad World Endurance Team, 69; **12** Maco Racing Team, 60.5; **13** Team HRC, 35; **14** Motobox Kremer Racing #65, 32.5; **15** Kawasaki Racing Team Suzuka 8H, 28.

MotoE World Cup

Round 1, PORTIMAO, Portugal, 23-24 March 2024, 2.853-mile/4.592km circuit
Race 1 (7 laps, 19.973 miles/32.144km)
1 Nicholas Spinelli, ITA (Ducati), 12m 32.726s, 95.5mph/153.7km/h.
2 Hector Garzo, SPA (Ducati); **3** Mattia Casadei, ITA (Ducati); **4** Lukas Tulovic, GER (Ducati); **5** Kevin Zannoni, ITA (Ducati); **6** Massimo Roccoli, ITA (Ducati); **7** Andrea Mantovani, ITA (Ducati); **8** Kevin Manfredi, ITA (Ducati); **9** Chaz Davies, GBR (Ducati); **10** Armando Pontone, ITA (Ducati); **11** Maria Herrera, SPA (Ducati); **12** Matteo Ferrari, ITA (Ducati); **13** Alessio Finello, ITA (Ducati); **14** N/A; **15** N/A.
Fastest lap: Alessandro Zaccone, 1m 46.811s, 96.1mph/154.7km/h.

Race 2 (7 laps, 19.973 miles/32.144km)
1 Mattia Casadei, ITA (Ducati), 12m 31.599s, 95.6mph/153.9km/h.
2 Hector Garzo, SPA (Ducati); **3** Oscar Gutierrez, SPA (Ducati); **4** Eric Granado, BRA (Ducati); **5** Jordi Torres, SPA (Ducati); **6** Lukas Tulovic, GER (Ducati); **7** Kevin Zannoni, ITA (Ducati); **8** Matteo Ferrari, ITA (Ducati); **9** Andrea Mantovani, ITA (Ducati); **10** Massimo Roccoli, ITA (Ducati); **11** Miquel Pons, SPA (Ducati); **12** Alessandro Zaccone, ITA (Ducati); **13** Alessio Finello, ITA (Ducati); **14** Kevin Manfredi, ITA (Ducati); **15** Chaz Davies, GBR (Ducati).
Fastest lap: Gutierrez, 1m 46.313s, 96.6mph/155.4km/h.
Championship points: **1** Casadei, 41; **2** Garzo, 40; **3** Spinelli, 25; **4** Tulovic, 23; **5** Zannoni, 20; **6** Gutierrez, 16.

Round 2, LE MANS, France, 10-11 May 2024, 2.600-mile/4.185km circuit
Race 1 (8 laps, 20.804 miles/33.480km)
1 Nicholas Spinelli, ITA (Ducati), 13m 25.693s, 92.9mph/149.5km/h.
2 Kevin Zannoni, ITA (Ducati); **3** Mattia Casadei, ITA (Ducati); **4** Jordi Torres, SPA (Ducati); **5** Andrea Mantovani, ITA (Ducati); **6** Eric Granado, BRA (Ducati); **7** Oscar Gutierrez, SPA (Ducati); **8** Matteo Ferrari, ITA (Ducati); **9** Alessio Finello, ITA (Ducati); **10** Kevin Manfredi, ITA (Ducati); **11** Lukas Tulovic, GER (Ducati); **12** Armando Pontone, ITA (Ducati); **13** Chaz Davies, GBR (Ducati); **14** Maria Herrera, SPA (Ducati); **15** Miquel Pons, SPA (Ducati).
Fastest lap: Hector Garzo, 1m 39.882s, 93.7mph/150.8km/h.

Race 2 (8 laps, 20.804 miles/33.480km)
1 Nicholas Spinelli, ITA (Ducati), 13m 28.043s, 92.6mph/149.1km/h.
2 Mattia Casadei, ITA (Ducati); **3** Oscar Gutierrez, SPA (Ducati); **4** Alessandro Zaccone, ITA (Ducati); **5** Andrea Mantovani, ITA (Ducati); **6** Lukas Tulovic, GER (Ducati); **7** Miquel Pons, SPA (Ducati); **8** Matteo Ferrari, ITA (Ducati); **9** Kevin Zannoni, ITA (Ducati); **10** Alessio Finello, ITA (Ducati); **11** Kevin Manfredi, ITA (Ducati); **12** Chaz Davies, GBR (Ducati); **13** Massimo Roccoli, ITA (Ducati); **14** Maria Herrera, SPA (Ducati); **15** N/A.
Fastest lap: Spinelli, 1m 40.198s, 93.4mph/150.3km/h.
Championship points: **1** Casadei, 77; **2** Spinelli, 75; **3** Zannoni, 47; **4** Gutierrez, 41; **5** Garzo, 40; **6** Tulovic, 38.

Round 3, BARCELONA, Spain, 24-25 May 2024, 2.894-mile/4.657km circuit
Race 1 (7 laps, 20.256 miles/32.599km)
1 Oscar Gutierrez, SPA (Ducati), 12m 44.802s, 95.3mph/153.4km/h.
2 Eric Granado, BRA (Ducati); **3** Kevin Zannoni, ITA (Ducati); **4** Hector Garzo, SPA (Ducati); **5** Alessandro Zaccone, ITA (Ducati); **6** Mattia Casadei, ITA (Ducati); **7** Jordi Torres, SPA (Ducati); **8** Matteo Ferrari, ITA (Ducati); **9** Miquel Pons, SPA (Ducati); **10** Massimo Roccoli, ITA (Ducati); **11** Kevin Manfredi, ITA (Ducati); **12** Alessio Finello, ITA (Ducati); **13** Maria Herrera, SPA (Ducati); **14** Armando Pontone, ITA (Ducati); **15** Andrea Mantovani, ITA (Ducati).
Fastest lap: Gutierrez, 1m 48.025s, 96.4mph/155.1km/h.

Race 2 (7 laps, 20.256 miles/32.599km)
1 Kevin Zannoni, ITA (Ducati), 12m 42.300s, 95.6mph/153.9km/h.
2 Oscar Gutierrez, SPA (Ducati); **3** Alessandro Zaccone, ITA (Ducati); **4** Jordi Torres, SPA (Ducati); **5** Hector Garzo, SPA (Ducati); **6** Lukas Tulovic, GER (Ducati); **7** Andrea Mantovani, ITA (Ducati); **8** Matteo Ferrari, ITA (Ducati); **9** Miquel Pons, SPA (Ducati); **10** Kevin Manfredi, ITA (Ducati); **11** Massimo Roccoli, ITA (Ducati); **12** Alessio Finello, ITA (Ducati); **13** Maria Herrera, SPA (Ducati); **14** Chaz Davies, GBR (Ducati); **15** Armando Pontone, ITA (Ducati).
Fastest lap: Gutierrez, 1m 48.076s, 96.4mph/155.1km/h.
Championship points: **1** Zannoni, 88; **2** Casadei, 87; **3** Gutierrez, 86; **4** Spinelli, 75; **5** Garzo, 64; **6** Tulovic, 48.

Round 4, MUGELLO, Italy, 31 May-1 June 2024, 3.260-mile/5.245km circuit
Race 1 (7 laps, 22.618 miles/36.4km)
1 Mattia Casadei, ITA (Ducati), 13m 37.214s, 100.5mph/161.7km/h.
2 Alessandro Zaccone, ITA (Ducati); **3** Hector Garzo, SPA (Ducati); **4** Kevin Zannoni, ITA (Ducati); **5** Eric Granado, BRA (Ducati); **6** Andrea Mantovani, ITA (Ducati); **7** Massimo Roccoli, ITA (Ducati); **8** Matteo Ferrari, ITA (Ducati); **9** Miquel Pons, SPA (Ducati); **10** Nicholas Spinelli, ITA (Ducati); **11** Oscar Gutierrez, SPA (Ducati); **12** Alessio Finello, ITA (Ducati); **13** Kevin Manfredi, ITA (Ducati); **14** Chaz Davies, GBR (Ducati); **15** Maria Herrera, SPA (Ducati).
Fastest lap: Zaccone, 1m 55.617s, 101.5mph/163.3km/h.

Race 2 (7 laps, 22.618 miles/36.715km)
1 Kevin Zannoni, ITA (Ducati), 13m 37.434s, 100.4mph/161.6km/h.
2 Mattia Casadei, ITA (Ducati); **3** Eric Granado, BRA (Ducati); **4** Massimo Roccoli, ITA (Ducati); **5** Andrea Mantovani, ITA (Ducati); **6** Alessandro Zaccone, ITA (Ducati); **7** Matteo Ferrari, ITA (Ducati); **8** Hector Garzo, SPA (Ducati); **9** Nicholas Spinelli, ITA (Ducati); **10** Oscar Gutierrez, SPA (Ducati); **11** Miquel Pons, SPA (Ducati); **12** Jordi Torres, SPA (Ducati); **13** Alessio Finello, ITA (Ducati); **14** Kevin Manfredi, ITA (Ducati); **15** Armando Pontone, ITA (Ducati).
Fastest lap: Spinelli, 1m 55.621s, 101.5mph/163.3km/h.
Championship points: **1** Zannoni, 113; **2** Casadei, 107; **3** Gutierrez, 92; **4** Spinelli, 82; **5** Garzo, 72; **6** Granado, 59.

Round 5, ASSEN, The Netherlands, 28-29 June 2024, 2.822-mile/4.542km circuit
Race 1 (7 laps, 19.756 miles/31.794km)
1 Hector Garzo, SPA (Ducati), 11m 48.283s, 100.4mph/161.5km/h.
2 Oscar Gutierrez, SPA (Ducati); **3** Jordi Torres, SPA (Ducati); **4** Miquel Pons, SPA (Ducati); **5** Matteo Ferrari, ITA (Ducati); **6** Massimo Roccoli, ITA (Ducati); **7** Lukas Tulovic, GER (Ducati); **8** Alessio Finello, ITA (Ducati); **9** Chaz Davies, GBR (Ducati); **10** Kevin Manfredi, ITA (Ducati); **11** Maria Herrera, SPA (Ducati); **12** Armando Pontone, ITA (Ducati); **13** Kevin Zannoni, ITA (Ducati); **14** N/A; **15** N/A.
Fastest lap: Gutierrez, 1m 39.836s, 101.7mph/163.7km/h.

Race 2 (7 laps, 19.756 miles/31.794km)
1 Alessandro Zaccone, ITA (Ducati), 11m 46.902s, 100.6mph/161.9km/h.
2 Oscar Gutierrez, SPA (Ducati); **3** Hector Garzo, SPA (Ducati); **4** Lukas Tulovic, GER (Ducati); **5** Jordi Torres, SPA (Ducati); **6** Miquel Pons, SPA (Ducati); **7** Kevin Zannoni, ITA (Ducati); **8** Mattia Casadei, ITA (Ducati); **9** Matteo Ferrari, ITA (Ducati); **10** Massimo Roccoli, ITA (Ducati); **11** Alessio Finello, ITA (Ducati); **12** Eric Granado, BRA (Ducati); **13** Maria Herrera, SPA (Ducati); **14** Andrea Mantovani, ITA (Ducati); **15** Kevin Manfredi, ITA (Ducati).
Fastest lap: Zaccone, 1m 39.632s, 102.0mph/164.1km/h.
Championship points: **1** Casadei, 140; **2** Zannoni, 138; **3** Gutierrez, 137; **4** Garzo, 129; **5** Zaccone, 99; **6** Spinelli, 88.

Round 6, SACHSENRING, Germany, 5-6 July 2024, 2.281-mile/3.671km circuit
Race 1 (5 laps, 11.405 miles/18.355km)
1 Hector Garzo, SPA (Ducati), 7m 14.150s, 94.6mph/152.2km/h.
2 Alessandro Zaccone, ITA (Ducati); **3** Nicholas Spinelli, ITA (Ducati); **4** Matteo Ferrari, ITA (Ducati); **5** Jordi Torres, SPA (Ducati); **6** Miquel Pons, SPA (Ducati); **7** Lukas Tulovic, GER (Ducati); **8** Kevin Zannoni, ITA (Ducati); **9** Mattia Casadei, ITA (Ducati); **10** Alessio Finello, ITA (Ducati); **11** Andrea Mantovani, ITA (Ducati); **12** Maria Herrera, SPA (Ducati); **13** Massimo Roccoli, ITA (Ducati); **14** Chaz Davies, GBR (Ducati); **15** Kevin Manfredi, ITA (Ducati).
Fastest lap: Garzo, 1m 26.522s, 94.9mph/152.7km/h.

Race 2 (8 laps, 22.827 miles/29.368km)
1 Hector Garzo, SPA (Ducati), 12m 43.708s, 86.0mph/138.4km/h.
2 Nicholas Spinelli, ITA (Ducati); **3** Jordi Torres, SPA (Ducati); **4** Oscar Gutierrez, SPA (Ducati); **5** Alessandro Zaccone, ITA (Ducati); **6** Matteo Ferrari, ITA (Ducati); **7** Miquel Pons, SPA (Ducati); **8** Andrea Mantovani, ITA (Ducati); **9** Mattia Casadei, ITA (Ducati); **10** Lukas Tulovic, GER (Ducati); **11** Massimo Roccoli, ITA (Ducati); **12** Armando Pontone, ITA (Ducati); **13** Kevin Manfredi, ITA (Ducati); **14** Alessio Finello, ITA (Ducati); **15** Kevin Zannoni, ITA (Ducati).
Fastest lap: Garzo, 1m 34.452s, 86.9mph/139.9km/h.
Championship points: **1** Garzo, 179; **2** Casadei, 154; **3** Gutierrez, 150; **4** Zannoni, 147; **5** Zaccone, 130; **6** Spinelli, 124.

Round 7, RED BULL RING, Austria, 16-17 August 2024, 2.702-mile/4.348km circuit
Race 1 (7 laps, 18.912 miles/30.436km)
1 Oscar Gutierrez, SPA (Ducati), 11m 35.551s, 97.9mph/157.5km/h.
2 Hector Garzo, SPA (Ducati); **3** Mattia Casadei, ITA (Ducati); **4** Kevin Zannoni, ITA (Ducati); **5** Jordi Torres, SPA (Ducati); **6** Alessandro Zaccone, ITA (Ducati); **7** Andrea Mantovani, ITA (Ducati); **8** Lukas Tulovic, GER (Ducati); **9** Massimo Roccoli, ITA (Ducati); **10** Maria Herrera, SPA (Ducati); **11** Nicholas Spinelli, ITA (Ducati); **12** Alessio Finello, ITA (Ducati); **13** Chaz Davies, GBR (Ducati); **14** Kevin Manfredi, ITA (Ducati); **15** Armando Pontone, ITA (Ducati).
Fastest lap: Gutierrez, 1m 38.284s, 98.9mph/159.2km/h.

Race 2 (7 laps, 18.782 miles/30.436km)
1 Hector Garzo, SPA (Ducati), 11m 34.304s, 98.1mph/157.8km/h.
2 Kevin Zannoni, ITA (Ducati); **3** Mattia Casadei, ITA (Ducati); **4** Jordi Torres, SPA (Ducati); **5** Alessandro Zaccone, ITA (Ducati); **6** Matteo Ferrari, ITA (Ducati); **7** Lukas Tulovic, GER (Ducati); **8** Nicholas Spinelli, ITA (Ducati); **9** Andrea Mantovani, ITA (Ducati); **10** Eric Granado, BRA (Ducati); **11** Massimo Roccoli, ITA (Ducati); **12** Maria Herrera, SPA (Ducati); **13** Alessio Finello, ITA (Ducati); **14** Chaz Davies, GBR (Ducati); **15** Kevin Manfredi, ITA (Ducati).
Fastest lap: Casadei, 1m 38.461s, 98.7mph/158.9km/h.
Championship points: **1** Garzo, 224; **2** Casadei, 186; **3** Zannoni, 180; **4** Gutierrez, 175; **5** Zaccone, 151; **6** Spinelli, 137.

Round 8, MISANO, San Marino, 6-7 September 2024, 2.630-mile/4.226km circuit
Race 1 (8 laps, 20.878 miles/33.808km)
1 Mattia Casadei, ITA (Ducati), 13m 24.775s, 94.0mph/151.2km/h.
2 Alessandro Zaccone, ITA (Ducati); **3** Eric Granado, BRA (Ducati); **4** Hector Garzo, SPA (Ducati); **5** Jordi Torres, SPA (Ducati); **6** Matteo Ferrari, ITA (Ducati); **7** Lukas Tulovic, GER (Ducati); **8** Oscar Gutierrez, SPA (Ducati); **9** Nicholas Spinelli, ITA (Ducati); **10** Andrea Mantovani, ITA (Ducati); **11** Miquel Pons, SPA (Ducati); **12** Alessio Finello, ITA (Ducati); **13** Kevin Manfredi, ITA (Ducati); **14** Maria Herrera, SPA (Ducati); **15** Chaz Davies, GBR (Ducati).
Fastest lap: Kevin Zannoni, 1m 40.107s, 94.4mph/151.9km/h.

Race 2 (8 laps, 20.878 miles/33.808km)
1 Oscar Gutierrez, SPA (Ducati), 13m 29.676s, 93.4mph/150.3km/h.
2 Mattia Casadei, ITA (Ducati); **3** Eric Granado, BRA (Ducati); **4** Jordi Torres, SPA (Ducati); **5** Kevin Zannoni, ITA (Ducati); **6** Matteo Ferrari, ITA (Ducati); **7** Hector Garzo, SPA (Ducati); **8** Alessandro Zaccone, ITA (Ducati); **9** Andrea Mantovani, ITA (Ducati); **10** Miquel Pons, SPA (Ducati); **11** Nicholas Spinelli, ITA (Ducati); **12** Alessio Finello, ITA (Ducati); **13** Maria Herrera, SPA (Ducati); **14** Kevin Manfredi, ITA (Ducati); **15** Chaz Davies, GBR (Ducati).
Fastest lap: Ferrari, 1m 39.862s, 94.6mph/152.3km/h.

Final FIM MotoE World Championship points:

1	Hector Garzo	246
2	Mattia Casadei	231
3	Oscar Gutierrez	208
4	Kevin Zannoni	191
5	Alessandro Zaccone	179
6	Jordi Torres	152

7 Nicholas Spinelli, 149; **8** Matteo Ferrari, 132; **9** Andrea Mantovani, 113; **10** Eric Granado, 112; **11** Lukas Tulovic, 111; **12** Miquel Pons, 94; **13** Massimo Roccoli, 88; **14** Alessio Finello, 70; **15** Kevin Manfredi, 56.

Isle of Man Tourist Trophy Races

ISLE OF MAN TOURIST TROPHY COURSE, 1-8 June 2024, 37.73-mile/60.72km circuit.

Monster Energy Supersport TT
Race 1 (4 laps, 150.92 miles/242.88km)
1 Michael Dunlop (Yamaha), 1h 11m 19.297s, 126.963mph/204.327km/h.
2 Davey Todd (Ducati), 1h 11m 27.871s; **3** Dean Harrison (Honda), 1h 11m 50.252s; **4** James Hillier (Kawasaki), 1h 12m 31.694s; **5** James Hind (Suzuki), 1h 12m 33.140s; **6** Joshua Brookes (Yamaha), 1h 12m 45.855s; **7** Paul Jordan (Honda), 1h 12m 48.035s; **8** Mike Browne (Yamaha), 1h 12m 49.556s; **9** Peter Hickman (Triumph), 1h 12m 52.580s; **10** Michael Evans (Triumph), 1h 13m 1.257s; **11** Dominic Herbertson (Yamaha), 1h 13m 5.018s; **12** David Johnson (Triumph), 1h 13m 29.108s; **13** Shaun Anderson (Suzuki), 1h 13m 46.573s; **14** Rob Hodson (Yamaha), 1h 14m 16.940s; **15** Ian Hutchinson (Honda), 1h 14m 28.231s.
Fastest lap: Dunlop (Yamaha), 17m 31.185s, 129.214mph/207.950km/h.
Supersport lap record: Dunlop (Yamaha), 17m 21.605s, 130.403mph/209.863km/h (2023).

3wheeling.media Sidecar TT
Race 1 (3 laps, 113.19 miles/182.16km)
1 Ryan Crowe/Callum Crowe (Honda LCR), 57m 14.976s, 118.628mph/190.913km/h.
2 Peter Founds/Jevan Walmsley (Honda DDM), 57m 41.871s; **3** Alan Founds/Rhys Gibbons (Yamaha LCR), 58m 56.251s; **4** Lewis Blackstock/Patrick Rosney (Yamaha LCR), 59m 5.252s; **5** Lee Crawford/Scott Hardie (Kawasaki LCR), 59m 5.788s; **6** Tim Reeves/Mark Wilkes (Honda LCR), 59m 13.527s; **7** Todd Ellis/Emmanuelle Clement (Yamaha CES), 59m 51.987s; **8** John Holden/Frank Claeys (Suzuki Christie), 1h 0m 51.952s; **9** John Saunders/James Saunders (Yamaha LCR), 1h 2m 22.690s; **10** Conrad Harrison/Ashley Moore (Yamaha Ireson), 1h 2m 54.487s; **11** Greg Lambert/Andrew Haynes (Honda LCR), 1h 3m 13.584s; **12** Shaun Chandler/Ben Chandler (Honda CES), 1h 3m 17.023s; **13** Robert Dawson/Matthew Sims (Honda LCR), 1h 3m 19.004s; **14** Rob Handcock/Basil Bevan (Suzuki Shelbourne), 1h 3m 48.678s; **15** Gary Gibson/Justin Sharp (Suzuki Shelbourne), 1h 4m 22.979s.
Fastest lap: Ryan Crowe/Callum Crowe (Honda LCR), 18m 53.789s, 119.800mph/192.799km/h.
Sidecar lap record: Ben Birchall/Tom Birchall (Honda LCR), 18m 45.850s, 120.645mph/194.159km/h (2023).

RST Superbike TT (6 laps, 226.38 miles/364.32km)
1 Peter Hickman (BMW), 1h 42m 56.114s, 131.955mph/212.361km/h.
2 Davey Todd (BMW), 1h 43m 1.954s; **3** Dean Harrison (Honda), 1h 43m 7.156s; **4** Michael Dunlop (Honda), 1h 43m 22.273s; **5** James Hillier (Honda), 1h 44m 55.042s; **6** John McGuinness (Honda), 1h 44m 57.929s; **7** Jamie Coward (Honda), 1h 44m 58.162s; **8** Mike Browne (Aprilia), 1h 47m 2.601s; **9** Michael Rutter (BMW), 1h 48m 28.596s; **10** Brian McCormack (BMW), 1h 48m 43.644s; **11** Julian Trummer (Honda), 1h 49m 8.331s; **12** Marcus Simpson (Honda), 1h 50m 30.085s; **13** Allann Venter (BMW), 1h 50m 33.986s; **14** James Chawke (Suzuki), 1h 51m 13.018s; **15** Samuel West (BMW), 1h 51m 13.104s.
Fastest lap: Dunlop (Honda), 16m 38.953s, 135.970mph/218.823km/h (new record).
Superbike TT previous lap record: Hickman (BMW), 16m 42.825s, 135.445mph/217.978km/h (2023).

Metzeler Supertwin TT
Race 1 (3 laps, 113.19 miles/182.16km)
1 Michael Dunlop (Paton), 56m 15.993s, 120.700mph/194.248km/h.
2 Peter Hickman (Yamaha), 56m 36.400s; **3** Dominic Herbertson (Paton), 56m 50.794s; **4** Jamie Coward (Kawasaki), 56m 56.289s; **5** Mike Browne (Aprilia), 57m 20.383s; **6** Davey Todd (Kawasaki), 58m 0.925s; **7** Michael Rutter (Yamaha), 58m 17.201s; **8** Joe Yeardsley (Paton), 58m 44.075s; **9** Allann Venter (Kawasaki), 59m 18.944s; **10** Pierre Yves Bian (Paton), 59m 24.230s; **11** Joshua Brookes (Yamaha), 59m 30.366s; **12** Michael Sweeney (Aprilia), 59m 32.119s; **13** Francesco Curinga (Paton), 59m 53.739s; **14** Julian Trummer (Aprilia), 59m 57.031s; **15** Tom Weeden (Aprilia), 1h 0m 2.680s.
Fastest lap: Dunlop (Paton), 18m 29.395s, 122.434mph/197.038km/h.
Supertwin (Lightweight) lap record: Dunlop (Paton), 18m 26.543s, 122.750mph/197.547km/h (2018).

RL360 Superstock TT
Race 1 (3 laps, 113.19 miles/182.16km)
1 Davey Todd (BMW), 51m 10.728s, 132.699mph/213.558km/h.
2 Peter Hickman (BMW), 51m 12.936s; **3** Michael Dunlop (Honda), 51m 30.676s; **4** Dean Harrison (Honda), 51m 34.286s; **5** James Hillier (Honda), 52m 6.877s; **6** Jamie Coward (Honda), 52m 11.465s; **7** John McGuinness (Honda), 52m 27.216s; **8** Conor Cummins (Honda), 52m 32.691s; **9** Dominic Herbertson (BMW), 52m 52.383s; **10** Mike Browne (Aprilia), 53m 3.236s; **11** Joshua Brookes (BMW), 53m 16.097s; **12** Paul Jordan (Honda), 53m 29.722s; **13** Ian Hutchinson (Honda), 53m 52.379s; **14** Rob Hodson (Honda), 53m 58.609s; **15** Shaun Anderson (Honda), 54m 3.767s.
Fastest lap: Hickman (BMW), 16m 45.088s, 135.140mph/217.487km/h.
Superstock lap record: Hickman (BMW), 16m 36.115s, 136.358mph/219.447km/h (2023, outright record).

3wheeling.media Sidecar TT
Race 2 (2 laps, 75.46 miles/121.44km)
1 Ryan Crowe/Callum Crowe (Honda LCR), 37m 49.274s, 119.711mph/192.656km/h.

2 Ben Birchall/Kevin Rousseau (Honda LCR), 38m 9.766s; 3 Dave Molyneux/Jake Roberts (Kawasaki DMR), 39m 22.931s; 4 Alan Founds/Rhys Gibbons (Yamaha LCR), 39m 29.810s; 5 Lewis Blackstock/Patrick Rosney (Yamaha LCR), 39m 34.557s; 6 Steve Ramsden/Mathew Ramsden (Honda LCR), 40m 54.688s; 7 John Saunders/James Saunders (Yamaha LCR), 41m 13.228s; 8 Wayne Lockey/Matthew Rostron (Honda LCR), 41m 17.148s; 9 Robert Dawson/Matthew Sims (Honda LCR), 41m 27.824s; 10 Conrad Harrison/Ashley Moore (Yamaha Ireson), 41m 43.819s; 11 Gary Gibson/Justin Sharp (Suzuki Shelbourne), 42m 8.554s; 12 Derek Lynch/Anthony McDonnell (Suzuki DMR), 42m 24.816s; 13 Renzo Van der Donckt/Vale Van der Donckt (Suzuki LCR), 42m 39.049s; 14 Shaun Chandler/Ben Chandler (Honda CES), 42m 57.485s; 15 Wiggert Kranenburg/Jermaine van Middegaal (Honda LCR), 43m 48.590s.
Fastest lap: Ryan Crowe/Callum Crowe (Honda LCR), 18m 48.748s, 120.335mph/193.660km/h.
Sidecar lap record: Ben Birchall/Tom Birchall (Honda LCR), 18m 45.850s, 120.645mph/194.159km/h (2023).

Monster Energy Supersport TT
Race 2 (2 laps, 75.46 miles/121.44km)
1 Michael Dunlop (Yamaha), 35m 18.593s, 128.225mph/206.358km/h.
2 Dean Harrison (Honda), 35m 22.482s, 3 Davey Todd (Ducati), 35m 24.825s, 4 Jamie Coward (Triumph), 35m 33.148s, 5 Peter Hickman (Triumph), 35m 35.377s, 6 James Hillier (Kawasaki), 35m 41.317s, 7 Mike Browne (Yamaha), 35m 51.040s, 8 Paul Jordan (Honda), 36m 11.129s, 9 Michael Evans (Triumph), 36m 32.064s, 10 Joshua Brookes (Yamaha), 36m 32.769s, 11 Shaun Anderson (Suzuki), 36m 36.107s, 12 Joe Yeardsley (Yamaha), 36m 48.698s, 13 Rob Hodson (Yamaha), 36m 49.567s, 14 Ian Hutchinson (Honda), 36m 59.279s, 15 Craig Neve (Triumph), 37m 14.543s.
Fastest lap: Dunlop (Yamaha), 17m 32.350s, 129.071mph/207.720km/h.
Supersport lap record: Dunlop (Yamaha), 17m 21.605s, 130.403mph/209.863km/h (2023).

PE Superstock TT
Race 2
Cancelled due to weather conditions.

Entire Cover insurance Supertwin TT
Race 2 (1 lap, 37.73 miles/60.72km)
1 Michael Dunlop (Paton), 18m 29.246s, 122.451mph/197.066km/h.
2 Peter Hickman (Yamaha), 18m 35.692s; 3 Mike Browne (Aprilia), 18m 43.681s; 4 Dominic Herbertson (Paton), 18m 47.030s; 5 Paul Jordan (Yamaha), 18m 56.382s; 6 Davey Todd (Kawasaki), 18m 57.980s; 7 Rob Hodson (Paton), 18m 58.330s; 8 Joshua Brookes (Yamaha), 19m 5.450s; 9 Adam McLean (Yamaha), 19m 5.949s; 10 Baz Furber (Yamaha), 19m 6.544s; 11 Stefano Bonetti (Paton), 19m 6.563s; 12 Pierre Yves Bian (Paton), 19m 10.396s; 13 Michael Rutter (Yamaha), 19m 22.386s; 14 Michael Sweeney (Aprilia), 19m 24.731s; 15 Michal Dokoupil (Aprilia), 19m 33.684s.
Fastest lap: Dunlop (Paton), 18m 29.246s, 122.451mph/197.066km/h.
Supertwin (Lightweight) lap record: Dunlop (Paton), 18m 26.543s, 122.750mph/197.547km/h (2018).

Milwaukee Senior TT (4 laps, 150.92 miles/242.88km)
1 Davey Todd (BMW), 1h 8m 9.761s, 132.847mph/213.797km/h.
2 Joshua Brookes (BMW), 1h 8m 48.846s; 3 Dean Harrison (Honda), 1h 9m 15.057s; 4 James Hillier (Honda), 1h 9m 52.433s; 5 John McGuinness (Honda), 1h 10m 19.913s; 6 Mike Browne (Aprilia), 1h 10m 27.078s; 7 Nathan Harrison (Honda), 1h 11m 17.499s; 8 Shaun Anderson (Suzuki), 1h 11m 17.903s; 9 Michael Rutter (BMW), 1h 11m 28.426s; 10 Paul Jordan (Honda), 1h 11m 31.658s; 11 Rob Hodson (Honda), 1h 11m 37.408s; 12 Ian Hutchinson (Honda), 1h 11m 56.405s; 13 Brian McCormack (BMW), 1h 12m 8.191s; 14 Julian Trummer (Honda), 1h 12m 33.966s; 15 Samuel West (BMW), 1h 12m 54.969s.
Fastest lap: Peter Hickman (BMW), 16m 42.252s, 135.523mph/218.103km/h (record).
Senior TT previous lap record: Hickman (BMW), 16m 42.367s, 135.507mph/218.077km/h (2023).

British Championships

CIRCUITO DE NAVARRA, 19-21 April 2024, 2.426-mile/3.904km circuit.
Bennetts British Superbike Championship, Round 1
Race 1 (20 laps, 48.520 miles/78.085km)
1 Ryan Vickers (Yamaha), 32m 33.607s, 89.41mph/143.89km/h.
2 Kyle Ryde (Yamaha); 3 Danny Kent (Yamaha); 4 Glenn Irwin (Ducati); 5 Rory Skinner (BMW); 6 Christian Iddon (Ducati); 7 Tommy Bridewell (Honda); 8 Max Cook (Kawasaki); 9 Charlie Nesbitt (Honda); 10 Jason O'Halloran (Kawasaki); 11 Leon Haslam (BMW); 12 Peter Hickman (BMW); 13 Fraser Rogers (Honda); 14 Lee Jackson (Honda); 15 Billy McConnell (Honda).
Fastest lap: Ryde, 1m 36.896s, 90.13mph/145.06km/h.

Race 2 (20 laps, 48.520 miles/78.085km)
1 Ryan Vickers (Yamaha), 32m 34.576s, 89.37mph/143.83km/h.
2 Danny Kent (Yamaha); 3 Kyle Ryde (Yamaha); 4 Leon Haslam (BMW); 5 Christian Iddon (Ducati); 6 Jason O'Halloran (Kawasaki); 7 Max Cook (Kawasaki); 8 Glenn Irwin (Ducati); 9 Charlie Nesbitt (Honda); 10 Peter Hickman (BMW); 11 Josh Brookes (BMW); 12 Lee Jackson (Honda); 13 Andrew Irwin (Honda); 14 Billy McConnell (Honda); 15 Storm Stacey (Kawasaki).
Fastest lap: Bridewell, 1m 36.907s, 90.12mph/145.04km/h.
Championship points: 1 Ryan Vickers, 36; 2 Danny Kent, 30; 3 Kyle Ryde, 30; 4 Christian Iddon, 21; 5 Glenn Irwin, 20; 6 Leon Haslam, 17.

Quattro Group British Supersport Championship, Round 1
Race 1 (12 laps, 29.112 miles/46.851km)
1 Luke Stapleford (Triumph), 20m 3.637s, 87.07mph/140.13km/h.
2 Davey Todd (Ducati); 3 Jack Kennedy (Honda); 4 Brad Perie (Kawasaki); 5 Rhys Irwin (Suzuki); 6 Harry Truelove (Suzuki); 7 Alastair Seeley (Yamaha); 8 Shane Richardson (Suzuki); 9 Matt Truelove (Suzuki); 10 Joe Francis (Ducati); 11 Benjamin Currie (Ducati); 12 Jack Nixon (Kramer); 13 Asher Durham (Kawasaki); 14 Jorel Boerboom (Kawasaki); 15 Sam Laffins (Kawasaki).
Fastest lap: Stapleford, 1m 39.394s, 87.87mph/141.41km/h.

Race 2 (18 laps, 43.668 miles/70.277km)
1 Benjamin Currie (Ducati), 30m 44.334s, 85.24mph/137.18km/h.
2 Luke Stapleford (Triumph); 3 Davey Todd (Ducati); 4 Brad Perie (Kawasaki); 5 Jack Kennedy (Honda); 6 Alastair Seeley (Yamaha); 7 Harry Truelove (Suzuki); 8 Joe Francis (Ducati); 9 Shane Richardson (Suzuki); 10 Asher Durham (Kawasaki); 11 Sam Laffins (Kawasaki); 12 Freddie Barnes (Yamaha); 13 Jorel Boerboom (Kawasaki); 14 Max Wadsworth (Triumph); 15 Owen Jenner (Kramer).
Fastest lap: Stapleford, 1m 39.561s, 87.72mph/141.18km/h.
Championship points: 1 Luke Stapleford, 47; 2 Davey Todd, 42; 3 Jack Kennedy, 36; 4 Brad Perie, 36; 5 Ben Currie, 30; 6 Alastair Seeley, 26.

R&G British Talent Cup, Round 1
Race 1 (14 laps, 33.964 miles/54.66km)
1 Julian Correa (Honda), 25m 78.740s, 78.74mph/126.72km/h.
2 Lucas Brown (Honda); 3 Ryan Frost (Honda); 4 Clayton Edmunds (Honda); 5 Harley McCabe (Honda); 6 Ronnie Harris (Honda); 7 Peter Willis (Honda); 8 Daniel Goodman (Honda); 9 Ben Jolliffe (Honda); 10 George Bowes (Honda); 11 Joshua Raymond Jr (Honda); 12 Harrison Mackay (Honda); 13 Alexander Rowan (Honda); 14 Scott McPhee (Honda); 15 Eli Banish (Honda).
Fastest lap: Amanuel Brinton, 1m 49.581s, 79.70mph/128.27km/h.

Race 2 (8 laps, 19.408 miles/31.234km)
1 Filip Surowiak (Honda), 14m 45.845s, 78.87mph/126.93km/h.
2 Julian Correa (Honda); 3 Amanuel Brinton (Honda); 4 Lucas Brown (Honda); 5 Mason Foster (Honda); 6 Ryan Frost (Honda); 7 Ollie Walker (Honda); 8 Ronnie Harris (Honda); 9 Charlie Huntingford (Honda); 10 Clayton Edmunds (Honda); 11 Jack Burrows (Honda); 12 Harrison Mackay (Honda); 13 Ben Jolliffe (Honda); 14 Alexander Rowan (Honda); 15 George Bowes (Honda).
Fastest lap: Surowiak, 1m 49.157s, 80.01mph/128.77km/h.

Race 3 (14 laps, 33.964 miles/54.66km)
1 Lucas Brown (Honda), 25m 48.745s, 78.95mph/127.06km/h.
2 Amanuel Brinton (Honda); 3 Mason Foster (Honda); 4 Filip Surowiak (Honda); 5 Ryan Frost (Honda); 6 Ronnie Harris (Honda); 7 Ollie Walker (Honda); 8 Clayton Edmunds (Honda); 9 Jack Burrows (Honda); 10 Charlie Huntingford (Honda); 11 Harley McCabe (Honda); 12 Peter Willis (Honda); 13 Harrison Mackay (Honda); 14 Ben Jolliffe (Honda); 15 Daniel Goodman (Honda).
Fastest lap: Brinton, 1m 49.499s, 79.76mph/128.36km/h.
Championship points: 1 Lucas Brown, 58; 2 Julian Correa, 45; 3 Filip Surowiak, 38; 4 Ryan Frost, 37; 5 Amanuel Brinton, 36; 6 Ronnie Harris, 28.
A
OULTON PARK, 4-6 May 2024, 2.692-mile/4.332km circuit.
Bennetts British Superbike Championship, Round 2
Race 1 (18 laps, 48.456 miles/77.982km)
1 Glenn Irwin (Ducati), 28m 22.971s, 102.43mph/164.85km/h.
2 Christian Iddon (Ducati); 3 Kyle Ryde (Yamaha); 4 Tommy Bridewell (Honda); 5 Ryan Vickers (Yamaha); 6 Danny Kent (Yamaha); 7 Jason O'Halloran (Kawasaki); 8 Rory Skinner (BMW); 9 Josh Brookes (BMW); 10 Leon Haslam (BMW); 11 Charlie Nesbitt (Honda); 12 Fraser Rogers (Honda); 13 Peter Hickman (BMW); 14 Lee Jackson (Honda); 15 Dean Harrison (Honda).
Fastest lap: Irwin, 1m 33.862s, 103.25mph/166.16km/h.

Race 2 (12 laps, 32.304 miles/51.988km)
1 Glenn Irwin (Ducati), 18m 53.385s, 102.60mph/165.12km/h.
2 Tommy Bridewell (Honda); 3 Christian Iddon (Ducati); 4 Danny Kent (Yamaha); 5 Kyle Ryde (Yamaha); 6 Jason O'Halloran (Kawasaki); 7 Josh Brookes (BMW); 8 Leon Haslam (BMW); 9 Ryan Vickers (Yamaha); 10 Max Cook (Kawasaki); 11 Lee Jackson (Honda); 12 Storm Stacey (Kawasaki); 13 Charlie Nesbitt (Honda); 14 Andrew Irwin (Honda); 15 Peter Hickman (BMW).
Fastest lap: Iddon, 1m 33.727s, 103.39mph/166.4km/h.

Race 3 (18 laps, 48.456 miles/77.982km)
1 Glenn Irwin (Ducati), 28m 20.762s, 102.56mph/165.05km/h.
2 Christian Iddon (Ducati); 3 Ryan Vickers (Yamaha); 4 Danny Kent (Yamaha); 5 Leon Haslam (BMW); 6 Tommy Bridewell (Honda); 7 Jason O'Halloran (Kawasaki); 8 Josh Brookes (BMW); 9 Max Cook (Kawasaki); 10 Storm Stacey (Kawasaki); 11 Lee Jackson (Honda); 12 Danny Buchan (Kawasaki); 13 Charlie Nesbitt (Honda); 14 Fraser Rogers (Honda); 15 Andrew Irwin (Honda).
Fastest lap: Iddon, 1m 33.712s, 103.41mph/166.43km/h.
Championship points: 1 Glenn Irwin, 74; 2 Ryan Vickers, 68; 3 Christian Iddon, 67; 4 Danny Kent, 64; 5 Kyle Ryde, 55; 6 Tommy Bridewell, 47.

Quattro Group British Supersport Championship, Round 2
Race 1 (12 laps, 32.304 miles/51.988km)
1 Luke Stapleford (Triumph), 19m 34.166s, 99.04mph/159.39km/h.
2 Benjamin Currie (Ducati); 3 Jack Kennedy (Honda); 4 Harry Truelove (Suzuki); 5 Eugene McManus (Ducati); 6 TJ Toms (Yamaha); 7 Rhys Irwin (Suzuki); 8 Brad Perie (Kawasaki); 9 Joe Francis (Ducati); 10 Alastair Seeley (Yamaha); 11 Shane Richardson (Suzuki); 12 Owen Jenner (Kramer); 13 Jack Nixon (Kramer); 14 Hikari Okubo (Honda); 15 Jamie Coward (Triumph).
Fastest lap: Stapleford, 1m 37.071s, 99.83mph/160.67km/h.

Race 2 (16 laps, 43.072 miles/69.318km)
1 Benjamin Currie (Ducati), 26m 10.432s, 98.73mph/158.89km/h.
2 Jack Kennedy (Honda); 3 Eugene McManus (Ducati); 4 Rhys Irwin (Suzuki); 5 Harry Truelove (Suzuki); 6 Alastair Seeley (Yamaha); 7 Shane Richardson (Suzuki); 8 Brad Perie (Kawasaki); 9 Matt Truelove (Suzuki); 10 Owen Jenner (Kramer); 11 Asher Durham (Kawasaki); 12 Hikari Okubo (Honda); 13 Joe Francis (Ducati); 14 Jack Nixon (Kramer); 15 Max Wadsworth (Triumph).
Fastest lap: Currie, 1m 37.377s, 99.52mph/160.16km/h.
Championship points: 1 Jack Kennedy, 78; 2 Ben Currie, 77; 3 Luke Stapleford, 72; 4 Harry Truelove, 60; 5 Brad Perie, 56; 6 Alastair Seeley, 46.

DONINGTON PARK GP, 17-19 May 2024, 2.487-mile/4.002km circuit.
Bennetts British Superbike Championship, Round 3
Race 1 (14 laps, 34.818 miles/56.034km)
1 Kyle Ryde (Yamaha), 20m 41.385s, 100.87mph/162.33km/h.
2 Tommy Bridewell (Honda); 3 Leon Haslam (BMW); 4 Danny Kent (Yamaha); 5 Glenn Irwin (Ducati); 6 Max Cook (Kawasaki); 7 Lee Jackson (Honda); 8 Jason O'Halloran (Kawasaki); 9 Charlie Nesbitt (Honda); 10 Josh Brookes (BMW); 11 Billy McConnell (Honda); 12 Franco Bourne (Honda); 13 Fraser Rogers (Honda); 14 Andrew Irwin (Honda); 15 Danny Buchan (Kawasaki).
Fastest lap: Christian Iddon, 1m 27.884s, 101.88mph/163.97km/h.

Race 2 (12 laps, 29.844 miles/48.029km)
1 Glenn Irwin (Ducati), 17m 40.802s, 101.16mph/162.80km/h.
2 Leon Haslam (BMW); 3 Tommy Bridewell (Honda); 4 Danny Kent (Yamaha); 5 Kyle Ryde (Yamaha); 6 Christian Iddon (Ducati); 7 Charlie Nesbitt (Honda); 8 Josh Brookes (BMW); 9 Andrew Irwin (Honda); 10 Fraser Rogers (Honda); 11 Dean Harrison (Honda); 12 Lee Jackson (Honda); 13 Lewis Rollo (Aprilia); 14 Luke Mossey (Kawasaki); 15 Alex Olsen (Honda).
Fastest lap: Kent, 1m 27.651s, 102.16mph/164.41km/h.

Race 3 (20 laps, 49.740 miles/80.049km)
1 Jason O'Halloran (Kawasaki), 29m 35.708s, 100.77mph/162.17km/h.
2 Tommy Bridewell (Honda); 3 Danny Kent (Yamaha); 4 Glenn Irwin (Ducati); 5 Kyle Ryde (Yamaha); 6 Leon Haslam (BMW); 7 Andrew Irwin (Honda); 8 Lee Jackson (Honda); 9 Christian Iddon (Ducati); 10 Max Cook (Kawasaki); 11 Charlie Nesbitt (Honda); 12 Fraser Rogers (Honda); 13 Dean Harrison (Honda); 14 Billy McConnell (Honda); 15 Storm Stacey (Kawasaki).
Fastest lap: Bridewell, 1m 27.868s, 101.90mph/164.00km/h.
Championship points: 1 Glenn Irwin, 115; 2 Danny Kent, 102; 3 Kyle Ryde, 95; 4 Tommy Bridewell, 93; 5 Christian Iddon, 84; 6 Leon Haslam, 82.

Quattro Group British Supersport Championship, Round 3
Race 1 (12 laps, 29.844 miles/48.029km)
1 Can Oncu (Kawasaki), 18m 10.024s, 98.45mph/158.44km/h.
2 Tom Booth-Amos (Triumph); 3 Benjamin Currie (Ducati); 4 Jack Kennedy (Honda); 5 TJ Toms (Yamaha); 6 Eugene McManus (Ducati); 7 Harry Truelove (Suzuki); 8 Ondrej Vostatek (Triumph); 9 Rhys Irwin (Suzuki); 10 Eunan McGlinchey (Kawasaki); 11 Alastair Seeley (Yamaha); 12 Brad Perie (Kawasaki); 13 Joe Francis (Ducati); 14 Owen Jenner (Kramer); 15 Shane Richardson (Suzuki).
Fastest lap: Oncu, 1m 30.048s, 99.44mph/160.03km/h.

Race 2 (15 laps, 37.305 miles/60.037km)
1 Tom Booth-Amos (Triumph), 22m 42.754s, 98.46mph/158.46km/h.
2 Can Oncu (Kawasaki); 3 Luke Stapleford (Triumph); 4 Benjamin Currie (Ducati); 5 Jack Kennedy (Honda); 6 TJ Toms (Yamaha); 7 Ondrej Vostatek (Triumph); 8 Brad Perie (Kawasaki); 9 Alastair Seeley (Yamaha); 10 Shane Richardson (Suzuki); 11 Owen Jenner (Kramer); 12 Eunan McGlinchey (Kawasaki); 13 Matt Truelove (Suzuki); 14 Max Wadsworth (Triumph); 15 Carter Brown (Yamaha).
Fastest lap: Oncu, 1m 30.076s, 99.41mph/159.98km/h.
Championship points: 1 Ben Currie, 115; 2 Jack Kennedy, 112; 3 Luke Stapleford, 92; 4 Harry Truelove, 72; 5 Brad Perie, 70; 6 Alastair Seeley, 59.

R&G British Talent Cup, Round 2
Race 1 (14 laps, 34.818 miles/56.034km)
1 Amanuel Brinton (Honda), 23m 31.039s, 88.74mph/142.81km/h.
2 Julian Correa (Honda); 3 Lucas Brown (Honda); 4 Ryan Frost (Honda); 5 Ronnie Harris (Honda); 6 Filip Surowiak (Honda); 7 Harley McCabe (Honda); 8 Clayton Edmunds (Honda); 9 George Bowes (Honda); 10 Ollie Walker (Honda); 11 Mason Foster (Honda); 12 Harrison Mackay (Honda); 13 Charlie Huntingford (Honda); 14 Joshua Raymond Jr (Honda); 15 Josh Bannister (Honda).
Fastest lap: Surowiak, 1m 39.816s, 89.70mph/144.37km/h.

Race 2 (11 laps, 27.357 miles/44.027km)
1 Ryan Frost (Honda), 18m 28.540s, 88.73mph/142.8km/h.
2 Lucas Brown (Honda); 3 Amanuel Brinton (Honda); 4 Ollie Walker (Honda); 5 Ronnie Harris (Honda); 6 Clayton Edmunds (Honda); 7 Harley McCabe (Honda); 8 Harrison Mackay (Honda); 9 George Bowes (Honda); 10 Scott McPhee (Honda); 11 Charlie Huntingford (Honda); 12 Peter Willis (Honda); 13 Alexander Rowan (Honda); 14 Daniel Goodman (Honda); 15 Josh Bannister (Honda).
Fastest lap: Brinton, 1m 39.379s, 90.10mph/145.00km/h.
Championship points: 1 Lucas Brown, 94; 2 Amanuel Brinton, 77; 3 Ryan Frost, 75; 4 Julian Correa, 65; 5 Ronnie Harris, 50; 6 Filip Surowiak, 48.

KNOCKHILL, 14-16 June 2024, 1.268-mile/2.042km circuit.
Bennetts British Superbike Championship, Round 4
Race 1 (25 laps, 31.673 miles/50.973km)
1 Tommy Bridewell (Honda), 20m 16.301s, 93.74mph/150.86km/h.
2 Rory Skinner (BMW); 3 Andrew Irwin (Honda); 4 Kyle Ryde (Yamaha); 5 Jason O'Halloran (Kawasaki); 6 Josh Brookes (BMW); 7 Danny Kent (Yamaha); 8 Lee Jackson (Honda); 9 Charlie Nesbitt (Honda); 10 Leon Haslam (BMW); 11 Danny Buchan (Kawasaki); 12 Storm Stacey (Kawasaki); 13 Fraser Rogers (Honda); 14 Luke Hedger (Kawasaki); 15 Franco Bourne (Honda).
Fastest lap: Bridewell, 47.946s, 95.13mph/153.09km/h.

Race 2 (20 laps, 25.338 miles/40.778km)
1 Rory Skinner (BMW), 17m 32.390s, 86.68mph/139.5km/h.
2 Christian Iddon (Ducati); 3 Tommy Bridewell (Honda); 4 Storm Stacey (Kawasaki); 5 Charlie Nesbitt (Honda); 6 Fraser Rogers (Honda); 7 Billy McConnell (Honda); 8 Glenn Irwin (Ducati); 9 Lee Jackson (Honda); 10 Max Cook (Kawasaki); 11 Lewis Rollo (Aprilia); 12 Josh Brookes (BMW); 13 Danny Buchan (Kawasaki); 14 Kyle Ryde (Yamaha); 15 Luke Hedger (Kawasaki).
Fastest lap: Danny Kent, 51.413s, 88.71mph/142.77km/h.

Race 3 (22 laps, 27.872 miles/44.856km)
1 Christian Iddon (Ducati), 19m 18.398s, 86.62mph/139.4km/h.
2 Tommy Bridewell (Honda); 3 Danny Kent (Yamaha); 4 Rory Skinner (BMW); 5 Billy McConnell (Honda); 6 Fraser Rogers (Honda); 7 Danny Buchan (Kawasaki); 8 Charlie Nesbitt (Honda); 9 Glenn Irwin (Ducati); 10 Lee Jackson (Honda); 11 Josh Brookes (BMW); 12 Luke Hedger (Kawasaki); 13 Storm Stacey (Kawasaki); 14 Lewis Rollo (Aprilia); 15 Kyle Ryde (Yamaha).
Fastest lap: Iddon, 52.005s, 87.70mph/141.14km/h.
Championship points: 1 Tommy Bridewell, 141; 2 Glenn Irwin, 130; 3 Danny Kent, 125; 4 Christian Iddon, 118; 5 Kyle Ryde, 110; 6 Leon Haslam, 88.

Quattro Group British Supersport Championship, Round 4
Race 1 (18 laps, 22.804 miles/36.699km)
1 Jack Kennedy (Honda), 14m 55.298s, 91.70mph/147.58km/h.
2 Luke Stapleford (Triumph); **3** Alastair Seeley (Yamaha); **4** Eugene McManus (Ducati); **5** Owen Jenner (Kramer); **6** Benjamin Currie (Ducati); **7** Rhys Irwin (Kawasaki); **8** Harry Truelove (Suzuki); **9** Shane Richardson (Suzuki); **10** Luke Jones (Ducati); **11** Adon Davie (Ducati); **12** Asher Durham (Kawasaki); **13** Oliver Barr (Yamaha); **14** Mikey Hardie (Kawasaki); **15** Jack Nixon (Kramer).
Fastest lap: Currie, 49.158s, 92.78mph/149.32km/h.

Race 2 (22 laps, 27.872 miles/44.856km)
1 Jack Kennedy (Honda), 19m 49.624s, 84.34mph/135.73km/h.
2 Benjamin Currie (Ducati); **3** Luke Stapleford (Triumph); **4** Alastair Seeley (Yamaha); **5** Owen Jenner (Kramer); **6** Shane Richardson (Suzuki); **7** Eunan McGlinchey (Kawasaki); **8** Oliver Barr (Yamaha); **9** Eugene McManus (Ducati); **10** Harry Truelove (Suzuki); **11** TJ Toms (Yamaha); **12** Asher Durham (Kawasaki); **13** Adon Davie (Ducati); **14** Sam Laffins (Kawasaki); **15** Carter Brown (Yamaha).
Fastest lap: Kennedy, 53.183s, 85.76mph/138.02km/h.
Championship points: 1 Jack Kennedy, 162; **2** Ben Currie, 153; **3** Luke Stapleford, 134; **4** Alastair Seeley, 97; **5** Harry Truelove, 84; **6** Eugene McManus, 78.

SNETTERTON, 5-7 July 2024, 2.969-mile/4.778km circuit.
Bennetts British Superbike Championship, Round 5
Race 1 (5 laps, 14.845 miles/23.891km)
1 Storm Stacey (Kawasaki), 10m 49.789s, 82.24mph/132.35km/h.
2 Lewis Rollo (Aprilia); **3** Kyle Ryde (Yamaha); **4** Jason O'Halloran (Kawasaki); **5** Glenn Irwin (Ducati); **6** Christian Iddon (Ducati); **7** Andrew Irwin (Honda); **8** Leon Haslam (BMW); **9** Ryan Vickers (Yamaha); **10** Franco Bourne (Honda); **11** Dean Harrison (Honda); **12** Tom Neave (Kawasaki); **13** Josh Brookes (BMW); **14** Louis Valleley (Kawasaki); **15** Danny Buchan (Kawasaki).
Fastest lap: Stacey, 2m 7.763s, 83.65mph/134.63km/h.

Race 2 (5 laps, 14.845 miles/23.891km)
1 Glenn Irwin (Ducati), 9m 5.477s, 97.96mph/157.65km/h.
2 Tommy Bridewell (Honda); **3** Christian Iddon (Ducati); **4** Kyle Ryde (Yamaha); **5** Andrew Irwin (Honda); **6** Danny Kent (Yamaha); **7** Ryan Vickers (Yamaha); **8** Jason O'Halloran (Kawasaki); **9** Charlie Nesbitt (Honda); **10** Josh Brookes (BMW); **11** Franco Bourne (Honda); **12** Lee Jackson (Honda); **13** Max Cook (Kawasaki); **14** Storm Stacey (Kawasaki); **15** Peter Hickman (BMW).
Fastest lap: G. Irwin, 1m 47.824s, 99.12mph/159.52km/h.

Race 3 (16 laps, 47.504 miles/76.450km)
1 Glenn Irwin (Ducati), 28m 56.592s, 98.47mph/158.47km/h.
2 Tommy Bridewell (Honda); **3** Christian Iddon (Ducati); **4** Danny Kent (Yamaha); **5** Kyle Ryde (Yamaha); **6** Andrew Irwin (Honda); **7** Josh Brookes (BMW); **8** Ryan Vickers (Yamaha); **9** Jason O'Halloran (Kawasaki); **10** Charlie Nesbitt (Honda); **11** Lee Jackson (Honda); **12** Max Cook (Kawasaki); **13** Franco Bourne (Honda); **14** Peter Hickman (BMW); **15** Storm Stacey (Kawasaki).
Fastest lap: Bridewell, 1m 47.768s, 99.17mph/159.6km/h.
Championship points: 1 Glenn Irwin, 177; **2** Tommy Bridewell, 173; **3** Christian Iddon, 156; **4** Kyle Ryde, 147; **5** Danny Kent, 147; **6** Jason O'Halloran, 108.

Quattro Group British Supersport Championship, Round 5
Race 1 (8 laps, 23.752 miles/38.225km)
1 Luke Jones (Ducati), 17m 40.797s, 80.60mph/129.71km/h.
2 Owen Jenner (Kramer); **3** Benjamin Currie (Ducati); **4** Asher Durham (Kawasaki); **5** Luke Stapleford (Triumph); **6** Matt Truelove (Suzuki); **7** Jorel Boerboom (Kawasaki); **8** Harry Truelove (Suzuki); **9** Eugene McManus (Ducati); **10** Oliver Barr (Yamaha); **11** Carter Brown (Yamaha); **12** Jack Nixon (Kramer); **13** Keo Walker (Triumph); **14** Harvey Claridge (Suzuki); **15** Charlie White (Ducati).
Fastest lap: Jack Kennedy, 2m 8.592s, 83.11mph/133.76km/h.

Race 2 (10 laps, 29.690 miles/47.781km)
1 Jack Kennedy (Honda), 18m 49.279s, 94.64mph/152.31km/h.
2 Benjamin Currie (Ducati); **3** Luke Stapleford (Triumph); **4** Harry Truelove (Suzuki); **5** Alastair Seeley (Yamaha); **6** Rhys Irwin (Kawasaki); **7** Shane Richardson (Suzuki); **8** TJ Toms (Yamaha); **9** Carter Brown (Yamaha); **10** Eugene McManus (Ducati); **11** Owen Jenner (Kramer); **12** Cameron Hall (Kawasaki); **13** Matt Truelove (Suzuki); **14** Harvey Claridge (Suzuki); **15** Oliver Barr (Yamaha).
Fastest lap: Stapleford, 1m 51.680s, 95.70mph/154.01km/h.
Championship points: 1 Ben Currie, 197; **2** Jack Kennedy, 187; **3** Luke Stapleford, 172; **4** Harry Truelove, 122; **5** Alastair Seeley, 113; **6** Eugene McManus, 94.

R&G British Talent Cup, Round 3
Race 1 (10 laps, 29.690 miles/47.781km)
1 Lucas Brown (Honda), 24m 17.920s, 73.31mph/117.98km/h.
2 Peter Willis (Honda); **3** Jack Burrows (Honda); **4** Amanuel Brinton (Honda); **5** Daniel Goodman (Honda); **6** Julian Correa (Honda); **7** Eli Banish (Honda); **8** George Bowes (Honda); **9** Alexander Rowan (Honda); **10** Mason Foster (Honda); **11** Ollie Walker (Honda); **12** Harrison Mackay (Honda); **13** Tyler King (Honda); **14** Clayton Edmunds (Honda); **15** Joshua Raymond Jr (Honda).
Fastest lap: Willis, 2m 24.238s, 74.10mph/119.25km/h.

Race 2 (12 laps, 35.628 miles/57.338km)
1 Amanuel Brinton (Honda), 25m 6.622s, 85.12mph/136.99km/h.
2 Lucas Brown (Honda); **3** Julian Correa (Honda); **4** Filip Surowiak (Honda); **5** Ryan Frost (Honda); **6** Mason Foster (Honda); **7** Bill Harris (Honda); **8** Harrison Mackay (Honda); **9** Harley McCabe (Honda); **10** George Bowes (Honda); **11** Josh Bannister (Honda); **12** Eli Banish (Honda); **13** Ollie Walker (Honda); **14** Clayton Edmunds (Honda); **15** Joshua Raymond Jr (Honda).
Fastest lap: Brinton, 2m 3.792s, 86.33mph/138.94km/h.
Championship points: 1 Lucas Brown, 139; **2** Amanuel Brinton, 115; **3** Julian Correa, 91; **4** Ryan Frost, 86; **5** Filip Surowiak, 61; **6** Ronnie Harris, 50.

BRANDS HATCH GP, 19-21 July 2024, 2.433-mile/3.916km circuit.
Bennetts British Superbike Championship, Round 6
Race 1 (20 laps, 48.660 miles/78.311km)
1 Ryan Vickers (Yamaha), 28m 38.129s, 101.96mph/164.09km/h.
2 Tommy Bridewell (Honda); **3** Andrew Irwin (Honda); **4** Glenn Irwin (Ducati); **5** Christian Iddon (Ducati); **6** Kyle Ryde (Yamaha); **7** Leon Haslam (BMW); **8** Lee Jackson (Honda); **9** Jason O'Halloran (Kawasaki); **10** Danny Buchan (Kawasaki); **11** Josh Brookes (BMW); **12** Max Cook (Kawasaki); **13** Luke Hedger (Kawasaki); **14** Billy McConnell (Honda); **15** Peter Hickman (BMW).
Fastest lap: Vickers, 1m 25.167s, 102.85mph/165.52km/h.

Race 2 (5 laps, 12.165 miles/19.578km)
1 Ryan Vickers (Yamaha), 7m 11.170s, 101.58mph/163.48km/h.
2 Tommy Bridewell (Honda); **3** Kyle Ryde (Yamaha); **4** Andrew Irwin (Honda); **5** Leon Haslam (BMW); **6** Christian Iddon (Ducati); **7** Lee Jackson (Honda); **8** Josh Brookes (BMW); **9** Franco Bourne (Honda); **10** Charlie Nesbitt (Honda); **11** Jason O'Halloran (Kawasaki); **12** Peter Hickman (BMW); **13** Max Cook (Kawasaki); **14** Storm Stacey (Kawasaki); **15** Lewis Rollo (Aprilia).
Fastest lap: Vickers, 1m 25.149s, 102.87mph/165.56km/h.

Race 3 (20, laps 48.660 miles/78.311km)
1 Ryan Vickers (Yamaha), 28m 36.586s, 102.06mph/164.25km/h.
2 Christian Iddon (Ducati); **3** Kyle Ryde (Yamaha); **4** Tommy Bridewell (Honda); **5** Andrew Irwin (Honda); **6** Lee Jackson (Honda); **7** Glenn Irwin (Ducati); **8** Jason O'Halloran (Kawasaki); **9** Charlie Nesbitt (Honda); **10** Leon Haslam (BMW); **11** Josh Brookes (BMW); **12** Max Cook (Kawasaki); **13** Peter Hickman (BMW); **14** Billy McConnell (Honda); **15** Danny Kent (Yamaha).
Fastest lap: Vickers, 1m 25.224s, 102.78mph/165.41km/h.
Championship points: 1 Tommy Bridewell, 217; **2** Glenn Irwin, 198; **3** Christian Iddon, 193; **4** Kyle Ryde, 185; **5** Danny Kent, 148; **6** Ryan Vickers, 146.

Quattro Group British Supersport Championship, Round 6
Race 1 (10 laps, 24.330 miles/39.155km)
1 Jack Kennedy (Honda), 14m 48.493s, 98.59mph/158.67km/h.
2 Benjamin Currie (Ducati); **3** Luke Stapleford (Triumph); **4** Alastair Seeley (Yamaha); **5** Richard Cooper (Yamaha); **6** Luke Jones (Ducati); **7** Harry Truelove (Suzuki); **8** TJ Toms (Yamaha); **9** Rhys Irwin (Kawasaki); **10** Shane Richardson (Suzuki); **11** Joe Sheldon-Shaw (Suzuki); **12** Eugene McManus (Ducati); **13** Carter Brown (Yamaha); **14** Eunan McGlinchey (Kawasaki); **15** Asher Durham (Kawasaki).
Fastest lap: Stapleford, 1m 28.050s, 99.48mph/160.10km/h.

Race 2 (16 laps, 38.928 miles/62.649km)
1 Jack Kennedy (Honda), 23m 36.283s, 98.96mph/159.26km/h.
2 Benjamin Currie (Ducati); **3** Richard Cooper (Yamaha); **4** Luke Stapleford (Triumph); **5** Harry Truelove (Suzuki); **6** Luke Jones (Ducati); **7** TJ Toms (Yamaha); **8** Alastair Seeley (Yamaha); **9** Carter Brown (Yamaha); **10** Rhys Irwin (Kawasaki); **11** Shane Richardson (Suzuki); **12** Eugene McManus (Ducati); **13** Joe Sheldon-Shaw (Suzuki); **14** Oliver Barr (Yamaha); **15** Owen Jenner (Kramer).
Fastest lap: Currie, 1m 27.903s, 99.65mph/160.37km/h.
Championship points: 1 Ben Currie, 241; **2** Jack Kennedy, 237; **3** Luke Stapleford, 210; **4** Harry Truelove, 150; **5** Alastair Seeley, 141; **6** Eugene McManus, 102.

R&G British Talent Cup, Round 4
Race 1 (14 laps, 34.062 miles/54.817km)
1 Ryan Frost (Honda), 22m 47.586s, 89.67mph/144.31km/h.
2 Filip Surowiak (Honda); **3** Lucas Brown (Honda); **4** Amanuel Brinton (Honda); **5** Julian Correa (Honda); **6** Harrison Mackay (Honda); **7** Ronnie Harris (Honda); **8** Harley McCabe (Honda); **9** George Bowes (Honda); **10** Clayton Edmunds (Honda); **11** Joshua Raymond Jr (Honda); **12** Scott McPhee (Honda); **13** Kyle Payne (Honda); **14** Mason Foster (Honda); **15** Bill Harris (Honda).
Fastest lap: Brinton, 1m 36.489s, 90.78mph/146.10km/h.

Race 2 (13 laps, 31.629 miles/50.902km)
1 Amanuel Brinton (Honda), 21m 6.725s, 89.89mph/144.66km/h.
2 Lucas Brown (Honda); **3** Filip Surowiak (Honda); **4** Ryan Frost (Honda); **5** Julian Correa (Honda); **6** Harley McCabe (Honda); **7** Harrison Mackay (Honda); **8** Ronnie Harris (Honda); **9** Scott McPhee (Honda); **10** Joshua Raymond Jr (Honda); **11** Kyle Payne (Honda); **12** Mason Foster (Honda); **13** Eli Banish (Honda); **14** Jack Burrows (Honda); **15** Josh Bannister (Honda).
Fastest lap: Brinton, 1m 36.026s, 91.22mph/146.81km/h.
Championship points: 1 Lucas Brown, 175; **2** Amanuel Brinton, 153; **3** Ryan Frost, 124; **4** Julian Correa, 113; **5** Filip Surowiak, 97; **6** Ronnie Harris, 67.

Silverstone MotoGP, 2-4 August 2024, 3.666-mile/5.900km circuit.
R&G British Talent Cup, Round 5
Race 1 (10 laps, 36.600 miles/59.000km)
1 Ryan Frost (Honda), 23m 36.900s, 93.1mph/149.9km/h.
2 Lucas Brown (Honda); **3** Julian Correa (Honda); **4** Amanuel Brinton (Honda); **5** Harrison Mackay (Honda); **6** Mason Foster (Honda); **7** Scott McPhee (Honda); **8** George Bowes (Honda); **9** Clayton Edmunds (Honda); **10** Ronnie Harris (Honda); **11** Kyle Payne (Honda); **12** Harley McCabe (Honda); **13** Filip Surowiak (Honda); **14** Joshua Raymond Jr (Honda); **15** Jack Burrows (Honda).
Fastest lap: Surowiak, 2m 20.390s, 94.01mph/151.31km/h.

Race 2 (10 laps, 36.600 miles/59.000km)
1 Filip Surowiak (Honda), 23m 39.185s, 93.0mph/149.6km/h.
2 Amanuel Brinton (Honda); **3** Lucas Brown (Honda); **4** Ryan Frost (Honda); **5** Julian Correa (Honda); **6** Mason Foster (Honda); **7** Clayton Edmunds (Honda); **8** Harrison Mackay (Honda); **9** Scott McPhee (Honda); **10** Kyle Payne (Honda); **11** Daniel Goodman (Honda); **12** Jack Burrows (Honda); **13** Joshua Raymond Jr (Honda); **14** Peter Willis (Honda); **15** Bill Harris (Honda).
Fastest lap: Correa, 2m 20.336s, 94.04mph/151.35km/h.
Championship points: 1 Lucas Brown, 211; **2** Amanuel Brinton, 186; **3** Ryan Frost, 162; **4** Julian Correa, 140; **5** Filip Surowiak, 125; **6** Mason Foster, 74.

THRUXTON, 9-11 August 2024, 2.356-mile/3.792km circuit.
Bennetts British Superbike Championship, Round 7
Race 1 (20 laps, 47.120 miles/75.832km)
1 Kyle Ryde (Yamaha), 25m 42.225s, 109.99mph/177.01km/h.
2 Ryan Vickers (Yamaha); **3** Jason O'Halloran (Kawasaki); **4** Tommy Bridewell (Honda); **5** Billy McConnell (Honda); **6** Leon Haslam (BMW); **7** Lee Jackson (Honda); **8** Max Cook (Kawasaki); **9** Christian Iddon (Ducati); **10** Peter Hickman (BMW); **11** Lewis Rollo (Aprilia); **12** Alex Olsen (Honda); **13** Storm Stacey (Kawasaki); **14** Glenn Irwin (Ducati); **15** Danny Buchan (Kawasaki).
Fastest lap: Cook, 1m 16.168s, 111.35mph/179.2km/h.

Race 2 (10 laps, 23.560 miles/37.916km)
1 Ryan Vickers (Yamaha), 13m 13.054s, 106.94mph/172.1km/h.
2 Max Cook (Kawasaki); **3** Danny Kent (Yamaha); **4** Josh Brookes (BMW); **5** Billy McConnell (Honda); **6** Christian Iddon (Ducati); **7** Tommy Bridewell (Honda); **8** Kyle Ryde (Yamaha); **9** Leon Haslam (BMW); **10** Storm Stacey (Kawasaki); **11** Lee Jackson (Honda); **12** Charlie Nesbitt (Honda); **13** Peter Hickman (BMW); **14** Andrew Irwin (Honda); **15** Danny Buchan (Kawasaki).
Fastest lap: Vickers, 1m 14.949s, 113.16mph/182.12km/h.

Race 3 (20 laps, 47.120 miles/75.832km)
1 Ryan Vickers (Yamaha), 25m 34.560s, 110.54mph/177.9km/h.
2 Danny Kent (Yamaha); **3** Billy McConnell (Honda); **4** Kyle Ryde (Yamaha); **5** Charlie Nesbitt (Honda); **6** Tommy Bridewell (Honda); **7** Lee Jackson (Honda); **8** Josh Brookes (BMW); **9** Andrew Irwin (Honda); **10** Leon Haslam (BMW); **11** Lewis Rollo (Aprilia); **12** Peter Hickman (BMW); **13** Christian Iddon (Ducati); **14** Storm Stacey (Kawasaki); **15** Glenn Irwin (Ducati).
Fastest lap: Nesbitt, 1m 15.845s, 111.82mph/179.97km/h.
Championship points: 1 Tommy Bridewell, 248; **2** Kyle Ryde, 223; **3** Christian Iddon, 213; **4** Glenn Irwin, 201; **5** Ryan Vickers, 198; **6** Danny Kent, 178.

Quattro Group British Supersport Championship, Round 7
Race 1 (5 laps, 11.780 miles/18.958km)
1 Luke Stapleford (Triumph), 6m 26.870s, 109.61mph/176.4km/h.
2 Jack Kennedy (Honda); **3** Alastair Seeley (Yamaha); **4** Benjamin Currie (Ducati); **5** Eugene McManus (Ducati); **6** Luke Jones (Ducati); **7** TJ Toms (Yamaha); **8** Dean Harrison (Honda); **9** Carter Brown (Yamaha); **10** Rhys Irwin (Kawasaki); **11** Shane Richardson (Suzuki); **12** Cameron Dawson (Kawasaki); **13** Joe Sheldon-Shaw (Suzuki); **14** Mikey Hardie (Kawasaki); **15** Lee Johnston (Triumph).
Fastest lap: Kennedy, 1m 16.384s, 111.03mph/178.70km/h.

Race 2 (18 laps, 42.408 miles/68.249km)
1 Jack Kennedy (Honda), 23m 14.747s, 109.45mph/176.14km/h.
2 Luke Stapleford (Triumph); **3** Benjamin Currie (Ducati); **4** Eugene McManus (Ducati); **5** Alastair Seeley (Yamaha); **6** Carter Brown (Yamaha); **7** Dean Harrison (Honda); **8** Cameron Dawson (Kawasaki); **9** Rhys Irwin (Kawasaki); **10** Owen Jenner (Kramer); **11** Shane Richardson (Suzuki); **12** Asher Durham (Kawasaki); **13** Joe Sheldon-Shaw (Suzuki); **14** Adon Davie (Ducati); **15** Lee Johnston (Triumph).
Fastest lap: Stapleford, 1m 16.830s, 110.39mph/177.66km/h.
Championship points: 1 Jack Kennedy, 284; **2** Ben Currie, 279; **3** Luke Stapleford, 257; **4** Alastair Seeley, 177; **5** Harry Truelove, 150; **6** Eugene McManus, 136.

R&G British Talent Cup, Round 6
Race 1 (14 laps, 32.984 miles/53.083km)
1 Marco Morelli (Honda), 19m 20.071s, 102.35mph/164.72km/h.
2 Ryan Frost (Honda); **3** Julian Correa (Honda); **4** Filip Surowiak (Honda); **5** Lucas Brown (Honda); **6** Ronnie Harris (Honda); **7** Harrison Mackay (Honda); **8** Mason Foster (Honda); **9** Joshua Raymond Jr (Honda); **10** Scott McPhee (Honda); **11** Clayton Edmunds (Honda); **12** Kyle Payne (Honda); **13** Daniel Goodman (Honda); **14** Bill Harris (Honda); **15** Ben Jolliffe (Honda).
Fastest lap: Morelli, 1m 21.763s, 103.73mph/166.94km/h.

Race 2 (12 laps, 28.272 miles/45.499km)
1 Marco Morelli (Honda), 16m 35.643s, 102.22mph/164.51km/h.
2 Filip Surowiak (Honda); **3** Julian Correa (Honda); **4** Lucas Brown (Honda); **5** Amanuel Brinton (Honda); **6** Ronnie Harris (Honda); **7** Harrison Mackay (Honda); **8** Clayton Edmunds (Honda); **9** Joshua Raymond Jr (Honda); **10** Scott McPhee (Honda); **11** Daniel Goodman (Honda); **12** Mason Foster (Honda); **13** Jack Burrows (Honda); **14** George Bowes (Honda); **15** Ben Jolliffe (Honda).
Fastest lap: Brinton, 1m 21.623s, 103.91mph/167.23km/h.
Championship points: 1 Lucas Brown, 235; **2** Amanuel Brinton, 197; **3** Ryan Frost, 182; **4** Julian Correa, 172; **5** Filip Surowiak, 158; **6** Ronnie Harris, 93.

CADWELL PARK, 24-26 August 2024, 2.180-mile/3.508km circuit.
Bennetts British Superbike Championship, Round 8
Race 1 (18 laps, 39.240 miles/63.151km)
1 Kyle Ryde (Yamaha), 26m 4.788s, 90.27mph/145.28km/h.
2 Lee Jackson (Honda); **3** Charlie Nesbitt (Honda); **4** Tommy Bridewell (Honda); **5** Glenn Irwin (Ducati); **6** Jason O'Halloran (Kawasaki); **7** Josh Brookes (BMW); **8** Leon Haslam (BMW); **9** Billy McConnell (Honda); **10** Danny Buchan (Kawasaki); **11** Storm Stacey (Kawasaki); **12** Peter Hickman (BMW); **13** Christian Iddon (Ducati); **14** Danny Kent (Yamaha); **15** Tom Ward (Honda).
Fastest lap: Jackson, 1m 28.253s, 90.93mph/146.34km/h.

Race 2 (12 laps, 26.160 miles/42.100km)
1 Tommy Bridewell (Honda), 17m 23.051s, 90.28mph/145.29km/h.
2 Kyle Ryde (Yamaha); **3** Lee Jackson (Honda); **4** Charlie Nesbitt (Honda); **5** Glenn Irwin (Ducati); **6** Ryan Vickers (Yamaha); **7** Josh Brookes (BMW); **8** Leon Haslam (BMW); **9** Christian Iddon (Ducati); **10** Jason O'Halloran (Kawasaki); **11** Danny Buchan (Kawasaki); **12** Billy McConnell (Honda); **13** Storm Stacey (Kawasaki); **14** Tom Ward (Honda); **15** Peter Hickman (BMW).
Fastest lap: Nesbitt, 1m 25.882s, 91.38mph/147.06km/h.

Race 3 (20, laps 43.600 miles/70.167km)
1 Kyle Ryde (Yamaha), 28m 52.399s, 90.60mph/145.81km/h.
2 Tommy Bridewell (Honda); **3** Lee Jackson (Honda); **4** Charlie Nesbitt (Honda); **5** Glenn Irwin (Ducati); **6** Josh Brookes (BMW); **7** Leon Haslam (BMW); **8** Christian Iddon (Ducati); **9** Peter Hickman (BMW); **10** Billy McConnell (Honda); **11** Danny Buchan (Kawasaki); **12** Danny Kent (Yamaha); **13** Storm Stacey (Kawasaki); **14** Max Cook (Kawasaki); **15** Bradley Perie (Kawasaki).

Fastest lap: Ryan Vickers, 1m 25.891s, 91.37mph/147.04km/h.
Championship points: **1** Tommy Bridewell, 294; **2** Kyle Ryde, 275; **3** Glenn Irwin, 234; **4** Christian Iddon, 231; **5** Ryan Vickers, 208; **6** Danny Kent, 184.

Quattro Group British Supersport Championship, Round 8
Race 1 (12 laps, 26.160 miles/42.1km)
1 Luke Stapleford (Triumph), 17m 53.221s, 87.75mph/141.22km/h.
2 Benjamin Currie (Ducati); **3** Harry Truelove (Suzuki); **4** Dean Harrison (Honda); **5** Eugene McManus (Ducati); **6** TJ Toms (Yamaha); **7** Rhys Irwin (Kawasaki); **8** Shane Richardson (Suzuki); **9** Alastair Seeley (Yamaha); **10** Matt Truelove (Suzuki); **11** Max Wadsworth (Triumph); **12** Owen Jenner (Kramer); **13** Joe Sheldon-Shaw (Suzuki); **14** Carter Brown (Yamaha); **15** Cameron Dawson (Kawasaki).
Fastest lap: Jack Kennedy, 1m 28.388s, 88.79mph/142.89km/h.

Race 2 (16 laps, 34.880 miles/56.134km)
1 Luke Stapleford (Triumph), 23m 50.082s, 87.80mph/141.3km/h.
2 Jack Kennedy (Honda); **3** Eugene McManus (Ducati); **4** TJ Toms (Yamaha); **5** Rhys Irwin (Kawasaki); **6** Harry Truelove (Suzuki); **7** Alastair Seeley (Yamaha); **8** Max Wadsworth (Triumph); **9** Cameron Dawson (Kawasaki); **10** Joe Sheldon-Shaw (Suzuki); **11** Matt Truelove (Suzuki); **12** Oliver Barr (Yamaha); **13** Cameron Hall (Kawasaki); **14** Owen Jenner (Kramer); **15** Asher Durham (Kawasaki).
Fastest lap: Kennedy, 1m 28.626s, 88.55mph/142.51km/h.
Championship points: **1** Luke Stapleford, 307; **2** Jack Kennedy, 306; **3** Ben Currie, 301; **4** Alastair Seeley, 197; **5** Harry Truelove, 184; **6** Eugene McManus, 172.

OULTON PARK, 13-15 September 2024, 2.692-mile/4.332km circuit.
Bennetts British Superbike Championship, Round 9 – Start of Showdown
Race 1 (18 laps, 48.456 miles/77.982km)
1 Kyle Ryde (Yamaha), 28m 29.529s, 102.04mph/164.22km/h.
2 Glenn Irwin (Ducati); **3** Lee Jackson (Honda); **4** Josh Brookes (BMW); **5** Ryan Vickers (Yamaha); **6** Leon Haslam (BMW); **7** Danny Kent (Yamaha); **8** Peter Hickman (BMW); **9** Jason O'Halloran (Kawasaki); **10** Max Cook (Kawasaki); **11** Rory Skinner (BMW); **12** Andrew Irwin (Honda); **13** Billy McConnell (Honda); **14** Storm Stacey (Kawasaki); **15** Bradley Perie (Kawasaki).
Fastest lap: Ryde, 1m 33.943s, 103.16mph/166.02km/h.

Race 2 (10 laps, 26.920 miles/43.324km)
1 Glenn Irwin (Ducati), 17m 42.973s, 91.17mph/146.72km/h.
2 Danny Kent (Yamaha); **3** Leon Haslam (BMW); **4** Tommy Bridewell (Honda); **5** Lewis Rollo (Aprilia); **6** Jason O'Halloran (Kawasaki); **7** Lee Jackson (Honda); **8** Storm Stacey (Kawasaki); **9** Andrew Irwin (Honda); **10** Fraser Rogers (Honda); **11** Billy McConnell (Honda); **12** Ryan Vickers (Yamaha); **13** Kyle Ryde (Yamaha); **14** Peter Hickman (BMW); **15** Max Cook (Kawasaki).
Fastest lap: G. Irwin, 1m 44.076s, 93.11mph/149.85km/h.

Race 3 (5 laps, 13.460 miles/21.662km)
1 Kyle Ryde (Yamaha), 8m 50.621s, 91.32mph/146.97km/h.
2 Tommy Bridewell (Honda); **3** Storm Stacey (Kawasaki); **4** Max Cook (Kawasaki); **5** Danny Kent (Yamaha); **6** Christian Iddon (Ducati); **7** Lee Jackson (Honda); **8** Andrew Irwin (Honda); **9** Glenn Irwin (Ducati); **10** Josh Brookes (BMW); **11** Peter Hickman (BMW); **12** Richard Kerr (Honda); **13** Leon Haslam (BMW); **14** Brayden Elliott (Kawasaki); **15** Luke Hedger (Kawasaki).
Fastest lap: Ryde, 1m 44.567s, 92.68mph/149.15km/h.
Championship points: **1** Tommy Bridewell, 334; **2** Kyle Ryde, 328; **3** Glenn Irwin, 289; **4** Christian Iddon, 245; **5** Danny Kent, 234; **6** Ryan Vickers, 228.

Quattro Group British Supersport Championship, Round 9
Race 1 (9 laps, 24.228 miles/38.991km)
1 Jack Kennedy (Honda), 14m 41.865s, 98.90mph/159.16km/h.
2 Luke Stapleford (Triumph); **3** Benjamin Currie (Ducati); **4** Harry Truelove (Suzuki); **5** Rhys Irwin (Kawasaki); **6** Eugene McManus (Ducati); **7** Dean Harrison (Honda); **8** TJ Toms (Yamaha); **9** Shane Richardson (Suzuki); **10** Lee Johnston (Triumph); **11** Richard Cooper (Yamaha); **12** Carter Brown (Yamaha); **13** Max Wadsworth (Triumph); **14** Joe Sheldon-Shaw (Suzuki); **15** Eugene McManus (Ducati).
Fastest lap: Kennedy, 1m 37.055s, 99.85mph/160.69km/h.

Race 2 (12 laps, 32.304 miles/51.988km)
1 Richard Cooper (Yamaha), 21m 40.253s, 89.44mph/143.94km/h.
2 Rhys Irwin (Kawasaki); **3** Luke Stapleford (Triumph); **4** Jack Kennedy (Honda); **5** Alastair Seeley (Yamaha); **6** Eugene McManus (Ducati); **7** Benjamin Currie (Ducati); **8** TJ Toms (Yamaha); **9** Dean Harrison (Honda); **10** Oliver Barr (Yamaha); **11** Carter Brown (Yamaha); **12** Lee Johnston (Triumph); **13** Jack Nixon (Kramer); **14** Harvey Claridge (Suzuki); **15** Joe Sheldon-Shaw (Suzuki).
Fastest lap: Irwin, 1m 45.423s, 91.92mph/147.94km/h.
Championship points: **1** Jack Kennedy, 349; **2** Luke Stapleford, 349; **3** Ben Currie, 333; **4** Alastair Seeley, 213; **5** Harry Truelove, 202; **6** Eugene McManus, 200.

R&G British Talent Cup, Round 7
Race 1 (12 laps, 32.304 miles/51.988km)
1 Ryan Frost (Honda), 21m 38.321s, 89.57mph/144.15km/h.
2 Julian Correa (Honda); **3** Lucas Brown (Honda); **4** Filip Surowiak (Honda); **5** Harrison Mackay (Honda); **6** Amanuel Brinton (Honda); **7** Harley McCabe (Honda); **8** Ronnie Harris (Honda); **9** George Bowes (Honda); **10** Scott McPhee (Honda); **11** Mason Foster (Honda); **12** Clayton Edmunds (Honda); **13** Alexander Rowan (Honda); **14** Charlie Barnes (Honda); **15** Ollie Walker (Honda).
Fastest lap: Frost, 1m 46.779s, 90.76mph/146.06km/h.

Race 2 (10 laps, 26.920 miles/43.324km)
1 Julian Correa (Honda), 20m 9.236s, 80.14mph/128.97km/h.
2 Filip Surowiak (Honda); **3** Amanuel Brinton (Honda); **4** Harley McCabe (Honda); **5** Ryan Frost (Honda); **6** Clayton Edmunds (Honda); **7** Jack Burrows (Honda); **8** Peter Willis (Honda); **9** George Bowes (Honda); **10** Alexander Rowan (Honda); **11** Harrison Mackay (Honda); **12** Scott McPhee (Honda); **13** Bill Harris (Honda); **14** Joshua Raymond Jr (Honda); **15** Finnan Wherity (Honda).
Fastest lap: Brinton, 1m 57.746s, 82.30mph/132.46km/h.
Championship points: 1 Lucas Brown, 251; **2** Amanuel Brinton, 223; **3** Ryan Frost, 218; **4** Julian Correa, 217; **5** Filip Surowiak, 191; **6** Harrison Mackay, 107.

DONINGTON PARK INTERNATIONAL, 27-29 September 2024, 2.822-mile/4.452km circuit.
Bennetts British Superbike Championship, Round 10
Race 1 (20 laps, 49.740 miles/80.049km)
1 Kyle Ryde (Yamaha), 29m 25.982s, 101.33mph/163.07km/h.
2 Tommy Bridewell (Honda); **3** Glenn Irwin (Ducati); **4** Andrew Irwin (Honda); **5** Danny Kent (Yamaha); **6** Charlie Nesbitt (Honda); **7** Ryan Vickers (Yamaha); **8** Lee Jackson (Honda); **9** Josh Brookes (BMW); **10** Christian Iddon (Ducati); **11** Leon Haslam (BMW); **12** Max Cook (Kawasaki); **13** Jason O'Halloran (Kawasaki); **14** Peter Hickman (BMW); **15** Rory Skinner (BMW).
Fastest lap: Bridewell, 1m 27.741s, 102.05mph/164.24km/h.

Race 2 (12 laps, 29.844 miles/48.029km)
1 Glenn Irwin (Ducati), 17m 39.870s, 101.25mph/162.95km/h.
2 Tommy Bridewell (Honda); **3** Kyle Ryde (Yamaha); **4** Danny Kent (Yamaha); **5** Charlie Nesbitt (Honda); **6** Andrew Irwin (Honda); **7** Lee Jackson (Honda); **8** Christian Iddon (Ducati); **9** Max Cook (Kawasaki); **10** Josh Brookes (BMW); **11** Ryan Vickers (Yamaha); **12** Jason O'Halloran (Kawasaki); **13** Peter Hickman (BMW); **14** Storm Stacey (Kawasaki); **15** Rory Skinner (BMW).
Fastest lap: G. Irwin, 1m 27.345s, 102.51mph/164.98km/h.

Race 3 (18 laps, 44.766 miles/72.044km)
1 Kyle Ryde (Yamaha), 26m 31.691s, 101.17mph/162.82km/h.
2 Danny Kent (Yamaha); **3** Ryan Vickers (Yamaha); **4** Glenn Irwin (Ducati); **5** Tommy Bridewell (Honda); **6** Andrew Irwin (Honda); **7** Charlie Nesbitt (Honda); **8** Max Cook (Kawasaki); **9** Lee Jackson (Honda); **10** Leon Haslam (BMW); **11** Josh Brookes (BMW); **12** Rory Skinner (BMW); **13** Storm Stacey (Kawasaki); **14** Bradley Perie (Kawasaki); **15** Lewis Rollo (Aprilia).
Fastest lap: Ryde, 1m 27.827s, 101.95mph/164.08km/h.
Championship points: **1** Kyle Ryde, 398; **2** Tommy Bridewell, 394; **3** Glenn Irwin, 352; **4** Danny Kent, 290; **5** Ryan Vickers, 265; **6** Christian Iddon, 261.

Quattro Group British Supersport Championship, Round 10
Race 1 (10 laps, 24.870 miles/40.024km)
1 Jack Kennedy (Honda), 15m 12.607s, 97.96mph/157.65km/h.
2 Benjamin Currie (Ducati); **3** TJ Toms (Yamaha); **4** Harry Truelove (Suzuki); **5** Eugene McManus (Ducati); **6** Lee Johnston (Triumph); **7** Owen Jenner (Kramer); **8** Alastair Seeley (Yamaha); **9** Dean Harrison (Honda); **10** Rhys Irwin (Kawasaki); **11** Eugene McManus (Ducati); **12** Cameron Dawson (Kawasaki); **13** Joe Sheldon-Shaw (Suzuki); **14** Oliver Barr (Yamaha); **15** Cameron Fraser (Suzuki).
Fastest lap: Kennedy, 1m 30.515s, 98.92mph/159.20km/h.

Race 2 (16 laps, 39.792 miles/64.039km)
1 Luke Stapleford (Triumph), 24m 19.342s, 98.08mph/157.84km/h.
2 Jack Kennedy (Honda); **3** Benjamin Currie (Ducati); **4** TJ Toms (Yamaha); **5** Eugene McManus (Ducati); **6** Rhys Irwin (Kawasaki); **7** Joe Sheldon-Shaw (Suzuki); **8** Dean Harrison (Honda); **9** Owen Jenner (Kramer); **10** Lee Johnston (Triumph); **11** Harry Truelove (Suzuki); **12** Shane Richardson (Suzuki); **13** Carter Brown (Yamaha); **14** Oliver Barr (Yamaha); **15** Max Wadsworth (Triumph).
Fastest lap: McManus, 1m 30.455s, 98.99mph/159.31km/h.
Championship points: **1** Jack Kennedy, 396; **2** Ben Currie, 375; **3** Luke Stapleford, 374; **4** Eugene McManus, 232; **5** Harry Truelove, 226; **6** Alastair Seeley, 225.

R&G British Talent Cup, Round 8
Race 1 (14 laps, 34.818 miles/56.034km)
1 Lucas Brown (Honda), 23m 35.821s, 88.44mph/142.33km/h.
2 Filip Surowiak (Honda); **3** Amanuel Brinton (Honda); **4** Harley McCabe (Honda); **5** Julian Correa (Honda); **6** Charlie Barnes (Honda); **7** George Bowes (Honda); **8** Jack Burrows (Honda); **9** Clayton Edmunds (Honda); **10** Alexander Rowan (Honda); **11** Mason Foster (Honda); **12** Scott McPhee (Honda); **13** Ben Jolliffe (Honda); **14** Bill Harris (Honda); **15** Ollie Walker (Honda).
Fastest lap: Brown, 1m 39.893s, 89.64mph/144.26km/h.

Race 2 (14 laps, 34.818 miles/56.034km)
1 Harley McCabe (Honda), 23m 30.736s, 88.76mph/142.2km/h.
2 Ryan Frost (Honda); **3** Julian Correa (Honda); **4** Amanuel Brinton (Honda); **5** Clayton Edmunds (Honda); **6** Alexander Rowan (Honda); **7** Mason Foster (Honda); **8** Scott McPhee (Honda); **9** Kyle Payne (Honda); **10** Ollie Walker (Honda); **11** Peter Willis (Honda); **12** Ben Jolliffe (Honda); **13** Daniel Goodman (Honda); **14** Josh Bannister (Honda); **15** Charlie Huntingford (Honda).
Fastest lap: Correa, 1m 39.814s, 89.71mph/144.37km/h.

Race 3 (14 laps, 34.818 miles/56.034km)
1 Ryan Frost (Honda), 23m 35.098s, 88.49mph/142.41km/h.
2 Harley McCabe (Honda); **3** Filip Surowiak (Honda); **4** Amanuel Brinton (Honda); **5** Julian Correa (Honda); **6** Harrison Mackay (Honda); **7** Scott McPhee (Honda); **8** Lucas Brown (Honda); **9** Mason Foster (Honda); **10** Peter Willis (Honda); **11** Charlie Barnes (Honda); **12** Clayton Edmunds (Honda); **13** Jack Burrows (Honda); **14** George Bowes (Honda); **15** Bill Harris (Honda).
Fastest lap: Frost, 1m 40.008s, 89.53mph/144.09km/h.
Championship points: **1** Lucas Brown, 284; **2** Amanuel Brinton, 265; **3** Ryan Frost, 263; **4** Julian Correa, 255; **5** Filip Surowiak, 227; **6** Harley McCabe 143.

BRANDS HATCH GP, 11-13 October 2024, 2.433-mile/3.916km circuit.
Bennetts British Superbike Championship, Round 11
Race 1 (20 laps, 48.660 miles/78.311km)
1 Danny Kent (Yamaha), 32m 30.732s, 89.81mph/144.54km/h.
2 Ryan Vickers (Yamaha); **3** Tommy Bridewell (Honda); **4** Kyle Ryde (Yamaha); **5** Peter Hickman (BMW); **6** Max Cook (Kawasaki); **7** Josh Brookes (BMW); **8** Lewis Rollo (Aprilia); **9** Storm Stacey (Kawasaki); **10** James Westmoreland (Honda); **11** Andrew Irwin (Honda); **12** Danny Buchan (Kawasaki); **13** Lee Jackson (Honda); **14** Luke Hedger (Kawasaki); **15** Brayden Elliott (Kawasaki).
Fastest lap: Kent, 1m 35.810s, 91.42mph/147.14km/h.

Race 2 (12 laps, 29.196 miles/46.986km)
1 Tommy Bridewell (Honda), 17m 9.030s, 102.15mph/164.39km/h.
2 Kyle Ryde (Yamaha); **3** Ryan Vickers (Yamaha); **4** Danny Kent (Yamaha); **5** Josh Brookes (BMW); **6** Andrew Irwin (Honda); **7** Max Cook (Kawasaki); **8** Peter Hickman (BMW); **9** Charlie Nesbitt (Honda); **10** Glenn Irwin (Ducati); **11** Leon Haslam (BMW); **12** Lee Jackson (Honda); **13** Storm Stacey (Kawasaki); **14** Billy McConnell (Honda); **15** Danny Buchan (Kawasaki).
Fastest lap: Bridewell, 1m 24.994s, 103.06mph/165.86km/h.

Race 3 (20 laps, 48.660 miles/78.311km)
1 Kyle Ryde (Yamaha), 28m 37.367s, 102.01mph/164.17km/h.
2 Tommy Bridewell (Honda); **3** Ryan Vickers (Yamaha); **4** Danny Kent (Yamaha); **5** Max Cook (Kawasaki); **6** Josh Brookes (BMW); **7** Glenn Irwin (Ducati); **8** Charlie Nesbitt (Honda); **9** Andrew Irwin (Honda); **10** Billy McConnell (Honda); **11** Peter Hickman (BMW); **12** Storm Stacey (Kawasaki); **13** Lewis Rollo (Aprilia); **14** Danny Buchan (Kawasaki); **15** Brayden Elliott (Kawasaki).
Fastest lap: Bridewell, 1m 24.759s, 103.34mph/166.32km/h.

Quattro Group British Supersport Championship, Round 11
Race 1 (3 laps, 7.299 miles/11.747km)
1 Jack Kennedy (Honda), 5m 18.054s, 82.62mph/132.96km/h.
2 Carter Brown (Yamaha); **3** Zak Corderoy (Yamaha); **4** Keo Walker (Triumph); **5** Oliver Barr (Yamaha); **6** Tom Tunstall (Ducati); **7** Eugene McManus (Ducati); **8** Joe Farragher (Kawasaki); **9** Adon Davie (Ducati); **10** Jef Van Calster (Ducati); **11** Max Morgan (Kawasaki); **12** Lucca Allen (Kalex); **13** Cameron Hall (Kawasaki); **14** Owen Jenner (Kramer); **15** Jamie Coward (Triumph).
Fastest lap: Dean Harrison, 1m 44.190s, 84.07mph/135.30km/h.

Race 2 (16 laps, 38.928 miles/62.649km)
1 Jack Kennedy (Honda), 23m 33.731s, 99.14mph/159.55km/h.
2 Luke Stapleford (Triumph); **3** Eugene McManus (Ducati); **4** Owen Jenner (Kramer); **5** Rhys Irwin (Kawasaki); **6** Dean Harrison (Honda); **7** Shane Richardson (Suzuki); **8** Oliver Barr (Yamaha); **9** Lee Johnston (Triumph); **10** Carter Brown (Yamaha); **11** Eugene McManus (Ducati); **12** Cameron Dawson (Kawasaki); **13** Zak Corderoy (Yamaha); **14** Harvey Claridge (Suzuki); **15** Harry Truelove (Suzuki).
Fastest lap: Kennedy, 1m 27.647s, 99.94mph/160.84km/h.

Final British Superbike Championship points:

1	Bradley Ray	1192
2	Glenn Irwin	1171
3	Tommy Bridewell	1141
4	Lee Jackson	1095
5	Jason O'Halloran	1087
6	Kyle Ryde	1077

7 Tarran Mackenzie, 1031; **8** Rory Skinner, 1017; **9** Peter Hickman, 283; **10** Danny Buchan, 272; **11** Leon Haslam, 205; **12** Tom Sykes, 187; **13** Andrew Irwin, 181; **14** Josh Brookes, 161; **15** Christian Iddon, 135.

Final British Supersport Championship points:

1	Jack Kennedy	401
2	Bradley Perie	359
3	Harry Truelove	275
4	Lee Johnston	257
5	Jamie van Sikkelerus	229
6	Luke Stapleford	200

7 Rhys Irwin, 155; **8** Eugene McManus, 153; **9** Damon Rees, 145; **10** Luke Jones, 135; **11** Jamie Perrin, 124; **12** Ash Barnes, 73; **13** Max Ingham, 55; **14** Caolán Irwin, 55; **15** Scott Swann, 52.

Final British Talent Cup points:

1	Johnny Garness	336
2	Carter Brown	232
3	Harrison Crosby	181
4	Rhys Stephenson	177
5	Lucas Brown	151
6	Harrison Dessoy	143

7 Evan Belford, 142; **8** Kiyano Veijer, 138; **9** Ryan Hitchcock, 103; **10** Matthew Ruisbroek, 98; **11** Harley McCabe, 95; **12** Julian Correa, 92; **13** Sullivan Mounsey, 88; **14** Harrison Mackay, 85; **15** Bailey Stuart-Campbell, 74.

Final British Superbike Championship points:

1	Kyle Ryde	487
2	Tommy Bridewell	486
3	Glenn Irwin	382
4	Danny Kent	373
5	Ryan Vickers	349
6	Christian Iddon	261

7 Lee Jackson, 251; **8** Josh Brookes, 249; **9** Leon Haslam, 228; **10** Andrew Irwin, 226; **11** Charlie Nesbitt, 223; **12** Max Cook, 203; **13** Jason O'Halloran, 187; **14** Storm Stacey, 141; **15** Peter Hickman, 120.

Final British Supersport Championship points:

1	Jack Kennedy	466
2	Luke Stapleford	404
3	Ben Currie	375
4	Eugene McManus	279
5	Harry Truelove	230
6	Alastair Seeley	225

7 Rhys Irwin, 222; **8** TJ Toms, 184; **9** Shane Richardson, 146; **10** Carter Brown, 111; **11** Dean Harrison, 102; **12** Oliver Barr, 86; **13** Luke Jones, 75; **14** Brad Perie, 70; **15** Richard Cooper, 66.

Final British Talent Cup points:

1	Lucas Brown	284
2	Amanuel Brinton	265
3	Ryan Frost	263
4	Julian Correa	255
5	Filip Surowiak	227
6	Harley McCabe	143

7 Clayton Edmunds, 120; **8** Harrison Mackay, 117; **9** Mason Foster, 112; **10** Ronnie Harris, 101; **11** Scott McPhee, 78; **12** George Bowes, 77; **13** Jack Burrows, 58; **14** Peter Willis, 58; **15** Ollie Walker, 53.

Supersport World Championship

Round 1, PHILLIP ISLAND, Australia, 23-25 February 2024, 2.762mile/4.445km circuit
Race 1 (18 laps, 49.716 miles/80.010km)
1 Yari Montella, ITA (Ducati), 28m 54.554s, 103.184mph/166.058km/h.
2 Stefano Manzi, ITA (Yamaha); **3** Marcel Schroetter, GER (MV Agusta); **4** Federico Caricasulo, ITA (MV Agusta); **5** Oliver Bayliss, AUS (Ducati); **6** Bahattin Sofuoglu, TUR (MV Agusta); **7** Jorge Navarro, ESP (Triumph); **8** John McPhee, GBR (Triumph); **9** Lucas Mahias, FRA (Yamaha); **10** Tom Toparis, AUS (Yamaha); **11** Yeray Ruiz, ESP (Yamaha); **12** Anupab Sarmoon, THA (Yamaha); **13** Marcel Brenner, SUI

(Kawasaki); **14** Ondrej Vostatek, CZE (Triumph); **15** Khairul Idham Bin Pawi, MAS (Honda).
Fastest lap: Montella, 1m 31.271s, 108.941mph/175.324km/h.

Race 2 (9 laps, 24.858 miles/40.005km)
1 Yari Montella, ITA (Ducati), 13m 54.138s, 107.283mph/172.655km/h.
2 Marcel Schroetter, GER (MV Agusta); **3** Adrian Huertas, ESP (Ducati); **4** Federico Caricasulo, ITA (MV Agusta); **5** Valentin Debise, FRA (Yamaha); **6** Bahattin Sofuoglu, TUR (MV Agusta); **7** Lucas Mahias, FRA (Yamaha); **8** John McPhee, GBR (Triumph); **9** Lorenzo Baldassarri, ITA (Ducati); **10** Oliver Bayliss, AUS (Ducati); **11** Yeray Ruiz, ESP (Yamaha); **12** Jorge Navarro, ESP (Triumph); **13** Thomas Booth-Amos, GBR (Triumph); **14** Niki Tuuli, FIN (Ducati); **15** Anupab Sarmoon, THA (Yamaha).
Fastest lap: Schroetter, 1m 31.53s, 108.633mph/174.828km/h.
Championship points: 1 Montella, 50; **2** Schroetter, 36; **3** Caricasulo, 26; **4** Manzi, 20; **5** Sofuoglu, 20; **6** Bayliss, 17.

Round 2, CATALUNYA, Spain, 22-24 March 2024, 2.875-mile/4.627km circuit
Race 1 (18 laps, 52.087 miles/83.826km)
1 Adrian Huertas, ESP (Ducati), 31m 47.366s, 98.310mph/158.215km/h.
2 Stefano Manzi, ITA (Yamaha); **3** Marcel Schroetter, GER (MV Agusta); **4** Yari Montella, ITA (Ducati); **5** Valentin Debise, FRA (Yamaha); **6** Federico Caricasulo, ITA (MV Agusta); **7** Jorge Navarro, ESP (Triumph); **8** Can Oncu, TUR (Kawasaki); **9** Andrea Antonelli, ITA (Ducati); **10** Bahattin Sofuoglu, TUR (MV Agusta); **11** Yeray Ruiz, ESP (Yamaha); **12** John McPhee, GBR (Triumph); **13** Thomas Booth-Amos, GBR (Triumph); **14** Glenn Van Straalen, NED (Yamaha); **15** Lorenzo Dalla Porta, ITA (Yamaha).
Fastest lap: Navarro, 1m 45.333s, 98.900mph/159.164km/h.

Race 2 (6 laps, 17.362 miles/27.942km)
1 Stefano Manzi, ITA (Yamaha), 10m 32.356s, 98.844mph/159.074km/h.
2 Marcel Schroetter, GER (MV Agusta); **3** Lucas Mahias, FRA (Yamaha); **4** Yari Montella, ITA (Ducati); **5** Valentin Debise, FRA (Yamaha); **6** Bahattin Sofuoglu, TUR (MV Agusta); **7** Jorge Navarro, ESP (Triumph); **8** Federico Caricasulo, ITA (MV Agusta); **9** Can Oncu, TUR (Kawasaki); **10** Glenn Van Straalen, NED (Yamaha); **11** Oliver Bayliss, AUS (Ducati); **12** Tom Edwards, AUS (Ducati); **13** Yeray Ruiz, ESP (Yamaha); **14** Lorenzo Dalla Porta, ITA (Yamaha); **15** Thomas Booth-Amos, GBR (Triumph).
Fastest lap: Adrian Huertas, 1m 44.432s, 99.753mph/160.537km/h.
Championship points: 1 Montella, 76; **2** Schroetter, 72; **3** Manzi, 65; **4** Caricasulo, 44; **5** Huertas, 41; **6** Sofuoglu, 36.

Round 3, ASSEN, The Netherlands, 19-21 April 2024, 2.822-mile/4.542km circuit
Race 1 (18 laps, 50.801 miles/81.756km)
1 Adrian Huertas, ESP (Ducati), 32m 12.002s, 94.660mph/152.340km/h.
2 Stefano Manzi, ITA (Yamaha); **3** Valentin Debise, FRA (Yamaha); **4** Glenn Van Straalen, NED (Yamaha); **5** Tom Edwards, AUS (Ducati); **6** Federico Caricasulo, ITA (MV Agusta); **7** Jorge Navarro, ESP (Triumph); **8** Bahattin Sofuoglu, TUR (MV Agusta); **9** Lucas Mahias, FRA (Yamaha); **10** Luke Power, AUS (MV Agusta); **11** John McPhee, GBR (Triumph); **12** Marcel Schroetter, GER (MV Agusta); **13** Anupab Sarmoon, THA (Yamaha); **14** Simone Corsi, ITA (Ducati); **15** Andrea Antonelli, ITA (Ducati).
Fastest lap: Caricasulo, 1m 40.176s, 101.439mph/163.250km/h.

Race 2 (18 laps, 50.801 miles/81.756km)
1 Glenn Van Straalen, NED (Yamaha), 34m 12.199s, 89.116mph/143.418km/h.
2 Adrian Huertas, ESP (Ducati); **3** Niki Tuuli, FIN (Ducati); **4** Andrea Antonelli, ITA (Ducati); **5** Bahattin Sofuoglu, TUR (MV Agusta); **6** Kaito Toba, JPN (Honda); **7** Yari Montella, ITA (Ducati); **8** Marcel Schroetter, GER (MV Agusta); **9** Can Oncu, TUR (Kawasaki); **10** Twan Smits, NED (Yamaha); **11** Jorge Navarro, ESP (Triumph); **12** Piotr Biesiekirski, POL (Ducati); **13** Simone Corsi, ITA (Ducati); **14** Anupab Sarmoon, THA (Yamaha); **15** Gabriele Giannini, ITA (Kawasaki).
Fastest lap: Sofuoglu, 1m 45.814s, 95.865mph/154.280km/h.
Championship points: 1 Huertas, 86; **2** Montella, 85; **3** Manzi, 85; **4** Schroetter, 84; **5** Sofuoglu, 55; **6** Caricasulo, 54.

Round 4, MISANO, Italy, 14-16 June 2024, 2.626-mile/4.226km circuit
Race 1 (18 laps, 47.266 miles/76.068km)
1 Adrian Huertas, ESP (Ducati), 29m 30.653s, 96.100mph/154.658km/h.
2 Yari Montella, ITA (Ducati); **3** Stefano Manzi, ITA (Yamaha); **4** Valentin Debise, FRA (Yamaha); **5** Jorge Navarro, ESP (Ducati); **6** Marcel Schroetter, GER (MV Agusta); **7** Federico Caricasulo, ITA (MV Agusta); **8** Oliver Bayliss, AUS (Ducati); **9** Niki Tuuli, FIN (Ducati); **10** Glenn Van Straalen, NED (Yamaha); **11** Luca Ottaviani, ITA (MV Agusta); **12** Tom Edwards, AUS (Ducati); **13** Federico Fuligni, ITA (Ducati); **14** Lorenzo Baldassarri, ITA (Triumph); **15** Lucas Mahias, FRA (Yamaha).
Fastest lap: Huertas, 1m 37.404s, 97.052mph/156.191km/h.

Race 2 (15 laps, 40.016 miles/64.400km)
1 Adrian Huertas, ESP (Ducati), 24m 58.358s, 96.144mph/154.729km/h.
2 Yari Montella, ITA (Ducati); **3** Valentin Debise, FRA (Yamaha); **4** Stefano Manzi, ITA (Yamaha); **5** Jorge Navarro, ESP (Ducati); **6** Marcel Schroetter, GER (MV Agusta); **7** Federico Caricasulo, ITA (MV Agusta); **8** Niki Tuuli, FIN (Ducati); **9** Andrea Antonelli, ITA (Ducati); **10** Thomas Booth-Amos, GBR (Triumph); **11** Simone Corsi, ITA (Ducati); **12** Luca Ottaviani, ITA (MV Agusta); **13** Oliver Bayliss, AUS (Ducati); **14** Glenn Van Straalen, NED (Yamaha); **15** Piotr Biesiekirski, POL (Ducati).
Fastest lap: Huertas, 1m 37.114s, 97.288mph/156.570km/h.
Championship points: 1 Huertas, 136; **2** Montella, 125; **3** Manzi, 114; **4** Schroetter, 104; **5** Debise, 78; **6** Caricasulo, 72.

Round 5, DONINGTON PARK, UK, 12-14 July 2024, 2.500-mile/4.023km circuit
Race 1 (19 laps, 47.496 miles/76.437km)
1 Adrian Huertas, ESP (Ducati), 28m 22.889s, 100.409mph/161.592km/h.
2 Stefano Manzi, ITA (Yamaha); **3** Yari Montella, ITA (Ducati); **4** Jorge Navarro, ESP (Ducati); **5** Valentin Debise, FRA (Yamaha); **6** Bahattin Sofuoglu, TUR (MV Agusta); **7** Thomas Booth-Amos, GBR (Triumph); **8** Oliver Bayliss, AUS (Ducati); **9** Niki Tuuli, FIN (Ducati); **10** Lucas Mahias, FRA (Yamaha); **11** Tom Edwards, AUS (Ducati); **12** Glenn Van Straalen, NED (Yamaha); **13** Simone Corsi, ITA (Ducati); **14** Lorenzo Baldassarri, ITA (Triumph); **15** Can Oncu, TUR (Kawasaki).
Fastest lap: Huertas, 1m 28.861s, 101.178mph/162.830km/h.

Race 2 (12 laps, 29.997 miles/48.276km)
1 Adrian Huertas, ESP (Ducati), 17m 50.208s, 100.906mph/162.392km/h.
2 Yari Montella, ITA (Ducati); **3** Jorge Navarro, ESP (Ducati); **4** Stefano Manzi, ITA (Yamaha); **5** Thomas Booth-Amos, GBR (Triumph); **6** Niki Tuuli, FIN (Ducati); **7** Glenn Van Straalen, NED (Yamaha); **8** Valentin Debise, FRA (Yamaha); **9** Oliver Bayliss, AUS (Ducati); **10** Lucas Mahias, FRA (Yamaha); **11** Marcel Schroetter, GER (MV Agusta); **12** Can Oncu, TUR (Kawasaki); **13** Simone Corsi, ITA (Ducati); **14** Lorenzo Baldassarri, ITA (Triumph); **15** Federico Caricasulo, ITA (MV Agusta).
Fastest lap: Montella, 1m 28.637s, 101.529mph/163.395km/h.
Championship points: 1 Huertas, 186; **2** Montella, 161; **3** Manzi, 147; **4** Schroetter, 109; **5** Debise, 97; **6** Navarro, 96.

Round 6, MOST, Czech Republic, 19-21 July 2024, 2.617-mile/4.212km circuit
Race 1 (19 laps, 49.727 miles/80.028km)
1 Adrian Huertas, ESP (Ducati), 30m 15.092s, 98.627mph/158.725km/h.
2 Valentin Debise, FRA (Yamaha); **3** Stefano Manzi, ITA (Yamaha); **4** Yari Montella, ITA (Ducati); **5** Federico Caricasulo, ITA (MV Agusta); **6** Lucas Mahias, FRA (Yamaha); **7** Marcel Schroetter, GER (MV Agusta); **8** Thomas Booth-Amos, GBR (Triumph); **9** Glenn Van Straalen, NED (Yamaha); **10** Niki Tuuli, FIN (Ducati); **11** Can Oncu, TUR (Kawasaki); **12** Oliver Bayliss, AUS (Ducati); **13** Ondrej Vostatek, CZE (Triumph); **14** Steven Odendaal, RSA (Yamaha); **15** Lorenzo Baldassarri, ITA (Triumph).
Fastest lap: Manzi, 1m 34.834s, 99.370mph/159.920km/h.

Race 2 (19 laps, 49.727 miles/80.028km)
1 Adrian Huertas, ESP (Ducati), 30m 17.046s, 98.521mph/158.554km/h.
2 Stefano Manzi, ITA (Yamaha); **3** Yari Montella, ITA (Ducati); **4** Valentin Debise, FRA (Yamaha); **5** Jorge Navarro, ESP (Ducati); **6** Federico Caricasulo, ITA (MV Agusta); **7** Glenn Van Straalen, NED (Yamaha); **8** Niki Tuuli, FIN (Ducati); **9** Marcel Schroetter, GER (MV Agusta); **10** Can Oncu, TUR (Kawasaki); **11** Simone Corsi, ITA (Ducati); **12** Ondrej Vostatek, CZE (Triumph); **13** Lorenzo Baldassarri, ITA (Triumph); **14** Steven Odendaal, RSA (Yamaha); **15** Oliver Bayliss, AUS (Ducati).
Fastest lap: Manzi, 1m 35.083s, 99.252mph/159.730km/h.
Championship points: 1 Huertas, 236; **2** Montella, 190; **3** Manzi, 183; **4** Debise, 130; **5** Schroetter, 125; **6** Navarro, 107.

Round 7, PORTIMAO, Portugal, 9-11 August 2024, 2.853mile/4.592km circuit
Race 1 (17 laps, 48.507 miles/78.064km)
1 Yari Montella, ITA (Ducati), 29m 24.538s, 98.963mph/159.266km/h.
2 Adrian Huertas, ESP (Ducati); **3** Stefano Manzi, ITA (Yamaha); **4** Jorge Navarro, ESP (Ducati); **5** Federico Caricasulo, ITA (MV Agusta); **6** Valentin Debise, FRA (Yamaha); **7** Marcel Schroetter, GER (MV Agusta); **8** Lucas Mahias, FRA (Yamaha); **9** Glenn Van Straalen, NED (Yamaha); **10** Niki Tuuli, FIN (Ducati); **11** Can Oncu, TUR (Kawasaki); **12** Lorenzo Baldassarri, ITA (Triumph); **13** Simone Corsi, ITA (Ducati); **14** Kaito Toba, JPN (Honda); **15** John McPhee, GBR (Triumph).
Fastest lap: Montella, 1m 43.246s, 99.513mph/160.150km/h.

Race 2 (17 laps, 48.507 miles/78.064km)
1 Yari Montella, ITA (Ducati), 29m 36.763s, 98.282mph/158.170km/h.
2 Stefano Manzi, ITA (Yamaha); **3** Valentin Debise, FRA (Yamaha); **4** Federico Caricasulo, ITA (MV Agusta); **5** Lucas Mahias, FRA (Yamaha); **6** Glenn Van Straalen, NED (Yamaha); **7** Can Oncu, TUR (Kawasaki); **8** Marcel Schroetter, GER (MV Agusta); **9** John McPhee, GBR (Triumph); **10** Thomas Booth-Amos, GBR (Triumph); **11** Simone Corsi, ITA (Ducati); **12** Adrian Huertas, ESP (Ducati); **13** Andrea Antonelli, ITA (Ducati); **14** Lorenzo Dalla Porta, ITA (Yamaha); **15** Oliver Bayliss, AUS (Ducati).
Fastest lap: Huertas, 1m 43.578s, 99.171mph/159.601km/h.
Championship points: 1 Huertas, 260; **2** Montella, 240; **3** Manzi, 219; **4** Debise, 156; **5** Schroetter, 142; **6** Navarro, 120.

Round 8, MAGNY-COURS, France, 6-8 September 2024, 2.741mile/4.411km circuit
Race 1 (12 laps, 32.890 miles/52.932km)
1 Niki Tuuli, FIN (Ducati), 21m 46.488s, 90.629mph/145.853km/h.
2 Federico Caricasulo, ITA (MV Agusta); **3** Glenn Van Straalen, NED (Yamaha); **4** Adrian Huertas, ESP (Ducati); **5** Can Oncu, TUR (Kawasaki); **6** Yari Montella, ITA (Ducati); **7** Tom Edwards, AUS (Ducati); **8** Jorge Navarro, ESP (Ducati); **9** Thomas Booth-Amos, GBR (Triumph); **10** Valentin Debise, FRA (Yamaha); **11** Oliver Bayliss, AUS (Ducati); **12** Lorenzo Dalla Porta, ITA (Yamaha); **13** Alvaro Diaz, ESP (Yamaha); **14** Anupab Sarmoon, THA (Yamaha); **15** Khairul Idham Bin Pawi, MAS (Honda).
Fastest lap: Oncu, 1m 43.122s, 95.684mph/153.988km/h.

Race 2 (19 laps, 52.076 miles/83.809km)
1 Yari Montella, ITA (Ducati), 31m 54.069s, 97.946mph/157.629km/h.
2 Stefano Manzi, ITA (Yamaha); **3** Adrian Huertas, ESP (Ducati); **4** Thomas Booth-Amos, GBR (Triumph); **5** Jorge Navarro, ESP (Ducati); **6** Glenn Van Straalen, NED (Yamaha); **7** Corentin Perolari, FRA (Honda); **8** Niki Tuuli, FIN (Ducati); **9** Can Oncu, TUR (Kawasaki); **10** Marcel Schroetter, GER (MV Agusta); **11** Oliver Bayliss, AUS (Ducati); **12** John McPhee, GBR (Triumph); **13** Kaito Toba, JPN (Honda); **14** Tom Edwards, AUS (Ducati); **15** Piotr Biesiekirski, POL (Ducati).
Fastest lap: Manzi, 1m 40.027s, 98.644mph/158.753km/h.
Championship points: 1 Huertas, 289; **2** Montella, 275; **3** Manzi, 239; **4** Debise, 162; **5** Schroetter, 148; **6** Navarro, 139.

Round 9, CREMONA, Italy, 20-22 September 2024, 2.341-mile/3.768km circuit
Race 1 (20 laps, 46.827 miles/75.360km)
1 Adrian Huertas, ESP (Ducati), 30m 53.327s, 90.958mph/146.383km/h.
2 Stefano Manzi, ITA (Yamaha); **3** Yari Montella, ITA (Ducati); **4** Marcel Schroetter, GER (MV Agusta); **5** Thomas Booth-Amos, GBR (Triumph); **6** Lucas Mahias, FRA (Yamaha); **7** John McPhee, GBR (Triumph); **8** Ondrej Vostatek, CZE (Triumph); **9** Niki Tuuli, FIN (Ducati); **10** Bahattin Sofuoglu, TUR (MV Agusta); **11** Tom Edwards, AUS (Ducati); **12** Borja Gomez Rus, ESP (Kawasaki); **13** Alvaro Diaz, ESP (Yamaha); **14** Miquel Pons, ESP (Yamaha); **15** Anupab Sarmoon, THA (Yamaha).
Fastest lap: Huertas, 1m 32.213s, 91.406mph/147.103km/h.

Race 2 (20 laps, 46.827 miles/75.360km)
1 Stefano Manzi, ITA (Yamaha), 30m 53.855s, 90.933mph/146.342km/h.
2 Adrian Huertas, ESP (Ducati); **3** Thomas Booth-Amos, GBR (Triumph); **4** Marcel Schroetter, GER (MV Agusta); **5** Valentin Debise, FRA (Yamaha); **6** Federico Caricasulo, ITA (MV Agusta); **7** Jorge Navarro, ESP (Ducati); **8** Can Oncu, TUR (Kawasaki); **9** Ondrej Vostatek, CZE (Triumph); **10** Niki Tuuli, FIN (Ducati); **11** Bahattin Sofuoglu, TUR (MV Agusta); **12** Simone Corsi, ITA (Ducati); **13** Luca Ottaviani, ITA (MV Agusta); **14** Oliver Bayliss, AUS (Ducati); **15** Glenn Van Straalen, NED (Yamaha).
Fastest lap: Yari Montella, 1m 32.117s, 91.501mph/147.256km/h.
Championship points: 1 Huertas, 334; **2** Montella, 291; **3** Manzi, 284; **4** Schroetter, 174; **5** Debise, 173; **6** Caricasulo, 148.

Round 10, ARAGON, Spain, 27-29 September 2024, 3.155-mile/5.077km circuit
Race 1 (15 laps, 47.321 miles/76.155km)
1 Adrian Huertas, ESP (Ducati), 28m 20.283s, 100.192mph/161.243km/h.
2 Stefano Manzi, ITA (Yamaha); **3** Valentin Debise, FRA (Yamaha); **4** Yari Montella, ITA (Ducati); **5** Jorge Navarro, ESP (Ducati); **6** Lucas Mahias, FRA (Yamaha); **7** Can Oncu, TUR (Kawasaki); **8** Federico Caricasulo, ITA (MV Agusta); **9** Glenn Van Straalen, NED (Yamaha); **10** Bahattin Sofuoglu, TUR (MV Agusta); **11** Marcel Schroetter, GER (MV Agusta); **12** Oliver Bayliss, AUS (Ducati); **13** Andrea Antonelli, ITA (Ducati); **14** Niki Tuuli, FIN (Ducati); **15** Piotr Biesiekirski, POL (Ducati).
Fastest lap: Manzi, 1m 52.797s, 100.685mph/162.036km/h.

Race 2 (15 laps, 47.321 miles/76.155km)
1 Yari Montella, ITA (Ducati), 28m 20.800s, 100.161mph/161.194km/h.
2 Stefano Manzi, ITA (Yamaha); **3** Jorge Navarro, ESP (Ducati); **4** Valentin Debise, FRA (Yamaha); **5** Adrian Huertas, ESP (Ducati); **6** Thomas Booth-Amos, GBR (Triumph); **7** Marcel Schroetter, GER (MV Agusta); **8** Lucas Mahias, FRA (Yamaha); **9** Federico Caricasulo, ITA (MV Agusta); **10** Glenn Van Straalen, NED (Yamaha); **11** Can Oncu, TUR (Kawasaki); **12** Borja Gomez Rus, ESP (Kawasaki); **13** Simone Corsi, ITA (Ducati); **14** Oliver Bayliss, AUS (Ducati); **15** Steven Odendaal, RSA (Triumph).
Fastest lap: Debise, 1m 52.862s, 100.627mph/161.943km/h.
Championship points: 1 Huertas, 370; **2** Montella, 329; **3** Manzi, 324; **4** Debise, 202; **5** Schroetter, 188; **6** Navarro, 175.

Round 11, ESTORIL, Portugal, 11-13 October 2024, 2.598-mile/4.182km circuit
Race 1 (18 laps, 46.774 miles/75.276km)
1 Yari Montella, ITA (Ducati), 30m 18.316s, 92.606mph/149.035km/h.
2 Adrian Huertas, ESP (Ducati); **3** Stefano Manzi, ITA (Yamaha); **4** Lucas Mahias, FRA (Yamaha); **5** Federico Caricasulo, ITA (MV Agusta); **6** Marcel Schroetter, GER (MV Agusta); **7** Simone Corsi, ITA (Ducati); **8** Bo Bendsneyder, NED (MV Agusta); **9** Glenn Van Straalen, NED (Yamaha); **10** Bahattin Sofuoglu, TUR (Yamaha); **11** Ondrej Vostatek, CZE (Triumph); **12** Oliver Bayliss, AUS (Ducati); **13** Piotr Biesiekirski, POL (Ducati); **14** Kaito Toba, JPN (Honda); **15** Thomas Booth-Amos, GBR (Triumph).
Fastest lap: Montella, 1m 40.266s, 93.301mph/150.153km/h.

Race 2 (18 laps, 46.774 miles/75.276km)
1 Stefano Manzi, ITA (Yamaha), 30m 13.035s, 92.876mph/149.470km/h.
2 Adrian Huertas, ESP (Ducati); **3** Valentin Debise, FRA (Yamaha); **4** Lucas Mahias, FRA (Yamaha); **5** Bo Bendsneyder, NED (MV Agusta); **6** Federico Caricasulo, ITA (MV Agusta); **7** Glenn Van Straalen, NED (Yamaha); **8** Bahattin Sofuoglu, TUR (Yamaha); **9** Jorge Navarro, ESP (Ducati); **10** Marcel Schroetter, GER (MV Agusta); **11** Simone Corsi, ITA (Ducati); **12** Ondrej Vostatek, CZE (Triumph); **13** Yeray Ruiz, ESP (Yamaha); **14** Andrea Antonelli, ITA (Ducati); **15** Lorenzo Baldassarri, ITA (Triumph).
Fastest lap: Manzi, 1m 40.063s, 93.490mph/150.457km/h.
Championship points: 1 Huertas, 410; **2** Manzi, 365; **3** Montella, 354; **4** Debise, 218; **5** Schroetter, 204; **6** Caricasulo, 184.

Round 12, JEREZ, Spain, 18-20 October 2024, 2.748mile/4.423km circuit
Race 1 (17 laps, 46.722 miles/75.191km)
1 Stefano Manzi, ITA (Yamaha), 29m 21.734s, 95.472mph/153.648km/h.
2 Yari Montella, ITA (Ducati); **3** Adrian Huertas, ESP (Ducati); **4** Marcel Schroetter, GER (MV Agusta); **5** Lucas Mahias, FRA (Yamaha); **6** Thomas Booth-Amos, GBR (Triumph); **7** Bo Bendsneyder, NED (MV Agusta); **8** John McPhee, GBR (Triumph); **9** Andrea Antonelli, ITA (Ducati); **10** Lorenzo Baldassarri, ITA (Triumph); **11** Glenn Van Straalen, NED (Yamaha); **12** Simone Corsi, ITA (Ducati); **13** Yeray Ruiz, ESP (Yamaha); **14** Kaito Toba, JPN (Honda); **15** Khairul Idham Bin Pawi, MAS (Honda).
Fastest lap: Federico Caricasulo, 1m 42.568s, 96.462mph/155.241km/h.

Race 2 (17 laps, 46.722 miles/75.191km)
1 Stefano Manzi, ITA (Yamaha), 29m 21.666s, 95.476mph/153.654km/h.
2 Valentin Debise, FRA (Yamaha); **3** Bo Bendsneyder, NED (MV Agusta); **4** Adrian Huertas, ESP (Ducati); **5** Marcel Schroetter, GER (MV Agusta); **6** Jorge Navarro, ESP (Ducati); **7** Lucas Mahias, FRA (Yamaha); **8** Yari Montella, ITA (Ducati); **9** Bahattin Sofuoglu, TUR (Yamaha); **10** Simone Corsi, ITA (Ducati); **11** Thomas Booth-Amos, GBR (Triumph); **12** Glenn Van Straalen, NED (Yamaha); **13** Andrea Antonelli, ITA (Ducati); **14** Kaito Toba, JPN (Honda); **15** Yeray Ruiz, ESP (Yamaha).
Fastest lap: Huertas, 1m 42.985s, 96.072mph/154.613km/h.

Final World Supersport Championship points:

1	Adrian Huertas, ESP	439
2	Stefano Manzi, ITA	415
3	Yari Montella, ITA	382
4	Valentin Debise, FRA	238
5	Marcel Schroetter, GER	228
6	Jorge Navarro, ESP	192

7 Federico Caricasulo, ITA, 184; **8** Glenn Van Straalen, NED, 165; **9** Lucas Mahias, FRA, 155; **10** Thomas Booth-Amos, GBR, 120; **11** Niki Tuuli, FIN, 118; **12** Bahattin Sofuoglu, TUR, 103; **13** Can Oncu, TUR, 92; **14** Oliver Bayliss, AUS, 76; **15** Simone Corsi, ITA, 60.